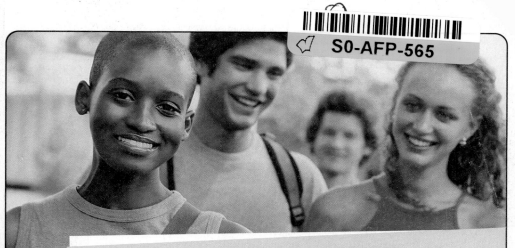

Why Do You Need This New Edition?

Six good reasons why you should buy this new Fourth Edition of *American Destiny*!

1. This edition is tied more closely than ever to the innovative website, MyHistoryLab, which helps you save time and improve results as you study history (www.myhistorylab.com). MyHistoryLab icons now appear throughout the textbook, connecting the main narrative of each chapter to a powerful array of MyHistoryLab resources, including primary source documents, analytical video segments, interactive maps, and more. Also tied to each chapter of the textbook, a powerful and personalized Study Plan is available on MyHistoryLab that will help you build a deeper and more critical understanding of the subject.

2. The new edition strengthens the guiding principle of the textbook—to survey American history in a way that bridges the present and the past, showing the relevance of history to contemporary readers. For example, the essays that open each chapter connect a major topic of the chapter to experiences that pertain to many readers. For the Fourth Edition these essays are either entirely new or have been thoroughly updated; nearly all pertain to events or developments since 2008.

3. Other elements designed to bridge the present and the past, such as the *American Lives* and *Re-Viewing the Past* essays, have also been thoroughly revised. Most of these essays are entirely new to the Fourth Edition.

4. The maps and graphs in this book have been completely reworked to convey new ideas and to enhance comprehension. Many entirely new maps have been created to illuminate important themes, including a stronger global emphasis.

5. Each chapter has been revised to reflect new scholarship, to offer important new perspectives, and to streamline and sharpen the writing. For instance, the Prologue and first few chapters reflect new insights concerning the "pre-historic" period. These chapters also feature a more detailed comparison of the civilizations of the Americas with those of the "Old World"—Europe, Africa, and Asia. An almost entirely new chapter, "From Boomers to Millennials" (Chapter 31), draws an explicit comparison between the social and cultural foundations of young modern Americans and their parents; it especially explores the culture of consumption and the impact of the Internet.

6. To facilitate study and review, each chapter now ends with a set of review questions, and a list of key terms that are defined in a new glossary.

PEARSON

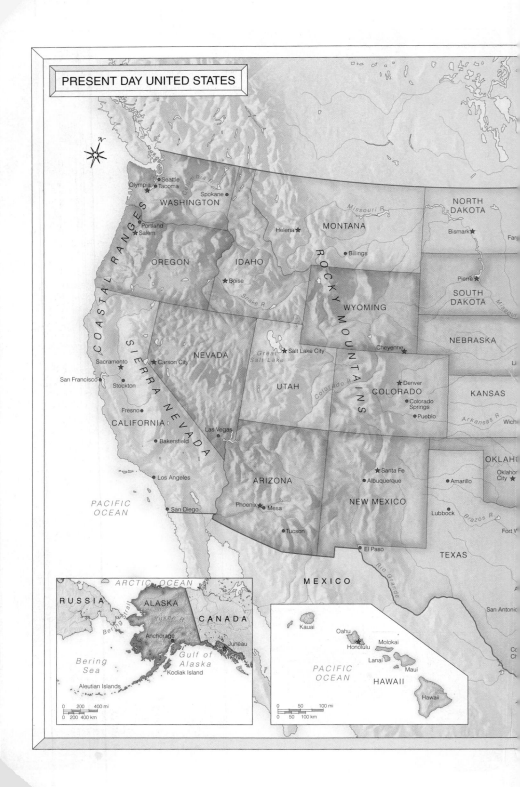

PRESENT DAY UNITED STATES

N

WASHINGTON
- Seattle
- Olympia ★
- Tacoma
- Spokane

OREGON
- Portland
- Salem ★

COASTAL RANGES

Columbia R.

IDAHO
- Boise ★

Snake R.

MONTANA
- Helena ★
- Billings

Missouri R.

NORTH DAKOTA
- Bismark ★
- Far

SOUTH DAKOTA
- Pierre ★

Missouri R.

ROCKY MOUNTAINS

WYOMING
- Cheyenne ★

NEBRASKA
- Li

NEVADA
- Carson City ★
- Sacramento ★
- Stockton

SIERRA NEVADA

Great Salt Lake

- Salt Lake City ★

UTAH

Colorado R.

COLORADO
- Denver ★
- Colorado Springs
- Pueblo

KANSAS

Arkansas R.

Wich

CALIFORNIA
- San Francisco
- Fresno
- Bakersfield
- Las Vegas
- Los Angeles
- San Diego

PACIFIC OCEAN

ARIZONA
- Phoenix ★
- Mesa
- Tucson

NEW MEXICO
- Santa Fe ★
- Albuquerque
- El Paso

- Amarillo
- Lubbock

OKLAHOMA
- Oklahoma City ★

Brazos R.

Fort W

TEXAS

Rio Grande

MEXICO

San Antonio

Co
Ch

(Alaska inset)

ARCTIC OCEAN

RUSSIA

Bering Strait

ALASKA
- Anchorage

Yukon R.

CANADA
- Juneau

Bering Sea

Gulf of Alaska

- Kodiak Island

Aleutian Islands

| 0 | 200 | 400 mi |
| 0 | 200 | 400 km |

(Hawaii inset)

- Kauai
- Oahu
- Honolulu ★
- Molokai
- Lanai
- Maui
- Hawaii

PACIFIC OCEAN

HAWAII

| 0 | 50 | 100 mi |
| 0 | 50 | 100 km |

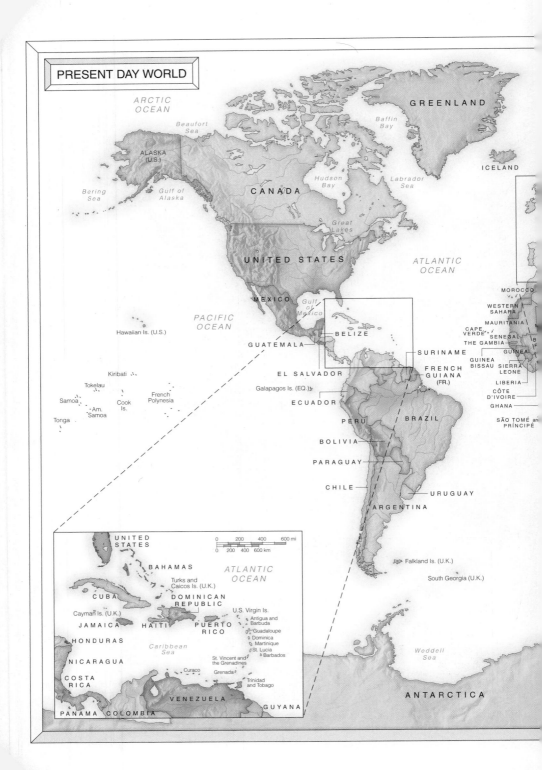

PRESENT DAY WORLD

ARCTIC
OCEAN

GREENLAND

Beaufort
Sea

Baffin
Bay

ALASKA
(U.S.)

ICELAND

Bering
Sea

Gulf of
Alaska

CANADA

Hudson
Bay

Labrador
Sea

Great
Lakes

ATLANTIC
OCEAN

UNITED STATES

MOROCCO

MEXICO

Gulf
of
Mexico

WESTERN
SAHARA

PACIFIC
OCEAN

Hawaiian Is. (U.S.)

MAURITANIA

BELIZE

CAPE
VERDE

SENEGAL
THE GAMBIA

GUATEMALA

SURINAME

GUINEA

Kiribati

EL SALVADOR

FRENCH
GUIANA
(FR.)

GUINEA
BISSAU

SIERRA
LEONE

Tokelau

French
Polynesia

Galapagos Is. (EQ.)

CÔTE
D'IVOIRE

Samoa

Cook
Is.

ECUADOR

GHANA

Am.
Samoa

PERU

BRAZIL

SÃO TOMÉ and
PRÍNCIPE

Tonga

BOLIVIA

PARAGUAY

CHILE

URUGUAY

ARGENTINA

Falkland Is. (U.K.)

South Georgia (U.K.)

UNITED
STATES

0   200   400   600 mi

0   200   400 600 km

Weddell
Sea

BAHAMAS

ATLANTIC
OCEAN

Turks and
Caicos Is. (U.K.)

CUBA

DOMINICAN
REPUBLIC

Cayman Is. (U.K.)

U.S. Virgin Is.

Antigua and
Barbuda

ANTARCTICA

JAMAICA

HAITI

PUERTO
RICO

Guadaloupe

HONDURAS

Caribbean
Sea

Dominica

Martinique

St. Lucia

Barbados

NICARAGUA

St. Vincent and
the Grenadines

COSTA
RICA

Curaco

Grenada

VENEZUELA

Trinidad
and Tobago

PANAMA

COLOMBIA

GUYANA

AMERICAN DESTINY

NARRATIVE OF A NATION

VOLUME TWO

FOURTH EDITION

MARK C. CARNES

Ann Whitney Olin Professor of History
Barnard College, Columbia University

JOHN A. GARRATY

Gouverneur Morris Professor of History, Emeritus
Columbia University

PEARSON

Boston Columbus Indianapolis New York San Francisco Upper Saddle River
Amsterdam Cape Town Dubai London Madrid Milan Munich Paris Montréal Toronto
Delhi Mexico City São Paulo Sydney Hong Kong Seoul Singapore Taipei Tokyo

Editorial Director: Craig Campanella
Editor in Chief: Dickson Musslewhite
Executive Editor: Ed Parsons
Editorial Assistants: Alex Rabinowitz,
   Emily Tamburri
Director of Marketing: Brandy Dawson
Senior Marketing Manager: Maureen E. Prado
   Roberts
Marketing Assistant: Samantha Bennett
Senior Managing Editor: Ann Marie McCarthy
Senior Project Manager: Debra A. Wechsler
AV Project Manager: Mirella Signoretto
Operations Specialist: Christina Amato
Senior Art Director: Maria Lange
Text Designer: GEX Publishing Services

Cover Designer: Art-Tronic Design
Cover Art: Zakim Bridge illuminated at dusk,
   Boston, USA. © Allan Baxter/Photodisc/
   Getty Images
Director of Media and Assessment: Brian Hyland
Media Editor: Andrea Messineo
Media Project Manager: Tina Rudowski
Full-Service Project Management: GEX Publishing
   Services
Composition: GEX Publishing Services
Printer/Binder: Courier/Kendallville
Cover Printer: Lehigh-Phoenix Color /
   Hagerstown
Text Font: 10/12 Minion Pro

Credits and acknowledgments borrowed from other sources and reproduced, with permission, in this textbook appear on appropriate page within text (or starting on page C-1).

Library of Congress Cataloging-in-Publication Data
Carnes, Mark C. (Mark Christopher), 1950-
   American destiny : narrative of a nation / Mark C. Carnes, John A. Garraty. — 4th ed.
      p. cm.
   Includes bibliographical references and index.
   ISBN-13: 978-0-205-79041-8
   ISBN-10: 0-205-79041-0
   ISBN-13: 978-0-205-79039-5 (v. 1)
   ISBN-10: 0-205-79039-9 (v. 1)
   [etc.]
1. United States—History. I. Garraty, John A. (John Arthur), 1920-2007. II. Title.

E178.6.C33 2012
973—dc22

                        2011015068
10 9 8 7 6 5 4 3 2 1

Combined Volume
ISBN 10: 0-205-79041-0
ISBN 13: 978-0-205-79041-8
Examination Copy
ISBN 10: 0-205-00149-1
ISBN 13: 978-0-205-00149-1
Volume 1
ISBN 10: 0-205-79039-9
ISBN 13: 978-0-205-79039-5
Volume 2
ISBN 10: 0-205-79040-2
ISBN 13: 978-0-205-79040-1

PEARSON

Brief Contents

Contents

MAPS

GRAPHS   PAGE

AMERICAN LIVES   PAGE

RE-VIEWING THE PAST   PAGE

Preface

"A New American Destiny begins"—so trumpeted a liberal newspaper after the election of Barack Obama as president in 2008. Shortly after his inauguration a conservative newsletter asked, "What is Barack Obama making of our American destiny?" Its reply was brusque: "a hash."

Despite their divergent views on the merits of the new president, both publications assumed that the United States **had** a "destiny." The term "destiny" refers to an inevitable course of events. The liberal newspaper believed that the United States was predestined to embrace diversity while the conservative paper regarded the nation as foreordained to promote traditional religious values. Some contend, by contrast, that history moves in no preset direction.

This book takes no stand on these issues. But it does agree that Americans have long **assumed** a national destiny, such as John Louis O'Sullivan's 1845 editorial proclaiming it "our manifest destiny" for Americans to spread throughout North America; or Daniel Webster's terse repudiation of the looming sectional crisis: "One country, one constitution, one destiny"; or Walt Whitman's celebration, after that crisis had erupted in civil war, of "one common indivisible destiny for ALL"; or Franklin D. Roosevelt's reference during the Great Depression to his generation's "rendezvous with destiny"; or the letter from a Birmingham jail by African American leader Martin Luther King, Jr. in which he declared that "our destiny is tied up with America's destiny."

But if Americans have commonly accepted the concept of a national purpose, they have endlessly debated where the nation was headed and the nature of the force impelling it there. Some have discerned the hand of God lifting the nation up—or perhaps hurling it down. Others have claimed that the nation's destiny was dictated by accident of geography or economics, by the "laws" of social evolution or the "spirit" of democratic liberalism, by the "patterns" of demography or "processes" of modernity, and so on.

This book maintains that no single model explains the complexity of American history. Because historians are poor prophets, we make no attempt to peer into the future. For us, the concept of an American destiny refers to a vague notion that has long exerted a hold on the American imagination.

The subtitle—"Narrative of a Nation"—may also strike readers as provocative. Some contend that the diverse peoples of the United States cannot be encompassed within the analytical boundaries of a single nation. Thus we have not attempted to write a history of "the American people": No book can possibly do justice to all its infinite variations of identity—racial, gender-related, and cultural. Rather, we describe how the voices and actions of its many peoples have produced a particular political structure—the United States—and how that nation has influenced the lives of everyone.

"Relevant History"

This narrative seeks to speak directly to students. Each of the features serves to connect past and present, a bridge to help students relate the people and events of history to their own lives.

Chapter Openers

To that end, every chapter opens with questions that pertain to many readers: Chapter 6—on Jeffersonian Democracy—begins: "Do you have too much debt?" The essay that follows examines the problem of credit card debt among college students today and shows how similar concerns occupied Jefferson and his followers. Chapter 18, on society and culture during the late nineteenth century, opens with: "Have you ever been kicked out of a mall?" The succeeding paragraphs show how much more of our lives are played out in public spaces compared to a century ago. Such questions bridge present and past; they connect our lives to those of our forebears.

Re-Viewing the Past

Because movies on historical themes often figure prominently in how we think about the past, ten of the chapters include *Re-Viewing the Past* essays, which contrast Hollywood's rendering of history with what really happened. The selected movies range from those with obvious "historical" themes, such as *The Alamo* and *Saving Private Ryan*, to popular movies whose historical themes are less well known, such as *Chicago*, a musical based on the actual story of women who murdered their lovers.

American Lives

Ten of the chapters include *American Lives* essays, ranging from Sojourner Truth, a slave who became a preacher and reformer, to contemporary figures such as Bill Gates and Barack Obama. These essays focus on the young adulthood of such figures; we hope that readers of the same age will in this way find it easier to relate to them.

New to This Edition

- Each chapter has been revised to reflect new scholarship, offer new perspectives, and streamline and sharpen the prose. An almost entirely new chapter, "From Boomers to Millennials" (Chapter 31), draws an explicit comparison between the social and cultural foundations of young modern Americans and their parents; it especially explores the culture of consumption and the impact of the Internet.
- The essays that introduce each chapter are either entirely new or have been updated; nearly all pertain to events or developments since 2008.
- The Prologue and first few chapters reflect new insights unearthed (literally) by archaeologists and anthropologists concerning the "pre-historic" period. These chapters also feature a more detailed comparison of the civilizations of the Americas with those of the "Old World"—Europe, Africa, and Asia.
- This edition includes several new *American Lives*: Davy Crockett—perhaps the first person who became famous for being famous; Charlotte Perkins Gilman, a visionary who perceived that women's legal and political emancipation was largely dependent on their gaining paid work; civil rights leader Martin Luther King, Jr.; Barack Obama, the first African American to be elected president; and three randomly selected heroes who were killed in the recent wars in Afghanistan and Iraq.

- This edition also includes three new *Re-Viewing the Past* essays. *Black Robe* thoughtfully explores the interaction of Indians and colonists in the seventeenth century. Two versions of *The Alamo*: The first, released in 1960, stars John Wayne; the second (2004) tells a different story with Billy Bob Thornton as Davy Crockett. The widely acclaimed *There Will Be Blood* presents Daniel Day Lewis's searing performance as an unscrupulous wildcatting oilman loosely based on the life of Edward Doheny, who opened up the major oil fields of California and Mexico early in the twentieth century.
- The maps in this book have been completely reworked to convey new ideas and to enhance comprehension.
- Nearly every chapter now includes at least one "conceptual" table illuminating key themes and topics.
- To encourage and facilitate study and review, each chapter now ends with a set of review questions, and a list of key terms that are defined in a new glossary.

Supplements for
Instructors and Students

Supplements for Qualified College Adopters	Supplements for Students
MyHistoryLab (www.myhistorylab.com) **Save Time. Improve Results.** MyHistoryLab is a dynamic website that provides a wealth of resources geared to meet the diverse teaching and learning needs of today's instructors and students. MyHistoryLab's many accessible tools will encourage students to read their text and help them improve their grade in their course.	**MyHistoryLab** (www.myhistorylab.com) **Save Time. Improve Results.** MyHistoryLab is a dynamic website that provides a wealth of resources geared to meet the diverse teaching and learning needs of today's instructors and students. MyHistoryLab's many accessible tools will encourage you to read your text and help you improve your grade in your course.
Instructor's Resource Manual with Test Bank Available at the Instructor's Resource Center, at **www.pearsonhighered.com/irc**, the Instructor's Resource Manual with Test Bank contains chapter outlines, summaries, key points and vital concepts, and information on audio-visual resources that can be used in developing and preparing lecture presentations. The Test Bank includes multiple-choice questions and essay questions and is text-specific.	**CourseSmart** www.coursesmart.com CourseSmart eTextbooks offer the same content as the printed text in a convenient online format— with highlighting, online search, and printing capabilities. You **save 60% over the list price** of the traditional book.
PowerPoint Presentation Available at the Instructor's Resource Center, at **www.pearsonhighered.com/irc**, the PowerPoints contain chapter outlines and full-color images of maps and art. They are text-specific and available for download.	**Library of American Biography Series** www.pearsonhighered.com/educator/series/Library-of-American-Biography/10493.page Pearson's renowned series of biographies spotlighting figures who had a significant impact on American history. Included in the series are Edmund Morgan's *The Puritan Dilemma: The Story of John Winthrop*, B. Davis Edmund's *Tecumseh and the Quest for Indian Leadership*, J. William T. Young's, *Eleanor Roosevelt: A Personal and Public Life*, John R. M. Wilson's *Jackie Robinson and the American Dilemma*, and Sandra Opdycke's *Jane Addams and Her Vision For America*.
MyTest Available at **www.pearsonmytest.com**, MyTest is a powerful assessment generation program that helps instructors easily create and print quizzes and exams. Questions and tests can be authored online, allowing instructors ultimate flexibility and the ability to efficiently manage assessments anytime, anywhere! Instructors can easily access existing questions and edit, create, and store using simple drag-and-drop and Word-like controls.	**Penguin Valuepacks** www.pearsonhighered.com/penguin A variety of Penguin-Putnam texts is available at discounted prices when bundled with *The American Nation, 14/e*. Texts include Benjamin Franklin's *Autobiography and Other Writings*, Nathaniel Hawthorne's *The Scarlet Letter*, Thomas Jefferson's *Notes on the State of Virginia*, and George Orwell's *1984*.

Supplements for Qualified College Adopters	Supplements for Students
Retreiving the American Past Available through the Pearson Custom Library (**www.pearsoncustom.com, keyword search | rtap**), the *Retrieving the American Past* (RTAP) program lets you create a textbook or reader that meets your needs and the needs of your course. RTAP gives you the freedom and flexibility to add chapters from several best-selling Pearson textbooks, in addition to *The American Nation, 14/e*, and/or 100 topical reading units written by the History Department of The Ohio State University, all under one cover. Choose the content you want to teach in depth, in the sequence you want, at the price you want your students to pay.	**A Short Guide to Writing About History, 7/e** Written by Richard Marius, late of Harvard University, and Melvin E. Page, East Tennessee State University, this engaging and practical text helps students get beyond merely compiling dates and facts. Covering both brief essays and the documented resource paper, the text explores the writing and researching processes, identifies different modes of historical writing, including argument, and concludes with guidelines for improving style. **ISBN-10: 0205673708; ISBN-13: 9780205673704**
	Longman American History Atlas This full-color historical atlas designed especially for college students is a valuable reference tool and visual guide to American history. This atlas includes maps covering the scope of American history from the lives of the Native Americans to the 1990s. Produced by a renowned cartographic firm and a team of respected historians, the *Longman American History Atlas* will enhance any American history survey course. **ISBN: 0321004868; ISBN-13: 9780321004864**
	Study Card for American History This timeline of major events in American social, political, and cultural history distills course information to the basics, helping you quickly master the fundamentals and prepare for exams. **ISBN: 0321292324; ISBN-13: 9780321292322**

MyHistoryLab

The Moment You Know

Educators know it. Students know it. It's that inspired moment when something that was difficult to understand suddenly makes perfect sense. MyHistoryLab has been designed and refined with a single purpose in mind: to help history teachers create that moment of understanding with their students.

Features of MyHistoryLab

MyHistoryLab provides **engaging experiences** that personalize, stimulate, and measure learning for each student.

- **Closer Look tours**—walk students through a variety of images, maps, and primary sources in detail, helping them to uncover their meaning and understand their context.
- **A History Bookshelf**—enables students to read, download, or print up to 100 of the most commonly assigned history works, like Thomas Paine's, *Common Sense*, Booker T. Washington's, *Up From Slavery*, and Andrew Carnegie's *Autobiography*.
- The **Pearson eText**—lets students access their textbook anytime, anywhere, and any way they want—including listening online or downloading to their iPad.
- A **personalized study plan** for each student, based on a chapter Pre-Test, arranges content from less complex thinking—like remembering basic facts—to more complex critical thinking—like understanding connections and analyzing the past. This layered approach promotes better critical-thinking skills, and helps students succeed in the course and beyond.
- **Assessment** tied to every chapter enables both instructors and students to track progress and get immediate feedback. With results flowing into a powerful gradebook, the assessment program helps instructors identify student challenges early—and find the best resources with which to help students.
- An **assignment calendar** allows instructors to assign graded activities, with specific deadlines, and measure student progress.
- **ClassPrep** collects the very best class presentation resources in one convenient online destination, so instructors can keep students engaged throughout every class.
- **Audio Files**—Full audio of the entire text is included to suit the varied learning styles of today's students. In addition there are audio clips of speeches, readings, and music that provide another engaging way to experience history.
- **Text and Visual Documents**—Over 1,500 primary source documents, images, and maps are available organized by chapter in the text. Primary source documents are also available in the MyHistoryLibrary and can be searched by author, title, theme, and topic. Many of these documents include critical thinking questions.
- **Lecture and Archival Videos**—Lectures by leading scholars on provocative topics give students a critical look at key points in history. Videos of speeches, news footage,

key historical events, and other archival video take students back to the moment in history.

- **MySearchLab**—This website provides students access to a number of reliable sources for online research, as well as clear guidance on the research and writing process.
- **Gradebook**—Students can follow their own progress and instructors can monitor the work of the entire class. Automated grading of quizzes and assignments helps both instructors and students save time and monitor their results throughout the course.

NEW In-text References to MyHistoryLab Resources

Read, View, See, Watch, Hear, Study, and Review Icons integrated in the text connect resources on MyHistoryLab to specific topics within the chapters. The icons are not exhaustive; many more resources are available than those highlighted in the book, but the icons draw attention to some of the most high-interest resources available on MyHistoryLab.

Read the **Document**

Points students to primary and secondary source documents related to the chapter.

View the **Image**

Identifies primary and secondary source images, including photographs, fine art, and artifacts to provide students with a visual perspective on history.

See the **Map**

Directs students to atlas and interactive maps; these present both broad overviews and detailed examinations of historical developments.

Watch the **Video**

Notes pertinent archival videos and videos of Pearson History authors that probe various topics.

Hear the **Audio**

Marks audio clips from historically significant songs and speeches that enrich students' engagement with history.

Study and **Review**

Alerts students to study resources for each chapter of the textbook available online through www.myhistorylab.com. These resources include practice tests and flashcards.

Acknowledgments

I THANK THE MANY FRIENDS, colleagues, and students who have helped me in writing this edition of *American Destiny*. My debt to John A. Garraty—teacher, colleague, co-author—warrants many paragraphs of acknowledgment. But his scorn for wordiness obliges me to acknowledge that he taught me the art of writing.

Mary Elin Korchinsky has lived this book (and nearly everything else) with me. My journey with her is a joy. For this edition, our particular challenge has been to relate the American nation's past to college students today. Much of the creativity in the chapters that follow—"Do you vote for *American Idol*?" "Do you illegally download?" "Do you space out during political debates?"—was a product of her special genius.

I especially thank E. Ward Smith for guidance through the murky depths of modern banking and finance. And I thank Prakhar Sharma for similarly leading me through the shrouded landscape of contemporary Iraq and Afghanistan.

Modern publishing, too, is a world of labyrinthine complexity. I thank the expert team at Pearson for sharing their mastery of its many arcane and demanding arts: Yolanda de Rooy, Roberta Meyer, Craig Campanella, Ed Parsons, Debra Wechsler, Mirella Signoretto, Maria Lange, Marisa Taylor, Brandy Dawson, Maureen Prado Roberts, and Alex Rabinowitz. Although they left me plenty of thread to find my way out, they also showed good sense in sometimes getting behind me and pushing. For that, and everything else, I am grateful.

I also thank:

Armando C. Alonzo, Texas A & M University
Andrew Bagley, Phillips Community College
Mary E. Barnes, Blinn College
Mack Bean, Blinn College
Thomas Born, Blinn College
Robert Brooks, Tyler Junior College
Dale Carnagey, Blinn College
Carrie Coston, Blinn College
Shannon Cross, Tyler Junior College
Alan Harazin, Holyoke Community College
Billy Hathorn, Laredo Community College
Peter Jones, Tyler Junior College
Gene Kirkpatrick, Tyler Junior College
Martha Kline, Blinn College
Alan Lehman, Blinn College
Jan McCauley, Tyler Junior College

Nora McMillan, San Antonio College
Horacio Salinas, Jr., Laredo Community College
Malcolum Saunders, University of the South Pacific
Kenneth McCullough, Blinn College
Dennis M. Nilsen, Molloy College
Jeff Owens, Tyler Junior College
Kahne Parsons, Tyler Junior College
Madeleine Ross, Tyler Junior College
James R. Sisson, Central Texas College
Herbert Sloan, Barnard College
Isaac Solis, Navarro College
Brian Steele, University of Alabama at Birmingham
Tracy Teslow, University of Cincinnati
Hubert P. van Tuyll, Augusta State University
Larry Watson, Blinn College
Stan Watson, Tyler Junior College
Don Whatley, Blinn College
Geoffrey Willbanks, Tyler Junior College

I thank the families of the American heroes, featured in Chapter 32, for sharing the stories of their children who served and died in the wars in Afghanistan and Iraq.

My daughter, Stephanie, read the book carefully and critically, and her comments have proven invaluable. My goal of connecting with younger readers was surely influenced by her own immense capacity for sharing love with her parents. This book is dedicated to her—in acknowledgment of that special gift and so many others.

Mark C. Carnes

Barnard College, Columbia University

About the Authors

MARK C. CARNES received his undergraduate degree from Harvard and his PhD in history from Columbia University. He has chaired both the history and American studies departments at Barnard College, Columbia University, where he serves as the Ann Whitney Olin Professor of History. Carnes and Garraty were General Editors of the 26-volume *American National Biography*, for which they were awarded the Waldo Leland Prize of the American Historical Association. Carnes has published numerous books on American social and cultural history, including *Secret Ritual and Manhood in Victorian America* (1989), *Past Imperfect: History According to the Movies* (1995), *Novel History: Historians and Novelists Confront America's Past* (2001), and *Invisible Giants: 50 Americans That Shaped the Nation but Missed the History Books* (2002). Carnes also pioneered the *Reacting to the Past* pedagogy, winner of the Theodore Hesburgh Award, sponsored by TIAA-CREF, as the outstanding pedagogical innovation in the nation (2004). In *Reacting to the Past*, college students play elaborate games, set in the past, their roles informed by classic texts. (For more on *Reacting*, see: www.barnard.edu/reacting.) In 2005 the American Historical Association named Carnes the recipient of the William Gilbert Prize for the best article on teaching history.

The late John A. Garraty, formerly Gouverneur Morris Professor Emeritus of History at Columbia University, received his PhD from Columbia University and an LHD from Michigan State University. He authored and edited scores of books, among them biographies of Silas Wright, Henry Cabot Lodge, Woodrow Wilson, George W. Perkins, and Theodore Roosevelt. Garraty's *The New Commonwealth*, included in the new *American Nation* series, challenged earlier dismissals of what was commonly known as "the Gilded Age." His *The Great Depression* argued that political leaders throughout the world happened upon "solutions" much like those proposed by Franklin D. Roosevelt. Garraty was co-General Editor with Mark Carnes of the *American National Biography*.

Reconstruction and the South

15

((•—⌐Hear the Audio Chapter 15 at myhistorylab.com

Has your family overcome adversity?

WITH NEARLY $3 BILLION IN ASSETS, OPRAH WINFREY IS THE RICHEST self-made woman in America. Her great-great-grandfather, Constantine Winfrey, was an illiterate slave in Sanford, Mississippi. On gaining his freedom in 1865, he owned little more than a strong back and a knowledge of cotton farming. But within fifteen years, he had learned to read and write and was owner of several farms and over 100 acres of land.

Whoopi Goldberg, another prominent black woman TV host and actress, is the great-great-granddaughter of William Washington and Elsa Tucker, slaves who were living in Alachua County, Florida when Lee surrendered at Appomattox. Over the next decade, the couple fulfilled the demanding provisions of the Southern Homestead Act, passed by the Republican-dominated Congress in 1866.

Chris Rock, comedian and actor, is the great-great-grandson of Julius Caesar Tingman, a slave in South Carolina. In March 1865, a few weeks after Sherman had marched through South Carolina, Tingman joined the U.S. Colored Troops in the Union army. Three years later, at the age of twenty-four, he was elected to the "reconstructed" South Carolina legislature.

Such accounts add another dimension to the usual narrative of the Reconstruction era (1865–1877). The period began with the liberal readmission of southern states to the Union as proposed by Lincoln and his successor, Andrew Johnson. Once readmitted, southern states restricted the rights of former slaves through a series of "**Black Codes**." A furious Republican Congress overturned white southern rule through a series of laws and constitutional amendments that empowered former slaves—and their Republican allies. A white backlash, often violent, followed Republican rule.

•••⌐Read the Document
The Mississippi Black Code, at myhistorylab.com

Ultimately, white political power was restored, and a corrupt bargain secured the presidency for the Republican, Hayes. When Hayes removed Union troops from the South in 1877, Reconstruction was over.

Deprived of federal assistance, former slaves were obliged to make do on their own. Many failed. Only 10 percent of freed slaves acquired farms. But the ancestors of Oprah Winfrey, Whoopi Goldberg, Chris Rock, and many others prove that *some* former slaves succeeded, almost entirely through their own efforts. Harvard historian Louis Henry

Gates, Jr., whose *In Search of Our Roots* (2009) recounted their stories and many similar ones, hoped that someday such accounts would move history "from our kitchens or parlors into the texts, ultimately changing the official narrative of American history itself." This chapter describes the era's bitter wrangles and recriminations, its political failures and disappointments, but it also shows that many survived and even flourished during these difficult years.

The Assassination of Lincoln

On April 5, 1865, Abraham Lincoln visited Richmond. The fallen capital lay in ruins, sections blackened by fire, but the president was able to walk the streets unmolested and almost unattended. Everywhere African Americans crowded around him worshipfully; some fell to their knees as he passed, crying "Glory, Hallelujah," hailing him as a messiah. Even white townspeople seemed to have accepted defeat without resentment.

A few days later, in Washington, Lincoln delivered an important speech on Reconstruction, urging compassion and open-mindedness. On April 14 he held a Cabinet meeting at which postwar readjustment was considered at length. That evening, while Lincoln was watching a performance of the play *Our American Cousin* at Ford's Theater, an actor, John Wilkes Booth, slipped into his box and shot him in the back of the head with a small pistol. Early the next morning, without having regained consciousness, Lincoln died.

Richmond, Virginia lies in ruins in April, 1865 at the time of Lincoln's visit—and a few days before his assassination.

The murder was part of a complicated plot organized by die-hard pro-Southerners. One of Booth's accomplices went to the home of Secretary of State William Seward and stabbed him—Seward recovered from his wounds. A third conspirator, assigned to kill Vice President Andrew Johnson, changed his mind and fled Washington. Seldom have fanatics displayed so little understanding of their own interests, for with Lincoln perished the South's best hope for a mild peace. After his body had been taken home to Illinois, the national mood hardened; apparently the awesome drama was still unfolding—retribution and a final humbling of the South were inevitable.

Presidential Reconstruction

Despite its bloodiness, the Civil War had caused less intersectional hatred than might have been expected. The legal questions related to bringing the defeated states back into the Union, however, were extremely complex. Since Southerners believed that secession was legal, logic should have compelled them to argue that they were out of the Union and would thus have to be formally readmitted. Northerners should have taken the contrary position, for they had fought to prove that secession was illegal. Yet the people of both sections did just the opposite. Senator Charles Sumner and Congressman Thaddeus Stevens, who in 1861 had been uncompromising expounders of the theory that the Union was indissoluble, now insisted that the Confederate states had "committed suicide" and should be treated like "conquered provinces."

The process of readmission began in 1862, when Lincoln reappointed provisional governors for those parts of the South that had been occupied by federal troops. On December 8, 1863, he issued a proclamation setting forth a general policy. With the exception of high Confederate officials and a few other special groups, all Southerners could reinstate themselves as United States citizens by taking a simple loyalty oath. When, in any state, a number equal to 10 percent of those voting in the 1860 election had taken this oath, they could set up a state government. Under this **Ten Percent Plan**, such governments had to be republican in form, must recognize the "permanent freedom" of the slaves, and must provide for black education. The plan, however, did not require that blacks be given the right to vote.

President Andrew Johnson poses regally with carefully manicured fingernails. Although Johnson hated southern aristocrats, he sometimes craved their approval.

The Ten Percent Plan reflected Lincoln's lack of vindictiveness and his political wisdom. He realized that any government based on such a small minority of the population would be, as he put it, merely "a tangible nucleus which the remainder . . . may rally around as fast as it can," a sort of puppet regime, like the paper government established in those sections of Virginia under federal control.[1] The regimes established under this plan in Tennessee, Louisiana, and Arkansas bore, in the president's mind, the same relation to finally reconstructed states that an egg bears to a chicken. "We shall sooner have the fowl by hatching it than by smashing it," he remarked. He knew that eventually representatives of the southern states would again be sitting in Congress, and he wished to lay the groundwork for a strong Republican party in the section. Yet he realized that Congress had no intention of seating representatives from the "10 percent" states at once.

The Radicals in Congress disliked the Ten Percent Plan, partly because of its moderation and partly because it enabled Lincoln to determine Union policy toward the recaptured regions. In July 1864 they passed the **Wade-Davis Bill**, which provided for constitutional conventions only after a majority of the others in a southern state had taken a loyalty oath. Confederate officials and anyone who had "voluntarily borne arms against the United States" were barred from voting in the election or serving at the convention. Besides prohibiting slavery, the new state constitutions would have to repudiate Confederate debts. Lincoln disposed of the Wade-Davis Bill with a pocket veto and that's where matters stood when Andrew Johnson became president following the assassination.

Lincoln had picked Johnson for a running mate in 1864 because he was a border-state Unionist Democrat and something of a hero as a result of his courageous service as military governor of Tennessee. His political strength came from the poor whites and yeomen farmers of eastern Tennessee, and he was fond of extolling the common man and attacking "stuck-up aristocrats."

Johnson was a Democrat, but because of his record and his reassuring penchant for excoriating southern aristocrats, the Republicans in Congress were ready to cooperate with him. "Johnson, we have faith in you," said Senator Ben Wade, author of the Wade-Davis Bill, the day after Lincoln's death. "By the gods, there will be no trouble now in running the government!"

Johnson's reply, "Treason must be made infamous," delighted the Radicals, but the president proved temperamentally unable to work with them. Like Randolph of Roanoke, his antithesis intellectually and socially, opposition was his specialty; he soon alienated every powerful Republican in Washington.

Radical Republicans listened to Johnson's diatribes against secessionists and the great planters and assumed that he was anti-southern. Nothing could have been further from the truth. He had great respect for states' rights and he shared most of his poor white Tennessee constituents' contempt of blacks. "Damn the negroes, I am fighting these traitorous aristocrats, their masters," he told a friend during the war. "I wish to God," he said on another occasion, "every head of a family in the United States had one slave to take the drudgery and menial service off his family."

The new president did not want to injure or humiliate all white Southerners. He issued an amnesty proclamation only slightly more rigorous than Lincoln's. It assumed, correctly

---

[1] By approving the separation of the western counties that had refused to secede, this government had provided a legal pretext for the creation of West Virginia in 1863.

enough, that with the war over most southern voters would freely take the loyalty oath; thus it contained no 10 percent clause. More classes of Confederates, including those who owned taxable property in excess of $20,000, were excluded from the general pardon. By the time Congress convened in December 1865, all the southern states had organized governments, ratified the **Thirteenth Amendment** abolishing slavery, and elected senators and representatives. Johnson promptly recommended these new governments to the attention of Congress.

Republican Radicals

Peace found the Republicans in Congress no more united than they had been during the war. A small group of "ultra" Radicals were demanding immediate and absolute civil and political equality for blacks; they should be given, for example, the vote, a plot of land, and access to a decent education. Senator Sumner led this faction. A second group of Radicals, headed by Thaddeus Stevens in the House and Ben Wade in the Senate, agreed with the ultras' objectives but were prepared to accept half a loaf if necessary to win the support of less radical colleagues.

Nearly all Radicals distinguished between the "natural" God-given rights described in the Declaration of Independence, and social equality. The moderate Republicans wanted to protect the former slaves from exploitation and guarantee their basic rights but were unprepared to push for full political equality. A handful of Republicans sided with the Democrats in support of Johnson's approach, but all the rest insisted at least on the minimal demands of the moderates. Thus Johnsonian Reconstruction was doomed.

Johnson's proposal had no chance in Congress for reasons having little to do with black rights. The Thirteenth Amendment had the effect of increasing the representation of the southern states in Congress because it made the Three-fifths Compromise meaningless (see Chapter 5). Henceforth those who had been slaves would be counted as whole persons in apportioning seats in the House of Representatives. If Congress seated the Southerners, the balance of power might swing to the Democrats. To expect the Republicans to surrender power in such a fashion was unrealistic. Former Copperheads gushing with extravagant praise for Johnson put them instantly on guard.

Congress Rejects Johnsonian Reconstruction

The Republicans in Congress rejected Johnsonian Reconstruction. Quickly they created a joint committee on Reconstruction, headed by Senator William P. Fessenden of Maine, a moderate, to study the question of readmitting the southern states.

The committee held public hearings that produced much evidence of the mistreatment of blacks. Colonel George A. Custer, stationed in Texas, testified: "It is of weekly, if not of daily occurrence that Freedmen are murdered." The nurse Clara Barton told a gruesome tale about a pregnant woman who had been brutally whipped. Others described the intimidation of blacks by poor whites. The hearings strengthened the Radicals, who had been claiming all along that the South was perpetuating slavery under another name.

President Johnson's attitude speeded the swing toward the Radical position. While the hearings were in progress, Congress passed a bill expanding and extending the **Freedmen's Bureau**, which had been established in March 1865 to care for refugees. The bureau, a branch of the war department, was already exercising considerable coercive and supervisory power in the South. Now Congress sought to add to its authority in order to protect the black population. Although the bill had wide support, Johnson vetoed it, arguing that it was an unconstitutional extension of military authority in peacetime. Congress then passed a Civil Rights Act that, besides declaring specifically that blacks were citizens of the United States, denied the states the power to restrict their rights to testify in court, to make contracts for their labor, and to hold property. In other words, it put teeth in the Thirteenth Amendment.

Once again the president refused to go along, although his veto was sure to drive more moderates into the arms of the Radicals. On April 9, 1866, Congress repassed the Civil Rights Act by a two-thirds majority, the first time in American history that a major piece of legislation became law over the veto of a president. This event marked a revolution in the history of Reconstruction. Thereafter Congress, not President Johnson, had the upper hand.

In the clash between the president and Congress, Johnson was his own worst enemy. His language was often intemperate, his handling of opponents inept, his analysis of southern conditions incorrect. He had assumed that the small southern farmers who made up the majority in the Confederacy shared his prejudices against the planter class. They did not, as their choices in the postwar elections demonstrated.

*•◦•⎯*Read the **Document**

Southern Skepticism of the Freedmen's Bureau at **myhistorylab.com**

The president also misread northern opinion. He believed that Congress had no right to pass laws affecting the South before southern representatives had been readmitted to Congress. However, in the light of the refusal of most southern whites to grant any real power or responsibility to the freedmen (an attitude that Johnson did not condemn), the public would not accept this point of view. Johnson placed his own judgment over that of the overwhelming majority of northern voters, and this was a great error, morally and tactically. By encouraging white Southerners to resist efforts to improve the lot of blacks, Johnson played into the hands of the Radicals.

The Radicals encountered grave problems in fighting for their program. Northerners might object to the Black Codes and to seating "rebels" in Congress, but few believed in racial equality. Between 1865 and 1868, Wisconsin, Minnesota, Connecticut, Nebraska, New Jersey, Ohio, Michigan, and Pennsylvania all rejected bills granting blacks the vote.

The Radicals were in effect demanding not merely equal rights for freedmen but extra rights; not merely the vote but special protection of that right against the pressure that southern whites would surely apply to undermine it. This idea flew in the face of conventional American beliefs in equality before the law and individual self-reliance. Such protection would involve interference by the federal government in local affairs, a concept at variance with American practice. Events were to show that the Radicals were correct—that what amounted to a political revolution in state–federal relations was essential if blacks were to achieve real equality. But in the climate of that day their proposals encountered bitter resistance, and not only from white Southerners.

Thus, while the Radicals sought partisan advantage in their battle with Johnson and sometimes played on war-bred passions in achieving their ends, they were taking large political risks in defense of genuinely held principles.

The Fourteenth Amendment

In June 1866 Congress submitted to the states a new amendment to the Constitution. The **Fourteenth Amendment** was, in the context of the times, a truly radical measure. Never before had newly freed slaves been granted significant political rights. For example, in the British Caribbean sugar islands, where slavery had been abolished in the 1830s, stiff property qualifications and poll taxes kept freedmen from voting. The Fourteenth Amendment was also a milestone along the road to the centralization of political power in the United States because it reduced the power of all the states. In this sense it confirmed the great change wrought by the Civil War: the growth of a more complex, more closely integrated social and economic structure requiring closer national supervision. Few people understood this aspect of the amendment at the time.

●●●—⌐Read the **Document**

13th, 14th, and 15th Amendments at **myhistorylab.com**

First the amendment supplied a broad definition of American citizenship: "All persons born or naturalized in the United States, and subject to the jurisdiction thereof, are citizens of the United States and of the State wherein they reside." Obviously this included blacks. Then it struck at discriminatory legislation like the Black Codes: "No State shall make or enforce any law which shall abridge the privileges or immunities of citizens of the United States; nor shall any State deprive any person of life, liberty, or property, without due process of law." The next section attempted to force the southern states to permit blacks to vote. If a state denied the vote to any class of its adult male citizens, its representation was to be reduced proportionately. Under another clause, former federal officials who had served the Confederacy were barred from holding either state or federal office unless specifically pardoned by a two-thirds vote of Congress. Finally, the Confederate debt was repudiated.

While the amendment did not specifically outlaw segregation or prevent a state from disenfranchising blacks, the southern states would have none of it. Without them the necessary three-fourths majority of the states could not be obtained.

President Johnson vowed to make the choice between the Fourteenth Amendment and his own policy the main issue of the 1866 congressional elections. He embarked on "a swing around the circle" to rally the public to his cause. He failed dismally. Northern women objected to the implication in the amendment that black men were more fitted to vote than white women, but a large majority of northern voters was determined that African Americans must have at least formal legal equality. The Republicans won better than two-thirds of the seats in both houses, together with control of all the northern state governments. Johnson emerged from the campaign discredited, the Radicals stronger and determined to have their way. The southern states, Congressman James A. Garfield of Ohio said in February 1867, have "flung back into our teeth the magnanimous offer of a generous nation. It is now our turn to act."

The Reconstruction Acts

Had the southern states been willing to accept the Fourteenth Amendment, coercive measures might have been avoided. Their recalcitrance and continuing indications that local authorities were persecuting blacks finally led to the passage, on March 2, 1867, of the First Reconstruction Act. This law divided the former Confederacy—exclusive of Tennessee, which had ratified the Fourteenth Amendment—into five military districts, each controlled by a major general. It gave these officers almost dictatorial power to protect the civil rights of "all persons," maintain order, and supervise the administration of justice. To rid themselves of military rule, the former states were required to adopt new state constitutions guaranteeing blacks the right to vote and disenfranchising broad classes of ex-Confederates. If the new constitutions proved satisfactory to Congress, and if the new governments ratified the Fourteenth Amendment, their representatives would be admitted to Congress and military rule ended. Johnson's veto of the act was easily overridden.

Although drastic, the Reconstruction Act was so vague that it proved unworkable. Military control was easily established. But in deference to moderate Republican views, the law had not spelled out the process by which the new constitutions were to be drawn up. Southern whites preferred the status quo, even under army control, to enfranchising blacks and retiring their own respected leaders. They made no effort to follow the steps laid down in the law. Congress therefore passed a second act, requiring the military authorities to register voters and supervise the election of delegates to constitutional conventions. A third act further clarified procedures.

See the Map
Reconstruction at **myhistorylab.com**

Still white Southerners resisted. The laws required that the constitutions be approved by a majority of the registered voters. Simply by staying away from the polls, whites prevented ratification in state after state. At last, in March 1868, a full year after the First Reconstruction Act, Congress changed the rules again. The constitutions were to be ratified by a majority of the voters. In June 1868 Arkansas, having fulfilled the requirements, was readmitted to the Union, and by July a sufficient number of states had ratified the Fourteenth Amendment to make it part of the Constitution. But it was not until July 1870 that the last southern state, Georgia, qualified to the satisfaction of Congress.

Congress Supreme

To carry out this program in the face of determined southern resistance required a degree of single-mindedness over a long period seldom demonstrated by an American legislature. The persistence resulted in part from the suffering and frustrations of the war years. The refusal of the South to accept the spirit of even the mild reconstruction designed by Johnson goaded the North to ever more overbearing efforts to bring the ex-Confederates to heel. President Johnson's stubbornness also influenced the Republicans. They became obsessed with the need to defeat him. The unsettled times and the large Republican majorities, always threatened by the possibility of a Democratic resurgence if "unreconstructed" southern congressmen were readmitted, sustained their determination.

These considerations led Republicans to attempt a kind of grand revision of the federal government, one that almost destroyed the balance between judicial, executive, and legislative power established in 1789. A series of measures passed between 1866 and 1868 increased the authority of Congress over the army, over the process of amending the Constitution, and over Cabinet members and lesser appointive officers. Even the Supreme Court was affected. Its size was reduced and its jurisdiction over civil rights cases limited. Finally, in a showdown caused by emotion more than by practical considerations, the Republicans attempted to remove President Johnson from office.

The chief issue was the Tenure of Office Act of 1867, which prohibited the president from removing officials who had been appointed with the consent of the Senate without first obtaining Senate approval. In February 1868 Johnson "violated" this act by dismissing Secretary of War Edwin M. Stanton, who had been openly in sympathy with the Radicals for some time. The House, acting under the procedure set up in the Constitution for removing the president, promptly impeached him before the bar of the Senate, Chief Justice Salmon P. Chase presiding.

In the trial, Johnson's lawyers easily established that he had removed Stanton only in an effort to prove the Tenure of Office Act unconstitutional. They demonstrated that the act did not protect Stanton to begin with, since it gave Cabinet members tenure "during the term of the President by whom they may have been appointed," and Stanton had been appointed in 1862, during Lincoln's first term!

Nevertheless the Radicals pressed the charges (eleven separate articles) relentlessly. Tremendous pressure was applied to the handful of Republican senators who were unwilling to disregard the evidence.

Seven of them resisted to the end, and the Senate failed by a single vote to convict Johnson. This was probably fortunate. The trial weakened the presidency, but if Johnson had been forced from office on such flimsy grounds, the independence of the executive might have been permanently undermined. Then the legislative branch would have become supreme.

The Fifteenth Amendment

The failure of the impeachment did not affect the course of Reconstruction. The president was acquitted on May 16, 1868. A few days later, the Republican National Convention nominated General Ulysses S. Grant for the presidency. At the Democratic convention Johnson had considerable support, but the delegates nominated Horatio Seymour, a former governor of New York. In November Grant won an easy victory in the Electoral College, 214 to 80, but the popular vote was close: 3 million to 2.7 million. Although he would probably have carried the Electoral College in any case, Grant's margin in the popular vote was supplied by southern blacks enfranchised under the Reconstruction acts, about 450,000 of whom supported him. A majority of white voters probably preferred Seymour. Since many citizens undoubtedly voted Republican because of personal admiration for General Grant, the election statistics suggest that a substantial white majority opposed the policies of the Radicals.

The Reconstruction acts and the ratification of the Fourteenth Amendment achieved the purpose of enabling black Southerners to vote. The Radicals, however, were

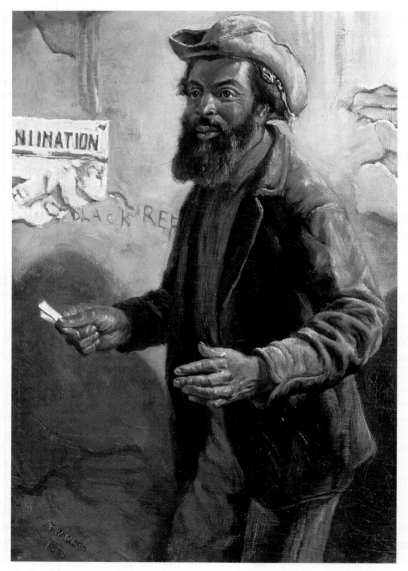

Thomas Waterman Wood, a Northerner, painted this hopeful interpretation of Reconstruction, *His First Vote* (1868).

not satisfied; despite the unpopularity of the idea in the North, they wished to guarantee the right of blacks to vote in every state. Another amendment seemed the only way to accomplish this objective, but passage of such an amendment appeared impossible. The Republican platform in the 1868 election had smugly distinguished between blacks voting in the South.

However, after the election had demonstrated how important the black vote could be, Republican strategy shifted. Grant had carried Indiana by fewer than 10,000 votes and lost New York by a similar number. If blacks in these and other closely divided states had voted, Republican strength would have been greatly enhanced.

Suddenly Congress blossomed with suffrage amendments. After considerable bickering over details, the **Fifteenth Amendment** was sent to the states for ratification in February 1869. It forbade all the states to deny the vote to anyone "on account of race, color, or previous condition of servitude." Once again nothing was said about denial of the vote on the basis of sex, which caused feminists, such as Elizabeth Cady Stanton, to be even more outraged than they had been by the Fourteenth Amendment.

Most southern states, still under federal pressure, ratified the amendment swiftly. The same was true in most of New England and in some western states. Bitter battles were waged in Connecticut, New York, Pennsylvania, and the states immediately north of the Ohio River, but by March 1870 most of them had ratified the amendment and it became part of the Constitution.

When the Fifteenth Amendment went into effect, President Grant called it "the greatest civil change and . . . the most important event that has occurred since the nation came to life." The American Anti-Slavery Society formally dissolved itself, its work apparently completed. "The Fifteenth Amendment confers upon the African race the care of its own destiny," Radical Congressman James A. Garfield wrote proudly after the amendment was ratified.

"Black Republican" Reconstruction: Scalawags and Carpetbaggers

The Radicals had at last succeeded in imposing their will on the South. Throughout the region former slaves had real political influence; they voted, held office, and exercised the "privileges" and enjoyed the "immunities" guaranteed them by the Fourteenth Amendment. Nearly all voted Republican.

The spectacle of blacks not five years removed from slavery in positions of power and responsibility attracted much attention. But the real rulers of the "black Republican" governments were white: the **scalawags**—Southerners willing to cooperate with the Republicans because they accepted the results of the war and wished to advance their own interests—and the **carpetbaggers**—Northerners who went to the South as idealists to help the freed slaves as employees of the federal government, or more commonly as settlers hoping to improve themselves.

Although scalawags were by far the more numerous, the carpetbaggers were a particularly varied lot. Most had mixed motives for coming south and personal gain was certainly among them. But so were opposition to slavery and the belief that blacks deserved to be treated decently and given a chance to get ahead in the world.

Many northern blacks became carpetbaggers: former Union soldiers, missionaries from northern black churches, and also teachers, lawyers, and other members of the small northern black professional class. Many of these became officeholders, but like southern black politicians their influence was limited.

That blacks should fail to dominate southern governments is certainly understandable. They lacked experience in politics and were mostly poor and uneducated. They were nearly everywhere a minority. Those blacks who held office during Reconstruction tended to be better educated and more prosperous than most southern blacks.

In South Carolina and elsewhere, blacks proved in the main to be able and conscientious public servants. Even at the local level, where the quality of officials was usually poor, there was little difference in the degree of competence displayed by white and black officeholders. In power, the blacks were not vindictive; by and large they did not seek to restrict the rights of ex-Confederates.

Not all black legislators and administrators were paragons of virtue. In South Carolina, despite their control of the legislature, they broke up into factions repeatedly and failed to press for laws that would improve the lot of poor black farm workers. Waste and corruption were common during Reconstruction governments. Half the budget of Louisiana in some years went for salaries and "mileage" for representatives and their staffs. A South Carolina legislator was voted an additional $1,000 in salary after he lost that sum betting on a horse race.

However, the corruption must be seen in perspective. The big thieves were nearly always white; blacks got mostly crumbs. Furthermore, graft and callous disregard of the public interest characterized government in every section and at every level during the decade after Appomattox. Big-city bosses in the North embezzled sums that dwarfed the most brazen southern frauds. The New York City Tweed Ring probably made off with more money than all the southern thieves, black and white, combined. While the

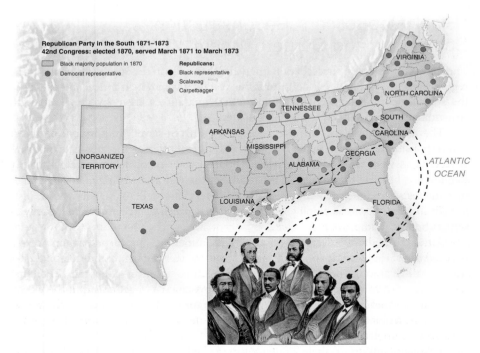

Republicans Win in Deep South The six black members of the House of Representatives in 1871 are from left to right: Benjamin Turner, Robert De Large, Josiah Wells, Jefferson Long, Joseph Rainey, Robert Brown Elliott. Each is linked to his district; the member in the blue coat—center—is not connected to a "black" dot. A special Republican primary replaced him with a scalawag.

evidence does not justify the southern corruption, it suggests that the unique features of Reconstruction politics—black suffrage, military supervision, and carpetbagger and scalawag influence—do not explain it.

In fact, the Radical southern governments accomplished a great deal. They spent money freely but not entirely wastefully. Tax rates zoomed, but the money financed the repair and expansion of the South's dilapidated railroad network, rebuilt crumbling levees, and expanded social services. Before the Civil War, southern planters possessed a disproportionate share of political as well as economic power, and they spent relatively little public money on education and public services of all kinds.

During Reconstruction an enormous gap had to be filled, and it took money to fill it. The Freedmen's Bureau made a major contribution. Northern religious and philanthropic organizations also did important work. Eventually, however, the state governments established and supported hospitals, asylums, and systems of free public education that, while segregated, greatly benefited everyone, whites as well as blacks. Much state money was also spent on economic development: land reclamation, repairing and expanding the war-ravaged railroads, maintaining levees.

> **Watch the Video**
> *The Schools that the Civil War & Reconstruction created* at **myhistorylab.com**

The Ravaged Land

The South's grave economic problems complicated the rebuilding of its political system. The section had never been as prosperous as the North, and wartime destruction left it desperately poor by any standard. In the long run the abolition of slavery released immeasurable quantities of human energy previously stifled, but the immediate effect was to create confusion. Freedom to move without a pass, to "see the world," was one of the former slaves' most cherished benefits of emancipation. Understandably, many at first equated legal freedom with freedom from having to earn a living, a tendency reinforced for a time by the willingness of the Freedmen's Bureau to provide rations and other forms of relief in war-devastated areas. Most, however, soon accepted the fact that they must earn a living; a small plot of land of their own ("40 acres and a mule") would complete their independence.

This objective was forcefully supported by the relentless Congressman Thaddeus Stevens, whose hatred of the planter class was pathological. "The property of the chief rebels should be seized," he stated. If the lands of the richest "70,000 proud, bloated and defiant rebels" were confiscated, the federal government would obtain 394 million acres. Every adult male ex-slave could easily be supplied with 40 acres. The beauty of his scheme, Stevens insisted, was that "nine-tenths of the [southern] people would remain untouched." Dispossessing the great planters would make the South "a safe republic," its lands cultivated by "the free labor of intelligent citizens." If the plan drove the planters into exile, "all the better."

Although Stevens's figures were faulty, many Radicals agreed with him. "We must see that the freedmen are established on the soil," Senator Sumner declared. "The great plantations, which have been so many nurseries of the rebellion, must be broken up, and the freedmen must have the pieces." Stevens, Sumner, and others who wanted to give land to the freedmen weakened their case by associating it with the idea of punishing the former rebels; the average American had too much respect for property rights to support a policy of confiscation.

The former slaves had either to agree to work for their former owners or strike out on their own. White planters, influenced by the precipitous decline of sugar production in Jamaica and other Caribbean islands that had followed the abolition of slavery there, expected freed blacks to be incapable of self-directed effort. If allowed to become independent farmers, they would either starve to death or descend into barbarism. Of course the blacks did neither. True, the output of cotton and other southern staples declined precipitously after slavery was abolished. Observers soon came to the conclusion that a free black produced much less than a slave had produced. "You can't get only about two-thirds as much out of 'em now as you could when they were slaves," an Arkansas planter complained.

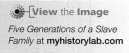

View the Image

Five Generations of a Slave Family at **myhistorylab.com**

However, the decline in productivity was not caused by the inability of free blacks to work independently. They simply chose no longer to work like slaves. They let their children play instead of forcing them into the fields. Mothers devoted more time to childcare and housework, less to farm labor. Elderly blacks worked less.

Noting these changes, white critics spoke scornfully of black laziness and shiftlessness. "You cannot make the negro work without physical compulsion," was the common view. Even General Oliver O. Howard, head of the Freedmen's Bureau, used the phrase "wholesome compulsion" in describing the policy of forcing blacks to sign exploitive labor contracts. Moreover, studies show that emancipated blacks earned almost 30 percent more than the value of the subsistence provided by their former masters.

Sharecropping and the Crop-Lien System

Before the passage of the Reconstruction acts, plantation owners tried to farm their land with gang labor, the same system as before, only now paying wages to the former slaves. But blacks did not like working for wages because it kept them under the direction of whites and thus reminded them of slavery. They wanted to be independent, to manage not merely their free time but their entire lives for themselves.

Quite swiftly, a new agricultural system known as **sharecropping** emerged. Instead of cultivating the land by gang labor as in antebellum times, planters broke up their estates into small units and established on each a black family. The

Read the Document

A Sharecrop Contract at **myhistorylab.com**

planter provided housing, agricultural implements, draft animals, seed, and other supplies, and the family provided labor. The crop was divided between them, usually on a fifty-fifty basis. If the landlord supplied only land and housing, the laborer got a larger share. This was called share tenancy.

Sharecropping gave blacks the day-to-day control of their lives that they craved and the hope of earning enough to buy a small farm. Many former slaves succeeded, as evidenced by the accounts narrated at the outset of this chapter. Oprah Winfrey's great-great-grandfather bought several plots of land and eventually moved a schoolhouse to his property so that black children in Sanford, Mississippi, could get an education. But not all managed to climb the first rungs into the middle class. As late as 1880 blacks owned less than 10 percent of the agricultural land in the South, although they made up more than half of the region's farm population.

Many white farmers in the South were also trapped by the sharecropping system and by white efforts to keep blacks in a subordinate position. New fencing laws kept them from grazing livestock on undeveloped land, a practice common before the Civil War. But the main cause of southern rural poverty for whites as well as for blacks was the lack of enough capital to finance the sharecropping system. Like their colonial ancestors, the landowners had to borrow against October's harvest to pay for April's seed. Thus the **crop-lien system** developed.

Under the crop-lien system, both landowner and sharecropper depended on credit supplied by local bankers, merchants, and storekeepers for everything from seed, tools, and fertilizer to overalls, coffee, and salt. Crossroads stores proliferated, and a new class of small merchants appeared. The prices of goods sold on credit were high, adding to the burden borne by the rural population. The small southern merchants were almost equally victimized by the system, for they also lacked capital, bought goods on credit, and had to pay high interest rates.

Seen in broad perspective, the situation is not difficult to understand. The South, drained of every resource by the war, was competing for funds with the North and West, both vigorous and expanding and therefore voracious consumers of capital. Reconstruction, in the literal sense of the word, was accomplished chiefly at the expense of the standard of living of the producing classes. The crop-lien system and the small

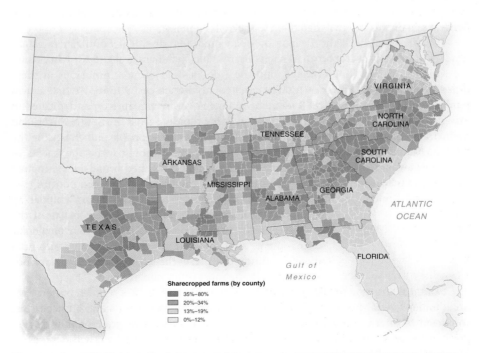

Sharecropping, 1880 Sharecropping became especially common in areas outside of the cotton belt—eastern Texas, upland Alabama, and North Carolina.

storekeeper were only agents of an economic process dictated by national, perhaps even worldwide, conditions.

Compared with the rest of the country, progress was slow. Just before the Civil War cotton harvests averaged about 4 million bales. During the conflict, output fell to about half a million, and the former Confederate states did not enjoy a 4-million-bale year again until 1870. In contrast, national wheat production in 1859 was 175 million bushels and in 1878, 449 million. About 7,000 miles of railroad were built in the South between 1865 and 1879; in the rest of the nation nearly 45,000 miles of track were laid.

But in the late 1870s, cotton production revived. It soon regained, and thereafter long retained, its title as "king" of the southern economy. This was true in large measure because of the crop-lien system.

The White Backlash

Radical southern governments could sustain themselves only as long as they had the support of a significant proportion of the white population, for except in South Carolina and Louisiana, the blacks were not numerous enough to win elections alone. The key to survival lay in the hands of the wealthy merchants and planters, mostly former Whigs. People of this sort had nothing to fear from black economic competition. Taking a broad view, they could see that improving the lot of the former slaves would benefit all classes.

Southern white Republicans used the Union League of America, a patriotic club founded during the war, to control the black vote. Employing secret rituals, exotic symbols, and other paraphernalia calculated to impress unsophisticated people, they enrolled the freedmen in droves and marched them to the polls en masse.

Powerless to check the League by open methods, dissident Southerners established a number of secret terrorist societies, bearing such names as the **Ku Klux Klan**, the Knights of the White Camelia, and the Pale Faces. The most notorious of these organizations was the Klan, which originated in Tennessee in 1866. At first it was purely a social club, but by 1868 it had been taken over by vigilante types dedicated to driving blacks out of politics, and it was spreading rapidly across the South. Sheet-clad nightriders roamed the countryside, frightening the impressionable and chastising the defiant. Klansmen, using a weird mumbo jumbo and claiming to be the ghosts of Confederate soldiers, spread horrendous rumors and published broadsides designed to persuade the freedmen that it was unhealthy for them to participate in politics.

When intimidation failed, the Klansmen resorted to force. After being whipped by one group in Tennessee, a recently elected justice of the peace reported, "They said they had nothing particular against me . . . but they did not intend any nigger to hold office." In hundreds of cases the KKK murdered their opponents, often in the most gruesome manner.

●●●Read the Document

Accounts from Victims of the Ku Klux Klan at **myhistorylab.com**

Congress struck at the Klan with three **Force Acts** (1870–1871), which placed elections under federal jurisdiction and imposed fines and prison sentences on persons convicted of interfering with any citizen's exercise of the franchise. Troops were dispatched to areas where the Klan was strong, and by 1872 the federal authorities had arrested enough Klansmen to break up the organization.

Nevertheless the Klan contributed substantially to the destruction of Radical regimes in the South. Its depredations weakened the will of white Republicans (few of whom really believed in racial equality), and it intimidated many blacks. The fact that the army had to be called in to suppress it was a glaring illustration of the weakness of the Reconstruction governments.

Gradually it became respectable to intimidate black voters. Beginning in Mississippi in 1874, terrorism spread through the South. Instead of hiding behind masks and operating in the dark, these terrorists donned red shirts, organized into military companies, and paraded openly. Mississippi redshirts seized militant blacks and whipped them publicly. Killings were frequent. When blacks dared to fight back, heavily armed whites put them to rout. In other states similar results followed.

Before long the blacks learned to stay home on election day. One by one, "Conservative" parties—Democratic in national affairs—took over southern state governments. Intimidation was only a partial explanation of this development. The increasing solidarity of whites, northern and southern, was equally significant.

The North had subjected the South to control from Washington while preserving state sovereignty in the North itself. In the long run this discrimination proved unworkable. Many Northerners had supported the Radical policy only out of irritation with President Johnson. After his retirement their enthusiasm waned. The war was fading into the past and with it the worst of the anger it had generated.

Northern voters could still be stirred by references to the sacrifices Republicans had made to save the Union and by reminders that the Democratic party was the organization of rebels, Copperheads, and the Ku Klux Klan. "If the Devil himself were at the helm of the ship of state," wrote the novelist Lydia Maria Child in 1872, "my conscience would not allow me to aid in removing him to make room for the Democratic party." Yet emotional appeals could not convince Northerners that it was still necessary to maintain a large army in the South. In 1869 the occupying forces were down to 11,000 men. After Klan disruption and intimidation had made a farce of the 1874 elections in Mississippi, Governor Ames appealed to Washington for help. President Grant's attorney general, Edwards Pierrepont, refused to act. "The whole public are tired out with these autumnal outbreaks in the South," he told Ames. "Preserve the peace by the forces of your own state."

Nationalism was reasserting itself. Had not Washington and Jefferson been Virginians? Was not Andrew Jackson Carolina-born? Since most Northerners had little real love or respect for African Americans, their interest in racial equality flagged once they felt reasonably certain that blacks would not be re-enslaved if left to their own devices in the South.

Another, much subtler force was also at work. The prewar Republican party had stressed the common interest of workers, manufacturers, and farmers in a free and mobile society, a land of equal opportunity where all could work in harmony. Southern whites had insisted that laborers must be disciplined if large enterprises were to be run efficiently. By the 1870s, as large industrial enterprises developed in the northern states, the thinking of business leaders changed—the southern argument began to make sense to them, and they became more sympathetic to the southern demand for more control over "their" labor force.

An 1872 Grant campaign poster of "Our Three Great Presidents" at best got it about two-thirds right.

Grant as President

Other matters occupied the attention of northern voters. The expansion of industry and the rapid development of the West, stimulated by a new wave of railroad building, loomed more important to many than the fortunes of the former slaves. Beginning in 1873, when a stock market panic struck at public confidence, economic difficulties plagued the country and provoked another debate over the tariff.

Grant's most serious weakness as president was his failure to deal effectively with economic and social problems, what injured him and the Republicans most was his inability to cope with government corruption. The worst of the scandals did not become public knowledge during Grant's first term. However, in 1872 Republican reformers, alarmed by rumors of corruption and disappointed by Grant's failure to press for civil service reform, organized the Liberal Republican party and nominated Horace Greeley, the able but eccentric editor of the *New York Tribune*, for president.

The Liberal Republicans were mostly well-educated, socially prominent types—editors, college presidents, economists, along with a sprinkling of businessmen and politicians. Their liberalism was of the laissez-faire variety; they were for low tariffs and sound money, and against what they called "class legislation," meaning measures benefiting particular groups, whether labor unions or railroad companies or farm organizations. Nearly all had supported Reconstruction at the start, but by the early 1870s most were including southern blacks among the special interests that ought to be left to their own devices. Their observation of urban corruption and of unrestricted immigration led them to disparage universal suffrage, which, one of them said, "can only mean in plain English the government of ignorance and vice."

The Democrats also nominated Greeley in 1872, although he had devoted his political life to flailing the Democratic party in the *Tribune*. That surrender to expediency, together with Greeley's temperamental unsuitability for the presidency, made the campaign a fiasco for the reformers. Grant triumphed easily, with a popular majority of nearly 800,000.

Nevertheless, the defection of the Liberal Republicans hurt the Republican party in Congress. In the 1874 elections, no longer hampered as in the presidential contest by Greeley's notoriety and Grant's fame, the Democrats carried the House of Representatives. It was clear that the days of military rule in the South were ending. By the end of 1875 only three southern states—South Carolina, Florida, and Louisiana—were still under Republican control.

The Republican party in the South was "dead as a doornail," a reporter noted. He reflected the opinion of thousands when he added, "We ought to have a sound sensible republican . . . for the next President as a measure of safety; but only on the condition of absolute noninterference in Southern local affairs, for which there is no further need or excuse."

The Disputed Election of 1876

Against this background the presidential election of 1876 took place. Since corruption in government was the most widely discussed issue, the Republicans passed over their most attractive political personality, the dynamic James G. Blaine, Speaker of the House of Representatives, who had been connected with some chicanery involving railroad securities. Instead they nominated Governor Rutherford B. Hayes of Ohio, a former general with an untarnished reputation. The Democrats picked Governor Samuel J. Tilden of New York, a wealthy lawyer who had attracted national attention for his part in breaking up the Tweed Ring in New York City.

In November early returns indicated that Tilden had carried New York, New Jersey, Connecticut, Indiana, and all the southern states, including Louisiana, South Carolina, and Florida, where Republican regimes were still in control. This seemed to give him 203 electoral votes to Hayes's 165, and a popular plurality in the neighborhood of 250,000 out of more than 8 million votes cast. However, Republican leaders had anticipated the possible loss of Florida, South Carolina, and Louisiana and were prepared to use their control of the election machinery in those states to throw out sufficient Democratic ballots to alter the results if doing so would change the national outcome. Realizing that the electoral votes of those states were exactly enough to elect their man, they telegraphed their henchmen on the scene, ordering them to go into action. The local Republicans then invalidated Democratic ballots in wholesale lots and filed returns showing Hayes the winner. Naturally the local Democrats protested vigorously and filed their own returns.

The Constitution provides (Article II, Section 1) that presidential electors must meet in their respective states to vote and forward the results to "the Seat of the Government." There, it adds, "the President of the Senate shall, in the Presence of the Senate and House of Representatives, open all the Certificates, and the Votes shall then be counted." But who was to do the counting? The House was Democratic, the Senate Republican; neither would agree to allow the other to do the job. On January 29, 1877, scarcely a month before inauguration day, Congress created an electoral commission to decide the disputed cases. The commission consisted of five senators (three Republicans and two Democrats), five representatives (three Democrats and two Republicans), and five justices of the Supreme Court (two Democrats, two Republicans, and one "independent" judge, David Davis).

Since it was a foregone conclusion that the others would vote for their party no matter what the evidence, Davis would presumably swing the balance in the interest of fairness.

But before the commission met, the Illinois legislature elected Davis senator. He had to resign from the Court and the commission. Since independents were rare even on the Supreme Court, no neutral justice was available to replace him. The vacancy went to Associate Justice Joseph P. Bradley of New Jersey, a Republican.

Evidence presented before the commission revealed a disgraceful picture of corruption. On the one hand, in all three disputed states Democrats had clearly cast a majority of the votes; on the other, it was unquestionable that many blacks had been forcibly prevented from voting.

In truth, both sides were shamefully corrupt. The governor of Louisiana was reported

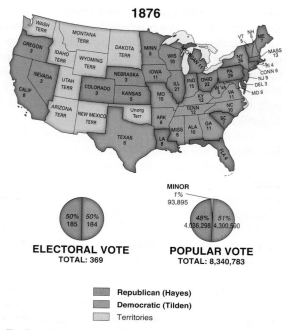

1876

ELECTORAL VOTE
TOTAL: 369

50% 185 | 50% 184

POPULAR VOTE
TOTAL: 8,340,783

MINOR
1%
93,895

48% 4,036,298 | 51% 4,300,590

- Republican (Hayes)
- Democratic (Tilden)
- Territories

The Republicans Gain the Presidency, the White South Loses the Union Army, 1877 By 1876 white Democrats had regained political control in much of the South, giving Tilden 203 electoral votes to the Republican Hayes's 185. But Republican election officials in South Carolina, Florida, and Louisiana invalidated thousands of Democratic votes, which seemingly gave the election to Tilden. In 1877 a congressional commission finalized a deal giving the presidency to Hayes, who would withdraw the Union army from the South.

willing to sell his state's electoral votes for $200,000. The Florida election board was supposed to have offered itself to Tilden for the same price. "That seems to be the standard figure," Tilden remarked ruefully.

The Democrats had some hopes that Justice Bradley would be sympathetic to their case, for he was known to be opposed to harsh Reconstruction policies. On the eve of the commission's decision in the Florida controversy, he was apparently ready to vote in favor of Tilden. But the Republicans subjected him to tremendous political pressure. When he read his opinion on February 8, it was for Hayes. Thus, by a vote of eight to seven, the commission awarded Florida's electoral votes to the Republicans.

Grant, a Republican and a Union war hero, won easily in 1868 and 1872 because ex-Confederates, many of whom had voted Democratic, were barred from the polls. By 1876, however, white Democrats had regained political control in much of the South, creating the electoral stalemate that led to the Compromise of 1877.

The rest of the proceedings was routine. The commission assigned all the disputed electoral votes (including one in Oregon where the Democratic governor had seized on a technicality to replace a single Republican elector with a Democrat) to Hayes.

Democratic institutions, shaken by the South's refusal to go along with the majority in 1860 and by the suppression of civil rights during the rebellion, and further weakened by military intervention and the intimidation of blacks in the South during Reconstruction, seemed now a farce. According to Tilden's campaign manager, angry Democrats in fifteen states, chiefly war veterans, were readying themselves to march on Washington to force the inauguration of Tilden. Tempers flared in Congress, where some spoke ominously of a filibuster that would prevent the recording of the electoral vote and leave the country, on March 4, with no president at all.

The Compromise of 1877

Forces for compromise had been at work behind the scenes in Washington for some time. Although northern Democrats threatened to fight to the last ditch, many southern Democrats were willing to accept Hayes if he would promise to remove the troops and allow the southern states to manage their internal affairs by themselves. Ex-Whig planters and merchants who had reluctantly abandoned the carpetbag governments and who sympathized with Republican economic policies hoped that by supporting Hayes they might contribute to the restoration of the two-party system that had been destroyed in the South during the 1850s.

Tradition has it that a great compromise between the sections was worked out during a dramatic meeting at the Wormley Hotel[2] in Washington on February 26. Actually the negotiations were drawn out and informal, and the Wormley conference was but one of many. With the tacit support of many Democrats, the electoral vote was counted by the president of the Senate on March 2, and Hayes was declared elected, 185 votes to 184.

Like all compromises, the **Compromise of 1877** was not entirely satisfactory; like most, it was not honored in every detail. Hayes recalled the last troops from South Carolina and Louisiana in April. He appointed a former Confederate general, David M. Key of Tennessee, postmaster general and delegated to him the congenial task of finding Southerners willing to serve their country as officials of a Republican administration. But the alliance of ex-Whigs and northern Republicans did not flourish; the South remained solidly Democratic. The major significance of the compromise, one of the great intersectional political accommodations of American history, was that it ended Reconstruction and inaugurated a new political order in the South. More than the Constitutional amendments and federal statutes, this new regime would shape the destinies of the four million freedmen.

For many former slaves, this future was to be bleak. Forgotten in the North, manipulated and then callously rejected by the South, rebuffed by the Supreme Court, voiceless in national affairs, they and their descendants were condemned in the interests of sectional harmony to lives of poverty, indignity, and little hope. But many other former slaves managed to thrive during the last third of the nineteenth century. Their hard work, discipline, and financial savvy elevated them into a property-owning middle class whose existence—more than Union armies—marked the end of slavery.

Watch the Video

The Promise and Failure of Reconstruction at **myhistorylab.com**

---

[2]Ironically, the hotel was owned by James Wormley, reputedly the wealthiest black person in Washington.

Table 15.1   Two Phases of Reconstruction: 1863–1877

Phase	Measure	Consequence
1. Presidential Reconstruction: Accommodation with white South		
	Lincoln's Ten-Percent Plan (1863)	Re-admits Southern states when 10 percent of 1860 voters profess loyalty to Union
	Lincoln vetoes Wade-Davis Bill (1864)	Retains 10 percent "easy-admission" policy
	Andrew Johnson pardons many Confederates and recommends admission of all former Confederate states	By 1866, all southern states are readmitted
	Southern states pass Black Codes (1864–1865) sharply restricting rights of former slaves	Outrages Republicans
2. Radical Reconstruction: Republicans gain power in Congress		
	Thirteenth Amendment (1865)	Ends Slavery
	Freedmen's Bureau (1865) established as branch of war department	Promotes education and economic opportunities for former slaves and destitute whites
	Congress passes Civil Rights Act over Johnson's veto (1866)	Republicans in Congress dominate federal government Washington
	Reconstruction Act of 1867	Divides South into five military districts, each under command of Union general
	Tenure of Office Act (1867)	Prohibits president from removing high officials
	Johnson impeached for firing Secretary of State Stanton	Johnson is tried but not removed from office

Table 15.1   Two Phases of Reconstruction: 1863–1877 (Continued)

Fourteenth Amendment (passed 1866, ratified 1868)	Requires that all citizens have "equal protection" of laws
Republican Grant elected president (1868)	Further increases Republican domination
Fifteenth Amendment (passed 1869, ratified 1870)	Prohibits voting restrictions on basis of race
Force Acts (1870-1871)	Federal control of elections in South

Milestones

1863	Lincoln announces "Ten Percent Plan" for Reconstruction	**1868**	Fourth Reconstruction Act requires a majority of Southern voters to ratify state constitutions
1865	Federal government sets up Freedmen's Bureau to ease transition from slavery to freedom		Senate acquits Johnson
	General Lee surrenders at Appomattox Court House		States ratify Fourteenth Amendment extending rights to freed slaves
	Abraham Lincoln is assassinated		Ulysses S. Grant is elected president
	Andrew Johnson becomes president		Ku Klux Klan uses intimidation and force throughout South
	Johnson issues amnesty proclamation	**1870**	States ratify Fifteenth Amendment granting black suffrage
	States ratify Thirteenth Amendment abolishing slavery	**1870–1871**	Force Act destroys Ku Klux Klan
1865–1866	Southern states enact Black Codes	**1872**	Liberal Republican party nominates Horace Greeley for president
1866	Civil Rights Act passes over Johnson's veto		Grant is reelected president
	Johnson campaigns for his Reconstruction policy	**1876**	Rutherford B. Hayes runs against Samuel Tilden in disputed presidential election
1867	First Reconstruction Act puts former Confederacy under military rule	**1877**	Electoral Commission awards disputed votes to Rutherford B. Hayes who becomes president
	Tenure of Office Act protects Senate appointees		Hayes agrees to Compromise of 1877 ending Reconstruction
1868	House of Representatives impeaches Johnson		

✓●┤Study and **Review** at **www.myhistorylab.com**

Review Questions

1. The introduction to this chapter—which cites the success of some randomly-chosen figures during Reconstruction—can be easily dismissed: Extraordinary people can prevail against any odds. What gains did most former slaves achieve during Reconstruction? Which federal policies and actions promoted their prospects?

2. What strategies did white Southerners use to control slaves after the Thirteenth Amendment had ended slavery?

3. Why did the Republicans in Congress disagree with Lincoln? With Andrew Johnson? In what sense did the Republican Congress come to "dominate" the political process?

4. What were the economic consequences of Reconstruction?

5. How did Reconstruction come to an end?

Key Terms

Black Codes *409*
carpetbaggers *419*
Compromise
    of 1877 *429*
crop-lien system *423*
Fifteenth
    Amendment *419*
Force Acts *424*

Fourteenth
    Amendment *415*
Freedmen's
    Bureau *414*
Ku Klux Klan *424*
Radical
    Republicans *412*
scalawags *419*

sharecropping *422*
Ten Percent Plan *411*
Thirteenth
    Amendment *413*
Wade-Davis Bill *412*

((•—[Hear the Audio Chapter 16 at myhistorylab.com

Do you live on land stolen from Indians?

IN 2010 THE CENSUS BUREAU REPORTED THAT BUFFALO COUNTY, South Dakota was the poorest in the nation, with well over half its residents below the poverty level. Buffalo County contains the Crow Creek Indian reservation. Six of the other ten poorest counties in the nation also consist of Indian reservations. Nationwide, nearly a quarter of all Indians live in poverty, twice the national average.

In 1988 Congress proposed to alleviate the plight of Native Americans with the Indian Gaming Regulatory Act. It allowed tribes to own casinos and other gambling operations. Within two decades, over 200 tribes had built 360 casinos and gaming establishments. By 2009, annual revenue from Indian casinos exceeded $25 billion, twice as much as the combined income of the National Football League (NFL) and Major League Baseball.

But little of the casino revenue has flowed to the poorest reservations. Foxwoods in Connecticut, the largest casino in the United States, generates about $1 billion annually, a windfall for the tiny Mashantucket Pequot tribe. But the Little Big Horn Casino, located in southeastern Montana near the battlefield where Custer lost his scalp, yielded a profit of only $100 a month during its first year of operation. Half of all reservation Indians live in Montana, Nevada, North and South Dakota, and Oklahoma, far from potential throngs of gamblers; those Indians remain mired in poverty.

Events that transformed the West after 1865 determined the plight of most Indians today. Ranchers and farmers acquired more Indian land. Railroad construction destabilized the habitat that sustained Indian life, especially the grazing lands of the buffalo, and brought still more settlers. The discovery of new deposits of gold, silver, and other valuable minerals caused miners and prospectors to swarm over and onto Indian lands. The federal government pushed Indians onto reservations, often on land unsuitable for cultivation, and sent troops to harass those who refused to abandon nomadic life. The new civilization that emerged in the West was increasingly controlled and organized by large-scale business enterprises.

By the turn of the twentieth century, the economic foundations of tribal life had been destroyed; relief, when it finally arrived many decades later, came in the form of slot machines. That so many Native Americans overcame the legacy of this past is testimony to their own initiative, and to traditional cultures characterized by both perseverance and adaptation.

The West after the Civil War

Although the image of the West as the land of great open spaces is accurate enough, after the Civil War the region contained several bustling cities. San Francisco, with a population approaching 250,000 in the late 1870s, had long outgrown its role as a rickety boomtown where the forty-niners bought supplies and squandered whatever wealth they had sifted from the streams of the Sierras. Though still an important warehouse and supply center, it had become the commercial and financial heart of the Pacific Coast and a center of light manufacturing, food processing, and machine shops. Denver, San Antonio, and Salt Lake City were far smaller, but growing rapidly and equally "urban."

Beginning in the mid-1850s a steady flow of Chinese migrated to the United States, most of them to the West Coast. About four or five thousand a year came, until the negotiation of the Burlingame Treaty of 1868, the purpose of which was to provide cheap labor for railroad construction crews. Thereafter the annual influx more than doubled, although before 1882 it exceeded 20,000 only twice. When the railroads were completed and the Chinese began to compete with native workers, a great cry of resentment went up on the west coast. Riots broke out in San Francisco in 1877. Chinese workers were called "groveling worms," "more slavish and brutish than the beasts that roam the fields." The California constitution of 1879 denied the right to vote to any "native of China" along with idiots, the insane, and persons convicted of "any infamous crime."

When Chinese immigration increased in 1882 to nearly 40,000, the protests reached such a peak that Congress passed the **Chinese Exclusion Act**, prohibiting all Chinese immigration for ten years. Later legislation extended the ban indefinitely.

Nevertheless, many parts of the West had as large a percentage of foreign-born residents as the populous eastern states—nearly a third of all Californians were foreign-born, as were more than 40 percent of Nevadans and more than half the residents of Idaho and Arizona. There were, of course, large populations of Spanish-speaking Americans of Mexican origin all over the Southwest. Chinese and Irish laborers were pouring into California by the thousands, and there were substantial numbers of Germans in Texas. Germans, Scandinavians, and other Europeans were also numerous on the High Plains east of the Rockies.

The Plains Indians

For 250 years the Indians had been driven back steadily, yet on the eve of the Civil War they still inhabited roughly half the United States. By the time of Hayes's inauguration, however, the Indians had been shattered as independent peoples, and in another decade the survivors were penned up on reservations, the government committed to a policy of extinguishing their way of life.

In 1860 the survivors of most of the eastern tribes were living peacefully in Indian Territory, what is now Oklahoma. In California the forty-niners had made short work of many of the local tribes. Elsewhere in the West—in the deserts of the Great Basin between the Sierras and the Rockies, in the mountains themselves, and on the semiarid, grass-covered plains between the Rockies and the edge of white civilization in eastern Kansas and Nebraska—nearly a quarter of a million Indians dominated the land.

In Charles Russell's *Trail of the Iron Horse* (1910) the steel rails stretch nearly to the sun, while wispy brushstrokes depict the Indians almost as ghosts.

By far the most important lived on the High Plains. From the Blackfoot of southwestern Canada and the Sioux of Minnesota and the Dakotas to the Cheyenne of Colorado and Wyoming and the Comanche of northern Texas, the plains tribes possessed a generally uniform culture. All lived by hunting the hulking American bison, or buffalo, which ranged over the plains by the millions.

Although they seemed the epitome of freedom, pride, and self-reliance, the Plains Indians had begun to fall under the sway of white power. They eagerly adopted the products of the more technically advanced culture—cloth, metal tools, weapons, and cheap decorations. However, the most important thing the whites gave them had nothing to do with technology: It was the horse.

Horses thrived on the plains and so did their masters. Mounted Indians could run down buffalo instead of stalking them on foot. They could move more easily over the country and fight more effectively too. They could acquire and transport more possessions and increase the size of their tepees, for horses could drag heavy loads.

The Indians also adopted modern weapons: the cavalry sword, which they particularly admired, and the rifle. Both added to their effectiveness as hunters and fighters. However, like the whites' liquor and diseases, horses and guns caused problems. The buffalo herds began to diminish, and warfare became bloodier and more frequent.

After the start of the gold rush the need to link the East with California meant that the tribes were pushed aside. Deliberately the government in Washington prepared the way. In 1851 Thomas Fitzpatrick—an experienced mountain man, a founder of the Rocky Mountain Fur Company, scout for the first large group of settlers to Oregon in 1841 and for American soldiers in California during the Mexican War, and now an Indian agent—summoned a great "council" of the tribes. About 10,000 Indians, representing nearly all the plains tribes, gathered that September at Horse Creek, thirty-seven miles east of Fort Laramie, in what is now Wyoming.

In the Fort Laramie Treaty of 1851, Fitzpatrick persuaded each tribe to accept definite limits to its hunting grounds. In return the Indians were promised gifts and annual payments. This policy, known as "concentration," was designed to cut down on intertribal warfare and—far more important—to enable the government to negotiate separately with each tribe. It was the classic strategy of divide and conquer.

Although it made a mockery of diplomacy to treat Indian tribes as though they were European powers, the United States maintained that each tribe was a sovereign nation, to be dealt with as an equal in solemn treaties. Both sides knew that this was not the case. When Indians agreed to meet in council, they were tacitly admitting defeat. They seldom drove hard bargains or broke off negotiations. Moreover, tribal chiefs had only limited power; young braves frequently refused to respect agreements made by their elders.

Indian Wars

The government showed little interest in honoring agreements with Indians. No sooner had the Kansas-Nebraska bill become law than the Kansas, Omaha, Pawnee, and Yankton Sioux tribes began to feel pressure for further concessions of territory. A gold rush into Colorado in 1859 sent thousands of greedy prospectors across the plains to drive the Cheyenne and Arapaho from land guaranteed them in 1851. By 1860 most of Kansas and Nebraska had been cleared. Thus it happened that in 1862, after federal troops had been pulled out of the West for service against the Confederacy, most of the Plains Indians rose up against the whites. For five years intermittent but bloody clashes kept the entire area in a state of alarm.

This was guerrilla warfare, with all its horror and treachery. In 1864 a party of Colorado militia under the command of Colonel J. M. Chivington fell on an unsuspecting Cheyenne community at Sand Creek and killed several hundred Indians. General Nelson A. Miles called this "Chivington massacre" the "foulest and most unjustifiable crime in the annals of America."

Robert Lindneux's *The Battle of Sand Creek*, 1864. Lindneux, born in 1871, did not witness what transpired at Sand Creek, Colorado. But although he used "battle" in the title of his painting, he depicted a massacre. "Kill and scalp all, big and little," Colonel J. M. Chivington, a minister in private life, told his men. The American flag (center right) was doubtless included as irony.

In turn the Indians slaughtered dozens of isolated white families, ambushed small parties, and fought many successful skirmishes against troops and militia. They achieved their most notable triumph in December 1866, when the Oglala Sioux, under their great chief Red Cloud, wiped out a party of eighty-two soldiers under Captain W. J. Fetterman. Red Cloud fought ruthlessly, but only when goaded by the construction of the Bozeman Trail, a road through the heart of the Sioux hunting grounds in southern Montana.[1]

●●●[Read the Document
Red Cloud's Speech at
myhistorylab.com

In 1867 the government tried a new strategy. The "concentration" policy had evidently not gone far enough. All the Plains Indians would be confined to two small reservations, one in the Black Hills of the Dakota Territory, the other in Oklahoma, and forced to become farmers. At two great conclaves held in 1867 and 1868 at Medicine Lodge Creek and Fort Laramie, the principal chiefs yielded to the government's demands and signed the 1868 Treaty of Fort Laramie.

Many Indians refused to abide by these agreements. With their whole way of life at stake, they raged across the plains like a prairie fire—and were almost as destructive.

That a relative handful of "savages," without central leadership, could hold off the cream of the army, battle-hardened in the Civil War, can be explained by the fact that the U.S. Army, usually with fewer than 20,000 soldiers, had to operate over a million square miles. Few Indian leaders were capable of organizing a campaign or following up an advantage. But the Indians made superb guerrillas. Every observer called them the best cavalry soldiers in the world. Armed with stubby, powerful bows capable of driving an arrow clear through a bull buffalo, they were a fair match for troops equipped with carbines and Colt revolvers.

If one concedes that no one could reverse the direction of history or stop the invasion of Indian lands, then some version of the "small reservation" policy would probably have been best for the Indians. Had they been guaranteed a reasonable amount of land and adequate subsidies and allowed to maintain their way of life, they might have accepted the situation and ceased to harass the whites.

Whatever chance that policy had was weakened by the government's poor administration of Indian affairs. In dealing with Indians, nineteenth-century Americans displayed a grave insensitivity. After 1849 the Department of the Interior supposedly had charge of tribal affairs. Most of its agents systematically cheated the Indians. "No branch of the national government is so spotted with fraud, so tainted with corruption . . . as this Indian Bureau," Congressman Garfield charged in 1869.

At about this time a Yale paleontologist, Othniel C. Marsh, who wished to dig for fossils on the Sioux reservation, asked Red Cloud for permission to enter his domain. The chief agreed on condition that Marsh, whom the Indians called Big Bone Chief, take back with him samples of the moldy flour and beef that government agents were supplying to his people. Appalled by what he saw on the reservation, Professor Marsh took the rotten supplies directly to President Grant and prepared a list of charges against the agents.

In 1874 gold was discovered in the Black Hills Indian reservation. By the next winter thousands of miners had invaded the reserved area. Already alarmed by the

---

[1]Fetterman had boasted that with eighty cavalrymen he could ride the entire length of the Bozeman Trail. When he tried, however, he blundered into an ambush.

Indian Wars, 1860–1890 The frequent battles, involving nearly all tribes, show that the Indians did not cede their lands: The lands were taken in battle.

approach of crews building the Northern Pacific Railroad, the Sioux once again went on the warpath. Joining with nontreaty tribes to the west, they concentrated in the region of the Bighorn River, in southern Montana Territory.

The summer of 1876 saw three columns of troops in the field against them. The commander of one column, General Alfred H. Terry, sent ahead a small detachment of the Seventh Cavalry under Colonel George A. Custer with orders to locate the Indians' camp and then block their escape route into the inaccessible Bighorn Mountains. Grossly underestimating the number of the Indians, Custer decided to attack directly with his tiny force of 264 men. At the Little Bighorn late in June he found himself surrounded by 2,500 Sioux under Rain-in-the-Face, Crazy Horse, and Sitting Bull. He and all his men died on the field.

Because it was so one-sided, "Custer's Last Stand" was not a typical battle, although it may be taken as symbolic of the Indian warfare of the period in the sense that it was characterized by bravery, foolhardiness, and a tragic waste of life. The battle greatly heartened the Indians, but it did not gain them their cause. That autumn, short of rations and hard-pressed by overwhelming numbers of soldiers, they surrendered and returned to the reservation.

The Destruction of Tribal Life

Thereafter, the fighting slackened. For this the building of transcontinental railroads and the destruction of the buffalo were chiefly responsible. Thousands of buffalo were butchered to feed the gangs of laborers engaged in building the Union Pacific Railroad. Thousands more fell before the guns of sportsmen. Buffalo hunting became a fad, and a brisk demand developed for buffalo rugs and mounted buffalo heads. Railroads made the Army a far more efficient force. Troops and supplies could be moved swiftly when trouble with the tribes erupted. The lines also contributed to the decimation of the buffalo by running excursion trains for hunters.

The discovery in 1871 of a way to make commercial use of buffalo hides completed the tragedy. In the next three years about 9 million head were killed; after another decade the animals were almost extinct. No more efficient way could have been found for destroying the Plains Indians. The disappearance of the bison left them starving and homeless.

By the 1880s, the advance of whites into the plains had become, in the words of one congressman, as irresistible "as that of Sherman's to the sea." Greed for land lay behind the pressure, but large numbers of disinterested people, including most of those who deplored the way the Indians had been treated in the past, believed that the only practical way to solve the "Indian problem" was to persuade the Indians to abandon their tribal culture and live on family farms. The "wild" Indian must be changed into a "civilized" member of "American" society.

To accomplish this goal Congress passed the **Dawes Severalty Act of 1887**. Tribal lands were to be split up into individual allotments. To keep speculators from wresting the allotments from the Indians while they were adjusting to their new way of life, the land could not be disposed of for twenty-five years. Funds were to be appropriated for educating and training the Indians, and those who accepted allotments—took up residence "separate from any tribe," and "adopted the habits of civilized life"— were to be granted U.S. citizenship.

●●●—[Read the **Document**

Secretary of the Interior's Report on Indian Affairs at **myhistorylab.com**

A mound of buffalo skulls. In 1870 an estimated 30 million buffalo roamed the plains; by 1900, there were fewer than 1,000. During an eight-month period between 1867 and 1868, William F. Cody (Buffalo Bill) killed 4,280 buffalo, which fed construction crews for the Union Pacific railroad. Tourists also took up buffalo hunting, often shooting them from trains. The depletion of the buffalo, which provided the Plains Indians with meat and hides, was a major source of conflict with whites.

The sponsors of the Severalty Act thought they were effecting a fine humanitarian reform. "We must throw some protection over [the Indian]," Senator Henry L. Dawes declared. "We must hold up his hand." But no one expected all the Indians to accept allotments at once, and for some years little pressure was put on any to do so.

The Dawes Act had disastrous results in the long run. It assumed that Indians could be transformed into small agricultural capitalists by an act of Congress. It shattered what was left of the Indians' culture without enabling them to adapt to white ways. Moreover, unscrupulous white men tricked many Indians into leasing their allotments for a pittance, and local authorities often taxed Indian lands at excessive rates. In 1934, the government returned to a policy of encouraging tribal ownership of Indian lands.

The story of U.S.–Indian relations in the nineteenth century concludes, predictably, with a sad coda. In 1890 the Teton Sioux, suffering from cold and hunger, took heart from the words of Wovoka, a prophet, who had said that the whites would disappear if the Sioux performed their "ghost dance" rituals. When the Ghost Dance movement spread, federal military authorities resolved to stamp it out. On December 14 they attempted to arrest Chief Sitting Bull, a legendary Sioux warrior. When he resisted, shots rang out and Sitting Bull was killed. His people left the reservation at Pine Ridge and fled into the Badlands. The soldiers pursued them and the Indians surrendered. As they were

Table 16.1 Key Federal Policies Affecting Indians

Policy	Year	Provisions	Consequences
Indian Removal Bill	1830	Indians surrender land east of Mississippi to settle in Oklahoma and elsewhere	Forcible removal of Indians from South
Treaty of Fort Laramie	1851	Indian tribes establish tribal boundaries over shared hunting grounds and ensure safe passage of westward-bound settlers through Indian territory	Discourages concerted action among Indian tribes; settlers encroach on Indian lands
Railroad land grants	1850–1871	Gives railroads lands to lay track throughout the West	Promotes settlement and further encroachment; hastens demise of buffalo
Treaty of Fort Laramie	1868	Concentrates Indians in reservations in the Dakotas and Oklahoma	Dissident Indians commence open warfare against U.S. government
Dawes Severalty Act	1887	Breaks Indian lands into small plots for Indian families or sale to whites	Weakens tribal authority; causes loss of Indian land
Indian Reorganization Act	1934	Rescinds Dawes	Increases tribal authority
Indian Gaming Regulatory Act	1988	Allows tribes to run federally regulated casinos and gambling operations	Generates huge revenue for a handful of eastern tribes, and little for the rest

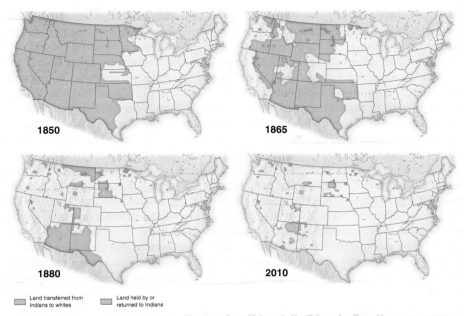

1850

1865

1880

2010

Land transferred from Indians to whites

Land held by or returned to Indians

Loss of Indian Lands, 1850–2010 This chapter describes the specific government policies, economic tendencies, and specific treaties that wrested land from the Indians. But the simplest explanation is that an aggressive, acquisitive, and militarily powerful people craved the West and they took it.

being disarmed, however, a scuffle broke out and the troops opened fire. Some 150 Sioux were killed, including many women and children. Thirty federal soldiers also died during the fighting at Wounded Knee.

The Lure of Gold and Silver in the West

The natural resources of the nation were exploited in these decades even more ruthlessly and thoughtlessly than were its human resources. From the mid-1850s to the mid-1870s thousands of gold-crazed prospectors fanned out through the Rockies, panning every stream and hacking furiously at every likely outcropping from the Fraser River country of British Columbia to Tucson in southern Arizona, from the eastern slopes of the Sierras to the Great Plains.

Gold and silver were scattered throughout the area, though usually too thinly to make mining profitable. Whenever anyone made a "strike," prospectors, the vast majority utterly without previous experience but driven by what a mining journal of the period called an "unhealthy desire" for sudden wealth, flocked to the site. For a few months the area teemed with activity. Then, usually, expectations faded in the light of reality: high prices, low yields, hardship, violence, and deception. A few found significant wealth, the rest only backbreaking labor and disappointment—that is, until tales of another strike sent them dashing feverishly across the land on another golden chase.

In June 1859 came the finds in Nevada, where the famous **Comstock Lode** yielded ores worth nearly $4,000 a ton. In 1861, while men in the settled areas were laying down their tools to take up arms, the miners were racing to the Idaho panhandle, hoping to become millionaires overnight. The next year the rush was to the Snake River valley, then in 1863 and 1864 to Montana. In 1874 to 1876 the Black Hills in the heart of the Sioux lands were inundated.

The sudden prosperity of the mining towns attracted every kind of shady character—according to one forty-niner "rascals from Oregon, pickpockets from New York, accomplished gentlemen from Europe, interlopers from Lima and Chile, Mexican thieves, gamblers from no particular spot, and assassins manufactured in Hell." Gambling dens, dance halls, saloons, and brothels mushroomed wherever precious metal was found.

Law enforcement was a constant problem. Storekeepers charged outrageous prices; claim holders "salted" worthless properties with nuggets in order to swindle gullible investors. Ostentation characterized the successful, mere swagger those who failed. During the administration of President Grant, Virginia City, Nevada, was at the peak of its vulgar prosperity, producing an average of $12 million a year in ore. Built on the richness of the Comstock Lode, Virginia City, Nevada had twenty-five saloons before it had 4,000 people. By the 1870s its mountainside site was disfigured by ugly, ornate mansions where successful mine operators ate from fine china and swilled champagne as though it were water.

Though marked by violence, fraud, greed, and lost hopes, the gold rushes had valuable results. The most obvious was the new metal itself, which bolstered the financial position of the United States during and after the Civil War. Quantities of European goods needed for the war effort and for postwar economic development were paid for with the yield of the new mines. Gold and silver also caused a great increase of interest in the West. A valuable literature appeared, part imaginative, part reportorial, describing the mining camps and the life of the prospectors. These works fascinated contemporaries. Mark Twain's *Roughing It* (1872), based in part on his experiences in the Nevada mining country, is the most famous example of this literature.

The mines also speeded the political organization of the West. Colorado and Nevada became territories in 1861, Arizona and Idaho in 1863, and Montana in 1864. Although Nevada was admitted before it had 60,000 residents, most of these territories did not become states for decades. But because of the miners, the framework for future development was early established.

Farmers Struggle to Keep Up

While miners were extracting the mineral wealth of the West, others were snapping up the region's choice farmland. Presumably the Homestead Act of 1862 was supposed to make it easier for poor families to acquire farms, thereby ending the reign of the speculator and the large landholder. The West, land reformers had assumed, would soon be dotted with 160-acre family farms.

They were doomed to disappointment. Most landless Americans were too poor to become farmers even when they could obtain land without cost. The expense of moving a family to the ever-receding frontier exceeded the means of many. As for the industrial workers for whom the free land was supposed to provide a "safety valve," they had neither the skills nor the inclination to become farmers. Homesteaders usually came from districts not far removed from frontier conditions.

The first settlers in western Kansas, Nebraska, and the Dakotas took up land along the rivers and creeks, where they found enough timber for home building, fuel, and fencing. Later arrivals had to build houses of the tough prairie sod and depend on hay, sunflower stalks, and buffalo dung for fuel.

Frontier farm families had always had to work hard and endure the hazards of storm, drought, and insect plagues, along with isolation and loneliness. But all these burdens were magnified on the prairies and the High Plains. Life was particularly hard for farm women, who, in addition to childcare and housework, performed endless farm chores,

Farming as Big Business

Immediately after the Civil War, Congress reserved 47.7 million acres of public land in the South for homesteaders, stopping all cash sales in the region. But in 1876 this policy was reversed and the land thrown open. Speculators flocked to the feast in such numbers that the Illinois Central Railroad ran special trains from Chicago to Mississippi and Louisiana.

The flat immensity of the land, combined with newly available farm machinery and the development of rail connections with the East, encouraged the growth of enormous corporation-controlled "bonanza" farms.

Bonanza farmers could buy supplies wholesale and obtain concessions from railroads and processors, but even the biggest organizations could not cope with prolonged drought, and most of the bonanza outfits failed in the dry years of the late 1880s. Those wise farmers who diversified their crops and cultivated their land intensively fared better in the long run, although even they could not hope to earn a profit in really dry years.

Despite the hazards of plains agriculture, the region became the breadbasket of America in the decades following the Civil War. By 1889 Minnesota topped the nation in wheat production, and ten years later four of the five leading wheat states lay west of the Mississippi. The plains also accounted for heavy percentages of the nation's other cereal crops, together with immense quantities of beef, pork, and mutton.

Like other exploiters of the nation's resources, farmers took whatever they could from the soil with little heed for preserving its fertility and preventing erosion. The consequent national loss was less apparent because it was diffuse and slow to assume drastic proportions, but it was nonetheless real.

Western Railroad Building

Further exploitation of land resources by private interests resulted from the government's policy of subsidizing western railroads. Here was a clear illustration of the conflict between the idea of the West as a national heritage to be disposed of to deserving citizens and the concept of the region as a cornucopia pouring forth riches to be gathered up and carted off. When it came to a choice between giving a particular tract to railroads or to homesteaders, the homesteaders nearly always lost out. On the other hand, the swift development of western railroads was essential if farmers, miners, and cattle ranchers were to prosper.

Unless the government had been willing to build the transcontinental lines itself—and this was unthinkable in an age dominated by belief in individual exploitation—some system of subsidy was essential. Private investors would not hazard the huge sums needed to lay tracks across hundreds of miles of rugged, empty country when traffic over the road could not possibly profit for many years. Most voters were wary of entrusting the dispensing of large sums to politicians. Grants of land seemed a sensible way of financing construction. The method avoided direct outlays of public funds, for the companies could pledge the land as security for bond issues or sell it directly for cash.

Federal land grants to railroads began in 1850 with those allotted to the Illinois Central. Over the next two decades about 49 million acres were given to various lines

Chinese work on a railway in the Far West. "Without them," Leland Stanford, president of the Central Pacific Railroad said, "it would be impossible to complete the western portion of this great national highway." Some Chinese were drawn from the gold fields farther north, and others were imported from China, under five-year contracts with the railroads, which paid them $10 or $12 a month.

indirectly in the form of grants to the states, but the most lavish gifts of the public domain were those made directly to builders of intersectional trunk lines. These roads received more than 155 million acres, although about 25 million acres reverted to the government because some companies failed to lay the required miles of track. About 75 percent of this land went to aid the construction of four transcontinental railroads: the Union Pacific–Central Pacific line, running from Nebraska to San Francisco, completed in 1869; the Atchison, Topeka, and Santa Fe, running from Kansas City to Los Angeles by way of Santa Fe and Albuquerque, completed in 1883; the Southern Pacific, running from San Francisco to New Orleans by way of Yuma and El Paso, completed in 1883; and the Northern Pacific, running from Duluth, Minnesota, to Portland, Oregon, completed in 1883.

The Pacific Railway Act of 1862 established the pattern for these grants. It gave the builders of the Union Pacific and Central Pacific railroads five square miles of public land on each side of their right-of-way for each mile of track laid. The land was allotted in alternate sections, forming a pattern like a checkerboard: the squares of one color representing railroad property, the other government property. Presumably this arrangement benefited the entire nation since half the land close to the railroad remained in public hands.

However, whenever grants were made to railroads, the adjacent government lands were not opened to homesteaders—on the theory that free land in the immediate vicinity of a line would prevent the road from disposing of its properties at good prices. In addition to the land granted the railroads, a wide zone of "indemnity" lands was reserved to allow the roads to choose alternative sites to make up for lands that settlers had already taken up within the checkerboard. Thus, homesteading was in fact prohibited near land-grant railroads. More than twenty years after receiving its immense grant, the Northern Pacific was still attempting to keep homesteaders from filing in the indemnity zone. President Cleveland finally put a stop to this in 1887, saying that he could find "no evidence" that "this vast tract is necessary for the fulfillment of the grant."

Historians have argued at length about the fairness of the land-grant system. Land-grant lines encouraged the growth of the West by advertising their property widely and by providing cheap transportation for prospective settlers and efficient shipping services for farmers. They were required by law to carry troops and handle government business free or at reduced rates, which saved the government millions over the years. At the same time the system imposed no effective restraints on how the railroads used the funds raised with federal aid. Being able to lay track with money obtained from land grants, the operators tended to be extravagant and often downright corrupt.

The construction of the Central Pacific in the 1860s illustrates how the system encouraged extravagance. The line was controlled by four businessmen: Collis P. Huntington, Leland Stanford, Mark Hopkins, and Charles Crocker. The Central Pacific and the Union Pacific were given, in addition to their land grants, loans in the form of government bonds—from $16,000 to $48,000 for each mile of track laid, depending on the difficulty of the terrain. The two competed with each other for the subsidies, the Central Pacific building eastward from Sacramento, the Union Pacific westward from Nebraska. They put huge crews to work grading and laying track, bringing up supplies over the already completed road. The Union Pacific employed Civil War veterans and Irish immigrants, while the Central employed Chinese immigrants.

This plan favored the Union Pacific. While the Central Pacific was inching up the gorges and granite of the mighty Sierras, the Union Pacific was racing across the level plains laying 540 miles of track between 1865 and 1867. Once beyond the Sierras, the Central Pacific would have easy going across the Nevada–Utah plateau country, but by then it might be too late to prevent the Union Pacific from making off with most of the government aid.

Crocker managed the Central Pacific construction crews. He wasted huge sums by working through the winter in the High Sierras. In 1866, over the most difficult terrain, he laid twenty-eight miles of track, at a cost of more than $280,000 a mile. Experts later estimated that 70 percent of this sum could have been saved had speed not been a factor.

Crocker's Herculean efforts paid off. The mountains were conquered, and then the crews raced across the Great Basin to Salt Lake City and beyond. The meeting of the rails—the occasion of a national celebration—took place at Promontory, north of Ogden, Utah, on May 10, 1869. Leland Stanford drove the final ceremonial golden spike with a silver hammer.[2] The Union Pacific had built 1,086 miles of track, the Central 689 miles.

In the long run the wasteful way in which the Central Pacific was built hurt the road severely. It was ill-constructed, over grades too steep and around curves too sharp, and burdened with debts that were too large. Such was the fate of nearly all the railroads constructed with the help of government subsidies.

The only transcontinental railroad built without land grants was the Great Northern, running from St. Paul, Minnesota, to the Pacific. Spending private capital, its guiding genius, James J. Hill, was compelled to build economically and to plan carefully. As a result, his was the only transcontinental line to weather the depression of the 1890s without going into bankruptcy.

---

[2]A mysterious "San Francisco jeweler" passed among the onlookers, taking orders for souvenir watch chains that he proposed to make from the spike at $5 each.

NAT LOVE

Nat Love, a slave, was born on a plantation in Davidson County, Tennessee sometime in 1854. Nat's father was a foreman on the plantation; his mother milked cows, cooked, and operated a loom.

After the Civil War, Love's father rented twenty acres from his former master. Nat spent Sundays at a horse farm, where he learned how to ride. Soon he was earning ten cents for every colt he "broke."

When Nat's father died, the family's circumstances became dire. He and his siblings went shoeless and their clothes were in tatters. Nat longed to escape from it all and see the world. His opportunity came when he won a horse in a raffle. In February 1869, he set out for the frontier. He was fifteen years old.

Months later, he arrived in Dodge City, Kansas, "a typical frontier city, with a great many saloons, dance halls, and gambling houses, and very little of anything else." At a camp outside of town, he asked a group of cowboys for a job. Eager to have some fun with the black "tenderfoot," they agreed if he could prove he could ride; then they put him on the wildest horse in camp. Love clung to the bucking bronco, much to everyone's astonishment. The boss hired him at $30 a month. He also gave Nat a saddle, a Colt 45 pistol and a new name—"Love" being unsuitable for a cowboy. Nat was now "Red River Dick."

Three days after the cowboys left Dodge, they were attacked by mounted Indians. "When I saw them coming after us and heard their blood curdling yell, I was too badly scared to run," Love recalled. Before the Indians were driven away by gunfire, they had killed one cowboy and made off with most of the horses and provisions. Love and the others walked to Texas.

Love then served with outfits that drove cattle to grazing ranges and markets throughout the West. Every spring and fall the ranchers staged a great roundup, driving in all the cattle to a central place, separating them by the brands, and culling steers for shipment to market. Love specialized as a brand reader. He "cut out" those belonging to his employer and drove them back to that herd.

Love's life was filled with adventure. In 1876, while Love was driving 500 steers from the Rio Grande to a ranch in the Shoshone mountains of Wyoming, Indians attacked and stampeded the cattle. The battle raged through the night. By morning, several score Indians were dead, most of them trampled by cattle. Another time, Love broke up a robbery of a Union Pacific railroad station. After he won a roping and riding competition in Deadwood, South Dakota, "Red River Dick" became known as "Deadwood Dick." Shortly afterward he was shot by Indians and captured. When he recovered, the chief offered him his daughter in marriage along with 100 ponies. Dick pretended to go along with the marriage, but then stole a horse and escaped.

By the late 1880s, the heyday of the cowboy had ended. Now railroads hauled cattle from the grazing ranges to slaughterhouses in Kansas City, Omaha, Chicago, and St. Louis. In 1889, Dick went to Denver and got married. The following year he found a job as a porter on the Pullman Railroad cars. He died in 1921.

Question for Discussion
■ Which factors perhaps promoted racial equality among ranch hands?

Nat Love, posed here with the requisite implements, claimed to have been the "Deadwood Dick" on whom a series of novels was based.

The Cattle Kingdom

While miners were digging out the mineral wealth of the West and railroaders were taking possession of much of its land, another group was exploiting endless acres of its grass. For twenty years after the Civil War cattlemen and sheep raisers dominated huge areas of the High Plains, making millions of dollars by grazing their herds on lands they did not own.

Watch the Video
Cowboys and Cattle at **myhistorylab.com**

The lack of markets and transportation explains why cattle, which existed in southern Texas by the millions, were lightly regarded. But conditions were changing. Industrial growth in the East was causing an increase in the urban population and a consequent rise in the demand for food. At the same time, the expansion of the railroad network made it possible to move cattle cheaply over long distances. As the iron rails inched across the plains, astute cattlemen began to do some elementary figuring. Longhorns could be had locally for $3 and $4 a head. In the northern cities they would bring ten times that much, perhaps even more. Why not round them up and herd them northward to the railroads, allowing them to feed along the way on the abundant grasses of the plains? The land was unoccupied and owned by the federal government. Anyone could drive cattle across it without paying a fee or asking anyone's permission.

In 1867 the drovers, inspired by a clever young Illinois cattle dealer named Joseph G. McCoy and other entrepreneurs, led their herds across unsettled grasslands to the Kansas Pacific line at Abilene, Kansas. They earned excellent profits, and during the next five years about 1.5 million head made the "long drive" over the Chisholm Trail to Abilene, where they were sold to ranchers, feedlot operators, and the agents of eastern meatpackers. Other shipping points sprang up as the railroads pushed

Read the Document
Chisholm Trail at **myhistorylab.com**

westward. According to the best estimates 10 million head were driven north before the practice ended in the mid-1880s. (For the story of one cowboy, see the American Lives essay on "Nat Love," p. 446.)

Open-Range Ranching

Soon cattlemen discovered that the hardy Texas stock could survive the winters of the northern plains. Attracted by the apparently limitless forage, they began to bring up herds to stock the vast regions where the buffalo had so recently roamed. By 1880 some 4.5 million head had spread across the sea of grass that ran from Kansas to Montana and west to the Rockies.

The prairie grasses offered ranchers a bonanza almost as valuable as the gold mines. Open-range ranching required actual ownership of no more than a few acres along some watercourse. In this semiarid region, control of water enabled a rancher to dominate all the surrounding area back to the divide separating his range from the next stream without investing a cent in the purchase of land. His cattle, wandering freely on the public domain, fattened on grass owned by all the people, were to be turned into beefsteak and leather for the profit of the rancher.

Theoretically, anyone could pasture stock on the open range, but without access to water it was impossible to do so. "I have 2 miles of running water," a cattleman said in testifying before the Public Land Commission. "That accounts for my ranch being where it is. The next water from me in one direction is 23 miles; now no man can have a ranch between these two places. I have control of the grass, the same as though I owned it." In the late 1870s one Colorado cattle baron controlled an area roughly the size of Connecticut and Rhode Island even though he owned only 105 small parcels that totaled about 15,500 acres.

With the demand for meat rising and transportation cheap, princely fortunes could be made in a few years. Capitalists from the East and from Europe began to pour funds into the business. Soon large outfits such as the Nebraska Land and Cattle Company, controlled by British investors, and the Union Cattle Company of Wyoming, a $3 million corporation, dominated the business, just as large companies had taken over most of the important gold and silver mines.

Unlike other exploiters of the West's resources, cattle ranchers did not at first injure or reduce any public resource. Grass eaten by their stock annually renewed itself; droppings from the animals enriched the soil. Furthermore, ranchers poached on the public domain because there was no reasonable way for them to obtain legal possession of the large areas necessary to raise cattle on the plains. Federal land laws made no allowance for the special conditions of the semiarid West.

A system to take account for those conditions was soon devised by Major John Wesley Powell, later the director of the United States Geological Survey. His *Report on the Lands of the Arid Region of the United States* (1879) suggested that western lands be divided into three classes: irrigable lands, timber lands, and "pasturage" lands. On the pasturage lands the "farm unit" ought to be at least 2,560 acres (four sections), Powell urged. Groups of these units should be organized into "pasturage districts" in which the ranchers "should have the right to make their own regulations for the division of lands, the use of the water . . . and for the pasturage of lands in common or in severalty."

Barbed-Wire Warfare

Congress refused to change the land laws in any basic way, and this had two harmful effects. First, it encouraged fraud: Those who could not get title to enough land honestly turned to subterfuge. The Desert Land Act (1877) allowed anyone to obtain 640 acres in the arid states for $1.25 an acre provided the owner irrigated part of it within three years. Since the original claimant could transfer the holding, the ranchers set their cowboys and other hands to filing claims, which were then signed over to them. Over 2.6 million acres were taken up under the act, and according to the best estimate, 95 percent of the claims were fraudulent—no sincere effort was made to irrigate the land.

Second, overcrowding became a problem that led to serious conflicts, even killings, because no one had uncontestable title to the land. The leading ranchers banded together in cattlemen's associations to deal with overcrowding and with such problems as quarantine regulations, water rights, and thievery. In most cases these associations devised effective and sensible rules, but their functions would better have been performed by the government.

To keep other ranchers' cattle from those sections of the public domain they considered their own, the associations and many individuals began to fence huge areas. This was possible only because of the invention in 1874 of barbed wire by Joseph F. Glidden, an

Illinois farmer. By the 1880s thousands of miles of the new fencing had been strung across the plains, often across roads and in a few cases around entire communities. "Barbed-wire wars" resulted, fought by rancher against rancher, cattleman against sheepman, herder against farmer. Posted signs gave dire warnings to trespassers. "The Son of a Bitch who opens this fence had better look out for his scalp," one such sign announced, another fine statement of the philosophy of the age.

By stringing so much wire the cattlemen were unwittingly destroying their own way of doing business. On a truly open range, cattle could fend for themselves, instinctively finding water during droughts, drifting safely downwind before blizzards. Barbed wire prevented their free movement. During winter storms these slender strands became as lethal as high-tension wires: the drifting cattle piled up against them and died by the thousands.

The boom times were ending. Overproduction was driving down the price of beef; expenses were on the rise; many sections of the range were badly overgrazed. The dry summer of 1886 left the stock in such poor condition as winter approached that the *Rocky Mountain Husbandman* urged its readers to sell their cattle despite the prevailing low prices rather than "endanger the whole herd by having the range overstocked."

Some ranchers took this advice; those who did not made a fatal error. Winter that year arrived early and with unparalleled fury. Blizzards raged and temperatures plummeted far below zero. Cattle crowded into low places only to be engulfed in giant snowdrifts; barbed wire took a fearful toll. When spring finally came, the streams were choked with rotting carcasses. Between 80 and 90 percent of all cattle on the range were dead.

That cruel winter finished open-range cattle-raising. The large companies were bankrupt; many independent operators became discouraged and sold out. When the industry revived, it was on a smaller, more efficiently organized scale. The fencing movement continued, but now ranchers enclosed only the land they actually owned. It then became possible to bring in pedigreed bulls to improve the breed. Cattle-raising, like mining before it, ceased to be an adventure in rollicking individualism and became a business.

By the late 1880s the bonanza days of the West were over. No previous frontier had caught the imagination of Americans so completely as the Great West, with its heroic size, its awesome emptiness, its massive, sculptured beauty. Most of what Walter Prescott Webb, author of the classic study *The Great Plains* (1931) called the "primary windfalls" of the region—the furs, the precious metals, the forests, the cattle, and the grass—had been snatched up by first comers and by individuals already wealthy. Big companies were taking over all the West's resources. The frontier was no more.

But the frontier never existed except as an intellectual construction among white settlers and those who wrote about them. To the Indians, the land was simply home. The "conquest of the frontier" was thus an appealing evasion: It transformed the harmful actions and policies of the nation into an expression of human progress, the march westward of "civilization."

See the **Map**

Resources and Conflict in the West at **myhistorylab.com**

"Civilization," though, was changing. The nation was becoming more powerful, richer, and larger, and its economic structure more complex and diversified as the West yielded its treasures. But the East, and especially eastern industrialists and financiers, were increasingly dominating the economy of the entire nation.

Milestones

1859	Discovery of the Comstock Lode lures miners west	1877	U.S. troops capture Chief Joseph of Nez Percé after 1,000-mile retreat
1864	Chivington massacre of Cheyenne	1878	Timber and Stone Act favors lumber companies
1869	Union Pacific Railroad completed Board of Indian Commissioners established	1879	Major Powell's *Report on the Lands of the Arid Region* suggests division of West
1873	Timber Culture Act encourages western forestation	1882	Chinese Exclusion Act bans Chinese immigrant workers for ten years
1876	Sioux slaughter Custer's cavalry at Battle of Little Bighorn	1886–1887	Blizzards end open-range ranching
1877	Desert Land Act favors ranchers	1887	Dawes Severalty Act splits tribal lands

✔●─ Study and Review at www.myhistorylab.com

Review Questions

1. The text suggests that if federal policy had been more tolerant, there would have been no need to drive Indians from so much of their land. What alternative policies might have succeeded and how?

2. In The *Comanche Empire* (2009), historian Pekka Hamalainen insists that the Comanche themselves managed to forge a mighty empire. Maps showing the steady loss of Indian lands (such as that on p. 441) deprive the Indians of their "agency" in history. In what ways did Indians leave their own imprint upon this period?

3. How did the treatment of African Americans during the last third of the nineteenth century compare with that of Indians?

4. The West has exerted a powerful hold on the American imagination. What explains the popularity of western themes in American life? How does the history compare with the popular image?

Key Terms

Chinese Exclusion Act   *434*
Comstock Lode   *441*

Dawes Severalty Act of 1887   *439*

An Industrial Giant Emerges

17

((•—[Hear the Audio Chapter 17 at myhistorylab.com

Do you save money at big box stores?

IN 2010 WALMART, WITH 2.1 MILLION EMPLOYEES, WAS THE LARGEST corporation in the history of the world. Its revenues of $405 billion exceeded the gross domestic product of Sweden and Saudi Arabia. The company's clout made it a frequent target of popular satire. A 2008 episode of *The Simpsons* was set at "Sprawl-Mart," where Homer was offered a job as Executive Greeter. "Is there a chance for advancement?" he asks. "No," the manager says. "You get to work overtime without us paying you extra."

Real-world critics of Walmart leveled similar charges. A labor union website described Walmart as a "death star" that "destroys all other economic activity in its path." Others complained that many Walmart employees qualified for public assistance.

In 2009 Walmart, whose motto is "Save Money Live Better," claimed that it saved $3,100 per American household. Former CEO Lee Scott credited Walmart with having "democratized consumption" in the United States by enabling "working-class families to buy former luxuries like inexpensive flat-screen televisions, down comforters and porterhouse steaks." A retailer helps society best by lowering prices, or so the company contended.

The debate over the human costs of corporate efficiencies echoes the one that accompanied the rise of powerful industrial combinations during the last third of the nineteenth century. Then, the power of the railroads enabled them to bring substantial benefits to thousands of communities; but this power also enabled the railroads to ruin those who opposed their will. Industrial corporations followed suit, especially in steel, iron, oil, and electricity, providing millions with new and improved products at lower prices. But the industrial behemoths also controlled political processes and often exploited workers. Reformers and labor leaders denounced this concentration of wealth and power. Some advocated regulation; others called for revolution. Then as now, defenders of big business pointed out its benefits: new technology, better products, lower prices.

The question remains: Does the efficiency generated by economic concentration justify its threat to smaller businesses and communities—and to democratic institutions?

Essentials of Industrial Growth

When the Civil War began, the country's industrial output, while important and increasing, did not approach that of major European powers. By the end of the century the United States had become far and away the colossus among world manufacturers, dwarfing the production of Great Britain and Germany. The world had never seen such a remarkable example of rapid economic growth. The value of American manufactured products rose from $1.8 billion in 1859 to over $13 billion in 1899.

American manufacturing flourished for many reasons. New natural resources were discovered and exploited steadily, thereby increasing opportunities. These opportunities, in turn, attracted the brightest and most energetic of a vigorous and expanding population. The growth of the country added constantly to the size of the national market, and protective tariffs shielded that market from foreign competition. Foreign capital, however, entered the market freely, in part because tariffs kept out so many foreign goods.

The dominant spirit of the time encouraged businessmen to maximum effort by emphasizing progress, yet it also produced a generation of Robber Barons. The energetic search for wealth led to corrupt business practices such as stock manipulation, bribery, and cutthroat competition and ultimately to "combinations in restraint of trade," a kind of American euphemism for monopoly.

The period witnessed rapid advances in basic science, and technicians created a bountiful harvest of new machines, processes, and power sources that increased productivity in many industries and created new industries as well. Agriculture was transformed by improved harvesters and binding machines, and combines capable of threshing and bagging 450 pounds of grain a minute. An 1886 report of the Illinois Bureau of Labor Statistics claimed that "new machinery has displaced fully 50 percent of the muscular labor formerly required to do a given amount of work in the manufacture of agricultural implements." Of course that also meant that many farm families were "displaced" from their homes and livelihoods, and it made farmers dependent on the vagaries of distant markets and powerful economic forces they could not control.

As a result of improvements in the milling of grain, packaged cereals appeared on the American breakfast table. The commercial canning of food, spurred by the "automatic line" canning factory, expanded so rapidly that by 1887 a writer in *Good Housekeeping* could say, "Housekeeping is getting to be ready made, as well as clothing." The Bonsack cigarette-rolling machine created a new industry that changed the habits of millions. George B. Eastman created still another with his development of mass-produced, roll photographic film and the simple but efficient Kodak camera. The perfection of the typewriter by the Remington company in the 1880s revolutionized office work. But even some of these inventions were mixed blessings. The harm done by cigarettes, for example, needs no explanation.

Railroads: The First Big Business

In 1866, returning from his honeymoon in Europe, thirty-year-old Charles Francis Adams Jr., (great-grandson of John Adams and grandson of John Quincy Adams), full of ambition and ready, as he put it, to confront the world "face to face," looked about in search of a career. "Surveying the whole field," he later explained, "I fixed on the railroad system as the most developing force and the largest field of the day, and determined to attach myself to it." Adams's judgment was acute: For the next twenty-five years the

The Union Railroad Station in Montgomery, Alabama, was designed by Henry Hobson Richardson, the nation's foremost architect in the late nineteenth century. Richardson borrowed ideas from the past, including arches that evoked ancient Rome. The building's massiveness and horizontal lines suggested the power and reach of the railroads: the American empire as built on steel rails.

railroads were probably the most significant element in American economic development, railroad executives the most powerful people in the country.

Railroads were important first as an industry in themselves. Fewer than 35,000 miles of track existed when Lee laid down his sword at Appomattox. In 1875 railroad mileage exceeded 74,000 and the skeleton of the network was complete. Over the next two decades the skeleton was fleshed out. In 1890 the mature but still-growing system took in over $1 billion in passenger and freight revenues. (The federal government's income in 1890 was only $403 million.) The value of railroad properties and equipment was more than $8.7 billion. The national railroad debt of $5.1 billion was almost five times the national debt of $1.1 billion. By 1900 the nation had 193,000 miles of track.

The emphasis in railroad construction after 1865 was on organizing integrated systems. The lines had high fixed costs: taxes, interest on their bonds, maintenance of track and rolling stock, and salaries of office personnel. A short train with half-empty cars required almost as many workers and as much fuel to operate as a long one jammed with freight or passengers. To earn profits the railroads had to carry as much traffic as possible. They therefore spread out feeder lines to draw business to their main lines the way the root network of a tree draws water into its trunk.

Before the Civil War, passengers and freight could travel by rail from beyond Chicago and St. Louis to the Atlantic coast, but only after the war did true interregional trunk lines appear. In 1867 the New York Central passed into the hands of "Commodore" Cornelius Vanderbilt, who had made a large fortune in the shipping business. Vanderbilt already controlled lines running from Albany to New York City; now he merged these properties with the New York Central. In 1873 he integrated the Lake Shore and Michigan

Southern into his empire and two years later the Michigan Central. At his death in 1877 the New York Central operated a network of over 4,500 miles of track between New York City and most of the principal cities of the Midwest.

While Vanderbilt was putting together the New York Central complex, Thomas A. Scott was fusing roads to Cincinnati, Indianapolis, St. Louis, and Chicago to his Pennsylvania Railroad, which linked Pittsburgh and Philadelphia. In 1871 the Pennsylvania line obtained access to New York; soon it reached Baltimore and Washington. By 1869 another important system, the Erie, extended from New York to Cleveland, Cincinnati, and St. Louis. Soon thereafter it too tapped the markets of Chicago and other cities. In 1874 the Baltimore and Ohio rail line also obtained access to Chicago.

The Civil War had highlighted the need for thorough railroad connections in the South. Shortly after the conflict the Chesapeake and Ohio opened a direct line from Norfolk, Virginia, to Cincinnati, Ohio. By the late 1880s, the Richmond and West Point Terminal Company controlled an 8,558-mile network. Like other southern trunk lines such as the Louisville and Nashville and the Atlantic Coast Line, this system was controlled by northern capitalists.

The trunk lines interconnected and thus had to standardize many of their activities. This in turn led to the standardization of other aspects of life. The present system of time zones was developed in 1883 by the railroads. The standard track gauge (four feet eight and one-half inches) was established in 1886. Standardized car coupling and braking mechanisms, standard signal systems, even standard methods of accounting were essential to the effective functioning of the network.

The lines sought to work out fixed rates for carrying different types of freight, charge more for valuable manufactured goods than for bulky products like coal or wheat, and they agreed to permit rate concessions to shippers when necessary to avoid hauling empty cars. In other words, they charged what the traffic would bear. However, by the 1880s the men who ran the railroads had come to recognize the advantages of cooperating with one another to avoid "senseless" competition. Railroad management was becoming a kind of profession, with certain standard ways of doing things, its own professional journals, and with regional organizations such as the Eastern Trunk Line Association and the Western Traffic Association.

To speed the settlement of new regions, the land-grant railroads sold land cheaply and on easy terms, for sales meant future business as well as current income. They offered reduced rates to travelers interested in buying farms and set up "bureaus of immigration" that distributed brochures describing the wonders of the new country. Their agents greeted immigrants at the eastern ports and tried to steer them to railroad property. They sent agents who were usually themselves immigrants—often ministers—all over Europe to recruit prospective settlers.

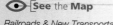

See the **Map**

Railroads & New Transportation Systems at **myhistorylab.com**

Iron, Oil, and Electricity

The transformation of iron manufacturing affected the nation almost as much as railroad development. Output rose from 920,000 tons in 1860 to 10.3 million tons in 1900, but the big change came in the development of ways to mass-produce steel. In its pure form (wrought iron) the metal is tough but relatively pliable: It bends under great stresses.

Ordinary cast iron, which contains large amounts of carbon and other impurities, is hard but brittle. Steel, which contains 1 or 2 percent carbon, combines the hardness of cast iron with the toughness of wrought iron. For nearly every purpose—structural girders for bridges and buildings, railroad track, machine tools, boiler plate, barbed wire—steel is immensely superior to other kinds of iron.

But steel was so expensive that it could not be used for bulky products until the invention in the 1850s of the Bessemer process, perfected independently by Henry Bessemer, an Englishman, and William Kelly of Kentucky. Bessemer and Kelly discovered that a stream of air directed into a mass of molten iron caused the carbon and other impurities to combine with oxygen and burn off. When measured amounts of carbon, silicon, and manganese were then added, the brew became steel. What had been a rare metal could now be produced by the hundreds and thousands of tons. In 1870, 77,000 tons of steel were manufactured; by 1890, that had expanded to nearly 5 million tons. Such growth would have been impossible without the huge supplies of iron ore in the United States and the coal necessary to fire the furnaces that refined it.

Pittsburgh, surrounded by vast coal deposits, became the iron and steel capital of the country, the Minnesota ores reaching it by way of steamers on the Great Lakes and rail lines from Cleveland. Other cities in Pennsylvania and Ohio were important producers, and a separate complex, centering on Birmingham, Alabama, developed to exploit local iron and coal fields.

The petroleum industry expanded even more spectacularly than iron and steel. Edwin L. Drake drilled the first successful well in Pennsylvania in 1859. During the Civil War,

This 1900 photograph of steel factories at night in Duquesne, near Pittsburgh, was tinted by hand.
Source: North Wind Picture Archives.

production ranged between 2 million and 3 million barrels a year. By 1890 the figure had leaped to about 50 million barrels.

Before the invention of the gasoline engine and the automobile, the most important petroleum product was kerosene, which was burned in lamps. Refiners heated crude oil in large kettles and, after the volatile elements had escaped, condensed the kerosene in coils cooled by water. The heavier petroleum tars were discarded.

Technological advances came rapidly. By the early 1870s, refiners had learned how to "crack" petroleum by applying high temperatures to the crude oil in order to rearrange its molecular structure, thereby increasing the percentage of kerosene yielded. By-products such as naphtha, gasoline (used in vaporized form as an illuminating gas), rhigolene (a local anesthetic), cymogene (a coolant for refrigerating machines), and many lubricants and waxes began to appear on the market. At the same time a great increase in the supply of crude oil drove prices down.

These circumstances put a premium on refining efficiency. Larger plants using expensive machinery and employing skilled technicians became more important. In the mid-1860s only three refineries in the country could process 2,000 barrels of crude oil a week; a decade later plants capable of handling 1,000 barrels a day were common.

Two other important new industries were the telephone and electric light businesses. Both were typical of the period, being products of technical advances and intimately related to the growth of a high-speed, urban civilization that put great stress on communication. The telephone was invented in 1876 by Alexander Graham Bell, who had been led to the study of acoustics through his interest in the education of the deaf. The invention soon proved its value. By 1900 there were almost 800,000 telephones in the country, twice the total for all Europe. The American Telephone and Telegraph Company, a consolidation of over 100 local systems, dominated the business.

When the Western Union Telegraph Company realized the importance of the telephone, it tried for a time to compete with Bell by developing a machine of its own. The man it commissioned to devise this machine was Thomas A. Edison, but Bell's patents proved unassailable. Edison had already made a number of contributions toward solving what he called the "mysteries of electrical force," including a multiplex telegraph capable of sending four messages over a single wire at the same time. At Menlo Park, New Jersey, he built the prototype of the modern research laboratory, where specific problems could be attacked on a mass scale by a team of trained specialists. During his lifetime he took out more than 1,000 patents dealing with machines as varied as the phonograph, the motion-picture projector, the storage battery, and the mimeograph.

Edison's most significant achievement was the incandescent lamp, or electric lightbulb. Others before him had experimented with the idea of producing light by passing electricity through a filament in a vacuum. Always, however, the filaments quickly burned out.

●●●[Read the **Document**

Edison, *The Success of the Electric Light* at myhistorylab.com

Edison tried hundreds of fibers before producing, in 1879, a carbonized filament that would glow brightly in a vacuum tube for as long as 170 hours without crumbling. At Christmastime he decorated the grounds about his laboratory with a few dozen of the new lights. People flocked by the thousands to see this miracle of the "Wizard of Menlo Park." The inventor boasted that soon he would be able to illuminate entire towns, even great cities like New York.

He was true to his promise. In 1882 his Edison Illuminating Company opened a power station in New York City and began to supply current for lighting to eighty-five consumers, including the *New York Times* and the banking house of J.P. Morgan and Company. Soon central stations were springing up everywhere until, by 1898, there were about 3,000 in the country.

The substitution of electric for steam power in factories was as liberating as that of steam for waterpower before the Civil War. Small, safe electric motors replaced dangerous and cumbersome mazes of belts and wheels. The electric power industry expanded rapidly. By the early years of the twentieth century almost 6 billion kilowatt-hours of electricity were being produced annually. Yet this was only the beginning.

Competition and Monopoly: The Railroads

During the post–Civil War era, expansion in industry went hand in hand with concentration. The principal cause of this trend, aside from the obvious economies resulting from large-scale production and the growing importance of expensive machinery, was the downward trend of prices after 1873. The deflation, which resulted mainly from the failure of the money supply to keep pace with the rapid increase in the volume of goods produced, affected agricultural goods as well as manufactures, and it lasted until 1896 or 1897.

Contemporaries believed that they were living through a "great depression." That label is misleading, for output expanded almost continuously, and at a rapid rate, until 1893, when production slumped and a true depression struck the country. Falling prices, however, kept a steady pressure on profit margins, and this led to increased production and thus to intense competition for markets.

According to the classical economists, competition advanced the public interest by keeping prices low and ensuring the most efficient producer the largest profit. Up to a point it accomplished these purposes in the years after 1865, but it also caused side effects that injured both the economy and society as a whole. Railroad managers, for instance, found it impossible to enforce "official" rate schedules and maintain their regional associations once competitive pressures mounted. In 1865 it had cost from ninety-six cents to $2.15 per 100 pounds, depending on the class of freight, to ship goods from New York to Chicago. In 1888 rates ranged from thirty-five cents to seventy-five cents.

Competition cut deeply into railroad profits, causing the lines to seek desperately to increase volume. It did so chiefly by reducing rates still more, on a selective basis. The competition gave rebates (secret reductions below the published rates) to large shippers in order to capture their business. Giving discounts to those who shipped in volume made economic sense: It was easier to handle freight in carload lots than in smaller units. So intense was the battle for business, however, that the railroads often made concessions to big customers far beyond what the economics of bulk shipment justified.

Railroad officials disliked rebating but found no way to avoid the practice. In extreme cases the railroads even gave large shippers drawbacks, which were rebates on the business of the shippers' competitors. Besides rebating, railroads issued passes to favored shippers, built sidings at the plants of important companies without charge, and gave freely of their landholdings to attract businesses to their territory.

To make up for losses forced on them by competitive pressures, railroads charged higher rates at waypoints along their tracks where no competition existed. Frequently it cost more to ship a product a short distance than a longer one. Rochester, New York, was served only by the New York Central. In the 1870s it cost thrity cents to transport a barrel of flour from Rochester to New York City, a distance of 350 miles. At the same time flour could be shipped from Minneapolis to New York, a distance of well over 1,000 miles, for only twenty cents a barrel.

Although cheap transportation stimulated the economy, few people benefited from cutthroat competition. Small shippers—and all businessmen in cities and towns with limited rail outlets—suffered; railroad discrimination speeded the concentration of industry in large corporations located in major centers. The instability of rates even troubled interests like the midwestern flour millers who benefited from the competitive situation, for it hampered planning. Nor could manufacturers who received rebates be entirely happy, since few could be sure that some other producer was not getting a larger reduction.

Probably the worst sufferers were the railroads themselves. The loss of revenue resulting from rate cutting, combined with inflated debts, put most of them in grave difficulty when faced with a downturn in the business cycle. In 1876 two-fifths of all railroad bonds were in default; three years later sixty-five lines were bankrupt.

Since the public would not countenance bankrupt railroads going out of business, these companies were placed in the hands of court-appointed receivers. The receivers, however, seldom provided efficient management and had no funds at their disposal for new equipment.

During the 1880s the major railroads responded to these pressures by building or buying lines in order to create interregional systems. These were the first giant corporations, capitalized in the hundreds of millions of dollars. Their enormous cost led to another wave of bankruptcies when a true depression struck in the 1890s.

The consequent reorganizations brought most of the big systems under the control of financiers, notably J. Pierpont Morgan and such other private bankers as Kuhn, Loeb of New York and Lee, Higginson of Boston.

⊙ View the Image
J.P. Morgan at **myhistorylab.com**

Critics called the reorganizations "Morganizations." Representatives of the bankers sat on the board of every line they saved and their influence was predominant. They consistently opposed rate wars, rebating, and other competitive practices. In effect, control of the railroad network became centralized, even though the companies maintained their separate existences and operated in a seemingly independent manner. When Morgan died in 1913, "Morgan men" dominated the boards of the New York Central; the Erie; the New York, New Haven, and Hartford; the Southern; the Pere Marquette; the Atchison, Topeka, and Santa Fe; and many other lines.

Competition and Monopoly: Steel

The iron and steel industry was also intensely competitive. Despite the trend toward higher production, demand varied erratically from year to year, even from month to month. In good times producers built new facilities, only to suffer heavy losses when demand declined. The forward rush of technology put a tremendous emphasis on efficiency; expensive plants quickly became obsolete. Improved transportation facilities allowed manufacturers in widely separated places to compete with one another.

The kingpin of the industry was Andrew Carnegie. Carnegie was born in Scotland and came to the United States in 1848 at the age of twelve. His first job, as a bobbin boy

This early 1900 photograph shows how steel mills spread along the riverfront of Pittsburgh, Pennsylvania.

in a cotton mill, brought him $1.20 a week, but his talents perfectly fitted the times and he rose rapidly: to Western Union messenger boy, to telegrapher, to private secretary, to railroad manager. He saved his money, made some shrewd investments, and by 1868 had an income of $50,000 a year.

At about this time he decided to specialize in the iron business. Carnegie possessed great talent as a salesman, boundless faith in the future of the country, an uncanny knack of choosing topflight subordinates, and enough ruthlessness to survive in the iron and steel jungle. Where other steel men built new plants in good times, he preferred to expand in bad times, when it cost far less to do so.

Carnegie grasped the importance of technological improvements. Slightly skeptical of the Bessemer process at first, once he became convinced of its practicality he adopted it enthusiastically. In 1875 he built the J. Edgar Thomson Steel Works, named after a president of the Pennsylvania Railroad, his biggest customer. He employed chemists and other specialists and was soon making steel from iron oxides that other manufacturers had discarded as waste. He was a merciless competitor. Carnegie sold rails by paying "commissions" to railroad purchasing agents, and he was not above reneging on a contract if he thought it profitable and safe to do so.

By 1890 the Carnegie Steel Company dominated the industry, and its output increased nearly tenfold during the next decade. Profits soared. Alarmed by his increasing control of the industry, the makers of finished steel products such as barbed wire and tubing considered pooling their resources and making steel themselves. Carnegie, his competitive temper aroused, threatened to manufacture wire, pipes, and other finished products. A colossal steel war seemed imminent.

However, Carnegie longed to retire in order to devote himself to philanthropic work. He believed that great wealth entailed social responsibilities and that it was a disgrace to die rich. When J.P. Morgan approached him through an intermediary with an offer to buy him out, he assented readily. In 1901 Morgan put together United States Steel, the "world's first billion-dollar corporation." This combination included all the Carnegie properties, the Federal Steel Company (Carnegie's largest competitor), and such important fabricators of finished products as the American Steel and Wire Company, the American Tin Plate Company, and the National Tube Company. Vast reserves of Minnesota iron ore and a fleet of Great Lakes ore steamers were also included. U.S. Steel was capitalized at $1.4 billion, about twice the value of its component properties but not necessarily an overestimation of its profit-earning capacity. The owners of Carnegie Steel received $492 million, of which $250 million went to Carnegie himself.

●●●—Read the Document
Carnegie, *Wealth* at
myhistorylab.com

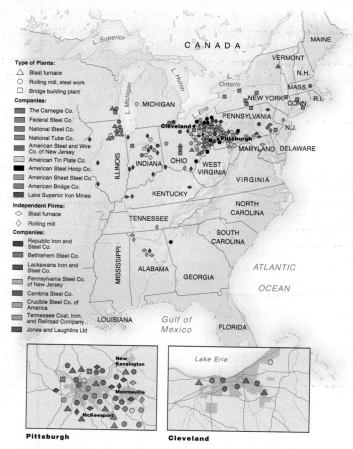

Firms Incorporated into U.S. Steel J.P. Morgan's consolidation that created U.S. Steel.

Competition and Monopoly: Oil

The pattern of fierce competition leading to combination and monopoly is well illustrated by the history of the petroleum industry. Irresistible pressures pushed the refiners into a brutal struggle to dominate the business. Production of crude oil, subject to the uncertainties of prospecting and drilling, fluctuated constantly and without regard for need. In general, output surged far ahead of demand.

By the 1870s the chief oil-refining centers were Cleveland, Pittsburgh, Baltimore, and the New York City area. Of these Cleveland was the fastest growing, chiefly because the New York Central and Erie railroads competed fiercely for its oil trade and the Erie Canal offered an alternative route.

The Standard Oil Company of Cleveland, founded in 1870 by a thirty-one-year-old merchant named John D. Rockefeller, emerged as the giant among the refiners. Rockefeller exploited every possible technical advance and employed fair means and foul to persuade competitors either to sell out or to join forces. By 1879 he controlled 90 percent of the nation's oil-refining capacity along with a network of oil pipelines and large reserves of petroleum in the ground.

Standard Oil emerged victorious from the competitive wars because Rockefeller and his associates were the toughest and most imaginative fighters as well as the most efficient refiners in the business. In addition to obtaining from the railroads a 10 percent rebate and drawbacks on its competitors' shipments, Standard Oil cut prices locally to force small independents to sell out or face ruin. Since kerosene was sold in grocery stores, Standard supplied its own outlets with meat, sugar, and other products at artificially low prices to help crush the stores that handled other brands of kerosene. The company employed spies to track down the customers of independents and offer them oil at bargain prices. Bribery was also a Standard practice; the reformer Henry Demarest Lloyd quipped that the company had done everything to the Pennsylvania legislature except refine it.

Although a bold planner and a daring taker of necessary risks, Rockefeller was far too orderly and astute to enjoy the free-swinging battles that plagued his industry. Born in an upstate New York village in 1839, he settled in Cleveland in 1855 and became a produce merchant. During the Civil War he invested in a local refinery and by 1865 was engaged full time in the oil business.

Having achieved his monopoly, Rockefeller stabilized and structured it by creating a new type of business organization, the trust. Standard Oil was an Ohio corporation, prohibited by local law from owning plants in other states or holding stock in out-of-state corporations. As Rockefeller and his associates took over dozens of companies with facilities scattered across the country, serious legal and managerial difficulties arose. How could these many organizations be integrated with Standard Oil of Ohio? Trusts

A Pennsylvania lawyer named Samuel C. T. Dodd came up with an answer to this question in 1879.[1] The stock of Standard of Ohio and of all the other companies that the Rockefeller interests had swallowed up was turned over to nine trustees, who were empowered to "exercise general supervision" over all the properties. In exchange, stockholders received trust certificates, on which dividends were paid. This seemingly simple device brought order to the petroleum business. Competition almost

---

[1]The trust formula was not "perfected" until 1882.

disappeared, prices steadied, and profits skyrocketed. By 1892 John D. Rockefeller was worth over $800 million.

The Standard Oil Trust was not a corporation. It had no charter, indeed no legal existence at all. For many years few people outside the organization knew that it existed. The form they chose persuaded Rockefeller and other Standard Oil officials that without violating their consciences, they could deny under oath that Standard Oil of Ohio owned or controlled other corporations "directly or indirectly through its officers or agents." The trustees controlled these organizations—and Standard of Ohio too!

After Standard Oil's duplicity was revealed during a New York investigation in 1888, the word *trust*, formerly signifying a fiduciary arrangement for the protection of the interests of individuals incompetent or unwilling to guard them themselves, became a synonym for monopoly. However, from the company's point of view, monopoly was not the purpose of the trust—that had been achieved before the device was invented. Centralization of the management of diverse and far-flung operations in the interest of efficiency was its chief function.

Competition and Monopoly: Retailing and Utilities

That utilities such as the telephone and electric lighting industries tended to form monopolies is not difficult to explain, for in such fields competition involved costly duplication of equipment and, particularly in the case of the telephone, loss of service efficiency. However, competitive pressures were strong in the early stages of their development. Since these industries depended on patents, Bell and Edison had to fight mighty battles in the courts with rivals seeking to infringe on their rights. A patent, Edison said bitterly, was "simply an invitation to a lawsuit."

The pattern of competition leading to dominance by a few great companies was repeated in many businesses. In life insurance an immense expansion took place after the Civil War. High-pressure salesmanship prevailed; agents gave rebates to customers by shaving their own commissions; companies stole crack agents from their rivals and raided new territories. They sometimes invested as much as 96 percent of the first year's premiums in obtaining new business. By 1900, after three decades of fierce competition, three giants dominated the industry—Equitable, New York Life, and Mutual Life, each with approximately $1 billion of insurance in force.

▶ Watch the Video
Rural Free Delivery Mail at
myhistorylab.com

American Ambivalence to Big Business

The expansion of industry and its concentration in fewer and fewer hands changed the way many people felt about the role of government in economic and social affairs. On the one hand, they professed to believe strongly in a government policy of noninterference, or **laissez-faire**. " 'Things regulate themselves' . . . means, of course, that God regulates them by his general laws," Professor Francis Bowen of Harvard wrote in his *American Political Economy* (1870).

Certain intellectual currents encouraged this type of thinking. Charles Darwin's *The Origin of Species* was published in 1859, and by the 1870s his theory of evolution was beginning to influence opinion in the United States. That nature had ordained a kind of inevitable progress, governed by the natural selection of those individual organisms best

A sneeze is captured on film—the first copyrighted movie (1894). In 1889 Thomas A. Edison conceived of a machine that would do for the eye what the phonograph did for the ear. Over the next two years, Edison invented two separate devices—a camera to take a rapid sequence of pictures and a machine to view them, called a kinetoscope. In 1893 he developed reliable film for his camera. The motion picture industry was born.

adapted to survive in a particular environment, seemed eminently reasonable to most Americans, for it fitted well with their own experiences. "Let the buyer beware; that covers the whole business," the sugar magnate Henry O. Havemeyer explained to an investigating committee. "You cannot wet-nurse people from the time they are born until the time they die. They have to wade and get stuck, and that is the way men are educated."

This reasoning was similar to that of the classical economists and was thus at least as old as Adam Smith's *Wealth of Nations* (1776). But it appeared to supply a hard scientific substitute for Smith's "invisible hand" as an explanation of why free competition advanced the common good.

Yale professor William Graham Sumner sometimes used the survival-of-the-fittest analogy in teaching undergraduates. "Professor," one student asked Sumner, "don't you believe in any government aid to industries?" "No!" Sumner replied, "It's root, hog, or die." The student persisted: "Suppose some professor of political science came along and took your job away from you. Wouldn't you be sore?" "Any other professor is welcome to try," Sumner answered promptly. "If he gets my job, it is my fault. My business is to teach the subject so well that no one can take the job away from me." Sumner's argument described what came to be known as **social Darwinism,** the belief that the activities of people, that is, their business and social relationships, were governed by the Darwinian principle that "the fittest" will always "survive" if allowed to exercise their capacities without restriction.

But the fact that Americans disliked powerful governments in general and strict regulation of the economy in particular had never meant that they objected to all government activity in the economic sphere. Banking laws, tariffs, internal-improvement legislation, and the granting of public land to railroads are only the most obvious of the economic regulations enforced in the nineteenth century by both the federal government and the states. Americans saw no contradiction between government activities of this type and the free enterprise philosophy.

The growth of huge industrial and financial organizations and the increasing complexity of economic relations frightened people yet made them at the same time greedy for more of the goods and services the new society was turning out. To many, the great new corporations and trusts resembled Frankenstein's monster—marvelous and powerful but a grave threat to society.

To some extent public fear of the industrial giants reflected concern about monopoly—much as some people today worry that Walmart may drive other retailers out of business. If Standard Oil dominated oil refining, it might raise prices inordinately at vast cost to consumers.

Far more important in causing resentment was the fear that the monopolists were destroying economic opportunity and threatening democratic institutions. It was not the wealth of tycoons like Carnegie and Rockefeller and Morgan so much as their influence that worried people. "The belief is common," wrote Charles Francis Adams's brother Henry as early as 1870, "that the day is at hand when corporations . . . will ultimately succeed in directing government itself."

Table 17.1   Defenders of Economic Consolidation

Defenders	Occupation	Argument
J. Pierpont Morgan	Wall Street financier	Excessive competition was wasteful and unstable; stable growth and efficiency required large business combinations
William Graham Sumner	Yale professor	Large corporations were those that were "fittest"—best-suited to prevail in the Darwinian world of capitalism
Andrew Carnegie	Steel manufacturer	Large corporations generated wealth, which could be channeled into charitable and other worthy causes

As criticism mounted, business leaders rose to their own defense. Rockefeller described in graphic terms the chaotic conditions that plagued the oil industry before the rise of Standard Oil: "It seemed absolutely necessary to extend the market for oil . . . and also greatly improve the process of refining so that oil could be made and sold cheaply, yet with a profit. We proceeded to buy the largest and best refining concerns and centralized the administration of them with a view to securing greater economy and efficiency." Carnegie, in an essay published in 1889, insisted that the concentration of wealth was necessary if humanity was to progress, softening this "Gospel of Wealth" by insisting that the rich must use their money "in the manner which . . . is best calculated to produce the most beneficial results for the community."

The voices of the critics were louder if not necessarily more influential. Many clergymen denounced unrestrained competition, which they considered un-Christian. The new class of professional economists tended to repudiate laissez-faire. State aid, Richard T. Ely of Johns Hopkins University wrote, "is an indispensable condition of human progress."

Reformers: George, Bellamy, Lloyd

The popularity of a number of radical theorists reflects public feeling in the period. In 1879 Henry George, a California journalist, published *Progress and Poverty*, a forthright attack on the uneven distribution of wealth in the United States. George argued that labor was the true and only source of capital. Observing the speculative fever of the West, which enabled landowners to reap profits merely by holding property while population increased, George proposed a property tax that would confiscate this "unearned increment." George's "single tax," as others called it, would bring in so much money that no other taxes would be necessary, and the government would have plenty of funds to establish badly needed social and cultural services. Single tax clubs sprang up throughout the nation, and *Progress and Poverty* became a best-seller.

Even more spectacular was the reception afforded *Looking Backward, 2000–1887*, a utopian novel written in 1888 by Edward Bellamy. This book, which sold over a million copies in its first few years, described a future America that was completely socialized, all economic activity carefully planned. Bellamy compared nineteenth-century

Edward Bellamy, author of the utopian novel *Looking Backward* (1888). Bellamy's socialism worried many. *The Household Encyclopedia* (1892) included this photograph of Bellamy in a section on phrenology, the "science" of ascertaining a person's character and intellectual traits from the shape of his or her cranium. Referring to Bellamy's, it concluded, "Large perceptive faculties; defective reasoning powers."

society to a lumbering stagecoach upon which the favored few rode in comfort while the mass of the people hauled them along life's route. The trend toward consolidation would continue, he predicted, until one monster trust controlled all economic activity. At this point everyone would realize that nationalization was essential.

A third influential attack on monopoly was that of Henry Demarest Lloyd, whose *Wealth Against Commonwealth* appeared in 1894. Lloyd, a journalist of independent means, devoted years to preparing a denunciation of the Standard Oil Company. Marshaling masses of facts and vivid examples of Standard's evildoing, he assaulted the trust at every point. In his zeal, Lloyd sometimes distorted and exaggerated the evidence; his forceful but uncomplicated arguments and his copious references to official documents made *Wealth Against Commonwealth* utterly convincing to thousands. The book was more than an attack on Standard Oil. Lloyd denounced the application of Darwin's concept of survival of the fittest to economic and social affairs, and he condemned laissez-faire policies as leading directly to monopoly.

The popularity of these books indicates that the trend toward monopoly in the United States worried many. But despite the drastic changes suggested in their pages, none of these writers questioned the underlying values of the middle-class majority. They insisted that reform could be accomplished without serious inconvenience to any individual or class.

Most of their millions of readers did not seriously consider trying to apply the reformers' ideas. Henry George ran for mayor of New York City in 1886 and lost narrowly to Abram S. Hewitt, a wealthy iron manufacturer, but even if he had won, he would have been powerless to apply the single tax to metropolitan property. The national discontent was apparently not as profound as the popularity of these works might suggest.

Reformers: The Marxists

By the 1870s the ideas of European socialists were beginning to penetrate the United States, and in 1877 a Socialist Labor party was founded. The first serious attempt to explain the ideas of German political philosopher Karl Marx to Americans was Laurence Gronlund's *The Cooperative Commonwealth*, which was published in 1884, two years before Marx's *Das Kapital* was translated into English.

Capitalism, Gronlund claimed, contained the seeds of its own destruction. The state ought to own all the means of production. Competition was "Established Anarchy," middlemen were "parasites," speculators "vampires." Yet like other harsh critics of that day, Gronlund expected the millennium to arrive in a peaceful, indeed orderly manner. The movement could accommodate "representatives of all classes," even "thoughtful" middlemen parasites.

The leading voice of the Socialist Labor party, Daniel De Leon, editor of the party's weekly publication, *The People*, was a different type. He was born in the West Indies, son of a Dutch army doctor stationed in Curaçao, and educated in Europe. He emigrated to the United States in the 1870s, where he was progressively attracted by the ideas of Henry George, then Edward Bellamy and the Knights of Labor, and finally Marx. While personally mild-mannered and kindly, when he put pen to paper he became a doctrinaire revolutionary. He excoriated American labor unions in *The People*, insisting that industrial workers could improve their lot only by adopting socialism and joining the

Table 17.2 Reformers Oppose Economic Consolidation

Reformers	Publication	Argument
Henry George	Author, *Progress and Poverty* (1879)	Labor was the source of wealth; but investors made money from *capital and property*. Governments should tax property, to help redistribute the unearned income of the wealthy.
Edward Bellamy	Author, *Looking Backward* (1888)	The trend toward industrial concentration would culminate in the government owning everything: an era of prosperity, stability, and cooperative planning would ensue.
Henry Demarest Lloyd	Author, *Wealth Against Commonwealth* (1894)	Concentration of power in corporations inevitably led to monopoly; the government must step in to prevent corporations from becoming behemoths.
Laurence Gronlund	Author, *The Cooperative Commonwealth* (1884)	Capitalism, including corporations, was doomed, as Marx had predicted; but the collapse of capitalism would not require a violent revolution.
Daniel De Leon	Editor, Socialist Labor, *The Weekly*	Capitalism, though doomed, would not fall without a fight; violent revolution was inevitable.

Socialist Labor party. He paid scant attention, however, to the practical needs or even to the opinions of rank-and-file working people. In 1891 he was the Socialist Labor party's candidate for governor of New York.

The Government Reacts to Big Business: Railroad Regulation

Political action related to the growth of big business came first on the state level and dealt chiefly with the regulation of railroads. Even before the Civil War, a number of New England states established railroad commissions to supervise lines within their borders; by the end of the century, twenty-eight states had such boards.

Strict regulation was largely the result of agitation by the **National Grange of the Patrons of Husbandry**. The Grange, founded in 1867 by Oliver H. Kelley, was created to provide social and cultural benefits for isolated rural communities. As it spread and grew in influence—fourteen states had Granges by 1872 and membership reached 800,000 in 1874—the movement became political too. "Granger" candidates won control of a number of state legislatures in the West and South. Granger-controlled legislatures established "reasonable" maximum rates and outlawed "unjust" discrimination. The legislature also set up a commission to enforce the laws and punish violators.

The railroads protested, insisting that they were being deprived of property without due process of law. In *Munn v. Illinois* (1877), a case that involved a grain elevator whose owner had refused to comply with a state warehouse act, the Supreme Court upheld the constitutionality of this kind of act. Any business that served a public interest, such as a railroad or a grain warehouse, was subject to state control, the justices ruled. Legislatures might fix maximum charges; if the charges seemed unreasonable to the parties concerned, they should direct their complaints to the legislatures or to the voters, not to the courts.

Regulation of the railroad network by the individual states was inefficient, and in some cases the commissions were incompetent and even corrupt. When the Supreme Court, in the case of *Wabash, St. Louis & Pacific Railroad v. Illinois* (1886), declared unconstitutional an Illinois regulation outlawing the long-and-short-haul evil, federal action became necessary. The railroad had charged twenty-five cents per 100 pounds for shipping goods from Gilman, Illinois, to New York City but only fifteen cents to ship goods from Peoria, which was eighty-six miles farther from New York. Illinois judges had held this to be illegal, but the Supreme Court decided that Illinois could not regulate interstate shipments.

Congress filled the gap created by the *Wabash* decision in 1887 by passing the **Interstate Commerce Act**. All charges made by railroads "shall be reasonable and just," the act stated. Rebates, drawbacks, the long-and-short-haul evil, and other competitive practices were declared unlawful, and so were their monopolistic counterparts—pools and traffic-sharing agreements. Railroads were required to publish

●●●─ Read the **Document**

Interstate Commerce Act at
myhistorylab.com

A farmer with a pitchfork, wearing a hat identifying him as a Granger, warns of an oncoming railroad train. But the American people—one reads a newspaper, another smokes a cigar, but most doze—are oblivious of the danger that will soon crush them.

schedules of rates and forbidden to change them without due public notice. Most important, the law established an Interstate Commerce Commission (ICC), the first federal regulatory board, to supervise the affairs of railroads, investigate complaints, and issue cease and desist orders when the roads acted illegally.

The new commission had less power than the law seemed to give it. It could not fix rates; it could only bring the roads to court when it considered rates unreasonably high. Such cases could be extremely complicated; applying the law "was like cutting a path through a jungle." With the truth so hard to determine and the burden of proof on the commission, the courts in nearly every instance decided in favor of the railroads.

Nevertheless, by describing so clearly the right of Congress to regulate private corporations engaged in interstate commerce, the Interstate Commerce Act challenged the philosophy of laissez-faire. Later legislation made the commission more effective. The commission also served as the model for a host of similar federal administrative authorities, such as the Federal Communications Commission (1934).

The Government Reacts to Big Business: The Sherman Antitrust Act

As with railroad legislation, the first antitrust laws originated in the states, but they were southern and western states with relatively little industry, and most of the statutes were vaguely worded and ill-enforced. Federal action came in 1890 with the passage of the **Sherman Antitrust Act**. Any combination "in the form of trust or otherwise" that was "in restraint of trade or commerce among the several states, or with foreign nations" was declared illegal. Persons forming such combinations were subject to fines of $5,000 and a year in jail. Individuals and businesses suffering losses because of actions that violated the law were authorized to sue in the federal courts for triple damages.

Where the Interstate Commerce Act sought to outlaw the excesses of competition, the Sherman Act was supposed to restore competition. If businessmen joined together to "restrain" (monopolize) trade in a particular field, they should be punished and their deeds undone. "The great thing this bill does," Senator George Frisbie Hoar of Massachusetts explained, "is to extend the common-law principle . . . to international and interstate commerce." This was important because the states ran into legal difficulties when they tried to use the common law to restrict corporations engaged in interstate activities.

The Supreme Court quickly emasculated the Sherman Act. In *United States v. E. C. Knight Company* (1895) it held that the American Sugar Refining Company had not violated the law by taking over a number of important competitors. Although the Sugar Trust now controlled about 98 percent of all sugar refining in the United States, it was not restraining trade. "Doubtless the power to control the manufacture of a given thing involves in a certain sense the control of its disposition," the Court said in one of the greatest feats of judicial understatement of all time. "Although the exercise of that power may result in bringing the operation of commerce into play, it does not control it, and affects it only incidentally and indirectly."

If the creation of the Sugar Trust did not violate the Sherman Act, it seemed unlikely that any other combination of manufacturers could be convicted under the law. However, in several cases in 1898 and 1899 the Supreme Court ruled that agreements to fix prices or divide markets did violate the Sherman Act. These decisions precipitated a wave of

Table 17.3 **Major Congressional and Supreme Court Decisions Concerning Corporations**

Case/Act	Year	Decision/Action	Consequence
Munn v. Illinois	1877	State legislatures can regulate economic enterprises	Expansion of state powers against powerful corporations and trusts
Wabash, St. Louis & Pacific Railroad v. Illinois	1886	State legislatures can NOT regulate interstate economic activity; only federal government can do that	Congress passes Interstate Commerce Act 1887, regulating railroad behavior
Interstate Commerce Act	1887	Federal government can regulate railroad rates and practices	Sets precedent for federal intervention in national economic matters
Sherman Antitrust Act	1890	The federal government can break up economic enterprises that are so big and powerful that they have a monopoly	Originally used to weaken labor unions; eventually allows government to break up large corporations
United States v. E. C. Knight	1895	Huge corporations that dominated markets can not be broken up if they do not also behave badly	Weakens Sherman Antitrust Act

outright mergers in which a handful of large companies swallowed up hundreds of smaller ones. Presumably mergers were not illegal. When, some years after his retirement, Andrew Carnegie was asked by a committee of the House of Representatives to explain how he had dared participate in the formation of the U.S. Steel Corporation, he replied, "Nobody ever mentioned the Sherman Act to me that I remember."

The Labor Union Movement

At the time of the Civil War only a small percentage of the American workforce was organized, and most union members were cigarmakers, printers, carpenters, and other skilled artisans, not factory hands. Aside from ironworkers, railroad workers, and miners, few industrial laborers belonged to unions. Nevertheless the union was the workers' response to the big corporation: a combination designed to eliminate competition for jobs and to provide efficient organization for labor.

After 1865 the growth of national craft unions, which had been stimulated by labor dissatisfaction during the Civil War, quickened perceptibly. In 1866 a federation of these organizations, the National Labor Union, was founded and by the early 1870s many new trades, notably in railroading, had been unionized.

Most of the leaders of these unions were visionaries who were out of touch with the practical needs and aspirations of workers. They opposed the wage system, strikes, and anything that increased the laborers' sense of being members of the working class. A major objective was the formation of worker-owned cooperatives.

Far more remarkable was the **Knights of Labor**, a curious organization founded in 1869 by a group of Philadelphia garment workers headed by Uriah S. Stephens. Like so many labor organizers of the period, Stephens was a reformer of wide interests rather than a man dedicated to the specific problems of industrial workers. He, his successor Terence V. Powderly, and many other leaders of the Knights would have been thoroughly at home in the labor organizations of the Jacksonian era. Like the Jacksonians, they supported political objectives that had no direct connection with working conditions, such as currency reform and the curbing of land speculation. They rejected the idea that workers must resign themselves to remaining wage earners. By pooling their resources, working people could advance up the economic ladder and enter the capitalist class. The leading Knights saw no contradiction between their denunciation of "soulless" monopolies and "drones" like bankers and lawyers and their talk of "combining all branches of trade in one common brotherhood." Such muddled thinking led the Knights to attack the wage system and to frown on strikes as "acts of private warfare."

> **View** the **Image**
> *Terence Powderly at Knights of Labor Convention* at **myhistorylab.com**

If the Knights had one foot in the past, they also had one foot in the future. They supported some startlingly advanced ideas. Rejecting the traditional grouping of workers by crafts, they developed a concept closely resembling modern industrial unionism. They welcomed blacks, women, and immigrants, and they accepted unskilled workers as well as artisans. The eight-hour day was one of their basic demands, their argument being that increased leisure would give workers time to develop more cultivated tastes and higher aspirations. Higher pay would inevitably follow.

Between 1882 and 1886 successful strikes by local "assemblies" against western railroads, including one against the hated Jay Gould's Missouri Pacific, brought recruits by the thousands. The membership passed 42,000 in 1882, 110,000 in 1885, and in 1886 it soared beyond the 700,000 mark. Alas, sudden prosperity was too much for the Knights. Its national leadership was unable to control local groups. A number of poorly planned strikes failed dismally, and the public was alienated by sporadic acts of violence and intimidation. Disillusioned recruits began to drift away.

Circumstances largely fortuitous caused the collapse of the organization. By 1886 the movement for the eight-hour day had gained wide support among workers, including many who did not belong to unions. Several hundred thousand were on strike in various parts of the country by May of that year. In Chicago, a center of the eight-hour movement, about 80,000 workers were involved, and a small group of anarchists was trying to take advantage of the excitement to win support.

When a striker was killed in a fracas at the McCormick Harvesting Machine Company, the anarchists called a protest meeting on May 4, at Haymarket Square. Police intervened to break up the meeting, and someone—his identity was never established—hurled a bomb into their ranks. Seven policemen were killed and many others injured.

The American Federation of Labor

Although the anarchists were the immediate victims of the resulting public indignation and hysteria, organized labor, especially the Knights, suffered heavily. No tie between the Knights and the bombing could be established, but the union had been closely connected with the eight-hour agitation, and the public tended to associate it with violence and radicalism. Its membership declined as suddenly as it had risen, and soon it ceased to exist as a force in the labor movement.

The Knights' place was taken by the **American Federation of Labor (AFL)**, a combination of national craft unions established in 1886. In a sense the AFL was a reactionary organization. Its principal leaders, Adolph Strasser and Samuel Gompers of the Cigarmakers Union, were, like the founders of the Knights of Labor, originally interested in utopian social reforms. They even toyed with the idea of forming a workers' political party. Experience, however, soon led them to concentrate on organizing skilled workers and fighting for "bread-and-butter" issues such as higher wages and shorter hours.

Strasser and Gompers paid great attention to building a strong organization of dues-paying members committed to unionism as a way of improving their lot. Rank-and-file AFL members were naturally eager to win wage increases and other benefits, but most also valued their unions for the companionship they provided, the sense of belonging to a group. Unions were a kind of club as well as a means of defending and advancing their members' material interests.

The chief weapon of the federation was the strike, which it used to win concessions from employers and to attract recruits. Gompers, president of the AFL almost continuously from 1886 until his death in 1924, encouraged workers to make "intelligent use of the ballot" in order to advance their interests. The federation avoided direct involvement in politics. "I have my own philosophy and my own dreams," Gompers once told a left-wing French politician, "but first and foremost I want to increase the workingman's welfare year by year. . . . The French workers waste their economic force by their political divisions."

On November 11, 1887, four anarchists were hanged in Chicago on charges they had thrown a bomb that had killed policemen at the Haymarket demonstration. The *Chicago Tribune* reported that after nooses were placed around the men's necks, and white hoods over their heads, "for a moment or two the men stood like ghosts." "Long live anarchy" one shouted.

Gompers's approach to labor problems produced solid, if unspectacular, growth for the AFL. Unions with a total of about 150,000 members formed the federation in 1886. By 1892 the membership had reached 250,000, and in 1901 it passed the million mark.

Labor Militancy Rebuffed

The stress of the AFL on the strike weapon reflected rather than caused the increasing militancy of labor. Workers felt themselves threatened from all sides: the growing size and power of their corporate employers; the substitution of machines for human skills; the invasion of foreign workers willing to accept substandard wages. At the same time they had tasted some of the material benefits of industrialization and had learned the advantages of concerted action.

The average employer behaved like a tyrant when dealing with his workers: He discharged them arbitrarily when they tried to organize unions; he hired scabs to replace strikers; he frequently failed to provide the most rudimentary protection against injury on the job. Some employers, Carnegie for example, professed to approve of unions, but almost none would bargain with labor collectively. To do so, they argued, would be to deprive workers of their freedom to contract for their own labor in any way they saw fit.

The industrialists of the period were not all ogres; they were as alarmed by the rapid changes of the times as their workers, and since they had more at stake materially, they were probably more frightened by the uncertainties. Deflation, technological change, and intense competition kept even the most successful under constant pressure.

The thinking of most employers was remarkably confused. They considered workers who joined unions "disloyal," and at the same time they treated labor as a commodity to be purchased as cheaply as possible. When labor was scarce, employers resisted demands for higher wages by arguing that the price of labor was controlled by its productivity; when it was plentiful, they justified reducing wages by referring to the law of supply and demand.

Thus capital and labor were often spoiling for a fight, frequently without fully understanding why. When labor troubles developed, they tended to be bitter, even violent. In 1877 a great railroad strike convulsed much of the nation. It began on the Baltimore and Ohio system in response to a wage cut and spread to other eastern lines and then throughout the West until about two-thirds of the railroad mileage of the country had been shut down. Violence broke out, rail yards were put to the torch, and dismayed and frightened businessmen formed militia companies to patrol the streets of Chicago and other cities. Eventually President Hayes sent federal troops to the trouble spots to restore order, and the strike collapsed. There had been no real danger of revolution, but the violence and destruction of the strike had been without precedent in America.

The disturbances of 1877 were a response to a business slump, those of the next decade a response to good times. Twice as many strikes occurred in 1886 as in any previous year. Even before the Haymarket bombing centered the country's attention on labor problems, the situation had become so disturbing that President Grover Cleveland, in the first presidential message devoted to labor problems, had urged Congress to create a voluntary arbitration board to aid in settling labor disputes— a remarkable suggestion for a man of Cleveland's conservative, laissez-faire approach to economic issues.

In 1892 a violent strike broke out among silver miners at Coeur d'Alene, Idaho, and a far more important clash shook Andrew Carnegie's Homestead steel plant near Pittsburgh when strikers attacked 300 private guards brought in to protect strikebreakers. Seven guards were killed at Homestead and the rest forced to "surrender" and march off ignominiously. The Homestead affair was part of a struggle between capital and labor in the steel industry. Steel producers insisted that the workers were holding back progress by resisting technological advances, while the workers believed that the company was refusing to share the fruits of more efficient operation fairly. The strike was precipitated by the decision of company officials to crush the union at all costs. The final defeat, after a five-month walkout, of the 24,000-member Amalgamated Association of Iron and Steel Workers, one of the most important elements in the AFL, destroyed unionism as an effective force in the steel industry and set back the progress of organized labor all over the country.

As in the case of the Haymarket bombing, the activities of radicals on the fringe of the dispute turned the public against the steelworkers. The boss of Homestead was Henry Clay Frick, a tough-minded foe of unions who was determined to "teach our employees a lesson." Frick made the decision to bring in strikebreakers and to employ Pinkerton detectives to protect them. During the course of the strike, Alexander Berkman, an anarchist, burst into Frick's office and attempted to assassinate him. Frick was only slightly wounded, but the attack brought him much sympathy and unjustly discredited the strikers.

The most important strike of the period took place in 1894. It began when the workers at George Pullman's Palace Car factory outside Chicago walked out in protest against wage cuts. Some Pullman workers belonged to the American Railway Union, headed by Eugene V. Debs. After the strike had dragged along for weeks, the union voted to refuse to handle trains with Pullman sleeper cars. The union was perfectly willing to handle mail trains, but the owners refused to run trains unless they were made up of a full complement of cars.

When Pullman cars were added to mail trains, the workers refused to move them. The resulting railroad strike tied up trunk lines running in and out of Chicago. The railroad owners appealed to President Cleveland to send troops to preserve order. On the pretext that the soldiers were needed to ensure the movement of the mails, Cleveland agreed. When Debs defied a federal injunction to end the walkout, he was jailed for contempt and the strike was broken.

Whither America, Whither Democracy?

Each year more of the nation's wealth and power seemed to fall into fewer hands. As with the railroads, other industries were being influenced, if not completely dominated, by bankers. The firm of J.P. Morgan and Company controlled many railroads; the largest steel, electrical, agricultural machinery, rubber, and shipping companies; two life insurance companies; and a number of banks. By 1913 Morgan and the Rockefeller National City Bank group between them could name 341 directors to 112 corporations worth over $22.2 billion. The "Money Trust," a loose but potent fraternity of financiers, seemed fated to become the ultimate monopoly.

Centralization unquestionably increased efficiency, at least in industries that used a great deal of expensive machinery to turn out goods for the mass market, and in those where close coordination of output, distribution, and sales was important. The public benefited immensely from the productive efficiency of the new empires. Living standards rose.

The crushing of the Pullman strike demonstrated the power of the courts to break strikes by issuing injunctions. And the courts seemed only concerned with protecting the interests of the rich and powerful. Particularly ominous for organized labor was the fact that the federal government based its request for the injunction that broke the strike on the Sherman Antitrust Act, arguing that the American Railway Union was a combination in restraint of trade. An indirect result of the Pullman strike was that while serving his sentence for contempt, Eugene Debs was visited by a number of prominent socialists who sought to convert him to their cause. One gave him a copy of Karl Marx's *Capital*, which he found too dull to finish, but he did read *Looking Backward* and *Wealth Against Commonwealth*. In 1897 he became a socialist.

Milestones

1859	First oil well is drilled in Pennsylvania	1886	Craft unions found American Federation of Labor (AFL)
	Charles Darwin publishes *The Origin of Species*	1887	Interstate Commerce Act regulates railroads
1868	Carnegie Steel Company is formed		
1869	George Westinghouse invents air brake	1888	Edward Bellamy publishes utopian *Looking Backward*
	Garment workers found Knights of Labor	1889	Philanthropist Andrew Carnegie publishes "Gospel of Wealth"
1870–1890	Railroad trunk lines are completed	1890	Sherman Antitrust Act outlaws monopolies
1876	Alexander Graham Bell invents telephone	1892	Seven Pinkerton guards are killed in Homestead steel strike
1877	Great railroad strike convulses nation		General Electric Company is formed
	Munn v. Illinois upholds state regulatory laws	1894	Eugene V. Debs leads American Railway Union in Pullman strike
1879	Thomas Edison invents electric light bulb		Henry Demarest Lloyd condemns laissez-faire in *Wealth Against the Commonwealth*
	Reformer Henry George publishes *Progress and Poverty*		
1884	Marxist Laurence Gronlund publishes *The Cooperative Commonwealth*	1895	*U.S. v. E.C. Knight Company* weakens Sherman Act
1886	Anarchists clash with police in Chicago's Haymarket bombing	1901	J.P. Morgan forms U.S. Steel, "world's first billion-dollar corporation"

✓●─[Study and **Review** at **www.myhistorylab.com**

Review Questions

1. The introduction asked whether the benefits of economic concentration outweighed its social and political costs. List the benefits and costs: Which argument is stronger?
2. What factors contributed to the nation's extraordinarily rapid industrial growth during the last third of the nineteenth century?
3. What technological developments had the greatest economic impact? Greatest social impact?
4. Who were the major critics of economic concentration in the late nineteenth century and how did they differ?
5. How did Congress respond to critics of monopoly? How did the Supreme Court respond to attempts to regulate the economy?

Key Terms

American Federation of Labor (AFL)   *472*
Interstate Commerce Act   *468*
Knights of Labor   *471*

laissez-faire   *462*
National Grange of the Patrons of Husbandry   *467*

Sherman Antitrust Act   *469*
social Darwinism   *464*

American Society in the Industrial Age

18

((•—⌐Hear the Audio Chapter 18 at myhistorylab.com

Have you been kicked out of a mall?

THE MALL OF AMERICA OUTSIDE MINNEAPOLIS, MINNESOTA, IS THE largest enclosed mall in the United States. It is also the nation's most popular tourist destination, visited by 42.5 million people in 2009.

This mall, like many others, was also once a popular hangout for young people. On Friday and Saturday nights, as many as 10,000 teenagers would gather there. But this practice ended in 1996, when the Mall of America instituted a 6:00 PM weekend curfew for teenagers under sixteen unless accompanied by an adult. Since then, hundreds of malls have adopted similar curfews.

Teenagers, who in 2009 bought $170 billion in merchandise, spend much of their free time in malls—over fifty minutes a day on the average. Many resent the curfews. Malls insist that as privately owned enterprises, they are exempt from First Amendment protections, such as freedom of speech and the right to assemble. Malls are not public property.

Yet recent malls have been designed to evoke the public spaces of the nineteenth-century city. The Mall of America includes an exhibition gallery, amusement park, wedding chapel, assembly hall, school, medical clinic, and a central "Rotunda" for staging "public events" ranging from gardening shows to Hulk Hogan wrestling matches.

In the late nineteenth century, city life was played out in spaces that really were public. Factory workers walked to work along crowded streets or jammed into streetcars or subways. Courting couples strolled through shopping districts or public parks. Children played in streets. "Little Italy" or "Chinatown" provided exotic attractions for all. Amusement parks and sporting events drew huge throngs.

But city life was not for all. In 1900, 50 percent more Americans lived in rural areas than in urban areas—even when "urban" was generously defined as holding more than 2,500 people. Why, asked sociologist Henry Fletcher in 1895, do "large masses of people, apparently against their own interests," abandon the nation's healthful and sociable rural areas and crowd into the nation's disease-ridden, anonymous cities?

Nineteenth-century cities, though noisy, chaotic, and often ill-governed, exerted a peculiar fascination. In cities, workers, even immigrants and young women, could more easily find jobs. Housing was cheap. Urban problems were daunting, but the immense aggregation of peoples and their resources constituted a limitless potential for uplift and reform.

Middle-Class Life

"This middle-class country had got a middle-class president, at last," Ralph Waldo Emerson had noted with satisfaction when Lincoln took office in 1861. Lincoln, in contrast to the presidents who had been wealthy planters or businessmen or high-ranking military men, was a self-made man who embraced middle-class values. Middle-class culture took the best aspects of romanticism—the enshrinement of human potential, the restless striving for personal betterment, the zest for competition and excitement— and tempered them with a passion for self-control and regularity.

But the Civil War sapped middle-class culture of its reforming zeal. The vital energy that invigorated antebellum reforms and had impelled the North to war became dissipated by that war. Afterwards, middle-class Americans focused their energies on building

The Breakfast (1911), by William McGregor Paxton, shows a middle-class husband, absorbed in the newspaper and in the world beyond the home. His wife, in a gorgeous dress, sits—very much a "bird in a gilded cage," the title of a popular song in 1900. The servant girl, face unseen, cleans up the cage.

Source: *The Breakfast*, William McGregor Paxton, American, 1911 The Metropolitan Museum of Art, New York, NY, U.S.A. Image copyright ©The Metropolitan Museum of Art.

institutions. American society and culture underwent a process of "incorporation," as the predominant form of the business world seeped deep into the American consciousness.

No institution was more central to middle-class life than the family. After the Civil War, it lost some of its moral fervor but gained a new substantiality. Increasingly family life was defined in terms of tangible goods. Modern scholars have often indicted this "culture of consumption" for its superficiality, a criticism commonly aired by patrician elites at the time. But no attack on middle-class culture and its conspicuous consumption surpassed the venom of Thorstein Veblen's *Theory of the Leisure Class* (1899). Veblen contended that consumers derived little real pleasure from their big homes and gaudy purchases; they were simply showing off their wealth. No one was ever satisfied with their wealth because everyone else was scrambling to get ahead of them. Everyone wanted more.   Still true today

Middle-class people regarded the matter differently. They conceived of the family as a refuge from the increasingly chaotic and unsavory aspects of urban life: A beautiful house that was filled with books, paintings, and musical instruments would inculcate the finer sensibilities and elevate the minds of its occupants. Better for children to find stimulation at home than to visit the vice districts or unsupervised amusements downtown. The abundant material culture of the "Victorian age" reflected not its superficiality but its solidity.

Skilled and Unskilled Workers

Wage earners, too, were drawn to urban areas. They felt the full force of the industrial tide, being affected in countless ways—some beneficial, others unfortunate. As manufacturing became more important, the number of manufacturing workers increased nearly ten-fold, from around 600,000 in 1860 to nearly 5 million in 1890. While workers lacked much sense of solidarity, they exerted a far larger influence on society at the turn of the century than they had in the years before the Civil War.

More efficient methods of production enabled them to increase their output, making possible a rise in their standard of living. The working day still tended to approximate the hours of daylight, but it was shortening perceptibly by the 1880s, at least in many occupations. In 1860 the average had been eleven hours, but by 1880 only one worker in four labored more than ten hours and radicals were beginning to talk about eight hours as a fair day's work.

Industrialization created problems for workers beyond the obvious one of earning enough money to support themselves. By and large, skilled workers improved their positions relatively, despite the increased use of machinery. Furthermore, when machines took the place of human skills, jobs became monotonous. Mechanization undermined both the artisans' pride and their bargaining power with employers. As expensive machinery became more important, the worker seemed of necessity less important. Machines controlled the pace of work and its duration. The time clock regulated the labor force more rigidly than the most exacting foreman. The length of the workday may have declined, but the pace of work and the danger involved in working around heavy, high-speed machinery increased accordingly.

Another problem for workers was that industrialization tended to accentuate swings of the business cycle. On the upswing something approaching full employment

This girl ran four spinning machines in a cotton mill in Whitnel, North Carolina. Only four feet, three inches tall, she earned forty-eight cents a day. Photographer Lewis Hine hoped that pictures such as this one (1908) would generate public support for child labor laws.

existed, but in periods of depression unemployment became a problem that affected workers without regard for their individual abilities. It is significant that the word *unemployment* (though not, of course, the condition itself) was a late-nineteenth-century invention.

Working Women

Women continued to supply a significant part of the industrial working force. But now many more of them were working outside their homes; the factory had almost completely replaced the household as the seat of manufacturing.[1] Such women had no choice but to leave the "domestic sphere" to make a living. Textile mills and "the sewing trades" absorbed a large percentage of women, but in all fields women were paid substantially lower wages than men. *Synthesis*

●◆●─ Read the **Document**

Massachusett Bureau of Statistics of Labor at myhistorylab.com

Women found many new types of work in these years. They made up the overwhelming majority of salespersons and cashiers in the big new department stores. Store managers considered women more polite, easier to control, and more honest than male workers, all qualities especially valuable in the huge emporiums.

Educated, middle-class women also dominated the new profession of nursing that developed alongside the expanding medical profession and the establishment of large urban hospitals. To nearly all doctors, to most men, and indeed to many women of that day, nursing seemed the perfect female profession since it required the same characteristics that women were thought to have by nature: selflessness, cleanliness, kindliness, tact, sensitivity, and submissiveness to male control. Typical was this remark of a contemporary authority: "Since God could not care for all the sick, he made women to nurse." Why it had not occurred to God to make more women physicians, or for that matter members of other prestigious professions like law and the clergy, this man did not explain, probably because it had not occurred to him either.

Middle-class women did replace men as teachers in most of the nation's grade schools, and they also replaced men as clerks and secretaries and operators of the new typewriters in government departments and in business offices. Most men with

---

[1]However, at least half of all working women were domestic servants.

the knowledge of spelling and grammar that these positions required had better opportunities and were uninterested in office work, so women high school graduates, of whom there was an increasing number, filled the gap.

Working-Class Family Life

Early social workers who visited the homes of industrial laborers in this period reported enormous differences in the standard of living of people engaged in the same line of work, differences related to such variables as health, intelligence, the wife's ability as a homemaker, the degree of the family's commitment to middle-class values, and pure luck. Some families spent most of their income on food; others saved substantial sums even when earning no more than $400 or $500 a year. Family incomes varied greatly among workers who received similar hourly wages, depending on the steadiness of employment and on the number of family members holding jobs.

Consider the cases of two families headed by railroad brakemen. One man brought home only $360 to house and feed a wife and eight children. Here is the report of a state official who interviewed the family: "Clothes ragged, children half-dressed and dirty. They all sleep in one room regardless of sex. . . . The entire concern is as wretched as could be imagined. Father is shiftless. . . . Wife is without ambition or industry."

The other brakeman and his wife had only two children, and he earned $484 in 1883. They owned a well-furnished house, kept a cow, and raised vegetables for home consumption. Although they were far from rich, they managed to put aside enough for insurance, reading matter, and a few small luxuries.

It depended on how you spent your money

Working-Class Attitudes

Social workers and government officials made many efforts in the 1880s and 1890s to find out how working people felt about all sorts of matters connected with their jobs. Their reports reveal a wide spectrum of opinion. To the question, asked of two Wisconsin carpenters, "What new laws, in your opinion, ought to be enacted?" one replied, "Keep down strikes and rioters. Let every man attend to his own business." But the other answered, "Complete nationalization of land and all ways of transportation. Burn all government bonds. A graduated income tax. . . . Abolish child labor and [pass] any other act that capitalists say is wrong."

Every variation of opinion between these extremes was expressed by working people in many sections and in many kinds of work. In 1881 a female textile worker in Lawrence, Massachusetts, said to an interviewer, "If you will stand by the mill, and see the people coming out, you will be surprised to see the happy, contented look they all have."

Despite such remarks and the general improvement in living standards, it is clear, if only from the large number of bitter strikes of the period, that there was a considerable dissatisfaction among industrial workers. Writing in 1885, the labor leader Terence V. Powderly reported that "a deep-rooted feeling of discontent pervades the masses."

The discontent had many causes. For some, poverty was still the chief problem, but for others, rising aspirations triggered discontent. Workers were confused about their destiny; the tradition that no one of ability need remain a hired hand died hard. They wanted to believe their bosses and the politicians when those worthies voiced the old slogans about a classless society and the community of interest of capital and labor. The rich were growing richer and more people were growing rich, but ordinary workers were better off too. However, the gap between the very rich and the ordinary citizen was widening. "The tendency . . . is toward centralization and aggregation," the Illinois Bureau of Labor Statistics reported in 1886. "This involves a separation of the people into classes, and the permanently subordinate status of large numbers of them."

Working Your Way Up

Americans in the late nineteenth century believed their society offered great opportunities for individual advancement, and to prove it they pointed to men like Andrew Carnegie and to other poor boys who accumulated large fortunes. How general was the rise from rags to riches (or even to modest comfort) is another question.

Americans had been on the move, mostly, of course, in a westward direction, since the colonial period, but studies of census records show that there was considerable geographic mobility in urban areas throughout the last half of the nineteenth century and into the twentieth. Most investigations reveal that only about half the people recorded in one census were still in the same place ten years later. The nation had a vast reservoir of rootless people. For many, the way to move up in the world was to move on.

In most of the cities studied, mobility was accompanied by some economic and social improvement. On the average, about a quarter of the manual laborers traced rose to middle-class status during their lifetimes, and the sons of manual laborers were still more likely to improve their place in society. In New York City about a third of the Italian and Jewish immigrants of the 1890s had risen from unskilled to skilled jobs a decade later.

Such progress was primarily the result of the economic growth the nation was experiencing and of the energy and ambition of the people, native-born and immigrant alike, who were pouring into the cities in such numbers. The public education system gave an additional boost to the upwardly mobile.

The history of American education after about 1870 reflects the impact of social and economic change. Although Horace Mann, Henry Barnard, and others had laid the foundations for state-supported school systems in the 1840s and 1850s (see Chapter 10), most of these systems became compulsory only after the Civil War, when the growth of cities provided the concentration of population and financial resources necessary for economical mass education. In the 1860s about half the children in the country were getting some formal education, but this did not mean that half the children were attending school at any one time. Sessions were short, especially in rural areas, and many teachers were poorly trained. President Calvin Coolidge noted in his autobiography that the one-room school he attended in rural Vermont in the 1880s was open only in slack seasons when the twenty-odd students were not needed in the fields. "Few, if any, of my teachers reached the standard now required," he wrote, adding that his own younger sister had obtained a teaching certificate and actually taught a class when she was only twelve.

Jacob Riis's photograph of a class on the Lower East Side of New York City. At Riis's death, Theodore Roosevelt called him "the staunchest, most efficient, friend the children of New York City have ever had."

Thereafter, steady growth and improvement took place. Attendance in the public schools increased from 6.8 million in 1870 to 15.5 million in 1900, a remarkable expansion even when allowance is made for the growth of the population. More remarkable still, during a time when prices were declining steadily, public expenditures for education nearly quadrupled. A typical elementary school graduate, at least in the cities, could count on having studied, besides the traditional "Three Rs," history, geography, a bit of science, drawing, and physical training.

Secondary education was still assumed to be only for those with special abilities and youths whose families did not require that they immediately become breadwinners. As late as 1890 fewer than 300,000 of the 14.3 million children attending public and private schools had progressed beyond the eighth grade and nearly a third of these were attending private institutions.

Education certainly helped young people to rise in the world, but progress from rags to real riches was far from common. Carnegies were rare. A study of the family backgrounds of 200 late-nineteenth-century business leaders revealed that nearly all of them grew up in well-to-do middle-class families. They were far better educated than the general run, and most were members of one or another Protestant church.

The unrealistic expectations inspired by the rags-to-riches myth more than the absence of real opportunity probably explains why so many workers, even when expressing dissatisfaction with life as it was, continued to subscribe to such middle-class values as hard work and thrift—that is, they continued to hope.

The "New" Immigration

Industrial expansion increased the need for labor, and this in turn powerfully stimulated immigration. Between 1866 and 1915 about 25 million foreigners entered the United States. Industrial growth alone does not explain the influx. The launching in 1858 of the English liner *Great Eastern*, which was nearly 700 feet from stem to stern and weighed about 19,000 tons, opened a new era in transatlantic travel. Although most immigrants traveled in steerage, which was cramped and almost totally lacking in anything that could be considered an amenity, the Atlantic crossing, once so hazardous, became safe and speedy with the perfection of the steamship. Competition between the great packet lines such as Cunard, North German Lloyd, and Holland-America drove down the cost of the passage, and advertising by the lines further stimulated traffic.

"Push" pressures as well as these "pull" factors had much to do with the new patterns of immigration. Improvements in transportation produced unexpected and disruptive changes in the economies of many European countries. Cheap wheat from the United States, Russia, and other parts of the world poured into Europe, bringing disaster to farmers throughout Europe. The spreading industrial revolution and the increased use of farm machinery led to the collapse of the peasant economy of central and southern Europe. For rural inhabitants this meant the loss of self-sufficiency, the fragmentation of landholdings, unemployment, and for many the decision to make a new start in the New World.

While immigrants continued to people the farms of America, industry absorbed an ever-increasing number of the newcomers. In 1870 one industrial worker in three was foreign-born. When congressional investigators examined twenty-one major industries

German and Irish Settlement in the Northeastern United States, 1870 In 1870, New York was the greatest immigrant city; its Irish population dwarfed that of Philadelphia or Boston. Its German population, too, greatly exceeded that of "German" cities such as Milwaukee and Chicago.

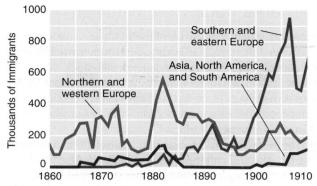

Immigration, 1860–1910 In this graph, Germany is counted as a part of northern and western Europe. Note the new immigration from southern and eastern Europe in the early 1900s.

early in the new century, they discovered that well over half of the labor force had not been born in the United States.

Before 1882, when—in addition to the Chinese—criminals, and persons adjudged mentally defective or liable to become public charges were excluded, entry into the United States was almost unrestricted. Indeed, until 1891 the Atlantic coast states, not the federal government, exercised whatever controls were imposed on newcomers. Even when federally imposed, medical inspection was perfunctory. Public health officials boasted that with "one glance" at each arrival, the inspectors could "take in six details, namely the scalp, face, neck, hands, gait and general condition, both mental and physical." Only those who failed this "test" were examined more closely. On average, only one immigrant in fifty was ultimately rejected.

> **Watch the Video**
> *Ellis Island Immigrants, 1903*
> at **myhistorylab.com**

> **View the Image**
> *Health Check at Ellis Island*
> at **myhistorylab.com**

Private agencies, philanthropic and commercial, served as a link between the new arrivals and employers looking for labor. Until the Foran Act of 1885 outlawed the practice, a few companies brought in skilled workers under contract, advancing them passage money and collecting it in installments from their paychecks, a system somewhat like the indentured servitude of colonial times. Numerous nationality groups assisted (and sometimes exploited) their compatriots by organizing "immigrant banks" that recruited labor in the old country, arranged transportation, and then housed the newcomers in boardinghouses in the United States while finding them jobs.

Beginning in the 1880s, the spreading effects of industrialization in Europe caused a shift in the sources of American immigration from northern and western to southern and eastern sections of the continent. In 1882, 789,000 immigrants entered the United States; more than 350,000 came from Great Britain and Germany, only 32,000 from Italy, and fewer than 17,000 from Russia. In 1907—the all-time peak year, with 1,285,000 immigrants— Great Britain and Germany supplied fewer than half as many as they had twenty-five years earlier, while the **new immigration** from southern and eastern Europe was supplying eleven times as many as then. Up to 1880, only about 200,000 southern and eastern Europeans had migrated to America. Between 1880 and 1910, approximately 8.4 million arrived.

> **See the Map**
> *Foreign-Born Population, 1890*
> at **myhistorylab.com**

New Immigrants Face New Nativism

The "new" immigrants, like the "old" Irish of the 1840s and 1850s, were mostly peasants. They also seemed more than ordinarily clannish; southern Italians typically called all people outside their families *forestieri*, "foreigners." Old-stock Americans thought them harder to assimilate, and in fact many were. Some Italian immigrants, for example, were unmarried men who had come to the United States to earn enough money to buy a farm back home. Such people made hard and willing workers but were not much concerned with being part of an American community.

These "birds of passage" were a substantial minority, but the immigrant who saved in order to bring his wife and children or his younger brothers and sisters to America was more typical. In addition, thousands of immigrants came as family groups and intended to remain. Some, like the eastern European Jewish migrants, were refugees who were almost desperately eager to become Americans, although of course they retained and nurtured much of their traditional culture.

Many "older" Americans concluded, wrongly but understandably, that the new immigrants were incapable of becoming good citizens and should be kept out. During the 1880s, large numbers of social workers, economists, and church leaders, worried by the problems that arose when so many poor immigrants flocked into cities already bursting at the seams, began to believe that some restriction should be placed on the incoming human tide.

Social Darwinists and people obsessed with pseudoscientific ideas about "racial purity" also found the new immigration alarming. Misunderstanding the findings of the new science of genetics, they attributed the social problems associated with mass immigration to supposed physiological characteristics of the newcomers. Forgetting that earlier Americans had accused pre–Civil War Irish and German immigrants of similar deficiencies, they decided that the peoples of southern and eastern Europe were racially inferior to "Nordic" and "Anglo-Saxon" types and ought to be kept out.

Workers, fearing the competition of people with low living standards and no bargaining power, spoke out against the "enticing of penniless and unapprised immigrants . . . to undermine our wages and social welfare." In 1883 the president of the Amalgamated Iron and Steel Workers told a Senate committee that Hungarian, Polish, Italian, and other immigrants "can live where I think a decent man would die; they can live on . . . food that other men would not touch." A Wisconsin iron worker put it this way: "Immigrants work for almost nothing and seem to be able to live on wind—something I can not do."

View the Image

Looking Backward at Immigrant Origins at
myhistorylab.com

Employers were not disturbed by the influx of people with strong backs willing to work hard for low wages. Nevertheless, by the late 1880s many employers were alarmed about the supposed radicalism of the immigrants. The Haymarket bombing focused attention on the handful of foreign-born extremists in the country and loosed a flood of unjustified charges that "anarchists and communists" were dominating the labor movement. **Nativism**, which had grown in the 1850s under the Know-Nothing banner and faded during the Civil War, now flared up again, and for similar reasons. Denunciations of "longhaired, wild-eyed, bad-smelling, atheistic, reckless foreign wretches," of "Europe's human and inhuman rubbish" crowded the pages of the nation's press.

These nativists, again like the pre–Civil War variety, disliked Catholics and other minority groups more than immigrants as such. The largest nativist organization of the period, the American Protective Association, founded in 1887, existed primarily to resist what its members called "the Catholic menace." The Protestant majority treated "new" immigrants as underlings, tried to keep them out of the best jobs, and discouraged their efforts to climb the social ladder. This prejudice functioned only at the social and economic level. But nowhere in America did prejudice lead to interference with religious freedom in the narrow sense. And neither labor leaders nor important industrialists, despite their misgivings about immigration, took a broadly antiforeigner position.

After the Exclusion Act of 1882 and the almost meaningless 1885 ban on importing contract labor, no further restrictions were imposed on immigration until the twentieth century. Strong support for a literacy test for admission developed in the 1890s, pushed by a new organization, the Immigration Restriction League. Since there was much more illiteracy in the southeastern quarter of Europe than in the northwestern, such a test would discriminate without seeming to do so on national or racial grounds. A literacy test bill passed both houses of Congress in 1897, but President Cleveland vetoed it. Such a "radical departure" from the "generous and free-handed policy" of the past, Cleveland said, was unjustified. He added, perhaps with tongue in cheek, that a literacy requirement would not keep out "unruly agitators," who were only too adept at reading and writing.

The Expanding City and Its Problems

Industrialization does not entirely explain the growth of nineteenth-century cities. All the large American cities began as commercial centers, and the development of huge metropolises like New York and Chicago would have been impossible without the national transportation network. But by the final decades of the century, the expansion of industry had become the chief cause of city growth. Thus the urban concentration continued; in 1890 one person in three lived in a city, by 1910 nearly one in two.

A steadily increasing proportion of the urban population was made up of immigrants. In 1890 the foreign-born population of Chicago almost equaled the total population of Chicago in 1880; a third of all Bostonians and a quarter of all Philadelphians were immigrants; and four out of five residents of New York City were either foreign-born or the children of immigrants.

After 1890 the immigrant concentration became even more dense. The migrants from eastern and southern Europe lacked the resources to travel to the agriculturally developing regions. As the concentration progressed it fed upon itself, for all the eastern cities developed many ethnic neighborhoods, in each of which immigrants of one nationality congregated. Lonely, confused, often unable to speak English, the Italians, the Greeks, the Polish and Russian Jews, and other immigrants tended to settle where their predecessors had settled.

Although ethnic neighborhoods were crowded, unhealthy, and crime-ridden, and many of the residents were desperately poor, they were not ghettos in the European sense, for those who lived there were not compelled by law to remain. Thousands "escaped" yearly to better districts. American ghettos were places where hopes and ambitions were fulfilled, where people worked hard and endured hardships in order to improve their own and their children's lot.

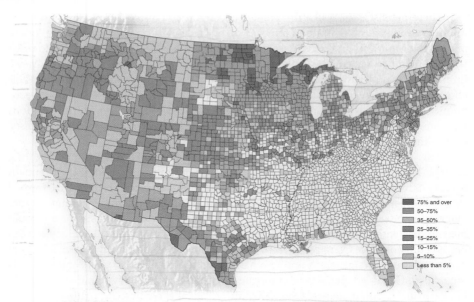

	75% and over
	50–75%
	35–50%
	25–35%
	15–25%
	10–15%
	5–10%
	Less than 5%

Percent of Foreign-Born Whites and Native Whites of Foreign or Mixed Parentage in Total Population, by Counties, 1910 In 1910, the South had the lowest proportion of immigrants; in Minnesota, Wisconsin, North Dakota, Massachusetts, Connecticut, Rhode Island, in the regions bordering Mexico, and in parts of the Rocky Mountains, over half of the population was immigrant.

Observing the immigrants' attachment to "foreign" values and institutions, numbers of "natives" accused the newcomers of resisting Americanization and blamed them for urban problems. The immigrants were involved in these problems, but the rapidity of urban expansion explains the troubles associated with city life far more fully than the high percentage of foreigners.

Teeming Tenements

The cities were suffering from growing pains. Sewer and water facilities frequently could not keep pace with skyrocketing needs. By the 1890s the tremendous growth of Chicago had put such a strain on its sanitation system that the Chicago River had become virtually an open sewer, and the city's drinking water contained such a high concentration of germ-killing chemicals that it tasted like creosote. In the 1880s all the sewers of Baltimore emptied into the sluggish Back Basin, and according to the journalist H. L. Mencken, every summer the city smelled "like a billion polecats." Fire protection became less and less adequate, garbage piled up in the streets faster than it could be carted away, and the streets themselves crumbled beneath the pounding of heavy traffic. Urban growth proceeded with such speed that new streets were laid out more rapidly than they could be paved. Chicago had more than 1,400 miles of dirt streets in 1890.

Substandard living quarters aggravated other evils such as disease and the disinte-gration of family life, with its attendant mental anguish, crime, and juvenile delinquency. The bloody New York City riots of 1863, though sparked by dislike of the Civil War draft

Impoverished immigrant families, like the one in this 1889 Jacob Riis photograph, often lived in tiny windowless rooms in crowded tenement districts. Riis devised a "flash bulb" for indoor photographs in poorly illuminated rooms like this one.

Source: Jacob A. Riis, *In Poverty Gap: An English Coal-Heaver's Home.* Courtesy of Museum of the City of New York.

and of blacks, reflected the bitterness and frustration of thousands jammed together amid filth and threatened by disease. A citizens' committee seeking to discover the causes of the riots expressed its amazement after visiting the slums "that so much misery, disease, and wretchedness can be huddled together and hidden . . . unvisited and unthought of, so near our own abodes."

New York City created a Metropolitan Health Board in 1866, and a state tenement house law the following year made a feeble beginning at regulating city housing. The magazine *Plumber and Sanitary Engineer* sponsored a contest to pick the best design for a **tenement**. The winner of the competition was James E. Ware, whose plan for a "dumbbell" apartment house managed to crowd from twenty-four to thirty-two four-room apartments on a plot of ground only 25 by 100 feet.

The unhealthiness of the tenements was notorious. No one knows exactly, but as late as 1900 about three-quarters of the residents of New York City's Lower East Side lacked indoor toilets and had to use backyard outhouses to relieve themselves. One noxious corner became known as the "lung block" because of the prevalence of tuberculosis among its inhabitants. In 1900 three out of five babies born in one poor district of Chicago died before their first birthday.

Slums bred criminals—the wonder was that they did not breed more. They also drove well-to-do residents into exclusive sections and to the suburbs. From Boston's

View the Image
New York City Tenements
at **myhistorylab.com**

Beacon Hill and Back Bay to San Francisco's Nob Hill, the rich retired into their cluttered mansions and ignored conditions in the poorer parts of town.

The Cities Modernize

Gradually the basic facilities of urban living were improved. Streets were paved, first with cobblestones and wood blocks and then with smoother, quieter asphalt. Gaslight, then electric arc lights, and finally Edison's incandescent lamps brightened the cities after dark, making law enforcement easier, stimulating night life, and permitting factories and shops to operate after sunset.

Urban transportation underwent enormous changes. Until the 1880s, horse-drawn cars running on tracks set flush with the street were the main means of urban public transportation. In 1860 New York City's horsecars were carrying about 100,000 passengers a day. But horsecars had serious drawbacks. Enormous numbers of horses were needed, and feeding and stabling the animals was costly. Their droppings (ten pounds per day per horse) became a major source of urban pollution. That is why the invention of the electric trolley car in the 1880s put an end to horsecar transportation. Trolleys were cheaper and less unsightly than horsecars and quieter than steam-powered trains.

A retired naval officer, Frank J. Sprague, installed the first practical electric trolley line in Richmond, Virginia, in 1887–1888. At once other cities seized on the trolley. Lines soon radiated outward from the city centers, bringing commuters and shoppers from the residential districts to the business district. Without them the big-city department stores could not have flourished as they did. By 1895 some 850 lines were busily hauling city dwellers over 10,000 miles of track, and mileage tripled in the following decade. As with other new enterprises, ownership of street railways quickly became centralized until a few big operators controlled the trolleys of more than 100 eastern cities and towns.

Streetcars changed the character of big-city life. Before their introduction urban communities were limited by the distances people could conveniently walk to work. The "walking city" could not easily extend more than twenty-one-and-a-half miles from its center. Streetcars increased this radius to six miles or more, which meant that the area of the city expanded enormously. Dramatic population shifts resulted as the better-off moved away from the center in search of air and space, abandoning the crumbling, jam-packed older neighborhoods to the poor. Thus economic segregation speeded the growth of ghettos. Older peripheral towns that had maintained some of the self-contained qualities of village life were swallowed up, becoming metropolitan centers.

As time passed, each new area, originally peopled by rising economic groups, tended to become crowded and then deteriorated. By extending their tracks beyond the developed areas, the streetcar companies further speeded suburban growth because they assured developers, bankers, builders, and middle-class home buyers of efficient transport to the center of town. By keeping fares low (five cents a ride was standard) the lines enabled poor people to "escape" to the countryside on holidays.

Leisure Activities: More Fun and Games

By bringing together large numbers of people, cities made possible many kinds of social activity difficult or impossible to maintain in rural areas. Cities remained unsurpassed as centers of artistic and intellectual life. New York was the outstanding example, as seen in its many theaters and in the founding of the American Museum of Natural History (1870), the Metropolitan Museum of Art (1870), and the Metropolitan Opera (1883), but other cities were equally hospitable to such endeavors. Boston's Museum of Fine Arts, for example, was founded in 1870 and the Boston Symphony in 1881.

Of course less sophisticated forms of recreation also flourished in the urban environment. From 1865 to 1885 the number of breweries in Massachusetts quadrupled. It is only a slight exaggeration to say that in crowded urban centers there was a saloon on every corner; during the last third of the century the number of saloons in the country tripled. Saloons were strictly male working-class institutions, usually decorated with pictures and other mementos of sports heroes, the bar perhaps under the charge of a retired pugilist.

Calvinist-inspired opposition to sports as a frivolous waste of valuable time was steadily evaporating, replaced among the upper and middle classes by the realization that games like golf and tennis were "healthy occupation[s] for mind and body." Bicycling became a fad, both as a means of getting from place to place in the ever-expanding cities and as a form of exercise and recreation.

The postwar era also saw the first important development of spectator sports, again because cities provided the concentrations of population necessary to support them. Curious relationships developed between upper- and working-class interests and between competitive sports as pure enjoyment for players and spectators and sports as something to bet on. Horse racing had strictly upper-class origins, but racetracks attracted huge crowds of ordinary people more intent on picking a winner than on improving the breed.

Professional boxing offers an even better example. It was in a sense a hobby of the rich, who sponsored favorite gladiators, offered prizes, and often wagered large sums on the matches. But the audiences were made up overwhelmingly of young working-class males, from whose ranks most of the fighters emerged. The gambling and also the brutality of the bloody, bare-knuckle character of the fights caused many communities to outlaw boxing, a fact that added to the appeal of the sport for some.

Three major team games—baseball, football, and basketball—developed in something approaching their modern form during the last quarter of the century. Various forms of what became baseball were played long before that time. Organized teams, in most cases made up of upper-class amateurs, first emerged in the 1840s, but the game only became truly popular during the Civil War, when it was a major form of camp recreation for the troops.

After the war professional teams began to appear (the first, the Cincinnati Red Stockings, paid players between $800 and $1,400 for the season), and in 1876 teams in eight cities formed the National League. The American League followed in 1901. After a brief period of rivalry, the two leagues made peace in 1903, the year of the first World Series.

Organized play led to codification of the rules and improvements in technique and strategy: for example, the development of "minor" leagues; impartial umpires calling balls and strikes and ruling on close plays; the use of catcher's masks and padded gloves; the invention of various kinds of curves and other erratic pitches (often enhanced by "doctoring" the ball). As early as the 1870s, baseball was being called "the national game" and losing all upper-class connotations. Important games

Luna Park at Coney Island was a vast living theater in which the strollers were both spectators and actors. At night, a quarter of a million electric lights turned Luna Park into what its designer, Frederic Thompson, called "a different world—a dream world, perhaps a nightmare world—where all is bizarre and fantastic."

attracted crowds in the tens of thousands; betting became a problem. Despite its urban origins, its broad green fields and dusty base paths gave the game a rural character that only recently has begun to fade away.

Nobody "invented" baseball, but both football and basketball owe their present form to individuals. James Naismith's invention of basketball is undisputed. In 1891, while a student at a YMCA school, he attached peach baskets to the edge of an elevated running track in the gymnasium and drew up what are still the basic rules of the game. The first basketball was a soccer ball. The game was popular from the start, but because it was played indoors it was not an important spectator sport until much later.

Football was not created by one person in the way that basketball was; it evolved out of English rugby. For many decades it remained almost entirely a college sport (and thus played almost entirely by upper- and middle-class types). Organized collegiate sports dated back to before the Civil War; the first intercollegiate matches were rowing races between Harvard and Yale students. The first intercollegiate football game occurred when Rutgers defeated Princeton in 1869, and by the 1880s college football had become extremely popular.

Much of the game's modern character, however, was the work of Walter Camp, the athletic director and football coach of Yale. Camp cut the size of teams from fifteen to eleven, and he invented the scrimmage line, the four-down system, and the key position of quarterback. He publicized the game in a series of books, ranging from *How to Coach a Team* (1886) to *Jack Hall at Yale* (1909). Camp's prestige was such that when he named his first All-American team after the 1889 season, no one challenged his judgment. Well into the twentieth century, the players that Camp selected were the All-Americans.

A football game pits Yale and Princeton in 1879. The field was not lined or bounded, and play consisted mostly of disorganized scrums.

Spectator sports had little appeal to women at this time and indeed for decades thereafter. And few women participated in organized athletics. Sports were "manly" activities; a woman might ride a bicycle, play croquet, and perhaps play a little tennis, but to display any concentrated interest in excelling in a sport was considered unfeminine.

Christianity's Conscience and the Social Gospel

The modernization of the great cities was not solving most of the social problems of the slums. As this fact became clear, a number of urban religious leaders began to take a hard look at the situation. Traditionally, American churchmen had insisted that where sin was concerned there were no extenuating circumstances. To the well-to-do they preached the virtues of thrift and hard work; to the poor they extended the possibility of a better existence in the next world; to all they stressed one's responsibility for one's own behavior—and thus for one's own salvation. Such a point of view brought meager comfort to residents of slums. Consequently, the churches lost influence in the poorer sections. Furthermore, as better-off citizens followed the streetcar lines out from the city centers, their church leaders followed them.

In New York, seventeen Protestant congregations abandoned the depressed areas of Lower Manhattan between 1868 and 1888. Catering thereafter almost entirely to middle-class and upper-class worshippers, the pastors tended to become even more conservative. No more strident defender of reactionary ideas existed than the pastor of Brooklyn's fashionable Plymouth Congregational Church, Henry Ward Beecher. Beecher, a younger brother of Harriet Beecher Stowe, the author of *Uncle Tom's Cabin*, attributed poverty to the improvidence of laborers who, he claimed, squandered their wages on liquor and tobacco. "No man in this land suffers from poverty," he said, "unless it be more than his fault—unless it be his sin." The best check on labor unrest was a plentiful supply of cheap immigrant labor, he told President Hayes. Unions were "the worst form of despotism and tyranny in the history of Christendom."

An increasing proportion of the residents of the blighted districts were Catholics, and the Roman church devoted much effort to distributing alms, maintaining homes for orphans and old people, and other forms of social welfare. But church leaders seemed unconcerned with the social causes of the blight; they were deeply committed to the idea that sin and vice were personal, while poverty was an act of God. They deplored the rising tide of crime, disease, and destitution among their coreligionists, yet they failed to see the connection between these evils and the squalor of the slums. "Intemperance is the great evil we have to overcome," wrote the president of the leading Catholic charitable organization, the Society of St. Vincent de Paul. "It is the source of the misery for at least three-fourths of the families we are called upon to visit and relieve."

The conservatism of most Protestant and Catholic clergymen did not prevent some earnest preachers from working directly to improve the lot of the city poor. Some followed the path blazed by Dwight L. Moody, a lay evangelist who became famous throughout America and Great Britain in the 1870s. A gargantuan figure weighing nearly 300 pounds, Moody conducted a vigorous campaign to persuade the denizens of the slums to cast aside their sinful ways. He went among them full of enthusiasm and God's love and made an impact no less powerful than that of George Whitefield during the Great Awakening of the eighteenth century or Charles Grandison Finney in the first part of the nineteenth. The evangelists founded mission schools in the slums and tried to provide spiritual and recreational facilities for the unfortunate. They were prominent in the establishment of American branches of the YMCA (1851) and the Salvation Army (1880).

However, many evangelists paid little heed to the causes of urban poverty and vice, believing that faith in God would enable the poor to transcend the material difficulties of

Dwight L. Moody, a lay preacher, saw the church he had built destroyed by the Chicago fire of 1871. But the fire also intensified his faith. His conversational manner appealed to working people, and his adherence to the literal word of the Bible provided them with an anchor in a sea of change.

life. For a number of Protestant clergymen who had become familiar with the slums, a different approach seemed called for. Slum conditions caused the sins and crimes of the cities; the wretched human beings who committed them could not be blamed, these ministers argued. They began to preach a **Social Gospel** that focused on improving living conditions rather than on saving souls. If people were to lead pure lives, they must have enough to eat, decent homes, and opportunities to develop their talents. Social Gospelers advocated civil service reform, child labor legislation, regulation of big corporations, and heavy taxes on incomes and inheritances.

The most influential preacher of the Social Gospel was probably Washington Gladden. At first, Gladden, who was raised on a Massachusetts farm, had opposed all government interference in social and economic affairs, but his experiences as a minister in Springfield, Massachusetts, and Columbus, Ohio, exposed him to the realities of life in industrial cities, and his views changed. In *Applied Christianity* (1886) and in other works he defended laborers' right to organize and strike and denounced the idea that supply and demand should control wage rates. He favored factory inspection laws, strict regulation of public utilities, and other reforms.

Nothing so well reveals the receptivity of the public to the Social Gospel as the popularity of Charles M. Sheldon's novel *In His Steps* (1896), one of America's all-time best-sellers. Sheldon, a minister in Topeka, Kansas, described what happened in the mythical city of Raymond when a group of leading citizens decided to live truly Christian lives, asking themselves "What would Jesus do?" before adopting any course of action. Naturally the tone of Raymond's society was immensely improved, but basic social reforms followed quickly. The Rectangle, a terrible slum area, "too dirty, too coarse, too sinful, too awful for close contact," became the center of a great reform effort. One of Raymond's "leading society heiresses" undertook a slum clearance project, and a concerted attack was made on drunkenness and immorality. The moral regeneration of the entire community was soon accomplished.

The Settlement Houses

Although millions read *In His Steps*, its effect, and that of other Social Gospel literature, was merely inspirational. On the practical level, a number of earnest souls began to grapple with slum problems by organizing what were known as **settlement houses**. These were community centers located in poor districts that provided guidance and services to all who would use them. The settlement workers, most of them idealistic, well-to-do young people, lived in the houses and were active in neighborhood affairs.

The prototype of the settlement house was London's Toynbee Hall, founded in the early 1880s; the first American example was the Neighborhood Guild, opened on the Lower East Side of New York in 1886 by Dr. Stanton Coit. By the turn of the century 100 had been established, the most famous being Jane Addams's Hull House in Chicago (1889), Robert A. Woods's South End House in Boston (1892), and Lillian Wald's Henry Street Settlement in New York (1893).

The settlement workers tried to interpret American ways to the new immigrants and to create a community spirit in order to teach, in the words of one of them, "right living through social relations." Unlike most charity workers, who acted out of a sense of upper-class responsibility toward the unfortunate, they expected to benefit morally

Table 18.1   Reformers and the Urban Poor

Person	Occupation	Action	Consequences
Jacob Riis, Lewis Hine	Photojournalists	Increased public awareness of poor immigrants' living conditions	Stimulated reform movements
Horace Mann	Educator	Favored state laws that supported public education	Increased proportion of young people in school
Dwight L. Moody	Lay evangelist	Encouraged people to consult the Bible for moral guidance and refrain from vice	Promoted spread of YMCA (1850) and Salvation Army (1880) in immigrant districts
Washington Gladden	Congregationalist minister	Persuaded people that they are obliged as Christians to improve conditions in the slums	Advanced the "social gospel"
Jane Addams, Robert Woods, and Lillian Wald	Settlement house organizers	Showed immigrants and impoverished people how to cope with urban conditions	Constructed playgrounds and provided social clubs, day-care centers, and schools

and intellectually themselves by experiencing a way of life far different from their own and by obtaining "the first-hand knowledge the college classroom cannot give."

Settlement workers soon discovered that practical problems absorbed most of their energies. They agitated for tenement house laws, the regulation of the labor of women and children, and better schools. They employed private resources to establish playgrounds in the slums, along with libraries, classes in everything from child nutrition and home management to literature and arts and crafts, social clubs, and day-care centers. When they observed that many poor families were so occupied with the struggle to survive that they were neglecting or even abandoning their children, they tried to place the children in foster homes in the country.

In Boston Robert A. Woods organized clubs to get the youngsters of the South End off the streets, helped establish a restaurant where a meal could be had for five cents, acted as an arbitrator in labor disputes, and lobbied for laws tightening up the franchises of public utility companies. In Chicago Jane Addams developed an outstanding cultural program that included classes in music and art and an excellent "little theater" group. Hull House soon boasted a gymnasium, a day nursery, and several social clubs. Addams also worked tirelessly and effectively for improved public services and for social legislation of all kinds. She even got herself appointed garbage inspector in her ward and hounded local landlords and the garbage contractor until something approaching decent service was established.

A few critics considered the settlement houses mere devices to socialize the unruly poor by teaching them the "punctilios of upper-class propriety," but almost everyone appreciated their virtues. By the end of the century the Catholics, laggard in entering the arena of practical social reform, were joining the movement, partly because they were losing many communicants to socially minded Protestant churches. The first Catholic-run settlement house was founded in 1898 in an Italian district of New York. Two years later Brownson House in Los Angeles, catering chiefly to Mexican immigrants, threw open its doors.

With all their accomplishments, the settlement houses seemed to be fighting a losing battle. "Private beneficence," Jane Addams wrote of Hull House, "is totally inadequate to deal with the vast numbers of the city's disinherited." Much as a tropical forest grows faster than a handful of men armed with machetes can cut it down, so the slums, fed by an annual influx of hundreds of thousands, blighted new areas more rapidly than settlement house workers could clean up old ones. It became increasingly apparent that the wealth and authority of the state must be brought to bear in order to keep abreast of the problem.

Civilization and Its Discontents

As the nineteenth century died, the majority of the American people, especially those comfortably well-off, the residents of small towns, the shopkeepers, and some farmers and skilled workers, remained confirmed optimists and uncritical admirers of their civilization. However, blacks, immigrants, and others who failed to share equitably in the good things of life, along with a growing number of humanitarian reformers, found little to cheer about and much to lament in their increasingly industrialized society. Giant monopolies flourished despite federal restrictions. The gap between rich and poor appeared to be widening while the slum spread its poison and the materially successful made a god of their success. Human values seemed in grave danger of being crushed by impersonal forces typified by the great corporations.

In 1871 Walt Whitman, usually so full of extravagant praise for everything American, had called his fellow countrymen the "most materialistic and money-making people ever known":

> I say we had best look our times and lands searchingly in the face, like a physician diagnosing some deep disease. Never was there, perhaps, more hollowness of heart than at present, and here in the United States.

By the late 1880s a well-known journalist could write to a friend, "The wheel of progress is to be run over the whole human race and smash us all." Others noted an alarming jump in the national divorce rate and an increasing taste for all kinds of luxury. "People are made slaves by a desperate struggle to keep up appearances," a Massachusetts commentator declared, and the economist David A. Wells expressed concern over statistics showing that heart disease and mental illness were on the rise. These "diseases of civilization," Wells explained, were "one result of the continuous mental and nervous activity which modern high-tension methods of business have necessitated."

Wells was a prominent liberal, but pessimism was no monopoly of liberals. A little later, Senator Henry Cabot Lodge of Massachusetts, himself a millionaire, complained of the "lawlessness" of "the modern and recent plutocrat" and his "disregard of the rights of others." Lodge spoke of "the enormous contrast between the sanguine mental attitude prevalent in my youth and that, perhaps wiser, but certainly darker view, so general today." His one-time Harvard professor, Henry Adams, was still more critical of the way his contemporaries had become moneygrubbers. "All one's friends," he complained, along with church and university leaders and other educated people, "had joined the banks to force submission to capitalism."

Of course intellectuals often tend to be critical of the world they live in, whatever its nature; Thoreau denounced materialism and the worship of progress in the 1840s as vigorously as any late-nineteenth-century prophet of gloom. But the voices of the dissatisfied were rising. Despite the many benefits that industrialization had made possible, it was by no means clear around 1900 that the American people were really better off under the new dispensation.

That the United States was fast becoming a modern nation no one disputed. Physician George M. Beard contended that "modern civilization" overloaded the human nervous system the way burning too many of Thomas Edison's lightbulbs overloaded an electrical circuit. On the other hand, Edward Bellamy saw the future as a "paradise of order, equity, and felicity." Most took a more balanced view, believing that the modern world encompassed new possibilities as well as perils. The future beckoned, and yet it also menaced.

Milestones

1858	English launch transatlantic liner *Great Eastern*	1885	Foran Act outlaws importing contract skilled labor
1870	Metropolitan Museum of Art and American Museum of Natural History open in New York City	1887	Nativists found American Protective Association
1876	Eight teams form National Baseball League	1888	Richmond, Virginia, opens first urban electric streetcar system
1880	American branch of Salvation Army is founded	1889	Jane Addams founds Hull House
			Yale's Walter Camp names first All-American football team
1880s	New immigration begins	1890s	Louis Sullivan's skyscrapers rise
1882	John L. Sullivan wins heavyweight boxing championship	1890	Jacob Riis publishes *How the Other Half Lives*
	Exclusion Act bans Chinese immigrants	1896	Charles M. Sheldon asks "What would Jesus do?" in best-selling *In His Steps*
1883	Roebling completes Brooklyn Bridge	1897	Cleveland vetoes Congress's literacy test bill

✓•⎯Study and **Review** at www.myhistorylab.com

Review Questions

1. The introduction to this chapter contrasts the appeal of cities in the late nineteenth century with their failures and limitations. Did people move into cities because they had no choice or because they wanted to do so? Were their lives better or worse in doing so?

2. What is the relationship between the rise of industry and economic consolidation, described in Chapter 17, to the rapid growth of cities described in this chapter?

3. How did the influx of immigrants into the cities affect relations among ethnic groups? Between immigrants and "natives"—nonimmigrant Americans?

4. How did the new forms of amusement and leisure differ from those in earlier, predominantly rural settings?

5. Which urban problems were most acute and what different solutions were proposed by the leading religious figures and social reformers?

Key Terms

nativism   486
new immigration   485
settlement houses   495

Social Gospel   495
tenement   489

19

Intellectual and Cultural Trends in the Late Nineteenth Century

((•—Hear the Audio Chapter 19 at myhistorylab.com

Is winning everything?

IN 2010 THE STATE OF CALIFORNIA CUT FUNDING FOR THE UNIVERSITY of California at Berkeley by several hundred million dollars, raised student fees 10 percent, and forced faculty and staff to take unpaid furloughs. Despite this, the university covered the nearly $6.4 million deficit generated by its intercollegiate athletics program. Campus supporters of the football program noted that two-thirds of the top NCAA football teams ran even larger deficits; the average was about $8 million.

Although some of Berkeley's faculty endorsed an "Academics First" petition, others applauded the chancellor's decision to pursue "competitive excellence" in all aspects of campus life. Berkeley's football team was mandated to compete "at the top levels of the Pacific Ten conference and in postseason and national championship play." To that end, Berkeley paid its head coach $1.5 million, about average for a Division I head coach.

This insistence on winning intercollegiate football originated in the late nineteenth century. At that time, a few colleges decided to pay coaches, recruited star prep school athletes, and charged spectators to watch the games. The game became faster and rougher. Soon the spectacle attracted huge audiences. Action often got out of hand and, lacking satisfactory protective equipment, many football players sustained serious injuries; each year, some were killed.

In 1892, William Rainey Harper, president of the University of Chicago, defended the high cost of winning football. "If the world can afford to sacrifice lives for commercial gain"—a reference to the victims of industrial accidents—"it can more easily afford to make similar sacrifices on the altar of vigorous and unsullied manhood." In 1896 Massachusetts Senator Henry Cabot Lodge told Harvard students that "the injuries incurred on the playing-field are part of the price which the English-speaking race has paid for being world-conquerors."

The rise of football in the 1890s symbolized a profound transformation in cultural and intellectual life. The religious sensibilities and gentlemanly precepts of an earlier age were yielding to a tougher, "more manly" mind-set. Life was a struggle, Darwin had proclaimed, in which the fittest prevailed and the losers vanished. In this "competition" for survival, power trounced sentiment. Ideas were valuable not because they espoused truths or evinced beauty, but because they left an imprint on the world. Art and literature functioned not to transcend life or prettify it but to lay bare its grim reality. This stern ethos unsettled many but also invigorated those who yearned to confront the world as it was.

Colleges and Universities

Industrialization altered the way Americans thought at the same time that it transformed their ways of making a living. Technological advances revolutionized the communication of ideas more drastically than they did the transportation of goods or the manufacture of steel. The materialism that permeated American attitudes toward business also affected contemporary education and literature, while Charles Darwin's theory of evolution influenced American philosophers, lawyers, and historians profoundly. This was especially true of the nation's institutions of higher education.

Between 1878 and 1898, the number of colleges and universities increased from about 350 to 500, and the student body roughly tripled. Despite this growth, less than 2 percent of the college-age population attended college, but the aspirations of the nation's youth were rising, and more and more parents had the financial means necessary for fulfilling them.

More significant than the expansion of the colleges were the alterations in their curricula and in the atmosphere permeating the average campus. In 1870 most colleges remained what they had been in the 1830s: small, limited in their offerings, and intellectually stagnant. Thereafter, change came like a flood tide: State universities proliferated; the federal government's land-grant program in support of training in "agriculture and the mechanic arts," established under the Morrill Act of 1862, came into its own; wealthy philanthropists poured fortunes into old

> •••−[Read **the Document**
> *The Morrill Act* at
> **myhistorylab.com**

institutions and founded new ones; educators introduced new courses and adopted new teaching methods; professional schools of law, medicine, education, business, journalism, and other specialties increased in number.

In the forefront of reform was Harvard, the oldest and most prestigious college in the country. In the 1860s it possessed an excellent faculty, but teaching methods were antiquated and the curriculum had remained almost unchanged since the colonial period. In 1869, however, a dynamic president, the chemist Charles W. Eliot, undertook a transformation of the college. Eliot introduced the elective system, gradually eliminating required courses and expanding offerings in such areas as modern languages, economics, and the laboratory sciences.

An even more important development in higher education was the founding of Johns Hopkins in 1876. This university was one of many established in the period by wealthy industrialists; its benefactor, the Baltimore merchant Johns Hopkins, had made his fortune in the Baltimore and Ohio Railroad. Its distinctiveness, however, was due to the vision of Daniel Coit Gilman, its first president.

Gilman modeled Johns Hopkins on the German universities, where meticulous research and freedom of inquiry were the guiding principles. In staffing the institution, he sought scholars of the highest reputation, scouring Europe as well as America in his search for talent and offering outstanding men high salaries for that time—up to $5,000 for a

> •••−[Read **the Document**
> Frederick Jackson Turner, *The Significance of the Frontier in American History (1893)* at
> **myhistorylab.com**

A physics lecture, circa 1890, at the University of Michigan. Note that women are segregated from men; but in the men's section white and black men are sitting together. Many of the Morrill Act universities admitted women.

professor, roughly ten times the income of a skilled artisan. Johns Hopkins specialized in graduate education. In the generation after its founding, it churned out a remarkable percentage of the most important scholars in the nation, including Woodrow Wilson in political science, John Dewey in philosophy, Frederick Jackson Turner in history, and John R. Commons in economics.

State and federal aid to higher education expanded rapidly. The Morrill Act, granting land to each state at a rate of 30,000 acres for each senator and representative, provided the endowments that gave many important modern universities, such as Illinois, Michigan State, and Ohio State, their start. While the federal assistance was earmarked for specific subjects, the land-grant colleges offered a full range of courses, and all received additional state funds. The land-grant universities adopted new ideas quickly. They were coeducational from the start, and most developed professional schools and experimented with extension work and summer programs.

Typical of the better state institutions was the University of Michigan, which reached the top rank among the nation's universities during the presidency of James B. Angell (1871–1909). Like Eliot at Harvard, Angell expanded the undergraduate curriculum and strengthened the law and medical schools. He encouraged graduate studies, seeking to make Michigan "part of the great world of scholars," and sought ways in which the university could serve the general community.

Important advances were made in women's higher education. Beginning with Vassar College, which opened its doors to 300 women students in 1865, the opportunity for young women to pursue serious academic work gradually expanded. Wellesley and Smith, both founded in 1875, completed the so-called Big Three women's colleges. Together with the already established Mount Holyoke (1837), and with Bryn Mawr (1885), Barnard (1889), and Radcliffe (1893), they became known as the Seven Sisters.

Not all the changes in higher education were beneficial. The elective system led to superficiality; students gained a smattering of knowledge of many subjects and mastered none. For example, 55 percent of the Harvard class of 1898 took elementary courses and no others during their four years of study. Intensive graduate work often produced narrowness of outlook and research monographs on trivial subjects. Attempts to apply the scientific method in fields such as history and economics often enticed students into making smug (and preposterous) claims to objectivity and definitiveness.

The gifts of rich industrialists sometimes came with strings, and college boards of trustees tended to be dominated by businessmen who sometimes attempted to impose their own social and economic beliefs on faculty members. Although few professors lost their positions because their views offended trustees, at many institutions trustees exerted constant nagging pressures that limited academic freedom and scholarly objectivity. At state colleges, politicians often interfered in academic affairs, even treating professorships as part of the patronage system.

As the number of college graduates increased, and as colleges ceased being primarily training institutions for clergymen, the influence of alumni on educational policies began to make itself felt, not always happily. Campus social activities became more important. Fraternities proliferated. Interest in organized sports first appeared as a laudable outgrowth of the general expansion of the curriculum, but soon athletic contests were playing a role all out of proportion to their significance. After football evolved as the leading intercollegiate sport (over 50,000 attended the Yale-Princeton game in 1893), it became a source of revenue that many colleges dared not neglect. Since students, alumni, and the public demanded winning teams, college administrators stooped to subsidizing student athletes, in extreme cases employing players who were not students at all. One exasperated college president quipped that the BA degree was coming to mean Bachelor of Athletics.

Watch the Video
College Football (1903) at **myhistorylab.com**

Thus higher education reflected American values, with all their strengths and weaknesses. A complex society required a more professional and specialized education for its youth; the coarseness and the rampant materialism and competitiveness of the era inevitably found expression in the colleges and universities.

Revolution in the Social Sciences

In the social sciences a close connection existed between the practical issues of the age and the achievements of the leading thinkers. The application of the theory of evolution to every aspect of human relations, the impact of industrialization on society—such topics were of intense concern to American economists, sociologists, and historians. An understanding of Darwin increased the already strong interest in studying the development of institutions and their interactions with one another. Controversies over trusts, slum conditions, and other problems drew scholars out of their towers and into practical affairs.

Among the economists something approaching a revolution took place in the 1880s. The classical school, which maintained that immutable natural laws governed all human behavior and which used the insights of Darwin only to justify unrestrained competition and laissez-faire, was challenged by a group of young economists who argued that as times changed, economic theories and laws must be modified in order to remain relevant. Richard T. Ely, another of the scholars who made Johns Hopkins a font of new ideas in the 1880s, summarized the thinking of this group in 1885. "The state [is] an educational and ethical agency whose positive aid is an indispensable condition of human progress," Ely proclaimed. Laissez-faire was outmoded and dangerous. Economic problems were basically moral problems; their solution required "the united efforts of Church, state and science." The proper way to study these problems was by analyzing actual conditions, not by applying abstract laws or principles.

This approach produced the so-called institutionalist school of economics, whose members made detailed, on-the-spot investigations of labor unions, sweatshops, factories, and mines. The study of institutions would lead both to theoretical insights and to practical social reform, they believed. John R. Commons, one of Ely's students at Johns Hopkins and later professor of economics at the University of Wisconsin, was the outstanding member of this school. His ten-volume *Documentary History of American Industrial Society* (1910–1911) reveals the institutionalist approach at its best.

A similar revolution struck sociology in the mid-1880s. Prevailing opinion up to that time rejected the idea of government interference with the organization of society. The influence of the English social Darwinist, Herbert Spencer, who objected even to public schools and the postal system, was immense. Spencer and his American disciples, among them Edward L. Youmans, editor of *Popular Science Monthly*, twisted the ideas of Darwin to mean that society could be changed only by the force of evolution, which moved with cosmic slowness. "You and I can do nothing at all," Youmans told the reformer Henry George. "It's all a matter of evolution. Perhaps in four or five thousand years evolution may have carried men beyond this state of things."

Read the **Document**

Herbert Spencer, Social Darwinism at **myhistorylab.com**

Progressive Education

Traditionally, American teachers had emphasized the three Rs and relied on strict discipline. Yet new ideas were attracting attention. According to a German educator, Johann Friedrich Herbart, teachers could best arouse the interest of their students by relating new information to what they already knew; good teaching called for professional training, psychological insight, enthusiasm, and imagination, not merely facts and a birch rod. At the same time, evolutionists were pressing for a kind of education that would help children to "survive" by adapting to the demands of their rapidly changing urban environment.

Forward-looking educators seized on these ideas because dynamic social changes were making the old system increasingly inadequate. Settlement house workers discovered that slum children needed training in handicrafts, citizenship, and personal hygiene as much as in reading and writing. They were appalled by the local schools, which suffered from the same diseases—filth, overcrowding, rickety construction—that plagued the tenements, and by school systems that were controlled by machine politicians who doled out teaching positions to party hacks and other untrained persons. They argued that school playgrounds, nurseries, kindergartens, and adult education programs were essential in communities where most women worked and many people lacked much formal education. The philosopher who summarized and gave direction to these forces was John Dewey, a professor at the University of Chicago. Dewey was concerned with the implications of evolution—indeed, of all science—for education.

"Education," Dewey insisted in *The School and Society* (1899), was "the fundamental method of social progress and reform." To seek to improve conditions merely by passing laws was "futile." Moreover, in an industrial society the family no longer performed many of the educational functions it had carried out in an agrarian society. Farm children learn about nature, about work, about human character in countless ways denied to children in cities. The school can fill the gap by becoming "an embryonic community . . . with types of occupations that reflect the life of the larger society." At the same time, education should center on the child, and new information should be related to what the child already knows. Finally, the school should become an instrument for social reform.

The School and Society created a stir, and Dewey immediately assumed leadership of what in the next generation was called progressive education. Although the gains made in public education before 1900 were more quantitative than qualitative and the philosophy dominant in most schools was not very different at the end of the century from that prevailing in Horace Mann's day, change was in the air. The best educators of the period were full of optimism, convinced that the future was theirs.

Law and History

Even jurisprudence, by its nature conservative and rooted in tradition, felt the pressure of evolutionary thought. In 1881 Oliver Wendell Holmes Jr. published *The Common Law*. Rejecting the ideas that judges should limit themselves to the mechanical explication of statutes and that law consisted only of what was written in law books, Holmes argued that "the felt necessities of the time" rather than precedent should determine the rules by which people are governed. "The life of the law has not been logic; it has been experience," he wrote.

Holmes went on to a long and brilliant judicial career, during which he repeatedly stressed the right of the people, through their elected representatives, to deal with contemporary problems in any reasonable way, unfettered by outmoded conceptions of the proper limits of government authority. Like the societies they regulated, laws should evolve as times and conditions changed, he said.

The new approach to knowledge did not always advance the cause of liberal reform. Historians in the graduate schools became intensely interested in studying the origins and evolution of political institutions. They concluded, after much "scientific" study of old charters and law codes, that the roots of democracy were to be found in the customs of the ancient tribes of northern Europe. This theory of the "Teutonic origins" of democracy, which has since been thoroughly discredited, fitted well with the prejudices of people of British stock, and it provided ammunition for those who favored restricting immigration and for those who argued that blacks were inferior beings.

Out of this work, however, came an essentially democratic concept, the frontier thesis of Frederick Jackson Turner, still another scholar trained at Johns Hopkins. Turner's essay "The Significance of the Frontier in American History" (1893) argued that the frontier experience, through which every section of the country had passed, had affected the thinking of the people and the shape of American institutions. The isolation of the frontier and the need during each successive westward advance to create civilization anew, Turner wrote, account for the individualism of Americans and the democratic character of their society. Nearly everything unique in our culture could be traced to the existence of the frontier, he claimed.

Turner, and still more his many disciples, made too much of his basic insights. Life on the frontier was not as democratic as Turner believed, and it certainly does not "explain" American development as completely as he said it did. Nevertheless, his work showed how important it was to investigate the evolution of institutions, and it encouraged historians to study social and economic, as well as purely political, subjects. If the

CHARLOTTE PERKINS GILMAN

In 1885, severe depression gripped twenty-five-year-old Charlotte Perkins Stetson. "Every morning the same helpless waking," she confided in her journal. "Retreat impossible, escape impossible." She had married the previous year and had just given birth to a daughter. But the infant gave her no pleasure. "I would hold her close—that lovely child!—and instead of love and happiness, feel only pain. The tears ran down my breast." Over the next few years, her depression worsened. She feared she was approaching "the edge of insanity."

Charlotte's life had not been easy. Shortly after she was born, her father abandoned the family. He visited every couple of years, and occasionally sent a check, but Charlotte, her brother, and her mother lacked regular income and lived with relatives, moving frequently. "What I do know is that my childhood had no father," she wrote. Charlotte's relationship with her mother was not much better. Shattered by her husband's abandonment, she refused to cuddle Charlotte as an infant lest the child become dependent on affection. They never were close. When she was an adolescent, Charlotte and her mother lived in a cooperative run by a spiritualist, a woman who claimed to communicate with spirits. One day Charlotte saw her taking grapes that were meant for the whole group. The woman accused Charlotte of thinking evil thoughts about her.

Charlotte's mother insisted that Charlotte apologize for her thoughts; Charlotte refused. "And what are you going to do about it?" she taunted. Her mother hit her. At that moment, "I was born," Charlotte recalled. "Neither she, nor any one, could *make* me do anything."

Charlotte devised a stern regimen to ensure her future independence. Every day she ran a mile and educated herself by drawing, reading, and writing. Never would she depend on anyone— especially a man. "I am not domestic and I don't want to be," she told a female confidante.

Her resolve weakened when she was courted by an aspiring young writer. They married and the baby soon followed. Charlotte's bouts of depression became more frequent and incapacitating. Finally she agreed to consult with neurologist S. Weir Mitchell,

Charlotte Perkins Stetson, shortly after her marriage, wrote, "You were called to serve humanity, and you cannot serve yourself. No good as a wife, no good as a mother, no good at anything. And you did it yourself!"

the nation's foremost expert on neurasthenia, a disease that especially afflicted well-to-do young women. Its chief symptoms were depression, listlessness, and invalidism.

Mitchell believed that women's nervous systems were attuned to childbearing and childrearing. Women who pursued education and careers would exhaust their nervous energy and become neurasthenic. Charlotte's condition, Mitchell assured her, resulted from her intellectual labors. His prescription was simple:

> Live as domestic a life as possible. Have your child with you all the time. Lie down an hour after each meal. Have but two hours' intellectual life a day. And never touch pen, brush, or pencil as long as you live.

For a time, Charlotte accepted his regimen. "I went home, followed those directions rigidly for months, and came perilously close to losing my mind," she noted. Then she decided to "cast off Dr. Mitchell bodily" and "do exactly as I pleased."

She separated from her husband, took her child to Pasadena, California, and wrote essays, editorials, and fiction.

In 1890 she finished "The Yellow Wallpaper," a story about a young wife who, suffering from depression, was confined by her doctor-husband to bed in an upstairs room, with servants tending to her every need. As she endlessly stared at her surroundings, the designs on the wallpaper changed shape; a figure appeared and wandered in and out of her consciousness. The wallpaper then grew bars that locked her into the room. Unable to escape through the bars, the woman chewed at the bed, fleeing ultimately into madness. The story was well-received as a literary horror story reminiscent of Edgar Allan Poe.

Having at last purged Mitchell from her psyche, Charlotte wrote incessantly and supported herself by giving lectures. She developed close and even intimate relationships with several women. When she sent her daughter to live with her father, newspapers denounced her for neglecting woman's proper function. Then she fell in love with Houghton Gilman, who accepted her refusal to embrace domesticity. "I *must not* focus on 'home duties' and entangle myself with them," she told him. They married in 1900.

Charlotte's first book, *Women and Economics* (1898), was a work of extraordinary creativity. A thoroughgoing Social Darwinist, Charlotte explained that marriage was founded on women's economic subjugation. Marx was wrong: Gender, not class, was the fundamental social distinction. The most important revolution would promote women's independence by allowing them to work outside the home.

In this and subsequent books and articles, Charlotte Perkins Gilman insisted that the domestic ideal had deprived society of women's creativity and ideas. Her own life was a case in point. With only four years of education, none after the age of fifteen, she achieved economic independence through her own heroic effort. Lacking alternative child-care arrangements, she sent her young child to live with her father so that she could pursue her life and work as an intellectual. The decision would psychologically scar both her and her daughter, but her work anticipated many of the themes of modern feminism.

claims of the new historians to objectivity and definitiveness were absurdly overstated, their emphasis on thoroughness, exactitude, and impartiality did much to raise standards in the profession.

Realism in Literature

When what Mark Twain called the Gilded Age began, American literature was dominated by the romantic mood. All the important writers of the 1840s and 1850s, except Hawthorne, Thoreau, and Poe, were still living. Longfellow stood at the height of his fame, and the lachrymose Susan Warner—"tears on almost every page"—continued to turn out stories in the style of her popular *The Wide, Wide World*. Romanticism, however, had lost its creative force; much of the popular writing in the decade after 1865 was sentimental trash pandering to the preconceptions of middle-class readers. Magazines like the *Atlantic Monthly* overflowed with stories about fair ladies worshiped from afar by stainless heroes, women coping selflessly with drunken husbands, and poor but honest youths rising through various combinations of virtue and diligence to positions of wealth and influence. Most writers of fiction tended to ignore the eternal conflicts inherent in human nature and the social problems of the age; polite entertainment and pious moralizing appeared to be their only objectives.

The patent unreality, even dishonesty, of contemporary fiction eventually caused a reaction. The most important forces giving rise to the Age of Realism were those that were transforming every other aspect of American life: industrialism, with its associ-ated complexities and social problems; the theory of evolution, which made people more aware of the force of the environment and the basic conflicts of existence; the new science, which taught dispassionate, empirical observation. Novelists undertook the examination of social problems such as slum life, the conflict between capital and labor, and political corruption. They created multidimensional characters, depicted persons of every social class, used dialect and slang to capture the flavor of particular types, and fashioned painstaking descriptions of the surroundings into which they placed their subjects. The romantic novel did not disappear. General Lew Wallace's *Ben Hur* (1880) and Frances Hodgson Burnett's *Little Lord Fauntleroy* (1886) were best-sellers. But by 1880 realism was the point of view of the finest literary talents in the country.

Mark Twain

While it was easy to romanticize the West, that region lent itself to the realistic approach. Almost of necessity, novelists writing about the West described coarse characters from the lower levels of society and dealt with crime and violence. The outstanding figure of western literature, the first great American realist, was Mark Twain.

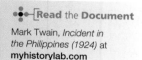
Read the Document

Mark Twain, *Incident in the Philippines (1924)* at **myhistorylab.com**

Twain, whose real name was Samuel L. Clemens, was born in 1835. He grew up in Hannibal, Missouri, on the banks of the Mississippi. After mastering the printer's trade and working as a riverboat pilot, he went west to Nevada in 1861. The wild, rough life of Virginia City fascinated him, but prospecting got him nowhere, and he became a reporter for the *Territorial Enterprise*. Soon he was publishing humorous stories about the local life under the nom de plume Mark Twain. In 1865, while working in California, he wrote "The Celebrated Jumping Frog of Calaveras County," a story that brought him national recognition. A tour of Europe and the Holy Land in 1867 to 1868 led to *The Innocents Abroad* (1869), which made him famous.

Twain's greatness stemmed from his keen reportorial eye and ear, his eagerness to live life to the full, his marvelous sense of humor, and his ability to be at once in society and outside it, and to love humanity yet be repelled by human vanity and perversity. He epitomized the zest and adaptability of his age and also its materialism. No contemporary pursued the almighty dollar more zealously. An inveterate speculator, he made a fortune with his pen and lost it in foolish business ventures.

> **Read the Document**
> Mark Twain, from *The Gilded Age* at **myhistorylab.com**

He was equally at home and equally successful on the Great River of his childhood, in the mining camps, and in the eastern bourgeois society of his mature years. But every prize slipped through his fingers. Twain died a dark pessimist, surrounded by adulation yet alone, an alien and a stranger in the land he loved and knew so well.

Whether directly, as in *The Innocents Abroad* and in his fascinating account of the world of the river pilot, *Life on the Mississippi* (1883), or when transformed by his imagination in works of fiction such as *Tom Sawyer* (1876) and *A Connecticut Yankee in King Arthur's Court* (1889), Mark Twain always put much of his own experience and feeling into his work. A story, he told a fellow author, "must be written with the blood out of a man's heart." His innermost confusions, the clash between his recognition of the pretentiousness and meanness of human beings and his wish to be accepted by society, added depths and overtones to his writing that together with his comic genius give it last-

> **Read the Document**
> Mark Twain, *To the Person Sitting in Darkness* (1901) at **myhistorylab.com**

ing appeal. He could not rise above the sentimentality and prudery of his generation entirely, for these qualities were part of his nature. He never dealt effectively with sexual love, for example, and often—even in *Huckleberry Finn*—contrived to end his tales on absurdly optimistic notes that ring false after so many brilliant pages portraying life as it is. On balance Twain's achievement was magnificent. Rough and uneven like the man himself, his works catch more of the spirit of the age he named than those of any other writer.

William Dean Howells

Twain's realism was far less self-conscious than that of his longtime friend William Dean Howells. Like Twain, Howells, who was born in Ohio in 1837, had little formal education. He learned the printer's trade from his father and became a reporter for the *Ohio State Journal*. After the Civil War he worked briefly for *The Nation* in New York and then moved to Boston, where he became editor of the *Atlantic Monthly*. In 1886 he returned to New York as editor of *Harper's*.

A long series of novels and much literary criticism poured from Howells's pen over the next thirty years. While he insisted on treating his material honestly, he was not at first a critic of society, being content to write about what he called "the smiling aspects" of life. Realism to Howells meant concern for the complexities of

In 1891 William Dean Howells championed the poetry of Emily Dickinson: "This poetry is as characteristic of our life as our business enterprise, our political turmoil, our demagogism, or our millionaires." Yet few of her poems appeared during her lifetime; arguably the most important poet of her age was unknown to that age.

individual personalities and faithful description of the genteel, middle-class world he knew best.

Besides a sharp eye and an open mind, Howells had a real social conscience. Gradually he became aware of the problems that industrialization had created. In 1885, in *The Rise of Silas Lapham*, he dealt with some of the ethical conflicts faced by businessmen in a competitive society. The harsh public reaction to the Haymarket bombing in 1886 stirred him, and he threw himself into a futile campaign to prevent the execution of the anarchist suspects. Thereafter he moved rapidly toward the left. In *A Hazard of New Fortunes* (1890), he attempted to portray the whole range of metropolitan life, weaving the destinies of a dozen interesting personalities from diverse sections and social classes.

His own works were widely read, and Howells was also the most influential critic of his time. He encouraged many important young American novelists, among them Stephen Crane, Theodore Dreiser, Frank Norris, and Hamlin Garland.

Some of these writers went far beyond Howells's realism to what they called naturalism. Many, like Twain and Howells, began as newspaper reporters. Working for a big-city daily in the 1890s was sure to teach anyone a great deal about the dark side of life. Naturalist writers believed that the human being was essentially an animal, a helpless creature whose fate was determined by environment. Their world was Darwin's world—mindless, without mercy or justice. They wrote chiefly about the most primitive emotions—lust, hate, and greed. In *Maggie, A Girl of the Streets* (1893), Stephen Crane described the seduction, degradation, and eventual suicide of a young woman, all set against the background of a sordid slum; in *The Red Badge of Courage* (1895), he captured the pain and humor of war. In *McTeague* (1899), Frank Norris told the story of a brutal, dull-witted dentist who murdered his greed-crazed wife with his bare fists.

Such stuff was too strong for Howells, yet he recognized its importance and befriended the younger writers in many ways. He found a publisher for *Maggie* after it had been rejected several times, and he wrote appreciative reviews of the work of Garland and Norris. Even Theodore Dreiser, who was contemptuous of Howells's writings and considered him hopelessly middle-class in point of view, appreciated his aid and praised his influence on American literature. Dreiser's first novel, *Sister Carrie* (1900), treated sex so forthrightly that it was withdrawn after publication.

Henry James

Henry James was very different in spirit and background from the tempestuous naturalists. Born to wealth, reared in a cosmopolitan atmosphere, twisted in some strange way while still a child and unable to achieve satisfactory relationships with women, James spent most of his mature life in Europe, writing novels, short stories, plays, and volumes of criticism. He was preeminently a realist, determined, as he once said, "to leave a multitude of pictures of my time" for the future to contemplate.

James dealt with social issues such as feminism and the difficulties faced by artists in the modern world, but he subordinated them to his interest in his subjects as individuals. *The American* (1877) told the story of the love of a wealthy American in Paris for a French noblewoman who rejected him because her family disapproved of his commercial background. *The Portrait of a Lady* (1881) described the disillusionment of an intelligent woman married to a charming but morally bankrupt man and her eventual decision to remain with him nonetheless. *The Bostonians* (1886) was a complicated and psychologically sensitive study of the varieties of female behavior in a seemingly uniform social situation.

James's reputation, greater today than in his lifetime, rests more on his highly refined accounts of the interactions of individuals and their environment and his masterful commentaries on the novel as a literary form than on his ability as a storyteller. Few major writers have been more long-winded, more prone to circumlocution. Yet few have been so dedicated to their art, possessed of such psychological penetration, or so successful in producing a large body of important work.

Realism in Art

American painters responded to the times as writers did, but with this difference: Despite the new concern for realism, the romantic tradition retained its vitality. Preeminent among the realists was Thomas Eakins, who was born in Philadelphia in 1844. Eakins studied in Europe in the late 1860s and was influenced by the great realists of the seventeenth century, Velasquez and Rembrandt. Returning to America in 1870, he passed the remainder of his life teaching and painting in Philadelphia.

The scientific spirit of the age suited Eakins perfectly. He mastered human anatomy; some of his finest paintings, such as *The Gross Clinic* (1875), are graphic illustrations of surgical operations. He was an early experimenter with motion pictures, using the camera to capture exactly the attitudes of human beings and animals in action. Like his friend Walt Whitman, whose portrait is one of his greatest achievements, Eakins gloried in the ordinary. But he had none of Whitman's weakness for self-delusion. His portraits are monuments to his integrity and craftsmanship: Never would he touch up a likeness to please his sitter.

Winslow Homer, a Boston-born painter best known for his brilliant watercolors, was also influenced by realist ideas. Homer was a lithographer as well as a master of the watercolor medium, yet he had had almost no formal training. During the Civil War, he worked as an artist-reporter for *Harper's Weekly*, and he continued to do magazine illustrations for some years thereafter. He roamed America, painting

Thomas Eakins's interest in science was as great as his interest in art. In the early 1880s he collaborated with photographer Eadweard Muybridge in serial-action photographic experiments and later devised a special camera for his anatomical studies. The accompanying picture (top) was taken with the Marey wheel. The impact of Eakins's photographic experiments is evident in *The Swimming Hole* (bottom), painted in 1883. At that time Eakins was director of the art school at the Pennsylvania Academy of the Fine Arts.
Source: (top) Philadelpia Museum of Art. Gift of Charles Bregler.

scenes of southern farm life, Adirondack campers, and, after about 1880, magnificent seascapes and studies of fishermen and sailors.

The careers of Eakins and Homer show that the late-nineteenth-century American environment was not uncongenial to first-rate artists. Nevertheless, at least two major American painters abandoned native shores for Europe. One was James A. McNeill Whistler, whose portrait of his mother, which he called *Arrangement in Grey and Black,* is probably the most famous canvas ever painted by an American. Whistler left the United States in 1855 when he was twenty-one and spent most of his life in Paris and London. "I shall come to America," he announced grandly, "when the duty on works of art is abolished!"

Whistler made a profession of eccentricity, but he was a talented and versatile artist. Spare and muted in tone, his paintings are more interesting as precise arrangements of color and space than as images of particular objects; they had considerable influence on the course of modern art.

The second important expatriate artist was Mary Cassatt, daughter of a wealthy Pittsburgh banker and sister of Alexander J. Cassatt, who was president of the Pennsylvania Railroad around the turn of the century. She went to Paris as a tourist and dabbled in art like many conventional young socialites, then was caught up in the impressionist movement and decided to become a serious painter. Her work is more French than American and was little appreciated in the United States before World War I.

The Pragmatic Approach

The theory of evolution posed an immediate challenge to religion: If Darwin was correct, the biblical account of the creation was apparently untrue and the idea that the human race had been formed in God's image was highly unlikely. A bitter controversy erupted, described by President Andrew D. White of Cornell in *The Warfare of Science with Theology in Christendom* (1896). While millions continued to believe in the literal truth of the Bible, among intellectuals, lay and clerical, victory went to the evolutionists because, in addition to the arguments of the geologists and the biologists, scholars were throwing light on the historical origins of the Bible, showing that its words were of human rather than divine inspiration.

If the account of the creation in Genesis could not be taken literally, the Bible remained a repository of wisdom and inspiration. Such books as John Fiske's *The Outlines of Cosmic Philosophy* (1874) provided religious persons with the comforting thesis that evolution, while true, was merely God's way of ordering the universe—as the liberal preacher Washington Gladden put it, "a most impressive demonstration of the presence of God in the world."

The effects of Darwinism on philosophy were less dramatic but in the end more significant. Fixed systems and eternal truths were difficult to justify in a world that was constantly evolving. By the early 1870s a few philosophers had begun to reason that ideas and theories mattered little except when applied to specifics.

"Nothing justifies the development of abstract principles but their utility in enlarging our concrete knowledge of nature," wrote Chauncey Wright, secretary of the American Academy of Arts and Sciences. This startling philosophy, known as **pragmatism**, was further developed by William James, brother of the novelist. James was one of the most remarkable persons of his generation. His *Principles of Psychology* (1890) may be said to have established that discipline as a modern science. His *Varieties of Religious Experience* (1902), which treated the subject from both psychological and philosophical points of view, helped thousands of readers

Table 19.1 Key Figures and Intellectual Currents

Intellectual	Chief Accomplishment	Major Ideas
Charles W. Eliot	Elective system at Harvard	Encouraged development of college majors and hiring of specialized faculty
Daniel Coit Gilman	Graduate education at Johns Hopkins	Brought German standards of research to the United States
Richard Ely	Founded "institutional school of economics"	Challenged theorists who focused on markets and advocated laissez-faire governmental policy
John Dewey	*The School and Society* (1899)	Insisted that meaningful social change was impossible without educational change
Oliver Wendell Holmes, Jr.	*The Common Law* (1881)	Demonstrated that law was not founded on historical precedent; legal principles evolved with society
Frederick Jackson Turner	"The Significance of the Frontier in American History" (1893)	Frontier conditions explained the individualism and democracy that characterized American society
Mark Twain	*Huckleberry Finn* (1884)	Lampooned the sentimentality and hypocrisy of Victorian culture
Charlotte Perkins Gilman	*Women and Economics* (1898)	Maintained that society was unjustly built upon women's economic dependence on men; social change depended on women finding meaningful paid work
William Dean Howells	*A Hazard of New Fortunes* (1890)	Promoted a realistic, nonsentimental look at society
Henry James	*The Portrait of a Lady* (1881)	Showed how literature could probe the depths and complexities of human relationships
Thomas Eakins	*The Gross Clinic* (1875)	Applied realistic perspectives to art
William James	*The Principles of Psychology* (1890)	Contended that the will, as influenced by psychological factors, was an independent force in human affairs

reconcile their religious faith with their increasing knowledge of psychology and the physical universe.

James's wide range and his verve and imagination as a writer made him by far the most influential philosopher of his time. He rejected the deterministic interpretation of Darwinism and all other one-idea explanations of existence. Belief in free will was one of his axioms; environment might influence survival, but so did the *desire* to survive, which existed independent of surrounding circumstances. Even truth was relative; it did not exist in the abstract but *happened* under particular circumstances. What a person thought helped to make thought occur, or come true. The mind, James wrote in a typically vivid phrase, has "a vote" in determining truth. Religion was true, for example, because people were religious.

Pragmatism brought Americans face-to-face with somber problems. While relativism made them optimistic, it also bred insecurity, for there could be no certainty, no comforting reliance on any eternal value in the absence of absolute truth. Pragmatism also seemed to suggest that the end justified the means, that what worked was more important than what ought to be. At the time of James's death in 1910, the *Commercial and Financial Chronicle* pointed out that the pragmatic philosophy was helpful to businessmen in making decisions. By emphasizing practice at the expense of theory, the new philosophy encouraged materialism, anti-intellectualism, and other unlovely aspects of the American character. And what place had conventional morality in such a system? Perhaps pragmatism placed too much reliance on the free will of human beings, ignoring their capacity for selfishness and self-delusion.

The people of the new century found pragmatism a heady wine. They would quaff it freely and enthusiastically—down to the bitter dregs.

The Knowledge Revolution

Improvements in public education and the needs of an increasingly complex society for every type of intellectual skill caused a veritable revolution in how knowledge was discovered, disseminated, and put to use. Nothing so well illustrates the desire for new information as the rise of the Chautauqua movement, founded by John H. Vincent, a Methodist minister, and Lewis Miller, an Ohio manufacturer of farm machinery. Vincent had charge of Sunday schools for the Methodist church. In 1874 he and Miller organized a two-week summer course for Sunday school teachers on the shores of Lake Chautauqua in New York. Besides instruction, they offered good meals, evening songfests around the campfire, and a relaxing atmosphere—all for $6 for the two weeks.

The forty young teachers who attended were delighted with the program, and soon the leafy shore of Lake Chautauqua became a city of tents each summer as thousands poured into the region from all over the country. The founders expanded their offerings to include instruction in literature, science, government, and economics. Famous authorities, including, over the years, six presidents of the United States, came to lecture to open-air audiences on every subject imaginable. Eventually Chautauqua supplied speakers to reading circles throughout the country; it even offered correspondence courses leading over a four-year period to a diploma, the program designed, in Vincent's words, to give "the college outlook" to persons who had not had the opportunity to obtain a higher education. Books were written specifically for the program, and a monthly magazine, the *Chautauquan*, was published.

Still larger numbers profited from the proliferation of public libraries. By the end of the century nearly all the states supported libraries. Private donors, led by the steel industrialist Andrew Carnegie, contributed millions to the cause. In 1900 over 1,700 libraries in the

The first commercially successful typewriter, manufactured in quantity beginning in 1874. It used the QWERTY keyboard found on later typewriters—and eventually found on computer keyboards.

United States had collections of more than 5,000 volumes.

Publishers tended to be conservative, but reaching the masses meant lowering intellectual and cultural standards, appealing to emotions, and adopting popular, sometimes radical, causes. Cheap, mass-circulation papers had first appeared in the 1830s and 1840s, the most successful being the *Sun*, the *Herald*, and the *Tribune* in New York; the *Philadelphia Public Ledger*; and the *Baltimore Sun*. None of them much exceeded a circulation of 50,000 before the Civil War. The first publisher to reach a truly massive audience was Joseph Pulitzer, a Hungarian-born immigrant who made a first-rate paper of the *St. Louis Post-Dispatch*. In 1883 Pulitzer bought the *New York World*, a sheet with a circulation of perhaps 20,000. Within a year he was selling 100,000 copies daily, and by the late 1890s the *World*'s circulation regularly exceeded 1 million.

Growth and ferment also characterized the magazine world. In 1865 there were about 700 magazines in the country, and by the turn of the century more than 5,000. Until the mid-1880s, few of the new magazines were in any way unusual. A handful of serious periodicals, such as the *Atlantic Monthly, Harper's*, and the *Century*, dominated the field. They were staid in tone and conservative in politics. Although they had great influence, none approached mass circulation because of the limited size of the upper-middle-class audience they aimed at.

Popular magazines rarely discussed the great issues that preoccupied intellectuals—the impact of Darwinism on law, sociology, and anthropology; the theories of John Dewey and the progressive educators; the import of realism in literature and art; the implications of pragmatism to psychology, philosophy, and theology. But some phenomena—such as the mania for college football—pressed forward because they represented so powerful a convergence of popular culture and intellectual trends.

Milestones

1862	Morrill Act establishes land-grant colleges	1886	William Dean Howells becomes editor of *Harper's*
1865	Vassar College is founded for women	1889	Edward W. Bok becomes editor of the *Ladies' Home Journal*
1869	Charles W. Eliot becomes Harvard's president	1890	William James publishes *Principles of Psychology*
1874	Chautauqua movement begins	1893	Frederick Jackson Turner publishes "Significance of the Frontier in American History"
1876	Johns Hopkins University is founded to specialize in graduate education		
1881	Oliver Wendell Holmes Jr. publishes *The Common Law*	1895	William Randolph Hearst purchases the *New York Journal*
	Henry James publishes *The Portrait of a Lady*	1898	Charlotte Perkins Gilman publishes *Women and Economics*
1883	Joseph Pulitzer purchases *New York World*	1899	John Dewey publishes *The School and Society*
1884	Mark Twain publishes *Huckleberry Finn*		
1886	Ottmar Mergenthaler invents linotype machine		

✓•⟨**Study** and **Review** at **www.myhistorylab.com**

Review Questions

1. The introductory essay argues that football was embraced by colleges and universities in the late nineteenth century because it reflected hard-nosed Darwinian concepts. What other aspects of late-nineteenth-century intellectual and cultural life were influenced by Darwinism? What intellectual trends and movements rejected social Darwinism?

2. What institutional developments transformed higher education during the last third of the nineteenth century?

3. How was popular culture at odds with intellectual trends in literature and the arts?

4. How did pragmatism—the belief that ideas must be judged by their consequences—challenge earlier outlooks on philosophy and morality?

Key Terms

pragmatism   *513*

20

From Smoke-Filled Rooms to Prairie Wildfire: 1877–1896

((•—Hear the Audio Chapter 20 at myhistorylab.com

Did you vote for an American Idol?

ON MAY 20, 2009, TWENTY-THREE-YEAR-OLD GUITAR-STRUMMING Kris Allen captivated the audience of *American Idol*·with his rendition of Keith Urban's "Kiss a Girl" and Bill Withers's "Ain't No Sunshine." By receiving a majority of the nearly 100 million "votes"—by telephone and text message—Allen became the *American Idol* for 2009.

Although pundits had for years grumbled that Americans cared more about pop stars on *American Idol* than about their president, this may not have been true in 2009. The producers of the show did not release the exact number of votes for Allen, but they did say the vote was close; probably he received no more than 55 million. Six months earlier, presidential candidates Barack Obama and John McCain received more votes than Allen, with 69 million and 60 million respectively.

A better comparison is of voter turnout for presidential elections nowadays and during the late nineteenth century. Since 1946, fewer than half of the eligible voters have on the average voted in presidential elections. By contrast, over three-fourths of eligible voters did so in presidential campaigns from 1876 to 1896—the highest rates in the nation's history.

This puzzles scholars, because the issues of that time seem inconsequential: Civil War soldiers' pensions, the tariff, paper money vs. gold and silver coins, and civil service reform. Perhaps the most volatile issue—the plight of former slaves—never attracted much notice because most politicians looked the other way. The other key issue—the minimal role of the federal government in the nation's industrial ascent—went without saying and, being unsaid, generated little controversy.

Why, then, did so many people vote? Local issues seem to have loomed large in most people's thinking. Public health, municipal services, and corruption all dominated the headlines. Then, during the 1890s, a nationwide industrial depression crushed many local manufacturing firms, just as an agricultural crisis was sweeping through the midsection of the nation.

Because the nation had become more tightly integrated, these economic upheavals jolted nearly every community. National policy and local issues converged, culminating in the extraordinary election of 1896, which brought over 80 percent of the electorate to the polls. In these years, politics had become the greatest show around.

Congress Ascendant

A succession of weak presidents occupied the White House during the last quarter of the nineteenth century. Although the impeachment proceedings against Andrew Johnson had failed, Congress dominated the government. Within Congress, the Senate generally overshadowed the House of Representatives. Critics called the Senate a "rich man's club," and it did contain many millionaires. However, the true sources of the Senate's influence lay in the long tenure of many of its members (which enabled them to master the craft of politics), in the fact that it was small enough to encourage real debate, and in its long-established reputation for wisdom, intelligence, and statesmanship.

The House of Representatives, on the other hand, was one of the most disorderly and inefficient legislative bodies in the world.

Desks slammed; members held private conversations, hailed pages, shuffled from place to place, clamored for the attention of the Speaker—and all the while some poor orator tried to discuss the question of the moment. Speaking in the House, one writer said, was like trying to address the crowd on a passing Broadway bus from the curb in front of the Astor House in New York. On one occasion in 1878 the adjournment of the House was held up for more than twelve hours because most of the members of an important committee were too drunk to prepare a vital appropriations bill for final passage.

The fundamental division between Democrats and Republicans was sectional, a result of the Civil War. The South, after the political rights of blacks had been drastically circumscribed, became heavily Democratic. Most of New England was solidly Republican. Elsewhere the two parties stood in fair balance, although the Republicans tended to have the advantage. A preponderance of the well-to-do, cultured Northerners were Republicans. Perhaps in reaction to this concentration, immigrants, Catholics, and other minority groups—except for blacks—tended to vote Democratic. But the

An 1887 cartoon indicting the Senate for closely attending to the Big (read, fat) Trusts rather than to the needs of the public (whose "entrance" to the Senate is "closed"). Drawn by Joseph Keppler, a caricaturist who was born and trained in Germany, this type of grotesque satire greatly influenced late-nineteenth-century American comic arts.

numerous exceptions weakened the applicability of these generalizations. German and Scandinavian immigrants usually voted Republican; many powerful business leaders supported the Democrats.

The bulk of the people—farmers, laborers, shopkeepers, white-collar workers—distributed their ballots fairly evenly between the two parties in most elections; the balance of political power after 1876 was almost perfect. Between 1856 and 1912 the Democrats elected a president only twice (1884 and 1892), but most contests were extremely close. Majorities in both the Senate and the House fluctuated continually. Between 1876 and 1896 the "dominant" Republican party controlled both houses of Congress and the presidency at the same time for only a single two-year period.

Recurrent Issues

Four questions obsessed politicians in these years. One was the "bloody shirt." The term, which became part of the language after a Massachusetts congressman dramatically displayed to his colleagues in the House the bloodstained shirt of an Ohio carpetbagger who had been flogged by terrorists in Mississippi, referred to the tactic of reminding the electorate of the northern states that the men who had precipitated the Civil War had been Democrats. Should Democrats regain power, former rebels would run the government and undo all the work accomplished at such sacrifice during the war. "Every man that endeavored to tear down the old flag," a Republican orator proclaimed in 1876, "was a Democrat. Every man that tried to destroy this nation was a Democrat. . . . The man that assassinated Abraham Lincoln was a Democrat. . . . Soldiers, every scar you have on your heroic bodies was given you by a Democrat." And every scoundrel or incompetent who sought office under the Republican banner waved the bloody shirt in order to divert the attention of northern voters from his own shortcomings. The technique worked so well that many decent candidates could not resist the temptation to employ it in close races.

Waving the bloody shirt was related intimately to the issue of the rights of African Americans. Throughout this period Republicans vacillated between trying to build up their organization in the South by appealing to black voters—which required them to make sure that blacks in the South could vote—and trying to win conservative white support by stressing economic issues such as the tariff.

The tariff was another perennial issue in post–Civil War politics. Despite considerable loose talk about free trade, almost no one in the United States except for a handful of professional economists, believed in eliminating duties on imports. Manufacturers desired protective tariffs to keep out competing products, and a majority of their workers were convinced that wage levels would fall if goods produced by cheap foreign labor entered the United States untaxed. Congressman William McKinley of Ohio stated the majority opinion in the clearest terms: high tariffs foster the growth of industry and thus create jobs. "Reduce the tariff and labor is the first to suffer," he said.

The tariff could have been a real political issue because American technology was advancing so rapidly that many industries no longer required protection from foreign competitors. The Democrats professed to believe in moderation, yet whenever party leaders tried to revise the tariff downward, Democratic congressmen from Pennsylvania, New York, and other industrial states sided with the Republicans. Many Republicans endorsed tariff reform in principle, but when particular schedules came up for discussion, most of them demanded the highest rates for industries in their own districts and traded votes shamelessly with colleagues representing other interests in order to get what they wanted. Every new tariff bill became an occasion for logrolling, lobbying, and outrageous politicking rather than for sane discussion and careful evaluation of the public interest.

A third political question in this period was currency reform. During the Civil War, the government, faced with obligations it could not meet by taxing or borrowing, suspended specie payments and issued about $450 million in paper money, originally printed in green ink. This currency, called greenbacks, did not command the full confidence of a people accustomed to money readily convertible into gold or silver. Greenbacks seemed to encourage inflation, for how could one trust the government not to print them in wholesale lots to avoid passing unpopular tax laws? Thus, when the war ended, strong sentiment developed for withdrawing the greenbacks from circulation and returning to a bullion standard—to coining money from silver and gold.

In fact, beginning during Reconstruction, prices declined sharply. The deflation increased the real income of bondholders and other creditors but injured debtors. Farmers were particularly hard-hit, for many of them had borrowed heavily during the wartime boom to finance expansion.

Many groups supported some kind of currency inflation. However, the major parties refused to confront each other over the currency question. While Republicans professed to be the party of sound money, most western Republicans favored expansion of the currency. Conservative Democrats favored deflation as much as Republicans did. Under various administrations steps were taken to increase or decrease the amount of money in circulation, but the net effect on the economy was not significant.

The final major political issue of these years was civil service reform. As American society grew larger and more complex, the government necessarily took on more functions. The need for professional administration increased. Corruption flourished; waste and inefficiency were the normal state of affairs.

Every honest observer could see the need for reform, but the politicians refused to surrender the power of dispensing government jobs to their lieutenants without regard for their qualifications. They argued that patronage was the lifeblood of politics, that parties could not function without armies of loyal political workers, and that the workers expected and deserved the rewards of office when their efforts were crowned with victory at the polls. When reformers suggested establishing the most modest kind of professional, nonpartisan civil service, politicians of both parties subjected them to every kind of insult and ridicule even though both the Democratic and Republican parties regularly wrote civil service reform planks into their platforms.

Party Politics: Sidestepping the Issues

With the Democrats invincible in the South and the Republicans predominant in New England and most of the states beyond the Mississippi, the outcome of presidential elections was usually determined in a handful of populous states: New York (together with its satellites, New Jersey and Connecticut), Ohio, Indiana, and Illinois. In every presidential election, Democrats and Republicans concentrated their heaviest guns on these states. Of the eighteen Democrats and Republicans nominated for president in the nine elections between 1868 and 1900, only three were not from New York, Ohio, Indiana, or Illinois, and all three lost.

With so much depending on so few, the level of political morality was abysmal. Mudslinging, character assassination, and plain lying were standard practice; bribery was routine. Drifters and other dissolute citizens were paid in cash—or more often in free drinks—to vote the party ticket. The names of persons long dead were solemnly inscribed in voting registers, their suffrages exercised by impostors.

Lackluster Presidents: From Hayes to Harrison

The leading statesmen of the period were disinterested in important contemporary questions, powerless to influence them, or content with things the way they were. Consider the presidents.

Rutherford B. Hayes, president from 1877 to 1881, came to office with a distinguished record. He attended Kenyon College and Harvard Law School before settling down to practice in Cincinnati. Although he had a family to support, he volunteered for service in the Union army within weeks after the first shell fell on Fort Sumter. "A just and necessary war," he called it in his diary. "I would prefer to go into it if I knew I was to die . . . than to live through and after it without taking any part."

In 1864 he was elected to Congress; four years later he became governor of Ohio, serving three terms altogether. The Republicans nominated him for president in 1876 because of his reputation for honesty and moderation, and his election, made possible by the Compromise of 1877, seemed to presage an era of sectional harmony and political probity.

Outwardly Hayes had a sunny disposition; inwardly, in his own words, he was sometimes "nervous to the point of disaster." Despite his geniality, he was utterly without political glamour. He played down the tariff issue. On the money question he was conservative. He approved the resumption of gold payments in 1879 and vetoed bills to expand the currency. He accounted himself a civil service reformer, being opposed to the collection of political contributions from federal officeholders.

Hayes complained about the South's failure to treat blacks decently after the withdrawal of federal troops, but he took no action. He worked harder for civil service reform, yet failed to achieve the "thorough, rapid, and complete" change he had promised. In most matters, he was content to "let the record show that he had made the requests."

Hayes's successor, James A. Garfield, fought at Shiloh and later at Chickamauga. In 1863 he won a seat in Congress, where his oratorical and managerial skills brought him to prominence in the affairs of the Republican party.

Garfield had been a compromise choice at the 1880 Republican convention. His election precipitated a great battle over patronage, the new president standing in a sort of no-man's land between contending factions within the party. In July 1881 an unbalanced office-seeker named Charles J. Guiteau shot Garfield in the Washington railroad station. The president died on September 19.

The assassination of Garfield elevated Chester A. Arthur to the presidency. A New York lawyer and abolitionist, Arthur became an early convert to the Republican party and rose rapidly in its local councils. In 1871 Grant gave him the juiciest political plum in the country, the collectorship of the Port of New York, which he held until removed by Hayes in 1878 for refusing to keep his hands out of party politics.

The vice presidency was the only elective position that Arthur had ever held. Before Garfield's death, he had paid little attention to questions like the tariff and

THE WOUNDED PRESIDENT—ASCERTAINING THE LOCATION OF THE BULLET.—From a Sketch by W. Shinkle.—[See Page 555.]

James A. Garfield lies mortally wounded. After failing to locate the bullet, surgeons called in Alexander Graham Bell, the famous inventor. Bell conceived of a device, pictured here, that anticipated the mine detector. Bell's machine failed to locate the bullet, however, perhaps because the metal bed springs interfered with its operation. Garfield died, either from the bullet or the surgeon's unsuccessful attempts to extricate it.

monetary policy, being content to take in fees ranging upward of $50,000 a year as collector of the port and to oversee the operations of the New York customs office, with its hordes of clerks and laborers. Of course, Arthur was an unblushing defender of the spoils system, though in fairness it must be said that he was personally honest and an excellent administrator.

The tragic circumstances of his elevation to the presidency sobered Arthur. Although he was a genial, convivial man, perhaps overly fond of good food and flashy clothes, he comported himself with dignity as president. He handled patronage matters with restraint, and he gave at least nominal support to the movement for civil service reform, which had been strengthened by the public's indignation at the assassination of Garfield. In 1883 Congress passed the **Pendleton Act**, "classifying" about 10 percent of all government jobs and creating the bipartisan Civil Service Commission to administer competitive examinations for these positions. The law made it illegal to force officeholders to make political contributions and empowered the president to expand the list of classified positions at his discretion.

> **Read the Document**
> Pendleton Civil Service Act at **myhistorylab.com**

The election of 1884 brought the Democrat Grover Cleveland to the White House. Cleveland grew up in western New York. After studying law, he settled in Buffalo. Although somewhat lacking in the social graces and in intellectual pretensions, he had a basic integrity that everyone recognized; when a group of reformers sought a candidate for mayor in 1881, he was a natural choice. His success in Buffalo led to his election as governor of New York in 1882.

In the governor's chair his no-nonsense attitude toward public administration endeared him to civil service reformers at the same time that his basic conservatism pleased businessmen. When he vetoed a popular bill to force a reduction of the fares charged by the New York City elevated railway on the ground that it was an unconstitutional violation of the company's franchise, his reputation soared. Here was a man who cared more for principle than for the adulation of the multitude, a man who was courageous, honest, hardworking, and eminently sound. The Democrats nominated him for president in 1884.

The election revolved around personal issues, for the platforms of the parties were almost identical. On the one hand, the Republican candidate, the dynamic James G. Blaine, had an immense following, but his reputation had been soiled by the publication of the "Mulligan letters," which connected him with the corrupt granting of congressional favors to the Little Rock and Fort Smith Railroad. On the other hand, it came out during the campaign that Cleveland, a bachelor, had fathered an illegitimate child. Instead of debating public issues, the Republicans chanted the ditty,

> *Ma! Ma! Where's my pa?*
> *Gone to the White House,*
> *Ha! Ha! Ha!*

to which the Democrats countered,

> *Blaine, Blaine, James G. Blaine,*
> *The continental liar from the State of Maine.*

Blaine lost more heavily in the mudslinging than Cleveland, whose quiet courage in saying "Tell the truth" when his past was brought to light contrasted favorably with Blaine's glib and unconvincing denials. A significant group of eastern Republicans, known as **mugwumps,** campaigned for the Democrats.[1] However, Blaine ran a strong race against a general pro-Democratic trend; Cleveland won the election by fewer than 25,000 votes. The change of 600 ballots in New York would have given that state, and the presidency, to his opponent.

Cleveland had little imagination and too narrow a conception of his powers and duties to be a dynamic president. He could defend a position against heavy odds, yet he lacked flexibility. He took a fairly broad view of the powers of the federal government, but he thought it unseemly to put pressure on Congress, believing in "the entire independence of the executive and legislative branches."

Toward the end of his term Cleveland bestirred himself and tried to provide constructive leadership on the tariff question. The government was embarrassed by a large revenue surplus, which Cleveland hoped to reduce by cutting the duties on necessities and on raw materials used in manufacturing. He devoted his entire annual message of December 1887 to the tariff, thereby focusing public attention on the subject. When worried Democrats reminded him that an election was coming up and that the tariff might cause a rift in the organization, he replied simply, "What is the use of being elected or re-elected, unless you stand for something?"

In that contest, Cleveland obtained a plurality of the popular vote, but his opponent, Benjamin Harrison, grandson of President William Henry Harrison, carried most of

---

[1]The mugwumps considered themselves reformers, but on social and economic questions nearly all of them were very conservative. They were sound-money proponents and advocates of laissez-faire. Reform to them consisted almost entirely of doing away with corruption and making the government more efficient.

President Grover Cleveland and Frances Folsom in 1888. The couple had married two years earlier; he was 48, and she, 21, the youngest First Lady. Her popularity blunted criticisms that Cleveland, a bachelor, had earlier fathered an illegitimate child. When he lost the 1888 election, his wife predicted that she would return as First Lady. Four years later, she did.

the key northeastern industrial states by narrow margins, thereby obtaining a comfortable majority in the electoral college, 233 to 168.

Although intelligent and able, Harrison was too reserved to make a good politician. During the Civil War he fought under Sherman at Atlanta and won a reputation as a stern, effective disciplinarian. In 1876 he ran unsuccessfully for governor of Indiana, but in 1881 was elected to the Senate.

Harrison believed ardently in protective tariffs. His approach to fiscal policy was conservative, though he was freehanded in the matter of veterans' pensions. Harrison professed to favor civil service reform, but fashioned an unimpressive record on the question. He appointed the vigorous young reformer Theodore Roosevelt to the Civil Service Commission and then proceeded to undercut him systematically. Before long the frustrated Roosevelt was calling the president a "cold blooded, narrow minded, prejudiced, obstinate, timid old psalm singing Indianapolis politician."

View the Image
Harrison and Morton Campaign Ad at **myhistorylab.com**

Under Harrison, Congress distinguished itself by expending, for the first time in a period of peace, more than $1 billion in a single session. It raised the tariff to an all-time high. The Sherman Antitrust Act was also passed.

Harrison had little to do with the fate of any of these measures. The Republicans lost control of Congress in 1890, and two years later Grover Cleveland swept back into power, defeating Harrison by more than 350,000 votes.

African Americans in the South after Reconstruction

Perhaps the most important issue of the last quarter of the nineteenth century was the fate of the former slaves after the withdrawal of federal troops from the South. Shortly after his inauguration in 1877, President Hayes made a goodwill tour of the South and he urged blacks to trust southern whites. That same year Governor Wade Hampton of South Carolina proposed to "secure to every citizen, the lowest as well as the highest, black as well as white, full and equal protection in the enjoyment of all his rights under the Constitution."

But the pledge was not kept. By December, Hayes was sadly disillusioned. "By state legislation, by frauds, by intimidation, and by violence of the most atrocious character, colored citizens have been deprived of the right of suffrage," he wrote in his diary. However, he did nothing to remedy the situation. Frederick Douglass called Hayes's policy "sickly conciliation."

Hayes's successors in the 1880s did no better. "Time is the only cure," President Garfield said, thereby confessing that he had no policy at all. President Arthur gave federal patronage to antiblack groups in an effort to split the Democratic South. In 1887 President Cleveland explained to a correspondent why he opposed "mixed [integrated] schools." Expert opinion, the president said, believed "that separate schools were of much more benefit for the colored people." Hayes, Garfield, and Arthur were Republicans, and Cleveland a Democrat; party made little difference. Both parties subscribed to hypocritical statements about equality and constitutional rights, and neither did anything to implement them.

For a time blacks were not totally disenfranchised in the South. Rival white factions tried to manipulate them, and corruption flourished as widely as in the machine-dominated wards of the northern cities. In the 1890s, however, the southern states, led by Mississippi, began to deprive blacks of the vote despite the Fifteenth Amendment. Poll taxes raised a formidable economic barrier, one that also disenfranchised many poor whites. Literacy tests completed the work; a number of states provided a loophole for illiterate whites by including an "understanding" clause whereby an illiterate person could qualify by demonstrating an ability to explain the meaning of a section of the state constitution when an election official read it to him. Blacks who attempted to take the test were uniformly declared to have failed it.

In Louisiana, 130,000 blacks voted in the election of 1896. Then the law was changed. In 1900 only 5,000 votes were cast by blacks. "We take away the Negroes' votes," a Louisiana politician explained, "to protect them just as we would protect a little child and prevent it from injuring itself with sharp-edged tools." Almost every Supreme Court decision after 1877 that affected blacks somehow nullified or curtailed their rights. The **civil rights cases** (1883) declared the Civil Rights Act of 1875 unconstitutional. Blacks who were refused equal accommodations or privileges by hotels, theaters, and other privately owned facilities had no recourse at law, the Court announced. The Fourteenth Amendment guaranteed their civil rights against invasion by the states, not by individuals.

Finally, in ***Plessy v. Ferguson*** (1896), the Court ruled that even in places of public accommodation, such as railroads and, by implication, schools, segregation was legal as long as facilities of equal quality were provided: "If one race be inferior to the other socially, the Constitution of the United States cannot put them upon the same plane." In a noble dissent in the Plessy case, Justice John Marshall Harlan protested this line of argument. "Our Constitution is color-blind," he said. "The two races in this country are indissolubly linked together, and the interests of both require that the common government of all shall not permit the seeds of race hatred to be planted under the sanction of law."

View the Image

Plessy v. Ferguson, 1896 at myhistorylab.com

Most Northerners supported the government and the Court. Newspapers presented a stereotyped, derogatory picture of blacks, no matter what the circumstances. Northern magazines, even high-quality publications such as *Harper's*, *Scribner's*, and the *Century*, repeatedly made blacks the butt of crude jokes.

A cartoon from *Judge* magazine in 1892 depicts Ku Klux Klansmen barring a black voter from the polls.

The restoration of white rule abruptly halted the progress in public education for blacks that the Reconstruction governments had made. Church groups and private foundations such as the Peabody Fund and the Slater Fund, financed chiefly by northern philanthropists, supported black schools after 1877. Among them were two important experiments in vocational training, Hampton Institute and Tuskegee Institute.

These schools had to overcome considerable resistance and suspicion in the white community; they survived only because they taught a docile philosophy, preparing students to accept second-class citizenship and become farmers and craftsmen. Since proficiency in academic subjects might have given the lie to the southern belief that blacks were intellectually inferior to whites, such subjects were avoided.

Booker T. Washington: A "Reasonable" Champion for African Americans

Since nearly all contemporary biologists, physicians, and other supposed experts on race were convinced that African Americans were inferior, white Americans generally accepted black inferiority as fact. By denying blacks decent educational opportunities and good jobs, the dominant race could use the blacks' resultant ignorance and poverty to justify the inferior facilities offered them.

Southern blacks reacted to this deplorable situation in a variety of ways. Some sought redress in racial pride and what would later be called black nationalism. Some became so disaffected that they tried to revive the African colonization movement. "Africa is our home," insisted Bishop Henry M. Turner, a huge, plainspoken man who had served as an army chaplain during the war and as a member of the Georgia legislature during Reconstruction. Another militant, T. Thomas Fortune, editor of the New York *Age* and founder of the Afro-American League (1887), called on blacks to demand full civil rights, better schools, and fair wages and to fight against discrimination of every sort. "Let us stand up like men in our own organization," he urged. "If others use . . . violence to combat our peaceful arguments, it is not for us to run away from violence."

For a time, militancy and black separatism won few adherents among southern blacks. For one thing, life was better than it had been under slavery. Segregation actually helped southern blacks who became barbers, undertakers, restaurateurs, and shopkeepers because whites were reluctant to supply such services to blacks. According to the most conservative estimates, the living standard of the average southern black more than doubled between 1865 and 1900. But this only made many southern whites more vindictive.

This helps explain the tactics of Booker T. Washington, one of the most extraordinary Americans of that generation. Washington had been born a slave in Virginia in 1856. Laboriously he obtained an education, supporting himself while a student by working as a janitor. In 1881, with the financial help of northern philanthropists, he founded Tuskegee Institute in Alabama. His experiences convinced Washington that blacks must lift themselves up by their own bootstraps but that they must also accommodate themselves to white prejudices. A persuasive speaker and a brilliant fund-raiser, he soon developed a national reputation as a "reasonable" champion of his race.

In 1895 Washington made a now-famous speech to a mixed audience at the Cotton States International Exposition in Atlanta. To the blacks he said, "Cast down your bucket where you are," by which he meant stop fighting segregation and second-class citizenship and concentrate on learning useful skills. Progress up the social and economic ladder would come not from "artificial forcing" but from self-improvement.

Booker T. Washington in his office at Tuskegee Institute, 1900. Washington chose a policy of accommodation. Washington did not urge blacks to accept inferiority and racial slurs but to ignore them. His own behavior was indeed subtle, even devious. In public he minimized the importance of civil and political rights. Behind the scenes he lobbied against restrictive measures, marshaled large sums of money to fight test cases in the courts, and worked hard in northern states to organize the black vote and make sure that black political leaders got a share of the spoils of office.

Washington asked the whites of what he called "our beloved South" to lend the blacks a hand in their efforts to advance themselves. If you will do so, he promised, you will be "surrounded by the most patient, faithful, law-abiding, and unresentful people that the world has seen."

This **Atlanta Compromise** delighted white Southerners and won Washington financial support in every section of the country. He became one of the most powerful men in the United States, consulted by presidents, in close touch with business and philanthropic leaders, and capable of influencing in countless unobtrusive ways the fate of millions of blacks.

Blacks responded to the compromise with mixed feelings. Accepting Washington's approach might relieve them of many burdens and dangers. But Washington was asking them to give up specific rights in return for vague promises of future help. The cost was high in surrendered personal dignity and lost hopes of obtaining real justice.

Washington's career illustrates the dilemma that American blacks have always faced: the choice between confrontation and accommodation. This choice was particularly difficult in the late nineteenth century.

City Bosses

Outside of the South, the main issue concerned municipal government.

The immigrants who flocked into American cities in the 1880s and early 1890s were largely of peasant stock, and having come from societies unacquainted with democracy, they had no experience with representative government. The tendency of urban workers to move frequently in search of better jobs further lessened the likelihood that they would develop political influence independently.

Furthermore, the difficulties of life in the slums bewildered and often overwhelmed newcomers, both native- and foreign-born. Hopeful, but passive and naive, they could hardly be expected to take a broad view of social problems when so beset by personal ones. This enabled shrewd urban politicians to take command of the city masses and march them in obedient phalanxes to the polls.

Most city machines were loose-knit neighborhood organizations headed by ward bosses, not tightly geared hierarchical bureaucracies ruled by a single leader. "Big Tim" Sullivan of New York's Lower East Side and "Hinky Dink" Kenna of Chicago were typical of the breed. Sullivan, Kenna, and others like them performed many useful services for people they liked to think of as their constituents. They found jobs for new arrivals and distributed food and other help to all in bad times. Anyone in trouble with the law could obtain at least a hearing from the ward boss, and often, if the crime was minor or due to ignorance, the difficulty was quietly "fixed" and the culprit was sent off with a word of caution. Informally, probably without consciously intending to do so, the bosses educated the immigrants in the complexities of American civilization, helping them to leap the gulf between the almost medieval society of their origins and the modern industrial world.

The price of such aid was unquestioning political support, which the bosses converted into cash. In New York, Sullivan levied tribute on gambling, had a hand in the liquor business, and controlled the issuance of peddlers' licenses. When he died in 1913, he was reputedly worth $1 million. Yet he and others like him were immensely popular; 25,000 grieving constituents followed Big Tim's coffin on its way to the grave.

The more visible and better-known city bosses played even less socially justifiable roles than the ward bosses. Their principal technique for extracting money from the public till was the kickback. To get city contracts, suppliers were made to pad their bills and, when paid for their work with funds from the city treasury, turn over the excess to the politicians. Similarly, operators of streetcar lines, gas and electricity companies, and other public utilities were compelled to pay huge bribes to obtain favorable franchises.

The most notorious of the nineteenth-century city bosses was William Marcy Tweed, whose "Tweed Ring" extracted tens of millions of dollars from New York City during the brief period of 1869–1871. He was swiftly jailed!

Despite their welfare work and their popularity, most bosses were essentially thieves. Efforts to romanticize them as the Robin Hoods of industrial society grossly distort the facts. However, the system developed and survived because too many middle-class city dwellers were indifferent to the fate of the poor. Except during occasional reform waves, few tried to check the rapaciousness of the politicos.

Many substantial citizens shared at least indirectly in the corruption. The owners of tenements were interested in crowding as many rent payers as possible into their buildings. Utility companies seeking franchises preferred a system that enabled them to buy favors. Honest citizens who had no selfish stake in the system and who were repelled by the sordidness of city government were seldom sufficiently concerned to do anything about it.

Many so-called urban reformers resented the boss system mainly because it gave political power to people who were not "gentlemen" or, as one reformer put it, to a "proletarian mob" of "illiterate peasants, freshly raked from Irish bogs, or Bohemian mines, or Italian robber nests."

Crops and Complaints

The vacuity of American politics may well have stemmed from the complacency of the middle-class majority. The country was growing; no foreign enemy threatened it; the poor were mostly recent immigrants, blacks, and others with little influence, who were easily ignored by those in comfortable circumstances. However, one important group in society suffered increasingly as the years rolled by: the farmers. Out of their travail came the force that finally, in the 1890s, brought American politics face to face with the problems of the age.

After the Civil War most farmers did well, but in the 1890s disaster struck. First came a succession of dry years and poor harvests. Then farmers in Australia, Canada, Russia, and Argentina took advantage of improvements in transportation to sell their produce in European markets that had relied on American foodstuffs. The price of wheat fell to about sixty cents a bushel. Cotton, the great southern staple, which sold for more than thirty cents a pound in 1866 and fifteen cents in the early 1870s, at times in the 1890s fell below six cents.

The tariff on manufactured goods appeared to aggravate the farmers' predicament, and so did the domestic marketing system, which enabled a multitude of middlemen to gobble up a large share of the profits of agriculture. The shortage of credit, particularly in the South, was an additional burden.

The downward swing of the business cycle in the early 1890s completed the devastation. Settlers who had paid more for their lands than they were worth and borrowed money at high interest rates to do so found themselves squeezed relentlessly. Thousands lost their farms and returned eastward, penniless and dispirited.

The Populist Movement

The agricultural depression triggered a new outburst of farm radicalism, the Alliance movement. Alliances were organizations of farmers' clubs, most of which had sprung up during the bad times of the late 1870s. The first Knights of Reliance group was founded in 1877 in Lampasas County, Texas. As the Farmers' Alliance, this organization gradually expanded in northeastern Texas, and after 1885 it spread rapidly throughout the cotton states. Alliance leaders stressed cooperation. Their co-ops bought fertilizer and other supplies in bulk and sold them at fair prices to members. They sought to market their crops cooperatively but could not raise the necessary capital from banks, with the result that some of them began to question the workings of the American financial and monetary system. They became economic and social radicals in the process.

Although the state alliances of the Dakotas and Kansas joined the Southern Alliance in 1889, for a time local prejudices and conflicting interests prevented the formation of a single national organization. But the farm groups emerged as a potent force in the 1890 elections.

In the South, Alliance-sponsored gubernatorial candidates won in Georgia, Tennessee, South Carolina, and Texas; eight southern legislatures fell under Alliance control, and forty-four representatives and three senators committed to Alliance objectives were sent to Washington. In the West, Alliance candidates swept Kansas, captured a majority in the Nebraska legislature, and accumulated enough seats in Minnesota and South Dakota to hold the balance of power between the major parties.

Such success, coupled with the reluctance of the Republicans and Democrats to make concessions to their demands, encouraged Alliance leaders to create a new national party. By uniting southern and western farmers, they succeeded in breaking the sectional barrier erected by the Civil War. If they could recruit industrial workers, perhaps a real political revolution could be accomplished. In February 1892, farm leaders, representatives of the Knights of Labor, and various professional reformers met at St. Louis. They organized the **People's (Populist) party**, and issued a call for a national convention to meet at Omaha in July.

That convention nominated General James B. Weaver of Iowa for president and drafted a platform that called for a graduated income tax and national ownership of railroads, the telegraph, and telephone systems. It also advocated a "subtreasury" plan that would permit farmers to keep nonperishable crops off the market when prices were low. Under this proposal the government would make loans in the form of greenbacks to farmers, secured by crops held in storage in federal warehouses. When prices rose, the farmers could sell their crops and repay the loans. To combat deflation further, the platform demanded the unlimited coinage of silver and an increase in the money supply "to no less than $50 per capita."

●●●|Read the **Document**

The People's Party Platform
at **myhistorylab.com**

To make the government more responsive to public opinion, the Populists urged the adoption of the initiative and referendum procedures and the election of U.S. senators by popular vote. To win the support of industrial workers, their platform denounced the use of Pinkerton detectives in labor disputes and backed the eight-hour day and the restriction of "undesirable" immigration.

The Populists saw themselves not as a persecuted minority but as a victimized majority betrayed by what would a century later be called the establishment. They were at most ambivalent about the free enterprise system, and they tended to attribute social and

In Kansas in 1893 a Populist governor and a Populist-controlled Senate invalidated the election of some Republicans in the Kansas House of Representatives, giving the Populists control of that body, too. The displaced Republicans, denied seats, smashed their way into the capitol building with this sledgehammer and ousted the Populists, who decided to meet in a separate building. Each proclaimed itself to be the true legislature and passed its own laws. Eventually the Kansas Supreme Court decided in favor of the Republican legislature and disbanded the Populist gathering.
Source: Kansas State Historical Society.

economic injustices not to built-in inequities in the system but to nefarious conspiracies organized by selfish interests in order to subvert the system.

The appearance of the new party was the most exciting and significant aspect of the presidential campaign of 1892, which saw Harrison and Cleveland refighting the election of 1888. The Populists put forth a host of colorful spellbinders: Tom Watson, a Georgia congressman whose temper was such that on one occasion he administered a beating to a local planter with the man's own riding crop; William A. Peffer, a senator from Kansas whose long beard and grave demeanor gave him the look of a Hebrew prophet; "Sockless Jerry" Simpson of Kansas, unlettered but full of grassroots shrewdness and wit, a former Greenbacker, and an admirer of the single tax doctrine of Henry George; and Ignatius Donnelly, the "Minnesota Sage," who claimed to be an authority on science, economics, and Shakespeare.

●●—Read the Document

Mary Elizabeth Lease, the Populist Crusader at **myhistorylab.com**

In the one-party South, Populist strategists sought to wean black farmers away from the ruling Democratic organization. Southern black farmers had their own Colored Farmers' Alliance, and even before 1892 their leaders had worked closely with the white alliances. Of course, the blacks would be useless to the party if they could not vote; therefore, white Populist leaders opposed the southern trend toward disfranchising African Americans and called for full civil rights for all.

The results proved disappointing. Tom Watson lost his seat in Congress, and Donnelly ran a poor third in the Minnesota gubernatorial race. The Populists did sweep Kansas. They elected numbers of local officials in other western states and cast over a million votes for General Weaver. But the effort to unite white and black farmers in the South failed miserably. Conservative Democrats, while continuing with considerable success to attract black voters, played on racial fears, insisting that the Populists sought to undermine white supremacy. Since most white Populists saw the alliance with blacks as at best a marriage of convenience, this argument had a deadly effect. Elsewhere, even in the old centers of the Granger movement, the party made no significant impression.

Mary Elizabeth Lease was a prominent Populist, noted for her rallying cry to "raise less corn and more hell."
Source: Kansas State Historical Society.

By standing firmly for conservative financial policies, Cleveland attracted considerable Republican support and won a solid victory over Harrison in the electoral college, 277 to 145. Weaver received twenty-two electoral votes.

Showdown on Silver

One conclusion that politicians reached after analyzing the 1892 election was that the money question, particularly the controversy over the coinage of silver, was of paramount interest to the voters. Despite the wide-ranging appeal of the Populist platform, most of Weaver's strength came from the silver-mining states.

In truth, the issue of gold versus silver was superficial; the important question was what, if anything, should be done to check the deflationary spiral. The declining price level benefited people with fixed incomes and injured most others. Industrial workers profited from deflation except when depression caused unemployment.

By the early 1890s, discussion of federal monetary policy revolved around the coinage of silver. Traditionally, the United States had been on a bimetallic standard. Both gold and silver were coined, the number of grains of each in the dollar being adjusted periodically to reflect the commercial value of the two metals. The discovery of numerous gold mines in

California in the 1840s and 1850s depressed the price of gold relative to silver. By 1861, a silver dollar could be melted down and sold for $1.03. No miner took silver to the mint to be stamped into coin. In a short time, silver dollars were withdrawn and only gold dollars circulated. However, an avalanche of silver from the mines of Nevada and Colorado gradually depressed the price until, around 1874, it again became profitable for miners to coin their bullion. Alas, when they tried to do so, they discovered that the Coinage Act of 1873, taking account of the fact that no silver had been presented to the mint in years, had demonetized the metal.

Silver miners denounced this as the "Crime of '73." Inflationists joined them in demanding a return to bimetallism. They knew that if more dollars were put into circulation, the value of each dollar would decline; that is, prices and wages would rise. Conservatives, still fighting the battle against inflationary greenback paper money, resisted strongly. The result was a series of compromises. In 1878 the **Bland-Allison Silver Purchase Act** authorized the buying of between $2 million and $4 million of silver a month at the market price, but this had little inflationary effect because the government consistently purchased the minimum amount. The commercial price of silver continued to fall. In 1890 the **Sherman Silver Purchase Act** required the government to buy 4.5 million *ounces* of silver monthly, but in the face of increasing supplies the price of silver fell still further. By 1894, a silver coin weighed thirty-two times more than a gold one.

L. Frank Baum, author of *The Wonderful Wizard of Oz* (1900) and a fan of William Jennings Bryan, perhaps wrote his story as an allegory of the 1896 election. Dorothy, wearing "silver" slippers (in the original), follows a "yellow brick road" (gold) on a crusade to free the Munchkins (the oppressed little people) from the Wicked Witch of the East (the rapacious corporations and financiers). Liberation is to come in Emerald City (greenbacks) through the intervention of a kindly, but ultimately ineffective wizard (Bryan). Only the entire people—Dorothy and entourage—can prevail against wickedness. Judy Garland starred as Dorothy in the film version of *The Wizard of Oz* (1939).

The compromises satisfied no one. Silver miners grumbled because their bullion brought in only half what it had in the early 1870s. Debtors noted angrily that because of the general decline in prices, the dollars they used to meet their obligations were worth more than twice as much as in 1865. Advocates of the gold standard feared that unlimited silver coinage would be authorized, "destroying the value of the dollar."

The Depression of 1893

Both the silverites and "gold bugs" warned of economic disaster if their policies were not followed. Then, in 1893, after the London banking house of Baring Brothers collapsed, a financial panic precipitated a worldwide industrial depression. In the United States hundreds of cotton mills and iron foundries closed, never to reopen. During the harsh winter of 1893–1894, millions were without jobs.

President Cleveland believed that the controversy over silver had caused the depression by shaking the confidence of the business community and that all would be well if the country returned to a single gold standard. He summoned a special session of Congress, and by exerting immense political pressure he obtained the repeal of the Sherman Silver Purchase Act in October 1893. All that this accomplished was to split the Democratic party, its southern and western wings deserting him almost to a man.

During 1894 and 1895, while the nation floundered in the worst depression it had ever experienced, a series of events further undermined public confidence. In the spring of 1894 several "armies" of the unemployed, the most imposing led by Jacob S. Coxey, an eccentric Ohio businessman, marched on Washington to demand relief. Coxey wanted the government to undertake a program of federal public works and other projects to hire unemployed workers to build roads.

When Coxey's group of demonstrators, perhaps 500 in all, reached Washington, he and two other leaders were arrested for trespassing on the grounds of the Capitol. Their followers were dispersed by club-wielding policemen. This callous treatment convinced many Americans that the government had little interest in the suffering of the people, an opinion strengthened when Cleveland, in July 1894, used federal troops to crush the Pullman strike.

The next year the Supreme Court handed down several reactionary decisions. In *United States v. E. C. Knight Company* it refused to employ the Sherman Antitrust Act to break up the Sugar Trust. The Court also denied a writ of habeas corpus to Eugene V. Debs of the American Railway Union, who was languishing in prison for disobeying a federal injunction during the Pullman strike.

On top of these indications of official conservatism came a desperate financial crisis. Throughout 1894 the Treasury's supply of gold dwindled as worried citizens exchanged greenbacks (now convertible into gold) for hard money and foreign investors cashed in large amounts of American securities. The government tried to sell bonds for gold to bolster the reserve, but the gold reserve continued to melt away. Early in 1895 it touched a low point of $41 million.

At this juncture a syndicate of bankers headed by J. P. Morgan turned the tide by underwriting a $62 million bond issue, guaranteeing that half the gold would come from Europe. This caused a great public outcry; the spectacle of the nation being saved from bankruptcy by a private banker infuriated millions.

As the presidential election of 1896 approached, the major parties found it impossible to continue straddling the money question. The Populist vote had increased by 42 percent

Table 20.1   The Supreme Court Supports Racial Segregation and Corporate Power

Civil Rights Cases	1883	Overturned Civil Rights Act of 1875	Limited Fourteenth Amendment to protecting blacks from deprivation of rights by *states*; allowed individuals to do so
Plessy v. Ferguson	1896	Upheld principle of "separate but equal" in public accommodations	Allowed southern states and municipalities to pass laws enforcing separation of whites and blacks
U.S. v. E. C. Knight Co.	1895	Refused to break up the Sugar Trust for being a monopoly	Rendered the Sherman Antitrust Act of 1890 nearly meaningless
In Re Debs	1895	Refused to free Eugene V. Debs, president of the American Railway Union who had been jailed for leading a strike	Enabled the government to use injunctions to stop strikes, thereby depriving union leaders of the chance to plead their case in court

in the 1894 congressional elections. Southern and western Democratic leaders feared that they would lose their following unless Cleveland was repudiated. Western Republicans, led by Senator Henry M. Teller of Colorado, were threatening to bolt to the Populists unless their party came out for silver coinage. After a generation of political equivocation, the major parties had to face an important issue squarely.

The Republicans, meeting to choose a candidate at St. Louis in June 1896, announced for the gold standard. "We are unalterably opposed to every measure calculated to debase our currency or impair the credit of our country," the platform declared. "We are therefore opposed to the free coinage of silver. . . . The existing gold standard must be maintained." The party then nominated Ohio's William McKinley for president. McKinley, best known for his staunch advocacy of the protective tariff yet highly regarded by labor, was expected to run strongly in the Midwest and the East.

The Democratic convention met in July in Chicago. The pro-gold Cleveland element made a hard fight, but the silverites swept them aside. The high point came when a youthful Nebraskan named William Jennings Bryan spoke for silver against gold, for western farmers against the industrial East.

"Burn down your cities and leave our farms," he said, "and your cities will spring up again as if by magic; but destroy our farms and the grass will grow in the streets of every city in the country." He ended with a marvelous figure of speech that set the tone for the coming campaign. "You shall not press down upon the brow of labor this crown of thorns," he warned, bringing his hands down suggestively to his temples. "You shall not crucify mankind upon a cross of gold!" Dramatically, he extended his arms to the side, the very figure of the crucified Christ.

The convention promptly adopted a platform calling for "the free and unlimited coinage of both silver and gold at the present legal ratio of 16 to 1" and went on to nominate Bryan, who was barely thirty-six, for president.

This action put tremendous pressure on the Populists. If they supported the Democrat Bryan, they risked losing their party identity; if they nominated another candidate, they would ensure McKinley's election. In part because the delegates could not find a person of stature willing to become a candidate against Bryan, the Populist convention nominated him, seeking to preserve the party identity by substituting Watson for the Democratic vice-presidential nominee, Arthur Sewall of Maine.

The Election of 1896

Never did a presidential campaign raise such intense emotions. The Republicans from the silver-mining states swung solidly behind Bryan. But many solid-money Democrats, especially in the Northeast, refused to accept the decision of the Chicago convention. Many others adopted the policy of Governor David B. Hill of New York, who said, "I am a Democrat still—very still." The extreme gold bugs, calling themselves National Democrats, nominated their own candidate, seventy-nine-year-old Senator John M. Palmer of Illinois. Palmer ran only to injure Bryan. "Fellow Democrats," he announced, "I will not consider it any great fault if you decide to cast your vote for William McKinley."

At the start the Republicans seemed to have everything in their favor. Bryan's youth and relative lack of political experience—two terms in the House—contrasted unfavorably with McKinley's distinguished war record, his long service in Congress and as governor of Ohio, and his reputation for honesty and good judgment. The severe depression operated in favor of the party out of power, although by repudiating Cleveland the Democrats escaped much of the burden of explaining away his errors. The newspapers came out almost unanimously for the Republicans. The Democrats had very little money and few well-known speakers to fight the campaign.

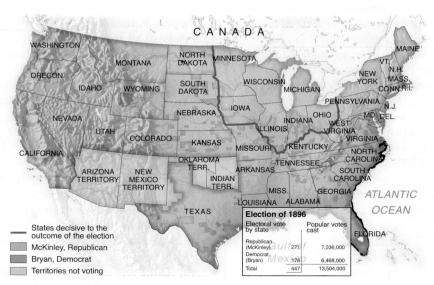

Election of 1896		
Electoral vote by state	Popular votes cast	
Republican (McKinley)	271	7,036,000
Democrat (Bryan)	176	6,468,000
Total	447	13,504,000

States decisive to the outcome of the election
McKinley, Republican
Bryan, Democrat
Territories not voting

Bryan vs. McKinley, 1896 Democrat/Populist Bryan carried much of the South and West, and most of the farming regions of the plains. But he failed to win over enough industrial workers to take states in the North.

But Bryan proved a formidable opponent. Casting aside tradition, he took to the stump personally, traveling 18,000 miles and making over 600 speeches. He was one of the greatest of orators, projecting an image of absolute sincerity without appearing fanatical or argumentative. At every major stop on his tour, huge crowds assembled. His energy was amazing, and his charm and good humor were unfailing. Everywhere he hammered away at the money question. Yet he did not totally neglect other issues. He was defending, he said, "all the people who suffer from the operations of trusts, syndicates, and combines."

McKinley's campaign was managed by a new type of politician, Marcus "Mark" Alonzo Hanna, an Ohio businessman. In a sense Hanna was a product of the Pendleton Civil Service Act. When deprived of the contributions of officeholders, the parties turned to business for funds, and Hanna was one of the first leaders with a foot in both camps. Politics fascinated him, and despite his wealth and wide interests, he was willing to labor endlessly at the routine work of political organization.

Before most Republicans realized how effective Bryan was on the stump, Hanna perceived the danger and sprang into action.

Certain that money was the key to political power, he raised an enormous campaign fund. When businessmen hesitated to contribute, he pried open their purses by a combination of persuasiveness and intimidation. Banks and insurance companies were "assessed" a percentage of their assets, big corporations a share of their receipts, until some $3.5 million had been collected.

Hanna disbursed these funds with efficiency and imagination. He sent 1,500 speakers into the doubtful districts and blanketed the land with 250 million pieces of campaign literature, printed in a dozen languages. "He has advertised McKinley as if he were a patent medicine," Theodore Roosevelt, never at a loss for words, exclaimed.

Incapable of competing with Bryan as a swayer of mass audiences, McKinley conducted a "front-porch campaign." This technique dated from the first Harrison-Cleveland election, when Harrison regularly delivered off-the-cuff speeches to groups of visitors representing special interests or regions in his hometown of Indianapolis. The system conserved the candidate's energies and enabled him to avoid the appearance of seeking the presidency too openly—which was still considered bad form—and at the same time allowed him to make headlines throughout the country.

Guided by the masterful Hanna, McKinley brought the front-porch method to perfection. Superficially the proceedings were delightfully informal. From every corner of the land, groups representing various regions, occupations, and interests descended on McKinley's unpretentious frame house in Canton, Ohio. Gathering on the lawn—the grass was soon reduced to mud, the fence stripped of pickets by souvenir hunters—the visitors paid their compliments to the candidate and heard him deliver a brief speech, while beside him on the porch his aged mother and adoring invalid wife listened with rapt attention. Then there was a small reception, during which the delegates were given an opportunity to shake their host's hand.

Despite the air of informality, these performances were carefully staged. The delegations arrived on a tightly coordinated schedule worked out by McKinley's staff and the railroads, which operated cut-rate excursion trains to Canton from all over the nation.

William Jennings Bryan's "Cross of Gold" speech inspired this cartoonist's caricature of it as "plagiarized from the Bible." Bryan's speech in favor of bimetallism was, in fact, studded with religious references. He described the unlimited coinage of silver and gold as a "holy cause" supported by those who built churches "where they praise their Creator."

THE SACRILEGIOUS CANDIDATE.

No man who drags into the dust the most sacred symbols of the Christian world is fit to be president of the United States.

McKinley was fully briefed on the special interests and attitudes of each group, and the speeches of delegation leaders were submitted in advance. Often his secretary amended these remarks, and on occasion McKinley wrote the visitors' speeches himself. His own talks were carefully prepared, each calculated to make a particular point. All were reported fully in the newspapers. Thus without moving from his doorstep, McKinley met thousands of people from every section of the country.

These tactics worked admirably. On election day McKinley collected 271 electoral votes to Bryan's 176, the popular vote being 7,036,000 to 6,468,000.

The Meaning of the Election

During the campaign, some frightened Republicans had laid plans for fleeing the country if Bryan were elected, and belligerent ones, such as Theodore Roosevelt, then police commissioner of New York City, readied themselves to meet the "social revolutionaries" on the battlefield. Victory sent such people into transports of joy. Most conservatives concluded that the way of life they so fervently admired had been saved for all time.

However heartfelt, such sentiments were not founded on fact. With workers standing beside capitalists and with the farm vote split, it cannot be said that the election divided the nation class against class or that McKinley's victory saved the country from revolution.

Far from representing a triumph for the status quo, the election marked the coming of age of modern America. The battle between gold and silver, which everyone had considered so vital, had little real significance. The inflationists seemed to have been beaten, but new discoveries of gold in Alaska and South Africa and improved methods of extracting gold from low-grade ores soon led to a great expansion of the money supply. In any case, within two decades the system of basing the volume of currency on bullion had been abandoned. Bryan and the "political" Populists who supported him, supposedly the advance agents of revolution, were oriented more toward the past than the future; their ideal was the rural America of Jefferson and Jackson.

McKinley, for all his innate conservatism, was capable of looking ahead toward the new century. His approach was national where Bryan's was basically parochial. Though never daring and seldom imaginative, McKinley was able to deal pragmatically with current problems. Before long, as the United States became increasingly an exporter of manufactures, he would even modify his position on the tariff. And no one better reflected the spirit of the age than Mark Hanna, the outstanding political realist of his generation. Far from preventing change, the outcome of the election of 1896 made possible still greater changes as the United States moved into the twentieth century.

Milestones

1872	Ulysses Grant is reelected president	1890	Sherman Silver Purchase Act requires government silver purchase
1873	Congress suspends the coining of silver ("Crime of '73")	1890–1900	Blacks are deprived of the vote in the South
1876	Rutherford B. Hayes is elected president	1892	People's (Populist) party is founded
1877	Farmers' Alliance movement is founded		Cleveland is elected president a second time
1878	Bland-Allison Act authorizes government silver purchases		
1879	Specie payments resume	1893	Sherman Silver Purchase Act is repealed
1880	James Garfield is elected president		
1881	Garfield is assassinated; Grover Cleveland becomes president	1893	Panic of 1893 causes industrial depression
1881	Booker T. Washington founds Tuskegee Institute for blacks	1894	Coxey's Army marches to Washington to demand relief
1883	Pendleton Act creates Civil Service Commission	1895	Supreme Court declares federal income tax unconstitutional (*Pollock v. Farmers' Loan and Trust Company*)
	Supreme Court Overturns Civil Rights Act of 1875 in the civil rights cases		
1884	Republicans support Democrats during Mugwump Movement		Booker T. Washington urges self-improvement in Atlanta Compromise Speech
	Grover Cleveland is elected president		
1887	Interstate Commerce Act regulates railroad rates		J. P. Morgan raises $62 million in gold for the U.S. Treasury
	Cleveland delivers tariff message	1896	William Jennings Bryan delivers "Cross of Gold" speech
1888	Benjamin Harrison is elected president		
	Englishman James Bryce analyzes American politics in *The American Commonwealth*		William McKinley is elected president
			Supreme Court upholds "separate but equal" in *Plessy v. Ferguson*

✓● Study and Review at www.myhistorylab.com

Review Questions

1. The introduction to this chapter suggests that Americans from 1877 to 1896 were as enthralled with politics as Americans are today with *American Idol*. And yet the chapter contends that the major parties took similar positions on the major issues. What explains the high voter turnouts of the era?

2. How did the urban bosses respond to the challenges confronting the cities?

3. How did the decisions of the Supreme Court aggravate race relations and give rise to political protest? What strategies did African American leaders consider in response to increased segregation?

4. Why did such a seemingly dull issue as currency reform generate such passion, culminating in William Jennings Bryan's crusade against "a cross of gold" in 1896? Why did the Populists fail to win the support of northern labor, and thus the election?

5. How has populism fared among historians? How is populism regarded by politicians today? Why?

Key Terms

Atlanta Compromise *529*
Bland-Allison Silver Purchase Act *534*
civil rights cases *526*

mugwumps *524*
Pendleton Act *523*
People's (Populist) party *531*

Plessy v. Ferguson *526*
Sherman Silver Purchase Act *534*

21 The Age of Reform

Are college students apathetic?

SOME THINK SO. IN 2007 *NEW YORK TIMES* COLUMNIST THOMAS Friedman proposed that they be known as Generation Q—for Quiet. That generation, he reported, was "too quiet, too online, for its own good, and for the country's own good."

In 2010 Gabrielle Grow, a senior at the University of California at Davis, offered an explanation in the *Huffington Post*: "From those who deem us apathetic, we have not only inherited a country up to its neck in debt but a society and lifestyle in which we are constantly expected to outperform each other. . . [An] intense course load combined with little free time leaves little room for political inquiry or investigation."

Other students challenged Friedman's stereotype through civic engagement of the old-fashioned sort, by rolling up their sleeves and helping out. In a 2009 UCLA survey, two-thirds of college seniors reported that they "occasionally" or "frequently" performed volunteer work. Over three-fourths said that they voted in the 2008 presidential election. In 2009 AmeriCorps, a federally sponsored public-service plan, received twice as many applications from college graduates as the previous year. That same year, more than 168,000 college students worked for Habitat for Humanity, far more than a decade earlier.

Today's college-age volunteers in many ways resemble their counterparts during the "age of reform" a century ago. Then, large numbers of young adults worked to improve society in various ways. They investigated tenements, factories, schools, municipal governments, and consumer goods. They promoted legislation to protect children from exploitative employers and to secure voting rights for women. They advocated conservation of natural resources. They swelled the ranks of the Socialist party, the Progressive party, and of more radical movements. In response to this sea change among younger voters, the Republican and Democratic parties embraced reforms that earlier generations had regarded as wild-eyed radicalism.

Roots of Progressivism

The progressives were never a single group seeking a single objective. The movement sprang from many sources. One was the fight against corruption and inefficiency in government, which began with the Liberal Republicans of the Grant era and was

Orchard Street, a tenement in lower Manhattan in New York City. The unpaved street, ankle-deep in mud, is lined with garbage. But while reformers deplored life in such slums, many who lived there enjoyed the sociability of the congested streets.

continued by the mugwumps of the 1880s. The struggle for civil service reform was only the first skirmish in this battle; the continuing power of corrupt political machines and the growing influence of large corporations and their lobbyists on municipal and state governments outraged thousands of citizens and led them to seek ways to make the machinery of government at all levels responsive to the majority rather than to special-interest groups. *Movements for social change*

Progressivism also had roots in the effort to regulate and control big business, which characterized the Granger and Populist agitation of the 1870s and 1890s. The failure of the Interstate Commerce Act to end railroad abuses and of the Sherman Antitrust Act to check the growth of large corporations became increasingly apparent after 1900. The return of prosperity after the depression of the 1890s encouraged reformers by removing the fear, so influential in the 1896 presidential campaign, that an assault on the industrial giants might lead to the collapse of the economy.

Between 1897 and 1904 the trend toward concentration in industry accelerated. Such new giants as Amalgamated Copper (1899), U.S. Steel (1901), and International Harvester (1902) attracted most of the attention, but even more alarming were the overall statistics. In a single year (1899) more than 1,200 firms were absorbed in mergers, the resulting combinations being capitalized at $2.2 billion. By 1904 there were 318 industrial combinations in the country with an aggregate capital of $7.5 billion. People who considered bigness inherently evil demanded that the huge new "trusts" be broken up or at least strictly controlled.

America was becoming more urban, more industrial, more mechanized, more centralized—in short, more complex. This trend put a premium on efficiency and cooperation. It seemed obvious to the progressives that people must become more socially minded, and the economy more carefully organized.

By attracting additional thousands of sympathizers to the general cause of reform, the return of prosperity after 1896 fueled the progressive movement. Good times made people more tolerant and generous. As long as profits were on the rise, the average employer did not object if labor improved its position too. Middle-class Americans who had been prepared to go to the barricades in the event of a Bryan victory in 1896 became conscience-stricken when they compared their own comfortable circumstances with those of the "huddled masses" of immigrants and native-born poor.

Giant industrial and commercial corporations undermined not so much the economic well-being as the ambitions and sense of importance of the middle class. The growth of large labor organizations worried such types. In general, character and moral values seemed less influential; organizations—cold, impersonal, heartless—were coming to control business, politics, and too many other aspects of life.

The middle classes could support reform measures without feeling that they were being very radical because they were resisting change and because the intellectual currents of the time harmonized with their ideas of social improvement and the welfare state. The new doctrines of the social scientists, the Social Gospel religious leaders, and the philosophers of pragmatism provided a salubrious climate for progressivism. Many of the thinkers who had formulated these doctrines in the 1880s and 1890s turned to the task of putting them into practice in the new century. Their number included the economist Richard T. Ely, the philosopher John Dewey, and the Baptist clergyman Walter Rauschenbusch, a civic reformer who wrote many books extolling the Social Gospel.

The Muckrakers

As the diffuse progressive army gradually formed its battalions, a new journalistic fad brought the movement into focus. For many years magazines had been publishing articles discussing current political, social, and economic problems. In the fall of 1902, *McClure's* began two particularly hard-hitting series of articles, one on Standard Oil by Ida Tarbell, the other on big-city political machines by Lincoln Steffens. When the editor, S. S. McClure, decided to include in the January 1903 issue an attack on labor gangsterism in the coal fields along with installments of the Tarbell and Steffens series, he called attention to the circumstance in a striking editorial.

Something was radically wrong with the "American character," McClure wrote. These articles showed that large numbers of American employers, workers, and politicians were fundamentally immoral. Lawyers were becoming tools of big business, judges were permitting evildoers to escape justice, the churches were materialistic, and educators seemed incapable of understanding what was happening.

McClure's editorial caused a sensation. The issue sold out quickly. Thousands of readers found their own vague apprehensions brought into focus. Some became active in progressive movements; still more lent passive support.

Other editors jumped to adopt the McClure formula. A small army of professional writers soon flooded the periodical press with denunciations of the insurance business, the drug business, college athletics, prostitution, sweatshop labor, political corruption, and dozens of other subjects. This type of article inspired Theodore Roosevelt, with his gift for vivid language, to compare the journalists to "the Man with the Muck-Rake" in John Bunyan's *Pilgrim's Progress*, whose attention was so fixed on the filth at his feet that he could not notice the "celestial crown" that was offered him in exchange. Roosevelt's characterization grossly misrepresented the literature of exposure, but the label *muckraking* was thereafter affixed to the type. Despite its literal connotations, **muckraker** became a term of honor.

The Progressive Mind

Unlike many earlier reformers, progressives believed that the source of society's evils lay in the structure of its institutions, not in the weaknesses or sinfulness of individuals. Therefore local, state, and national government must be made more responsive to the will of citizens who stood for the traditional virtues. In the South, many people who considered themselves progressives even argued that poll taxes and other measures designed to deny blacks the vote were reforms because they discouraged a class of people they considered unthinking and shiftless from voting.

When government had been thus reformed, then it must act; whatever its virtues, laissez-faire was obsolete. Businessmen, especially big businessmen, must be compelled to behave fairly, their acquisitive drives curbed in the interests of justice and equal opportunity for all. The weaker elements in society—women, children, the poor, the infirm—must be protected against unscrupulous power.

Despite its fervor and democratic rhetoric, progressivism was paternalistic, moderate, and often softheaded. Typical reformers of the period oversimplified complicated issues and treated their personal values as absolute standards of truth and morality. Thus progressives often acted at cross-purposes; at times some were even at war with themselves. This accounts for the diffuseness of the movement.

The progressives never challenged the fundamental principles of capitalism, nor did they attempt a basic reorganization of society. They would have little to do with the socialist brand of reform. Many progressives were anti-immigrant, and only a handful had anything to offer blacks, surely the most exploited group in American society.

A good example of the relatively limited radicalism of most progressives is offered by the experiences of progressive artists. Early in the century a number of painters, including Robert Henri, John Sloan, and George Luks, tried to develop a distinctively American style. They turned to city streets and the people of the slums for their models, and they depended more on inspiration and inner conviction than on careful craftsmanship to achieve their effects.

These artists of the **Ashcan School** were individualists, yet they supported political and social reform and were caught up in the progressive movement. Sloan was a socialist; Henri claimed to be an anarchist. Most saw themselves as rebels. But artistically the Ashcan painters were not very advanced. Their idols were long-dead European masters such as Hogarth, Goya, and Daumier. They were uninfluenced by the outburst of post-impressionist activity then taking place in Europe. To their dismay, when they included canvases by Matisse, Picasso, and other European artists in a show of their own works at the Sixty-Ninth Regiment Armory in New York City in 1913, the "advanced" Europeans got all the attention.

In 1900, Ashcan artist George Luks portrayed corporate monopolies and franchises as a monster preying on New York City.

"Radical" Progressives: The Wave of the Future

The hard times of the 1890s and the callous reactions of conservatives to the victims of that depression pushed many toward Marxian socialism. In 1900 the labor leader Eugene V. Debs ran for president on the Socialist ticket. He polled fewer than 100,000 votes. When he ran again in 1904 he got more than 400,000, and in later elections still more. Labor leaders hoping to organize unskilled workers in heavy industry were increasingly frustrated by the craft orientation of the American Federation of Labor, and some saw in socialism a way to win rank-and-file backing.

In 1905 Debs, William "Big Bill" Haywood of the Western Federation of Miners, Mary Harris "Mother" Jones (a former organizer for the United Mine Workers), Daniel De Leon of the Socialist Labor party, and a few others organized a new union: the **Industrial Workers of the World (IWW).** The IWW was openly anticapitalist. The preamble to its constitution began: "The working class and the employing class have nothing in common."

But the IWW never attracted many ordinary workers. Haywood, its most prominent leader, was usually a general in search of an army. His forte was attracting attention to spontaneous strikes by unorganized workers, not the patient recruiting of workers and the pursuit of practical goals. In 1912 he was closely involved in a bitter and, at times, bloody strike of textile workers in Lawrence, Massachusetts, which was settled with some benefit to the strikers; he was also involved in a failed strike the following winter and spring by silk workers in Paterson, New Jersey.

Other "advanced" European ideas affected the thinking and behavior of some important progressive intellectuals. Sigmund Freud's psychoanalytical theories attracted numbers of Americans. Many picked up enough of the vocabulary of psychoanalysis to discourse impressively about the significance of slips of the tongue, sublimation, and infant sexuality.

Some saw in Freud's ideas reason to effect a "revolution of manners and morals" that would have shocked (or at least embarrassed) Freud, who was personally quite conventional. They advocated easy divorce, trial marriage, and doing away with the double standard in all matters relating to sex. They rejected Victorian reticence and what they incorrectly identified as "puritan" morality out of hand, and they called for programs of sex education, especially the dissemination of information about methods of birth control.

Most large cities boasted groups of these "bohemian" thinkers, by far the most famous being the one centered in New York City's Greenwich Village. The dancer Isadora Duncan, the photographer Alfred Stieglitz, the novelist Floyd Dell, several of the Ashcan artists, and the playwright Eugene O'Neill rubbed shoulders with Big Bill Haywood of the IWW, the anarchist Emma Goldman, the psychoanalyst A. A. Brill, the militant feminist advocate of birth control Margaret Sanger, Max Eastman, and John Reed, a young Harvard graduate who was soon to become famous for his eyewitness account of the Russian Revolution in *Ten Days That Shook the World*.

Goldman, Haywood, Sanger, and a few others in this group were genuine radicals who sought basic changes in bourgeois society, but most of the Greenwich Village intellectuals were as much concerned with aesthetic as social issues. Nearly all of them came from middle-class backgrounds. They found the far-different world of the Italian and Jewish immigrants of the Village and its surrounding neighborhoods charming. But they did not become involved in the immigrants' lives the way the settlement house workers did. Their influence on their own times, therefore, was limited. They are historically important, however, because many of them were genuinely creative people and because many of the ideas and practices they advocated were adopted by later generations.

The creative writers of the era, applying the spirit of progressivism to the realism they had inherited from Howells and the naturalists, tended to adopt an optimistic tone. The poet Ezra Pound, for example, at this time talked grandly of an American renaissance and fashioned a new kind of poetry called imagism, which, while not appearing to be realistic, rejected all abstract generalizations and concentrated on concrete word pictures to convey meaning. "Little" magazines and experimental theatrical companies sprang to life by the dozen, each convinced that it would revolutionize its art. The poet Carl Sandburg, the best-known representative of the Chicago school, denounced the local plutocrats but sang the praises of the city they had made: "Hog Butcher for the World," "City of the Big Shoulders."

Most writers eagerly adopted Freudian psychology without understanding it. Freud's teachings seemed only to mean that they should cast off the restrictions of Victorian prudery; they ignored his essentially dark view of human nature. Theirs was an "innocent rebellion," exuberant and rather muddleheaded.

Rural Socialism Socialist strength extended far beyond the cities. Socialists in rural areas called for tenants to be allowed to work on state-owned plots of land. In 1912, Socialist candidates received nearly half the vote in southern Oklahoma.

Agrarian Socialism, Oklahoma, 1912

Percentage of presidential Socialist vote:
30
15

EMMA GOLDMAN

In January 1886 a sixteen-year-old Jewish girl named Emma Goldman arrived in New York City from St. Petersburg, Russia, where her parents ran a grocery store. As soon as immigration officials had approved her entry into the United States, she hurried on to Rochester, New York, where her half-sister lived. Like most immigrants she expected the United States to be a kind of paradise on earth.

After moving in with her half-sister's family, Emma got a job in a factory sewing coats and earning $2.50 a week. She paid her sister $1.50 a week for room and board and spent sixty cents a week to get to her job. But when she asked her employer for more money he told her to "look for work elsewhere. " She found a job at another factory that paid $4 a week.

In 1887 she married Jacob Kirshner, another Russian immigrant, but they soon divorced. In 1889 she took up with a group of radicals, most of them either socialists or anarchists. By this time Goldman was herself an ardent anarchist, convinced by her experiences that *all* governments repressed individual freedom and should be abolished.

In New York Emma fell in love with another Russian-born radical, Alexander Berkman. They started a kind of commune. Emma worked at home sewing shirts. Alexander found a job making cigars. They never married.

A "mug shot" of Emma Goldman, 1901. She was arrested so often that she took to carrying a book with her everywhere so that she would have something to read in jail if she were arrested.

The couple moved to New Haven, where Emma started a cooperative dressmaking shop. Then they moved to Springfield, Massachusetts, where, with Berkman's cousin, an artist, they opened a photography studio. When this business failed, they opened an ice cream parlor.

Nearly all immigrants of that period retained their faith in the promise of American life even after they discovered that the streets were not paved with gold. But Emma was so disappointed that she became a radical.

In 1892 when she and Berkman learned of the bloody battle between Pinkertons and strikers during the Homestead steel strike, they closed the ice cream parlor and plotted to assassinate Henry Clay Frick, the archvillain of the Homestead drama. Berkman went to Pittsburgh, where, posing as a representative of an agency that provided strikebreakers, he got into Frick's office. Pulling a pistol, Berkman aimed for Frick's head but the shot went wide and hit Frick in the shoulder. Berkman then stabbed Frick, but still the Homestead boss survived. Convicted of the attempt on Frick's life, Berkman was imprisoned for fourteen years.

The next year Goldman was herself arrested and sentenced to a year in jail for making an "incendiary" speech urging unemployed workers to distrust politicians. Upon her release, Goldman went to Vienna, where she trained as a nurse. When she returned to America, she worked as a midwife among the New York poor, an experience that made her an outspoken advocate of birth control. She also helped organize a theatrical group, managed a touring group of Russian actors, and lectured on theatrical topics. In 1901, Goldman was arrested on charges of inspiring Leon Czolgosz to assassinate President McKinley. Czolgosz had attended one of Goldman's lectures, but there was no direct connection between the two, and the charges against her were dropped.

In 1906 Goldman founded *Mother Earth*, an anarchist journal. When Alexander Berkman was released from prison later that year, she made him its editor. *Mother Earth* denounced governments, organized religion, and private property. By this time Goldman had become a celebrity. "She was considered a monster, an exponent of free love and bombs," recalled Margaret Anderson, editor of a literary magazine.

Now Goldman campaigned for freedom of speech and lectured in support of birth control. In 1915, after Margaret Sanger was arrested for disseminating information on birth control, Goldman did the same in public speeches. She was arrested and spent two weeks in jail.

Goldman regarded the Great War—and especially American entry in it—as a calamity beyond measure. In 1917 Goldman and Berkman were convicted of conspiring to persuade men not to register for the draft. They served two years in federal prison. In 1919 they were deported to Russia. Two years later, disillusioned with the Bolsheviks, Goldman left the Soviet Union.

"Red Emma" Goldman was not a typical American, but she was in many ways a typical American immigrant. She learned English and quickly became familiar with American ways. She worked hard and developed valuable skills. Gradually she moved up the economic ladder. And while she was critical of the United States, she was a typical immigrant also in insisting that she was an American patriot. "The kind of patriotism we represent," she said during her trial in 1917, "is the kind of patriotism which loves America with open eyes."

Questions for Discussion

- Why did most immigrants, on learning of the gap between the promise of America and its reality, not become radicals?
- Was Goldman a radical by birth or by acculturation?

Political Reform: Cities First

To most "ordinary" progressives, political corruption and inefficiency lay at the root of the evils plaguing American society, nowhere more obvious than in the nation's cities. Urban life's anonymity and complexity help explain why slavery did not flourish in cities, but also why the previously named vices did flourish. As the cities grew, their antiquated and boss-ridden administrations became more and more disgraceful.

City reformers could seldom destroy the machines without changing urban political institutions. Some cities obtained "home rule" charters that gave them greater freedom from state control in dealing with local matters. Many created research bureaus that investigated government problems in a scientific and nonpartisan manner. A number of middle-sized communities (Galveston, Texas, was the prototype) experimented with a system that integrated executive and legislative powers in the hands of a small elected commission, thereby concentrating responsibility and making it easier to coordinate complex activities. Out of this experiment came the city manager system, under which the commissioners appointed a professional manager to administer city affairs on a non-partisan basis. Dayton, Ohio, which adopted the plan after a flood devastated the town in 1913, offers the best illustration of the city manager system in the Progressive Era.

Once the political system had been made responsive to the desires of the people, the progressives hoped to use it to improve society itself. Many cities experimented with "gas and water socialism," taking over public utility companies and operating them as departments of the municipal government. Under "Golden Rule" Jones, Toledo established a minimum wage for city employees, built playgrounds and golf courses, and moderated its harsh penal code. Mayor Seth Low improved New York's public transportation system and obtained passage of the tenement house law of 1901. Mayor Tom Johnson forced a fare cut to three cents on the Cleveland street railways.

Political Reform: The States

To carry out this kind of change required the support of state legislatures since all municipal government depends on the authority of a sovereign state. Such approval was often difficult to obtain—local bosses were usually entrenched in powerful state machines, and rural majorities insensitive to urban needs controlled most legislatures. Therefore the progressives had to strike at inefficiency and corruption at the state level too.

During the first decade of the new century, Robert M. La Follette, one of the most remarkable figures of the age, transformed Wisconsin. He had served three terms as a Republican congressman (1885–1891) and developed a reputation as an uncompromising foe of corruption before being elected governor in 1900. That the people would always do the right thing if properly informed and inspired was the fundamental article of his political faith. "Machine control is based upon misrepresentation and ignorance," La Follette said. "Democracy is based upon knowledge."

Despite the opposition of railroad and lumbering interests, Governor La Follette obtained a direct primary system for nominating candidates, a corrupt practices act, and laws limiting campaign expenditures and lobbying activities. In power he became something of a boss himself. He made ruthless use of patronage, demanded absolute loyalty of his subordinates, and often stretched, or at least oversimplified, the truth when presenting complex issues to the voters.

La Follette was a consummate showman who never rose entirely above rural prejudices. He was prone to see a nefarious "conspiracy" organized by "the interests" behind even the mildest opposition to his proposals. But he was devoted to the cause of honest government. Realizing that some state functions called for specialized technical knowledge, he used commissions and agencies to handle such matters as railroad regulation, tax assessment, conservation, and highway construction. Wisconsin established a legislative reference library to assist lawmakers in drafting bills. For work of this kind, La Follette called on the faculty of the University of Wisconsin, enticing top-notch economists and political scientists into the public service and drawing freely on the advice of such outstanding social scientists as Richard T. Ely, John R. Commons, and E. A. Ross.

The success of these policies, which became known as the Wisconsin Idea, led other states to adopt similar programs. Reform administrations swept into office in Iowa and Arkansas (1901); Oregon (1902); Minnesota, Kansas, and Mississippi (1904); New York and Georgia (1906); Nebraska (1909); and New Jersey and Colorado (1910). In some cases the reformers were Republicans, in others Democrats, but in all the example of Wisconsin was influential. By 1910, fifteen states had established legislative reference services, most of them staffed by personnel trained in Wisconsin. The direct primary system, in which candidates were selected by voters rather than party bosses, became almost universal.

Some states went beyond Wisconsin in striving to make their governments responsive to the popular will. In 1902 Oregon began to experiment with the initiative, a system by which a bill could be forced on the attention of the legislature by popular petition, and the referendum, a method for allowing the electorate to approve measures rejected by their representatives and to repeal measures that the legislature had passed. Eleven states, most of them in the West, legalized these devices by 1914.

State Social Legislation

The first state laws aimed at social problems long preceded the Progressive Era, but most were either so imprecise as to be unenforceable or, like the Georgia law "limiting" textile workers to eleven hours a day, so weak as to be ineffective. In 1874 Massachusetts restricted the working hours of women and children to ten per day, and by the 1890s many other states, mostly in the East and Midwest, had followed suit. Illinois passed an eight-hour law for women workers in 1893.

As part of this trend, some states established special rules for workers in hazardous industries. In the 1890s several states limited the hours of railroad workers on the grounds that fatigue sometimes caused railroad accidents. Utah restricted miners to eight hours in 1896. In 1901 New York finally enacted an effective tenement house law, greatly increasing the area of open space on building lots and requiring toilets for each apartment, better ventilation systems, and more adequate fireproofing.

Before 1900 the collective impact of such legislation was not impressive. Powerful manufacturers and landlords often succeeded in defeating the bills or rendering them innocuous. The federal system further complicated the task of obtaining effective legislation. The Fourteenth Amendment to the Constitution, although enacted to protect the civil rights of blacks, imposed a revolutionary restriction on the states by forbidding them to "deprive any person of life, liberty, or property without due process of law." Since much state social legislation represented new uses of coercive power that conservative judges considered dangerous and unwise, the Fourteenth Amendment gave such judges

On March 25, 1911, as scores of young factory girls leaped to their deaths from the eighth, ninth, and tenth stories of the Triangle Shirtwaist Factory in New York City, eighteen-year-old Victor Gatto watched in horror. Thirty-three years later he painted this rendering of his nightmare, the bodies of the dead girls placed in order at the base of the building.
Source: Victor Joseph Gatto (1893–1965), *Triangle Fire: March 25, 1911.* c. 1944 (depicting 1911), oil on canvas, 19 × 28", Gift of Mrs. Henry L. Moses, 54.75. The Museum of the City of New York.

an excuse to overturn the laws that deprived employers of the "liberty" to choose how long their employees should work or the conditions of the workplace.

As stricter and more far-reaching laws were enacted, many judges, fearing a trend toward socialism and regimentation, adopted an increasingly narrow interpretation of state authority to regulate business. In 1905 the U.S. Supreme Court declared in the case of *Lochner v. New York* that a New York ten-hour act for bakers deprived the bakers of the liberty of working as long as they wished and thus violated the Fourteenth Amendment. Justice Oliver Wendell Holmes, Jr., wrote a famous dissenting opinion in this case. If the people of New York believed that the public health was endangered by bakers working long hours, he reasoned, it was not the Court's job to overrule them.

Nevertheless, the progressives continued to battle for legislation to use state power against business. Women played a particularly important part in these struggles. Sparked by the National Child Labor Committee, organized in 1904, reformers over the next ten years obtained laws in nearly every state banning the employment of young children and limiting the hours of older ones. Many of these laws were poorly enforced, yet when Congress passed a federal child labor law in 1916, the Supreme Court, in *Hammer v. Dagenhart* (1918), declared it unconstitutional.[1]

View the Image

Little Spinner in Globe Cotton Mill at **myhistorylab.com**

---

[1] A second child labor law, passed in 1919, was also thrown out by the Court, and a child labor amendment, submitted in 1924, failed to achieve ratification by the necessary three-quarters of the states.

By 1917 nearly all the states had placed limitations on the hours of women industrial workers, and about ten had set minimum wage standards for women. But once again federal action that would have extended such regulation to the entire country did not materialize. A minimum wage law for women in the District of Columbia was overturned by the Court in *Adkins v. Children's Hospital* (1923).

The passage of so much state social legislation sent conservatives scurrying to the Supreme Court for redress. Such persons believed that no government had the power to deprive either workers or employers of the right to negotiate any kind of labor contract they wished. The decision of the Supreme Court in *Lochner v. New York* seemed to indicate that the justices would adopt this point of view. When an Oregon law limiting women laundry workers to ten hours a day was challenged in *Muller v. Oregon* (1908), Florence Kelley and Josephine Goldmark of the Consumers' League persuaded Louis D. Brandeis to defend the statute before the Court.

The Consumers' League, whose slogan was "investigate, agitate, legislate," was probably the most effective of the many women's reform organizations of the period. With the aid of league researchers, Brandeis prepared a remarkable brief stuffed with economic and sociological evidence indicating that long hours damaged both the health of individual women and the health of society. This nonlegal evidence greatly impressed the justices, who upheld the constitutionality of the Oregon law.

Political Reform: The Woman Suffrage Movement

On the national level the Progressive Era saw the culmination of the struggle for **woman suffrage.** The shock occasioned by the failure of the Fourteenth and Fifteenth Amendments to give women the vote after the Civil War continued to embitter most leaders of the movement. But it resulted in a split among feminists. One group, the American Woman Suffrage Association (AWSA), focused on the vote question alone. The more radical National Woman Suffrage Association (NWSA), led by Elizabeth Cady Stanton and Susan B. Anthony, concerned itself with many issues of importance to women as well as suffrage. The NWSA put the immediate interests of women ahead of everything else. It was deeply involved in efforts to unionize women workers, yet it did not hesitate to urge women to be strikebreakers if they could get better jobs by doing so.

Aside from their lack of unity, feminists were handicapped in the late nineteenth century by widely held Victorian ideals: Sex was a taboo topic, and women were to be "pure" guardians of home and family. Even under the best of circumstances, dislike of male-dominated society is hard enough to separate from dislike of men. Most feminists, for example, opposed contraception, insisting that birth control by any means other than continence would encourage what they called masculine lust.

These ideas and prejudices enticed feminists into a logical trap. If women were morally superior to men—a tempting conclusion—giving women the vote would improve the character of the electorate. Society would benefit because politics would become less corrupt, war a thing of the past. "City housekeeping has failed," said

See the **Map**
Woman Suffrage Before the 19th Century at
myhistorylab.com

Another argument in support of woman suffrage claimed that women were intrinsically *better* than men. Note that this woman in the turn-of-the-century poster, crowned by a halo, has her clothes arranged in the shape of a cross.

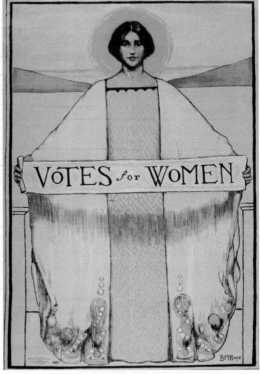

Jane Addams of Hull House in arguing for the reform of municipal government, "partly because women, the traditional housekeepers, have not been consulted."

By the early twentieth century there were signs of progress. In 1890 the two major women's groups combined as the **National American Woman Suffrage Association** (**NAWSA**). Stanton and Anthony were the first two presidents of the association, but new leaders were emerging, the most notable being Carrie Chapman Catt, a woman who combined superb organizing abilities and political skills with commitment to broad social reform. The NAWSA made winning the right to vote its main objective and concentrated on a state-by-state approach. Wyoming gave women the vote in 1869, and Utah, Colorado, and Idaho had been won over to woman suffrage by 1896.

The burgeoning of the progressive movement helped as middle-class recruits of both sexes adopted the suffrage cause. The 1911 referendum in California was crucial. Fifteen years earlier, California voters had rejected the measure. But in 1911, despite determined opposition from saloonkeepers, the proposal barely passed. Within three years, most other Western states fell into line. For the first time, large numbers of working-class women began to agitate for the vote. In 1917, bosses at New York City's Tammany Hall, who had engineered the defeat of woman suffrage in that state two years earlier, concluded that passage was inevitable and threw their support to the measure, which passed. The suffragists then shifted the campaign back to the national level, the lead taken by a new organization, the Congressional Union headed by Alice Paul and the wealthy reformer Alva Belmont. When President Wilson refused to support the idea of a constitutional amendment granting women the vote, militant women picketed the White House. A number of them were arrested and sentenced to sixty days in the workhouse. This roused a storm of criticism, and Wilson quickly pardoned the picketers. After some hesitation the NAWSA stopped concentrating on the state-by-state approach and began to campaign for a constitutional amendment. Pressure on Congress mounted steadily. The amendment finally won congressional approval in 1919. By 1920 the necessary three-quarters of the states had ratified the Nineteenth Amendment; the long fight was over.

19th ammendment = women's suffrage

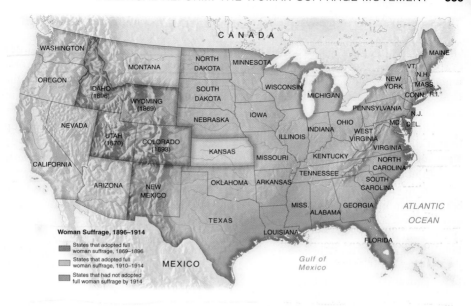

Woman Suffrage, 1896–1914

- States that adopted full woman suffrage, 1869–1896
- States that adopted full woman suffrage, 1910–1914
- States that had not adopted full woman suffrage by 1914

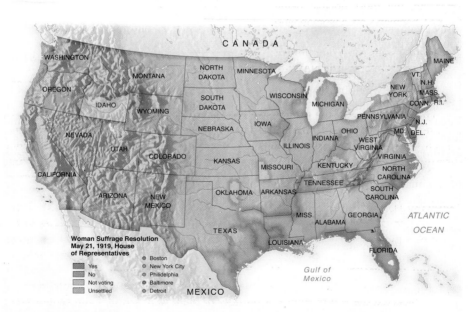

Woman Suffrage Resolution
May 21, 1919, House
of Representatives

- Yes
- No
- Not voting
- Unsettled

- Boston
- New York City
- Philidelphia
- Baltimore
- Detroit

The Advance of Woman Suffrage In 1869 Wyoming, still a territory, voted to give women the vote. The next year, after Mormon leader Brigham Young endorsed woman suffrage, Utah followed. Then came Colorado (1893) and Idaho (1896), frontier states that sought to attract women settlers. In 1911, by a margin of 3,587 votes, California endorsed woman suffrage, and within three years the remainder of the western states had done so, too. World War I stimulated support for the Woman Suffrage (Nineteenth) Amendment. The May 21, 1919, vote in the House of Representatives shows that most of the opposing votes came from southern congressmen who believed that woman suffrage would be the first step toward securing the vote for blacks.

Theodore Roosevelt: Cowboy in the White House

On September 6, 1901, an anarchist named Leon Czolgosz shot President McKinley during a public reception at the Pan-American Exposition at Buffalo, New York. Eight days later McKinley died and Theodore Roosevelt became president of the United States. His ascension to the presidency marked the beginning of a new era in national politics.

Although only forty-two, by far the youngest president in the nation's history up to that time, Roosevelt brought solid qualifications to the office. Son of a well-to-do New York merchant, he had graduated from Harvard in 1880 and studied law briefly at Columbia, though he did not obtain a degree. In addition to political experience that included three terms in the New York assembly, six years on the U.S. Civil Service Commission, two years as police commissioner of New York City, another as assistant secretary of the navy, and a term as governor of New York, he had been a rancher in the Dakota Territory and a soldier in the Spanish-American War. Politically, he had always been a loyal Republican. He rejected the mugwump heresy in 1884, and during the tempestuous 1890s he vigorously denounced populism, Bryanism, and "labor agitators."

Nevertheless, Roosevelt's elevation to the presidency alarmed many conservatives, and not without reason. He did not fit their conception, based on a composite image of the chief executives from Hayes to McKinley, of a president. He seemed too undignified, too energetic, too outspoken, too unconventional. It was one thing to have operated a cattle ranch, another to have captured a gang of rustlers at gunpoint; one thing to have run a metropolitan police force, another to have roamed New York slums in the small hours to catch patrolmen fraternizing with thieves and prostitutes; and one thing to have commanded a regiment, another to have killed a Spaniard personally.

Roosevelt worshiped aggressiveness and was extremely sensitive to any threat to his honor as a gentleman. When another young man showed some slight interest in Roosevelt's fiancée, he sent for a set of French dueling pistols. His teachers found him an interesting student, for he was intelligent and imaginative, if annoyingly argumentative.

Few individuals have rationalized or sublimated their feelings of inferiority as effectively as Roosevelt and to such good purpose. And few have been more genuinely warmhearted, more full of spontaneity, more committed to the ideals of public service and national greatness. As a political leader he was energetic and hard-driving. Conservatives and timid souls, sensing his aggressiveness even

Theodore Roosevelt addressing a crowd in Evanston, Illinois, in the early 1900s.

when he held it in check, distrusted Roosevelt's judgment. In fact his judgment was nearly always sound; responsibility usually tempered his aggressiveness.

When Roosevelt was first mentioned as a running mate for McKinley in 1900, he wrote, "The Vice Presidency is a most honorable office, but for a young man there is not much to do." As president it would have been unthinkable for him to preside over a caretaker administration devoted to maintaining the status quo. However, the reigning Republican politicos, basking in the sunshine of the prosperity that had contributed so much to their victory in 1900, distrusted anything suggestive of change.

Had Roosevelt been the impetuous hothead that conservatives feared, he would have plunged ahead without regard for their feelings and influence. Instead he moved slowly and often got what he wanted by using his executive power rather than by persuading Congress to pass new laws. His domestic program included some measure of control of big corporations, more power for the Interstate Commerce Commission (ICC), and the conservation of natural resources. By consulting congressional leaders and following their advice not to bring up controversial matters like the tariff and currency reform, he obtained a modest budget of new laws.

The Newlands Act (1902) funneled the proceeds from land sales in the West into federal irrigation projects. The Department of Commerce and Labor, which was to include a Bureau of Corporations with authority to investigate industrial combines and issue reports, was established. The Elkins Railroad Act of 1903 strengthened the ICC's hand against the railroads by making the receiving as well as the granting of rebates illegal and by forbidding the roads to deviate in any way from their published rates.

Roosevelt and Big Business

Roosevelt soon became known as a trustbuster, and in the sense that he considered the monopoly problem the most pressing issue of the times, this was accurate to an extent. But he did not believe in breaking up big corporations indiscriminately. Regulation seemed the best way to deal with large corporations because, he said, industrial giantism "could not be eliminated unless we were willing to turn back the wheels of modern progress."

With Congress unwilling to pass a stiff regulatory law, Roosevelt resorted to the Sherman Act to get at the problem. Although the Supreme Court decision in the Sugar Trust case (*E.C. Knight* [1895], see p. 469) seemed to have emasculated that law, in 1902 he ordered the Justice Department to bring suit against the Northern Securities Company.

He chose his target wisely. The Northern Securities Company controlled the Great Northern, the Northern Pacific, the Chicago, the Burlington, and the Quincy railroads. It had been created in 1901 after a titanic battle on the New York Stock Exchange between the forces of J. P. Morgan and James J. Hill and those of E. H. Harriman, who was associated with the Rockefeller interests. In their efforts to obtain control of the Northern Pacific, the rivals had forced its stock up to $1,000 a share, ruining many speculators and threatening to cause a panic.

Neither side could win a clear-cut victory, so they decided to put the stock of all three railroads in a holding company owned by the two groups. Since Harriman already controlled the Union Pacific and the Southern Pacific, the plan resulted in a virtual monopoly of western railroads. The public had been alarmed, for the merger seemed to typify the rapaciousness of the tycoons.

The announcement of the suit caused consternation in the business world. Morgan rushed to the White House. "If we have done anything wrong," he said to the president, "send your man to my man and they can fix it up." Roosevelt was not fundamentally opposed to this sort of agreement, but it was too late to compromise in this instance. Attorney General Philander C. Knox pressed the case vigorously, and in 1904 the Supreme Court ordered the dissolution of the Northern Securities Company.

Roosevelt then ordered suits against the meat packers, the Standard Oil Trust, and the American Tobacco Company. His stock among progressives rose, yet he had not embarrassed the conservatives in Congress by demanding new antitrust legislation.

The president went out of his way to assure cooperative corporation magnates that he was not against size per se. At a White House conference in 1905, Roosevelt and Elbert H. Gary, chairman of the board of U.S. Steel, reached a "gentlemen's agreement" whereby Gary promised "to cooperate with the Government in every possible way." The Bureau of Corporations would conduct an investigation of U.S. Steel, Gary allowing it full access to company records. Roosevelt in turn promised that if the investigation revealed any corporate malpractices, he would allow Gary to set matters right voluntarily, thereby avoiding an antitrust suit. He reached a similar agreement with the International Harvester Company two years later.

There were limits to the effectiveness of such arrangements. Standard Oil agreed to a similar détente and then reneged, refusing to turn over vital records to the bureau. The Justice Department brought suit against the company under the Sherman Act, and eventually the company was broken up at the order of the Supreme Court. Roosevelt would have preferred a more binding kind of regulation, but when he asked for laws giving the government supervisory authority over big combinations, Congress refused to act.

Roosevelt and the Coal Strike

Roosevelt made remarkable use of his executive power during the anthracite coal strike of 1902. In June the United Mine Workers (UMW), led by John Mitchell, laid down their picks and demanded higher wages, an eight-hour day, and recognition of the union. Most of the anthracite mines were owned by railroads. Two years earlier the miners had won a 10 percent wage increase in a similar strike, chiefly because the owners feared that labor unrest might endanger the election of McKinley. Now the coal companies were dead set against further concessions; when the men walked out, they shut down the mines and prepared to starve the strikers into submission.

The strike dragged on through summer and early fall. The miners conducted themselves with great restraint, avoiding violence and offering to submit their claims to arbitration. As the price of anthracite soared with the approach of winter, sentiment in their behalf mounted.

Roosevelt shared the public's sympathy for the miners, and the threat of a coal shortage alarmed him. Early in October he summoned both sides to a conference in Washington and urged them as patriotic Americans to sacrifice any "personal consideration" for the "general good." His action enraged the coal owners, for they believed he was trying to force them to recognize the union. They refused even to speak to the UMW representatives at the conference and demanded that Roosevelt end the strike by force and bring suit against the union under the Sherman Act. Mitchell, aware of the immense prestige that Roosevelt had conferred on the union by calling the conference, cooperated fully with the president.

Table 21.1   Major Supreme Court Rulings during the Progressive Era

Northern Securities Case	1904	Upheld antitrust ruling against railroad conglomerate
Lochner v. New York	1905	Overturned (progressive) New York law restricting the hours bakers could work; invoked the Fourteenth Amendment to protect bakers' "right" to work as long as they wished
Muller v. Oregon	1908	Affirmed the right of Oregon to limit the hours worked by women in laundries

The attitudes of management and of the union further strengthened public support for the miners. Even former president Grover Cleveland, who had used federal troops to break the Pullman strike, said that he was "disturbed and vexed by the tone and substance of the operators' deliverances." Encouraged by this state of affairs, Roosevelt took a bold step: He announced that unless a settlement was reached promptly, he would order federal troops into the anthracite regions, not to break the strike but to seize and operate the mines.

The threat of government intervention brought the owners to terms. A Cabinet member, Elihu Root, worked out the details with J. P. Morgan, whose firm had major interests in the Reading and other railroads. The miners would return to the pits and all issues between them and the coal companies would be submitted for settlement to a commission appointed by Roosevelt. Both sides accepted the arrangement, and the men went back to work. In March 1903 the commission granted the miners a 10 percent wage increase and a nine-hour workday.

To the public the incident seemed a perfect illustration of the progressive spirit—in Roosevelt's words, everyone had received a **Square Deal** In fact the results were by no means so clear-cut. The miners gained relatively little and the companies lost still less. The president was the main winner. The public acclaimed him as a fearless, imaginative, public-spirited leader. Without calling on Congress for support, he had expanded his own authority and hence that of the federal government. His action marked a major forward step in the evolution of the modern presidency.

TR's Triumphs

By reviving the Sherman Act, settling the coal strike, and pushing moderate reforms through Congress, Roosevelt ensured that he would be reelected president in 1904. Despite his resentment at Roosevelt's attack on the Northern Securities Company, J. P. Morgan contributed $150,000 to the Republican campaign. Other tycoons gave with equal generosity. Roosevelt swept the country, carrying even the normally Democratic border states of Maryland and Missouri.

Encouraged by the landslide and the increasing militancy of progressives, Roosevelt pressed for more reform legislation. His most imaginative proposal was a plan to make the District of Columbia a model progressive community. He suggested child labor and factory inspection laws and a slum clearance program, but Congress refused to act. Likewise, his request for a minimum wage for railroad workers was rejected.

Early in the twentieth century, when malnutrition was common, companies such as this one advertised that its pills could make people fatter. The Pure Food and Drug Act of 1906 fined manufacturers who made false claims for their products. A century later, in 2010, the *Seattle Post Intelligencer*, under the headline "Too Fat to Fight," reported that over a fourth of eighteen to twenty-four-year-old potential army recruits were rejected as unfit.

With progressive state governors demanding federal action and farmers and manufacturers, especially in the Midwest, clamoring for relief against discriminatory rates, Roosevelt was ready by 1905 to make railroad legislation his major objective. The ICC should be empowered to fix rates, not merely to challenge unreasonable ones. It should have the right to inspect the private records of the railroads since fair rates could not be determined unless the true financial condition of the roads were known.

Because these proposals struck at rights that businessmen considered sacrosanct, many congressmen balked. But Roosevelt applied presidential pressure, and in June 1906 the Hepburn bill became law. It gave the commission the power to inspect the books of railroad companies, to set maximum rates (once a complaint had been filed by a shipper), and to control sleeping car companies, owners of oil pipelines, and other firms engaged in transportation. Railroads could no longer issue passes freely—an important check on their political influence. In all, the **Hepburn Act** made the ICC a more powerful and more active body. Congress also passed meat inspection and pure food and drug legislation. In 1906 Upton Sinclair published *The Jungle,* a devastating exposé of the filthy conditions in the Chicago slaughterhouses. Sinclair was more interested in writing a socialist tract than he was in meat inspection, but his book, a best seller, raised a storm against the packers. After Roosevelt read *The Jungle* he sent two officials to Chicago to investigate. Their report was so shocking, he said, that its publication would "be well-nigh ruinous to our export trade in meat." He threatened to release the report unless Congress acted. After a fight, the meat inspection bill passed. The Pure Food and Drug Act, forbidding the manufacture and sale of adulterated and fraudulently labeled products, rode through Congress on the coattails of this measure.

To advanced liberals Roosevelt's achievements seemed limited when placed beside his professed objectives and his smug evaluations of what he had done. How could he be a reformer and a defender of established interests at the same time? Roosevelt found no difficulty in holding such a position. As one historian has said, "He stood close to the center and bared his teeth at the conservatives of the right and the liberals of the extreme left."

Roosevelt Tilts Left

As the progressive movement advanced, Roosevelt advanced with it. He never accepted all the ideas of what he called its "lunatic fringe," but he took steadily more liberal positions. He always insisted that he was not hostile to business interests, but when those interests sought to exploit the national domain, they had no more implacable foe. **Conservation** of natural resources was dear to his heart and probably his most significant achievement as president. He placed some 150 million acres of forest lands in federal reserves, and he strictly enforced the laws governing grazing, mining, and lumbering.

As Roosevelt became more liberal, conservative Republicans began to balk at following his lead. The sudden panic that struck the financial world in October 1907 speeded the trend. Government policies had no direct bearing on the panic, which began with a run on several important New York trust companies and spread to the Stock Exchange when speculators found themselves unable to borrow money to meet their obligations. In the emergency Roosevelt authorized the deposit of large amounts of government cash in New York banks. He informally agreed to the acquisition of the Tennessee Coal and Iron Company by U.S. Steel when the bankers told him that the purchase was necessary to end the panic. In spite of his efforts, conservatives insisted on referring to the financial collapse as "Roosevelt's panic," and they blamed the president for the depression that followed on its heels.

Roosevelt, however, turned left rather than right. In 1908 he came out in favor of federal income and inheritance taxes, stricter regulation of interstate corporations, and reforms designed to help industrial workers. He denounced "the speculative folly and the flagrant dishonesty" of "malefactors of great wealth," further alienating conservative, or Old Guard, Republicans. When the president began criticizing the courts, the last bastion of conservatism, he lost all chance of obtaining further reform legislation. As he said himself, during his last months in office "stagnation continued to rage with uninterrupted violence."

William Howard Taft: The Listless Progressive, or More Is Less

But Roosevelt remained popular and politically powerful; before his term ended, he chose William Howard Taft, his secretary of war, to succeed him and easily obtained Taft's nomination. William Jennings Bryan was again the Democratic candidate. Campaigning on Roosevelt's record, Taft carried the country by well over a million votes, defeating Bryan 321 to 162 in the Electoral College.

Taft was intelligent, experienced, and public spirited; he seemed ideally suited to carry out Roosevelt's policies. Born in Cincinnati in 1857, educated at Yale, he had served as an Ohio judge, as solicitor general of the United States under Benjamin Harrison, and

"GOODNESS GRACIOUS! I MUST HAVE BEEN DOZING!"

A hapless Taft is entangled in governmental yarn, while a disapproving Roosevelt looks on. "Goodness gracious! I must have been dozing," reads the caption, a reference to Taft's penchant for naps.

then as a federal circuit court judge before accepting McKinley's assignment to head the Philippine Commission in 1900. His success as civil governor of the Philippines led Roosevelt to make him secretary of war in 1904.

Taft supported the Square Deal loyally. This, together with his mentor's ardent endorsement, won him the backing of most progressive Republicans. Yet the Old Guard liked him too; although outgoing, he had none of the Roosevelt impetuosity and aggressiveness. His genial personality and his obvious desire to avoid conflict appealed to moderates.

However, Taft lacked the physical and mental stamina required of a modern chief executive. Although not lazy, he weighed over 300 pounds and needed to rest this vast bulk more than the job allowed. Campaigning bored him; speech making seemed a useless chore. The judicial life was his real love; intense partisanship dismayed and confused him. He was too reasonable to control a coalition and not ambitious enough to impose his will on others. He supported many progressive measures, but he never absorbed the progressive spirit.

Taft honestly wanted to carry out most of Roosevelt's policies. He enforced the Sherman Act vigorously and continued to expand the national forest reserves. He signed the Mann-Elkins Act of 1910 which empowered the ICC to suspend rate increases without waiting for a shipper to complain and established the Commerce Court to speed the settlement of railroad rate cases. An eight-hour day for all persons engaged in work on government contracts, mine safety legislation, and several other reform measures received his approval. He even summoned Congress into special session specifically to reduce tariff duties—something that Roosevelt had not dared to attempt.

But Taft had been disturbed by Roosevelt's sweeping use of executive power. "We have got to work out our problems on the basis of law," he insisted. Whereas Roosevelt had excelled at maneuvering around congressional opposition and at finding ways to accomplish his objectives without waiting for Congress to act, Taft adamantly refused to use such tactics. His restraint was in many ways admirable, but it reduced his effectiveness.

In 1910 Taft got into difficulty with the conservationists. Although he believed in husbanding natural resources carefully, he did not like the way Roosevelt had circumvented Congress in adding to the forest reserves. He demanded, and eventually obtained, specific legislation to accomplish this purpose. The issue that aroused the conservationists concerned the integrity of his secretary of the interior, Richard A. Ballinger. A less than ardent conservationist, Ballinger returned to the public domain certain waterpower sites that the Roosevelt administration had withdrawn on the legally questionable ground that they were to become ranger stations. Ballinger's action alarmed Chief Forester Gifford Pinchot, the darling of the conservationists. When Pinchot learned that Ballinger intended to validate the shaky claim of mining interests to a large tract of coal-rich land in Alaska, he launched an intemperate attack on the secretary.

In the Ballinger-Pinchot controversy Taft felt obliged to support his own man. The coal lands dispute was complex, and Pinchot's charges were exaggerated. It was certainly unfair to call Ballinger "the most effective opponent the conservation policies have yet had." When Pinchot, whose own motives were partly political, persisted in criticizing Ballinger, Taft dismissed him. He had no choice under the circumstances, but a more adept politician might have found some way of avoiding a showdown.

Breakup of the Republican Party

One ominous aspect of the Ballinger-Pinchot affair was that Pinchot was a close friend of Theodore Roosevelt. After Taft's inauguration, Roosevelt had gone off to hunt big game in Africa, bearing in his baggage an autographed photograph of his protégé and a touching letter of appreciation, in which the new president said, "I can never forget that the power I now exercise was a voluntary transfer from you to me." As soon as he emerged from the wilderness in March 1910, bearing more than 3,000 trophies, including nine lions, five elephants, and thirteen rhinos, he was caught up in the squabble between the progressive members of his party and its titular head. Pinchot met him in Italy, laden with injured innocence and a packet of angry letters from various progressives. TR's intimate friend Senator Henry Cabot Lodge, essentially a conservative, barraged him with messages, the gist of which was that Taft was lazy and inept and that Roosevelt should prepare to become the "Moses" who would guide the party "out of the wilderness of doubt and discontent" into which Taft had led it.

Roosevelt hoped to steer a middle course, but Pinchot's complaints impressed him. Taft had decided to strike out on his own, he concluded. Taft sensed the former president's coolness and was offended. He was egged on by his ambitious wife, who wanted him to stand clear of Roosevelt's shadow and establish his own reputation.

Perhaps the resulting rupture was inevitable. The Republican party was dividing into two factions, the progressives and the Old Guard. Forced to choose between them, Taft threw in his lot with the Old Guard. Roosevelt backed the progressives. Speaking at Osawatomie, Kansas, in August 1910 he came out for a comprehensive program of social legislation, which he called the **New Nationalism**. Besides attacking "special privilege" and the "unfair money-getting"

Read the Document

Roosevelt, *The New Nationalism* at **myhistorylab.com**

practices of "lawbreakers of great wealth," he called for a broad expansion of federal power. "The betterment we seek must be accomplished," he said, "mainly through the National Government."

The final break came in October 1911 when Taft ordered an antitrust suit against U.S. Steel. He was prepared to enforce the Sherman Act "or die in the attempt." But this initiative angered Roosevelt because the lawsuit focused on U.S. Steel's absorption of the Tennessee Coal and Iron Company, which Roosevelt had unofficially authorized during the panic of 1907. The government's antitrust brief made Roosevelt appear to have been either a proponent of the monopoly or, far worse, a fool who had been duped by the steel corporation. Early in 1912 he declared himself a candidate for the Republican presidential nomination.

Roosevelt plunged into the preconvention campaign with typical energy. He was almost uniformly victorious in states that held presidential primaries, carrying even Ohio, Taft's home state. However, the president controlled the party machinery and entered the national convention with a small majority of the delegates. Since some Taft delegates had been chosen under questionable circumstances, the Roosevelt forces challenged the right of 254 of them to their seats. The Taft-controlled credentials committee, paying little attention to the evidence, gave all but a few of the disputed seats to the president, who then won the nomination on the first ballot.

Roosevelt was understandably outraged by the ruthless manner in which the Taft "steamroller" had overridden his forces. When his leading supporters urged him to organize a third party, and when two of them, George W. Perkins, formerly a partner of the banker J. P. Morgan, and the publisher Frank Munsey, offered to finance the campaign, Roosevelt agreed to make the race.

In August, amid scenes of hysterical enthusiasm, the first convention of the Progressive party met at Chicago and nominated him for president. Announcing that he felt "as strong as a bull moose," Roosevelt delivered a stirring "confession of faith," calling for strict regulation of corporations, a tariff commission, national presidential primaries, minimum wage and workers' compensation laws, the elimination of child labor, and many other reforms.

Watch the Video
Bull Moose Campaign Speech
at **myhistorylab.com**

The Election of 1912

The Democrats made the most of the opportunity offered by the Republican schism. Had they nominated a conservative or allowed Bryan a fourth chance, they would probably have ensured Roosevelt's election. Instead, they nominated Woodrow Wilson, who had achieved a remarkable liberal record as governor of New Jersey.

Although as a political scientist Wilson had criticized the status quo and taken a pragmatic approach to the idea of government regulation of the economy, he had objected strongly to Bryan's brand of politics. In 1896 he voted for the Gold Democratic party candidate instead of Bryan. But by 1912, influenced partly by ambition and partly by the spirit of the times, he had been converted to progressivism. He called his brand of reform the **New Freedom**.

The federal government could best advance the cause of social justice, Wilson reasoned, by eradicating the special privileges that enabled the "interests" to flourish. Where

1912: Divided Republicans, Democratic Victory In 1912, when Theodore Roosevelt chose to run as a Progressive, he took away millions of votes from the Republican Taft. This ensured Democrat Woodrow Wilson's landslide election.

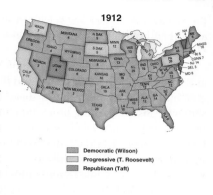

1912

Democratic (Wilson)
Progressive (T. Roosevelt)
Republican (Taft)

Roosevelt had lost faith in competition as a way of protecting the public against monopolies, Wilson insisted that competition could be restored. The government must break up the great trusts, establish fair rules for doing business, and subject violators to stiff punishments. Thereafter, the free enterprise system would protect the public from exploitation without destroying individual initiative and opportunity.

Roosevelt's reasoning was perhaps theoretically more sound. He called for a New Nationalism. Laissez-faire made less sense than it had in earlier times. The complexities of the modern world seemed to call for a positive approach, a plan, the close application of human intelligence to social and economic problems.

But being more in line with American experience than the New Nationalism, Wilson's New Freedom had much to recommend it. The danger that selfish individuals would use the power of the state for their own ends had certainly not disappeared, despite the efforts of progressives to make government more responsive to popular opinion. Any considerable expansion of national power, as Roosevelt proposed, would increase the danger and probably create new difficulties. Managing so complicated an enterprise as an industrialized nation was sure to be a formidable task for the federal government. Furthermore, individual freedom of opportunity merited the toleration of a certain amount of inefficiency.

To choose between the New Nationalism and the New Freedom, between the dynamic Roosevelt and the idealistic Wilson, was indeed difficult. Taft got the hard-core Republican vote but lost the progressive wing of the GOP to Roosevelt. Wilson had the solid support of both conservative and liberal Democrats. As a result, Wilson won an easy victory in the Electoral College, receiving 435 votes to Roosevelt's 88 and Taft's 8. The popular vote was Wilson, 6,286,000; Roosevelt, 4,126,000; and Taft, 3,484,000.

If partisan politics had determined the winner, the election was nonetheless an overwhelming endorsement of progressivism. The temper of the times was shown by the 897,000 votes for Eugene Debs, who was again the Socialist candidate. Altogether, professed liberals amassed over 11 million of the 15 million ballots cast. Wilson was a minority president, but he took office with a clear mandate to press forward with further reforms.

Wilson: The New Freedom

No one ever rose more suddenly or spectacularly in American politics than Woodrow Wilson. In the spring of 1910 he was president of Princeton University; he had never held or even run for public office. In the fall of 1912 he was president-elect of the United States. Yet if his rise was meteoric, in a very real sense he had devoted his life to preparing for it. As a student he became interested in political theory, dreaming of representing his state in the Senate. He studied law solely because he thought it the best avenue to public office, and when he discovered that he did not like legal work, he took a doctorate at Johns Hopkins in political science.

For years Wilson's political ambitions appeared doomed to frustration. He taught at Bryn Mawr, then at Wesleyan, and finally at his alma mater, Princeton. He wrote several influential books, among them *Congressional Government* and *The State*, and achieved an outstanding reputation as a teacher and lecturer. In 1902 he was chosen president of Princeton and soon won a place among the nation's leading educators. In time Wilson's educational ideas and his overbearing manner of applying them got him in trouble with some of Princeton's alumni and trustees. Although his university career was wrecked, the controversies, in which he appeared to be championing democracy and progress in the face of reactionary opponents, brought him at last to the attention of the politicians. Then, in a great rush, came power and fame.

Wilson was an immediate success as president. Since Roosevelt's last year in office, Congress had been almost continually at war with the executive branch and with itself. Legislative achievements had been few. Now a small avalanche of important measures received the approval of the lawmakers. In October 1913 the Underwood Tariff brought the first significant reduction of duties since before the Civil War. To compensate for the expected loss of revenue, the act provided for a graduated tax on personal incomes.

Two months later the Federal Reserve Act gave the country a central banking system for the first time since Jackson destroyed the Bank of the United States. The measure divided the nation into twelve banking districts, each under the supervision of a Federal Reserve bank, a sort of bank for bankers. All national banks in each district and any state banks that wished to participate had to invest 6 percent of their capital and surplus in the reserve bank, which was empowered to exchange paper money, called Federal Reserve notes, for the commercial and agricultural paper that member banks took in as security from borrowers. The volume of currency was no longer at the mercy of the supply of gold or any other particular commodity.

The nerve center of the system was the Federal Reserve Board in Washington, which appointed a majority of the directors of the Federal Reserve banks and had some control over rediscount rates. The board provided a modicum of public control over the banks, but the effort to weaken the power of the great New York banks by decentralizing the system proved ineffective. Nevertheless, a true central banking system was created.

When inflation threatened, the reserve banks could raise the rediscount rate, discouraging borrowing and thus reducing the amount of money in circulation. In bad times it could lower the rate, making it easier to borrow and injecting new dollars into the economy. Much remained to be learned about the proper management of the money supply, but the nation finally had a flexible yet safe currency.

In 1914 Congress passed two important laws affecting corporations. One created the Federal Trade Commission (FTC) to replace Roosevelt's Bureau of Corporations. In addition to investigating corporations and publishing reports, this nonpartisan board could issue cease-and-desist orders against "unfair" trade practices brought to light through its research. The law did not define the term *unfair*, and the commission's rulings could be taken on appeal to the federal courts, but the FTC was nonetheless a powerful instrument for protecting the public against the trusts.

The second measure, the Clayton Antitrust Act, made certain specific business practices illegal, including price discrimination that tended to foster monopolies; tying agreements, which forbade retailers from handling the products of a firm's competitors; and the creation of interlocking directorates as a means of controlling competing companies. The act exempted labor unions and agricultural organizations from the antitrust laws and curtailed the use of injunctions in labor disputes. The officers of corporations could be held individually responsible if their companies violated the antitrust laws.

The Democrats controlled both houses of Congress for the first time since 1890 and were eager to make a good record, but Wilson's imaginative and aggressive use of presidential power was decisive. He called the legislators into special session in April 1913 and appeared before them to lay out his program; he was the first president to address Congress in person since John Adams. Then he followed the course of administration bills closely. Administration representatives haunted the cloakrooms and lobbies of both houses. Cooperative congressmen began to receive notes of praise and encouragement, whereas recalcitrant ones received stern demands for support, often pecked out on the president's own portable typewriter.

Wilson explained his success by saying, only half humorously, that running the government was child's play for anyone who had managed the faculty of a university. Responsible party government was his objective; he expected individual Democrats to support the decisions of the party majority, and his idealism never prevented him from awarding the spoils of office to city bosses and conservative congressmen, as long as they supported his program. Nor did his career as a political theorist make him rigid and doctrinaire. In practice the differences between his New Freedom and Roosevelt's New Nationalism tended to disappear. The FTC and the Federal Reserve system represented steps toward the kind of regulated economy that Roosevelt advocated.

Table 21.2 Progressive Legislation (Federal)

Newlands Act	1902	Funneled revenues from sale of public lands to irrigation projects
Elkins Act	1903	Strengthened the ICC by making it illegal for railroads to deviate from published rates, such as by granting rebates
Hepburn Act	1906	Gave ICC the power to fix rates of railroads and other corporations involved in interstate commerce (such as corporations operating oil pipelines)
Pure Food and Durg Act	1906	Prohibited the fraudulent advertising, manufacturing, and selling of impure foods and drugs
Mann-Elkins Act	1910	Empowered ICC to suspend rate increases for railroads or telephone companies
Underwood Tariff	1913	Lowered tariff rates; introduced graduated tax on personal incomes
Federal Reserve Act	1913	Established federal supervision of banking system
Sixteenth Amendment	1913	Authorized federal income tax
Clayton Antitrust Act	1914	Exempted labor unions from antitrust laws and curtailed injunctions against labor leaders
Nineteenth Amendment	1920	Established woman suffrage

There were limits to Wilson's progressivism. He objected as strenuously to laws granting special favors to farmers and workers as to those benefiting the tycoons. When a bill was introduced in 1914 making low-interest loans available to farmers, he refused to support it. He considered the provision exempting unions from the antitrust laws equally unsound. Nor would he push for a federal law prohibiting child labor; such a measure would be unconstitutional, he believed. He also refused to back the constitutional amendment giving the vote to women.

By the end of 1914 Wilson's record, on balance, was positive but distinctly limited. The president believed that the major progressive goals had been achieved; he had no plans for further reform. Many other progressives thought that a great deal more remained to be done.

The Progressives and Minority Rights

On one important issue, race relations, Wilson was distinctly reactionary. With a mere handful of exceptions, the progressives exhibited strong prejudices against nonwhite people and against certain categories of whites as well. Many were as unsympathetic to immigrants from Asia and eastern and southern Europe as any of the "conservative" opponents of immigration in the 1880s and 1890s.

American Indians were also affected by the progressives' racial attitudes. Where the sponsors of the Dawes Act (1887) had assumed that Indians were inherently capable of adopting the ways of "civilized" people, in the progressive period the tendency was to write Indians off as fundamentally inferior and to assume that they would make second-class citizens at best. Francis Leupp, Theodore Roosevelt's commissioner of Indian affairs, put it this way in a 1905 report: "If nature has set a different physical stamp upon different races of men it is fair to assume that the variation . . . is manifested in mental and moral traits as well. . . . Nothing is gained by trying to undo nature's work." A leading muckraker, Ray Stannard Baker, who was far more sympathetic to blacks than most progressives, dismissed Indians as pathetic beings, "eating, sleeping, idling, with no more thought of the future than a white man's child."

In 1902 Congress passed the Dead Indian Land Act, which made it easier for Indians to sell allotments that they had inherited, and in 1906 another law further relaxed restrictions on land sales. Efforts to improve the education of Indian children continued, but most progressives assumed that only vocational training would help them. Theodore Roosevelt knew from his experiences as a rancher in the Dakota Territory that Indians could be as energetic and capable as whites, but he considered these "exceptional." As for the rest, it would be many generations before they could be expected to "move forward" enough to become "ordinary citizens," Roosevelt believed.

To say that African Americans did not fare well at the hands of progressives would be a gross understatement. White southerners, furious at Populist efforts to unite white and black farmers, imposed increasingly repressive measures after 1896. Segregation became more rigid, white opposition to black voting more monolithic. In 1900 the body of a Mississippi black was dug up by order of the state legislature and reburied in a segregated cemetery; in Virginia in 1902 the daughter of Robert E. Lee was arrested for riding in the black section of a railroad car.

On May 15, 1916, after deliberating for one hour, an all-white jury in Waco, Texas, found seventeen-year-old Jesse Washington guilty of bludgeoning a white woman to death. A mob rushed him out of the courtroom, chained him to a tree, and burned him to death. The story was chronicled by Patricia Bernstein in *The First Waco Horror* (2005).

Many progressive women, still smarting from the insult to their sex entailed in the Fourteenth and Fifteenth Amendments and eager to attract southern support for their campaign for the vote, adopted racist arguments. They contrasted the supposed corruption and incompetence of black voters with their own "purity" and intelligence. Southern progressives of both sexes argued that disfranchising blacks would reduce corruption by removing from unscrupulous white politicians the temptation to purchase black votes!

The typical southern attitude toward the education of blacks was summed up in a folk proverb: "When you educate a Negro, you spoil a good field hand." In 1910 only about 8,000 black children in the entire South were attending high schools. Despite the almost total suppression of black rights, lynchings persisted; between 1900 and 1914 more than 1,100 blacks were murdered by mobs, most (but not all) in the southern states. In the rare cases in which local prosecutors brought the lynchers to trial, juries almost without exception brought in verdicts of not guilty.

●●●—Read the Document

"Events in Paris, Texas," from Ida B. Wells, *A Red Record* at **myhistorylab.com**

Booker T. Washington was shaken by this trend, but he could find no way to combat it. The times were passing him by. He appealed to his white southern "friends" for help but got nowhere. Increasingly he talked about the virtues of rural life, the evils of big cities, and the uselessness of higher education for black people. By the turn of the century a number of young, well-educated blacks, most of them Northerners, were breaking away from his accommodationist leadership.

Black Militancy

William E. B. Du Bois was the most prominent of the militants. Du Bois was born in Great Barrington, Massachusetts, in 1868. His father, a restless wanderer of Negro and French Huguenot stock, abandoned the family, and young William grew up on the edge of poverty. Neither accepted nor openly rejected by the overwhelmingly white community, he devoted himself to his studies, showing such brilliance that his future education was ensured by scholarships: to Fisk University, then to Harvard, and then to the University of Berlin. In 1895 Du Bois became the first American black to earn a PhD in history from Harvard; his dissertation, *The Suppression of the African Slave Trade* (1896), remains a standard reference.

Like Washington, Du Bois wanted blacks to lift themselves up by their own bootstraps. They must establish their own businesses, run their own newspapers and colleges, and write their own literature; they must preserve their identity rather than seek to amalgamate themselves into a society that offered them only crumbs and contempt. At first he cooperated with Washington, but in 1903, in the essay "Of Mr. Booker T. Washington and Others," he subjected Washington's "attitude of adjustment and submission" to polite but searching criticism. Washington had asked blacks to give up political power, civil rights, and the hope of higher education, not realizing that "voting is necessary to modern manhood, that . . . discrimination is barbarism, and that black boys need education as well as white boys." Washington "apologizes for injustice," Du Bois charged. "He belittles the emasculating effects of caste distinctions, and opposes the higher training and ambitions of our brightest minds." Du Bois deemed this totally wrong: "The way for a people to gain their reasonable rights is not by voluntarily throwing them away."

Du Bois was not an uncritical admirer of the ordinary American black. He believed that "immorality, crime, and laziness" were common vices. He blamed the weaknesses of blacks on the treatment afforded them by whites, but his approach to the solution of racial problems was frankly elitist. "The Negro race," he wrote, "is going to be saved by its exceptional men," what he called the "talented tenth" of the black population. Whatever his prejudices, Du Bois exposed both the weaknesses of Washington's strategy and the callousness of white American attitudes. Accommodation was not working. Washington was praised, even lionized by prominent

Watch the Video
The conflict between Booker T. Washington & W.E.B Du Bois at **myhistorylab.com**

southern whites, yet when Theodore Roosevelt invited him to a meal at the White House they exploded with indignation, and Roosevelt, although not personally prejudiced, meekly backtracked, never repeating his "mistake." He defended his record by saying, "I have stood as valiantly for the rights of the negro as any president since Lincoln." That, sad to relate, was true enough.

Not mere impatience but despair led Du Bois and a few like-minded blacks to meet at Niagara Falls in July 1905 and to issue a stirring list of demands: the unrestricted right to vote, an end to every kind of segregation, equality of economic opportunity, higher education for the talented, equal justice in the courts, and an end to trade-union discrimination. This **Niagara movement** did not attract mass support, but it did stir the consciences of some whites, many of them the descendants of abolitionists, who were also becoming disenchanted by the failure of accommodation to provide blacks with real opportunity.

In 1909, the centennial of the birth of Abraham Lincoln, a group of these liberals, including the newspaperman Oswald Garrison Villard (grandson of William Lloyd Garrison), the social worker Jane Addams, the philosopher John Dewey, and the novelist William Dean Howells, founded the **National Association for the Advancement of Colored People (NAACP)**. The organization was dedicated to the eradication of racial discrimination. Its leadership was predominantly white in the early years, but Du Bois became a national officer and the editor of its journal, *The Crisis*.

A turning point had been reached. After 1909 virtually every important leader, white and black alike, rejected the Washington approach. More and more, blacks turned to the study of their past in an effort to stimulate pride in their heritage. In 1915 Carter G. Woodson founded the Association for the Study of Negro Life and History; the following year he began editing the *Journal of Negro History*, which became the major publishing organ for scholarly studies on the subject.

This militancy produced few results in the Progressive Era. Theodore Roosevelt behaved no differently than earlier Republican presidents; he courted blacks when he thought it advantageous, and turned his back when he did not. When he ran for president on the Progressive ticket in 1912, he pursued a "lily-white" policy, hoping to break the Democrats' monopoly in the South. By trusting in "[white] men of justice and of vision," Roosevelt argued in the face of decades of experience to the contrary, "the colored men of the South will ultimately get justice."

The southern-born Wilson was actively hostile to blacks. During the 1912 campaign he appealed to them for support and promised to "assist in advancing the interest of their race" in every possible way. Once elected, he refused even to appoint a privately financed commission to study the race problem. Southerners dominated his administration and Congress; as a result, blacks were further degraded.

These actions stirred such a storm that Wilson backtracked a little, but he never abandoned his belief that segregation was in the best interests of both races. "Wilson . . . promised a 'new freedom,'" one newspaperman complained. "On the contrary we are given a stone instead of a loaf of bread." Even Booker T. Washington admitted that his people were more "discouraged and bitter" than at any time in his memory.

Du Bois, who had supported Wilson in 1912, attacked administration policy in *The Crisis*. In November 1914 the militant editor of the *Boston Guardian*, William Monroe Trotter, a classmate of Du Bois at Harvard and a far more caustic critic of the Washington approach, led a delegation to the White House to protest the segregation policy of the government. When Wilson accused him of blackmail, Trotter lost his temper, and an ugly confrontation resulted. The mood of black leaders had changed completely.

By this time the Great War had broken out in Europe. Soon every American would feel its effects, blacks perhaps more than any other group. In November 1915, a year almost to the day after Trotter's clash with Wilson, Booker T. Washington died. One era had ended; a new one was beginning.

Many of the young Americans who had participated in the various crusades of the "age of reform" would soon embark on another crusade—but one of a very different character.

Milestones

1890	National American Woman Suffrage Association is founded	1908	*Muller v. Oregon* upholds law limiting women's work hours
1900	Robert La Follette is elected governor of Wisconsin		William Howard Taft is elected president
	McKinley is reelected president	1909	NAACP is founded
1901	McKinley is assassinated; Theodore Roosevelt becomes president	1910	Ballinger-Pinchot Affair deepens Roosevelt–Taft rift
1902	Roosevelt helps settle anthracite coal strike	1911	Roosevelt gives New Nationalism speech
	Oregon adopts initiative system for proposing legislation	1912	Roosevelt runs for president on Progressive ticket
1904	Northern Securities case revives Sherman Antitrust Act		Woodrow Wilson is elected president
	National Child Labor Committee is established	1913	Sixteenth Amendment authorizes federal income taxes
	Theodore Roosevelt is elected president		Seventeenth Amendment provides for direct election of U.S. senators
1905	Anticapitalist Industrial Workers of the World (IWW) is founded		Underwood Tariff Act reduces duties and imposes personal income tax
1906	Hepburn Act strengthens Interstate Commerce Commission		Federal Reserve Act gives the United States a central banking system again
	Upton Sinclair exposes Chicago slaughterhouses in *The Jungle*	1914	Federal Trade Commission is created to protect against trusts
1907	U.S. Steel absorbs Tennessee Coal and Iron Company		Clayton Antitrust Act regulates business
1908	Theodore Roosevelt convenes National Conservation Conference	1920	Nineteenth Amendment guarantees women the right to vote

✓•—Study and Review at www.myhistorylab.com

Review Questions

1. The introduction to this chapter compares volunteers today to young reformers early in the twentieth century. What were the similarities and differences?

2. List the ideas of the various progressive-thinking leaders and their movements. What attitudes and values did they share? Were these sufficiently coherent to constitute a "Progressive movement"?

3. How did the attitudes of the reformers and political activists compare with those of the people whose lives they meant to improve? How did immigrants, Native Americans, and workers respond to Progressive reforms?

4. In what ways was the Progressive Era especially challenging for African Americans?

5. How did the relationship between business and government change during the presidencies of Roosevelt, Taft, and Wilson? Did business oppose government regulation or favor it as a means of controlling competition and weakening radicalism?

Key Terms

Ashcan School *545*

Clayton Antitrust Act *566*

Conservation *561*

Federal Reserve Act *566*

Hepburn Act *560*

Industrial Workers of the World (IWW) *546*

muckraker *545*

National American Woman Suffrage Association (NAWSA) *554*

National Association for the Advancement of Colored People (NAACP) *571*

New Freedom *564*

New Nationalism *563*

Niagara movement *570*

Progressivism *543*

Square Deal *559*

Underwood Tariff *566*

woman suffrage *553*

22 From Isolation to Empire

Can you find Afghanistan on a map?

DURING THE PRESIDENTIAL CAMPAIGN OF 2000, REPUBLICAN CANDIDATE George W. Bush chastised the Clinton administration for sending troops to Haiti and the Balkans. "If we don't stop extending our troops all around the world in nation-building missions," Bush declared, "then we're going to have a serious problem coming down the road."

Few could have imagined that within two years, following the 9/11 attacks on the World Trade Center and the Pentagon, thousands of American troops would be patrolling the high mountains of the Hindu Kush, fighting enemies at places named Tora Bora and Mazar-e Sharif, and working to install a new government in Afghanistan. A National Geographic Society survey found that nearly half of Americans aged 18 to 24 knew that the fictional island for the *Survivor* TV series was located in the South Pacific, but five in six could not find Afghanistan on a map.

Yet by the summer of 2010, President Barack Obama had increased American troops in Afghanistan to nearly 100,000. "If I thought for a minute that America's vital interests were not at stake here in Afghanistan," he told American soldiers, "I would order all of you home right away." These vital interests in many ways originated during the late nineteenth and early twentieth centuries.

Until then, Americans had given little thought to foreign affairs. In 1888 Benjamin Harrison articulated a widely held belief when he said that the United States was "an apart nation" and should remain so.

But sentiment was shifting. Intellectuals and many others cited "Darwinian" principles, such as "survival of the fittest," to justify American expansion abroad. Missionaries called on Americans to help impoverished and ill-educated peoples elsewhere in the world. American businessmen, increasingly confident of their own powers, craved access to foreign resources and markets. Such factors converged in Cuba, prompting the United States to go to war with Spain.

In 1898 tens of thousands of American troops were dispatched to Cuba and, within a year, to the Philippines. For years thereafter, Americans at home would struggle to locate on globes and in atlases battle sites in places such as Balangiga, Pulang Lupa, and Kandahar. They still do.

Isolation or Imperialism?

If Americans had little concern for what was going on far beyond the seas, their economic interest in Latin America was great and growing, and in East Asia only somewhat less so. Whether one sees isolation or expansion as the hallmark of American foreign policy after 1865 depends on what part of the world one looks at.

The disdain of the people of the United States for Europe rested on several historical foundations. Faith in the unique character of American civilization—and the converse of that belief, suspicion of Europe's supposedly aristocratic and decadent society—formed the chief basis of this **isolationism**. Bitter memories of indignities suffered during the Revolution and the Napoleonic Wars and anger at the hostile attitude of the great powers toward the United States during the Civil War strengthened it. In an era before airplanes, the United States was virtually invulnerable to European attack and at the same time incapable of mounting an offensive against any European power. In turning their backs on Europe, Americans were taking no risk and passing up few opportunities.

Origins of the Large Policy: Coveting Colonies

The nation's interests elsewhere in the world gradually increased. During the Civil War, France had established a protectorate over Mexico, installing the Archduke Maximilian of Austria as emperor. In 1866 Secretary of State William H. Seward demanded that the French withdraw, and the United States moved 50,000 soldiers to the Rio Grande. While fear of American intervention was only one of many reasons for their action, the French pulled their troops out of Mexico during the winter of 1866–1867. Mexican nationalists promptly seized and executed Maximilian. In 1867, at the instigation of

Midway Island, an inhospitable atoll acquired in 1867, was valuable as a military base located midway between Pearl Harbor, another naval station, and East Asia. The acquisition of a Pacific empire during these years was a reason why Pearl Harbor and Midway became pivotal during the war in the Pacific in World War II.

Seward, the United States purchased Alaska from Russia for $7.2 million, ridding the continent of another foreign power.

In 1867 Seward acquired the Midway Islands in the western Pacific. He also made overtures toward annexing the Hawaiian Islands, and he looked longingly at Cuba. In 1870 President Grant submitted to the Senate a treaty annexing the Dominican Republic. He applied tremendous pressure in an effort to obtain ratification, thus forcing a "great debate" on extracontinental expansion. The distance of the Dominican Republic from the continent and its population of what one congressman called "semi-civilized, semi-barbarous men who cannot speak our language" made annexation unattractive. The treaty was rejected.

The internal growth that preoccupied Americans eventually led them to look outward. By the late 1880s the country was exporting a steadily increasing share of its agricultural and industrial output. Exports, only $450 million in 1870, passed the billion-dollar mark early in the 1890s. Imports increased at a rate only slightly less spectacular.

The character of foreign trade was also changing: Manufactures loomed ever more important among exports until in 1898 the country shipped abroad more manufactured goods than it imported. By this time American steelmakers could compete with producers anywhere in the world. When American industrialists became conscious of their ability to compete with Europeans in far-off markets, they took more interest in world affairs, particularly during periods of depression.

Shifting intellectual currents further altered the attitudes of Americans. Darwin's theories, applicable by analogy to international relations, gave the concept of manifest destiny a new plausibility. Darwinists like the historian John Fiske argued that the American democratic system of government was so clearly the world's "fittest" that it was destined to spread peacefully over "every land on the earth's surface." In *Our Country* (1885) Josiah Strong found racist and religious justifications for American expansionism, again based on the theory of evolution. The Anglo-Saxon race, centered now in the United States, possessed "an instinct or genius for colonization," Strong claimed.

The completion of the conquest of the American West encouraged Americans to consider expansion beyond the seas. "For nearly 300 years the dominant fact in American life has been expansion," declared Frederick Jackson Turner, propounder of the frontier thesis. "That these energies of expansion will no longer operate would be a rash prediction." Turner and writers who advanced other expansionist arguments were much influenced by foreign thinking. European liberals had tended to disapprove of colonial ventures, but in the 1870s and 1880s many of them were changing their minds. English liberals in particular began to talk and write about the "superiority" of English culture, to describe the virtues of the "Anglo-Saxon race," to stress a "duty" to spread Christianity among the heathen, and to advance economic arguments for overseas expansion.

European ideas were reinforced for Americans by their observation of the imperialist activities of the European powers in what would today be called underdeveloped areas. "While the great powers of Europe are steadily enlarging their colonial domination in Asia and Africa," James G. Blaine said in 1884, "it is the especial province of this country to improve and expand its trade with the nations of America." While Blaine emphasized commerce, the excitement and adventure of overseas enterprises appealed to many people even more than the economic possibilities or any sense of obligation to fulfill a supposed national, religious, or racial destiny.

Finally, military and strategic arguments were advanced to justify adopting a "large" policy. The powerful Union army had been demobilized rapidly after Appomattox; in the 1880s only about 25,000 men were under arms, their chief occupation fighting Indians in the West.

Half the navy, too, had been scrapped after the war, and the remaining ships were obsolete. While other nations were building steam-powered iron warships, the United States still depended on wooden sailing vessels. In 1867 a British naval publication accurately described the American fleet as "hapless, broken-down, tattered [and] forlorn."

Although no foreign power menaced the country, the decrepit state of the navy vexed many of its officers and led one of them, Captain Alfred Thayer Mahan, to develop a startling theory about the importance of sea power. According to him, history proved that a nation with a powerful navy and the overseas bases necessary to maintain it would be invulnerable in war and prosperous in time of peace. Applied to the current American situation, this meant that in addition to building a modern fleet, the United States should obtain a string of coaling stations and bases in the Caribbean, annex the Hawaiian Islands, and cut a canal across Central America. A more extensive colonial empire might follow, but these bases and the canal they would protect were essential first steps to ensure America's future as a great power.

Mahan attracted many influential disciples. One was Congressman Henry Cabot Lodge of Massachusetts, a prominent member of the Naval Affairs Committee. Lodge had married into a navy family and was close with the head of the new Naval War College, Commodore Stephen B. Luce. In 1883 he helped push through Congress an act authorizing the construction of three steel warships, and he consistently advocated expanding and modernizing the fleet. Elevated to the Senate in 1893, Lodge pressed for expansionist policies, basing his arguments on the

> ◉—View the **Image**
>
> *Uncle Sam Teaching the
> World* at **myhistorylab.com**

strategic concepts of Mahan. Lodge's friend Theodore Roosevelt was another ardent supporter of the "large" policy, but he had little influence until McKinley appointed him assistant secretary of the navy in 1897.

Toward an Empire in the Pacific

The interest of the United States in the Pacific and East Asia began in the late eighteenth century, when the first American merchant ship dropped anchor in Canton harbor. After the Treaty of Wanghia (1844), American merchants in China enjoyed many privileges and trade expanded rapidly.

The Hawaiian Islands were an important way station on the route to China, and by 1820 merchants and missionaries were making contacts there. As early as 1854 a movement to annex the islands existed, although it foundered because Hawaii insisted on being admitted to the Union as a state. Commodore Perry's expedition to Japan led to the signing of a commercial treaty (1858) that opened several Japanese ports to American traders.

American influence in Hawaii increased steadily; the descendants of missionary families, most of them engaged in raising sugar, dominated the Hawaiian monarchy. While they made no overt effort to make the islands an American colony, all the expansionist ideas of the era—manifest destiny, Darwinism, Josiah Strong's racist and religious assumptions, and the relentless force of American commercial interests—pointed them in that direction. In 1875 a reciprocity treaty admitted Hawaiian sugar to the United

The Course of Empire, 1867–1901 China was the focus of American imperial visions: Missionaries, most of them women, flocked into China, and American manufacturers craved access to the huge China market.

States free of duty in return for a promise to yield no territory to a foreign power. When this treaty was renewed in 1887, the United States obtained the right to establish a naval base at Pearl Harbor. In addition to occupying Midway, America obtained a foothold in the Samoan Islands in the South Pacific.

During the 1890s American interest in the Pacific area steadily intensified as a result of the situation in Hawaii. The McKinley Tariff Act of 1890, discontinuing the duty on raw sugar and compensating American producers of cane and beet sugar by granting them a bounty of two cents a pound, struck Hawaiian sugar growers hard, for it destroyed the advantage they had gained in the reciprocity treaty.

The following year the death of King Kalakaua brought Queen Liliuokalani, a determined nationalist, to the throne. Placing herself at the head of a "Hawaii for the Hawaiians" movement, she abolished the existing constitution under which the white minority had pretty much controlled the islands and attempted to rule as an absolute monarch. The resident Americans then staged a coup. In January 1893, with the connivance of the U.S. minister, John L. Stevens, who ordered 150 marines into Honolulu, they deposed Queen Liliuokalani and set up a provisional government.

Stevens recognized their regime at once, and the new government sent a delegation to Washington to seek a treaty of annexation.

In the closing days of the Harrison administration such a treaty was negotiated and sent to the Senate, but when Cleveland took office in March, he withdrew it.

The new president disapproved of the way American troops had been used to overthrow the monarchy and attempted to restore Queen Liliuokalani. But by now the new regime, backed by American businessmen, was firmly entrenched. Cleveland found himself unable to do anything.

Finally, in July 1898, after the outbreak of the Spanish-American War, Congress annexed the islands by joint resolution, a procedure requiring only a simple majority vote.

Toward an Empire in Latin America

Most of the arguments for extending American influence in the Pacific applied more strongly to Central and South America, where the United States had much larger economic interests and where the strategic importance of the region was clear.

As early as 1869 President Grant had come out for an American-owned canal across the isthmus of Panama, in spite of the fact that the United States had agreed in the Clayton-Bulwer Treaty with Great Britain (1850) that neither nation would "obtain or maintain for itself any exclusive control" over an inter-oceanic canal. In 1880, when the French engineer Ferdinand de Lesseps organized a company to build a canal across the isthmus, President Hayes announced that the United States would not permit a European power to control such a waterway.

When Cleveland returned to power in 1893, the possibility of trouble in Latin America seemed remote, for he had always opposed imperialistic ventures. Yet scarcely two years later the United States was again on the verge of war in South America as a result of a crisis in Venezuela, and before this issue was settled Cleveland had made the most powerful claim to American hegemony in the hemisphere ever uttered. The tangled borderland between Venezuela and British Guiana had long been in dispute, Venezuela demanding more of the region than it was entitled to and Great Britain making exaggerated claims and refusing to submit the question to arbitration. What made a crisis of the controversy was the political situation in the United States. With his party rapidly deserting him because of his stand on the silver question, and with the election of 1896 approaching, President Cleveland desperately needed a popular issue.

There was considerable anti-British feeling in the United States. By taking the Venezuelan side in the boundary dispute, Cleveland would be defending a weak neighbor against a great power, a position certain to evoke a popular response.

In July 1895 he ordered Secretary of State Richard Olney to send a near ultimatum to the British. By occupying the disputed territory, Olney insisted, Great Britain was invading Venezuela and violating the Monroe Doctrine. Unless Great Britain responded promptly by agreeing to arbitration, the president would call the question to the attention of Congress.

The note threatened war, but the British ignored it for months. They did not take the United States seriously as a world power. The American navy, although expanding, could not hope to stand up against the British, who had fifty battleships, twenty-five armored cruisers, and many smaller vessels. When Lord Salisbury, the prime minister and foreign secretary, finally replied, he rejected outright the argument that the Monroe Doctrine had any status under international law and refused to arbitrate what he called the "exaggerated pretensions" of the Venezuelans.

Cleveland was furious. On December 17, 1895, he asked Congress for authority to appoint an American commission to determine the correct line between British Guiana and Venezuela. When that had been done, he added, the United States should "resist by every means in its power" the appropriation by Great Britain of any territory "we have determined of right belongs to Venezuela." Congress responded at once, unanimously appropriating $100,000 for the boundary commission. Popular approval was almost universal.

In Great Britain government and people suddenly awoke to the seriousness of the situation. No one wanted a war with the United States over a remote patch of tropical real estate. In Europe, Britain was concerned about German economic competition and the increased military power of that nation. The immense potential strength of the United States could no longer be ignored. Why make an enemy of a nation of 70 million, already the richest industrial power in the world?

Great Britain agreed to arbitrate the boundary, and the war scare subsided. When the boundary tribunal awarded nearly all the disputed region to Great Britain, whatever ill feeling the surrender may have occasioned in that country faded away. Instead of leading to war, the affair marked the beginning of an era of Anglo-American friendship. It had the unfortunate effect, however, of adding to the long-held American conviction that the nation could get what it wanted in international affairs by threat and bluster—a dangerous illusion.

The Cuban Revolution

On February 10, 1896, scarcely a week after Venezuela and Great Britain had signed the treaty ending their dispute, General Valeriano Weyler arrived in Havana from Spain to take up his duties as governor of Cuba. His assignment to this post was occasioned by the guerrilla warfare that Cuban nationalist rebels had been waging for almost a year. Weyler, a tough and ruthless soldier, began herding the rural population into wretched **"reconcentration" camps** to deprive the rebels of food and recruits. Resistance in Cuba hardened.

The United States had been interested in Cuba since the time of John Quincy Adams and, were it not for Northern opposition to adding more slave territory, might well have obtained the island one way or another before 1860. When the Cubans revolted against Spain in 1868, considerable support for intervening on their behalf developed. Hamilton Fish, Grant's secretary of state, resisted this sentiment, and Spain managed to pacify the rebels in 1878 by promising reforms. But change was slow in coming—slavery was not abolished until 1886. The worldwide depression of the 1890s hit the Cuban economy hard, and when an American tariff act in 1894 jacked up the rate on Cuban sugar by 40 percent, thus cutting off Cuban growers from the American market, the resulting distress precipitated another revolt.

Public sympathy in the United States went to the Cubans, who seemed to be fighting for liberty and democracy against an autocratic Old World power. Most newspapers supported the rebels; labor unions, veterans' organizations, many Protestant clergymen, a great majority of American blacks, and important politicians in both major parties demanded that the United States aid their cause. Rapidly increasing American investments in Cuban sugar plantations, now approaching $50 million, were endangered by the fighting and by the social chaos sweeping across the island.

In April 1896 Congress adopted a resolution suggesting that the revolutionaries be granted the rights of belligerents. Since this would have been akin to formal recognition, Cleveland would not go that far, but he did exert diplomatic pressure on Spain to remove the causes of the rebels' complaints, and he offered the services of his government as mediator. The Spanish rejected the suggestion. For a time the issue subsided. The election of 1896 deflected American attention from Cuba, and then McKinley refused to take any action that might disturb Spanish-American relations. In Cuba General Weyler made some progress toward stifling rebel resistance.

American expansionists, however, continued to demand intervention, and the press kept resentment alive with tales of Spanish atrocities. McKinley remained adamant. Although he warned Spain that Cuba must be pacified, his tone was friendly and he issued no ultimatum. A new government in Spain relieved the situation by recalling Weyler and promising partial self-government to the Cubans. In a message to Congress in December 1897, McKinley urged that Spain be given "a reasonable chance to realize her expectations" in the island.

His hopes were doomed. The fighting in Cuba continued. When riots broke out in Havana in January 1898, McKinley ordered the battleship *Maine* to Havana harbor to protect American citizens.

Shortly thereafter Hearst's *New York Journal* printed a letter written to a friend in Cuba by the Spanish minister in Washington, Dupuy de Lôme. The letter had been stolen by a spy. De Lôme, an experienced but arrogant diplomat, failed to appreciate McKinley's efforts to avoid intervening in Cuba. In the letter he characterized the president as a *politicastro*, or "small-time politician," which was a gross error, and a "bidder for the admiration of the crowd," which was equally insulting though somewhat closer to the truth. Americans were outraged, and de Lôme's hasty resignation did little to soothe their feelings.

Then, on February 15, the *Maine* exploded and sank in Havana harbor, 260 of the crew perishing in the disaster. Interventionists in the United States accused Spain of having destroyed the ship and clamored for war. The willingness of Americans to blame Spain indicates the extent of anti-Spanish opinion in the United States by 1898. No one has ever discovered what actually happened. A naval court of inquiry decided that the vessel had been sunk by a submarine mine, but it now seems more likely that an internal explosion destroyed the *Maine*. The Spanish government could hardly have been foolish enough to commit an act that would probably bring American troops into Cuba.

Watch the Video
Burial of the *Maine* Victims at **myhistorylab.com**

With admirable courage, McKinley refused to panic; but he could not resist the wishes of millions of citizens that something be done to stop the fighting and allow the Cubans to determine their own fate. Spanish pride and Cuban patriotism had taken the issue of peace or war out of the president's hands. Spain could not put down the rebellion, and it would not yield to the nationalists' increasingly extreme demands. The Cubans, sensing that the continuing bloodshed aided their cause, refused to give the Spanish regime room to maneuver. After the *Maine* disaster, Spain might have agreed to an armistice had the rebels asked for one, and in the resulting negotiations it might well have given up the island. The rebels refused to make the first move. The fighting continued, bringing the United States every day closer to intervention.

The president faced a dilemma. Most of the business interests of the country, to which he was particularly sensitive, opposed intervention. Congress, however, seemed

The explosion of the *Maine* in Havana harbor, killing 260 men, caused much speculation in the newspapers and across the nation. Many Americans accused Spain of destroying the ship, a reaction that typified American sentiment toward the Spanish in 1898. What really caused the explosion remains unknown.
Source: ICHi-08428/Kurz & Allison/Chicago History Museum.

determined to act. When he submitted a restrained report on the sinking of the *Maine*, the Democrats in Congress, even most of those who had supported Cleveland's policies, accused him of timidity. Vice President Garret A. Hobart warned him that the Senate could not be held in check for long; should Congress declare war on its own, the administration would be discredited.

Finally, early in April, the president drafted a message asking for authority to use the armed forces "to secure a full and final termination of hostilities" in Cuba.

At the last moment the Spanish government seemed to yield; it ordered its troops in Cuba to cease hostilities. McKinley passed this information on to Congress along with his war message, but he gave it no emphasis and did not try to check the march toward war. To seek further delay would have been courageous but not necessarily wiser. Merely to stop fighting was not enough. The Cuban nationalists now insisted on full independence, and the Spanish politicians were unprepared to abandon the last remnant of their once-great American empire. If the United States took Cuba by force, the Spanish leaders might save their political skins; if they meekly surrendered the island, they were done for.

The "Splendid Little" Spanish-American War

On April 20, 1898, Congress, by joint resolution, recognized the independence of Cuba and authorized the use of the armed forces to drive out the Spanish. An amendment proposed by Senator Henry M. Teller disclaiming any intention of adding Cuban territory to the United States passed without opposition. Four days after passage of the **Teller Amendment**, Spain declared war on the United States.

Sailors on the USS *Oregon* watch the destruction of the Spanish cruiser, *Cristobal Colon*, during the Battle of Santiago, Cuba, July 3, 1898.

The Spanish-American War was fought to free Cuba, but the first action took place on the other side of the globe, in the Philippine Islands. Weeks earlier, Theodore Roosevelt, at the time assistant secretary of the navy, had alerted Commodore George Dewey, who was in command of the United States Asiatic Squadron located at Hong Kong, to move against the Spanish base at Manila if war came. Dewey had acted promptly, drilling his gun crews, taking on supplies, giving his gleaming white ships a coat of battle-gray paint, and establishing secret contacts with the Filipino nationalist leader, Emilio Aguinaldo. When word of the declaration of war reached him, Dewey steamed from Hong Kong across the South China Sea with four cruisers and two gunboats. On the night of April 30 he entered Manila Bay, and at daybreak he opened fire on the Spanish fleet at 5,000 yards. His squadron made five passes, each time reducing the range; when the smoke had cleared, all ten of Admiral Montojo's ships had been destroyed. Not a single American was killed in the engagement.

Dewey immediately asked for troops to take and hold Manila, for now that war had been declared, he could not return to Hong Kong or any other neutral port. McKinley took the fateful step of dispatching some 11,000 soldiers and additional naval support. On August 13 these forces, assisted by Filipino irregulars under Aguinaldo, captured Manila.

Watch the Video

Roosevelt's Rough Riders
at **myhistorylab.com**

Meanwhile, in Cuba, the United States had won a total victory. When the war began, the U.S. regular army consisted of about 28,000 men. This tiny force was bolstered by 200,000 hastily enlisted volunteers. Aggressive units like the regiment of "Rough Riders" raised by Theodore Roosevelt, who had resigned his Navy Department post to become a lieutenant colonel of volunteers, scrambled for space and supplies, shouldering aside other units to get what they needed.

Since a Spanish fleet under Admiral Pascual Cervera was known to be in Caribbean waters, no invading army could safely embark until the fleet could be located. On May 29 American ships found Cervera at Santiago harbor, on the eastern end of Cuba, and established a blockade. In June a 17,000-man expeditionary force landed at Daiquiri, east of Santiago, and pressed quickly toward the city. The Americans sweated through Cuba's torrid summer in heavy wool winter uniforms, ate "embalmed beef" out of cans, and fought mostly with old-fashioned rifles using black powder cartridges that marked the position of each soldier with a puff of smoke whenever he pulled the trigger. On July 1 they broke through undermanned Spanish defenses and stormed San Juan Hill, the intrepid Roosevelt in the van.

With Santiago harbor in range of American artillery, Admiral Cervera had to run the blockade. On July 3 his black-hulled ships, flags proudly flying, steamed forth from the harbor and fled westward along the coast. Five American battleships and two cruisers, commanded by Rear Admiral William T. Sampson and Commodore Winfield Scott Schley, ran them down. In four hours the entire Spanish force was destroyed. Damage to the American ships was superficial; only one American seaman lost his life in the engagement.

Spanish-American War: Caribbean Theater, 1898 After boarding in Tampa, American soldiers landed near Santiago, Cuba. They swiftly overran Spanish fortifications on the heights to the east of the city. When U.S. troops came within artillery range of Santiago Bay, the Spanish fleet fled. Soon the Spanish ships were intercepted and destroyed by the American navy.

The end then came abruptly. Santiago surrendered on July 17. A few days later, other U.S. troops completed the occupation of Puerto Rico. On August 12, one day before the fall of Manila, Spain agreed to get out of Cuba and to cede Puerto Rico and an island in the Marianas (Guam) to the United States. The future of the Philippines was to be settled at a formal peace conference, convening in Paris on October 1.

Developing a Colonial Policy

Although the Spanish resisted surrendering the Philippines at Paris, they had been so thoroughly defeated that they had no choice. The decision hung rather on the outcome of a conflict over policy within the United States. The war, won at so little cost militarily, produced problems far larger than those it solved.[1] The nation had become a great power in the world's eyes. European leaders had been impressed by the forcefulness of Cleveland's diplomacy in the Venezuela boundary dispute and by the efficiency displayed by the navy in the war. The annexation of Hawaii and other overseas bases intensified their conviction that the United States was determined to become a major force in international affairs.

But were the American people determined to exercise that force? The debate over taking the Philippine Islands throws much light on their attitudes. It was titillating for Americans to think of a world map liberally sprinkled with American flags and of the economic benefits that colonies might bring, but most citizens were not prepared to join in a worldwide struggle for power and influence. They entered blithely on adventures in far-off regions without facing the implications of their decision.

Since the United States had abjured any claim to Cuba, even though the island had long been desired by expansionists, logic dictated that a similar policy be applied to the Philippines. But expansionists were eager to annex the entire archipelago. Even before he had learned to spell the name, Senator Lodge was saying that "the Phillipines [sic] mean a vast future trade and wealth and power," offering the nation a greater opportunity "than anything that has happened . . . since the annexation of Louisiana."

President McKinley adopted a more cautious stance, but he too favored "the general principle of holding on to what we can get." A speaking tour of the Midwest in October 1898, during which he experimented with varying degrees of commitment to expansionism, convinced him that the public wanted the islands. Business opinion had shifted dramatically during the war. Business leaders were now calling the Philippines the gateway to the markets of East Asia.

The Anti-Imperialists

The war had produced a wave of unifying patriotic feeling. It greatly furthered reconciliation between the North and the South. But victory raised new divisive questions. An important minority objected strongly to the U.S. acquisition of overseas possessions.

The anti-imperialists insisted that since no one would consider statehood for the Philippines, it would be unconstitutional to annex them. It was a violation of the spirit of

---

[1] More than 5,000 Americans died as a result of the conflict, but fewer than 400 fell in combat. The others were mostly victims of yellow fever, typhoid, and other diseases.

While the good children (the states) sit at their seats, with the Indian off to the side, the unruly blacks—"Cuba," "Puerto Rico," "Hawaii," and "Philippines"—are lectured by Uncle Sam. Racist anti-imperialists argued, as did this cartoon in *Puck* in 1899, that the inclusion of other peoples would weaken the American nation.

the Declaration of Independence to govern a foreign territory without the consent of its inhabitants, Senator George Frisbie Hoar of Massachusetts argued; by taking over "vassal states" in "barbarous archipelagoes" the United States was "trampling . . . on our own great Charter, which recognizes alike the liberty and the dignity of individual manhood."

McKinley was not insensitive to this appeal to idealism and tradition, which was the fundamental element in the anti-imperialist argument. But he rejected it for several reasons.

Public opinion would not sanction restoring Spanish authority in the Philippines or allowing some other power to have them. That the Filipinos were sufficiently advanced and united socially to form a stable government if granted independence seemed unlikely. Senator Hoar believed that "for years and for generations, and perhaps for centuries, there would have been turbulence, disorder and revolution" in the islands if they were left to their own devices.

The president searched the depths of his soul and could find no solution but annexation. The state of public feeling made the decision easier, and he probably found the idea of presiding over an empire appealing. Certainly the commercial possibilities did not escape him. In the end it was with a heavy sense of responsibility that he ordered the American peace commissioners to insist on acquiring the Philippines. To salve the feelings of the Spanish the United States agreed to pay $20 million for the archipelago, but it was a forced sale, accepted by Spain under duress.

The peace treaty faced a hard battle in the U.S. Senate, where a combination of partisan politics and anticolonialism made it difficult to amass the two-thirds majority necessary for ratification. McKinley had shrewdly appointed three senators, including one

Democrat, to the peace commission. This predisposed many members of the upper house to approve the treaty, but the vote was close. William Jennings Bryan, titular head of the Democratic party, could probably have prevented ratification had he urged his supporters to vote nay. Although he was opposed to taking the Philippines, he did not do so. To reject the treaty would leave the United States technically at war with Spain and the fate of the Philippines undetermined; better to accept the islands and then grant them independence. The question should be decided, Bryan said, "not by a minority of the Senate but by a majority of the people" at the next presidential election. Perplexed by Bryan's stand, a number of Democrats allowed themselves to be persuaded by the expansionists' arguments and by McKinley's judicious use of patronage; the treaty was ratified in February 1899 by a vote of fifty-seven to twenty-seven.

The Philippine Insurrection

The national referendum that Bryan had hoped for never materialized. Bryan himself confused the issue in 1900 by making free silver a major plank in his platform, thereby driving conservative anti-imperialists into McKinley's arms. Moreover, early in 1899 the Filipino nationalists under Aguinaldo, furious because the United States would not withdraw, took up arms. A savage guerrilla war resulted, one that cost far more in lives and money than the "splendid little" Spanish-American conflict.

Neither side displayed much regard for the "rules" of war. Goaded by sneak attacks and instances of cruelty to captives, American soldiers, most of whom had little respect for Filipinos to begin with, responded in kind. (See American Lives, "Frederick Funston," pp. 590–591.) Civilians were rounded up, prisoners tortured, and property destroyed. Horrifying tales of rape, arson, and murder by U.S. troops filtered into the country, providing ammunition for the anti-imperialists. In fact, far more than 8,000 Filipinos lost their lives during the conflict, which raged for three years. More than 70,000 American soldiers had to be sent to the islands before the resistance was crushed, and about as many of them lost their lives as had perished in the Cuban conflict.

In 1900 McKinley sent a commission headed by William Howard Taft, a federal judge, to establish a government. Taft took an instant liking to the

●●●─ **Read** the **Document**
Twain, *Incident in the Philippines*
at **myhistorylab.com**

●─ **View** the **Image**
Filipino Guerrillas at
myhistorylab.com

Emilio Aguinaldo, shown here with his young son, commanded Filipino insurgents who worked with Commodore Dewey to help overthrow Spanish rule of the Philippines in 1898. He later took up arms against the United States in a brutal three-year struggle when President McKinley opposed granting independence to the islands.

Filipinos, and his policy of encouraging them to participate in the territorial government attracted many converts. In July 1901 he became the first civilian governor of the Philippines.

Actually, the reelection of McKinley in 1900 settled the Philippine question so far as most Americans were concerned. Anti-imperialists still claimed that it was unconstitutional to take over territories without the consent of the local population. Their reasoning, while certainly not unsound, was unhistorical. No American government had seriously considered the wishes of the American Indians, the French and Spanish settlers in Louisiana, the Eskimos of Alaska, or the people of Hawaii when it had seemed in the national interest to annex new lands.

Cuba and the United States

Nevertheless, grave constitutional questions arose as a result of the acquisitions that followed the Spanish-American War. McKinley acted with remarkable independence in handling the problems involved in expansion. He set up military governments in Cuba, Puerto Rico, and the Philippines without specific congressional authority. The Supreme Court, in what became known as the "insular cases," granted Congress permission to act toward the colonies much as it pleased.

While the most heated arguments raged over Philippine policy, the most difficult colonial problems concerned the relationship between the United States and Cuba. Despite the desire of most Americans to get out of Cuba, an independent government could not easily be created.

The insurgent government was feeble, corrupt, and oligarchic, the Cuban economy in a state of collapse, and life was chaotic. The first Americans entering Havana found the streets littered with garbage and the corpses of horses and dogs. All public services were at a standstill; it seemed essential for the United States, as McKinley said, to give "aid and direction" until "tranquillity" could be restored.

The problems were indeed knotty, for no strong local leader capable of uniting Cuba appeared. Even Senator Teller, father of the Teller Amendment, expressed concern lest "unstable and unsafe" elements gain control of the country. European leaders expected that the United States would eventually annex Cuba; and many Americans, including General Leonard Wood, who became military governor in December 1899, considered this the best solution. The desperate state of the people, the heavy economic stake of Americans in the region, and its strategic importance militated against withdrawal.

In the end the United States did withdraw, after doing a great deal to modernize sugar production, improve sanitary conditions, establish schools, and restore orderly administration. In November 1900 a Cuban constitutional convention met at Havana and proceeded without substantial American interference or direction to draft a frame of government. The chief restrictions imposed by this document on Cuba's freedom concerned foreign relations; at the insistence of the United States, it authorized American intervention whenever necessary "for the preservation of Cuban independence" and "the maintenance of a government adequate for the protection of life, property, and individual liberty." Cuba had to promise to make no treaty with a foreign power compromising its independence and to grant naval bases on its soil to the United States.

The Cubans, after some grumbling, accepted this arrangement, known as the Platt Amendment. It had the support of most American opponents of imperialism. The amendment was a true compromise: It safeguarded American interests while granting to the Cubans real self-government on internal matters. In May 1902 the United States turned over the reins of government to the new republic. The next year the two countries signed a reciprocity treaty tightening the economic bonds between them.

True friendship did not result. Although American troops occupied Cuba only once more, in 1906, and then at the specific request of Cuban authorities, the United States repeatedly used the threat of intervention to coerce the Cuban government. American economic penetration proceeded rapidly and without regard for the well-being of the Cuban peasants, many of whom lived in a state of peonage on great sugar plantations. Nor did the Americans' good intentions make up for their tendency to consider themselves innately superior to the Cubans and to overlook the fact that Cubans did not always wish to adopt American customs and culture.

The United States in the Caribbean and Central America

If the purpose of the Spanish-American War had been to bring peace and order to Cuba, the Platt Amendment was a logical step. The same purpose soon necessitated a further extension of the principle, for once the United States accepted the role of protector and stabilizer in parts of the Caribbean and Central America, it seemed desirable to supervise the entire region.

The Caribbean and Central American countries were economically underdeveloped, politically unstable, and desperately poor. Most of the people were uneducated peasants, many of whom were little better off than slaves. Rival cliques of wealthy families struggled for power, force being the usual method of effecting a change in government. Most of the meager income of the average Caribbean state was swallowed up by the military or diverted into the pockets of the current rulers.

Cynicism and fraud poisoned the relations of most of these nations with the great powers. European merchants and bankers systematically cheated their Latin American customers, who in turn frequently refused to honor their obligations. Foreign bankers floated bond issues on outrageous terms, while revolutionary governments in the region annulled concessions and repudiated debts with equal disdain for honest business dealing.

In 1902, shortly after the United States had pulled out of Cuba, trouble erupted in Venezuela, where a dictator, Cipriano Castro, was refusing to honor debts owed the citizens of European nations. To force Castro to pay up, Germany and Great Britain established a blockade of Venezuelan ports and destroyed a number of Venezuelan gunboats and harbor defenses. Under American pressure the Europeans agreed to arbitrate the dispute. For the first time, European powers had accepted the broad implications of the Monroe Doctrine. By this time Theodore Roosevelt had become president of the United States, and he quickly capitalized on the new

FREDERICK FUNSTON

On the night of March 22, 1901, as rain battered his campsite in the deep jungles of Luzon Island in the Philippines, Frederick Funston pondered what awaited him the next day. Ten miles to the north lay his prey, Emilio Aguinaldo, President of the Philippine Republic. For two years, the American army had been trying to capture Aguinaldo. But repeatedly Aguinaldo had slipped away. This time Funston was close. His ruse was working.

It had been a wild idea, something out of a boy's adventure story. He conceived it after capturing a Filipino messenger carrying coded documents. Funston's interrogation of the courier had been successful. The courier confirmed that Aguinaldo's secret headquarters was located in a remote area of Luzon.

Funston had chosen eighty Filipino scouts from the Macabebes, a tribe hostile to Aguinaldo. He outfitted them in the uniforms of Aguinaldo's army and trained them to pretend to be Filipino nationalists. These "nationalists" would escort five American "prisoners" (including Funston) for presentation to Aguinaldo.

Funston longed to be a hero. Ever since he was a child, he worried that he failed to measure up to his father. Edward "Foghorn" Funston had been an artillery officer during the Civil War and a fiery Republican congressman afterward. At six feet two and 200 pounds, he was regarded by all as an exemplar of nineteenth-century manhood. But Frederick, born in 1864, was only five feet four and slightly built. He compensated with bravado displays of martial manliness. He craved a military career, but though his father was a congressman, West Point rejected him: His grades were mediocre, and he was too small.

In 1886 he enrolled at the University of Kansas but didn't fit in. He devoted himself to the pursuit of the most desirable women on campus, all of whom spurned him. Increasingly he retreated from social situations, preferring to drink alone in his room, periodically bursting out in a drunken rage.

He dropped out of college. First, he explored an unmapped section of Death Valley in California. Then he volunteered to gather botanical samples in Alaska for the Department of Agriculture. When the department proposed that he command an entire expedition for the purpose, he flatly turned them down. Alone, he trekked into the frigid wastes of northern Alaska and remained there for the better part of a year. When he ran out of food he ate his sled dogs.

During those long, silent nights, Funston realized that he could hardly prove that he measured up if no one were around to take the measurements. He decided to become a soldier, not caring much against whom he fought. In 1895 he contacted a recruiter for the cause of Cuban independence and accepted a commission as an artillery officer in the rebel army.

In Cuba he was given command of a Hotchkiss cannon; he made up for his lack of gunnery skill by sneaking his cannon absurdly close to Spanish fortifications at night, often within 400 yards. As the sun rose, the Spaniards, aghast at what was sitting on their doorstep, fired everything they had at Funston's cannon. Funston calmly adjusted the sights, pulled the lanyard, and climbed upon the parapet, shouting

Frederick Funston: hero or antihero?

"Viva Cuba libre!" He was repeatedly wounded; once, a bullet pierced his lungs. When a severe hip wound became infected, he returned to the United States for medical assistance.

But he was not done with war. In 1898 Funston was given command of the Kansas regiments that had volunteered against Spain. To his dismay, they were sent to the Philippines, where the Spaniards had already ceased fighting. But after President McKinley decided to annex the Philippines, war broke out between the Americans and the Filipino nationalists. Funston finally got what he craved: sweeping charges, glorious victories, and newspaper feature stories. Yet the jokes persisted. Behind his back, his men called him the "Bantam General." The New York Times, in its coverage of a battle in which he won a Congressional Medal of Honor, ran the headline: "Daring Little Colonel Funston." The opening paragraph attributed Funston's courage to the fact that he was too small to hit.

But now, if he captured Aguinaldo, Funston, the little man, would become a great one.

On March 23, 1901, Funston's Macabebes and their five American "prisoners" met up with a contingent of Aguinaldo's army. Deceived, Aguinaldo's troops escorted Funston's band into the town of Palanan. Aguinaldo watched from a window above. When shots rang out, thinking the troops were firing a salute, he shouted, "Stop that foolishness. Don't waste ammunition!"

Then Funston burst into Aguinaldo's compound: "I am General Funston. You are a prisoner of war of the Army of the United States of America."

Dazed, Aguinaldo replied, "Is this not some joke?" Funston seized Aguinaldo, dragged him through the jungle to the coast, where the USS Vicksburg was waiting. It took them to American headquarters in Manila.

After being subjected to intense pressure by American officials, Aguinaldo renounced the Filipino revolution, swore allegiance to the United States, and called on his followers to do likewise. The Philippine-American conflict was virtually over. Frederick Funston had almost single-handedly won the war.

For a time, Funston was a sensation. He was promoted to brigadier general. Newspaper editors and politicians championed him for governor of Kansas or for vice president on a ticket headed by Theodore Roosevelt in 1904. But within a few years Funston all but vanished. Anti-imperialists pointed out that Funston's men had surrendered and then fired their weapons, and that the Macabebes had been wearing enemy uniforms; both actions violated international law. Worse, several reporters and some of his soldiers claimed that Funston had ordered the execution of Filipino prisoners. He was ordered to an inconsequential command in San Francisco.

One hundred years after Funston's capture of Aguinaldo, U.S. troops would again be tracking a rebel fugitive: Osama bin Laden, mastermind of the September 11, 2001, attacks on the World Trade Center and Pentagon. That virtually no one recalled Funston's single-handed pursuit and capture of Aguinaldo was one measure of how completely he had slipped from view.

But Funston's name resurfaced in 2010, after major earthquakes had triggered widespread looting in Haiti and Chile. The New York Times observed that when the 1906 earthquake destroyed much of San Francisco, General Frederick Funston had immediately marched his troops into the city and taken charge; sometimes, the Times noted, leaders must act decisively.

Question for Discussion

■ To catch Aguinaldo, Funston employed tactics of doubtful legality. A century later Americans have been accused of using torture and other unsavory methods to win "the war on terror." Are such techniques morally or legally wrong? Why or why not?

The United States in the Caribbean and Central America Puerto Rico was ceded by Spain to the United States after the Spanish-American War; the Virgin Islands were bought from Denmark; the Canal Zone was leased from Panama. The ranges of dates shown for Cuba, the Dominican Republic, Haiti, Nicaragua, and Panama cover those years during which the United States either had troops in occupation or in some other way (such as financial) had a protectorate relationship with that country.

European attitude. In 1903 the Dominican Republic defaulted on bonds totaling some $40 million. When European investors urged their governments to intervene, Roosevelt announced that under the Monroe Doctrine the United States could not permit foreign nations to intervene in Latin America. But, he added, Latin American nations should not be allowed to escape their obligations.

The president did not want to make a colony of the Dominican Republic. He therefore arranged for the United States to take charge of the Dominican customs service—the one reliable source of revenue in that poverty-stricken country. Fifty-five percent of the customs duties would be devoted to debt payment, the remainder turned over to the Dominican government to care for its internal needs. Roosevelt defined his policy, known as the Roosevelt Corollary to the Monroe Doctrine, in a message to Congress in December 1904. "Chronic wrongdoing" in Latin America, he stated with his typical disregard for the subtleties of complex affairs, might require outside intervention. Since, under the Monroe Doctrine, no other nation could step in, the United States must "exercise . . . an international police power."

In the short run this policy worked. Dominican customs were honestly collected for the first time and the country's finances put in order. The presence of American warships in the area provided a needed measure of political stability. In the long run, however, the Roosevelt Corollary caused a great deal of resentment in Latin America.

See the Map

Activities of the United States in the Caribbean at **myhistorylab.com**

The Open Door Policy in China

The insular cases, the Platt Amendment, and the Roosevelt Corollary established the framework for American policy both in Latin America and in East Asia. Coincidental with the Cuban rebellion of the 1890s, a far greater upheaval had convulsed the ancient empire of China. In 1894–1895 Japan easily defeated China in a war over Korea. Alarmed by Japan's aggressiveness, the European powers hastened to carve out for themselves new spheres of influence along China's coast. After the annexation of the Philippines, McKinley's secretary of state, John Hay, urged on by business leaders fearful of losing out in the scramble to exploit the Chinese market, tried to prevent the further absorption of China by the great powers.

For the United States to join in the dismemberment of China was politically impossible because of anti-imperialist feeling, so Hay sought to protect American interests by clever diplomacy. In a series of "Open Door" notes (1899) he asked the powers to agree to respect the trading rights of all countries and to impose no discriminatory duties within their spheres of influence.

The replies to the Open Door notes were at best noncommittal, yet Hay blandly announced in March 1900 that the powers had "accepted" his suggestions! Thus he could claim to have prevented the breakup of the empire and protected the right of Americans to do business freely in its territories. In reality nothing had been accomplished; the imperialist nations did not extend their political control of China only because they feared that by doing so they might precipitate a major war among themselves. Nevertheless, Hay's action marked a revolutionary departure from the traditional American policy of isolation, a bold advance into the complicated and dangerous world of international power politics.

Within a few months of Hay's announcement the **Open Door policy** was put to the test. Chinese nationalists, angered by the spreading influence of foreign governments, launched the so-called Boxer Rebellion. They swarmed into Peking and drove foreigners behind the walls of their legations, which were placed under siege. For weeks, until an international rescue expedition (which included 2,500 American soldiers) broke through to free them, the fate of the foreigners was unknown. Fearing that the Europeans would use the rebellion as a pretext for further expropriations, Hay sent off another round of Open Door notes announcing that the United States believed in the preservation of "Chinese territorial and administrative entity" and in "the principle of equal and impartial trade with all parts of the Chinese Empire." This broadened the Open Door policy to include all China, not merely the European spheres of influence.

Hay's diplomacy was superficially successful. But once again European jealousies and fears rather than American cleverness were responsible. When the Japanese, mistrusting Russian intentions in Manchuria, asked Hay how he intended to implement his policy, he replied meekly that the United States was "not prepared . . . to enforce these views." The United States was being caught up in the power struggle in East Asia without having faced the implications of its actions.

In time the country would pay a heavy price for this unrealistic attitude, but in the decade following 1900 its policy of diplomatic meddling worked fairly well. Japan attacked Russia in a quarrel over Manchuria, smashing the Russian fleet in 1905 and winning a series of battles on the mainland. Japan was not prepared for a long war,

Grace Service, a YMCA missionary, explained that these porters worked at the base of Mount Omei in Szechwan, China, a favorite site for Buddhist pilgrims. Upper-class Chinese women's feet were bound to keep them small. The deformities that resulted limited the distance they could walk, so they hired men such as these to carry them to the summit.

however, and suggested to President Roosevelt that an American offer to mediate would be favorably received.

Eager to preserve the balance of power in East Asia, which enabled the United States to exert influence without any significant commitment of force, Roosevelt accepted the hint. In June 1905 he invited the belligerents to a conference at Portsmouth, New Hampshire. At the conference the Japanese won title to Russia's sphere around Port Arthur and a free hand in Korea, but when they demanded Sakhalin Island and a large money indemnity, the Russians balked. Unwilling to resume the war, the Japanese settled for half of Sakhalin and no money.

The Treaty of Portsmouth was unpopular in Japan, and the government managed to place the blame on Roosevelt, who had supported the compromise. Ill feeling against Americans increased in 1906 when the San Francisco school board, responding to local opposition to the influx of cheap labor from Japan, instituted a policy of segregating Asian children in a special school. Japan protested, and President Roosevelt persuaded the San Franciscans to abandon segregation in exchange for his pledge to cut off further Japanese immigration. He accomplished this through a "Gentlemen's Agreement" (1907) in which the Japanese promised not to issue passports to laborers seeking to come to America. Discriminatory legislation based specifically on race was thus avoided. However, the atmosphere between the two countries remained charged. Japanese resentment at American racial prejudice was great; many Americans talked fearfully of the "yellow peril."

Roosevelt did not appreciably increase American naval and military strength in East Asia, nor did he stop trying to influence the course of events in the area, and he took no step toward withdrawing from the Philippines. He sent the fleet on a world cruise to demonstrate its might to Japan but knew well that this was mere bluff. "The 'Open Door' policy," he advised his successor, "completely disappears as soon as a powerful nation determines to disregard it." Nevertheless he allowed the belief to persist in the United States that the nation could influence the course of East Asian history without risk or real involvement.

The Panama Canal

In the Caribbean region American policy centered on building an interoceanic canal across Central America. The first step was to get rid of the old Clayton-Bulwer Treaty with Great Britain, which barred the United States from building a canal on its own. In 1901 Lord Pauncefote, the British ambassador, and Secretary of State John Hay negotiated an agreement abrogating the Clayton-Bulwer pact and giving the United States the right to build and defend a canal connecting the Pacific Ocean with the Caribbean Sea.

One possible canal route lay across the Colombian province of Panama, where the French-controlled New Panama Canal Company had taken over the franchise of the old De Lesseps company. Only fifty miles separated the oceans in Panama. The terrain, however, was rugged and unhealthy. While the French company had sunk much money into the project, it had little to show for its efforts aside from some rough excavations. A second possible route ran across Nicaragua. This route was about 200 miles long but was relatively easy since much of it traversed Lake Nicaragua and other natural waterways.

President McKinley appointed a commission to study the alternatives. It reported that the Panamanian route was technically superior, but recommended building in

An electron microscopic photo of a mosquito that carried yellow fever. Major Walter Reed of the U.S. army proved that yellow fever was not spread directly among humans, but from the bites of infected mosquitoes. The virus then multiplied in the human bloodstream. Headache, backache, fever, and vomiting ensued. Liver cells were destroyed, resulting in jaundice—thus the name "yellow fever." American surgeon William Crawford Gorgas worked to eliminate yellow fever by destroying the breeding grounds of these mosquitoes. The last yellow fever outbreak in the United States struck New Orleans and parts of the South in 1905.

The U.S. Panama Canal Following many negotiations, construction of the Panama Canal began in 1904. After many delays and hardships, it was completed in 1914.

Nicaragua because the New Panama Canal Company was asking $109 million for its assets, which the commission valued at only $40 million. Lacking another potential purchaser, the French company lowered its price to $40 million, and after a great deal of clever propagandizing by Philippe Bunau-Varilla, a French engineer with heavy investments in the company, President Roosevelt settled on the Panamanian route.

In January 1903 Secretary of State Hay negotiated a treaty with Colombia. In return for a ninety-nine-year lease on a zone across Panama six miles wide, the United States agreed to pay Colombia $10 million and an annual rent of $250,000. The Colombian senate, however, unanimously rejected this treaty. It demanded $15 million directly from the United States, plus one-fourth of the $40 million U.S. payment to the New Panama Canal Company.

A little more patience might have produced a mutually satisfactory settlement, but Roosevelt looked on the Colombians as highwaymen who were "mad to get hold of the $40,000,000 of the Frenchmen." When Panamanians, egged on by the French company, staged a revolution against Colombia in November 1903, he ordered the cruiser *Nashville* to Panama. Colombian government forces found themselves looking down the barrels of the guns of the *Nashville* and shortly thereafter eight other American warships. The revolution succeeded.

Roosevelt instantly recognized the new Republic of Panama. Secretary Hay and the new "Panamanian" minister, Bunau-Varilla, then negotiated a treaty granting the United States a zone ten miles wide in perpetuity, on the same terms as those rejected by Colombia. Within the Canal Zone the United States could act as "the sovereign of the territory . . . to the entire exclusion of . . . the Republic of Panama." The United States guaranteed the independence of the republic. The New Panama Canal Company then received its $40 million, including a substantial share for Bunau-Varilla.

Historians have condemned Roosevelt for his actions, and with good reason. It was not that he fomented the Panamanian revolution, for he did not. Separated from the government at Bogotá by an impenetrable jungle, the people of Panama province had long wanted to be free of Colombian rule. He sinned, rather, in his disregard of Latin American sensibilities. He referred to the Colombians as "dagoes" and insisted that he was defending "the interests of collective civilization" when he overrode their opposition to his plans.

If uncharitable, Roosevelt's analysis was not entirely inaccurate, yet it did not justify his haste in taking Panama under his wing. Throughout Latin America, especially as nationalist sentiments grew stronger, Roosevelt's intolerance and aggressiveness in the canal incident bred resentment and fear.

Table 22.1 Path to Empire, 1885–1901

Josiah Strong, *Our Country*	1885	Applied social Darwinism—"survival of the fittest"—to justify American expansion
A. T. Mahan, *The Influence of Seapower upon History*	1890	Endorsed naval power to ensure prosperity and national security
United States helped sugar planters depose Queen Liliuokalani	1893	Major step toward annexation of Hawaii
United States intervened in British dispute with Venezuela over land claims	1895	Reaffirmed the Monroe Doctrine claim to American supervision of Latin America
USS *Maine* exploded in Havana harbor	1898	Generated public pressure for war against Spain
Defeat of Spain	1898	Opened former Spanish colonies to U.S. annexation and economic penetration
U.S. annexation of Philippines	1899	United States became formal empire
"Open Door" Policy	1899	United States asserted trading rights in China
Roosevelt intervened on behalf of Panamanian independence	1903	Advanced expansive rights in Central America
Roosevelt Corollary	1904	Asserted U.S. right to military intervention in Latin America
Taft's Dollar Diplomacy	1909–1913	Encouraged U.S. government-supported investment abroad
Panama Canal opened	1914	Allowed U.S. warships to travel swiftly between Atlantic and Pacific

The first vessels passed through the canal in 1914—and American hegemony in the Caribbean expanded. Yet even in that strategically vital area there was more show than substance to American strength. The navy ruled Caribbean waters largely by default, for it lacked adequate bases in the region. In 1903, as authorized by the Cuban constitution, the United States obtained an excellent site for a base at Guantanamo Bay, but before 1914 Congress appropriated only $89,000 to develop it.

The tendency was to try to influence outlying areas without actually controlling them. Roosevelt's successor, William Howard Taft, called this policy **dollar diplomacy**, his reasoning being that economic penetration would bring stability to underdeveloped areas and power and profit to the United States without the government's having to commit troops or spend public funds.

Under Taft the State Department won a place for American bankers in an international syndicate engaged in financing railroads in Manchuria. When Nicaragua defaulted on its foreign debt in 1911, the department arranged for American bankers to reorganize Nicaraguan finances and manage the customs service. Although the government truthfully insisted that it did not "covet an inch of territory south of the Rio Grande," dollar diplomacy provoked further apprehension in Latin America. Efforts to establish similar arrangements in Honduras, Costa Rica, and Guatemala all failed. In Nicaragua orderly administration of the finances did not bring internal peace. In 1912, 2,500 American marines and sailors had to be landed to put down a revolution.

Economic penetration proceeded briskly. American investments in Cuba reached $500 million by 1920, and smaller but significant investments were made in the Dominican Republic and in Haiti. In Central America the United Fruit Company accumulated large holdings in banana plantations, railroads, and other ventures. Other firms plunged heavily into Mexico's rich mineral resources.

Imperialism without Colonies

If one defines imperialism narrowly as a policy of occupying and governing foreign lands, American imperialism lasted for an extremely short time. With trivial exceptions, all the American colonies—Hawaii, the Philippines, Guam, Puerto Rico, the Guantanamo base, and the Canal Zone—were obtained between 1898 and 1903. In retrospect it seems clear that the urge to own colonies was only fleeting; the legitimate questions raised by the anti-imperialists and the headaches connected with the management of overseas possessions soon produced a change of policy.

The objections of protectionists to the lowering of tariff barriers, the shock of the Philippine insurrection, and a growing conviction that the costs of colonial administration outweighed the profits affected American thinking. Hay's Open Door notes marked the beginning of the retreat from imperialism as thus defined, while the Roosevelt Corollary and dollar diplomacy signaled the consolidation of a new policy. Elihu Root summarized this policy as it applied to the Caribbean nations in 1905: "We do not want to take them for ourselves. We do not want any foreign nations to take them for themselves. We want to help them."

Yet imperialism can be given a broader definition. Although the United States did not seek colonies, it pursued a course that promoted American economic penetration of underdeveloped areas without the trouble of owning and controlling them. American statesmen regarded American expansion as beneficial to all concerned. They genuinely believed that they were exporting democracy along with capitalism and industrialization.

Dollar diplomacy had two main objectives, the avoidance of violence and the economic development of Latin America; it paid small heed to how peace was maintained and how the fruits of development were distributed. The policy was self-defeating, for in the long run stability depended on the support of local people, and this was seldom forthcoming.

By the eve of World War I the United States had become a world power and had assumed what it saw as a duty to guide the development of many countries with traditions far different from its own. The national psychology, if such a term has any meaning, remained fundamentally isolationist. Americans understood that their wealth and numbers made their nation strong and that geography made it virtually invulnerable. Thus they proceeded to do what they wanted to do in foreign affairs, limited more by their humanly flexible consciences than by any rational analysis of the probable consequences. This policy seemed safe enough—in 1914.

See the **Map**

World Colonial Empires, 1900
at **myhistorylab.com**

Milestones

1850	Britain and United States sign Clayton-Bulwer Treaty concerning interoceanic canal	1898	Theodore Roosevelt leads Rough Riders at Battle of San Juan Hill
			United States annexes Hawaii
1858	Commercial treaty with Japan opens several ports to American trade	1899	Hay's Open Door policy safeguards United States' access to China trade
1867	United States buys Alaska from Russia		United States annexes Philippines and becomes an empire
1871	Treaty of Washington settles *Alabama* claims		
		1900	Platt Amendment gives United States naval stations and right to intervene in Cuba
1875	Reciprocity treaty increases U.S. influence in Hawaii		
1885	Josiah Strong justifies expansionism in *Our Country*	1901	Hay-Pauncefote Treaty gives United States rights to build interoceanic canal
1890	A. T. Mahan fuels American imperialism in *The Influence of Sea Power*		
			Supreme Court's insular cases give Congress free reign over colonies
1893	United States helps sugar planters depose Queen Liliuokalani of Hawaii	1902	Europeans accept Monroe Doctrine during Venezuela bond dispute
1895	United States supports Venezuela in European border dispute over British Guiana	1904	Roosevelt Corollary to Monroe Doctrine gives United States "international police power"
1898	*Maine* explodes in Havana harbor		
	Spanish-American war breaks out	1907	"Gentlemen's Agreement" curtails Japanese immigration
	Dewey defeats Spanish fleet at Manila Bay	1914	Panama Canal opens

✓●—Study and Review at www.myhistorylab.com

Review Questions

1. The introduction to this chapter holds that American soldiers are fighting in Afghanistan in part because of American imperialism after 1890. Could Americans then have avoided imperial expansion? What factors impelled them to support imperialism?

2. On what issues did the anti-imperialists and the imperialists agree? And how did they differ?

3. How did American involvement in the Caribbean differ from the United States' approach to China and East Asia?

4. Why did McKinley choose to annex the Philippines? Was his decision a wise one?

5. How did the Roosevelt Corollary modify the Monroe Doctrine? How did Taft's policies differ from those of Roosevelt?

6. Was American imperialism from 1890–1910 chiefly beneficial or harmful to other nations? To the United States?

Key Terms

dollar diplomacy *597*
isolationism *575*
Open Door policy *593*

Platt Amendment *589*
"reconcentration"
   camps *580*

Teller Amendment *582*

Woodrow Wilson and the Great War

23

((•—[Hear the Audio Chapter 23 at myhistorylab.com

Do you know someone with TBI?

IN 2008 TOGGLE, A CHARACTER IN GARY TRUDEAU'S *DOONESBURY* comic strip, was driving a Humvee in Iraq when it was blown up by an improvised explosive device (IED). Toggle was hospitalized with traumatic brain injury (TBI), a buffeting of the brain caused by the shock waves of an explosion. By 2010 over 5,000 service members had been diagnosed with TBI, about a quarter of all combat casualties. "The Iraq war," the *Washington Post* observed, "has brought back one of the worst afflictions of World War I trench warfare: shell shock."

During World War I millions of men hunkered down in trenches surrounded by thickets of barbed wire. Before a major offensive, attacking armies hurled millions of artillery shells to pulverize such defenses. The casualties were staggering; many of the wounded suffered from shell shock—some 80,000 in the British army alone. Most never returned to active duty.

Just as American soldiers at the outset of the twenty-first century could not have imagined that they would be the victims of powerful explosions in Afghanistan and Iraq, few Americans in the early twentieth century thought it possible that they would get caught up in a war in Europe. To be sure, in the early 1900s Americans heard ominous rumblings from across the Atlantic Ocean. But even as European rivals spoke of war, none of it had much to do with American imperial interests in the Pacific and the Caribbean. But history unfolds in unpredictable ways.

In 1914 a spark ignited the powder keg of ethnic tensions in the Balkans. Soon, much of Europe was in flames. As the armies of the major powers became bogged down in a bloody stalemate, nonbelligerent nations were drawn into the conflagration. Woodrow Wilson, who had campaigned as a peace candidate, later called on the United States to go to war. Eventually he embraced it with an almost religious zeal. He recruited workers, farmers, financiers, manufacturers, minorities, and women to help in the war effort. He stamped out dissent. He also sought to take advantage of the transformations wrought by the war to promote various reforms—including the creation of an international body to mediate future conflicts. The tragedy of the Wilson years was that none of it turned out quite as he had imagined.

Wilson's "Moral" Diplomacy

Wilson did not lead the nation to war; both he and the nation stumbled into it without meaning to. Part of the reason was that Wilson's foreign relations, though well-intentioned, were often confused. He knew that the United States had no wish to injure any foreign state and assumed that all nations would recognize this fact and cooperate. Like nineteenth-century Christian missionaries, he wanted to spread the gospel of American democracy, to lift and enlighten the unfortunate and the ignorant—but in his own way.

Wilson set out to raise the moral tone of American foreign policy by denouncing dollar diplomacy. To seek special economic concessions in Latin America was "unfair" and "degrading." The United States would deal with Latin American nations "upon terms of equality and honor."

Yet Wilson sometimes failed to live up to his promises. Because of the strategic importance of the Panama Canal, he was unwilling to tolerate "unrest" anywhere in the Caribbean. Within months of his inauguration he was pursuing the same tactics employed by Roosevelt and Taft. The Bryan-Chamorro Treaty of 1914, which gave the United States an option to build a canal across Nicaragua, made that country virtually an American protectorate and served to maintain in power an unpopular dictator, Adolfo Díaz.

A much more serious example of missionary diplomacy occurred in Mexico. In 1911 a liberal coalition overthrew the dictator Porfirio Díaz, who had been exploiting the resources and people of Mexico for the benefit of a small class of wealthy landowners, clerics, and military men since the 1870s. Francisco Madero became president.

Perhaps inspired by progressive reforms in the United States, Madero proposed a liberal constitution for Mexico. But British oil magnates, who controlled most of Mexico's chief export, conspired with Victoriano Huerta, a general in Madero's army. In 1913 Huerta assassinated Madero and seized power. Britain promptly recognized Huerta's government.

The American ambassador urged Wilson to do so too, but he refused. His sympathies were with the government of Madero, whose murder had horrified him. "I will not recognize a government of butchers," he said. Wilson instead brought enormous pressure to bear against Huerta. He demanded that Huerta hold free elections as the price of American mediation in the continuing civil war. Huerta refused. The tense situation exploded in April 1914, when a small party of American sailors was arrested in the port of Tampico, Mexico. Wilson used the affair as an excuse to send troops into Mexico.

The invasion took place at Veracruz, where Winfield Scott had launched the

In 1911, Francisco Madero overthrew Mexican dictator Porfirio Diaz and established a constitutional government.

assault on Mexico City in 1847. Instead of surrendering the city, the Mexicans resisted, suffering 400 casualties before falling back. This bloodshed caused dismay throughout Latin America. Huerta, hard-pressed by Mexican opponents, fled from power.

Wilson now made a monumental blunder. He threw his support to Francisco "Pancho" Villa, one of Huerta's generals. But Villa was little more than an ambitious bandit whose only objective was personal power. In October 1915, realizing his error, Wilson abandoned Villa and backed another Mexican rebel, who drove Villa to the northern border of Mexico. In 1916 Villa stopped a train in northern Mexico and killed sixteen American passengers in cold blood. Then he crossed into New Mexico and burned the town of Columbus, killing nineteen.

Having learned the perils of intervening in Mexican politics, Wilson would have preferred to bear even this assault in silence; but public opinion forced him to send American troops under General John J. Pershing across the border in pursuit of Villa.

Villa proved impossible to catch. Cleverly he drew Pershing deeper and deeper into Mexico, which challenged Mexican sovereignty. Several clashes occurred between Pershing's men and Mexican regulars, and for a brief period in June 1916 war seemed imminent. Wilson now acted bravely and wisely. Early in 1917 he recalled Pershing's force, leaving the Mexicans to work out their own destiny.

Missionary diplomacy in Mexico had produced mixed, but in the long run beneficial, results. His bungling bred anti-Americanism in Mexico; but his opposition to Huerta strengthened the real revolutionaries, enabling the constitutionalists to consolidate power.

Europe Explodes in War

On June 28, 1914, in the Austro-Hungarian provincial capital of Sarajevo, Gavrilo Princip, a young student, assassinated the Archduke Franz Ferdinand, heir to the imperial throne. Princip was a member of the Black Hand, a Serbian terrorist organization. He was seeking to further the cause of Serbian nationalism. Instead his rash act precipitated a general European war. Within little more than a month, following a complex series of diplomatic challenges and responses, two great coalitions, the **Central Powers** (chiefly Germany, Austria-Hungary, and Ottoman Turkey) and the **Allied Powers** (chiefly Great Britain, France, and Russia), were locked in a brutal struggle that brought one era in world history to a close and inaugurated another.

> **Watch the Video**
> *The outbreak of WWI* at
> **myhistorylab.com**

The outbreak of this Great War caught Americans psychologically unprepared; few understood its significance. President Wilson promptly issued a proclamation of neutrality and asked the nation to be "impartial in thought." The almost unanimous reaction of Americans, aside from dismay, was that the conflict did not concern them.

Although most Americans hoped to keep out of the war, nearly everyone was partial to one side or the other. People of German or Austrian descent, about 8 million in number, and the nation's 4.5 million Irish Americans, motivated chiefly by hatred of the British, sympathized with the Central Powers. The majority of the people, however, influenced by bonds of language and culture, preferred an Allied victory, and when the Germans launched a mighty assault across neutral Belgium in an effort to outflank the French armies, many Americans were outraged.

As the war progressed, the Allies—especially Britain—cleverly exploited American prejudices by publishing exaggerated tales of German atrocities against Belgian civilians. A supposedly impartial study of these charges by the widely respected James Bryce, author of *The American Commonwealth,* portrayed the Germans as ruthless barbarians. The Germans also conducted a propaganda campaign in the United States, but they labored under severe handicaps and won few converts.

Freedom of the Seas

Propaganda did not basically alter American attitudes; far more important were questions arising out of trade and commerce. Under international law, neutrals could trade freely with any belligerent. Americans were prepared to do so, but because the British fleet dominated the North Atlantic, they could not. The situation was similar to the one that had prevailed during the Napoleonic Wars. The British declared nearly all commodities, even foodstuffs, to be contraband of war. They forced neutral merchant ships into British or French ports in order to search them for goods headed for the enemy. Many cargoes were confiscated, often without payment. American firms that traded with the Central Powers were "blacklisted," which meant that no British subject could deal with them. When Americans protested, the British answered that in a battle for survival, they dared not adhere to old-fashioned rules of international law.

Had the United States insisted that Great Britain abandon these "illegal" practices, as the Germans demanded, no doubt it could have had its way. The British foreign secretary, Sir Edward Grey, later admitted, "The ill-will of the United States meant certain defeat. The object of diplomacy, therefore, was to secure the maximum of blockade that could be enforced without a rupture with the United States." It is ironic that an embargo, which failed so ignominiously in Jefferson's day, would have been almost instantly effective if applied at any time after 1914, for American supplies were vital to the Allies.

Wilson faced a dilemma. To allow the British to make the rules meant siding against the Central Powers. Yet to insist on the old rules meant siding against the Allies because that would have deprived them of much of the value of their naval superiority. *Nothing* the United States might do would be truly impartial.

The immense expansion of American trade with the Allies made an embargo unthinkable. While commerce with the Central Powers fell to a trickle, that with the Allies soared from $825 million in 1914 to over $3.2 billion in 1916. An attempt to limit this commerce would have raised a storm; to have eliminated it would have caused a catastrophe. Munitions makers and other businessmen did not want the United States to enter the war. Neutrality suited their purposes admirably.

Britain and France soon exhausted their ready cash, and by early 1917 they had borrowed well over $2 billion. Although these loans violated no principle of international law, they fastened the United States more closely to the Allies' cause.

During the first months of the Great War, the Germans were not especially concerned about neutral trade or American goods because they expected to crush the Allied armies quickly. When their first swift thrust into France was blunted along the Marne River, only twenty miles from Paris, and the war became a bloody stalemate, they began to challenge the Allies' control of the seas. Unwilling to risk their battleships and cruisers against the much larger British fleet, they resorted to a new weapon, the submarine, commonly known as the U-boat (for *Unterseeboot*). German submarines played a role in World War I not unlike that of American privateers in the Revolution and the War of 1812: They ranged the seas stealthily in search of merchant ships. However, submarines could not operate under the ordinary rules of war, which required that a raider stop its prey, examine its papers and cargo, and give the crew and passengers time to get off in lifeboats before sending it to the bottom. U-boats when surfaced were vulnerable to the deck guns that many merchant ships carried; they could even be sunk by ramming, once they had stopped and put out a boarding party. Therefore, they commonly launched their torpedoes from below the surface without warning, often resulting in a heavy loss of life.

●●●—[Read the Document
Adolf K.G.E. Von Spiegal, *U-boat 202 (1919)* at **myhistorylab.com**

In February 1915 the Germans declared the waters surrounding the British Isles a zone of war and announced that they would sink without warning all enemy merchant ships encountered in the area. Since Allied vessels sometimes flew neutral flags to disguise their identity, neutral ships entering the zone would do so at their own risk. This statement was largely bluff, for the Germans had only a handful of submarines at sea; but they were feverishly building more.

Wilson—perhaps too hurriedly, considering the importance of the question—warned the Germans that he would hold them to "strict accountability" for any loss of American life or property resulting from violations of "acknowledged [neutral] rights on the high seas." He did not distinguish clearly between losses incurred through the destruction of *American* ships and those resulting from the sinking of other vessels. If he meant to hold the Germans responsible for injuries to Americans on *belligerent* vessels, he was changing international law as arbitrarily as the Germans were. Secretary of State Bryan, who opposed Wilson vigorously on this point, stood on sound legal ground when he said, "A ship carrying contraband should not rely upon passengers to protect her from attack—it would be like putting women and children in front of an army."

Correct or not, Wilson's position reflected the attitude of most Americans. It seemed barbaric to them that defenseless civilians should be killed without warning; Americans refused to surrender their "rights" as neutrals to cross the North Atlantic on any ship they wished. The depth of their feeling was demonstrated when, on May 7, 1915, the submarine *U-20* sank the British liner *Lusitania* off the Irish coast. This caused a profound and emotional reaction in the United States. The sinking of the *Lusitania* evoked the sinking of HMS *Titanic* three years earlier, after it had struck an iceberg in

NOTICE!

TRAVELLERS intending to embark on the Atlantic voyage are reminded that a state of war exists between Germany and her allies and Great Britain and her allies; that the zone of war includes the waters adjacent to the British Isles; that, in accordance with formal notice given by the Imperial German Government, vessels flying the flag of Great Britain, or of any of her allies, are liable to destruction in those waters and that travellers sailing in the war zone on ships of Great Britain or her allies do so at their own risk.

IMPERIAL GERMAN EMBASSY
WASHINGTON, D. C., APRIL 22, 1915.

Three weeks before the *Lusitania* was torpedoed, this notice appeared in the classified sections of Washington newspapers.

Titanic

James Cameron's *Titanic* (1997) was a block-buster. He made audiences feel what it was like to be on the ship. What sent a shiver down the spine was the knowledge that real people had experienced what was being depicted on the screen.

Cameron well understood the audience's craving to relive a true story. The movie opens with footage of the actual HMS *Titanic* on the floor of the Atlantic, fish gliding silently through its barnacle-encrusted wreckage. Cameron also spent scores of millions of dollars devising computer-enhanced techniques to ensure that his *Titanic* looked like the one that went down in the North Atlantic on the night of April 14–15, 1912.

But Cameron's *Titanic* was more than a disaster movie. It was also the story of two young people who fall in love. The romance begins when Jack (Leonardo DiCaprio), a struggling artist, spots Rose (Kate Winslet), a wealthy socialite, climbing over the railing and peering despondently into the water below. Obliged to marry a contemptuous (and contemptible) snob, she is miserable. Jack, from a lower deck, scrambles up and persuades her to forgo the plunge.

As a reward for saving Rose, Jack is invited to dine with Rose's table. At dinner, Rose appraises Jack more carefully—and is impressed. He looks good in a tuxedo, displays plenty of moxie, and possesses artistic talent ("Jack, you see things!").

When the ship has its close encounter of the icy kind, Jack—young, vital, alive—perishes in the frigid waters. But he has imparted to Rose a gift of love, and thus of life. This tale of young lovers, held apart by society, is a nautical "Romeo and Juliet," a brief, pure instant of love, tragically ended by death.

If Cameron's *Titanic* is a love story for the ages, it was also frozen in a particular place and in a particular time. Much as Cameron spent millions to show the ship as it really was, he took similar pains to give a convincing rendering of New York society, especially its clothing, silverware, and social conventions.

Of the latter, the most significant for the story are the elaborate rituals of Victorian courtship. Rose seeks to break free from her impending marriage partly because she despises her fiancé, but also because marriage to him constitutes the final, irreversible step into the gilded cage of a society lady. Jack's presence at dinner with the "best" of society underscores the shallow materialism of this upper crust and its preoccupation with wealth, its absurd rules of etiquette, and its repressive attitudes toward sexuality. Viewers of the movie, looking through Rose's eyes, may wonder how such rituals ever came to be.

Some had existed for centuries. The idealization of courtly love and pure womanhood was a commonplace of medieval literature. In the early nineteenth century novelist Jane Austen described the subtle interplay of money and romance in England. But the rituals of New York society in the Gilded Age were characterized by sumptuous and public displays of wealth—glittering balls and extravagant "Grand Tours" of Europe.

This new mode of courtship was largely the creation of Mrs. John Jacob Astor, wife of one of New York's wealthiest business-men, and her friends. After the Civil War, industrialization and urbanization were generating new wealth and destroying the old at a dizzying pace. While prominent businessmen and investment bankers were devising institutions to impose order on this creative industrial chaos, their wives were regulating its social elite. They endeavored to determine who should be admitted to New York's "best" families—and who should not. They concluded that it was not enough to be rich; the elite of the nation must also adhere to high standards of etiquette and decorum. Society women possessed immense power.

Leonardo DiCaprio and Kate Winslet as lovers on the *Titanic*.

Although the system was created and supervised by mature women, it demanded the compliance of adolescent girls. The process began when a wealthy mother took her daughter on a round of visits to society women, to whom they would present their "calling cards." If mother and daughter were judged suitable, they would be invited in for tea; if the girl behaved with decorum (and if her father's assets proved sound), she would be invited to balls and other formal events. At or near her sixteenth birthday, her parents would hold a ball in her honor—in New York the event usually took place at Delmonico's restaurant—marking her "debut" into society. She wore a white gown symbolizing her virginity. A male relative presented her formally to the prominent women. Now she could accept male suitors from "society."

This highly stylized—almost tribal—ritual brought young women to the threshold of womanhood. Marriage awaited beyond the door. Many eagerly anticipated the acquisition of adult status and the social power it entailed. Others regarded this rite with terror. (Novelist Edith Wharton remembered her debut as a "long cold agony of shyness.") In the early twentieth century, some young women began to rebel. Elsie Clews, daughter of a Wall Street banker, refused to wear corsets. When her mother wasn't looking, she took off her veil and white gloves. She subsequently scandalized Newport—the fashionable Rhode Island summer resort for society's wealthy—by going swimming with a young man without a chaperone (but not without a bathing suit).

To her mother's dismay, Clews delayed marriage and went to Barnard College; eventually she became a respected anthropologist (Elsie Clews Parsons).

Kate Winslet's "Rose" was, like Elsie Clews, a prematurely "modern" woman. But Clews dispensed with the rituals of courtship, not its substance. Even in the waning years of the Victorian era, few wealthy young women succumbed to impoverished men, however earnest and appealing.

Victorian courtship was necessarily protracted. Young women did not unburden themselves to strangers; and even to friends, especially of the opposite sex, the process of revealing one's inner feelings unfolded slowly, often after a series of tests and trials. One person's tentative disclosure invited a reciprocal response. Letters and diaries show that, over time, these personal revelations often led to sexual intimacies. Nowadays many people regard Victorian marriages as unfeeling and stiff, but many Victorians maintained that their personal intimacies were the more delicious for having been long delayed.

Cameron's *Titanic* looks like the past; but the heart of the movie is Jack and Rose's whirlwind romance. While Rose's story addresses some of the anxieties of young society women, it more closely resembles the courtship patterns of Hollywood today than the experiences of young people at the beginning of the last century.

Questions for Discussion

- Jack and Rose "hooked up," to use modern slang. Why was such behavior improbable among young women of wealthy families in the late nineteenth century?
- What other behaviors in the film seem anachronistic?

The *Titanic* carried only twenty lifeboats, a reason why so many perished in 1912. The *Lusitania* (above) carried forty-eight lifeboats, but it sank so quickly that many went unused.

the northern Atlantic; first-person accounts rendered the tragedy all the more vivid to Americans. When it was learned that nearly 1,200 persons, including 128 Americans, lost their lives when the *Lusitania* went down (nearly as many as had perished on the *Titanic*), Americans were outraged. (For more on the *Titanic*, see Re-Viewing the Past, pp. 606–607.)

Wilson demanded that Germany disavow the sinking, indemnify the victims, and promise to stop attacking passenger vessels. When the Germans quibbled about these points, he responded with further diplomatic correspondence rather than with an ultimatum.

In one sense this was sound policy. The Germans pointed out that they had published warnings in American newspapers saying they considered the *Lusitania* subject to attack, that the liner was carrying munitions, and that on past voyages it had flown the American flag to deceive German U-boat captains. However, after dragging the controversy out for nearly a year, Germany apologized and agreed to pay an indemnity. After the torpedoing of the French channel steamer *Sussex* in March 1916 had produced another stiff American protest, the Germans at last promised, in the *Sussex* pledge, to stop sinking merchant ships without warning.

Theodore Roosevelt urged Wilson to commit the United States to war with Germany; Wilson's refusal to do so incensed him. In November 1915 Wilson, in a belated nod to such criticisms, pressed for increased military and naval expenditures.

The Election of 1916

Wilson had won the presidency in 1912 only because the Republican party had split in two. In late 1915 he sought to broaden his support by winning over the progressives. In January 1916 he appointed Louis D. Brandeis to the Supreme Court. In addition to being an advanced progressive, Brandeis was the first Jewish Justice appointed to the Court. Wilson's action won him many friends among people who favored fair treatment for minority groups. In July Wilson bid for the farm vote by signing the Farm Loan Act to provide low-cost loans based on agricultural credit. Shortly thereafter, he approved the Keating-Owen Child Labor Act barring goods manufactured by the labor of children under 16 from interstate commerce, and a workers' compensation act for federal employees. He persuaded Congress to pass the Adamson Act establishing an eight-hour day for railroad workers, and he modified his position on the tariff by approving the creation of a tariff commission.

Each of these actions represented a sharp reversal. In 1913 Wilson had considered Brandeis too radical even for a Cabinet post. The new farm, labor, and tariff laws were all examples of the kind of "class legislation" he had refused to countenance in 1913 and 1914. Wilson was putting into effect much of the progressive platform of 1912. Although the progressive convention came out for the Republican nominee, Associate Justice Charles Evans Hughes, who had compiled a record as a progressive governor of New York, many other progressives supported Wilson.

The key issue in the campaign was American policy toward the warring powers. Wilson intended to stress preparedness, which he was now wholeheartedly supporting. However, during the Democratic convention, the delegates shook the hall with cheers whenever orators referred to the president's success in keeping the country out of the war. "He Kept Us Out of War" became the Democratic slogan.

The combination of progressivism and the peace issue placed the Democrats on substantially equal terms with the Republicans. In the end, personal factors probably tipped the balance. Hughes was very stiff and an ineffective speaker; he offended a number of important politicians, especially in crucial California, where he inadvertently snubbed the popular progressive governor, Hiram Johnson; and he equivocated on a number of issues. Nevertheless, on election night he appeared to have won, having carried nearly all the East and Midwest. Late returns gave Wilson California, however, and with it victory by the narrow margin of 277 to 254 in the Electoral College. He led Hughes in the popular vote, 9.1 million to 8.5 million.

The Road to War

Wilson's own feelings were more genuinely neutral than at any other time during the war, for the Germans had stopped sinking merchant ships without warning and the British had irritated him repeatedly by their arbitrary restrictions on neutral trade. He drafted a note to the belligerents asking them to state the terms on which they would agree to lay down their arms. Unless the fighting ended soon, he warned, neutrals and belligerents alike would be so ruined that peace would be meaningless.

When neither side responded encouragingly, Wilson, on January 22, 1917, delivered a moving speech aimed at "the people of the countries now at war" more than at their governments. Any settlement imposed by a victor, he declared, would breed hatred and more wars. There must be "peace without victory," based on the principles that all nations were equal and that every nationality should determine its own form of government. He mentioned, albeit vaguely, disarmament and freedom of the seas, and he suggested the creation of some kind of international organization to preserve world peace. This noble appeal met a tragic fate. The Germans had already decided to renounce the Sussex pledge and unleash their submarines against all vessels headed for Allied ports. After February 1, any ship in the war zone would be attacked without warning. Possessed now of more than 100 U-boats, the German military leaders had convinced themselves that they could starve the British people into submission and reduce the Allied armies to impotence by cutting off the flow of American supplies. The United States would probably declare war, but the Germans believed that they could overwhelm the Allies before the Americans could get to the battlefields in force. In 1917, after the German military leaders had made this decision, events moved relentlessly, almost uninfluenced by the actors who presumably controlled the fate of the world:

Watch the Video

American entry into WWI at **myhistorylab.com**

February 3: Housatonic is torpedoed. Wilson announces to Congress that he has severed diplomatic relations with Germany.

February 24: Walter Hines Page, United States ambassador to Great Britain, transmits to the State Department an intercepted German dispatch (the "Zimmermann telegram") revealing that Germany has proposed a secret alliance with Mexico; Mexico will receive, in the event of war with the United States, "the lost territory in Texas, New Mexico, and Arizona."

February 25: Cunard liner *Laconia* is torpedoed; two American women perish.

February 26: Wilson asks Congress for authority to arm American merchant ships.

March 1: Zimmermann telegram is released to the press.

March 4: President Wilson takes oath of office, beginning his second term.

March 9: Wilson, acting under his executive powers, orders the arming of American merchantmen.

March 12: Revolutionary provisional government is established in Russia. *Algonquin* is torpedoed.

March 15: Czar Nicholas II of Russia abdicates.

March 16: City of Memphis, *Illinois*, and *Vigilancia* are torpedoed.

March 21: New York World, a leading Democratic newspaper, calls for declaration of war on Germany. Wilson summons Congress to convene in a special session on April 2.

March 25: Wilson calls up the National Guard.

April 2: Wilson asks Congress to declare war. Germany is guilty of "throwing to the winds all scruples of humanity," he says. America must fight, not to conquer, but for "peace and justice. . . . The world must be made safe for democracy."

April 4, 6: Congress declares war—the vote, 82–6 in the Senate, 373–50 in the House.

The bare record conceals Wilson's agonizing search for an honorable alternative to war. To admit that Germany posed a threat to the United States meant confessing that interventionists had been right all along. To go to war meant, besides sending innocent Americans to their deaths, allowing "the spirit of ruthless brutality [to] enter into the very fibre of our national life."

Read the Document

United States Declaration of War (1917) at **myhistorylab.com**

The president's Presbyterian conscience tortured him. He lost sleep, appeared gray and drawn. In the end Wilson could salve his conscience only by giving intervention an

Read the Document

President Wilson's War Message to Congress (1917) at **myhistorylab.com**

idealistic purpose: the war had become a threat to humanity. Unless the United States threw its weight into the balance, Western civilization itself might be destroyed.

Mobilizing the Economy

America's entry into the Great War determined its outcome. The Allies were running out of money and supplies; their troops, decimated by nearly three years in the trenches, were exhausted, disheartened, and rebellious. In February and March 1917, U-boats sent over a million tons of Allied shipping to the bottom of the Atlantic. The outbreak of the Russian Revolution in March 1917, at first lifting the spirits of the Western democracies, led to the Bolshevik takeover under Lenin. The Russian armies collapsed; by December 1917 Russia was out of the war and the Germans were moving masses of men and equipment from the eastern front to France. Without the aid of the United States, the Allies would likely have sued for peace according to terms dictated from Berlin. Instead American men and supplies helped contain the Germans' last drives and then push them back to final defeat.

It was a close thing, for the United States entered the war little better prepared to fight than it had been in 1898. The conversion of American industry to war production had to be carried out without prearrangement. Confusion and waste resulted. The hurriedly designed shipbuilding program was an almost total fiasco. The gigantic Hog Island yard in Maine, which employed at its peak over 34,000 workers, completed its first vessel only after the war ended. Airplane, tank, and artillery construction programs developed too slowly to affect the war. The big guns that backed up American soldiers in 1918 were made in France and Great Britain; of the 8.8 million rounds of artillery ammunition fired by American troops, a mere 8,000 were manufactured in the United States. Congress authorized the manufacture of 20,000 airplanes, but only a handful, mostly British-designed planes made in America, got to France.

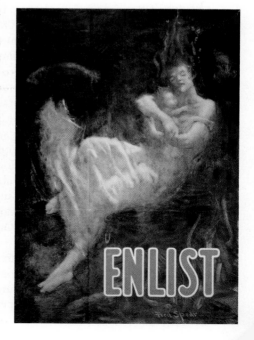

The problem of mobilization was complicated. It took Congress six weeks of hot debate merely to decide on conscription. Only in September 1917, nearly six months after the declaration of war, did the first draftees reach the training camps, and it is hard to see how Wilson could have speeded this process. He wisely supported the professional soldiers, who insisted that he resist the appeals of politicians who wanted to raise volunteer units, even rejecting, at considerable political cost, Theodore Roosevelt's offer to raise an entire army division.

"Enlist"—a poster by Fred Spear, published in June 1915 by the Boston Committee of Public Safety— evoked the drowning deaths of women and children on the *Lusitania*.

Wilson was a forceful and inspiring war leader once he grasped what needed to be done. He displayed both determination and unfailing patience in the face of frustration and criticism. Raising an army was only a small part of the job. The Allies had to be supplied with food and munitions, and immense amounts of money had to be collected.

After several false starts, Wilson placed the task in the hands of the **War Industries Board (WIB)**. The board was given almost dictatorial power to allocate scarce materials, standardize production, fix prices, and coordinate American and Allied purchasing. Evaluating the mobilization effort raises interesting historical questions. The antitrust laws were suspended and producers were encouraged, even compelled, to cooperate with one another. Government regulation went far beyond what the New Nationalists had envisaged in 1912.

As for the New Freedom variety of laissez-faire, it had no place in a wartime economy. The nation's railroads, strained by immensely increased traffic, became progressively less efficient. A monumental tie-up in December and January 1917–1918 finally persuaded Wilson to appoint Secretary of the Treasury William G. McAdoo director-general of the railroads, with power to run the roads as a single system. McAdoo's Railroad Administration pooled all railroad equipment, centralized purchasing, standardized accounting practices, and raised wages and passenger rates.

Wilson accepted the kind of government-industry agreement that he had denounced in 1912. Prices were set by the WIB at levels that allowed large profits—U.S. Steel, for example, despite high taxes, cleared over half a billion dollars in two years. It is at least arguable that producers would have turned out just as much even if compelled to charge lower prices.

Mobilization required close cooperation between business and the military. However, the army, suspicious of civilian institutions, resisted cooperating with them. Wilson finally compelled the War Department to place officers on WIB committees, laying the foundation for what was later to be known as the "industrial-military complex," an alliance between business and military leaders.

The history of industrial mobilization was the history of the entire home-front effort in microcosm: Marvels were performed, but the task was so gigantic and unprecedented that a full year passed before an efficient system had been devised, and many unforeseen results occurred.

The problem of mobilizing agricultural resources was solved more quickly, and this was fortunate because in April 1917 the British had on hand only a six-week supply of food Wilson appointed as food administrator Herbert Hoover; Hoover, a mining engineer, had headed the Belgian Relief Commission earlier in the war. Acting under powers granted by the Lever Act of 1917, Hoover set the price of wheat at $2.20 a bushel in order to encourage production. He established a government corporation to purchase the entire American and Cuban sugar crops, which he then doled out to American and British refiners. To avoid rationing he organized a campaign to persuade consumers to conserve food voluntarily. One slogan ran "If U fast U beat U boats"; another, "Serve beans by all means."

Without subjecting its own citizens to serious inconvenience, the United States increased food exports from 12.3 million tons to 18.6 million tons. Farmers, of course, profited greatly. Their real income went up nearly 30 percent between 1915 and 1918.

Workers in Wartime

With the army siphoning so many men from the labor market and with immigration reduced to a trickle, unemployment disappeared and wages rose. Although the cost of living soared, imposing hardships on people with fixed incomes, the boom produced unprecedented opportunities.

Americans, always a mobile people, pulled up their roots in record numbers. Disadvantaged groups, especially African Americans, were particularly attracted by jobs in big-city factories. Early in the conflict, the government began regulating the wages and hours of workers building army camps and manufacturing uniforms. In April 1918 Wilson created the National War Labor Board, headed by former president Taft and Frank P. Walsh, a prominent lawyer, to settle labor disputes. The board considered more than 1,200 cases and prevented many strikes. The War Labor Policies Board, chaired by Felix Frankfurter of the Harvard Law School, set wages-and-hours standards for each major war industry. Since these were determined in consultation with employers and representatives of labor, they speeded the unionization of workers by compelling management, even in antiunion industries like steel, to deal with labor leaders. Union membership rose by 2.3 million during the war.

However, the wartime emergency roused the public against strikers. While he opposed strikes that impeded the war effort, Wilson set great store in preserving the individual worker's freedom of action. It would be "most unfortunate . . . to relax the laws by which safeguards have been thrown about labor," he said. "We must accomplish the results we desire by organized effort rather than compulsion."

Paying for the War

Wilson managed the task of financing the war effectively. The struggle cost the United States about $33.5 billion, not counting pensions and other postwar expenses. About $7 billion of this was lent to the Allies,[1] but since this money was spent largely in America, it contributed to the national prosperity.

Over two-thirds of the cost of the war was met by borrowing. Five Liberty and Victory Loan drives, spurred by advertising, parades, and other appeals to patriotism, persuaded people to open their purses. Industrialists, eager to instill in their employees a sense of personal involvement in the war effort, conducted campaigns in their plants. In addition to borrowing, the government collected about $10.5 billion in taxes during the war. A steeply graduated income tax took more than 75 percent of the incomes of the wealthiest citizens. A 65 percent excess-profits tax and a 25 percent inheritance tax were also enacted. Thus although many individuals made fortunes from the war, its cost was distributed far more equitably than during the Civil War.

Americans also contributed generously to philanthropic agencies engaged in war work. Most notable, perhaps, was the great 1918 drive of the United War Work Council, an interfaith religious group, which raised over $200 million mainly to finance recreational programs for the troops overseas.

---

[1] In 1914 Americans owed foreigners about $3.8 billion. By 1919 Americans were owed $12.5 billion by Europeans alone.

Propaganda and Civil Liberties

Wilson was preeminently a teacher and preacher, a specialist in the transmission of ideas and ideals. He excelled at mobilizing public opinion and inspiring Americans to work for the better world he hoped would emerge from the war. In April 1917 he created the Committee on Public Information (CPI), headed by the journalist George Creel. Soon 75,000 speakers were deluging the country with propaganda prepared by hundreds of CPI writers. They pictured the war as a crusade for freedom and democracy, the Germans as a bestial people bent on world domination.

A large majority of the nation supported the war enthusiastically. But thousands of persons—German Americans and Irish Americans, for example; people of pacifist leanings such as Jane Addams, the founder of Hull House; and some who thought both sides in the war were wrong—still opposed American involvement. Creel's committee and a number of unofficial "patriotic" groups allowed their enthusiasm for the conversion of the hesitant to become suppression of dissent. People who refused to buy war bonds were often exposed to public ridicule and even assault. Those with German names were persecuted without regard for their views; some school boards outlawed the teaching of the German language; sauerkraut was renamed "liberty cabbage." A cartoonist pictured Senator Robert La Follette, who had opposed entering the war, receiving an Iron Cross from the German militarists, and the faculty of his own University of Wisconsin voted to censure him.

●●○─ Read the **Document**

Buffington, *Friendly Words to the Foreign Born* at **myhistorylab.com**

Although Wilson spoke in defense of free speech, his actions opposed it. He signed the **Espionage Act** of 1917, which imposed fines of up to $10,000 and jail sentences ranging to twenty years on persons convicted of aiding the enemy or obstructing recruiting, and he authorized the postmaster general to ban from the mails any material that seemed treasonable or seditious.

In May 1918, again with Wilson's approval, Congress passed the **Sedition Act,** which made "saying anything" to discourage the purchase of war bonds a crime, with the proviso that investment counselors could still offer "bona fide and not disloyal advice" to clients. The law also made it illegal to "utter, print, write, or publish any disloyal, profane, scurrilous, or abusive language" about the government, the Constitution, or the uniform of the army or navy. Socialist periodicals such as The Masses were suppressed, and Eugene V. Debs, formerly a candidate for president, was sentenced to ten years in prison for making an anti-war speech. Ricardo Flores Magón, an anarchist, was sentenced to twenty

Eugene V. Debs ("Convict #9653") was imprisoned for speaking against the war. In 1920 he ran as the Socialist candidate for president from the Atlanta federal prison, receiving nearly a million votes.

Table 23.1 Suppression of Liberties during World War I

Federal Action	Year	Consequence
Espionage Act	1917	Prohibited words or actions that would aid the enemy or obstruct recruiting efforts
Sedition Act	1918	Prohibited people from "saying anything" that might discourage purchase of war bonds or otherwise undermine the federal government or the Constitution
Schenck v. United States	1919	Supreme Court upheld limitations on free speech during times of "clear and present danger" to the nation

years in jail for publishing a statement criticizing Wilson's Mexican policy, an issue that had nothing to do with the war.

These laws went far beyond what was necessary to protect the national interest. Citizens were jailed for suggesting that the draft law was unconstitutional and for criticizing private organizations like the Red Cross and the YMCA.

The Supreme Court upheld the constitutionality of the Espionage Act in *Schenck v. United States* (1919), a case involving a man who had mailed circulars to draftees urging them to refuse to report for induction into the army. Free speech has its limits, Justice Oliver Wendell Holmes, Jr., explained. When there is a "clear and present danger" that a particular statement would threaten the national interest, it can be repressed by law. In peacetime Schenck's circulars would be permissible, but not in time of war.

The "clear and present danger" doctrine did not prevent judges and juries from interpreting the espionage and sedition acts broadly, and although in many instances higher courts overturned their decisions, this usually did not occur until after the war. The wartime repression far exceeded anything that happened in Great Britain and France. In 1916 the French novelist Henri Barbusse published *Le Feu (Under Fire)*, a graphic account of the horrors and purposelessness of trench warfare. In one chapter Barbusse described a pilot flying over the trenches on a Sunday, observing French and German soldiers at Mass in the open fields, each worshiping the same God. Yet *Le Feu* circulated freely in France and even won the coveted Prix Goncourt.

Wartime Reforms

The American mobilization experience was part and product of the Progressive Era. Many progressives believed that the war was creating the sense of common purpose that would stimulate the people to act unselfishly to benefit the poor and to eradicate social evils. Patriotism and public service seemed at last united. Secretary of War Newton D. Baker, a prewar urban reformer, expressed this attitude in supporting a federal child labor law: "We cannot afford, when we are losing boys in France, to lose children in the United States."

Men and women of this sort worked for a dozen causes only remotely related to the war effort. The women's suffrage movement was brought to fruition, as was the campaign against alcohol. Both the Eighteenth Amendment, outlawing alcoholic beverages, and the Nineteenth, giving women the vote, were adopted at least in part because of the war. Reformers began to talk about health insurance. The progressive campaign against prostitution and venereal disease gained strength, winning the enthusiastic support both of persons worried about inexperienced local girls being seduced by the soldiers and of those concerned lest prostitutes lead innocent soldiers astray. One of the latter type claimed to have persuaded "over 1,000 fallen women" to promise not to go near any army camps.

The effort to wipe out prostitution around military installations was a cause of some misunderstanding with the Allies, who provided licensed facilities for their troops as a matter of course. When the premier of France offered to supply prostitutes for American units in his country, Secretary Baker is said to have remarked, "For God's sake . . . don't show this to the President or he'll stop the war." Apparently Baker had a rather peculiar sense of humor. After a tour of the front in France, he assured an American women's group that life in the trenches was "far less uncomfortable" than he had thought and that not a single American doughboy was "living a life which he would not be willing to have [his] mother see him live."

Women and Blacks in Wartime

Although a number of prominent feminists were pacifists, most supported the war enthusiastically, moved by patriotism and the belief that opposition to the war would doom their hopes of gaining the vote. They also expected that the war would open up many kinds of high-paying jobs to women. To some extent it did; about a million women replaced men in uniform, but the numbers actually engaged in war industries were small (about 6,000 found jobs making airplanes, for example), and the gains were fleeting. When the war ended, most women who were engaged in industrial work either left their jobs voluntarily or were fired to make room for returning veterans. Some women went overseas as nurses, and a few served as ambulance drivers and YMCA workers.

Most unions were unsympathetic to the idea of enrolling women, and the government did little to encourage women to do more for the war effort than prepare bandages, knit warm clothing for soldiers, participate in food conservation programs, and encourage people to buy war bonds. The final report of another wartime agency, issued in 1919, admitted that

Women workers at the Dupont factory in Old Hickory, Tennessee, in 1917, form smokeless gunpowder into long strips, which will then be cut for use in artillery shells and other armaments.

few women war workers had been paid as much as men and that women had been promoted more slowly than men, were not accepted by unions, and were discharged promptly when the war ended.

The wartime "great migration" of southern blacks to northern cities where jobs were available brought them important economic benefits. Between 1870 and 1890 only about 80,000 blacks moved to northern cities. Compared with the influx from Europe and from northern farms, this number was inconsequential. The black proportion of the population of New York City, for example, fell from over 10 percent in 1800 to under 2 percent in 1900.

Watch the Video

The Great Migration at myhistorylab.com

Around the turn of the century, as the first postslavery generation reached maturity and as southern repression increased, the northward movement quickened—about 200,000 blacks migrated between 1890 and 1910. Then, after 1914, the war boom drew blacks north in a flood. Agents of northern manufacturers flocked into the cotton belt to recruit them in wholesale lots. Half a million made the move between 1914 and 1919. The African American population of New York City rose from 92,000 to 152,000; that of Chicago from 44,000 to 109,000; and that of Detroit from 5,700 to 41,000.

Life for the newcomers was difficult; many whites resented them; workers feared them as potential strikebreakers yet refused to admit them into their unions. In East St. Louis, Illinois, where employers had brought in large numbers of blacks in an attempt to discourage local unions from striking for higher wages, a bloody riot erupted during the summer of 1917 in which nine whites and an undetermined number of blacks were killed. As in peacetime, the Wilson administration was at worst antagonistic and at best indifferent to blacks' needs and aspirations.

Nevertheless, the blacks who moved north during the war were, as a group, infinitely better off than those they left behind. Many earned good wages and were accorded at least some human rights. They were not treated by the whites as equals, or even in most cases entirely fairly, but they could vote, send their children to decent schools, and within reasonable limits do and say what they pleased without fear of humiliation or physical attack.

There were two black regiments in the regular army and a number of black national guard units when the war began, and once these outfits were brought up to combat strength, no more volunteers were accepted. At first no blacks were conscripted; Southerners in particular found the thought of giving large numbers of guns to blacks and teaching them how to use them most disturbing. However, blacks were soon drafted, and once they were, a larger proportion of them were taken than whites. One Georgia draft board exempted more than 500 of 815 white registrants and only 6 of the 202 blacks in its jurisdiction before its members were relieved of their duties. After a riot in Texas in which black soldiers killed seventeen white civilians, black recruits were dispersed among many camps for training to lessen the possibility of trouble.

In the military service, all blacks were placed in segregated units. Only a handful were commissioned as officers. Despite the valor displayed by black soldiers in the Civil War and the large role they played in the Spanish-American War, where five blacks had won the Congressional Medal of Honor, most even those sent overseas, were assigned to labor battalions working as stevedores and common laborers. But many fought and died for their country. Altogether about 200,000 served overseas.

W. E. B. Du Bois supported the war wholeheartedly. He praised Wilson for making, at last, a strong statement against lynching, which had increased to a shocking extent during the previous decade. He even went along with the fact that the handful of black officer candidates were trained in a segregated camp. "Let us," he wrote in the Crisis, "while the war lasts, forget our special grievances and close ranks shoulder to shoulder with our fellow citizens and the allied nations that are fighting for democracy."

Many blacks condemned Du Bois's accommodationism, but most saw the war as an opportunity to demonstrate their patriotism and prove their worth. For the moment the prevailing mood was one of optimism. If winning the war would make the world safe for democracy, surely blacks in the United States would be better off when it was won. Whether or not this turned out to be so was (and still is) a matter of opinion.

Americans: To the Trenches and Over the Top

All activity on the home front had one ultimate objective: defeating the Central Powers on the battlefield. This was accomplished. The navy performed with special distinction. In April 1917, German submarines sank more than 870,000 tons of Allied shipping; after April 1918, monthly losses never reached 300,000 tons. The decision to send merchant ships across the Atlantic in convoys screened by destroyers made the reduction possible. Checking the U-boats was essential because of the need to transport American troops to Europe. Slightly more than 2 million soldiers made the voyage safely. Those who crossed on fast ocean liners were in little danger as long as the vessel maintained high speed and followed a zigzag course, a lesson learned from the *Lusitania*, whose

The Western Front, 1918 The Germans launched their great offensive in the spring and summer of 1918 with the goal of taking Paris. American troops helped hold the line at Château-Thierry and Belleau Woods. Several months later, a half million American soldiers participated in the counteroffensive that drove the Germans back to the Meuse River.

captain had neglected both precautions. Those who traveled on slower troop transports benefited from the protection of destroyers and also from the fact that the Germans concentrated on attacking supply ships. They continued to believe that inexperienced American soldiers would not be a major factor in the war.

The first units of the American Expeditionary Force (AEF), elements of the regular army commanded by General John J. Pershing, reached Paris on Independence Day, 1917. They took up positions on the front near Verdun in October. Not until the spring of 1918, however, did the "doughboys" play a significant role in the fighting, though their mere presence boosted French and British morale.

In March 1918 the Germans launched a great spring offensive, their armies strengthened by thousands of veterans who had been freed from the eastern front by the collapse of Russia. By late May they had reached a point on the Marne River near the town of Château-Thierry, only fifty miles from Paris. Early in June the AEF fought its first major engagements, driving the Germans back from Château-Thierry and Belleau Wood.

In this fighting only about 27,500 Americans saw action, and they suffered appalling losses. Nevertheless, when the Germans advanced again in the direction of the Marne in mid-July, 85,000 Americans were in the lines that withstood their charge. Then, in the major turning point of the war, the Allied armies counterattacked. Some 270,000 Americans participated, helping to flatten the German bulge between Reims and Soissons. By late August the American First Army, 500,000 strong, was poised before the Saint-Mihiel bulge, a deep extension of the German lines southeast of Verdun. On September 12 this army, buttressed by French troops, struck and in two days wiped out the salient.

Late in September began the greatest American engagement of the war. No fewer than 1.2 million doughboys plunged into the Argonne Forest. For over a month of indescribable horror they inched ahead through the tangle of the Argonne and the formidable defenses of the Hindenburg line, while to the west, French and British armies staged similar drives. In this one offensive the AEF suffered 120,000 casualties. Finally, on November 1, they broke the German center and raced toward the vital Sedan-Mézières railroad. On November 11, with Allied armies advancing on all fronts, the Germans signed the armistice, ending the fighting.

Preparing for Peace

The fighting ended on November 11, 1918, but the shape of the postwar world remained to be determined. European society had been shaken to its foundations. Confusion reigned. People wanted peace yet burned for revenge. Millions faced starvation. Other millions were disillusioned by the seemingly purposeless sacrifices of four years of horrible war. Communism—to some an idealistic promise of human betterment, to others a commitment to rational economic and social planning, to still others a danger to individual freedom, toleration, and democracy—having conquered Russia, threatened to envelop Germany and much of the defunct Austro-Hungarian Empire, perhaps even the victorious Allies. How could stability be restored? How could victory be made worth its enormous cost?

Woodrow Wilson had grasped the significance of the war while most statesmen still thought that triumph on the battlefield would settle everything automatically. As early as January 1917 he had realized that victory would be wasted if the winners permitted themselves the luxury of vengeance. Such a policy would disrupt the balance of power and lead to economic and social chaos. The victors must build a better society, not punish those they believed had destroyed the old one.

In a speech to Congress on January 8, 1918, Wilson outlined a plan, known as the **Fourteen Points**, designed to make the world "fit and safe to live in." The peace treaty should be negotiated in full view of world opinion, not in secret. It should guarantee the freedom of the seas to all nations, in war as in peacetime. It should tear down barriers to international trade, provide for a drastic reduction of armaments, and establish a colonial system that would take proper account of the interests of the native peoples concerned. European boundaries should be redrawn so that no substantial group would have to live under a government not of its own choosing.

More specifically, captured Russian territory should be restored, Belgium evacuated, Alsace-Lorraine returned to France, the heterogeneous nationalities of Austria-Hungary accorded autonomy. Italy's frontiers should be adjusted "along clearly recognizable lines of nationality," the Balkans made free, Turkey divested of its subject peoples, and an independent Polish state (with access to the Baltic Sea) created. To oversee the new system, Wilson insisted, "a general association of nations must be formed under specific covenants for the purpose of affording mutual guarantees of political independence and territorial integrity to great and small states alike."

Wilson's Fourteen Points for a fair peace lifted the hopes of people everywhere. After the guns fell silent, however, the vagueness and inconsistencies in his list became apparent. Complete national self-determination was impossible in Europe; there were too many regions of mixed population for every group to be satisfied. Self-determination, like the war itself, also fostered the spirit of nationalism that Wilson's dream of international organization, a league of nations, was designed to de-emphasize. Furthermore, the Allies had made territorial commitments to one another in secret treaties that ran counter to the principle of self-determination, and they were not ready to give up all claims to Germany's colonies. Freedom of the seas in wartime posed another problem; the British flatly refused to accept the idea. In every Allied country, millions rejected the idea of a peace without indemnities. They expected to make the enemy pay for the war.

Wilson assumed that the practical benefits of his program would compel opponents to fall in line. He had the immense advantage of seeking nothing for his own country and the additional strength of being leader of the one important nation to emerge from the war richer and more powerful than it had been in 1914.

Yet this combination of altruism, idealism, and power was his undoing; it intensified his tendency to be overbearing and undermined his judgment. He had never found it easy to compromise. Now, believing that the fate of humanity hung on his actions, he was unyielding. Always a preacher, he became in his own mind a prophet—almost, one fears, a kind of god.

In the last weeks of the war Wilson proved to be a brilliant diplomat, first dangling the Fourteen Points before the German people to encourage them to overthrow Kaiser Wilhelm II and sue for an armistice, then sending Colonel House to Paris to persuade Allied leaders to accept the Fourteen Points as the basis for the peace. When the Allies raised objections, House made small concessions, but by hinting that the United States might make a separate peace with Germany, he forced them to agree. Under the armistice, Germany had to withdraw behind the Rhine River and surrender its submarines, together with quantities of munitions and other materials. In return it received the assurance of the Allies that the Wilsonian principles would prevail at the Paris peace conference.

Wilson then came to a daring decision: He would personally attend the conference as a member of the United States Peace Commission. This was a precedent-shattering step, for no president had ever left American territory while in office.

Wilson probably erred in going to Paris, but not because of the novelty or possible illegality of the act. By going, he was turning his back on obvious domestic problems. Western farmers believed that they had been discriminated against during the war, since wheat prices had been controlled while southern cotton had been allowed to rise unchecked from seven cents a pound in 1914 to thirty-five cents in 1919. The administration's drastic tax program had angered many businessmen. Labor, despite its gains, was restive in the face of reconversion to peacetime conditions.

Wilson had increased his political difficulties by making a partisan appeal for the election of a Democratic Congress in 1918. Republicans, who had in many instances supported his war program more loyally than the Democrats, considered the action a gross affront. The appeal failed; the Republicans won majorities in both houses. Wilson appeared to have been repudiated at home at the very moment that he set forth to represent the nation abroad. Most important, Wilson intended to break with the isolationist tradition and bring the United States into a league of nations. Such a revolutionary change would require explanation; he should have undertaken a major campaign to convince the American people of the wisdom of this step.

The Paris Peace Conference and the Versailles Treaty

Wilson arrived in Europe a world hero. When the conference settled down to its work, control quickly fell into the hands of the so-called Big Four: Wilson, Prime Minister David Lloyd George of Great Britain, Premier Georges Clemenceau of France, and Prime Minister Vittorio Orlando of Italy. Wilson stood out in this group but did not dominate it. His principal advantage in the negotiations was his untiring industry. He alone of the leaders tried to master all the complex details of the task.

The seventy-eight-year-old Clemenceau cared only for one thing: French security. He viewed Wilson cynically, saying that since mankind had been unable to keep God's Ten Commandments, it was unlikely to do better with Wilson's Fourteen Points. Lloyd George's approach was pragmatic and almost cavalier.

Europe before the Great War In 1914, five countries dominated Europe: the German Empire, France, Great Britain, Austria-Hungary, and Russia.

Europe after the Great War The Versailles Treaty and other postwar settlements punished the losers, especially Germany and Austria-Hungary, transferring their lands to newly-created nations in eastern Europe, such as Poland, Czechoslovakia, and Yugoslavia.

He sympathized with much that Wilson was trying to accomplish but found the president's frequent sermonettes about "right being more important than might, and justice being more eternal than force" incomprehensible. "If you want to succeed in politics," Lloyd George advised a British statesman, "you must keep your conscience well under control." Orlando, clever, cultured, a believer in international cooperation but inflexible where Italian national interests were concerned, was not the equal of his three colleagues in influence. He left the conference in a huff when they failed to meet all his demands.

The conference labored from January to May 1919 and finally brought forth the Versailles Treaty. American liberals whose hopes had soared at the thought of a peace based on the Fourteen Points found the document abysmally disappointing.

The peace settlements failed to carry out the principle of self-determination completely. They gave Italy a large section of the Austrian Tyrol, though the area contained 200,000 people who considered themselves Austrians. Other German-speaking groups were incorporated into the new states of Poland and Czechoslovakia.

The victors forced Germany to accept responsibility for having caused the war—an act of senseless vindictiveness as well as a gross oversimplification—and to sign a "blank check," agreeing to pay for all damage to civilian properties and even future pensions and other indirect war costs. This reparations bill, as finally determined, amounted to $33 billion. Instead of attacking imperialism, the treaty attacked German imperialism; instead of seeking a new international social order based on liberty and democracy, it created a great-power entente designed to crush Germany and to exclude Bolshevik Russia from the family of nations.

Wilson himself backtracked on his pledge to honor the right of self-determination. For centuries, most Arabs had lived under the Turkish rulers of the Ottoman Empire. When the Ottoman Empire joined Germany and Austria-Hungary in World War I, Arab nationalists looked to the Allies and eventually worked out a deal with Britain. In return for Arab military support against the Ottoman Empire and the Germans, Britain would endorse Arab independence after the war. Wilson seemingly concurred, for Point Twelve of his Fourteen Points called for the "autonomous development" of Arab peoples. But in 1917 the British issued the Balfour Declaration in support of "a national home" for the Jewish people in Palestine, land mostly occupied by Palestinian Arabs. How could Palestinian Arabs be granted independence if Palestine was to become the home of Jewish settlers?

In the postwar negotiations, Britain retreated from its earlier promise to the Arabs. Wilson, too, had second thoughts about granting the Arab peoples self-determination.

Ottoman Empire and the Arab World, 1914 In 1914, the Ottoman Empire, also known as Turkey, controlled much of the Arab world, stretching from the Persian Gulf to the Red Sea.

Secretary of State Lansing worried about the "danger of putting such ideas into the minds of certain races," particularly the "Mohammedans [Muslims] of Syria and Palestine." Wilson reluctantly deleted explicit references to self-determination from the postwar settlements. Rather than grant the Arab peoples independence, Britain and France themselves seized Arab lands that had been ruled by the Turks. This land grab was "legalized" through the device of a mandate to rule the region issued by the League of Nations.

Similarly, Ho Chi Minh, a young Vietnamese nationalist, was embittered by the failure at Versailles to deliver his people from French colonial rule. He decided to become a communist revolutionary. The repercussions of Arab and Vietnamese discontent, though far removed from American interests at the time, would be felt in full force much later.

To those who had taken Wilson's "peace without victory" speech and the Fourteen Points literally, the Versailles Treaty seemed an abomination. The complaints of the critics were individually reasonable, yet their conclusions were not entirely fair. The new map of Europe left fewer people on "foreign" soil than in any earlier period of history. Although the Allies seized the German colonies, they were required, under the mandate system, to render the **League of Nations** annual accounts of their stewardship and to prepare the inhabitants for eventual independence. Above all, Wilson had persuaded the powers to incorporate the League of Nations in the treaty.

Wilson expected the League of Nations to make up for all the inadequacies of the Versailles Treaty. Once the League had begun to function, problems like freedom of the seas and disarmament would solve themselves, he argued, and the relaxation of trade barriers would surely follow. The League would arbitrate international disputes, act as a central body for registering treaties, and employ military and economic sanctions against aggressor nations. Each member promised (Article 10) to protect the "territorial integrity" and "political independence" of all other members. No nation could be made

Dismantling the Ottoman Empire, 1919–1920 The Ottoman Empire was the biggest loser at Versailles: It lost everything apart from Turkey itself; but the Arab nationalists lost as well, because Britain and France, through League-appointed mandates, took control of Syria, Transjordan, Palestine, and Mesopotamia (Iraq).

to go to war against its will, but Wilson emphasized that all were morally obligated to carry out League decisions. By any standard, Wilson had achieved a remarkably moderate peace, one full of hope for the future. Except for the war guilt clause and the heavy reparations imposed on Germany, he could be justly proud of his work.

The Senate Rejects the League of Nations

When Wilson returned from France, he finally directed his attention to the task of winning public approval of his handiwork. A large majority of the people probably favored the League of Nations in principle, though few understood all its implications or were entirely happy with every detail. Wilson had persuaded the Allies to accept certain changes in the original draft to mollify American opposition. No nation could be forced to accept a colonial mandate, and "domestic questions" such as tariffs, the control of immigration, and the Monroe Doctrine were excluded from League control.

Many senators found these modifications insufficient. Even before the peace conference ended, thirty-seven Republican senators signed a manifesto, devised by Henry Cabot Lodge of Massachusetts, opposing Wilson's League and demanding that the question of an international organization be put off until "the urgent business of negotiating peace terms with Germany" had been completed. Wilson rejected this suggestion icily. Further alterations were out of the question. Thus the stage was set for a monumental test of strength between the president and the Republican majority in the Senate.

Partisanship, principle, and prejudice clashed mightily in this contest. A presidential election loomed. Should the League prove a success, the Republicans wanted to be able to claim a share of the credit, but Wilson had refused to allow them to participate

Despite Wilson's serving as mother hen, the League of Nations never hatched.

in drafting the document. This predisposed all of them to favor changes. Politics aside, genuine alarm at the possible sacrifice of American sovereignty to an international authority led many Republicans to urge modification of the League covenant, or constitution. Yet the noble purpose of the League made many reluctant to reject it entirely. The intense desire of the people to have an end to the long war made Republican leaders hesitate before voting down the Versailles Treaty, and they could not reject the League without rejecting the treaty.

Wilson could count on the Democratic senators almost to a man, but he had to win over many Republicans to obtain the two-thirds majority necessary for ratification. Republican opinion divided roughly into three segments. At one extreme were some dozen "irreconcilables," led by the shaggy-browed William E. Borah of Idaho, an able and kindly person of progressive leanings but an uncompromising isolationist. Borah claimed that he would vote against the League even if Jesus Christ returned to earth to argue in its behalf, and most of his followers were equally inflexible. At the other extreme stood another dozen "mild" reservationists who were in favor of the League but who hoped to alter it in minor ways, chiefly for political purposes. In the middle were the "strong" reservationists, senators willing to go along with the League only if American sovereignty were fully protected and if it were made clear that their party had played a major role in fashioning the final document.

Senator Lodge, the leader of the Republican opposition, was an intensely partisan individual. He possessed a keen intelligence, a mastery of parliamentary procedure, and, as chairman of the Senate Foreign Relations Committee, a great deal of power. Although not an isolationist, he had little faith in the League. He also had a profound distrust of Democrats, especially Wilson, whom he considered a hypocrite and a coward. While perfectly ready to see the country participate actively in world affairs, Lodge insisted that its right to determine its own best interests in every situation be preserved. When a Democratic president tried to ram the Versailles Treaty down the Senate's throat, he fought him with every weapon he could muster.

Lodge belonged to the strong reservationist faction. His own proposals, known as the Lodge Reservations, fourteen in number to match Wilson's Fourteen Points, limited U.S. obligations to the League and stated in unmistakable terms the right of Congress to decide when to honor these obligations. Some of the reservations were mere quibbles. Others, such as the provision that the United States would not endorse Japan's seizure of Chinese territory, were included mainly to embarrass Wilson by pointing out compromises he had made at Versailles. The most important reservation applied to Article Ten of the League

Read the Document

Henry Cabot Lodge's Objections to the Treaty of Versailles at **myhistorylab.com**

covenant, which committed signatories to protect the political independence and territorial integrity of all member nations. Wilson had rightly called Article Ten "the heart of the Covenant." One of Lodge's reservations made it inoperable so far as the United States was concerned "unless in any particular case the Congress . . . shall by act or joint resolution so provide."

Lodge performed brilliantly, if somewhat unscrupulously, in uniting the three Republican factions behind his reservations. He got the irreconcilables to agree to them by conceding their right to vote against the final version in any event, and he held the mild reservationists in line by modifying some of his demands and stressing the importance of party unity. Reservations—as distinct from amendments—would not have to win the formal approval of other League members. In addition, the Lodge proposals dealt forthrightly with the problem of reconciling traditional concepts of national sovereignty with the new idea of world cooperation. Supporters of the League could accept them without sacrifice of principle. Wilson, however, refused to agree.

This foolish intransigence seems almost incomprehensible in a man of Wilson's intelligence and political experience. In part his hatred of Lodge accounts for it, in part his faith in his League. His physical condition in 1919 also played a role. At Paris he had suffered a violent attack of indigestion that was probably a symptom of a minor stroke. Thereafter, many observers noted small changes in his personality, particularly increased stubbornness and a loss of good judgment. Instead of making concessions, the president set out early in September on a nationwide speaking crusade to rally support for the League. In three weeks, Wilson traveled some 10,000 miles by train and gave forty speeches, some of them brilliant. On September 25, after an address in Pueblo, Colorado, he collapsed. A few days later, in Washington, he suffered a severe stroke that partially paralyzed his left side.

For nearly two months the president was almost totally cut off from affairs of state, leaving supporters of the League leaderless while Lodge maneuvered the reservations through the Senate. Gradually, popular attitudes toward the League shifted. The arguments of the irreconcilables persuaded many citizens that Wilson had made too sharp a break with America's isolationist past and that the Lodge Reservations were therefore necessary. Other issues connected with the reconversion of society to a peacetime basis increasingly occupied the public mind.

A coalition of Democratic and moderate Republican senators could easily have carried the treaty. That no such coalition was organized was Wilson's fault. Lodge obtained the simple majority necessary to add his reservations to the treaty merely by keeping his own party united. When the time came for the final roll call on November 19, Wilson, bitter and emotionally distraught, urged the Democrats to vote for rejection. "Better a thousand times to go down fighting than to dip your colors to dishonorable compromise," he explained to his wife. Thus the amended treaty failed, thirty-five to fifty-five, the irreconcilables and the Democrats voting against it. Lodge then allowed the original draft without his reservations to come to a vote. Again the result was defeat, thirty-eight to fifty-three. Only one Republican cast a ballot for ratification.

Dismayed but not yet crushed, friends of the League in both parties forced reconsideration of the treaty early in 1920. Neither Lodge nor Wilson would yield an inch. Lodge, who had little confidence in the effectiveness of any league of nations, was under no compulsion to compromise. Wilson, who believed that the League was the world's best hope, did have such a compulsion. Yet he would not compromise either, and this ensured the treaty's defeat.

Wilson's behavior is further evidence of his physical and mental decline. Had he died or stepped down, the treaty, with reservations, would almost certainly have been ratified. When the Senate balloted again in March, half the Democrats voted for the treaty with the Lodge Reservations. The others, mostly southern party regulars, joined the irreconcilables. Together they mustered thirty-five votes, seven more than the one-third that meant defeat.

The Red Scare

Business boomed in 1919 as consumers spent wartime savings on cars, homes, and other goods that had been in short supply during the conflict. But temporary shortages caused inflation; by 1920 the cost of living stood at more than twice the level of 1913. Workers demanded that their wages be increased as well. The unions, grown strong during the war, struck for wage increases. Over four million workers, one in five in the labor force, were on strike at some time during 1919.

The activities of radicals in the labor movement led millions of citizens to associate unionism and strikes with the new threat of communist world revolution. Although there were only a relative handful of communists in the United States, Russia's experience persuaded many that a tiny minority of ruthless revolutionaries could take over a nation of millions if conditions were right. Communists appointed themselves the champions of workers; labor unrest attracted them magnetically. When strikes broke out, some accompanied by violence, many people interpreted them as communist-inspired preludes to revolution.

But organized labor in America had seldom been truly radical. The Industrial Workers of the World (IWW) had made little impression in most industries. But some labor leaders had been attracted to socialism, and many Americans failed to distinguish between the common ends sought by communists and socialists and the entirely different methods by which they proposed to achieve those ends. When a general strike paralyzed Seattle in February 1919, the fact that a procommunist had helped organize it sent shivers down countless conservative spines. When the radical William Z. Foster began a drive to organize the steel industry at about this time, the fears became more intense. In September 1919 a total of 343,000 steelworkers walked off their jobs, and in the same month the Boston police went on strike. Violence marked the steel strike, and the suspension of police protection in Boston led to looting and fighting that ended only when Governor Calvin Coolidge called out the National Guard.

During the same period a handful of terrorists caused widespread alarm by attempting to murder various prominent persons, including John D. Rockefeller, Justice Oliver Wendell Holmes Jr., and Attorney General A. Mitchell Palmer. Although the terrorists were anarchists and anarchism had little in common with communism, many citizens lumped all extremists together and associated them with a monstrous assault on society.

What aroused the public even more was the fact that most radicals were not American citizens. Wartime fear of alien saboteurs easily transformed itself into peacetime terror of foreign radicals. In place of Germany, the enemy became the lowly immigrant, usually an Italian or a Jew or a Slav and usually an industrial worker. In this muddled way, radicalism, unionism, and questions of racial and national origins combined to make many Americans believe that their way of life was in imminent danger. That few immigrants were radicals, that most workers had no interest in communism, and that the extremists themselves were faction-ridden and irresolute did not affect conservative thinking. From all over the country came demands that radicals be ruthlessly suppressed. Thus the **"red scare"** was born.

Attorney General Palmer was the key figure in the resulting purge. He had been a typical progressive, a supporter of the League of Nations and such reforms as woman suffrage and child labor legislation. But pressure from Congress and his growing conviction that the communists really were a menace led him to join the "red hunt." Soon he was saying of the radicals, "Out of the sly and crafty eyes of many of them leap cupidity, cruelty, insanity, and crime; from their lopsided faces, sloping brows, and misshapen features may be recognized the unmistakable criminal type."

In August 1919, Palmer established within the Department of Justice the General Intelligence Division, headed by J. Edgar Hoover, to collect information about clandestine radical activities. In November, Justice Department agents in a dozen cities swooped down on the meeting places of an anarchist organization known as the Union of Russian Workers. More than 650 persons, many of them unconnected with the union, were arrested but in only forty-three cases could evidence be found to justify deportation.

Nevertheless, the public reacted so favorably that Palmer, thinking now of winning the 1920 Democratic presidential nomination, planned an immense roundup of communists. He obtained 3,000 warrants, and on January 2, 1920, his agents, reinforced by local police and self-appointed vigilantes, struck simultaneously in thirty-three cities.

About 6,000 persons were taken into custody, many of them citizens and therefore not subject to the deportation laws, many others unconnected with any radical cause. Some were held incommunicado for weeks while the authorities searched for evidence against them. In a number of cases, individuals who went to visit prisoners were themselves thrown behind bars on the theory that they too must be communists. Hundreds of suspects were jammed into filthy "bullpens," beaten, and forced to sign "confessions."

The public tolerated these wholesale violations of civil liberties because of the supposed menace of communism. Gradually, however, protests began to be heard, first from lawyers and liberal magazines, then from a wider segment of the population. No revolutionary outbreak had taken place. Of 6,000 seized in the Palmer raids, only 556 proved liable to deportation. The widespread ransacking of communists' homes and meeting places produced mountains of inflammatory literature but only three pistols.

Palmer, attempting to maintain the crusade, announced that the radicals planned a gigantic terrorist demonstration for May Day, 1920. In New York and other cities thousands of police were placed on round-the-clock duty; federal troops stood by anxiously. But the day passed without even a rowdy meeting. Suddenly Palmer appeared ridiculous. The red scare swiftly subsided.

The Election of 1920

Wilson still hoped for vindication at the polls in the presidential election, which he sought to make a "great and solemn referendum" on the League. He would have liked to run for a third term, but in his enfeebled condition he attracted no support among Democratic leaders. The party nominated James M. Cox of Ohio.

Cox favored joining the League, but the election did not produce the referendum on the new organization that Wilson desired. The Republicans, whose candidate was another Ohioan, Senator Warren G. Harding, equivocated shamelessly on the issue.

The election turned on other matters, largely emotional. Disillusioned by the results of the war, many Americans had their fill of idealism. They wanted, apparently, to end the long period of moral uplift and reform agitation that had begun under Theodore Roosevelt and return to what Harding called "normalcy."

To the extent that the voters were expressing opinions on Wilson's League, their response was overwhelmingly negative. Senator Harding, a strong reservationist, swept the country, winning over 16.1 million votes to Cox's 9.1 million. In July 1921, Congress formally ended the war with the Central Powers by passing a joint resolution.

The defeat of the League was a tragedy both for Wilson, whose crusade for a world order based on peace and justice ended in failure, and for the world, which was condemned to endure another, still more horrible and costly war. Perhaps this dreadful outcome could not have been avoided. Had Wilson compromised and Lodge behaved like a statesman instead of a politician, the United States would have joined the League, but it might well have failed to respond when called on to meet its obligations. As events soon demonstrated, the League powers acted timidly and even dishonorably when challenged by aggressor nations.

Yet it might have been different had the Senate ratified the Versailles Treaty. What was lost when the treaty failed was not peace but the possibility of peace, a tragic loss indeed.

Milestones

Year	Event	Year	Event
1914	United States invades Veracruz, Mexico	1918	Sedition Act limits freedom of speech
	Great War begins in Europe		Wilson announces Fourteen Points
1915	German U-boat torpedoes *Lusitania*		Republicans gain control of both houses of Congress
1916	Wilson appoints Louis D. Brandeis to Supreme Court		Armistice ends the Great War
	Adamson Act gives railroad workers eight-hour day	1918–1919	Flu epidemic kills 600,000 Americans
	"Pancho" Villa burns Columbus, New Mexico	1919	Steel workers strike
	Wilson is reelected president		Red scare culminates in Palmer raids
1917	Germany resumes unrestricted submarine warfare		Big Four meet at Paris Peace Conference
	Russian Revolution begins		Senate rejects Versailles Treaty and League of Nations
	United States declares war on Central Powers		Wilson wins Nobel Peace Prize, suffers massive stroke
	Bernard Baruch heads War Industries Board	1920	Senate again rejects Versailles Treaty and League of Nations
	Former President Taft heads War Labor Board		Warren Harding is elected president

✓•—Study and Review at **www.myhistorylab.com**

Review Questions

1. The chapter's introduction draws a parallel between the American efforts to fight terrorism in Afghanistan and Iraq and Woodrow Wilson's crusade to make the world "safe for democracy." Does the history of American involvement in World War I teach any "lessons" about foreign wars?

2. Why did Woodrow Wilson recommend neutrality at the outset of the European war and why did he change his mind?

3. Did progressivism play a role in leading the United States into World War I? Did it shape how the war was waged?

4. What problems did the United States encounter in mobilizing for war? How did the war effort contribute to the growth of the American state?

5. How did the war affect minorities and women? How did it restrict dissent and labor?

6. What were the arguments for and against American ratification of the League of Nations?

Key Terms

Allied Powers *603*
Central Powers *603*
Espionage Act *614*

Fourteen Points *620*
League of Nations *623*
"red scare" *628*

Sedition Act *614*
War Industries Board (WIB) *612*

Postwar Society and Culture: Change and Adjustment

24

((•─Hear the Audio Chapter 24 at myhistorylab.com

Do you drink too much?

MANY COLLEGE STUDENTS DRINK—A LOT. IN 2008 THE NATIONAL CENTER on Addiction and Substance Abuse (CASA) at Columbia University found that 44 percent of college students were binge-drinkers and that nearly one in four fulfilled the medical criteria for substance abuse. In 2010 the National Institute on Alcohol Abuse and Alcoholism reported that alcohol annually caused nearly 100,000 sexual assaults and date rapes and 1,700 deaths of college students.

"It's time to get the 'high' out of higher education," declared Joseph A. Califano, president of CASA and former U.S. secretary of health, education, and welfare. He blamed college administrators for condoning a "college culture of abuse." Campaigns to promote responsible drinking accomplished little, he noted. The only effective strategy was campus-wide prohibition.

But such words caused many to bristle. In 2010, after Iowa City banned those under twenty-one from bars, the *Daily Iowan* at the University of Iowa claimed that "harsh restrictions on alcohol drive the behavior underground, pushing young people to use more hard liquor in unsupervised private house parties." "Let's not repackage the Prohibition Era of the 1920s," the article concluded. When the University of Hawaii considered banning alcohol at the football stadium, another professor cited the nation's experience with Prohibition eighty years earlier. "You cannot root out the drinking of alcohol by outlawing it," he added.

The Prohibition Era was in many ways a response to unsettling social changes. The flood of immigration during the early 1900s had strained the nation's social fabric, especially in cities. Young women were challenging traditional gender roles. African Americans were leaving the South in droves and demanding rights that had been long deferred. Gays were becoming visible—at least to each other. Movies and radio, and even artists and writers, stimulated a rebellious youth culture. Advertising encouraged people to lose themselves in the delights of consumption.

These transformations also elicited opposition. The federal government curtailed immigration and cracked down on foreign-born radicals. The Ku Klux Klan reemerged to intimidate immigrants and blacks. Traditionalists inveighed against the enticements of popular culture and decline in faith. Prohibition was only the most visible expression of a reaction against social and cultural change.

Closing the Gates to New Immigrants

In 1921 Congress, reflecting a widespread prejudice against a huge influx of eastern and southern European immigrants, passed an emergency act establishing a quota system. Each year 3 percent of the number of foreign-born residents of the United States in 1910 (about 350,000 persons) might enter the country. Each country's quota was based on the number of its nationals in the United States in 1910. This meant that only a relative handful of the total would be from southern and eastern Europe. In 1924 the quota was reduced to 2 percent and the base year shifted to 1890, thereby lowering further the proportion of southern and eastern Europeans admitted.

In 1929 Congress established a system that allowed only 150,000 immigrants a year to enter the country. Each national quota was based on the supposed origins of the entire white population of the United States in 1920, not merely on the foreign-born.

The system was complicated and unscientific, for no one could determine with accuracy the "origins" of millions of citizens. More seriously, it ignored America's long history of constantly changing ethnic diversity. The motto *E Pluribus Unum*—Out of Many, One—conceived to represent the unity of the original thirteen states, applied even more appropriately to the blending of different cultures into one nationality. The new law sought to freeze the mix.

The law reduced actual immigration to far below 150,000 a year. Between 1931 and 1939, for example, only 23,000 British immigrants came to the United States, far below Britain's annual quota of 65,000. Meanwhile, hundreds of thousands of southern and eastern Europeans waited for admission.

The United States had closed the gates. The **National Origins Act** caused the foreign-born percentage of the population to fall from about 13 percent in 1920 to 4.7 percent in 1970. Instead of an open, cosmopolitan society eager to accept, in Emma Lazarus's stirring line, the "huddled masses yearning to breathe free," America now became committed to preserving a homogeneous, "Anglo-Saxon" population.

Distaste for the "new" immigrants from eastern Europe, many of whom were Jewish, expanded into a more general anti-Semitism in the 1920s. American Jews, whether foreign-born or native, were subjected to increasing discrimination, not because they were slow in adopting

"Give me your tired, your poor, your huddled masses yearning to breathe free, the wretched refuse of your teeming shore"—these words of Emma Lazarus, inscribed at the base of the Statue of Liberty, tell only part of the story. Most immigrants were young and hopeful, like this family at Ellis Island; many were resolute and ambitious. The restriction of immigration during the 1920s, conceived to exclude misfits, also deprived the nation of people such as these.

American ways but because many of them were getting ahead in the world somewhat more rapidly than expected. Prestigious colleges like Harvard, Yale, and Columbia that had in the past admitted Jews based on their academic records now imposed unofficial but effective quotas. Medical schools also established quotas, and no matter how talented, most young Jewish lawyers and bankers could find places only in so-called "Jewish" firms.

New Urban Social Patterns

The census of 1920 revealed that for the first time a majority of Americans (54 million in a population of 106 million) lived in "urban" rather than "rural" places. These figures are somewhat misleading because the census classified anyone in a community of 2,500 or more as urban. Of the 54 million "urban" residents in 1920, over 16 million lived in villages and towns of fewer than 25,000 persons and the evidence suggests strongly that a large majority of them held ideas and values more like those of rural citizens than like those of city dwellers. But the truly urban Americans, the one person in four who lived in a city of 100,000 or more, were increasing steadily in number and influence. More than 19 million persons moved from farms to cities in the 1920s, and the population living in centers of 100,000 or more increased by about a third.

The urban environment transformed family structure, educational opportunities, and dozens of other aspects of human existence. Indeed, since most of the changes in the relations of husbands, wives, and children that had occurred in the nineteenth century were related to the fact that people were leaving farms to work in towns and cities, these trends continued and were intensified in the early twentieth century as more and more people settled in urban centers.

Earlier differences between working-class and middle-class family structures persisted. In 1920 about a quarter of the American women who were working were married, but less than 10 percent of all married women were working. Middle-class married women who worked were nearly all either childless or highly paid professionals who were able to employ servants. Most male skilled workers now earned enough to support a family in

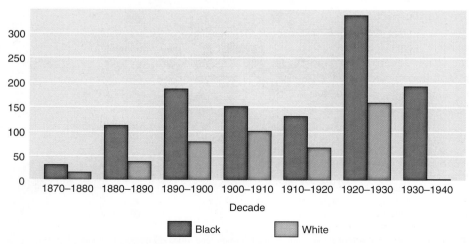

Black and White Out-Migration from Virginia and North and South Carolina, 1870–1940

modest comfort so long as they could work steadily, but an unskilled laborer still could not. Wives in most such families helped out, usually by taking in laundry or sewing.

By the 1920s the idea of intrafamily democracy had emerged. In such families, husbands and wives would deal with each other as equals; given existing conditions, this meant sharing housework and childcare, downplaying male authority, and stressing mutual satisfaction in sexual and other matters. On the one hand, they should be friends and lovers, not merely housekeepers, earners of money, and producers of children. On the other hand, advocates of these companionate relationships believed that there was nothing particularly sacred about marriage; divorce should be made easier for couples that did not get along, provided they did not have children.

Much attention was given to "scientific" child-rearing. Childcare experts agreed that routine medical examinations and good nutrition were of central importance, but they were divided about how the socialization and psychological development of the young should be handled. One school stressed rigid training. Children could be "spoiled" by indulgence; toilet training should begin early in infancy; thumb sucking should be suppressed; too much kissing could turn male youngsters into "mama's boys." Another school favored a more permissive approach. Toilet training could wait; parents should pay attention to their children's expressed needs, not impose a generalized set of rules on them.

Population Losses in the South The graph shows that whites and especially blacks were leaving the South in large numbers, especially during the 1920s. The map shows that while many urban areas in the South gained population, most rural areas lost population.

The growth of large cities further loosened social constraints on sexuality. Amidst the sea of people that surged down the streets or into the subways, the solitary individual acquired a freedom derived from anonymity. (For further perspective on urban life, see Re-Viewing the Past, *Chicago*, pp. 638–639.) Homosexuals, in particular, developed a set of identifying signals and fashioned a distinctive culture in parks, cafeterias, nightclubs, and rooming houses of big cities.

The Younger Generation

The 1920s has been described as the Jazz Age, the era of "flaming youth," when young people danced to syncopated "African" rhythms, careened about the countryside in automobiles in search of pleasure and forgetfulness, and made gods of movie stars and professional athletes. This view of the period bears a superficial resemblance to reality. "Younger people," one observer noted in 1922, were attempting "to create a way of life free from the bondage of an authority that has lost all meaning." But if they differed from their parents and grandparents, it was primarily because young people were adjusting to more profound and more rapid changes in their world than their grandparents could have imagined.

Trends that were barely perceptible during the Progressive Era now reached avalanche proportions. This was particularly noticeable in relationships between the sexes. Courtship, for example, was transformed. In the late nineteenth century, a typical young man "paid a call" on a female friend. He met and conversed with her parents, perhaps over coffee and cookies. The couple remained at home, the parents nearby if not actually participating in what was essentially a social event held in a private place.

By the 1920s paying calls was being replaced by *dating*; the young man called only to "pick up" his "date," to go off, free of parental supervision, to whatever diversion they wished. There is no question that for young people of the 1920s, relations between the sexes were becoming more relaxed and uninhibited. Respectable young women smoked cigarettes, something previously done in public only by prostitutes and bohemian types. They cast off heavy corsets, wore lipstick and "exotic" perfumes, and shortened both their hair and their skirts, the latter rising steadily from instep to ankle to calf to knee and beyond as the decade progressed. For decades female dressmakers and beauty salon proprietors had sold their own beauty products. By 1920, however, new cosmetic corporations, managed primarily by men, appropriated the products and marketing strategies of local women entrepreneurs and catered to national mass markets.

Freudian psychology and the more accessible ideas of the British "sexologist" Havelock Ellis reached steadily deeper into the popular psyche. Since sex was "the central function of life," Ellis argued, it must be "simple and natural and pure and good." Bombarded by these exciting ideas, to say nothing of their own inclinations, young people found casting off their inhibitions more and more tempting.

Conservatives bemoaned what they described as the breakdown of moral standards, the fragmentation of the family, and the decline of parental authority—all with some reason. Nevertheless, society was not collapsing. Much of the rebelliousness of the young, like their particular style of dress, was faddish in nature, in a sense a kind of youthful conformity. This was particularly true of college students. Elaborate rituals governed every aspect of their extracurricular life, which was consuming a steadily larger share of most students' time and energy. Fraternity and sorority initiations, "proms," attendance at Saturday afternoon football games, styles of dress, and college slang, seemingly aspects of independence and free choice, were nearly everywhere shaped and controlled by peer pressure.

But young people's new ways of relating to one another, while influenced by the desire to conform, were not mere fads and were not confined to people under thirty. This can be seen most clearly in the birth control movement, the drive to legalize the use of contraceptives.

The "New" Woman

The young people of the 1920s were more open about sex and perhaps more sexually precocious than the young had been before the war. This does not mean that most of them engaged in sexual intercourse before marriage or that they tended to marry earlier. Single young people might "believe in" birth control, but relatively few (at least by modern standards) had occasion to practice it. Contraception was a concern of married people, and particularly of married women.

The leading American proponent of birth control in the 1920s, actually the person who coined the term, was Margaret Sanger. Before the war she was a political radical, a friend of Eugene Debs, "Big Bill" Haywood, and the anarchist Emma Goldman. Gradually, however, her attention focused on the plight of the poor women she encountered while working as a nurse; many of these women, burdened by large numbers of children, knew nothing about contraception. Sanger began to write articles and pamphlets designed to enlighten them, but when she did so she ran afoul of the Comstock Act of 1873, an anti-obscenity law that banned the distribution of information about contraception from the mail. She was frequently in trouble with the law, but she was persistent to the edge of fanaticism. In 1921 she founded the American Birth Control League and two years later a research center. (Not until the 1960s, however, did the Supreme Court determine that the right to use contraceptives was guaranteed by the Constitution.)

●●●─ Read the **Document**

Margaret Sanger, *Happiness in Marriage* at **myhistorylab.com**

Other gender-based restrictions and limitations of particular importance to women also seemed to be breaking down. The divorce laws had been modified in most states. More women were taking jobs, attracted by the expanding demand for clerks, typists, salespeople, receptionists, telephone operators, and similar service-oriented occupations. Over 10.6 million women were working by the end of the decade, in contrast with 8.4 million in 1920. The Department of Labor's Women's Bureau, outgrowth of a wartime agency, was founded in 1920 and was soon conducting investigations of the working conditions women faced in different industries and how various laws affected them.

But most of these gains were illusory. Relaxation of the strict standards of sexual morality did not eliminate the double standard. More women worked, but most of the jobs they held were still menial or of a kind that few men wanted: domestic service, elementary school teaching, clerical work, selling behind a counter. When they competed for jobs with men, women usually received much lower wages. Women's Bureau studies demonstrated this repeatedly; yet when the head of the bureau, Mary Anderson, tried to get employers to raise women's wages, most of them first claimed that the men had families to support, and when she reminded them that many female employees also had family responsibilities, they told her that there was a "tacit understanding" that women were to make less than men.

More women graduated from college, but the colleges placed more emphasis on subjects like home economics that seemed designed to make them better housewives rather than professional nutritionists or business executives. As one Vassar College

This photograph of Margaret Sanger was taken during her trial in January 1917. Having opened the nation's first birth control clinic in Brooklyn, New York, she was convicted of disseminating information on contraception and served thirty days in prison. Friends had advised Sanger to dress conservatively and affect a persona of motherhood. Despite her demure clothing, her eyes express her characteristic assertiveness.

administrator (a woman!) said, colleges should provide "education for women along the lines of their chief interests and responsibilities, motherhood and the home."

The 1920s proved disillusioning to feminists, who now paid a price for their single-minded pursuit of the right to vote in the Progressive Era. After the ratification of the Nineteenth Amendment, many activists, assuming the battle won, lost interest in agitating for change. They believed that the suffrage amendment had given them the one weapon needed to achieve whatever women still lacked. In fact, it soon became apparent that women did not vote as a bloc. Many married women voted for the candidates their husbands supported.

When radical feminists discovered that voting did not automatically bring true equality, they founded the National Woman's Party (NWP) and began campaigning for an equal rights amendment. Their dynamic leader, Alice Paul, disdained specific goals such as disarmament, ending child labor, and liberalized birth control. Total equality for women was the one objective. The party considered protective legislation governing the hours and working conditions of women discriminatory. This caused the so-called social feminists, who believed that children and working women needed the protection provided by such laws, to break away.

The NWP never attracted a wide following, but only partly because of the split with the social feminists. Many of the younger radical women were primarily concerned with their personal freedom to behave as they wished; politics did not interest them. But a more important reason was that nearly all the radicals failed to see that questions of gender—the attitudes that men and women *were taught* to take toward each other—stood in the way of sexual equality. Many more women joined the more moderate League of Women Voters, which attempted to mobilize support for a broad spectrum of reforms, some of which had no specific connection to the interests of women as such. The entire women's movement lost momentum. The battle for the equal rights amendment persisted through the 1930s, but it was lost. By the end of that decade the movement was moribund.

Popular Culture: Movies and Radio

The postwar decade saw immense changes in popular culture. Unlike the literary flowering of the era (see pp. 646–648), these changes seemed in tune with the times, not a reaction against them. This was true in part because they were products as much of technology as of human imagination.

Chicago

Chicago (2003) is a tale of illicit sex, booze, and "all that jazz." The characters played by Renée Zellweger and Catherine Zeta-Jones aspire to cabaret stardom. Each is married, each is jilted, and each shoots her wayward lover because "he had it coming." The newspapers gleefully promote the stories. From prison, while awaiting trial for murder, the women compete to garner the most headlines, courting the fame that will boost their careers. Richard Gere, who plays their celebrity lawyer, "razzle dazzles" all Chicago (including the juries) and gets the women acquitted. Chicago is a musical. It does not claim to be history. The movie, however, is based on a true story; and both the movie and the story illuminate important aspects of the Roaring Twenties.

On March 11, 1924, Walter Law, an automobile salesman, was found dead from a gunshot wound to the head. A pistol and an empty bottle of gin were on the floor. The car was registered to Belva Gaertner, a twice-divorced cabaret singer known as Belle Brown. Police hurried to her rooming house and peppered her with questions.

"We went driving, Mr. Law and I," she told them. She explained that they had stopped at the Bingham "café," bought a bottle of gin (illegally, since this was during Prohibition), and drove around town. "I don't know what happened next," she declared. During the interrogation Gaertner paced nervously, perhaps for good reason: Her clothes were soaked with blood. The police charged her with murder.

On April 3, police received a phone call from Beulah Annan, a young married woman who worked in a laundry. She said that a man had attempted to rape her and that she had shot him. Police raced to her apartment, where they found Harry Kalstedt dead from a gunshot wound. Annan insisted that she had acted in self-defense, and her husband supported her story. But police hammered away at the fact that Kalstedt had

worked at the same laundry as Annan, and that he had been shot in the back. Annan eventually confessed that the two had been having an affair. When he threatened to dump her, she shot him. For two hours, as he lay dying, she drank cocktails and listened to a recording of "Hula Lou," a foxtrot about a Hawaiian girl "with more sweeties than a dog has fleas."

Maurine Watkins, a young reporter, covered both stories for the Chicago Tribune. Murder had long been a staple of local journalism, but Watkins recognized the extraordinary appeal of this story: jazz, booze, and two comely "lady murderesses," as Watkins termed them. While awaiting trial in prison, the women provided Watkins with delicious quotes.

Gaertner told Watkins that she was innocent. "No woman can love a man enough to kill him," she explained. "There are always plenty more. " When the grand jury ruled that she could be tried for murder, Gaertner was irritated. "That was bum," she snapped. She called the jurors "narrow-minded old birds—bet they never heard a jazz band in their lives. Now, if I'm tried, I want worldly men, broad-minded men, men who know what it is to get out a bit. Why, no one like that would convict me!"

Watkins described Gaertner as "stylish" and "classy" but called Annan the "prettiest woman ever accused of murder in Chicago"—"young, slender, with bobbed auburn hair; wide set, appealing blue eyes, upturned nose; translucent skin, faintly, very faintly, rouged, an ingenuous smile. Refined features, intelligent expression—an 'awfully nice girl.'" This account appeared on the front page.

During the trial, Annan's attorney pointed to "this frail little girl, struggling with a drunken brute." On May 25, after deliberating less than two hours, the all-male jury acquitted her of the crime. Two weeks after Annan's trial, Gaertner was also found not

Catherine Zeta-Jones and Renée Zellweger from the movie *Chicago*.

Beulah Annan, "lady murderess."
Source: DN-0076798/*Chicago Daily News*/Chicago Historical Society.

guilty. "Another pretty woman gone free," muttered the prosecutor.

Unlike the movie's "lady murderesses," Annan and Gaertner did not team up in a cabaret act. Annan had a nervous breakdown, was institutionalized, and died in 1928. Of Gaertner's subsequent life, little is known. Watkins abandoned journalism and entered Yale drama school. In 1926 she wrote *Chicago*, a comedy derived from the Gaertner and Annan trials, and it ran on Broadway for 172 performances. The next year Cecil B. De Mille adapted the play as a silent movie. In 1975 director Bob Fosse bought the rights to *Chicago* and created the Broadway musical on which the 2003 movie was based.

The "lady murderesses" became part of the lore of the Roaring Twenties; the story seemed to confirm the fears of traditionalists. One minister warned about jazz's "wriggling movement and sensuous stimulation" of the body's "sensory center." Silk stockings, skirts that exposed knees, and straight dresses that de-emphasized the waist further suggested that women's bodies were not meant solely for childbirth. The movie makes all of these points with suitable salaciousness.

The movie also reiterates widespread concerns about city life. Several months after the acquittal of Gaertner and Annan, *Literary Digest* warned "country girls" of the moral dangers of large cities. Such fears echoed the judgments of sociologists, especially those of "the Chicago school" of urban sociology, headed by Robert Park of the University of Chicago. The Chicago sociologists contended that large cities disrupted traditional bonds of family and community and fostered crime and deviance. In *The Gold Coast and the Slum* (1929), sociologist Harvey Zorbaugh maintained that life in much of downtown Chicago was "the direct antithesis of all we are accustomed to think of as normal in society." Big-city life was characterized by a "laxity of conventional standards, and of personal and social disorganization."

Scholars now recognize that the portrait of urban city life as propounded by "the Chicago school"—and by movies such as *Chicago*—was overdrawn. Urbanization did not shatter family and ethnic ties. Neighborliness and community persisted even in blighted tenement districts. Few people cast off social conventions, much less succumbed to murderous impulses. In short, Belva Gaertner and Beulah Annan were good copy, and stories such as theirs helped make that celebrated decade roar, but most folks painted the town less vividly, if at all.

Questions for Discussion

- Compare the photograph of Beulah Annan with those of actresses Catherine Zeta-Jones and Renée Zellweger. What are the similarities and differences and what do they suggest about Hollywood's rendering of the past?
- Why would Hollywood take pains to depict the visual aspects of the past accurately?

The first motion pictures were made around 1900, but the medium only came into its own after the Great War. The early films, such as the eight-minute epic *The Great Train Robbery* (1903), were brief, action-packed, and unpretentious. Professional actors and most educated people viewed them with amused contempt. But their success was instantaneous with recent immigrants and many other slum dwellers. In 1912 there were nearly 13,000 movie houses in the United States, more than 500 in New York City alone.

By the mid-1920s the industry, centered in Hollywood, California, was the fourth largest in the nation in capital investment. Movie "palaces" seating several thousand people sprang up in the major cities. Daily ticket sales averaged more than 10 million. With the introduction of talking movies, *The Jazz Singer* (1927) being the first of significance, and color films a few years later, the motion picture reached technological maturity. Costs and profits mounted; by the 1930s million-dollar productions were common.

Many movies were still tasteless trash catering to the prejudices of the multitude. Sex, crime, war, romantic adventure, broad comedy, and luxurious living were the main themes, endlessly repeated in predictable patterns. Critics charged that the movies were destroying the legitimate stage (which underwent a sharp decline), corrupting the morals of youth, and glorifying the materialistic aspects of life.

Nevertheless the motion picture made positive contributions to American culture. Beginning with D. W. Griffith's *Birth of a Nation* (1915), filmmakers created an entirely new theatrical art. Movies enabled dozens of established actors to reach wider audiences and developed many first-rate new ones. As the medium matured, it produced many dramatic works of high quality. At its best the motion picture offered a breadth and power of impact superior to anything on the traditional stage.

Charlie Chaplin was the greatest film star of the era. His characterization of the sad-eyed little tramp with his toothbrush moustache and cane, tight coat, and baggy trousers became famous throughout the world. Chaplin's films were superficially unpretentious. But his work proved both universally popular and enduring; he was perhaps the greatest comic artist of all time. The animated cartoon, perfected by Walt Disney in the 1930s, was a lesser but significant cinematic achievement; Mickey Mouse, Donald Duck, and other Disney cartoon characters gave endless delight to millions of children.

Even more pervasive than the movies in its effects on the American people was radio. Wireless transmission of sound was developed in the late nineteenth century by many scientists in Europe and the United States. During the war radio was put to important military uses and was strictly controlled, but immediately thereafter the airwaves were thrown open.

Radio was briefly the domain of hobbyists, thousands of "hams" broadcasting in indiscriminate fashion. Even under these conditions, the manufacture of radio equipment became a big business. In 1920 the first commercial station (KDKA in Pittsburgh) began broadcasting, and by the end of 1922 over 500 stations were in operation. In 1926 the National Broadcasting Company, the first continent-wide network, was created.

It took little time for broadcasters to discover the power of the new medium. When one pioneer interrupted a music program to ask listeners to phone in requests, the station received 3,000 calls in an hour. The immediacy of radio explained its tremendous impact. As a means of communicating the latest news, it had no peer; beginning with the broadcast of the 1924 presidential nominating conventions, all major public events were covered live. Advertisers seized on radio too; it proved to be as effective a way to sell soap as to transmit news.

In 1927 Congress limited the number of stations and parceled out wavelengths to prevent interference. Further legislation in 1934 established the Federal Communications Commission (FCC), with power to revoke the licenses of stations that failed to operate in the public interest. But the FCC placed no effective controls on programming or on advertising practices.

The Golden Age of Sports

The extraordinary popularity of sports in the postwar period can be explained in a number of ways. People had more money to spend and more free time to fill. Radio was bringing suspenseful, play-by-play accounts of sports contests into millions of homes, thus encouraging tens of thousands to want to see similar events. New means of persuasion developed by advertisers to sell lipstick, breakfast cereal, and refrigerators were applied with equal success to sporting events and to the athletes who participated in them.

There had been great athletes before; indeed probably the greatest all-around athlete of the twentieth century was Jim Thorpe, a Sac and Fox Indian who won both the pentathlon and the decathlon at the 1912 Olympic Games, made Walter Camp's All-American football team in 1912 and 1913, then played major league baseball for several years before becoming a pioneer founder and player in the National Football League. But what truly made the 1920s a golden age was a coincidence—the emergence in a few short years of a remarkable collection of what today would be called superstars.

In football there was the University of Illinois's Harold "Red" Grange, who averaged over ten yards a carry during his college career and who in one incredible quarter during the 1924 game between Illinois and Michigan carried the ball four times and scored a touchdown each time, gaining in the process 263 yards.

During the same years William "Big Bill" Tilden dominated tennis, winning the national singles title every year from 1920 to 1925 along with nearly every other tournament he entered. Beginning in 1923, Robert T. "Bobby" Jones ruled over the world of golf with equal authority, his climactic achievement being his capture of the amateur and open championships of both the United States and Great Britain in 1930.

A few women athletes dominated their sports during this golden age in similar fashion. In tennis Helen Wills was three times United States singles champion and the winner of the women's singles at Wimbledon eight times in the late 1920s and early 1930s. The swimmer Gertrude Ederle, holder of eighteen world records by the time she was seventeen, swam the English Channel on her second attempt, in 1926. She was not only the first woman to do so, but she did it faster than any of the four men who had previously made it across.

However, the sports star among stars was "the Sultan of Swat," baseball's Babe Ruth. Ruth not only dominated baseball, he changed it from a game ruled by pitchers and low scores to one in which hitting was more greatly admired. Originally himself a brilliant pitcher, his incredible hitting ability made him more valuable in the outfield, where he could play every day. Before Ruth, John "Home Run" Baker was the most famous slugger; his greatest annual home run total was 12, achieved shortly before the Great War. Ruth hit twenty-nine in 1919 and fifty-four in 1920, his first year with the New York Yankees. By 1923 he was so feared that pitchers intentionally walked him more than half the times he appeared at the plate.

Newly built Yankee Stadium on opening day of the 1923 baseball season. Babe Ruth hit his first home run and soon Yankee Stadium was dubbed "the House that Ruth Built." That year, perhaps his best, Ruth hit forty-one home runs, batted .393, and drew 170 walks. He got on base more than half the times he appeared at the plate. Ruth's feats matched the colossal appearance of Yankee Stadium, whose arches evoked the imperial grandeur of ancient Rome.

The achievements of these and other outstanding athletes had a cumulative effect. New stadiums were built, and they were filled by "the largest crowds that ever witnessed athletic sports since the fall of Rome."

Urban–Rural Conflicts: Fundamentalism

These were buoyant times for people in tune with the times. However, the tensions and hostilities of the 1920s exaggerated an older rift in American society—the conflict between urban and rural ways of life. To many among the scattered millions who tilled the soil and among the millions who lived in towns and small cities, the new city-oriented culture seemed sinful, overly materialistic, and unhealthy.

Yet there was no denying its fascination. Made even more aware of the appeal of the city by radio and the automobile, farmers and townspeople coveted the comfort and excitement of city life at the same time that they condemned its vices. Rural society proclaimed the superiority of its ways at least in part to protect itself from temptation. Change, omnipresent in the postwar world, must be resisted even at the cost of individualism and freedom.

One expression of this resistance was a resurgence of religious fundamentalism. Although it was especially prevalent among Baptists and Methodists, fundamentalism was primarily an attitude of mind, profoundly conservative, rather than a religious idea. Fundamentalists rejected the theory of evolution as well as advanced hypotheses on the origins of the universe.

What made crusaders of the fundamentalists was their resentment of modern urban culture. The teaching of evolution must be prohibited, they insisted. Throughout the 1920s they campaigned vigorously for laws banning discussion of Darwin's theory in textbooks and classrooms. By 1929 five southern states had passed laws prohibiting the teaching of evolution in the public schools.

Their greatest asset in this crusade was William Jennings Bryan. After leaving Wilson's Cabinet in 1915 he devoted much time to religious and moral issues, but without applying himself conscientiously to the study of these difficult questions. He went about the country charging that "they"—meaning the mass of educated Americans— had "taken the Lord away from the schools." He denounced the use of public money to undermine Christian principles, and he offered $100 to anyone who would admit to being descended from an ape. His immense popularity in rural areas assured him a wide audience, and no one came forward to take his money.

The fundamentalists won a minor victory in 1925, when Tennessee passed a law forbidding instructors in the state's schools and colleges to teach "any theory that denies the story of the Divine Creation of man as taught in the Bible." The bill passed both houses by big majorities; few legislators wished to expose themselves to charges that they did not believe the Bible.

On learning of the passage of this act, the American Civil Liberties Union announced that it would finance a test case challenging its constitutionality if a Tennessee teacher would deliberately violate the statute. Urged on by friends, John T. Scopes, a young biology teacher in Dayton, reluctantly agreed to do so. He was arrested. A battery of nationally known lawyers came forward to defend him, and the state obtained the services of Bryan himself. The **Scopes trial**, also known as the "Monkey Trial," became an overnight sensation.

Clarence Darrow, chief counsel for the defendant, stated the issue clearly. "Scopes isn't on trial," he said, "civilization is on trial. No man's belief will be safe if they win." The comic aspects of the trial obscured this issue. Scopes's conviction was a foregone conclusion; after the jury rendered its verdict, the judge fined him $100.

Nevertheless, the trial exposed the danger of the fundamentalist position. The high point came when Bryan agreed to testify as an expert witness on the Bible. In a sweltering courtroom, the lanky, rough-hewn Darrow cross-examined the aging champion of fundamentalism, exposing his childlike faith and his disdain for the science of the day. "I believe in a God that can make a whale and can make a man and make both do what He pleases," Bryan explained.

The Monkey Trial ended badly for nearly everyone concerned. Scopes moved away from Dayton; the judge,

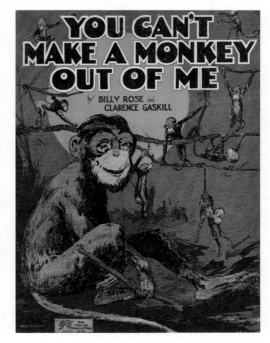

The Scopes trial was a media sensation; it even gave rise to popular songs, such as this one by Billy Rose.

John Raulston, was defeated when he sought reelection; Bryan died in his sleep a few days after the trial. But fundamentalism continued to flourish, not only in the nation's backwaters but also in many cities, brought there by rural people in search of work. In retrospect, even the heroes of the Scopes trial—science and freedom of thought—seem somewhat less stainless than they did to liberals at the time. The account of evolution in the textbook used by Scopes was hopelessly deficient and laced with bigotry, yet it was advanced as unassailable fact. In a section on the "Races of Man," for example, it described Caucasians as "the highest type of all . . . represented by the civilized white inhabitants of Europe and America."

Urban–Rural Conflicts: Prohibition

The conflict between the countryside and the city was fought on many fronts, and in one sector the rural forces achieved a quick victory. This was the Eighteenth Amendment, ratified in 1919, which prohibited the manufacture, transportation, and sale of alcoholic beverages. Although there were some big-city advocates of prohibition, the Eighteenth Amendment, in the words of one historian, marked a triumph of the "Corn Belt over the conveyor belt."

The temperance movement had been important since the age of Jackson; it was a major issue in many states during the Gilded Age, and by the Progressive Era powerful organizations like the Anti-Saloon League and the Women's Christian Temperance Union were seeking to have drinking outlawed entirely. Indeed, prohibition was a typical progressive reform, moralistic, backed by the middle class, and aimed at frustrating "the interests"—in this case the distillers.

World War I aided the prohibitionists by increasing the need for food. The Lever Act of 1917 outlawed the use of grain in the manufacture of alcoholic beverages, primarily as a conservation measure. The prevailing dislike of foreigners helped the dry cause still more: Beer drinking was associated with Germans. State and local laws had made a large part of the country dry by 1917. National prohibition became official in January 1920.

This "experiment noble in purpose," as Herbert Hoover called it, achieved a number of socially desirable results. It reduced the annual national consumption of alcohol from 2.6 gallons per capita in the period just before the war to less than 1 gallon in the early 1930s. Arrests for drunkenness fell off sharply, as did deaths from alcoholism. Fewer workers squandered their wages on drink. If the drys had been willing to legalize beer and wine, the experiment might have worked. Instead, by insisting on total abstinence, they drove thousands of moderates to violate the law. Strict enforcement became impossible, especially in the cities.

In areas where sentiment favored prohibition strongly, liquor remained difficult to find. Elsewhere, anyone with sufficient money could obtain it easily. Smuggling became a major business, *bootlegger* a household word. Private individuals busied themselves learning how to manufacture "bathtub gin." Many druggists issued prescriptions for alcohol with a free hand. The manufacture of wine for religious ceremonies was legal, and consumption of sacramental wine jumped by 800,000 gallons during the first two years of prohibition. The saloon disappeared, replaced by the speakeasy, a supposedly secret bar or club operating under the benevolent eye of the local police.

That the law was often violated does not mean that it was ineffective any more than violations of laws against theft and murder mean that those laws are ineffective.

Although gangsters such as Alphonse "Scarface Al" Capone of Chicago were engaged in the liquor traffic, their "organizations" existed before the passage of the Eighteenth Amendment. But prohibition widened already serious rifts in the social fabric of the country. Organized crime became more powerful. Besides undermining public morality by encouraging hypocrisy, prohibition almost destroyed the Democratic party as a national organization. Democratic immigrants in the cities hated it, but southern Democrats sang its praises, often while continuing to drink (the humorist Will Rogers quipped that Mississippi would vote dry "as long as the voters could stagger to the polls").

The hypocrisy of prohibition had a particularly deleterious effect on politicians, a class seldom famous for candor. Members of Congress catered to the demands of the powerful lobby of the Anti-Saloon League yet failed to grant adequate funds to the Prohibition Bureau. Nearly all the prominent leaders, Democrat and Republican, from Wilson and La Follette to Hoover and Franklin D. Roosevelt, equivocated shamelessly on the liquor question. By the end of the decade almost every competent observer recognized that prohibition at least needed to be overhauled, but the well-organized and powerful dry forces rejected all proposals for modifying it.

((•—[Hear the Audio
Prohibition is a Failure at
myhistorylab.com

The Ku Klux Klan

The most horrible manifestation of the social malaise of the 1920s was the revival of the Ku Klux Klan. This new Klan, founded in 1915 by William J. Simmons, a former preacher, admitted only native-born white Protestants. The distrust of foreigners, blacks, Catholics, and Jews implicit in this regulation explains why it flourished in the social climate that spawned religious fundamentalism, immigration restriction, and prohibition. In a little over a year the Klan enrolled 100,000 recruits, and by 1923 they claimed the astonishing total of 5 million.

A Ku Klux Klan initiation ceremony photographed in Kansas in the 1920s. During its peak influence at mid-decade, Klan endorsement was essential to political candidates in many areas of the West and Midwest. Campaigning for reelection in 1934, an Indiana congressman testified, "I was told to join the Klan, or else."
Source: Kansas State Historical Society.

Simmons gave his society trappings and mystery calculated to attract gullible and bigoted people who yearned to express their frustrations and hostilities without personal risk. Klansmen masked themselves in white robes and hoods and enjoyed a childish mumbo jumbo of magnificent-sounding titles and dogmas. They burned crosses in the night, organized mass demonstrations to intimidate people they disliked, and put pressure on businessmen to fire black workers from better-paying jobs.

The Klan had relatively little appeal in the Northeast or in metropolitan centers in other parts of the country, but it found many members in mid-sized cities and in the small towns and villages of midwestern and western states. The rationale was an urge to return to an older, supposedly finer America and to stamp out all varieties of nonconformity. Klansmen persecuted gamblers, "loose" women, violators of the prohibition laws, and anyone who happened to differ from them on religious questions or who belonged to a "foreign race."

The very success of the Klan led to its undoing. Factionalism sprang up, and rival leaders squabbled over the large sums that had been collected from the membership. The cruel and outrageous behavior of the organization roused both liberals and conservatives in every part of the country. And of course its victims joined forces against their tormentors. When the powerful leader of the Indiana Klan, a middle-aged reprobate named David C. Stephenson, was convicted of assaulting and causing the death of a young woman, the rank and file abandoned the organization in droves. The Klan remained influential for a number of years, but it ceased to be a dynamic force after 1924. By 1930 it had only some 9,000 members.

●●●—Read the **Document**

Creed of Klanswomen at
myhistorylab.com

Literary Trends

The literature of the 1920s reflects the disillusionment of the intellectuals. The wasteful horrors of the Great War and then the antics of the fundamentalists and the cruelty of the red-baiters and the Klan turned them into critics of society. Many intellectuals deplored the 1927 execution of Nicola Sacco and Bartolomeo Vanzetti, Italian immigrants (and anarchists) who were deprived of a fair trial in a murder case. They included the poet Edna St. Vincent Millay, the playwright Maxwell Anderson, and the novelists Upton Sinclair and John Dos Passos. After the war the poet Ezra Pound dropped his talk of an American Renaissance and wrote instead of a "botched civilization."

●●●—Read the **Document**

Bartolomeo Vanzetti,
Court Statement at
myhistorylab.com

The symbol of what some called the "lost generation," in his own mind as well as to his contemporaries and to later critics, was F. Scott Fitzgerald. Born to modest wealth in St. Paul, Minnesota, in 1896, Fitzgerald attended Princeton and served in the army during the Great War. He rose to sudden fame in 1920 when he published *This Side of Paradise*, a somewhat sophomoric novel that appealed powerfully to college students and captured the fears and confusions of the lost generation. In *The Great Gatsby* (1925), a more mature work, Fitzgerald depicted a modern millionaire—coarse, unscrupulous, jaded, in love with another man's wife. Gatsby's tragedy lay in his dedication to a woman who, Fitzgerald made clear, did not merit his passion.

The tragedy of *The Great Gatsby* was related to Fitzgerald's own. Pleasure-loving and extravagant, he squandered the money earned by *This Side of Paradise*. When *The Great Gatsby* failed to sell as well, he turned to writing potboilers. "I really worked hard as hell last winter," he told the critic Edmund Wilson, "but it was all trash and it nearly broke my heart." While some of his later work, particularly *Tender Is the Night* (1934), is first-class, he descended into the despair of alcoholism and ended his days as a Hollywood scriptwriter.

Many young American writers and artists became expatriates in the 1920s. They flocked to Rome, Berlin, and especially Paris, where they could live cheaply and escape what seemed to them the "conspiracy against the individual" prevalent in their own country. Some made meager livings as journalists, translators, and editors, perhaps turning an extra dollar from time to time by selling a story or a poem to an American magazine or a painting to a tourist.

Ernest Hemingway was the most talented of the expatriates. He had served in the Italian army during the war and been grievously wounded (in spirit as well as in body). He settled in Paris in 1922 to write. His first novel, *The Sun Also Rises* (1926), portrayed the café world of the expatriate and the rootless desperation, amorality, and sense of outrage at life's meaninglessness that obsessed so many in those years. In *A Farewell to Arms* (1929) he drew on his military experiences to describe the confusion and horror of war.

Hemingway's books were best-sellers and he became a legend in his own time. Few novelists have been as capable of suggesting powerful emotions and action in so few words. Mark Twain and Stephen Crane were his models; Gertrude Stein, a writer and revolutionary genius, his teacher. But his style was his own—direct, simple, taut, sparse:

> I went out the door and down the hall to the room where Catherine was to be after the baby came. I sat in a chair there and looked at the room. I had the paper in my coat that I had bought when I went out for lunch and I read it. . . . After a while I stopped reading and turned off the light and watched it get dark outside. *(A Farewell to Arms)*

Source: Reprinted with the permission of Scribner, a Division of Simon & Schuster, Inc., from *A Farewell to Arms* by Ernest Hemingway. Copyright © 1929 by Charles Scribner's Son's; copyright renewed 1956 by Ernest Hemingway. All rights reserved.

This kind of writing, evoking rather than describing emotion, fascinated readers and inspired hundreds of imitators; it made a permanent mark on world literature. What Hemingway had to say was of less universal interest. He wrote about bullfights, hunting and fishing, and violence; while he did so with masterful penetration, these themes placed limits on his work that he never transcended. The critic Alfred Kazin summed up Hemingway in a sentence: "He brought a major art to a minor vision of life."

Edith Wharton was of the New York aristocracy. She was educated by tutors and governesses and never went to college. She traveled frequently to Europe, eventually chose to live there, and took up writing. After co-authoring a book on home decoration, she wrote novels on marriage and manners in some ways reminiscent of Henry James. In Paris at the outset of the Great War, she threw herself into war-related charities. But while the shock of the war jolted Fitzgerald and Hemingway into the vanguard of innovation, she retreated from the jangling energy of postwar life and culture. The product of her retreat, *The Age of Innocence* (1920), offered a penetrating portrait of an unsettlingly serene if vanished world. The Nation remarked that Wharton had described the wealthy of old New York "as familiarly as if she loved them and as lucidly as if she hated them."

Although neither was the equal of Hemingway, Fitzgerald, or Wharton, two other writers of the 1920s deserve mention: H. L. Mencken and Sinclair Lewis. Each reflected the distaste of intellectuals for the climate of the times. Mencken, a Baltimore newspaperman and founder of one of the great magazines of the era, the *American Mercury*, was a thoroughgoing cynic. He coined the word *booboisie* to define the complacent, middle-class majority, and he fired superbly witty broadsides at fundamentalists, prohibitionists, and "Puritans." "Puritanism," he once said, "is the haunting fear that someone, somewhere, may be happy."

But Mencken was never indifferent to the many aspects of American life that roused his contempt. Politics at once fascinated and repelled him, and he assailed the statesmen of his generation with magnificent impartiality:

[On Coolidge]: "A cheap and trashy fellow, deficient in sense and almost devoid of any notion of honor—in brief, a dreadful little cad."

[On Hoover]: "Lord Hoover is no more than a pious old woman, a fat Coolidge."

Source: H. L. Mencken

Mencken's diatribes, while amusing, were not profound. In perspective he seems more a professional iconoclast than a constructive critic; like both Fitzgerald and Hemingway, he was something of a perennial adolescent. However, he consistently supported freedom of expression of every sort.

Sinclair Lewis was probably the most popular American novelist of the 1920s. Like Fitzgerald, his first major work brought him instant fame and notoriety—and for the same reason. *Main Street* (1920) portrayed the smug ignorance and bigotry of the American small town so accurately that even Lewis's victims recognized themselves; his title became a symbol for provinciality and middle-class meanness of spirit. In *Babbitt* (1922), he created what many people considered the typical businessman of the 1920s, gregarious, a "booster," blindly orthodox in his political and social opinions, a slave to every cliché, and full of loud self-confidence, but under the surface a bumbling, rather timid fellow who would have liked to be better than he was but dared not try. Lewis went on to dissect the medical profession in *Arrowsmith* (1925), religion in *Elmer Gantry* (1927), and fascism in *It Can't Happen Here* (1935).

The "New Negro"

The postwar reaction brought despair for many blacks. Aside from the barbarities of the Klan, they suffered from the postwar middle-class hostility to labor. The increasing presence of southern blacks in northern cities also caused conflict. Some 393,000 settled in New York, Pennsylvania, and Illinois in the 1920s, most of them in New York City, Philadelphia, and Chicago. The black population of New York City more than doubled between 1920 and 1930.

In earlier periods blacks in northern cities had tended to live together, but in small neighborhoods scattered over large areas. Now the tendency was toward concentration in what came to be called ghettos.

Even in small northern cities where they made up only a tiny proportion of the population, blacks were badly treated. When Robert S. and Helen M. Lynd made their classic sociological analysis of "Middletown" (Muncie, Indiana), they discovered that although black and white children attended the same schools, the churches, the larger movie houses, and other places of public accommodation were segregated. The local YMCA had a gymnasium where high school basketball was played, but the secretary refused to allow any team with a black player to use it. Even the news in Muncie was segregated. Local papers chronicled the affairs of the black community—roughly 5 percent of the population— under the heading "In Colored Circles."

Coming after the hopes inspired by wartime gains, the disappointments of the 1920s produced a new militancy among many blacks. In 1919 W. E. B. Du Bois wrote in *The Crisis*, "We are cowards and jackasses if . . . we do not marshal every ounce of our brain and brawn to fight . . . against the forces of hell in our own land." He increased his commitment to black nationalism, organizing a series of Pan African Conferences in an effort—futile, as it turned out—to create an international black movement.

Du Bois never made up his mind whether to work for integration or black separatism. Such ambivalence never troubled Marcus Garvey, a West Indian whose Universal Negro Improvement Association attracted hundreds of thousands of followers in the early 1920s. Garvey had nothing but contempt for whites, for light-skinned blacks like Du Bois, and for organizations such as the NAACP, which sought to bring whites and blacks together to fight segregation and other forms of prejudice. "Back to Africa" was his slogan; the black man must "work out his salvation in his motherland."

Garvey's message was naive, but it served to build racial pride among the masses of poor and unschooled blacks. He organized black businesses of many sorts, including a company that manufactured black dolls. He established a corps of Black Cross nurses and a Black Star Line Steamship Company to transport blacks back to Africa.

More sophisticated black leaders like Du Bois detested Garvey, whom they thought something of a charlatan. In 1923 Garvey's steamship line went into bankruptcy. He was convicted of defrauding the thousands of his supporters who had invested in its stock and was sent to prison. Nevertheless, his message, if not his methods, helped to create the "New Negro," proud of being black and prepared to resist both mistreatment and white ideas. The ghettos produced compensating advantages for blacks. One effect, not fully utilized until later, was to increase their political power by enabling them to elect representatives to state legislatures and

A painting from Jacob Lawrence's Migration Series (1940–1941).
Source: Gift of Mrs. David M. Levy. (28.1942.20). ©The Museum of Modern Art/Artists Rights Society/Art Resource, NY.

The Making of Black Harlem In 1911, African Americans lived mostly in a dozen-block region of Harlem; by 1930, they had created a predominantly black city of well over 100 city blocks.

Congress, and to exert considerable influence in closely contested elections. More immediately, city life stimulated self-confidence; despite their horrors, the ghettos offered economic opportunity, political rights, and freedom from the everyday debasements of life in the South. The ghetto was a black world where black men and women could be themselves.

Black writers, musicians, and artists found in the ghettos both an audience and the "spiritual emancipation" that unleashed their capacities. Jazz, the great popular music of the age, was largely the creation of black musicians working in New Orleans before the turn of the century. By the 1920s it had spread throughout the country and to most of the rest of the world. White musicians and white audiences took it up—in a way it became a force for racial tolerance and understanding.

Harlem, the largest black community in the world, became in the 1920s a cultural capital, center of the **Harlem Renaissance**. Black newspapers and magazines flourished along with theatrical companies and libraries. Du Bois opened *The Crisis* to young writers and artists, and a dozen "little" magazines sprang up. Langston Hughes, one of the most talented poets of the era, described the exhilaration of his first arrival in this city within a city, a magnet for every black intellectual and artist: "Harlem! I . . . dropped my bags, took a deep breath, and felt happy again." In 1925 Zora Neale Hurston joined with Hughes to create a literary magazine, and celebrated the lives of ordinary black workers.

With some exceptions, African American writers like Hughes and Hurston did not share in the disillusionment that afflicted so many white intellectuals. The persistence of prejudice angered them and made them militant. But to be militant, one must be at some

◉ Watch the Video

The Harlem Renaissance at **myhistorylab.com**

Zora Neale Hurston, a major figure of the Harlem Renaissance, wrote eighteen novels—many of which were made into movies.

level hopeful. Sociologists and psychologists (for whom the ghettos were indispensable social laboratories) were demonstrating that environment rather than heredity was preventing black economic progress. Together with the achievements of creative blacks, which for the first time were being appreciated by large numbers of white intellectuals, these discoveries seemed to herald the eventual disappearance of racial prejudice. The black, Alain Locke wrote in *The New Negro* (1925), "lays aside the status of beneficiary and ward for that of a collaborator and participant in American civilization." Alas, as Locke and other black intellectuals were soon to discover, this prediction, like so many made in the 1920s, did not come to pass.

Economic Expansion

Despite the turmoil of the times and the dissatisfactions expressed by some of the nation's best minds, the 1920s was an exceptionally prosperous decade. Business boomed, real wages rose, unemployment declined. The United States was as rich as all Europe; perhaps 40 percent of the world's total wealth lay in American hands. Little wonder that business leaders and other conservatives described the period as a "new era."

The prosperity rested on many bases, one of which was the friendly, hands-off attitude of the federal government, which bolstered the confidence of the business community. The Federal Reserve Board kept interest rates low, a further stimulus to economic growth. The continuing mechanization and rationalization of industry provided a more fundamental stimulus to the economy. From heavy road-grading equipment and concrete mixers to devices for making cigars and glass tubes, from pneumatic tools to the dial telephone, machinery was replacing human hands at an ever more rapid rate. Industrial output almost doubled between 1921 and 1929 without any substantial increase in the industrial labor force.

Most important, American manufacturing was experiencing a remarkable improvement in efficiency. The method of breaking down the complex processes of production into many simple operations and the use of interchangeable parts were nineteenth-century innovations; in the 1920s they were adopted on an almost universal scale. The moving assembly line which carried the product to the worker, first devised by Henry Ford in his automobile plant in the decade before World War I, speeded production and reduced costs. In ten years the hourly output of Ford workers quadrupled.

The Age of the Consumer

The growing ability of manufacturers to produce goods meant that great effort had to be made to create new consumer demands. Advertising and salesmanship were raised almost to the status of fine arts. Bruce Barton, one of the advertising "geniuses" of the era, wrote a best-selling book, *The Man Nobody Knows* (1925), in which he described Jesus as the "founder of modern business," the man who "picked up twelve men from the bottom ranks . . . and forged them into an organization that conquered the world."

Producers concentrated on making their goods more attractive and on changing models frequently to entice buyers into the market. The practice of selling goods on the installment plan helped bring expensive items within the reach of the masses. Inventions and technological advances created new or improved products: radios, automobiles, electric appliances such as vacuum cleaners and refrigerators, gadgets like cigarette lighters, and new forms of entertainment like motion pictures.

Undoubtedly the automobile had the single most important impact on the nation's economy in the 1920s. Although well over a million cars a year were being regularly produced by 1916, the real expansion of the industry came after 1921. Output reached 3.6 million in 1923 and fell below that figure only twice during the remainder of the decade. By 1929, 23 million private cars clogged the highways, an average of nearly one per family.

Watch the Video

The rise and fall of the automobile economy at **myhistorylab.com**

The auto industry created companies that manufactured tires and spark plugs and other products. It triggered a gigantic road-building program: There were 387,000 miles of paved roads in the United States in 1921, and 662,000 miles in 1929. Thousands of persons found employment in filling stations, roadside stands, and other businesses catering to the motoring public. The tourism industry profited, and the shift of population from the cities to the suburbs accelerated.

The automobile made life more mobile yet also more encapsulated. It changed recreational patterns and family life. In addition, it profoundly affected the way Americans thought. It gave them a freedom never before imagined. The owner of the most rickety jalopy could travel farther, faster, and far more comfortably than a monarch of old with his purebloooded steeds and gilded coaches.

These benefits were real and priceless. Cars also became important

Would women believe the claims of cosmetics advertisements? "Kissproof" promised to make a woman's lips "pulsate with the very spirit of reckless, irrepressible youth." In a 1927 survey of housewives in Columbus, Ohio, Pond's Company found that two-thirds of the women could not even recall the company's advertisements. Younger women, however, were more impressionable. When the J. Walter Thompson advertising agency asked Vassar students to describe cosmetics, they unconsciously used the exact phrases from advertising copy—proof of its power.

FREE —Send coupon for 8 x 10 Art Print of this beautiful painting—the Kissproof Girl. Printed in 13 colors, mailed flat for framing.

NEW

Kissproof the waterproof rouge . . . in a startling jade green case

50¢

Waterproof it stays on!

Kissproof

symbols. They gave their owners the feeling of power and status that a horse gave to a medieval knight. According to some authorities the typical American cared more about owning an automobile than a house.

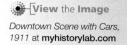

Downtown Scene with Cars, 1911 at **myhistorylab.com**

In time there were undesirable, even dangerous results of the automotive revolution: roadside scenery disfigured by billboards, gas stations, and other enterprises aimed at satisfying the traveler's needs; horrendous traffic jams; soaring accident rates; air pollution; and the neglect of public transportation, which was an important cause of the deterioration of inner cities. All these disadvantages were noticed during the 1920s, but in the springtime of the new industry they were discounted. The automobile seemed an unalloyed blessing—part toy, part tool, part symbol of American freedom, prosperity, and individualism.

Henry Ford

The person most responsible for the growth of the automobile industry was Henry Ford, a self-taught mechanic from Greenfield, Michigan. Ford was neither a great inventor nor one of the true automobile pioneers. Ford's first brilliant insight was to "get the prices down to the buying power." Through mass production, cars could be made cheaply enough to put them within reach of the ordinary citizen. In 1908 he designed the Model T Ford, a simple, tough box on wheels. In a year he proved his point by selling 11,000 Model Ts. Relentlessly cutting costs and increasing efficiency with the assembly line system, he expanded production at an unbelievable rate. By 1925 he was turning out more than 9,000 cars a day, one approximately every ten seconds, and the price of the Model T had been reduced below $300.

Ford's second insight was the importance of high wages in stimulating output (and selling more automobiles). The assembly line simplified the laborer's task and increased the pace of work; at the same time it made each worker much more productive. Jobs became boring and fatiguing, and absenteeism and labor turnover became serious problems. To combat this difficulty, in 1914 Ford established the $5 day, an increase of about $2 over prevailing wages. The rate of turnover in his plant fell 90 percent, and although critics charged that he recaptured his additional labor costs by speeding up the line, his policy had a revolutionary effect on wage rates. Later he raised the minimum to $6 and then to $7 a day.

Ford's profits soared along with sales; since he owned the entire company, he became a billionaire. He also became an authentic folk hero: his homespun style, his dislike of bankers and sophisticated society, and his intense individualism endeared him to millions. He stood as a symbol of the wonders of the American system—he had given the nation a marvelous convenience at a low price, at the same time enriching himself and raising the living standards of his thousands of employees.

Unfortunately, Ford had the defects of his virtues in full measure. He paid high wages but refused to deal with any union and he employed spies to investigate the private lives of his workers, and gangsters and thugs to enforce plant discipline. When he discovered a worker driving any car but a Ford, he had him dismissed. So close was the supervision in the factory that workers devised the "Ford whisper," a means of talking without moving one's lips.

Success made Ford stubborn. The Model T remained essentially unchanged for nearly twenty years. Other companies, notably General Motors, were soon turning out better vehicles for very little more money. Customers, increasingly affluent and style-conscious, began to shift to Chevrolets and Chryslers. Finally, in 1927, Ford shut down all operations for eighteen months in order to retool for the Model A. His competitors rushed in during this period to fill the vacuum. Although his company continued to make a great deal of money, Ford never regained the dominant position he had held for so long.

Ford was enormously uninformed, yet—because of his success and the praise the world heaped on him—he did not hesitate to speak out on subjects far outside his area of competence, from the evils of drink and tobacco to medicine and international affairs. He developed political ambitions and published virulent anti-Semitic propaganda. He said he would not give five cents for all the art in the world.

While praising his talents as a manufacturer, historians have not dealt kindly with Ford the man, in part no doubt because he once said, "History is more or less the bunk."

The Airplane

Henry Ford was also an early manufacturer of airplanes, and while the airplane industry was not economically important in the 1920s, its development in that decade laid the basis for changes in lifestyles and attitudes at least as momentous as those produced by the automobile. The invention of the internal combustion gasoline engine, with its extremely high ratio of power to weight, made the airplane possible, which explains why the early experiments with "flying machines" took place at about the same time that the prototypes of the modern automobile were being manufactured. Wilbur and Orville Wright made their famous flight at Kitty Hawk, North Carolina, in 1903, five years before Ford produced his Model T. Another pair of brothers, Malcolm and Haimes Lockheed, built their Model G, one of the earliest commercial planes in 1913.

The great event of the decade for aviation, still an achievement that must strike awe in the hearts of reflective persons, was Charles A. Lindbergh's nonstop flight from New York to Paris in May 1927. It took more than thirty-three hours for Lindbergh's single-engine *Spirit of St. Louis* to cross the Atlantic, a formidable physical achievement for the pilot as well as an example of skill and courage. When the public learned that the intrepid "Lucky Lindy" was handsome, modest, uninterested in converting his new fame into cash, and a model of propriety (he neither drank nor smoked), his role as American hero was ensured. It was a role Lindbergh detested—one biographer has described him as "by nature solitary"—but could not avoid.

Lindbergh's flight enormously increased public interest in flying, but it was a landmark in aviation technology as well. The day of routine passenger flights was at last about to dawn. In July 1927, a mere two months after the *Spirit of St. Louis* touched down at Le Bourget Field in France, William E. Boeing of Boeing Air Transport began flying passengers and mail between San Francisco and Chicago, using the M–40, a plane of his own design and manufacture. Early in 1928 he changed the company name to United Aircraft and Transport. Two years later Boeing produced the first all-metal low-wing plane and, in 1933, the twin-engine 247, a prototype for many others.

In retrospect the postwar era seems even more a period of transition than it appeared to most people at the time. Rarely had change come so swiftly, and rarely had old and new existed side by side in such profusion. Creativity and reaction, hope and despair, freedom and repression—the modern world in all its unfathomable complexity was emerging.

Milestones

1903	Wright brothers fly at Kitty Hawk, NC	1926	Gertrude Ederle swims English Channel
1908	Henry Ford designs Model T automobile		Ernest Hemingway publishes *The Sun Also Rises*
1914	Ford establishes $5 day for autoworkers		
1919	Eighteenth Amendment outlaws alcoholic beverages (Prohibition)	1927	Charles Lindbergh flies solo across Atlantic
	Nineteenth Amendment gives women right to vote		Sacco and Vanzetti are executed
1920	Sinclair Lewis publishes *Main Street*		*The Jazz Singer*, first motion picture with sound, is released
	First commercial radio station, KDKA, Pittsburgh, begins broadcasting		Jack Dempsey loses heavyweight boxing title to Gene Tunney
1920s	Black culture flourishes in Harlem Renaissance		Babe Ruth hits sixty home runs
1921	Margaret Sanger founds American Birth Control League	1928	John B. Watson publishes *The Psychological Care of Infant and Child*
1924	Ku Klux Klan membership peaks		
1925	Scopes is convicted for teaching evolution	1929	Capone's gang kills Moran's in Valentine's Day Massacre
	F. Scott Fitzgerald publishes *The Great Gatsby*		

✔•⎯Study and Review at www.myhistorylab.com

Review Questions

1. The introduction suggests that the prohibition of alcohol encouraged people to flaunt other conventions. To what extent were the cultural shifts of the 1920s a rebellion against tradition?

2. How did traditionalists respond to these social and cultural transformations? Was the fundamental tension, as the chapter suggests, between rural and urban cultures? Or was it between classes or ethnic groups?

3. How did technological changes such as radio, the automobile, and the airplane influence culture? How did "mass culture" touch the lives of Americans? Did it improve life or diminish it?

4. How did the 1920s liberate women, African Americans, and minorities?

Key Terms

Harlem Renaissance *650*   National Origins Act *632*   Scopes trial *643*

25 From "Normalcy" to Economic Collapse: 1921–1933

((•—[Hear the Audio **Chapter 25 at myhistorylab.com**

Will you get a job?

IN JUNE, 2009 KYLE DALEY GRADUATED FROM UCLA WITH A 3.5 AVERAGE. He applied for 600 jobs, mostly entry-level positions in large corporations. He got two interviews but no job. He was not alone. In 2010 the Labor Department reported that nearly 11 percent of recent college graduates were without jobs, the highest rate on record. Because two-thirds had taken out student loans averaging $23,200, many considered bankruptcy.

Daley and his age cohort had grown up during the most prosperous decades the American nation had ever witnessed. But it all came crashing down in 2008. The enormous hot-air balloon that was the U.S. housing market burst. Worldwide financial markets, tethered to U.S. mortgages, fell precipitously. Major investment firms declared bankruptcy. Massive layoffs ensued. "I don't remember any time, maybe even the Great Depression, when things went down so fast," observed Paul Volker, the eighty-one-year-old former chairman of the Federal Reserve.

The Great Depression had similarly been preceded by an era of economic prosperity. In 1924 Commerce Secretary Herbert Hoover had proclaimed "a new era" in which cutthroat competition was being superseded by cooperative associations of producers. This heralded "infinite possibilities of moral progress." Such words perhaps sounded hollow, coming in the wake of a Harding administration disgraced by scandal. By 1924 Calvin Coolidge was president, to be succeeded by Hoover in 1929; both presided over a nation that basked in the dawn of a prosperous new era, though a few dark war clouds could be seen in the distance. Many Americans, giddy over their stock market winnings, placed more and more bets on Wall Street. When it all went bust in 1929, many found themselves mired in the depths of the Great Depression.

Harding and "Normalcy"

Warren G. Harding was a newspaperman by trade, publisher of the *Marion Star*, with previous political experience as a legislator and lieutenant governor in his home state, Ohio, and as a U.S. senator. No president, before or since, looked more like a statesman; few were less suited for running the country.

656

Harding's genial nature and lack of strong convictions made him attractive to many of the politicos after eight years of the headstrong Wilson. During the campaign he exasperated sophisticates by his ignorance and imprecision. He coined the famous vulgarism *normalcy* as a substitute for the word *normality*, and committed numerous other blunders. Senator Lodge, ordinarily a stickler for linguistic exactitude, replied acidly that he found Harding a paragon by comparison with Wilson, "a man who wrote English very well without ever saying anything." A large majority of the voters, untroubled by the candidate's lack of erudition, shared Lodge's confidence that Harding would be a vast improvement over Wilson.

Harding has often been characterized as lazy and incompetent. In fact, he was hardworking and politically shrewd; his major weaknesses were indecisiveness and an unwillingness to offend. He turned the most important government departments over to efficient administrators of impeccable reputation: Charles Evans Hughes, the secretary of state; Herbert Hoover in the Commerce Department; Andrew Mellon in the Treasury; and Henry C. Wallace in Agriculture. He kept track of what these men did but seldom initiated policy in their areas. However, Harding gave many lesser offices, and a few of major importance, to the unsavory "Ohio Gang" headed by Harry M. Daugherty, whom he made attorney general.

The president was too kindly, too well-intentioned, and too unambitious to be dishonest. He appointed corrupt officials like Daugherty, Secretary of the Interior Albert B. Fall, Director of the Mint "Ed" Scobey, and Charles R. Forbes, head of the new Veterans Bureau, out of a sense of personal obligation or because they were old friends who shared his taste for poker and liquor. Before 1921 he had enjoyed holding office. In the lonely eminence of the White House, however, he found only misery. "The White House is a prison," he complained. "I can't get away from the men who dog my footsteps. I am in jail."

"The Business of the United States is Business"

Secretary of the Treasury Mellon, multimillionaire banker and master of the aluminum industry, dominated the administration's domestic policy. Mellon set out to lower the taxes of the rich, reverse the low-tariff policies of the Wilson period, return to the laissez-faire philosophy of McKinley, and reduce the national debt by cutting expenses and administrating the government more efficiently.

In principle his program had considerable merit. Tax rates designed to check consumer spending in time of war and to raise the huge sum needed to defeat the Central Powers were undoubtedly hampering economic expansion in the early 1920s. Certain industries that had sprung up in the United States during the Great War were suffering from German and Japanese competition now that the fighting had ended. Rigid regulation necessary during a national crisis could well be dispensed with in peacetime. And efficiency and economy in government are always desirable.

Yet Mellon carried his policies to unreasonable extremes. He proposed eliminating inheritance taxes and reducing the tax on high incomes by two-thirds, but he opposed lower rates for taxpayers earning less than $66,000 a year, apparently not realizing that economic expansion required greater mass consumption as well. Freeing the rich from "oppressive" taxation, he argued, would enable them to invest

Big oil's plans to drill in the Teapot Dome oil reserves led to a major scandal in the Harding administration. (See also Re-Viewing the Past, *There Will Be Blood*, pp. 660–661.)

more in potentially productive enterprises, the success of which would create jobs for ordinary people. Mellon succeeded in balancing the budget and reducing the national debt by an average of over $500 million a year. So committed were the Republican leaders to retrenchment that they even resisted the demands of veterans, organized in the politically potent American Legion, for an "adjusted compensation" bonus.

That the business community heartily approved the policies of Harding and Coolidge is not surprising. Both presidents were uncritical advocates of the business point of view. "We want less government in business and more business in government," Harding pontificated, to which Coolidge added, "The business of the United States is business." Harding and Coolidge used their power of appointment to convert regulatory bodies like the Interstate Commerce Commission (ICC) and the Federal Reserve Board into pro-business agencies that ceased almost entirely to restrict the activities of the industries they were

●◄●─[Read the Document

Purinton, *Big Ideas from Big Business* at **myhistorylab.com** supposed to be controlling. The ICC became almost the reverse of what it had been in the Progressive Era.

The Harding Scandals

At least Mellon was honest. The Ohio gang used its power in the most corrupt way imaginable. Jesse Smith, a crony of Attorney General Daugherty, was what today would be called an influence peddler. When he was exposed in 1923, he committed suicide. Charles R. Forbes of the Veterans Bureau siphoned millions of dollars appropriated for the construction of hospitals into his own pocket. When he was found out, he fled to Europe. Later he returned, stood trial, and was sentenced to two years in prison. His assistant, Charles F. Cramer, committed suicide. Daugherty himself was implicated in the fraudulent return of German assets seized by the alien property custodian to their original owners. He escaped imprisonment only by refusing to testify on the ground that he might incriminate himself.

The worst scandal involved Secretary of the Interior Albert B. Fall, a former senator. In 1921 Fall arranged with the complaisant Secretary of the Navy Edwin Denby for the transfer to the Interior Department of government oil reserves being held for the future use of the navy. He then leased these properties to private oil companies. Edward L. Doheny's Pan-American Petroleum Company got the Elk Hills reserve in California; the Teapot Dome reserve in Wyoming was turned over to Harry F. Sinclair's Mammoth Oil Company. When critics protested, Fall explained that it was necessary to develop the Elk Hills and Teapot Dome properties because adjoining private drillers were draining off the navy's oil. Nevertheless, in 1923 the Senate ordered a full-scale investigation, conducted by Senator Thomas J. Walsh of Montana. It soon came out that Doheny had "lent" Fall $100,000 in hard cash, handed over secretly in a "little black bag." Sinclair had given Fall over $300,000 in cash and negotiable securities. (For more on Doheny and Fall, see Re-Viewing the Past, *There Will Be Blood*, pp. 660–661.)

Although the three culprits in the **Teapot Dome scandal** escaped conviction on the charge of conspiring to defraud the government, Sinclair was sentenced to nine months in jail for contempt of the Senate and for tampering with a jury, and Fall was fined $100,000 and given a year in prison for accepting a bribe. In 1927 the Supreme Court revoked the leases and the two reserves were returned to the government.

●●●—Read the Document

Executive Orders and Senate Resolutions on Teapot Dome at **myhistorylab.com**

The public still knew little of the scandals when, in June 1923, Harding left Washington on a speaking tour that included a visit to Alaska. His health was poor and his spirits low, for he had begun to understand how his "Goddamn friends" had betrayed him. On the return trip from Alaska, he suffered a heart attack. He died in San Francisco on August 2.

Few presidents have been more deeply mourned by the people at the moment of their passing. Harding's kindly nature, his very ordinariness, increased his human appeal. Three million people viewed his coffin as it passed across the country. When the scandals came to light, sadness turned to scorn and contempt.

There Will Be Blood

In 2008 Daniel Day-Lewis won the Academy Award for his portrayal of Daniel Plainview in *There Will Be Blood,* a movie about wildcatting oil exploration in California in the early 1900s. Day-Lewis portrayed Plainview as a remorseless predator who lied with fluency and cheated with sincerity. He coaxed and coerced property owners into granting him oil leases on his own terms. When he didn't get what he wanted, he lashed out in violence.

Day-Lewis's Plainview fixed his coal-black eyes onto people like a fighter-pilot locking onto a target. A reviewer for the *New York Times* called Day-Lewis's performance "among the greatest I've ever seen." Day-Lewis filled Plainview "with so much rage and purpose you wait for him to blow," the reviewer added.

By the usual conventions of Hollywood, the evil Plainview would be vanquished by a white-hatted hero. But in *There Will Be Blood* no good guys ride to the rescue because there were no good guys: *Everyone* is after money.

In the absence of a conflict between good and evil, the movie turns on the question: What made Plainview so bad? Certainly, he was long-suffering. The movie begins with him in a mine shaft, hacking away at rock with a pick and scrabbling through the shards on his hands and knees, looking without success for a glint of gold or silver. When he fell down the shaft and broke his leg, he climbed out by himself. These powerfully discouraging scenes, which take up the first twenty minutes of the movie, include no dialogue whatsoever: Plainview's struggle was a solitary one.

This provides a motivational clue. Plainview hated everyone—with the exception of his son. "I see the worst in people," he declared. "I've built my hatreds up over the years, little by little." He crushed enemies not because he craved wealth but because he could not abide anyone getting the better of him. Which raises the larger question: Were the obsessions of Daniel Plainview characteristic of the industrial and financial magnates of the age?

Plainview, "born in Fond du Lac, Wisconsin," was based on California oil magnate, Edward L. Doheny, himself born in Fond du Lac. The son of a poor Irish immigrant, Doheny left home at a young age and prospected for gold and silver in New Mexico. He had little luck. His wife and children went hungry; she became an alcoholic and committed suicide. In 1891 Doheny gave up prospecting and went to Los Angeles to find a job. One day he spotted a man with a cart whose wheels were coated in tar. Doheny asked what had happened, and the man mentioned a tar pit at the corner of Patton and State Streets, near what is now Dodger Stadium.

Doheny acquired the oil rights to the area and began digging, shoveling dirt and tar into buckets and hauling it to the surface. At the depth of 155 feet, he was nearly killed by toxic fumes; then he studied a diagram of an oil rig and built a crude derrick. He used a sharpened eucalyptus tree as the drill. At 460 feet, he struck oil. Within a few years, he had built scores of derricks throughout Los Angeles. The growth of the city that became synonymous with the automobile was literally fueled by the oil that lay beneath it.

Doheny's first oil strike at Signal Hill near Los Angeles.

Edward L. Doheny, California oil magnate.

Daniel Day-Lewis as Daniel Plainview.

By 1920 southern California had become the world's leading oil-producer, and Doheny had become rich.

There Will Be Blood omitted the next stage in Doheny's life. In 1900 he went to Mexico and worked out a deal with the dictator Profirio Diaz for the oil rights to some promising regions of the undeveloped country. In 1910, Doheny hit several enormous gushers; soon his company was the largest oil producer in the world. His chief competitor in Mexico was Weetman Pearson, an English engineer and builder who had also wangled a lucrative deal out of Diaz.

Doheny was a tough and even ruthless businessman; he made many enemies. But it was not until the 1920s that he attained notoriety. He was among the oilmen who secured from Albert B. Fall, Harding's interior secretary, the right to drill in oil fields that were kept as an emergency reserve for the navy. On learning that Fall was in financial difficulties, Doheny sent his son Ned to Fall's apartment with $100,000 in cash. Fall accepted the money.

Several years later Doheny and his son were among those indicted for bribing Fall. In a Senate hearing Doheny professed his innocence. He had not bribed a government official; he had helped a friend. The amount of the gift—$100,000—was "a bagatelle to me," the equivalent of "the ordinary individual" giving $25 to a down-and-out neighbor. The statement drew gasps from the audience. Doheny, though acquitted, became the era's exemplar of greed and corruption.

There Will Be Blood ends with Plainview living alone in an enormous mansion. When an old antagonist stops by, seeking a hand-out, Plainview, drunk and enraged, murders him. The scene was filmed in the actual Beverly Hills mansion that Doheny had built for his son. In 1929 a deranged family friend who lived in the mansion shot and killed Ned before turning the gun on himself. It was some measure of Doheny's shattered reputation that rumors long circulated that Doheny had himself murdered both men. One recent historian has argued that Doheny was responsible for the deaths if only because his greed poisoned everything around him.

There Will Be Blood came out just before the great financial collapse of 2008–2009, when wildcatting financiers inflicted several trillion dollars' damage upon the global economy. It is tempting to see in such behavior a heart of darkness, such as the film imputed to Doheny. But we must remember that while Doheny was no paragon of propriety, he was no murderer. In painting him with the oily hues of a Daniel Plainview, Hollywood transformed the oil magnate into caricature. Indeed, Hollywood's search for box-office gushers is itself reminiscent of Day-Lewis's character. And if, like Plainview, it plays fast and loose with the literal truth, can it really be blamed?

Questions for Discussion

- Doheny pursued wealth with obsessive determination. In *Wall Street* (1987), the character Gordon Gekko declares that "Greed is good." How does greed promote economic growth? How does it become a destructive force?
- Did Doheny benefit society and, if so, how? How did he harm it?

Coolidge Prosperity

Had he lived, Harding might well have been defeated in 1924 because of the scandals. Vice President Coolidge, unconnected with the troubles and not the type to surround himself with cronies of any kind, seemed the ideal person to clean out the corrupt officials. Coolidge was a taciturn, extremely conservative New Englander with a long record in Massachusetts. He preferred to follow public opinion and hope for the best.

Coolidge defused his predecessor's scandals by replacing Harding's Attorney General Daugherty with Harlan Fiske Stone, dean of the Columbia University Law School. Soon Coolidge became the darling of the conservatives. His admiration for businessmen and his devotion to laissez-faire knew no limit. Andrew Mellon, whom he kept on as secretary of the Treasury, became his mentor in economic affairs.

Coolidge won the 1924 Republican nomination easily. The Democrats, badly split, required 103 ballots to choose a candidate. The southern wing, dry, anti-immigrant, pro-Klan, had fixed on William G. McAdoo, Wilson's secretary of the Treasury. The eastern, urban, wet element supported Governor Alfred E. Smith of New York, child of the slums, a Catholic who had compiled a distinguished record in social welfare legislation. After days of futile politicking, the party compromised on John W. Davis, a conservative corporation lawyer closely allied with the Morgan banking interests.

Dismayed by the conservatism of Coolidge and Davis, Robert M. La Follette, backed by the farm bloc, the Socialist party, the American Federation of Labor, and numbers of intellectuals, entered the race as the candidate of a new Progressive party. The Progressives adopted a neopopulist platform calling for the nationalization of railroads, the direct election of the president, the protection of labor's right to bargain collectively, and other reforms.

The situation was the opposite of 1912, when one conservative had run against two liberals and had been swamped. Coolidge received 15.7 million votes, Davis 8.4 million, La Follette 4.8 million. Conservatism was clearly the dominant mood of the country.

While Coolidge reigned, complacency was the order of the day. "Mr. Coolidge's genius for inactivity is developed to a very high point," the correspondent Walter Lippmann wrote. "It is a grim, determined, alert inactivity, which keeps Mr. Coolidge occupied constantly."[1] "The country," the president reported to Congress in 1928, "can regard the present with satisfaction, and anticipate the future with optimism."

Peace without a Sword

Presidents Harding and Coolidge handled foreign relations in much the same way they managed domestic affairs. Harding deferred to senatorial prejudice against executive domination in the area and let Secretary of State Charles Evans Hughes make policy. Coolidge adopted a similar course. In directing foreign relations, they faced the obstacle of a resurgent isolationism. The bloodiness of the Great War convinced millions that the only way to be sure it would not happen again was to "steer clear" of "entanglements." That these famous words had been used by Washington and Jefferson in vastly different contexts did not deter the isolationists of the 1920s from

---

[1]Coolidge was physically delicate, plagued by chronic stomach trouble. He required ten or eleven hours of sleep a day.

attributing to them the same authority they gave to Scripture. On the other hand, far-flung American economic interests, as well as the need for both raw materials for industry and foreign markets for America's growing surpluses of agricultural and manufactured goods, made close attention to and involvement in developments all over the world unavoidable.

Isolationist sentiments, therefore, did not deter the government from seeking to advance American interests abroad. The Open Door concept remained predominant; the State Department worked to obtain opportunities in underdeveloped countries for exporters and investors, hoping both to stimulate the American economy and to bring stability to "backward" nations. Although this policy sometimes roused local resentments because of the tendency of the United States to support entrenched elites while the mass of peasants and city workers lived in poverty, it also resulted in a further retreat from active interventionism.

The first important diplomatic event of the period revealed a great deal about American foreign policy after the Great War. During the war, Japan had greatly increased its influence in East Asia, especially in Manchuria, the northeastern province of warlord-dominated China. To maintain the Open Door in China, it would be necessary to check Japanese expansion. But there was little hope of restoring the old spheres of influence, which the mass of Chinese people bitterly resented. In addition, Japan, the United States, and Great Britain were engaged in expensive naval building programs, a competition none of them really wanted but from which all dared not withdraw unilaterally.

In November 1921, hoping to reach a general agreement with China, Japan, and the Europeans that would keep China open to the commerce of all and slow the armaments race, Secretary of State Hughes convened a conference in Washington. By the following February the Washington Conference had drafted three major treaties and a number of lesser agreements.

In the Five-Power Treaty, the United States, Great Britain, France, Japan, and Italy agreed to stop building battleships for ten years and to reduce their fleets of battleships to a fixed ratio, with Great Britain and the United States limited to 525,000 tons, Japan to 315,000 tons, and France and Italy to 175,000 tons. The new ratio was expected to produce a balance of forces in the Pacific.

The Four-Power Treaty, signed by the United States, Great Britain, Japan, and France, committed these nations to respect one another's interests in the islands of the Pacific and to confer in the event that any other country launched an attack in the area.

All the conferees signed the Nine-Power Treaty, agreeing to respect China's independence and to maintain the Open Door. On the surface, this was of monumental importance to the United States since it seemed to mean that Japan had given up its territorial ambitions on the Asian mainland and that both the Japanese and the Europeans had formally endorsed the Open Door concept.

The treaties, however, were uniformly toothless. The signers of the Four-Power Treaty agreed only to consult in case of aggression in the Pacific; they made no promises to help one another or to restrict their own freedom of action. As President Harding assured the Senate, "there [was] no commitment to armed force, no alliance, no written or moral obligation to join in defense."

The naval disarmament treaty said nothing about the number of other warships that the powers might build, about the far more important question of land and air forces, or about the underlying industrial and financial structures that controlled the ability of the nations to make war. In addition, the 5:5:3 ratio actually enabled the Japanese to dominate the western Pacific. It made the Philippine Islands indefensible and exposed Hawaii to possible attack. In a sense these American bases became hostages of Japan. Yet Congress was so unconcerned about Japanese sensibilities that it refused to grant any immigration quota to Japan under the National Origins Act of 1924, even though the formula applied to other nations would have allowed only 100 Japanese a year to enter the country. The law, Secretary Hughes warned, produced in Japan "a sense of injury and antagonism instead of friendship and cooperation."

Hughes did not think war a likely result, but Japanese resentment of "white imperialism" played into the hands of the military party in that nation. Many Japanese army and navy officers considered war with the United States inevitable.

As for the key Nine-Power Treaty, Japan did not abandon its territorial ambitions in China, and China remained so riven by conflict among the warlords and so resentful of the "imperialists" that the economic advantages of the Open Door turned out to be small indeed.

The United States entered into all these agreements without realizing their full implications and not really prepared to play an active part in East Asian affairs. The Japanese soon realized that the United States would not do much to defend its interests in China.

The Peace Movement

The Americans of the 1920s wanted peace but would neither surrender their prejudices nor build the defenses necessary to make it safe to indulge these passions.

Peace societies flourished, among them the Carnegie Endowment for International Peace, designed "to hasten the abolition of war, the foulest blot upon our civilization," and the Woodrow Wilson Foundation, aimed at helping "the liberal forces of mankind throughout the world . . . who intend to promote peace by the means of justice."

So great was the opposition to international cooperation that the United States refused to accept membership on the World Court, although this tribunal could settle disputes only when the nations involved agreed. Too many peace lovers believed that their goal could be attained simply by pointing out the moral and practical disadvantages of war.

The culmination of this illusory faith in preventing war by criticizing it came with the signing of the Kellogg-Briand Pact in 1928. The treaty was born in the fertile brain of French Foreign Minister Aristide Briand, who was eager to collect allies against possible attack by a resurgent Germany. In 1927 Briand proposed to Secretary of State Frank B. Kellogg that their countries agree never to go to war with each other. Kellogg found the idea as repugnant as any conventional alliance, but American isolationists and pacifists found the suggestion fascinating. To extricate himself from this situation, Kellogg suggested that the pact be broadened to include all nations. Now Briand was angry. Like Kellogg, he saw how meaningless such a treaty would be, especially when Kellogg insisted that it be hedged with a proviso that "every nation is free at all times . . . to defend its territory from attack and it alone is competent to decide when circumstances require war in self-defense." Nevertheless, Briand too found public pressures irresistible. In August 1928, at Paris, diplomats from fifteen nations bestowed upon one another an "international kiss," condemning "recourse to war for the solution of international controversies" and renouncing war "as an instrument of national policy." Seldom has so unrealistic a promise been made by so many intelligent people. Yet most Americans considered the Kellogg-Briand Pact a milestone in the history of civilization: The Senate, habitually so suspicious of international commitments, ratified it eighty-five to one.

The Good Neighbor Policy

The conflict between the desire to avoid foreign entanglements and the desire to advance American economic interests is well-illustrated by events in Latin America. In dealing with this part of the world, Harding and Coolidge performed neither better nor worse than Wilson had. In the face of continued radicalism and instability in Mexico, which caused Americans with interests in land and oil rights to suffer heavy losses, President Coolidge acted with forbearance. The Mexicans were able to complete their social and economic revolution in the 1920s without significant interference by the United States.

Under Coolidge's successor, Herbert Hoover, the United States began at last to treat Latin American nations as equals. Hoover reversed Wilson's policy of trying to teach them "to elect good men." The Clark Memorandum (1930), written by Undersecretary of State J. Reuben Clark, disassociated the right of intervention in Latin America from the Roosevelt Corollary. The corollary had been an improper extension of the Monroe Doctrine, Clark declared. The right of the United States to intervene depended rather on "the doctrine of self-preservation."

The distinction seemed slight to Latin Americans, but since it seemed unlikely that the existence of the United States could be threatened in the area, it was important. By 1934 the marines who had been occupying Nicaragua, Haiti, and the Dominican Republic had all been withdrawn and the United States had renounced the right to intervene in Cuban affairs. Instead of functioning as the policeman for the region, the United States would be its "**good neighbor**." Unfortunately, the United States did little to try to improve social and economic conditions in the Caribbean region, so the underlying envy and resentment of "rich Uncle Sam" did not disappear.

The Totalitarian Challenge

The futility and danger of isolationism were exposed in September 1931 when the Japanese, long dominant in Chinese Manchuria, marched their army in and converted the province into a puppet state named Manchukuo. This violated both the Kellogg-Briand and Nine-Power pacts. China, now controlled by General Chiang Kai-shek, appealed to the League of Nations and to the United States for help. Neither would intervene. When League officials asked about the possibility of American cooperation in some kind of police action, President Hoover refused to consider either economic or military reprisals.

The League sent a commission to Manchuria to investigate. Henry L. Stimson, Hoover's secretary of state, announced (the Stimson Doctrine) that the United States would never recognize the legality of seizures made in violation of American treaty rights. This served only to irritate the Japanese.

In January 1932 Japan attacked Shanghai. When the League at last officially condemned their aggressions, the Japanese withdrew from the organization and extended their control of northern China. The lesson of Manchuria was not lost on Adolf Hitler, who became chancellor of Germany on January 30, 1933.

In surveying the diplomatic events of 1920–1929, it is easy to condemn the United States and the European democracies for their unwillingness to stand up for principles, their refusal to resist when Japan and later Germany and Italy embarked

The League of Nations covenant, the Kellogg Pact, the Nine-Power Treaty—all were mere scraps of paper. They did nothing to prevent Japan's invasion of Manchuria in 1931.

on the aggressions that led to World War II. It is also proper to place some of the blame for the troubles of the era on the United States and the European democracies, which controlled much of the world's resources and were primarily interested in holding on to what they had.

War Debts and Reparations

The democracies did not take a strong stand against Japan in part because they were quarreling about other matters. Particularly divisive was the controversy over war debts—those of Germany to the Allies and those of the Allies to the United States. The United States had lent more than $10 billion to its comrades-in-arms. Since most of this money had been spent on weapons and other supplies in the United States, it might well have been considered part of America's contribution to the war effort. The public, however, demanded full repayment—with interest. "These were loans, not contributions," Secretary of the Treasury Mellon firmly declared. The total, to be repaid over a period of sixty-two years, amounted to more than $22 billion.

The Allies tried to load their obligations to the United States, along with the other costs of the war, on the backs of the Germans. They demanded that the Germans pay reparations amounting to $33 billion. If this sum were collected, they declared, they could rebuild their economies and obtain the international exchange needed to pay their debts to the United States. But Germany was reluctant even to try to pay such huge reparations, and when Germany defaulted, so did the Allies.

Everyone shared the blame: the Germans because they resorted to a runaway inflation that reduced the mark to less than one trillionth of its prewar value, at least in part in hopes of avoiding their international obligations; the Americans because they refused to recognize the connection between the tariff and the debt question; and the Allies because they made little effort to pay even a reasonable proportion of their obligations.

In 1924 an international agreement, the Dawes Plan, provided Germany with a $200 million loan designed to stabilize its currency. Germany agreed to pay about $250 million a year in reparations. In 1929 the Young Plan further scaled down the reparations bill. In practice, the Allies paid the United States about what they collected from Germany. Since Germany got the money largely from private American loans, the United States would have served itself and the rest of the world far better had it written off the war debts at the start. In any case, in the late 1920s Americans stopped lending money to Germany, the Great Depression struck, Germany defaulted on its reparations payments, and the Allies then gave up all pretense of meeting their obligations to the United States. The last token payments were made in 1933. All that remained was a heritage of mistrust and hostility.

The Election of 1928

Meanwhile, dramatic changes had occurred in the United States. The climax of Coolidge prosperity came in 1928. The president decided not to run again, and Secretary of Commerce Hoover, whom he detested, easily won the Republican nomination. Hoover was the intellectual leader, almost the philosopher, of the New Era. American capitalists, he believed, had learned to curb their selfish instincts.

Although stiff, uncommunicative, and entirely without experience in elective office, Hoover made an admirable candidate in 1928. His roots in the Midwest and West (Iowa-born, he was raised in Oregon and educated at Stanford University in California) neatly balanced his outstanding reputation among eastern business tycoons. He took a "modern" approach to both capital and labor; businessmen should cooperate with one another and with their workers too. He opposed both unionbusting and trustbusting. His

Herbert Hoover relaxes during the 1928 presidential campaign. "That man has been offering me advice for the last five years," President Coolidge said of his secretary of commerce, "all of it bad."

career as a mining engineer had given him a wide knowledge of the world, yet he had become highly critical of Europe.

The Democrats, having had their fill of factionalism in 1924, could no longer deny the nomination to Governor Al Smith. Superficially, Smith was Hoover's antithesis. Born and raised in New York's Lower East Side slums, he had been schooled in machine politics by Tammany Hall. He was a Catholic, Hoover a Quaker, a wet where Hoover supported prohibition; he dealt easily with people of every race and nationality, while Hoover had little interest in and less knowledge of African Americans and immigrants. However, like Hoover, Smith managed to combine a basic conservatism with humanitarian concern for the underprivileged. As adept in administration as Hoover, he was equally uncritical of the American capitalist system.

View the Image

A Heavy Load for Al (1928) at
myhistorylab.com

In the election Hoover triumphed, 444 to 87 in the Electoral College, 21.4 million to 14 million in the popular vote. All the usually Democratic border states and even North Carolina, Florida, and Texas went to the Republicans, along with the entire West and the Northeast save for Massachusetts and Rhode Island.

After this defeat the Democratic party appeared on the verge of extinction. Nothing could have been further from the truth. The religious question and his big-city roots had hurt Smith, but the chief reason he lost was prosperity—and the good times were soon to end. Hoover's overwhelming victory also concealed a political realignment that was taking place. Working-class voters in the cities, largely Catholic and unimpressed by Coolidge prosperity, had swung heavily to the Democrats. In 1924 the twelve largest cities had been solidly Republican; in 1928 all went Democratic. In agricultural states like Iowa, Smith ran far better than Davis had in 1924, for Coolidge's vetoes of bills designed to raise farm prices had caused considerable resentment. A new coalition of urban workers and dissatisfied farmers was in the making.

Economic Problems

The American economic system of the 1920s had grave flaws. Certain industries did not share in the good times. The coal business, suffering from the competition of petroleum, entered a period of decline. Cotton and woolen textiles also lagged because of the competition of new synthetics, principally rayon. Industry began to be plagued by falling profit margins and chronic unemployment.

The movement toward consolidation in industry, somewhat checked during the latter part of the Progressive Era, resumed; by 1929, 200 corporations controlled nearly half the nation's corporate assets. General Motors, Ford, and Chrysler turned out nearly 90 percent of all American cars and trucks. Four tobacco companies produced over 90 percent of the cigarettes. One percent of all financial institutions controlled 46 percent of the nation's banking business. Most large manufacturers, aware that bad public relations resulting from the unbridled use of monopolistic power outweighed any immediate economic gain, sought stability and "fair" prices rather than the maximum profit possible at the moment. "Regulated" competition was the order of the day, oligopoly the typical situation. The trade association movement flourished; producers formed voluntary organizations to exchange information, discuss policies toward government and the public, and "administer" prices in their industry. Usually the largest corporation, such as U.S. Steel in the iron and steel business, became the "price leader," its competitors, some themselves giants, following slavishly.

The success of the trade associations depended in part on the attitude of the federal government, for such organizations might well have been attacked under the antitrust laws. Their defenders, including President Harding, argued that the associations made business more efficient and prevented violent gyrations of prices and production. Secretary of Commerce Hoover put the facilities of his department at the disposal of the associations. After Coolidge became president, the antitrust division of the Justice Department itself encouraged the trade associations to cooperate in ways that had previously been considered violations of the Sherman Act.

Even more important to the trade associations were the good times. With profits high and markets expanding, the most powerful producers could afford to share the bounty with smaller, less efficient competitors.

The weakest element in the economy was agriculture. Farm prices slumped and farmers' costs mounted. Besides having to purchase expensive machinery in order to compete, farmers were confronted by high foreign tariffs and in some cases quotas on the importation of foodstuffs. As crop yields per acre rose, chiefly because of the increased use of chemical fertilizers, agricultural prices fell further.

Despite the efforts of the farm bloc, the government did little to improve the situation. President Harding opposed direct aid to agriculture as a matter of principle. During his administration Congress strengthened the laws regulating railroad rates and grain exchanges and made it easier for farmers to borrow money, but it did nothing directly to increase agricultural income. Nor did the high tariffs on agricultural produce have much effect. Being forced to sell their surpluses abroad, farmers found that world prices depressed domestic prices despite the tariff wall.

Thus the unprecedented prosperity rested on unstable foundations. The problem was mainly one of maldistribution of resources. Productive capacity raced ahead of buying power. Too large a share of the profits was going into too few pockets. The 27,000 families with the highest annual incomes in 1929 received as much money as the 11 million with annual incomes of under $1,500, the minimum sum required at that time to maintain a family decently. High earnings and low taxes permitted huge sums to pile up in the hands of individuals who did not invest the money productively. A good deal of it went into stock market speculation, which led to the "big bull market" and eventually to the Great Depression.

The Stock Market Crash of 1929

In the spring of 1928, prices on the New York Stock Exchange, already at a historic high, began to surge. As the presidential campaign gathered momentum, the market increased its upward pace, stimulated by the candidates' efforts to outdo each other in praising the marvels of the American economic system. A few conservative brokers expressed alarm, warning that most stocks were grossly overpriced. The majority scoffed at such talk.

During the first half of 1929 stock prices climbed still higher. A mania for speculation swept the country, thousands of small investors putting their savings in common stocks. Then, in September the market wavered. Amid volatile fluctuations stock averages eased downward. Most analysts contended that the stock exchange was "digesting" previous

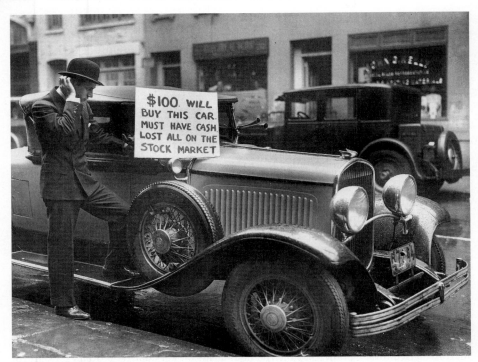

Walter Thompson saw his assets evaporate during the stock market collapse in 1929. Desperate for cash (like nearly everyone else) he offered his snappy roadster for $100.

gains. A Harvard economist expressed the prevailing view when he said that stock prices had reached a "permanently high plateau" and would soon resume their advance.

On October 24 a wave of selling sent prices spinning. Nearly 13 million shares changed hands—a record. Bankers and politicians rallied to check the decline, as they had during the Panic of 1907. But on October 29, the bottom seemed to drop out. More than 16 million shares were sold, prices plummeting. The boom was over.

Hoover and the Depression

The collapse of the stock market did not cause the Depression; stocks rallied late in the year, and business activity did not begin to decline significantly until the spring of 1930. The Great Depression was a worldwide phenomenon caused chiefly by economic imbalances resulting from the chaos of the Great War. In the United States too much wealth had fallen into too few hands, with the result that consumers were unable to buy all the goods produced. The trouble came to a head mainly because of the easy-credit policies of the Federal Reserve Board and the Mellon tax structure, which favored the rich. Its effects were so profound and prolonged because the politicians (and for that matter the professional economists) did not fully understand what was happening or what to do about it.

The chronic problem of underconsumption operated to speed the downward spiral. Unable to rid themselves of mounting inventories, manufacturers closed plants and laid off workers, thereby causing demand to shrink further. Automobile output fell from 4.5 million units in 1929 to 1.1 million in 1932. When Ford closed his Detroit plants in 1931, some 75,000 workers lost their jobs, and the decline in auto production affected a host of suppliers and middlemen as well.

The financial system cracked under the strain. More than 1,300 banks closed their doors in 1930, 3,700 more during the next two years. Each failure deprived thousands of persons of funds that might have been used to buy goods; when the Bank of the United States in New York City became insolvent in December 1930, 400,000 depositors found their savings immobilized. And of course the industrial depression worsened the depression in agriculture by further reducing the demand for American foodstuffs. Every economic indicator reflected the collapse. New investments declined from $10 billion in 1929 to $1 billion in 1932, and the national income fell from over $80 billion to under $50 billion in the same brief period. Unemployment, under 1 million at the height of the boom, rose to at least 13 million.

President Hoover was an intelligent man, experienced in business matters and knowledgeable in economics. Secretary of the Treasury Mellon believed that the economy should be allowed to slide unchecked until the cycle had found its bottom. "Let the slump liquidate itself," Mellon urged. "Liquidate labor, liquidate stocks, liquidate the farmers. . . . People will work harder, live a more moral life. Values will be adjusted, and enterprising people will pick up the wrecks from less competent people." Hoover realized that such a policy would cause unbearable hardship for millions. He rejected Mellon's advice to let the Depression run its course.

Hoover's program for ending the Depression evolved gradually. At first he called on businessmen to maintain prices and wages. The government should cut taxes in order to increase consumers' spendable income, institute public works programs to stimulate production and create jobs for the unemployed, lower interest rates to make it easier for businesses to borrow in order to expand, and make loans to banks and industrial corporations threatened with collapse and to homeowners unable to meet mortgage payments. The president also proposed measures making it easier for farmers to borrow money, and he suggested that the government should support cooperative farm marketing schemes designed to solve the problem of overproduction. He called for an expansion of state and local relief programs and urged all who could afford it to give more to charity. Above all he tried to restore public confidence: The economy was basically healthy; the Depression was only a minor downturn; prosperity was "just around the corner."

Although Hoover's plans were theoretically sound, they failed to check the economic slide, in part because of curious limitations in his conception of how they should be implemented. He placed far too much reliance on his powers of persuasion and the willingness of citizens to act in the public interest without legal compulsion. He urged manufacturers to maintain wages and keep their factories in operation, but the manufacturers soon slashed wages and curtailed output sharply. He permitted the Federal Farm Board to establish semipublic stabilization corporations with authority to buy up surplus wheat and cotton, but he refused to consider crop or acreage controls. The stabilization corporations poured out hundreds of millions of dollars without checking falling agricultural prices because farmers increased production faster than the corporations could buy up the excess for disposal abroad.

Hoover resisted proposals to shift responsibility from state and local agencies to the federal government, despite the fact—soon obvious—that they lacked the resources to cope with the emergency. By 1932 the federal government, with Hoover's approval, was spending $500 million a year on public works projects, but because of the decline in state and municipal construction, the total public outlay fell nearly $1 billion below what it had been in 1930. More serious was his refusal, on constitutional grounds, to allow federal funds to be used for the relief of individuals.

Unfortunately the Depression was drying up the sources of private charities just as the demands on these organizations were expanding. State and municipal agencies were swamped just when their capacities to tax and borrow were shrinking. By 1932 more than 40,600 Boston families were on relief (compared with 7,400 families in 1929); in Chicago 700,000 persons—40 percent of the workforce—were unemployed. Only the national government possessed the power and the credit to deal adequately with the crisis.

Yet Hoover would not act. He set up a committee to coordinate local relief activities but insisted on preserving what he called "the principles of individual and local responsibility." For the federal government to take over relief would "lead to the super-state where every man becomes the servant of the state and real liberty is lost."

Federal loans to commercial enterprises were constitutional, he believed, because the money could be put to productive use and eventually repaid. When drought destroyed the crops of farmers in the South and Southwest in 1930, the government lent them money to buy seed and even food for their livestock, but Hoover would permit no direct relief for the farmers themselves. In 1932 he approved the creation of the Reconstruction Finance Corporation (RFC) to lend money to banks, railroads, and insurance companies. The RFC represented an important extension of national authority, yet it was thoroughly in line with Hoover's philosophy. Its loans, secured by solid collateral, were commercial transactions, not gifts; the agency did almost nothing for individuals in need of relief. The same could be said of the Glass-Steagall Banking Act of 1932, which eased the tight credit situation by permitting Federal Reserve banks to accept corporate stocks and bonds as security for loans. The public grew increasingly resentful of the president's doctrinaire adherence to principle while breadlines lengthened and millions of willing workers searched fruitlessly for jobs.

As time passed and the Depression worsened, Hoover put more stress on the importance of balancing the federal budget, reasoning that since citizens had to live within their limited means in hard times, the government should set a good example. This policy was counterproductive; by reducing its expenditures the government made the Depression worse, which reduced federal revenue further. By June 1931 the budget was nearly $500 million in the red.

Hoover understood the value of pumping money into a stagnant economy. He might have made a virtue of necessity. The difficulty lay in the fact that nearly all "informed" opinion believed that a balanced budget was essential to recovery. The most prestigious economists insisted on it, and so did business leaders, labor leaders, and even most socialists.

Much of the contemporary criticism of Hoover and a good deal of that heaped on him by later historians was unfair. Yet his record as president shows that he was too rigidly wedded to a particular theory of government to cope effectively with the problems of the day. Since these problems were in a sense insoluble, flexibility and a willingness to experiment were essential to any program aimed at restoring prosperity. Hoover lacked these qualities. He was

▶ Watch the Video

Prosperity of the 1920s and the Great Depression at **myhistorylab.com**

his own worst enemy, being too uncompromising to get on well with the politicians and too aloof to win the confidence and affection of ordinary people. He had too much faith in himself and his plans. When he failed to achieve the results he anticipated, he attracted, despite his devotion to duty and his concern for the welfare of the country, not sympathy but scorn.

The Economy Hits Bottom

During the spring of 1932, as the economy sounded the depths, thousands of Americans faced starvation. In Philadelphia during an eleven-day period when no relief funds were available, hundreds of families existed on stale bread, thin soup, and garbage. In the nation as a whole, only about one-quarter of the unemployed were receiving any public aid. Many people were evicted, and they often gathered in ramshackle communities constructed of packing boxes, rusty sheet metal, and similar refuse on swamps, garbage dumps, and other wasteland. People began to call these places "Hoovervilles."

View the Image
Depression Breadlines in New York City at **myhistorylab.com**

Thousands roamed the countryside begging and scavenging for food. At the same time, food prices fell so low that farmers burned corn for fuel. Iowa and Nebraska farmers organized "farm holiday" movements, refusing to ship their crops to market in protest against the thirty-one-cent-a-bushel corn and thirty-eight-cent wheat. They blocked roads and rail lines, dumped milk, overturned trucks, and established picket lines to enforce their boycott.

The national mood ranged from apathy to resentment. In 1931 federal immigration agents and local groups in the Southwest began rounding up Mexican-Americans and deporting them. Some of those returned to Mexico had entered the United States illegally; others had come in properly. Unemployed Mexicans were ejected because they might become public charges, those with jobs because they were presumably taking bread from the mouths of citizens.

In June and July 1932, 20,000 Great War veterans marched on Washington to demand immediate payment of their "adjusted compensation" bonuses. When Congress rejected their appeal, some 2,000 refused to leave, settling in a jerrybuilt camp of shacks and tents at Anacostia Flats, a swamp bordering the Potomac. President Hoover, alarmed, charged incorrectly that the **Bonus Army** was largely composed of criminals and radicals and sent troops into the Flats to disperse it with bayonets, tear gas, and tanks. The

View the Image
Burning Bonus Army Shacks, 1932 at **myhistorylab.com**

task was accomplished amid much confusion; fortunately no one was killed. The protest had been aimless and not entirely justified, yet the spectacle of the U.S. government chasing unarmed veterans with tanks appalled the nation.

The unprecedented severity of the Depression led some persons to favor radical economic and political changes. The disparity between the lots of the rich and the poor, always a challenge to democracy, became more striking and engendered considerable bitterness. "Unless something is done to provide employment," two labor leaders warned Hoover, "disorder . . . is sure to arise. . . . There is a growing demand that the entire business and social structure be changed because of the general dissatisfaction with the present system."

Evicted from their homes, many unemployed people gravitated to vacant industrial property, where they erected hovels from scraps of lumber, tarpaper, and cardboard. This shantytown is outside of Seattle.

The communist party gained few converts among farmers and industrial workers, but a considerable number of intellectuals, alienated by the trends of the 1920s, responded positively to the communists' emphasis on economic planning and the total mobilization of the state to achieve social goals. Even the cracker-barrel humorist Will Rogers was impressed by reports of the absence of serious unemployment in Russia. "All roads lead to Moscow," the former muckraker Lincoln Steffens wrote.

The Depression and Its Victims

Depression is a word used by economists but also by psychologists, and the depression of the 1930s had profound psychological effects on its victims as well as the obvious economic ones. Almost without exception people who lost their jobs first searched energetically for new ones, but when they remained unemployed for more than a few months they sank gradually into despair. E. Wight Bakke, a Yale sociologist who interviewed hundreds of unemployed men in the United States and England during the Depression, described the final stage of decline as "permanent readjustment," by which he meant that the long-term jobless simply gave up. The settlement house worker Lillian Wald came to a similar conclusion. Unemployed people at her famous Henry Street settlement, she noticed, had lost both "ambition and pride."

Simple discouragement alone does not explain why so many of the jobless reacted this way. People who had worked all their adult lives often became ashamed of themselves when they could not find a job. Professor Bakke reported that half the unemployed people in New Haven that he interviewed never applied for public assistance no matter how desperate their circumstances. The Depression affected the families of the jobless in many ways. It caused a dramatic drop in the birthrate, from 27.7 per thousand population in 1920 to 18.4 per thousand in the early 1930s, the lowest in American history. Sometimes it strengthened family ties. Some unemployed men spent more time with their children and helped their wives with cooking and housework. Others, however, became impatient when their children demanded attention, refused to help around the house, sulked, or took to drink.

The influence of wives in families struck by unemployment tended to increase, and in this respect women suffered less psychologically from the Depression. They were usually too busy trying to make ends meet to become apathetic. But the way they used this influence varied. Some wives were sympathetic, others scornful, when the "breadwinner" came home with empty hands. If there is any generalization about the effects of the Depression on family relations it is probably an obvious one—where relationships were close and loving they became stronger, where they were not, the results could be disastrous.

The Election of 1932

As the end of his term approached, President Hoover seemed to grow daily more petulant and pessimistic. The Depression, coming after twelve years of Republican rule, probably ensured a Democratic victory in any case, but his attitude as the election neared alienated many voters and turned defeat into rout.

Confident of victory, the Democrats chose Governor Franklin Delano Roosevelt of New York as their presidential candidate. Roosevelt owed his nomination chiefly to his success as governor. Under his administration, New York had led the nation in providing relief for the needy and had enacted an impressive program of old-age pensions, unemployment insurance, and conservation and public power projects. In 1928, while Hoover was carrying New York against Smith by a wide margin, Roosevelt won election by 25,000 votes. In 1930 he swept the state by a 700,000-vote majority, double the previous record. He also had the advantage of the Roosevelt name (he was a distant cousin of the inimitable TR), and his sunny, magnetic personality contrasted favorably with that of the glum and colorless Hoover.

Roosevelt was far from being a radical. Although he had supported the League of Nations while campaigning for the vice presidency in 1920, during the 1920s he had not seriously challenged the basic tenets of Coolidge prosperity. He never had much difficulty adjusting his views to prevailing attitudes. His life before the Depression gave little indication that he understood the aspirations of ordinary people or had any deep commitment to social reform.

Roosevelt was born to wealth and social status in Dutchess County, New York, in 1882. He was educated at the exclusive Groton School and then at Harvard. Ambition as much as the desire to render public service motivated his career in politics; even after an attack of polio in 1921 had badly crippled both his legs, he refused to abandon his

A vigorous-looking Franklin D. Roosevelt campaigns for the presidency in 1932. His vice-presidential running mate, John N. Garner, and the conveniently placed post allowed the handicapped candidate to stand when greeting voters along the way.

hopes for high office. During the 1920s he was a hardworking member of the liberal wing of his party. He supported Smith for president in 1924 and 1928.

Roosevelt was a marvelous campaigner. Like every great political leader, he took as much from the people as he gave them, understanding the causes of their confusion and sensing their needs. "I have looked into the faces of thousands of Americans," he told a friend. "They have the frightened look of lost children. . . . They are saying: 'We're caught in something we don't understand; perhaps this fellow can help us out.'"

On matters such as farm policy, the tariff, and government spending, Roosevelt equivocated, contradicted himself, or remained silent. Nevertheless Roosevelt's basic position was unmistakable. There must be a "re-appraisal of values," a "New Deal." Instead of adhering to conventional limits on the extent of federal power, the government should do whatever was necessary to protect the unfortunate and advance the public good. Lacking concrete answers, Roosevelt advocated a point of view rather than a plan: "The country needs bold, persistent experimentation. It is common sense to take a method and try it. If it fails, admit it frankly and try another. But above all, try something."

The popularity of this approach was demonstrated in November. Hoover, who had lost only eight states in 1928, won only six, all in the Northeast, in 1932. Roosevelt amassed 22.8 million votes to Hoover's 15.8 million and carried the Electoral College, 472 to 59.

●●●─ Read the Document

Hoover, New York Campaign Speech at **myhistorylab.com**

During the interval between the election and Roosevelt's inauguration in March 1933, the Great Depression reached its nadir. The holdover "lame duck" Congress, last of its kind, proved incapable of effective action.[2] President Hoover, perhaps understandably, hesitated to institute changes without the cooperation of his successor. Roosevelt, for equally plausible reasons, refused to accept responsibility before assuming power officially. The nation, curiously apathetic in the face of so much suffering, drifted aimlessly, like a sailboat in a flat calm.

---

[2]The Twentieth Amendment (1933) provided for convening new Congresses in January instead of the following December. It also advanced the date of the president's inauguration from March 4 to January 20.

Milestones

1921–1922	Washington Conference tries to slow arms race	1930	Clark Memorandum renounces Roosevelt Corollary to Monroe Doctrine
1923	President Harding dies; Coolidge becomes president		Hawley-Smoot tariff raises duties on foreign manufactures
	Teapot Dome and other Harding scandals are exposed		Ten-year Dust Bowl begins in South and Midwest
1924	Dawes Plan restructures German reparations payments	1931	Japan invades Manchuria
	National Origins Act establishes immigration quotas		Hoover imposes moratorium on war debts
	Coolidge is elected president	1932	Federal troops disperse Bonus Army marchers in Washington, DC
1928	Fifteen nations sign Kellogg-Briand Pact to "outlaw" war		Reconstruction Finance Corporation (RFC) lends to banks, railroads, insurance companies
	Herbert Hoover is elected president		Franklin Delano Roosevelt is elected president
1929	New York Stock Exchange crash ends big bull market; Great Depression begins		
	Young Plan further reduces German reparations	1933	Japan withdraws from League of Nations

✓ Study and Review at www.myhistorylab.com

Review Questions

1. The introduction draws a parallel between the crash of the stock market in 1929 and the U.S. mortgage market in 2008–2009 as explanations of subsequent economic crises. What were the main differences?
2. What were the similarities in the policies of Harding, Coolidge, and Hoover? The differences?
3. What factors explained the prosperity of the 1920s? In what ways was that prosperity shaky?
4. During the 1920s and early 1930s, what role did the United States play in Latin America? In the worsening situations in Europe and Asia?
5. How did the election of 1932 constitute a political "revolution"?

Key Terms

Bonus Army   *673*

"good neighbor"   *665*

Teapot Dome scandal   *659*

((•—Hear the Audio Chapter 26 at myhistorylab.com

Do you have health insurance?

IN MARCH 2010, CONGRESS NARROWLY PASSED A MAJOR HEALTH reform law. It requires most employers to provide employees with health insurance and allows parents to extend coverage of their children to age twenty-six. It also creates a fund of nearly a trillion dollars to pay for health insurance for many people not covered by employer-paid policies until 2020.

President Barack Obama compared the battle to the one waged by Franklin D. Roosevelt sixty-five years earlier over guaranteed incomes for the elderly. "When FDR proposed Social Security, he was accused of being a Socialist," Obama observed. Michelle Bachmann, a Republican congresswoman from Minnesota, opposed the health insurance proposal for that very reason: "If you look at FDR and Barack Obama, this is really the final leap to socialism."

President Franklin D. Roosevelt signed the Social Security Act in 1935, the cornerstone of his New Deal to counteract the Great Depression. Other New Deal initiatives sought to put the unemployed to work on government projects; to use federal funds to help farmers by raising the price of agricultural products; to reorganize banks, and to alter federal regulation of corporations.

These measures generated opposition. Conservatives regarded much of the New Deal as an unconstitutional infringement of private rights; populists and Marxists denounced the New Deal as a band-aid that failed to address the root causes of poverty. But times were bad. The nation was in desperate trouble. Through it all, Roosevelt won the allegiance of voters who regarded him almost as an economic savior and the New Deal as gospel.

The Hundred Days

As the date of Franklin Roosevelt's inauguration approached, the banking system completely disintegrated and a financial panic swept the land. Depositors lined up before the doors of even the soundest institutions, desperate to withdraw their savings. Hundreds of banks were forced to close. In February, to check the panic, the governor of Michigan declared a "bank holiday," shutting every bank in the state for eight days.

Maryland, Kentucky, California, and a number of other states followed suit; by inauguration day four-fifths of the states had suspended all banking operations. Other issues loomed, especially war clouds over Europe and east Asia, but few Americans could look much beyond their own immediate, and increasingly dire, economic prospects.

Watch the Video
FDR's Inauguration at
myhistorylab.com

Something drastic had to be done. The most conservative business leaders were as ready for government intervention as the most advanced radicals. Partisanship, while not disappearing, was for once subordinated to broad national needs. A sign of this change came in February, even before Roosevelt took office, when Congress submitted to the states the Twenty-First Amendment, putting an end to prohibition. Before the end of the year the necessary three-quarters of the states had ratified it, and the prohibition era was over.

It was unquestionably Franklin D. Roosevelt who provided the spark that reenergized the American people. His inaugural address reassured the country and at the same time stirred it to action. "The only thing we have to fear is fear itself. . . . This Nation asks for action, and action now. . . . I assume unhesitatingly the leadership of this great army of our people. . . ." Many such lines punctuated the brief address, which captured the heart of the country; almost half a million letters of congratulation poured into the White House. When Roosevelt summoned Congress into a special session on March 9, the legislators outdid one another to enact his proposals into law. In the following "hundred days" serious opposition, in the sense of an organized group committed to resisting the administration, simply did not exist.

Roosevelt had the power and the will to act but no comprehensive plan of action. He and his eager congressional collaborators proceeded in a dozen directions at once, often at cross-purposes with themselves and one another. One of the first administration measures was the Economy Act, which reduced the salaries of federal employees by 15 percent and cut various veterans' benefits. Such belt-tightening measures could only make the Depression worse. But most **New Deal** programs were designed to stimulate the economy. All in all, an impressive body of new legislation was placed on the statute books.

On March 5 Roosevelt declared a nationwide bank holiday and placed an embargo on the exportation of gold. To explain the complexities of the banking problem to the public, Roosevelt delivered the first of his "fireside chats" over a national radio network. "I want to talk for a few minutes with the people of the United States about banking," he explained. His warmth and steadiness reassured millions. A plan for

A 1933 banner celebrates the repeal of prohibition.

reopening the banks under Treasury Department licenses was devised, and soon most of them were functioning again, public confidence in their solvency restored.

In April Roosevelt took the country off the gold standard, hoping thereby to cause prices to rise. Before the session ended, Congress established the Federal Deposit Insurance Corporation (FDIC) to guarantee bank deposits. It also forced the separation of investment banking and commercial banking concerns while extending the power of the Federal Reserve Board over both types of institutions, and it created the Home Owners Loan Corporation (HOLC) to refinance mortgages and prevent foreclosures. It passed the Federal Securities Act requiring promoters to make public full financial information about new stock issues and giving the Federal Trade Commission the right to regulate such transactions.

The National Recovery Administration (NRA)

Problems of unemployment and industrial stagnation had high priority during the hundred days. Congress appropriated $500 million for relief of the needy, and it created the **Civilian Conservation Corps (CCC)** to provide jobs for men between the ages of eighteen and twenty-five in reforestation and other conservation projects. To stimulate industry, Congress passed one of its most controversial measures, the National Industrial Recovery Act (NIRA). Besides establishing the Public Works Administration with authority to spend $3.3 billion, this law permitted manufacturers to draw up industry-wide codes of "fair business practices." Under the law producers could agree to raise prices and limit production without violating the antitrust laws. The law gave workers the protection of minimum wage and maximum hours regulations and guaranteed them the right "to organize and bargain collectively through representatives of their own choosing," an immense stimulus to the union movement.

The NIRA was a variant on the idea of the corporate state. This concept envisaged a system of industry-wide organizations of Capitalists and workers (supervised by the government) that would resolve conflicts internally, thereby avoiding wasteful economic competition and dangerous social clashes. It was an outgrowth of the trade association idea, although Hoover, who had supported voluntary associations, denounced it because of its compulsory aspects. It was also similar to experiments being carried out by the fascist dictator Benito Mussolini in Italy and by the Nazis in Adolf Hitler's Germany. It did not, of course, turn America into a fascist state, but it did herald an increasing concentration of economic power in the hands of interest groups, both industrialists' organizations and labor unions.

The act created a government agency, the **National Recovery Administration (NRA)**, to supervise the drafting and operation of the business codes. Drafting posed difficult problems, first because each industry insisted on tailoring the agreements to its special needs and second because most manufacturers were unwilling to accept all the provisions of Section 7a of the law, which guaranteed workers the right to unionize and bargain collectively. Many employers were more interested in the monopolistic aspects of the act than in boosting wages and encouraging unionization. In practice, the largest manufacturers in each industry drew up the codes.

The NRA did not end the Depression. There was a brief upturn in the spring of 1933, but the expected revival of industry did not take place; in nearly every case the dominant producers in each industry used their power to raise prices and limit production rather than to hire more workers and increase output.

Beginning with the cotton textile code, however, the agreements succeeded in doing away with the centuries-old problem of child labor in industry. They established the principle of federal regulation of wages and hours and led to the organization of thousands of workers, even in industries where unions had seldom been significant. Within a year John L. Lewis's United Mine Workers expanded from 150,000 members to half a million. About 100,000 automobile workers joined unions, as did a comparable number of steelworkers.

Labor leaders used the NIRA to persuade workers that Roosevelt wanted them to join unions—which was something of an overstatement. In 1935, because the craft-oriented AFL had displayed little enthusiasm for enrolling unskilled workers on an industry-wide basis, John L. Lewis, together with officials of the garment trade unions, formed the Committee for Industrial Organization (CIO) and set out to rally workers in each of these mass-production industries into one union without regard for craft lines. Since a union containing all the workers in a factory was easier to organize and direct than separate craft unions, this was a far more effective way of unionizing factory labor. The AFL expelled these unions, however, and in 1938 the CIO became the Congress of Industrial Organizations. Soon it rivaled the AFL in size and importance.

View the **Image**

PWA in Action Poster at **myhistorylab.com**

The Agricultural Adjustment Administration (AAA)

Roosevelt was more concerned about the plight of the farmers than that of any other group because he believed that the nation was becoming overcommitted to industry. The Agricultural Adjustment Act of May 1933 combined compulsory restrictions on production with government payments to growers of wheat, cotton, tobacco, pork, and a few other staple crops. The object was to lift agricultural prices to "parity" with industrial prices, the ratio in most cases being based on the levels of 1909–1914, when farmers had been reasonably prosperous. In return for withdrawing part of their land from cultivation, farmers received "rental" payments from the **Agricultural Adjustment Act (AAA)**.

Since the 1933 crops were growing when the law was passed, Secretary of Agriculture Henry A. Wallace, son of Harding's secretary of agriculture and himself an experienced farmer and plant geneticist, decided to pay farmers to destroy the crops in the field. Cotton planters plowed up 10 million acres, receiving $100 million in return. Thereafter, limitation of acreage proved sufficient to raise some agricultural prices. Tobacco growers benefited, and so did those who raised corn and hogs. The price of wheat also rose, though more because of bad harvests than because of the AAA program. But dairy farmers and cattlemen were hurt by the law, as were the railroads (which had less freight to haul) and, of course, consumers. Many farmers insisted that the NRA was raising the cost of manufactured goods more than the AAA was raising the prices they received for their crops.

A far more serious weakness of the program was its effect on tenant farmers and sharecroppers, many of whom lost their livelihoods when owners took land out of production to obtain AAA payments. In addition many landowners substituted machinery for labor. In the Cotton Belt

Read the **Document**

An Attack on New Deal Farm Policies at **myhistorylab.com**

farmers purchased more than 100,000 tractors during the 1930s. Each could do the work of several tenant or sharecropping families. Yet acreage restrictions and mortgage relief helped thousands of others. The AAA was a drastic change of American policy, but foreign producers of coffee, sugar, tea, rubber, and other staples had adopted the same techniques of restricting output and subsidizing growers well before the United States did.

The Dust Bowl

A protracted drought compounded the plight of the farmers, especially in dry sections of the Midwest. During the first third of the twentieth century, midwestern farmers perfected dryland techniques. This entailed "dragging" the fields after rainfall to improve absorption, raking them repeatedly to eliminate water-devouring weeds, and plowing the soil deeply and frequently to allow rain to sink in quickly. The use of tractors, combines, plows, and trucks during the 1920s made possible this intensive working of the fields. Farmers planted the driest areas in winter wheat, which required little moisture; in Nebraska and Iowa, most farmers planted corn.

Then came the dust storms. During the winter of 1933–1934, bitter cold killed off the winter wheat and heavy storms pulverized the soil. By March 1934 driving winds whipped across the Great Plains. In April storms from the Dakotas belched great clouds of dust through Nebraska and Kansas. In May, after the fields had been plowed, more windstorms scattered the seeds and topsoil.

The summer of 1934 was dry, especially in the Dakotas and western Kansas. These farmers were accustomed to dry weather, but the topsoil had been loosened through dryland farming. Strong winds scooped up the dried-out dirt and blew it in

A huge dust cloud engulfs Dodge City, Kansas in 1935.
Source: Kansas State Historical Society.

heaving clouds throughout the plains. Dust, forced into people's lungs, induced "dust pneumonia," a respiratory ailment that sometimes proved fatal.

The winds devastated wheat and corn. Over 30 percent of the crops in much of North Dakota, South Dakota, Nebraska, Kansas, and the Oklahoma panhandle failed. Two years later, another drought produced similar results. Coming in the midst of the Great Depression, this second calamity proved more than many farmers could bear. Tens of thousands abandoned their farms.

The Tennessee Valley Authority (TVA)

Although Roosevelt could do little about the midwestern droughts, he did propose a major initiative to alter the economic infrastructure of the upper South. During the Great War the government had constructed a hydroelectric plant at Muscle Shoals, Alabama, to provide power for factories manufacturing synthetic nitrate explosives. After 1920 farm groups and public power enthusiasts, led by Senator George W. Norris of Nebraska, had blocked administration plans to turn these facilities over to private Capitalists, but their efforts to have the site operated by the government had been defeated by presidential vetoes.

During his first hundred days, Roosevelt proposed a **Tennessee Valley Authority (TVA)** to implement a broad experiment in social planning. Besides expanding the hydroelectric plants at Muscle Shoals and developing nitrate manufacturing in order to produce cheap fertilizers, he envisioned a coordinated program of soil conservation, reforestation, and industrialization.

⊙ See the Map

The Tennessee Valley Authority at **myhistorylab.com**

Over the objections of private power companies, Congress passed the TVA Act in May 1933. This law created a board authorized to build dams, power plants, and transmission lines and to sell fertilizers and electricity to individuals and local communities. The board could undertake flood control, soil conservation, and reforestation projects and improve the navigation of the river. Although the TVA never became the comprehensive regional planning organization some of its sponsors had anticipated, it improved the standard of living of millions of inhabitants of the valley.

The Tennessee Valley Authority Although the Tennessee Valley Authority (TVA) never fully became the regional planning organization its sponsors had anticipated, the TVA nevertheless was able to expand the hydroelectric plants at Muscle Shoals, Alabama, and build dams, power plants, and transmission lines to service the surrounding area.

Table 26.1 First New Deal and First Hundred Days (March–June, 1933)

Legislation	Purpose
Banking Act	Provided federal loans to private bankers
Beer-Wine Revenue Act	Repealed Prohibition
Civilian Conservation Corps (CCC)	Created jobs for unemployed young men
Federal Emergency Relief Act (FERA)	Gave federal money to states and localities to provide relief of poor
Agricultural Adjustment Act (AAA)	Raised farm prices by restricting production
Tennessee Valley Authority (TVA)	Massive construction project that generated employment—and electricity—in Tennessee Valley
National Industrial Recovery Act (NIRA)	Created structure for business and labor to cooperate to make particular industries more profitable

The New Deal Spirit

By the end of the hundred days a large majority of the country labeled the New Deal a solid success. Considerable recovery had taken place, but more basic was the fact that Roosevelt had infused his administration with a spirit of bustle and optimism.

Although Roosevelt was not much of an intellectual, his openness to suggestion made him eager to draw on the ideas and energies of experts of all sorts. New Deal agencies soon teemed with college professors and young lawyers without political experience.

The New Deal lacked any consistent ideological base. Theorists never impressed Roosevelt much. His New Deal drew on the old populist tradition, as seen in its antipathy to bankers and its willingness to adopt schemes for inflating the currency; on the New Nationalism of Theodore Roosevelt, in its dislike of competition and its de-emphasis of the antitrust laws; and on the ideas of social workers trained in the Progressive Era. Techniques developed by the Wilsonians also found a place in the system: Louis D. Brandeis had considerable influence on Roosevelt's financial reforms, and New Deal labor policy was an outgrowth of the experience of the War Labor Board of 1917–1918.

Within the administrative maze that Roosevelt created, rival bureaucrats battled to enforce their views. The "spenders," led by Tugwell, clashed with those favoring strict economy, who gathered around Lewis Douglas, director of the budget. Roosevelt mediated between the factions. Washington became a battleground for dozens of special interest groups: the Farm Bureau Federation, the unions, the trade associations, and the silver miners. While the system was superior to that of Roosevelt's predecessors—who had allowed one interest, big business, to predominate—it slighted the unorganized majority. The NRA aimed frankly at raising the prices paid by consumers of manufactured goods; the AAA processing tax came ultimately from the pocketbooks of ordinary citizens.

The Unemployed

At least 9 million persons were still without work in 1934. Yet the Democrats confounded the political experts, including their own, by increasing their already large majorities in both houses of Congress in the 1934 elections. All the evidence indicates

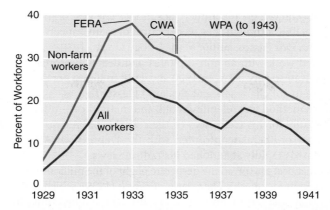

Unemployment and Federal Action, 1929–1941 Unemployment of non-farm workers reached nearly 40 percent by early 1933. The Federal Emergency Relief Act (FERA) and Civil Works Administration (CWA) (both in 1933) and the Works Progress Administration (WPA) (1935) put millions back to work.

that most of the jobless continued to support the administration. Their loyalty can best be explained by Roosevelt's unemployment policies.

In May 1933 Congress had established the Federal Emergency Relief Administration (FERA) and given it $500 million to be dispensed through state relief organizations. Roosevelt appointed Harry L. Hopkins, an eccentric but brilliant and dedicated social worker, to direct the FERA. Hopkins insisted that the unemployed needed jobs, not handouts. In November he persuaded Roosevelt to create the Civil Works Administration (CWA) and swiftly put 4 million people to work building and repairing roads and public buildings, teaching, decorating the walls of post offices with murals, and utilizing their special skills in dozens of other ways.

In May 1935 Roosevelt put Hopkins in charge of the **Works Progress Administration (WPA)**. By the time this agency was disbanded in 1943 it had found employment for 8.5 million people. Besides building public works, the WPA made important cultural contributions. It developed the Federal Theatre Project, which put actors, directors, and stagehands to work; the Federal Writers' Project, which turned out valuable guidebooks, collected local lore, and published about 1,000 books and pamphlets; and the Federal Art Project, which employed painters and sculptors. In addition, the National Youth Administration created part-time jobs for more than 2 million high school and college students.

At no time during the New Deal years did unemployment fall below 10 percent of the workforce, and in some places it was much higher. WPA did not go far enough, chiefly because Roosevelt could not escape his fear of drastically unbalancing the budget. The president also hesitated to undertake projects that might compete with private enterprises. Yet his caution did him no good politically; the business interests he sought to placate were becoming increasingly hostile to the New Deal.

Literature during the Depression

Some American novelists found Soviet communism attractive and wrote "proletarian" novels in which ordinary workers were the heroes, and stylistic niceties gave way to the rough language of the street and the factory. Most of these books are of little artistic merit, and none achieved great commercial success. The best of the Depression writers avoided the party line, although they were critical of many aspects of American life.

One was John Dos Passos, author of the trilogy *U.S.A.* (1930–1936), a massive, intricately constructed work with an anti-capitalist and deeply pessimistic point of view. It portrayed American society between 1900 and 1930 in broad perspective, interweaving the stories of five major characters and a galaxy of lesser figures.

Dos Passos's method was relentless, cold, and methodical—utterly realistic. He displayed no sympathy for his characters or their world. *U.S.A.* was a monument to the despair and anger of liberals confronted with the Depression. After the Depression, however, Dos Passos rapidly abandoned his radical views.

The novel that best portrayed the desperate plight of the millions impoverished by the Depression was John Steinbeck's *The Grapes of Wrath* (1939), which described the fate of the Joads, an Oklahoma farm family driven by drought and bad times to abandon their land and become migratory laborers in California. Steinbeck captured the patient bewilderment of the downtrodden, the brutality bred of fear that characterized their exploiters, and the furious resentments of the radicals of the 1930s. He depicted the parching blackness of the Oklahoma dust bowl, the grandeur of California, the backbreaking toil of the migrant fruit pickers, and the ultimate indignation of a people repeatedly degraded.

William Faulkner, probably the finest American novelist of the era, responded in still another way. Between 1929 and 1932, he burst into prominence with four major novels: *The Sound and the Fury, As I Lay Dying, Sanctuary*, and *Light in August*.

Faulkner was essentially a pessimist. His characters continually experience emotions too intense to be bearable, often too profound and too subtle for the natures he had given them. Nevertheless his stature was beyond question, and unlike so many other novelists of the period he maintained a high level in his later years.

Three Extremists: Long, Coughlin, and Townsend

Roosevelt's moderation and the desperation of the poor roused extremists both on the left and on the right. The most formidable was Louisiana's Senator Huey Long, the "Kingfish." Raised on a farm in northern Louisiana, Long was successively a traveling salesman, a lawyer, state railroad commissioner, governor, and, after 1930, U.S. senator. By 1933 his rule in Louisiana was absolute. Long was certainly a demagogue—yet the plight of all poor people concerned him deeply. More important, he tried to do something about it.

As a reformer, Long stood in the populist tradition; he hated bankers and "the interests." He believed that poor people, regardless of color, should have a chance to earn a decent living and get an education. His arguments were simplistic, patronizing, possibly insincere, but effective. "Don't say I'm working for niggers," he told one northern journalist. "I'm for the poor man—all poor men. Black and white, they all gotta have a chance. . . . 'Every Man a King'—that's my slogan."

Long had supported the New Deal at the start. But partly because he thought Roosevelt too conservative and partly because of his own ambition, he soon broke with the administration. While Roosevelt was probably more hostile to the big financiers than to any other interest, Long denounced him as "a phoney" and a stooge of Wall Street.

By 1935 Long's "Share Our Wealth" movement had a membership of over 4.6 million. His program called for the confiscation of family fortunes of more than $5 million and a tax of 100 percent on incomes over $1 million a year, the money to be used to buy every family a "homestead" (a house, a car, and other necessities) and provide an annual family income of $2,000 to $3,000, plus old-age pensions, educational benefits, and veterans' pensions. As the 1936 election approached, he planned to organize a third party to split the liberal vote. He assumed that the Republicans would win the election and so botch the job of fighting the Depression that he could sweep the country in 1940.

Less powerful than Long but more widely influential was Father Charles E. Coughlin, the "Radio Priest." A genial Canadian of Irish lineage, Coughlin in 1926 began broadcasting a weekly religious message over station WJR in Detroit. His mellifluous voice attracted a huge national audience, and the Depression gave him a secular cause. In 1933 he had been an eager New Dealer, but his dislike of New Deal financial policies—he believed that inflating the currency would end

Read the Document
Coughlin, *A Third Party (1936)*
at **myhistorylab.com**

the Depression—and his need for ever more sensational ideas to hold his radio audience led him to turn against the New Deal. By 1935 he was calling Roosevelt a "great betrayer and liar."

Although Coughlin's National Union for Social Justice was especially appealing to Catholics, it attracted people of every faith, particularly in the lower-middle-class districts of the big cities. He attacked bankers, New Deal planners, Roosevelt's farm program, and the alleged sympathy of the administration for Communists and Jews, both of which Coughlin denounced in his weekly talks. His program resembled fascism more than any leftist philosophy, but he posed a threat, especially in combination with Long, to the continuation of Democratic rule.

Charles E. Coughlin, the "Radio Priest," was the father of conservative "talk radio."

Another rapidly growing movement alarmed the Democrats in 1934–1935: Dr. Francis E. Townsend's campaign for "old-age revolving pensions." Townsend, a retired California physician, had an oversimplified and therefore appealing "solution" to the nation's troubles. He advocated paying every person aged sixty years and over a pension of $200 a month, the only conditions being that the pensioners not hold jobs and that they spend the entire sum within thirty days. Their purchases, he argued, would stimulate production, thereby creating new jobs and revitalizing the economy. A stiff transactions tax, collected whenever any commodity changed hands, would pay for the program.

Economists quickly pointed out that with about 10 million persons eligible for the Townsend pensions, the cost would amount to $24 billion a year—roughly half the national income. But among the elderly the scheme proved extremely popular. Although most Townsendites were anything but radical politically, their plan, like Long's "Share Our Wealth" scheme, would have revolutionized the distribution of wealth in the country. The movement marked the emergence of a new force in American society. With medical advances lengthening the average life span, the percentage of old people in the population was rising. The breakdown of close family ties in an increasingly mobile society now caused many of these citizens to be cast adrift to live out their last years poor, sick, idle, and alone.

With the possible exception of Long, the extremists had little understanding of practical affairs. Collectively, however, they represented a threat to Roosevelt; their success helped to make the president see that he must move boldly to restore good times or face serious political trouble in 1936.

Political imperatives had much to do with Roosevelt's decisions, and the influence of Justice Brandeis and his disciples, notably Felix Frankfurter, was great. They urged Roosevelt to abandon his probusiness programs, especially the NRA, and stress restoring competition and taxing corporations more heavily. The fact that most businessmen were turning away from him encouraged the president to accept this advice; so did the Supreme Court's decision in *Schecter v. United States* (May 1935), which declared the National Industrial Recovery Act unconstitutional. (The case involved the provisions of the NRA Live Poultry Code; the Court voided the act on the grounds that Congress had delegated too much legislative power to the code authorities and that the defendants, four brothers engaged in slaughtering chickens in New York City, were not engaged in interstate commerce.)

The Second New Deal

Existing laws had failed to end the Depression. Conservatives roundly denounced Roosevelt, and extremists were luring away some of his supporters. Voters, heartened by the partial success of early New Deal measures, were clamoring for further reforms. But the Supreme Court had declared many key New Deal measures unconstitutional. For these many reasons, Roosevelt, in June 1935, launched what historians call the Second New Deal.

There followed the "second hundred days," one of the most productive periods in the history of American legislation. The National Labor Relations Act—commonly known as the **Wagner Act**—gave workers the right to bargain collectively and prohibited employers from interfering with union organizational activities in their factories. A National Labor Relations Board (NLRB) was established to supervise plant elections and designate successful unions as official bargaining agents when a majority of the workers approved.

Monopoly, patented in 1935, was an instant best-seller: Players risk all their assets in an attempt to secure a real estate monopoly—and thus great wealth.

It was difficult to force some big corporations to bargain "in good faith," as the law required, but the NLRB could conduct investigations of employer practices and issue cease and desist orders when "unfair" activities came to light.

The **Social Security Act** of August 1935 set up a system of old-age insurance, financed partly by a tax on wages (paid by workers) and partly by a tax on payrolls (paid by employers). It created a state-federal system of unemployment insurance, similarly financed. Liberal critics considered this Social Security system inadequate because it did not cover agricultural workers, domestics, self-employed persons, and some other groups particularly in need of its benefits. Health insurance was not included, and because the size of pensions depended on the amount earned, the lowest-paid workers could not count on much support after reaching sixty-five. Yet the law was of major significance. Over the years the pension payments were increased and the classes of workers covered expanded.

The Rural Electrification Administration (REA), created by executive order, also began to function during this remarkable period. The REA lent money at low interest rates to utility companies and to farmer cooperatives interested in bringing electricity to rural areas. When the REA went into operation, only one farm in ten had electricity; by 1950 only one in ten did not.

Another important measure was the Wealth Tax Act of August 1935, which raised taxes on large incomes considerably. Estate and gift taxes were also increased. Stiffer

Table 26.2 Second New Deal (1935–1938)

Legislation	Purpose
Emergency Relief Appropriations Act (1935)	Created Works Progress Administration (WPA) to give jobs to blacks, white-collar workers, and even artists and writers
Rural Electrification Administration (1935)	Extended electric power lines to rural areas
Social Security Act (1935)	Devised system to provide unemployment insurance and pensions for elderly
Wagner Act (1935)	Guaranteed the rights of unions to organize and negotiate for members
Fair Labor Standards Act (1938)	Set minimum hourly wages and maximum hours of work

taxes on corporate profits reflected the Brandeis group's desire to penalize corporate giantism. Much of the opposition to other New Deal legislation arose from the fact that after these changes in the tax laws were made, the well-to-do had to bear a larger share of the cost of *all* government activities.

Herbert Hoover epitomized the attitude of conservatives when he called the New Deal "the most stupendous invasion of the whole spirit of Liberty that the nation has witnessed." Undoubtedly many opponents of the New Deal sincerely believed that it was undermining the foundations of American freedom. The cost of the New Deal also alarmed them. By 1936 some members of the administration had fallen under the influence of the British economist John Maynard Keynes, who argued that the world Depression could be conquered if governments would deliberately unbalance their budgets by reducing interest rates and taxes and by increasing expenditures to stimulate consumption and investment.

Roosevelt never accepted Keynes's theories; he conferred with the economist in 1934 but could not grasp the "rigmarole of figures" with which Keynes deluged him. Nevertheless the imperatives of the Depression forced him to spend more than the government was collecting in taxes; thus he adopted in part the Keynesian approach. Conservative businessmen considered him financially irresponsible, and the fact that deficit spending seemed to be good politics made them seethe with rage.

The Election of 1936

The election of 1936 loomed as a showdown. The GOP candidate, Governor Alfred M. Landon of Kansas, was a former follower of Theodore Roosevelt, a foe of the Ku Klux Klan in the 1920s, and a believer in government regulation of business. But he was a poor speaker and against the charm and political astuteness of Roosevelt, Landon's arguments—chiefly that he could administer the government more efficiently than the president—made little impression.

On election day the country gave the president a tremendous vote of confidence. He carried every state but Maine and Vermont. The Republicans elected only eighty-nine members of the House of Representatives and their strength in the Senate fell to sixteen, an all-time low. In dozens of city and state elections, Democratic candidates also made large gains. Both Roosevelt's personality and his program had captivated the land. He seemed irresistible, the most powerfully entrenched president in the history of the United States.

Roosevelt did not win in 1936 because of the inadequacies of his foes. Having abandoned his efforts to hold the businessmen, whom he now denounced as "economic royalists," he appealed for the votes of workers and the underprivileged. The new labor unions gratefully poured thousands of dollars into the campaign to reelect him. Black voters switched to the Democrats in record numbers. Farmers liked Roosevelt because of his evident concern for their welfare. Countless elderly persons backed Roosevelt out of gratitude for the Social Security Act.

Roosevelt Tries to Undermine the Supreme Court

On January 20, in his second inaugural address, Roosevelt spoke of the plight of millions of citizens "denied the greater part of what the very lowest standards of today call the necessities of life." A third of the nation, he added without exaggeration, was "ill-housed, ill-clad, ill-nourished." He interpreted his landslide victory as a mandate for further reforms, and with his prestige and his immense congressional majorities, nothing appeared to stand in his way. Nothing, that is, except the Supreme Court.

Throughout Roosevelt's first term the Court had stood almost immovable against increasing the scope of federal authority and broadening the general power of government, state as well as national, to cope with the exigencies of the Depression. Of the nine justices, only Louis Brandeis, Benjamin N. Cardozo, and Harlan Fiske Stone viewed the New Deal sympathetically. Four others—James C. McReynolds, Willis Van Devanter, Pierce Butler, and George Sutherland—were intransigent conservatives. Chief Justice Charles Evans Hughes and Justice Owen J. Roberts, while more open-minded, tended to side with the conservatives on many questions.

Much of the early New Deal legislation, pushed through Congress at top speed during the hundred days, had been drafted without proper regard for the Constitution. Even the liberal justices considered the National Industrial Recovery Act unconstitutional.

In 1937 all the major measures of the second hundred days appeared doomed. The Wagner Act had little chance of winning approval, experts predicted. Lawyers were advising employers to ignore the Social Security Act, so confident that the Court would declare it unconstitutional.

Faced with this situation, Roosevelt decided to ask Congress to shift the balance on the Court by increasing the number of justices, thinly disguising the purpose of his plan by making it part of a general reorganization of the judiciary. A member of the Court who reached the age of seventy would have the option of retiring at full pay. Should such a justice choose not to retire, the president was to appoint an additional justice, up to a maximum of six, to ease the burden of work for the aged jurists who remained on the bench.

Roosevelt knew that this measure would run into resistance, but he expected that the huge Democratic majorities in Congress could override any opposition and that the public would back him solidly. No astute politician had erred so badly in estimating the effects of an action since Stephen A. Douglas introduced the Kansas-Nebraska bill in 1854.

Although polls showed the public fairly evenly divided on the "court-packing" bill, the opposition was vocal and influential. To the expected denunciations of conservatives were added the complaints of liberals fearful that the principle of court packing might in the future be used to subvert civil liberties. Opposition in Congress was immediate and intense; many who had cheerfully supported every New Deal bill came out against the plan. Chief Justice Hughes released a devastating critique; even the liberal Brandeis—the oldest judge on the court—rejected the bill out of hand.

For months Roosevelt stubbornly refused to concede defeat, but in July 1937 he had to yield. Minor administrative reforms of the judiciary were enacted, but the size of the Court remained unchanged.

The struggle did result in saving the legislation of the Second New Deal. Alarmed by the threat to the Court, Justices Hughes and Roberts beat a strategic retreat on a series of specific issues. While the debate was raging in Congress, they sided with the liberals in upholding first a minimum wage law of the state of Washington that was little different from a New York act the Court had recently rejected, then the Wagner Act, and then the Social Security Act. In May Justice Van Devanter retired and Roosevelt replaced him with Senator Hugo Black of Alabama, a New Dealer. The conservative justices thereupon gave up the fight, and soon Roosevelt was able to appoint enough new judges to give the Court a large pro-New Deal majority. No further measure of significance was declared unconstitutional during his presidency. The Court fight hurt Roosevelt severely. When the president summoned a special session of Congress in November 1937 and submitted a program of "must" legislation, not one of his bills was passed.

The New Deal Winds Down

With unemployment high, wages low, and workers relatively powerless against their employers, most Americans had liked New Deal labor legislation and sympathized with the industrial unions whose growth it stimulated. The NRA, the Wagner Act, and the CIO's organization of industries like steel and automobiles changed the power structure within the economy. What amounted to a revolution in the lives of wage earners had occurred. Unionization had meant fair methods of settling disputes about work practices and a measure of job security based on seniority for tens of thousands of workers. The CIO in particular had done much to increase the influence of labor in politics and to bring blacks and other minorities into the labor movement.

In 1937 a series of "sit-down strikes" broke out, beginning at the General Motors plant in Flint, Michigan. The tolerant attitude of the Roosevelt administration ensured the strikers against government intervention. Fearful that all-out efforts to clear their plants would result in the destruction of expensive machinery, most employers capitulated to the workers' demands. All the automobile manufacturers but Henry Ford quickly came to terms with the United Automobile Workers.

The major steel companies, led by U.S. Steel, recognized the CIO and granted higher wages and a forty-hour week. The auto and steel unions alone boasted more than 725,000 members by late 1937; other CIO units conquered the rubber industry, the electrical industry, the textile industry, and many more.

These gains and the aggressive way in which the unions pursued their objectives gave many members of the middle class second thoughts concerning the justice of labor's demands. Sit-down strikes, the disregard of unions for the "rights" of nonunion workers, and the violence that accompanied some strikes seemed to many not merely unreasonable but also a threat to social order. The enthusiasm of such people for all reform cooled rapidly.

While the sit-down strikes and the Court fight were going on, the New Deal suffered another heavy blow. Business conditions had been gradually improving since 1933. Heartened by the trend, Roosevelt cut back sharply on the relief program in June 1937, with disastrous results. Between August and October the economy slipped downward like sand through a chute. Stock prices plummeted; unemployment rose by 2 million; industrial production slumped. This "Roosevelt recession" further damaged the president's reputation.

In April 1938 Roosevelt again committed himself to heavy deficit spending. At his urging Congress passed a $3.75 billion public works bill. Two major pieces of legislation were also enacted at about this time. A new AAA program set marketing quotas and acreage limitations for growers of staples like wheat, cotton, and tobacco and authorized the Commodity Credit Corporation to lend money to farmers on their surplus crops.

The second measure, the Fair Labor Standards Act, abolished child labor and established a national minimum wage of 40 cents an hour and a maximum workweek of 40 hours, with time and a half for overtime. Although the law failed to cover many of the poorest-paid types of labor, its passage meant wage increases for 750,000 workers. In later years many more classes of workers were brought within its protection, and the minimum wage was repeatedly increased.

These measures further alienated conservatives without dramatically improving economic conditions. The resistance of many Democratic members of Congress to additional economic and social "experiments" hardened. As the 1938 elections approached, Roosevelt decided to go to the voters in an effort to strengthen party discipline and reenergize the New Deal. He singled out a number of conservative Democratic senators, notably Walter F. George of Georgia, Millard F. Tydings of Maryland, and "Cotton Ed" Smith of South Carolina, and tried to "purge" them by backing other Democrats in the primaries.

The purge failed. Southern voters liked Roosevelt but resented his interference in local politics. Smith dodged the issue of liberalism by stressing the question of white supremacy. Tydings emphasized Roosevelt's "invasion" of Maryland. All three senators were easily renominated and then reelected in November. In the nation at large the Republicans made important gains for the first time since Roosevelt had taken office. The Democrats maintained nominal control of both houses of Congress, but the conservative coalition, while unable to muster the votes to do away with accomplished reforms, succeeded in blocking additional legislation.

Significance of the New Deal

After World War II broke out in 1939, the Great Depression was swept away on a wave of orders from the beleaguered European democracies. For this prosperity, Roosevelt received much undeserved credit. Despite the aid given to the jobless, the generation of workers born between 1900 and 1910 who entered the 1930s as unskilled laborers had their careers permanently stunted by the Depression. Far fewer rose to middle-class status than at any time since the 1830s and 1840s.

Roosevelt's willingness to experiment with different means of combating the Depression made sense because no one really knew what to do; however, his uncertainty about the ultimate objectives of the New Deal was counterproductive. He vacillated

To hold back immense volumes of water, the Hoover Dam, seen from above, consisted of 2.5 million cubic yards of concrete which, at the base, was thicker than two football fields set end-to-end. It was built through the New Deal.

between seeking to stimulate the economy by deficit spending and trying to balance the budget, between a narrow "America first" economic nationalism and a broad-gauged international approach, between regulating monopolies and trust-busting, and between helping the underprivileged and bolstering those already strong.

Roosevelt's fondness for establishing new agencies to deal with specific problems vastly increased the federal bureaucracy, indirectly added to the influence of lobbyists, and made it more difficult to monitor government activities. His cavalier attitude toward constitutional limitations on executive power, which he justified as being necessary in a national emergency, set in motion trends that so increased the prestige and authority of the presidency that the balance among the executive, legislative, and judicial branches was threatened.

Yet these are criticisms after the fact. Because of New Deal decisions, many formerly unregulated areas of American life became subject to federal authority: the stock exchange, agricultural prices and production, labor relations, old-age pensions, relief of the needy. By encouraging the growth of unions, the New Deal probably helped workers obtain a larger share of the profits of industry. By putting a floor under the income of many farmers, it checked the decline of agricultural living standards, though not that of the agricultural population. The Social Security program, with all its inadequacies, lessened the impact of bad times on an increasingly large proportion of the population and provided immense psychological benefits to all.

⊙ Watch the Video
Responding to the Great Depression: Whose New Deal? at **myhistorylab.com**

Women as New Dealers: The Network

Largely because of the influence of Eleanor Roosevelt and Molly Dewson, head of the Women's Division of the Democratic National Committee, the Roosevelt administration employed far more women in positions of importance than any earlier one. Secretary of Labor Frances Perkins, the first woman appointed to a Cabinet post, had been active in labor relations for more than twenty years, as secretary of the Consumers' League during the progressive period, as a factory inspector immediately after the war, and as chair of the New York State Industrial Commission. As secretary of labor she helped draft

New Deal labor legislation and kept Roosevelt informed on various labor problems outside the government.

Through her newspaper column "My Day" and as a speaker on public issues, Eleanor Roosevelt became a major political force, especially in the area of civil rights, where the administration needed constant prodding.

She particularly identified with efforts to obtain better treatment for blacks, in and out of government. Her best-known action occurred in 1939 after the Daughters of the American Revolution (DAR) refused to permit the use of their Washington auditorium for a concert by the black contralto Marian Anderson. Eleanor Roosevelt resigned from the DAR in protest, and after the president arranged for Anderson to sing at the Lincoln Memorial, she persuaded a small army of dignitaries to sponsor the concert. An interracial crowd of 75,000 people attended the performance. The *Chicago Defender*, an influential black newspaper, noted that the First Lady "stood like the Rock of Gibraltar against pernicious encroachments on the rights of minorities."

Blacks during the New Deal

The shift of black voters from the Republican to the Democratic party during the New Deal years was one of the most significant political turnarounds in American history. In 1932 when things were at their worst, fewer African Americans defected from the Republican party than the members of any other traditionally Republican group. Four years later, however, blacks voted for Roosevelt in overwhelming numbers.

Blacks supported the New Deal for the same reasons that whites did, but how the New Deal affected blacks in general and racial attitudes specifically are more complicated questions. Claiming that he dared not antagonize southern congressmen, whose votes he needed for his recovery programs, Roosevelt did nothing about civil rights before 1941 and relatively little thereafter. For the same reason, many southern white liberals hesitated to support racial integration for fear that other liberal causes could be injured as a result.

Many of the early New Deal programs treated blacks as second-class citizens. They were often paid at lower rates than whites under NRA codes and the early farm programs shortchanged black tenants and sharecroppers. TVA developments were rigidly segregated, and almost no blacks got jobs in TVA offices. Because the Social Security Act excluded agricultural laborers and domestic servants, it did nothing for hundreds of thousands of poor black workers or for Mexican American farmhands in the Southwest. In 1939 unemployment was twice as high among blacks as among whites, and whites' wages were double the level of blacks' wages.

The fact that members of racial minorities got less than they deserved did not keep most of them from becoming New Dealers: Half a loaf was more than any American government had given blacks since the time of Ulysses S. Grant.

In the labor movement the new CIO unions accepted black members, and this was particularly significant because these unions were organizing industries—steel, automobiles, and mining among others—that employed large numbers of blacks. Thus, while black Americans suffered horribly during the Depression, New Deal efforts to counteract its effects brought them some relief and a measure of hope. And this became

Black sharecroppers evicted from their tenant farms were photographed by Arthur Rothstein along a Missouri road in 1939. Rothstein was one of a group of outstanding photographers who created a unique "sociological and economic survey" of the nation between 1936 and 1942 under the aegis of the Farm Security Administration.

increasingly true with the passage of time. During Roosevelt's second term, blacks found far less to criticize than had been the case earlier.

A New Deal for Indians

New Deal policy toward American Indians built on earlier trends but carried them further. During the Harding and Coolidge administrations more Indian land had passed into the hands of whites, and agents of the Bureau of Indian Affairs had tried to suppress elements of Indian culture that they considered "pagan" or "lascivious." In 1924 Congress finally granted citizenship to all Indians, but it was still generally agreed by whites that Indians should be treated as wards of the state. Assimilation had failed; Indian languages and religious practices, patterns of family life, Indian arts and crafts had all resisted generations of efforts to "civilize" the tribes.

Government policy took a new direction in 1933 when President Roosevelt named John Collier commissioner of Indian affairs. In the 1920s Collier had studied the Indians of the Southwest and been appalled by what he learned. He became executive secretary of the American Indian Defense Association and, in 1925, editor of a reform-oriented magazine, *American Indian Life*. By the time he was appointed commissioner, the Depression had reduced perhaps a third of the 320,000 Indians living on reservations to penury.

Collier tried to revive the spirits of these people. He was particularly eager to encourage the revival of tribal governments that could represent the Indians in dealings with the United States government and function as community service centers.

In part because of Collier's urging, Congress passed the Indian Reorganization Act of 1934. This law did away with the Dawes Act allotment system and enabled Indians to establish tribal governments with powers like those of cities, and it encouraged Indians to return individually owned lands to tribal control. About 4 million of the 90 million acres of Indian land lost under the allotment system were returned to the tribes.

In truth the problem was more complicated than Collier had imagined. Indians who owned profitable allotments, such as those in Oklahoma who held oil and mineral rights, did not relish turning over their land to tribal control. All told, 77 of 269 tribes voted against communal holdings.

Collier resigned in 1945, and in the 1950s Congress "terminated" most government efforts aimed at preserving Indian cultures. Nevertheless, like so many of its programs, the New Deal's Indian policy was a bold effort to deal constructively with a long-standing national problem.

The Role of Roosevelt

How much of the credit for New Deal policies belongs personally to Franklin D. Roosevelt is debatable. He had little to do with many of the details and some of the broad principles behind the New Deal. His knowledge of economics was skimpy, his understanding of many social problems superficial, and his political philosophy distressingly vague. The British leader Anthony Eden described him as "a conjurer, skillfully juggling with balls of dynamite, whose nature he failed to understand."

Nevertheless, every aspect of the New Deal bears the brand of Roosevelt's remarkable personality. Roosevelt constructed the coalition that made the program possible; his humanitarianism made it a reform movement of major significance. Although

A miner greets the president. Franklin's "first-class temperament" compensated for his "second-class intellect," Justice Oliver Wendell Holmes famously observed.

considered by many a terrible administrator because he encouraged rivalry among his subordinates, assigned different agencies overlapping responsibilities, failed to discharge many incompetents, and frequently put off making difficult decisions, he was in fact one of the most effective chief executives in the nation's history.

Like Andrew Jackson, Roosevelt maximized his role as leader of all the people. His informal biweekly press conferences kept the public in touch with developments and himself in tune with popular thinking. His "fireside chats" convinced millions that he was personally interested in each citizen's life and welfare, as in a way he was. At a time when the size and complexity of the government made it impossible for any one person to direct the nation's destiny, Roosevelt managed the minor miracle of personifying that government to 130 million people.

While the New Deal was still evolving, contemporaries recognized Roosevelt's right to a place beside Washington, Jefferson, and Lincoln among the great presidents. Yet as his second term drew toward its close, some of his most important work still lay in the future.

The Triumph of Isolationism

Franklin Roosevelt was at heart an internationalist, but like most world leaders in the 1930s, he placed revival of his own country's limping economy ahead of general world recovery. In April 1933 he took the United States off the gold standard, hoping that devaluing the dollar would make it easier to sell American goods abroad. The following month the World Economic Conference met in London. Delegates from sixty-four nations sought ways to increase world trade, perhaps by a general reduction of tariffs and the stabilization of currencies. After flirting with the idea of currency stabilization, Roosevelt threw a bombshell into the conference by announcing that the United States would not return to the gold standard. His decision increased international ill feeling, and the conference collapsed.

Against this background, vital changes in American foreign policy took place. Unable to persuade the country to take positive action against aggressors, internationalists like Secretary of State Stimson had begun in 1931 to work for a discretionary arms embargo law to be applied by the president in time of war against whichever side had broken the peace. By early 1933 Stimson had obtained Hoover's backing for an embargo bill, as well as the support of President-elect Roosevelt. First the munitions manufacturers and then the isolationists pounced on it, and in the resulting debate it was amended to make the embargo apply to *all* belligerents.

Stimson's policy would have permitted arms shipments to China but not to Japan, which might have discouraged the Japanese from attacking. As amended, the embargo would have automatically applied to both sides, thus removing the United States as an influence in the conflict. Although Roosevelt accepted the change, the internationalists in Congress did not, and when they withdrew their support the measure died.

The danger of another world war mounted steadily as Germany, Italy, and Japan repeatedly resorted to force to achieve their expansionist aims. In March 1935 Hitler instituted universal military training and denounced the settlement at Versailles. In May Mussolini massed troops in Italian Somaliland, using a trivial border clash as a pretext for threatening the ancient kingdom of Ethiopia.

Congress responded by passing a series of **neutrality acts** to prevent the United States from being drawn into a wider war. The Neutrality Act of 1935 forbade the sale of munitions to all belligerents whenever the president should proclaim that a state of war existed. Americans who took passage on belligerent ships after such a proclamation had been issued would do so at their own risk. Roosevelt would have preferred a discretionary embargo or no new legislation at all, but he dared not rouse the ire of the isolationists by vetoing the bill.

In October 1935 Italy invaded Ethiopia and Roosevelt invoked the new neutrality law. Secretary of State Cordell Hull asked American exporters to support a "moral embargo" on the sale of oil and other products not covered by the act. His plea was ignored; oil shipments to Italy tripled between October and January. Italy quickly overran and annexed Ethiopia. In February 1936 Congress passed a second neutrality act forbidding all loans to belligerents.

Then, in the summer of 1936, civil war broke out in Spain. The rebels, led by the reactionary General Francisco Franco and strongly backed by Italy and Germany, sought to overthrow the somewhat leftist Spanish Republic. Here, clearly, was a clash between democracy and fascism, and the neutrality laws did not apply to civil wars. However, Roosevelt now became more fearful of involvement than some isolationists. The president believed that American interference might cause the conflict in Spain to become a global war, and he was wary of antagonizing the substantial number of American Catholics who were sympathetic to the Franco regime. At his urging Congress passed another neutrality act broadening the arms embargo to cover civil wars.

Isolationism now reached its peak. A public opinion poll revealed in March 1937 that 94 percent of the people thought American policy should be directed at keeping out of all foreign wars rather than trying to prevent wars from breaking out. In April Congress passed still another neutrality law. It continued the embargo on munitions and loans, forbade Americans to travel on belligerent ships, and gave the president discretionary authority to place the sale of other goods to belligerents on a cash-and-carry basis. This played into the hands of the aggressors. While German planes and cannons were turning the tide in Spain, the United States was denying the hard-pressed Spanish loyalists even a case of cartridges.

In January 1938 the House narrowly defeated the Ludlow amendment, which would have prohibited Congress from declaring war without the prior approval of the nation's voters.

President Roosevelt, in part because of domestic problems such as the Supreme Court packing struggle and the wave of sit-down strikes, and in part because of his own vacillation, seemed to have lost control over the formulation of American foreign policy. The American people, like wild creatures before a forest fire, were rushing in blind panic from the conflagration.

War Again in Asia and Europe

There were limits beyond which Americans would not go. In July 1937 the Japanese resumed their conquest of China, pressing ahead on a broad front. Roosevelt believed that invoking the neutrality law would only help the well-armed Japanese. Taking advantage of the fact that neither side had formally declared war, he allowed the shipment of arms and supplies to both sides.

Roosevelt came gradually to the conclusion that resisting aggression was more important than keeping out of war, but when he did, the need to keep the country united

In 1939 Hitler reviews goose-stepping troops during a celebration of his 50th birthday.

led him at times to be less than candid in his public statements. Hitler's annexation of Austria in March 1938 caused him deep concern. The Nazis' vicious anti-Semitism had caused many of Germany's 500,000 Jewish citizens to seek refuge abroad. Now 190,000 Austrian Jews were under Nazi control. When Roosevelt learned that the Germans were burning synagogues, expelling Jewish children from schools, and otherwise mistreating innocent people, he said that he "could scarcely believe that such things could occur." But public opinion opposed changing the immigration law so that more refugees could be admitted, and the president did nothing.

In September 1938 Hitler demanded that Czechoslovakia cede the German-speaking Sudetenland to the Reich. British Prime Minister Neville Chamberlain and French Premier Edouard Daladier, in a conference with Hitler at Munich, yielded to Hitler's threats and promises and persuaded the Czechs to surrender the region. Roosevelt failed again to speak out. But when the Nazis seized the rest of Czechoslovakia in March 1939, Roosevelt called for "methods short of war" to demonstrate America's determination to check the fascists.

When Hitler threatened Poland in the spring of 1939, demanding the free city of Danzig and the Polish Corridor separating East Prussia from the rest of Germany, and when Mussolini invaded Albania, Roosevelt urged Congress to repeal the 1937 neutrality act so that the United States could sell arms to Britain and France in the event of war. Congress refused.

In August 1939 Germany and the Soviet Union signed a nonaggression pact, prelude to their joint assault on Poland. On September 1 Hitler's troops invaded Poland, at last provoking Great Britain and France to declare war. Roosevelt immediately asked Congress to repeal the arms embargo. In November, in a vote that followed party lines closely, the Democratic majority pushed through a law permitting the sale of arms and other contraband on a cash-and-carry basis. Short-term loans were authorized, but American vessels were forbidden to carry any products to the belligerents. Since the Allies controlled the seas, cash-and-carry gave them a tremendous advantage.

The German attack on Poland effected a basic change in American thinking. Keeping out of the war remained an almost universal hope, but preventing a Nazi victory became the ultimate, if not always conscious, objective of many citizens. In Roosevelt's case it was perfectly conscious, although he dared not express his feelings candidly because of isolationist strength in Congress and the country. He moved slowly, responding to rather than directing the course of events.

Poland fell in less than a month; then, Hitler loosed his armored divisions. Between April 9 and June 22 he taught the world the awful meaning of *Blitzkrieg*— lightning war, spearheaded by tanks and supporting aircraft. Denmark, Norway, the Netherlands, Belgium, and France were successively overwhelmed. The British army, pinned against the sea at Dunkirk, saved itself from annihilation only by fleeing across the English Channel. After the French submitted to his harsh terms on June 22, Hitler controlled nearly all of western Europe.

Roosevelt responded to these disasters in a number of ways. In the fall of 1939, reacting to warnings from Albert Einstein and other scientists that the Germans were trying to develop an atomic bomb, he committed federal funds to a top-secret atomic bomb program, which came to be known as the **Manhattan Project**. Even as the British and French were falling back, he sold them, without legal authority, surplus government arms. When Italy entered the war against France, the president called the invasion a stab in the back. During the first five months of 1940 he asked Congress to appropriate over $4 billion for national defense. To strengthen national unity he named Henry L. Stimson secretary of war[1] and another Republican, Frank Knox, secretary of the navy.

After the fall of France, Hitler attempted to bomb and starve the British into submission. The epic air battles over England during the summer of 1940 ended in a decisive defeat for the Nazis, but the Royal Navy, which had only about 100 destroyers, could not control German submarine attacks on shipping. In this desperate hour, Prime Minister Winston Churchill, who had replaced Chamberlain in May 1940, asked Roosevelt for fifty old American destroyers to fill the gap.

Japanese Expansion, 1920–1941 The Japanese empire, which conquered Korea early in the twentieth century, seized Manchuria in 1931; Jehol, north of Beijing, in 1933; and the rest of China after 1937.

German Expansion, 1936–1939 In March 1936, Hitler's forces reoccupied the Rhineland. In 1938 Germany annexed Austria and wrested the Sudetenland from Czechoslovakia, and in 1939 occupied the remaining Czech lands.

---

[1]Stimson had held this post from 1911 to 1913 in the Taft Cabinet!

The navy had 240 destroyers in commission and more than fifty under construction. But direct loan or sale of the vessels would have violated both international and American laws. Any attempt to obtain new legislation would have roused fears that the United States was going down the path that had led it into World War I. Long delay if not outright defeat would have resulted. Roosevelt therefore arranged to "trade" the destroyers for six British naval bases in the Caribbean. In addition, Great Britain leased bases in Bermuda and Newfoundland to the United States.

The destroyers-for-bases deal was a masterful achievement. It helped save Great Britain, and at the same time it circumvented isolationist prejudices since the president could present it as a shrewd bargain that bolstered America's defenses. A string of island bastions in the Atlantic was more valuable than fifty old destroyers.

Lines were hardening throughout the world. In September 1940, despite last-ditch isolationist resistance, Congress enacted the first peacetime draft in American history. Some 1.2 million draftees were summoned for one year of service, and 800,000 reservists were called to active duty. That same month Japan signed a mutual-assistance pact with Germany and Italy. This Rome-Berlin-Tokyo coalition—the **Axis Powers**—fused the conflicts in Europe and Asia, turning the struggle into a global war.

A Third Term for FDR

In the midst of these events the 1940 presidential election took place. Roosevelt was easily renominated. Vice President Garner, who had become disenchanted with Roosevelt and the New Deal, did not seek a third term; at Roosevelt's dictation, the party chose Secretary of Agriculture Henry A. Wallace to replace him.

By using concern about the European war to justify running for a tradition-breaking third term, Roosevelt brought down on his head the hatred of conservative Republicans and the isolationists of both major parties, just when they thought they would be rid of him. The Republicans nominated the darkest of dark horses, Wendell L. Willkie of Indiana, the utility magnate who had led the fight against the TVA in 1933.

Despite his political inexperience and Wall Street connections, Willkie made an appealing candidate. He was an energetic, charming, openhearted man. His rough-hewn, rural manner (one Democrat called him "a simple, barefoot Wall Street lawyer") won him wide support in farm districts. Willkie had difficulty, however, finding issues on which to oppose Roosevelt. The New Deal reforms were too popular and too much in line with his own thinking to invite attack. He believed as strongly as the president that America could no longer ignore the Nazi threat.

In the end Willkie focused his campaign on Roosevelt's conduct of foreign relations. While rejecting the isolationist position, Willkie charged that Roosevelt intended to make the United States a participant in the war. Roosevelt retorted (disingenuously, since he knew he was not a free agent in the situation), "I have said this before, but I shall say it again and again and again: Your boys are not going to be sent into any foreign wars." In November Roosevelt carried the country handily, though by a smaller majority than in 1932 or 1936. The popular vote was 27 million to 22 million, the electoral count 449 to 82.

The Undeclared War

The election encouraged Roosevelt to act more boldly. When Prime Minister Churchill informed him that the cash-and-carry system would no longer suffice because Great Britain was rapidly exhausting its financial resources, he decided at once to provide the British with whatever they needed. Instead of proposing to lend them money, a step certain to rouse memories of the vexatious war debt controversies, he devised the lend-lease program, one of his most ingenious and imaginative creations.

First he delivered a "fireside chat" that stressed the evil intentions of the Nazis and the dangers that a German victory would create for America. Aiding Britain should be looked at simply as a form of self-defense. When the radio talk provoked a favorable public response, Roosevelt went to Congress in January 1941 with a plan calling for the expenditure of $7 billion for war materials that the president could sell, lend, lease, exchange, or transfer to any country whose defense he deemed vital to that of the United States. After two months of debate, Congress gave him what he had asked for.

Although the wording of the **Lend-Lease Act** obscured its immediate purpose, the saving of Great Britain, the president was frank in explaining his plan. He did not minimize the dangers involved, yet his mastery of practical politics was never more in evidence. To counter Irish American prejudices against the English, he pointed out that the Irish Republic would surely fall under Nazi domination if Hitler won the war. He coupled his demand for heavy military expenditures with his enunciation of the idealistic "Four Freedoms"—freedom of speech, freedom of religion, freedom from want, and freedom from fear—for which, he said, the war was being fought.

After the enactment of lend-lease, aid short of war was no longer seriously debated. The American navy began to patrol the North Atlantic, shadowing German submarines and radioing their locations to British warships and planes. In April 1941 U.S. forces occupied Greenland; in May the president declared a state of unlimited national emergency. After Hitler invaded the Soviet Union in June, Roosevelt moved slowly, for anti-Soviet feeling in the United States was intense.[2] But it was obviously to the nation's advantage to help any country that was resisting Hitler's armies. In November, $1 billion in lend-lease aid was put at the disposal of the Soviet Union.

Meanwhile, Iceland was occupied in July 1941, and the draft law was extended in August—by the margin of a single vote in the House of Representatives. In September the German submarine *U–652* fired a torpedo at the destroyer *Greer* in the North Atlantic. The *Greer*, which had provoked the attack by tracking *U–652* and flashing its position to a British plane, avoided the torpedo and dropped nineteen depth charges in an effort to sink the submarine.

Roosevelt announced that the *Greer* had been innocently "carrying mail to Iceland." He called the U-boats "the rattlesnakes of the Atlantic" and ordered the navy to "shoot on sight" any German craft in the waters south and west of Iceland and to convoy merchant vessels as far as that island. After the sinking of the destroyer *Reuben James* on October 30, Congress voted to allow the arming of American merchant ships and to permit them to carry cargoes to Allied ports. For all practical purposes, though not yet officially, the United States had gone to war.

---

[2]During the 1930s the Soviet Union took a far firmer stand against the fascists than any other power, but after joining Hitler in swallowing up Poland, it attacked and defeated Finland during the winter of 1939–1940 and annexed the Baltic states. These acts virtually destroyed the small communist movement in the United States.

Cinderella Man

As *Cinderella Man* (2005) opens, boxer James J. Braddock (Russell Crowe) lands a right-hook that sends his opponent sprawling to the canvas—a knockout. Braddock raises his hands in triumph. The crowd roars and a jazz band blares.

When Braddock arrives at his home in New Jersey, his wife, Mae (Renée Zellweger) leaps into his arms. "I'm so proud of you," she says. Three children mob their father. Later, as Braddock prepares for bed, he sets his gold watch and thick wallet onto a polished wood dresser. The year is 1928.

Abruptly, the scene dissolves. A cheap, unfinished dresser comes into focus. The watch and wallet are gone. Braddock, unshaven, looks wearily around a squalid hovel. The children, on mattresses in shadows, cough and wheeze. The year is 1933.

Braddock, like much of the nation, has fallen on hard times, his savings wiped out by the Depression. Worse, he has broken his powerful right hand and, desperate for money, resumed boxing before it healed. He tries to work at the dockyards but often there is no work to be had. The grocer refuses credit. The milkman stops deliveries. The power company shuts off the gas and electricity. His children, underfed and chilled, become sick. Braddock returns to Madison Square Garden, hat in hand, and begs for money. He also applies and receives federal assistance—welfare—at $6.40 a week. Compared to Braddock, Cinderella had it easy.

Then Braddock's agent, an unlikely fairy godmother, shows up with an extraordinary proposition. A huge, young bruiser and leading contender for the heavyweight title—"Corn" Griffin—had been scheduled to fight the next evening at Madison Square Garden. But Griffin's opponent has backed out at the last minute. Rather than cancel the fight, Madison Square Garden has offered Braddock $250 to serve as Griffin's punching bag. Desperate, Braddock accepts.

What happens the next day—June 14, 1934—is the stuff of fairy tales. Braddock borrows boxing boots and heads to Madison Square Garden. When Braddock enters the ring, his robe bears another boxer's name.

After the opening bell, Griffin, a thick-necked bull of a man, charges Braddock and pounds him mercilessly. Braddock, sustained only by raw courage—and a tough chin, survives the first two rounds. Then, in the third, he surprises Griffin with a thunderous hook, knocking the giant out cold.

Because Griffin was the top contender, Braddock himself is placed on the list of contenders. He proceeds to score one upset after another until he's next in line to face Max Baer (Craig Bierko), the heavyweight champion whose fearsome right has killed two boxers. The manager of Madison Square Garden requires Braddock to sign a waiver absolving it of responsibility should Braddock also perish at Baer's hands.

On June 13, 1935, the night of the fight, as Mae goes to church to pray, reporters speculate on whether Braddock can last a single round. The betting odds against Braddock are the worst in memory. But a movie named after a fairy tale must have a happy ending, and *Cinderella Man* comes through. After fifteen harrowing rounds, Braddock wins a unanimous decision. In 364 days, he has gone from impoverished "bum" to heavyweight champion of the world.

"This is a true story," declared director Ron Howard. Yet fairy tales, by definition, are make-believe; and Hollywood, by reputation, believes in nothing as fervently as the dollar. Thus viewers are entitled to ask: Does *Cinderella Man* tell the actual story of James J. Braddock?

The surprising answer, given the implausibility of the plot, is yes, up to a point. And that point begins with the Baer-Braddock fight: Madison Square Garden did not warn Braddock of the danger of fighting Baer or oblige him to sign a waiver. Also, the fight was no slugfest. The *New York Times* dubbed

Russell Crowe and Renée Zellweger embrace in *Cinderella Man*.

it "one of the worst heavyweight championship contests" in boxing history. Reporters assumed that Baer failed to take the early rounds seriously, lost others on foolish fouls, and realized too late that he was behind. Baer, too, was no unfeeling monster. Most interesting is the movie's error of omission, or, more precisely, of suppression. It makes no mention of the fact that Baer proudly trumpeted his Jewish ancestry. Baer had a large Star of David stitched onto his trunks, an image that appears in the movie once, briefly and from a distance.

Why did director Howard evade the truth about Baer? The likely answer is that Howard knew that fairy tales require villains as well as heroes. *Cinderella Man's* Braddock looms larger for slaying the Big Bad Baer.

In fact, the real enemy was the Great Depression. Braddock understood this. When asked how he managed to turn his career around, he explained, "I was fighting for milk." Damon Runyon, the writer who first called Braddock "Cinderella Man," recognized that the boxer's story took on mythic proportions because it encapsulated the aspirations of an entire nation.

But the movie misses the point that many ethnic groups had their own boxing champions. After Braddock had upset Griffin, he fought Joe Louis, the Brown Bomber. While the movie rightly shows Irish Americans praying for Braddock, it neglects the millions of African Americans who also gathered around radios, praying for Louis. Jewish fans, similarly, identified with Baer, cherishing his 1933 defeat of the German boxer, Max Schmeling, Hitler's favorite. When Braddock defeated Baer, many Jews were devastated.

Madison Square Garden, keenly aware of the ethnic appeal of boxing, worked hard to ensure that nearly every major immigrant group had someone to cheer for on fight night. Boxing promoters were among the first to learn that in sports, as in entertainment more generally, segregation did not pay.

Cinderella Man depicts, with considerable accuracy, a simple and good man's triumph over adversity. His story was, indeed, the stuff of myth. But in its earnest attempt to universalize Braddock's appeal, the movie obscures the ethnic divisions that characterized so much of American life during the first half of the twentieth century.

Question for Discussion

- Do you think the Depression encouraged solidarity among Americans of different races and ethnicities, because everyone could empathize with each other's suffering? Or did it exacerbate tensions by pitting different groups against each other in search of scarce jobs?

Milestones

1933	FDR becomes president
	Hitler is elected German chancellor
	FDR proclaims Good Neighbor Policy
	Banking Act gives FDR broad powers
	Civilian Conservation Corps (CCC) employs 250,000 young men
	Federal Emergency Relief Act (FERA) funds relief programs
	Agricultural Adjustment Act (AAA) seeks relief for farmers
	Tennessee Valley Authority (TVA) plans dams and power plants
	National Industrial Recovery Act (NIRA) establishes Public Works Administration (PWA) and National Recovery Administration (NRA)
	Banking Act establishes Federal Deposit Insurance Corporation (FDIC)
	Civil Works Administration puts 4 million to work
	Twenty-First Amendment ends prohibition
1934	Indian Reorganization Act gives tribes more autonomy
	Securities and Exchange Commission (SEC) regulates stocks and bonds
	Federal Communications Commission (FCC) regulates interstate and foreign communication
	Federal Housing Administration (FHA) gives housing loans
1935	Emergency Relief Appropriation Act creates Works Project Administration (WPA)
	Rural Electrification Administration brings electricity to farms

1935	Supreme Court rules NIRA unconstitutional in *Schechter v. United States*
	National Labor Relations Act (Wagner-Connery) encourages unionization
	Social Security Act guarantees pensions and other benefits
	Neutrality Act forbids wartime arms sales to belligerents
	Italy invades and annexes Ethiopia
	Walter Millis publishes isolationist *The Road to War: America, 1914–1917*
1936	FDR is reelected president in record landslide
	Supreme Court declares AAA unconstitutional
1937	Roosevelt tries to pack Supreme Court
	Japanese in China seize Beijing, Shanghai, Nanking
1938	Fair Labor Standards Act abolishes child labor, sets minimum wage
	House of Representatives defeats Ludlow (isolationist) Amendment
	Britain and France appease Hitler at Munich
1939	Germany invades Poland; World War II begins
1940	Hitler conquers Denmark, Norway, the Netherlands, Belgium, France
	FDR is reelected to third term
	Axis Powers sign Rome-Berlin-Tokyo pact
	Isolationists form America First Committee
1941	Lend-Lease Act helps Britain

✓●⌐Study and Review at www.myhistorylab.com

Review Questions

1. The introduction of this chapter compares the 2010 health insurance law with that establishing Social Security in 1935. In what ways is the comparison an apt one? How did the measures and times differ? Was Social Security a form of socialism?

2. Compare the First and Second New Deals. What were the similarities and differences?

3. What was the impact of the Great Depression on art, literature, and popular culture? How did it affect women and minority groups? Labor?

4. How did the New Deal expand the role of the federal government?

5. Why did Asia and Europe slip into war in the 1930s? How did the United States respond during that decade and why?

Key Terms

Agricultural Adjustment
  Act (AAA) *681*
Axis Powers *702*
Blitzkrieg 701
Civilian Conservation
  Corps (CCC) *680*
Lend-Lease Act *703*

Manhattan Project *701*
National Recovery
  Administration
  (NRA) *680*
neutrality acts *698*
New Deal *679*
Social Security Act *689*

Tennessee Valley
  Authority (TVA) *683*
Wagner Act *688*
Works Progress
  Administration
  (WPA) *685*

27 War and Peace: 1941–1945

Hear the **Audio** Chapter 27 at myhistorylab.com

Does the war in Afghanistan touch your life?

ALTHOUGH ALL YOUNG AMERICAN MEN ARE REQUIRED TO REGISTER for the military draft, none has actually been drafted since the 1970s. (Registration exists in the event of a national military emergency.) In place of conscription, the Department of Defense has recruited all-volunteer military services. In times of peace, most generals prefer a volunteer army: Professional soldiers are better trained and often more attentive to orders; but in times of war, when recruiting officers struggle to fill quotas and tours-of-duty are extended, many generals call for a return to the draft.

By 2010, a heated debate among officers surfaced in the *Armed Forces Journal*. Most defended the professional army, noting that the quality of recruits was higher than in two decades. But other officers called for a return to the "citizen soldiers" envisioned by Washington and Jefferson. One reason was that wars fought by conscripts ensured that the nation as a whole engaged in the war effort. The *Seattle Times* observed that although the Iraq war had gone on far longer than World War II, "life for most Americans has clicked along without personal loss or even higher federal taxes." "Marines are at war," one general complained, "America is at the mall."

Such remarks underscored how different the current conflicts in Iraq and Afghanistan are from World War II, a monstrous global war among advanced industrial nations. Of every five American males between the ages of twenty and twenty-five, four served in World War II. At the beginning of World War II, 4 million Americans paid income tax; by its end, 43 million did so. Over 85 million Americans—half the nation's population—spent $185 billion to buy war bonds. Food and gasoline were rationed. World War II required the mobilization of the entire nation.

World War II transformed society, too. In the absence of so many young men, women assumed new roles and worked at different types of jobs. African Americans, Hispanics, American Indians, and other minorities found new opportunities even as they encountered persistent discrimination. Americans of Japanese extraction were relocated against their will to isolated camps. Technological change—culminating in the atom bomb—transformed everyone's lives. It was a war unlike any other.

The Road to Pearl Harbor

Neither the United States nor Japan wanted war. Roosevelt considered Germany by far the more dangerous enemy and was alarmed by the possibility of simultaneously fighting German armies in Europe and Japanese forces in the Pacific. In the spring of 1941 Secretary of State Cordell Hull conferred in Washington with the Japanese ambassador, Kichisaburo Nomura, in an effort to resolve their differences. Hull showed little appreciation of the political and military situation in East Asia. He demanded that Japan withdraw from China.

Japan might well have accepted limited annexations in the area in return for the removal of American trade restrictions, but Hull insisted on total withdrawal, to which even the moderates in Japan would not agree. When Hitler invaded the Soviet Union, thereby removing the threat of Russian intervention in East Asia, Japan decided to complete its conquest of China and occupy French Indochina even at the risk of war with the United States. Roosevelt retaliated in July 1941 by freezing Japanese assets in the United States and clamping an embargo on oil.

Now the ultranationalist war party in Japan assumed control. Nomura was instructed to tell Hull that Japan would refrain from further expansion if the United States and Great Britain would cut off all aid to China and lift the economic blockade. Japan promised to pull out of Indochina once "a just peace" had been established with China. When the United States rejected these demands, the Japanese prepared to attack the Dutch East Indies, British Malaya, and the Philippines. To immobilize the U.S. Pacific fleet, they planned a surprise air assault on the Hawaiian naval base at Pearl Harbor.

Japan's surprise attack on Pearl Harbor on December 7, 1941, killed more than 2,400 American sailors and soldiers and thrust the United States into World War II. President Roosevelt asked Congress for a declaration of war the next day, calling the attack "a date that will live in infamy."

An American cryptanalyst, Colonel William F. Friedman, had cracked the Japanese diplomatic code: The Japanese were making plans to attack in early December. But in the hectic rush of events, both military and civilian authorities failed to make effective use of the information collected. They expected the blow to fall somewhere in East Asia, possibly the Philippines.

The garrison at Pearl Harbor was alerted against "a surprise aggressive move in any direction." The commanders there, Admiral Husband E. Kimmel and General Walter C. Short, believing an attack impossible, took precautions only against Japanese sabotage. Thus when planes from Japanese aircraft carriers swooped down upon Pearl Harbor on the morning of December 7, they found easy targets. In less than two hours they reduced the Pacific fleet to a smoking ruin: two battleships destroyed, six others heavily battered, nearly a dozen lesser vessels put out of action. More than 150 planes were wrecked; over 2,400 soldiers and sailors were killed and 1,100 wounded.

Never had American armed forces suffered a more devastating or shameful defeat. Although the official blame was placed chiefly on Admiral Kimmel and General Short, responsibility for the disaster was widespread. Military and civilian officials in Washington had failed to pass on all that they knew to Hawaii or even to one another.

On December 8 Congress declared war on Japan. Formal war with Germany and Italy was still not inevitable—isolationists were far more ready to resist the "yellow peril" in Asia than to fight in Europe. The Axis Powers, however, honored their treaty obligations to Japan and on December 11 declared war on the United States. America was now fully engaged in another great war, World War II.

Mobilizing the Home Front

World War II placed immense strains on the American economy and produced immense results. About 15 million men and women entered the armed services; they, and in part the millions more in Allied uniforms, had to be fed, clothed, housed, and supplied with equipment ranging from typewriters and paper clips to rifles, grenades, tanks, and airplanes. Congress granted wide emergency powers to the president. However, while the Democrats retained control of both houses throughout the war, their margins were relatively narrow. A coalition of conservatives in both parties frequently prevented the president from having his way and exercised close control over expenditures.

Roosevelt was an inspiring war leader but not a very good administrator. The squabbling and waste characteristic of the early New Deal period made relatively little difference—what mattered then was raising the nation's spirits and keeping people occupied; efficiency was less than essential, however desirable. But in wartime, the nation's fate, perhaps that of the entire free world, depended on delivering weapons and supplies to the battlefronts.

Roosevelt's greatest accomplishment was his inspiring of industrialists, workers, and farmers with a sense of national purpose. In this respect his function duplicated his earlier role in fighting the Depression, and he performed it with even greater success.

The tremendous economic expansion can be seen in the official production statistics. In 1939 the United States was still mired in the Great Depression. The gross national product amounted to about $91.3 billion. In 1945, after allowing for changes in the price level, it was $166.6 billion. Manufacturing output nearly doubled and agricultural output rose

22 percent. In 1939 the United States turned out fewer than 6,000 airplanes, in 1944 more than 96,000. Shipyards produced 237,000 tons of vessels in 1939, 10 million tons in 1943.

This growth was especially notable in the South and Southwest. This region got a preponderance of the new army camps built for the war as well as a large share of the new defense plants. Southern productive capacity increased by about 50 percent, and southern per capita output, while still low, crept closer to the national average.

Wartime experience proved that the Keynesian economists were correct in saying that government spending would spark economic growth. About 8 million people were unemployed in June 1940. After Pearl Harbor, unemployment virtually disappeared, and by 1945 the civilian workforce had increased by nearly 7 million. Military mobi-

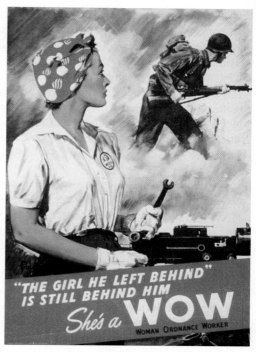

"THE GIRL HE LEFT BEHIND" IS STILL BEHIND HIM She's a **WOW** WOMAN ORDNANCE WORKER

A poster encourages women to work in munitions to support the war effort.

lization had begun well before December 1941, by which time 1.6 million men were already under arms. Economic mobilization proceeded much more slowly, mainly because the president refused to centralize authority. For months after Pearl Harbor various civilian agencies squabbled with the military over everything from the allocation of scarce raw materials to the technical specifications of weapons. Roosevelt refused to settle these conflicts.

The War Economy

Yet by early 1943 the nation's economic machinery had been converted to a wartime footing and was functioning effectively. Supreme Court Justice James F. Byrnes resigned from the Court to become a sort of "economic czar." His Office of War Mobilization had complete control over priorities and prices. Rents, food prices, and wages were strictly regulated, and items in short supply were rationed to consumers. While wages and prices had soared during 1942, after April 1943 they leveled off. Thereafter the cost of living scarcely changed until controls were lifted after the war.

Wages and prices remained in fair balance. Overtime work fattened paychecks, and a new stress in labor contracts on paid vacations, premium pay for night work, and various forms of employer-subsidized health insurance were added benefits. The war effort had almost no adverse effect on the standard of living of

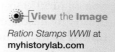

View the **Image**
Ration Stamps WWII at
myhistorylab.com

the average citizen, a vivid demonstration of the productivity of the American economy. The manufacture of automobiles ceased and pleasure driving became next to impossible because of gasoline rationing, but most civilian activities went on much as they had before Pearl Harbor. While items such as meat, sugar, and shoes were rationed, they were doled out in amounts adequate for the needs of most persons.

The federal government spent twice as much money between 1941 and 1945 as in its entire previous history. This made heavy borrowing necessary. The national debt, which stood at less than $49 billion in 1941, increased by more than that amount each year between 1942 and 1945 and totaled nearly $260 billion when the war ended. However, more than 40 percent of the total was met by taxation, a far larger proportion than in any earlier war.

This policy helped to check inflation by siphoning off money that would otherwise have competed for scarce consumer goods. Heavy excise taxes on amusements and luxuries further discouraged spending, as did the government's war bond campaigns, which persuaded patriotic citizens to lend part of their income to Uncle Sam. High taxes on incomes (up to 94 percent) and on excess profits (95 percent) convinced people that no one was profiting inordinately from the war effort.

The income tax, which had never before touched the mass of white-collar and industrial workers, was extended downward until nearly everyone had to pay it. To collect efficiently the relatively small sums paid by most persons, Congress adopted the payroll-deduction system proposed by Beardsley Ruml, chairman of the Federal Reserve Bank of New York. Employers withheld the taxes owed by workers from their paychecks and turned the money over to the government.

The steeply graduated tax rates, combined with a general increase in the income of workers and farmers, effected a substantial shift in the distribution of wealth in the United States. The poor became richer, while the rich, if not actually poorer, collected a smaller proportion of the national income. The wealthiest 1 percent of the population had received 13.4 percent of the national income in 1935 and 11.5 percent in 1941. In 1944 this group received 6.7 percent.

War and Social Change

World War II altered the patterns of American life in many ways. Never was the population more fluid. The millions who put on uniforms found themselves transported first to training camps in every section of the country and then to battlefields scattered from Europe and Africa to the far reaches of the Pacific. Burgeoning new defense plants, influenced by a government policy of locating them in "uncongested areas," drew other millions to places like Hanford, Washington, and Oak Ridge, Tennessee, where great atomic energy installations were constructed, and to the aircraft factories of California and other states. As in earlier periods the trend was from east to west and from the rural south to northern cities.

During the war the marriage rate rose steeply, from 75 per thousand adult women in 1939 to 118 in 1946. Many young couples felt the need to put down roots before the husbands went off to risk death in distant lands. The population of the United States had increased by only 3 million during the Depression decade of the 1930s; during the next *five* years it rose by 6.5 million.

Minorities in Time of War: Blacks, Hispanics, and Indians

The war affected black Americans in many ways. Several factors helped improve their lives. One was their own growing tendency to demand fair treatment. Another was the reaction of Americans to Hitler's barbaric treatment of millions of Jews, an outgrowth of his doctrine of "Aryan" superiority. These barbarities compelled millions of white citizens to reexamine their views about race. If the nation expected African Americans to risk their lives for the common good, how could it continue to treat them as second-class citizens? Black leaders pointed out the inconsistency between fighting for democracy abroad and ignoring it at home.

Blacks in the armed forces were treated more fairly than they had been in World War I. They were enlisted for the first time in the air force and the marines, and they were given more responsible positions in the army and navy. Altogether about a million served, about half of them overseas. The extensive and honorable performance of these units could not be ignored by the white majority.

However, segregation in the armed services was maintained. The navy continued to confine black and Hispanic sailors to demeaning, noncombat tasks, and black soldiers were often provided with inferior recreational facilities and otherwise mistreated in and around army camps, especially those in the South. However, economic realities operated significantly to the advantage of black civilians. More of them had been unemployed in proportion to their numbers than any other group; now the labor shortage brought employment for all. More than 5 million blacks moved from rural areas to cities between 1940 and 1945 in search of work. At least a million of them found defense jobs in the North and on the West Coast, often developing valuable skills that had been difficult for blacks to acquire before the war because of the discriminatory policies of trade unions and many employers. The black population of Los Angeles, San Francisco, Denver, Buffalo, Milwaukee, and half a dozen other large industrial cities more than doubled in that brief period. The migrants were

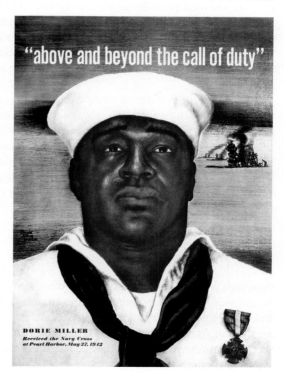

"above and beyond the call of duty"

DORIE MILLER
Received the Navy Cross
at Pearl Harbor, May 27, 1942

A poster commemorates Doris "Dorie" Miller, a mess attendant aboard the USS *West Virginia* at Pearl Harbor. Before the ship sank, Miller manned an antiaircraft machine gun and shot down several Japanese planes. He won the Navy Cross for courage, the first awarded to an African American.

mostly forced to live in urban ghettoes, but their very concentration (and the fact that outside the South blacks could vote freely) made them important politically.

Watch the Video

The desegregation of the military and blacks in combat at **myhistorylab.com**

However, prejudice and mistreatment of blacks did not cease. In areas around defense plants white resentment of the black "invasion" mounted. By 1943, 50,000 new blacks had crowded into Detroit. A wave of strikes disrupted production at U.S. Rubber and several former automobile plants where white workers laid down their tools to protest the hiring of blacks. In June a race riot marked by looting and bloody fighting raged for three days. By the time federal troops restored order, twenty-five blacks and nine whites had been killed. Rioting also erupted in New York and many other cities.

In Los Angeles the attacks were upon Hispanic residents. Wartime employment needs resulted in a reversal of the Depression policy of forcing Mexicans out of the Southwest, and many thousands flocked north in search of work. Most had to accept menial jobs. But work was plentiful, and they, as well as resident Spanish-speaking Americans, experienced rising living standards.

Blacks became increasingly embittered. Roy Wilkins, head of the NAACP, put it this way in 1942: "No Negro leader with a constituency can face his members today and ask full

Read the Document

Randolph, *Why Should We March* at **myhistorylab.com**

support for the war in the light of the atmosphere the government has created." Many black newspaper editors were so critical of the administration that conservatives demanded they be indicted for sedition.

Roosevelt would have none of that, but the militants annoyed him; he felt that they should hold their demands in abeyance until the war had been won. Apparently he failed to realize the depth of black anger, and in this he was no different from the majority of whites. A revolution was in the making, yet in 1942 a poll revealed that a solid majority of whites still believed that black Americans were satisfied with their place in society. The riots of 1943 undoubtedly disabused some of them of this illusion.

Concern about national unity did lead to a reaction against the New Deal policy of encouraging Indians to preserve their ancient cultures and develop self-governing communities. There was even talk of going back to the allotment system and trying to assimilate Indians into the larger society. In fact, the war encouraged assimilation in several ways. More than 24,000 Indians served in the armed forces, an experience that brought them into contact with new people, new places, and new ideas. Many thousands more left the reservations to work in defense industries in cities all over the country.

The Treatment of German and Italian Americans

Although World War II affected the American people far more drastically than had World War I, it produced much less intolerance and fewer examples of the repression of individual freedom of opinion. People seemed able to distinguish between Italian fascism and Italian Americans and between the government of Nazi Germany and Americans of German descent in a way that had escaped their parents. The fact that few Italian Americans admired Mussolini and that nearly all German Americans were vigorously anti-Nazi helps explain this. So does the fact that both groups were well-organized and prepared to use their considerable political power if necessary to protect themselves from abuse. Nevertheless, U.S. military authorities arrested some 14,000 Germans and Italians as security risks.

Americans went to war in 1941 without illusions and without enthusiasm, determined to win but expecting only to preserve what they had. They therefore found it easier to tolerate dissent, to view the dangers they faced realistically, and to concentrate on the real foreign enemy without venting their feelings on domestic scapegoats. The nation's 100,000 conscientious objectors met with little hostility.

Internment of Japanese Americans

The relatively tolerant treatment of most Americans of German and Italian descent makes the nation's policies toward American citizens of Japanese extraction all the more difficult to comprehend. Generals on the West Coast were understandably unnerved by the Japanese attack on Pearl Harbor and warned that people of Japanese descent might engage in sabotage or espionage for Japan. "The Japanese race is an enemy race," General John L. Dewitt claimed. The 112,000 Americans of Japanese ancestry, the majority of them native-born citizens, were "potential enemies." "The very fact that no sabotage has taken place to date," Dewitt observed, "is a disturbing and confirming indication that such action will be taken." Secretary of War Stimson proposed the relocation of the West Coast people of Japanese extraction, including American citizens, to **internment camps** in Wyoming, Arizona, and other interior states.

The Japanese were properly indignant but also baffled, in some cases hurt more than angry. "We didn't feel Japanese. We felt American," one woman, the mother of three small children, recalled many years later. Some Japanese Americans challenged military authorities. Gordon Hirabayashi, an American citizen and senior at the University of Washington, refused to report for transportation to an internment camp. After being convicted and sentenced to prison, he decided to appeal. Previous Supreme Courts had ruled that the government could deprive Americans of their freedoms during war only when the "military necessity" was compelling. By the time the Supreme Court ruled on his and similar cases, the Japanese military had been thrown back in the Pacific; no

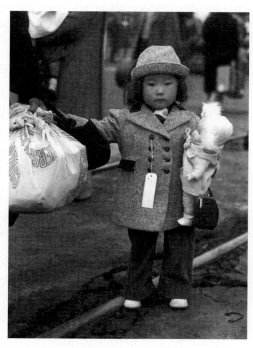

A Japanese girl in California, tagged for relocation to an internment camp, clutches her doll.

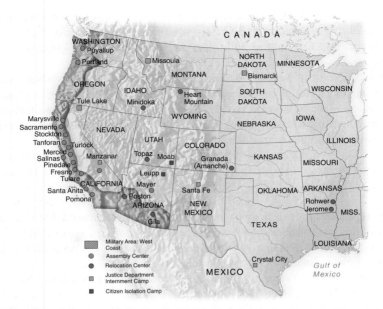

Japanese Relocation from the West Coast, 1942–1945 Japanese and Japanese Americans who lived in the West Coast Military Area were ordered to report to various "assembly centers," from which they were then deported to inland internment or isolation camps.

invasion was even conceivable. Yet the justices worried that if they declared the internment policy to be unconstitutional, they would appear, "out of step" with the nation, as Justice Felix Frankfurter put it. In June 1943, the Court upheld the conviction of Hirabayashi. Finally, in *Ex parte Endo*, it forbade the internment of loyal Japanese American citizens. Unfortunately the latter decision was not handed down until December 1944.

Women's Contributions to the War Effort

With economic activity on the rise and millions of men going off to war, a sudden need for more women workers developed. The trends of the 1920s—more women workers and more of them married—soon accelerated. By 1944, 6.5 million additional women had entered the workforce, and at the peak of war production in 1945, more than 19 million women were employed, many of them in well-paying industrial jobs. Additional thousands were serving in the armed forces: 100,000 in the Women's Auxiliary Army Corps, others in navy, marine, and air corps auxiliaries.

View the Image

Rosie the Riveter at **myhistorylab.com**

At first there was considerable resistance to what was happening. About one husband in three objected in principle to his wife taking a job. Many employers in so-called heavy industry and in other fields traditionally dominated by men doubted that women could handle such tasks. Unions frequently made the same point, usually without much evidence.

These male attitudes lost force in the face of the escalating demand for labor. That employers usually did not have to pay women as much as men made them attractive, as did the fact that they were not subject to the draft. A breakthrough occurred when the big Detroit automobile manufacturers agreed to employ women on their wartime production lines. Soon women were working not only as riveters and cab drivers but also as welders, as machine tool operators, and in dozens of other occupations formerly the exclusive domain of men.

Women took wartime jobs for many reasons other than the obvious economic ones. Patriotism, of course, was important, but so were the excitement of entering an entirely new world, the desire for independence, even loneliness. "It's thrilling work, and exciting, and something women have never done before," one woman reported. She was talking about driving a taxi.

Black women workers had a particularly difficult time: employers often hesitating to hire them because they were black, and black men looking down on them because they were women. But the need for willing hands was infinite. Sybil Lewis of Sapula, Oklahoma, went to Los Angeles and found a job as a waitress in a black restaurant. Then she responded to a notice of a training program at Lockheed Aircraft, took the course, and became a riveter making airplane gas tanks. When an unfriendly foreman gave her a less attractive assignment, she moved on to Douglas Aircraft. By 1943 she was working as a welder in a shipyard.

Few wartime jobs were easy, and for women there were special burdens, not the least of which was the prejudice of many of the men they worked with. For married women there was housework to do after a long day. One War Manpower Commission bureaucrat figured out that Detroit defense plants were losing 100,000 woman-hours a month because of employees taking a day off to do the family laundry. Although the government made some effort to provide day-care facilities, there were never nearly enough; this was one reason why relatively few women with small children entered the labor market during the war.

Newly married wives of soldiers and sailors (known generally as "war brides") often followed their husbands to training camps, where life was often as difficult as it was around defense plants. Whatever their own behavior, war brides quickly learned that society applied a double standard to infidelity, especially when it involved a man presumably risking his life in some far-off land. There was a general relaxation of sexual inhibitions, part of a decades-long trend but accelerated by the war. So many hasty marriages, followed by long periods of separation, also brought a rise in divorces, from about 170 per thousand marriages in 1941 to 310 per thousand in 1945.

Of course "ordinary" housewives also had to deal with shortages, ration books, and other inconveniences during the war. In addition most took on other duties and bore other burdens, such as tending "victory gardens" and preserving their harvests, using crowded public transportation when there was no gas for the family car, mending and patching old clothes when new ones were unavailable, participating in salvage drives, and doing volunteer work for hospitals, the Red Cross, or various civil defense and servicemen's centers.

Allied Strategy: Europe First

Only days after Pearl Harbor, Prime Minister Churchill and his military chiefs met in Washington with Roosevelt and his advisers. In every quarter of the globe, disaster threatened. The Japanese were gobbling up East Asia. Hitler's armies, checked outside Leningrad and Moscow, were preparing for a massive attack in the direction of Stalingrad, on the

⊙►See the **Map**

World War II in Europe
at **myhistorylab.com**

Volga River. German divisions under General Erwin Rommel were beginning a drive across North Africa toward the Suez Canal. U-boats were taking a heavy toll in the North Atlantic. British and American leaders believed that eventually they could muster enough force to smash their enemies, but whether or not the troops already in action could hold out until this force arrived was an open question.

The decision of the strategists was to concentrate first against the Germans. Japan's conquests were in remote and, from the point of view of the **Allies**, relatively unimportant regions. If the Soviet Union surrendered, Hitler's position in Europe might prove impregnable.

American leaders wanted to attack German positions in France, at least by 1943. The Soviets, with their backs to the wall and bearing the full weight of the German war machine, heartily agreed. Churchill, however, was more concerned with protecting Britain's overseas possessions than with easing the pressure on the Soviet Union. He advocated instead air bombardment of German industry combined with an attempt to drive the Germans out of North Africa, and his argument carried the day.

During the summer of 1942 Allied planes began to bomb German cities. In a crescendo through 1943 and 1944, British and American bombers pulverized the centers of Nazi might. While air attacks did not destroy the German army's capacity to fight, they hampered war production, tangled communications, and brought the war home to

The firebombing of Hamburg (painted here by Floyd Davis, who flew with the Anglo American mission in 1943) killed 50,000 and destroyed Hamburg.

the German people. Humanitarians deplored the heavy loss of life among the civilian population, but the response of the realists was that Hitler had begun indiscriminate bombing, and victory depended on smashing the German war machine.

In November 1942 an Allied army commanded by General Dwight D. Eisenhower struck at French North Africa. After the fall of France, the Nazis had set up a puppet regime in those parts of France not occupied by their troops, with head-quarters at Vichy in central France. This collaborationist Vichy government controlled French North Africa. But the North African commandant, Admiral Jean Darlan, agreed to switch sides when Eisenhower's forces landed. After a brief show of resistance, the French surrendered.

Eisenhower now pressed forward quickly against the Germans in North Africa. In February 1943 at Kasserine Pass in the desert south of Tunis, American tanks met Rommel's Afrika Korps. The battle ended in a standoff, but with British troops closing in from their Egyptian bases to the East, the Germans were soon trapped and crushed. In May, after Rommel had been recalled to Germany, his army surrendered.

In July 1943, while air attacks on Germany continued and the Russians slowly pushed the Germans back from the gates of Stalingrad, the Allies invaded Sicily from

The Liberation of Europe After November, 1942, Allied armies pushed the German-Italian armies back on three fronts: the Soviets, from the East; and American-British armies from North Africa and then, after the Normandy invasion, from France.

Africa. In September they advanced to the Italian mainland. Mussolini had already fallen from power and his successor, Marshal Pietro Badoglio, surrendered. However, the German troops in Italy threw up an almost impregnable defense across the rugged Italian peninsula. The Anglo American army inched forward, paying heavily for every advance. Monte Cassino, halfway between Naples and Rome, did not fall until May 1944, the capital itself not until June; months of hard fighting remained before the country was cleared of Germans. The Italian campaign was an Allied disappointment even though it weakened the enemy.

Germany Overwhelmed

By the time the Allies had taken Rome, the mighty army needed to invade France had been collected in England under Eisenhower's command. On **D-Day**, June 6, 1944, the assault forces stormed ashore at five points along the coast of Normandy, supported by a great armada and thousands of planes and paratroops. Against fierce but ill-coordinated German resistance, they established a beachhead: Within a few weeks a million troops were on French soil. (See Re-Viewing the Past, *Saving Private Ryan*, pp. 722–723.)

Thereafter victory was assured, though nearly a year of hard fighting lay ahead. In August the American Third Army under General George S. Patton erupted southward into Brittany and then veered east toward Paris. Another Allied army invaded France from the Mediterranean in mid-August and advanced rapidly north. Free French troops were given the honor of liberating Paris on August 25. Belgium was cleared by British and Canadian units a few days later. By mid-September the Allies were fighting on the edge of Germany itself.

The front now stretched from the Netherlands along the borders of Belgium, Luxembourg, and France all the way to Switzerland. If the Allies had mounted a massive assault at any one point, the struggle might have been brought to a quick conclusion. Although the two armies were roughly equal in size, the Allies had complete control of the air and twenty times as many tanks as the foe. The pressure of the advancing Russians on the eastern front made it difficult for the Germans to reinforce their troops in the west. But General Eisenhower believed a concentrated attack was too risky. He prepared instead for a general advance.

While he was regrouping, the Germans on December 16 launched a counterattack, planned by Hitler himself, against the Allied center in the Ardennes Forest. The Germans hoped to break through to the Belgian port of Antwerp, thereby splitting the Allied armies in two. The plan was foolhardy and therefore unexpected, and it almost succeeded. The Germans drove a salient ("the bulge") about fifty miles into Belgium. But once the element of surprise had been overcome, their chance of breaking through to the sea was lost. Eisenhower concentrated first on preventing them from broadening the break in his lines and then on blunting the point of their advance. By late January 1945 the old line had been reestablished.

The Battle of the Bulge cost the United States 77,000 casualties and delayed Eisenhower's offensive, but it exhausted the Germans' last reserves. The Allies then pressed forward to the Rhine, winning a bridgehead on the far bank of the river on March 7. Thereafter, one German city fell almost daily. With the Soviets racing westward against crumbling resistance, the end could not be long delayed. In April, American and Soviet

Table 27.1 Turning Points of the War in Europe

Summer 1942	British bombing of German cities brings war home to Germany
November 1942	U.S./British invasion of North Africa, defeat of Rommel
February 1943	Germans turned back at Stalingrad, beginning of German retreat from Soviet Union
July 1943	U.S./British invasion of Sicily
June 1944	D-Day: U.S./British invasion of northern France
January 1945	Battle of the Bulge: Last-ditch German offensive defeated
May 8, 1945	Germany surrenders

forces made contact at the Elbe River. A few days later, with Soviet shells reducing his capital to rubble, Hitler, by then probably insane, took his own life in his Berlin air raid shelter. On May 8 Germany surrendered.

As the Americans drove swiftly forward in the late stages of the war, they began to overrun Nazi concentration camps where millions of Jews and others had been murdered. The Americans were horrified by what they discovered, but they should not have been surprised. Word of this holocaust, in which 12 million people (half of them Jews) were slaughtered, had reached the United States much earlier. At first the news had been dismissed as propaganda, then discounted as grossly exaggerated. Hitler was known to hate Jews and to have persecuted them, but that he could order the murder of millions of innocent people, even children, seemed beyond belief. By 1943, however, the truth could not be denied.

Little could be done about those already in the camps, but there were thousands of refugees in occupied Europe who might have been spirited to safety. President Roosevelt declined to make the effort; he refused to bomb the Auschwitz death camp in Poland or the rail lines used to bring victims to its gas chambers on the grounds that the destruction of German soldiers and military equipment took precedence over any other objective. Thus, when American journalists entered the camps with the advancing troops, saw the heaps of still-unburied corpses, and talked with the emaciated survivors, their reports caused a storm of protest in America.

Watch the Video

Nazi Murder Mills at myhistorylab.com.
WARNING: This clip is very graphic.

The Naval War in the Pacific

Defeating Germany first had not meant abandoning the Pacific region entirely to the Japanese. While armies were being trained and matériel accumulated for the European struggle, much of the available American strength was diverted to maintaining vital communications in East Asia and preventing further Japanese expansion.

See the **Map**

World War II in the Pacific at **myhistorylab.com**

Saving Private Ryan

Steven Spielberg's *Saving Private Ryan* (1998), starring Tom Hanks, has been widely praised as the most realistic combat movie ever made. This judgment is based chiefly on its re-creation of the June 6, 1944, Allied assault on Omaha Beach during the invasion of Normandy. The camera focuses on Hanks, rain dripping from his helmet, huddled in a crowded landing vessel. Explosions rumble in the distance. The ship plows through heavy seas toward a blackened brow of land. Around him, men vomit. Explosions become louder and sharper. Nearby ships strike mines and blow up; others are obliterated by shell-fire. Hanks's landing craft lurches to avoid the mayhem. Like hail against a tin roof, gunfire riddles the landing craft. Some of the men are hit, and the others hunch lower, still vomiting. A deafening din envelops the ship as its bow opens. A curtain of bullets cuts down the men in front. Hanks and several others leap into the sea, but the ship has stopped far short of the beach. They sink. As bullets tear through the water, ripping into those still submerged, Hanks struggles to the surface. He swims, weaponless, toward the beach.

He has crossed the threshold of hell, and over the next fifteen minutes viewers descend with him the rest of the way.

Saving Private Ryan differs from other combat films not in the graphic horror of the bloodshed, but in its randomness. The audience expects Hanks to survive the opening scenes of the movie in which he stars, and he does. But all other bets are off: a valiant exploit, a kind gesture, a handsome face—none of these influences the grim lottery of battle. A medic frenziedly works on a severely wounded man, injecting morphine, compressing arteries, and binding wounds. Then more bullets splatter his patient beyond recognition. "Why can't you bastards give us a chance?" the medic screams. That is the point: When huge armies converge, hurling high explosives and steel at each other, one's chances of survival are unaffected by ethics or aesthetics.

But having made this point with heart-pounding emphasis, the movie subverts it. Hanks, unnerved and dispirited, initially hunkers down in the relative safety of the seawall. But then he does his job, rallying his men. They blast a hole through obstacles, crawl toward the concrete fortifications above, penetrate trench defenses, blow up bunkers, and seize the hill. Many perish in the effort; Hanks, an infantry captain, is among the survivors.

Then comes a new mission that occupies the remainder of the movie. George C. Marshall, U.S. Army Chief of Staff, has learned of a Mrs. Ryan who has been notified on a single day that three of her sons were killed in action. Her fourth son, James, a private in the 101st Airborne, has just parachuted into Normandy behind German lines. Marshall orders that Private Ryan be returned to safety. This mission is given to Hanks and his platoon. They march inland, encounter snipers, ambushes, and, in the final scenes, a large detachment of German armored vehicles. But they also find Ryan (played by Matt Damon).

Along the way, the movie asks many provocative questions, such as whether war improves those who fight. "I think this is all good for me, sir," one earnest soldier confides to Hanks. "Really," Hanks says with a faint smile, "how is that?" The soldier cites Ralph Waldo Emerson: "War educates the senses. Calls into action the will. Perfects the physical constitution." "Emerson had a way of finding the bright side," Hanks deadpans. Hanks's hand twitches uncontrollably, a physical manifestation of a disordered soul. War, demonstrably, has not made men better.

Except in one way: Hanks and his men have repeatedly demonstrated a willingness to give up their lives for others. Indeed, the movie's central dilemma concerns the moral arithmetic of sacrifice. Is it right to risk eight men to save one? To send a thousand men to near certain death in an initial assault at Omaha Beach to improve the chances of

Actual photograph of American troops approach code-named Omaha Beach at Normandy.

Tom Hanks, Matt Damon, and Edward Burns in *Saving Private Ryan.*

those that follow? To make one generation endure hell so that another may have freedom? The movie provides no ready answers. But in nearly the final scene it does issue a challenge. Hanks, mortally wounded, is lying amidst the corpses of his platoon, and he beckons to Ryan, who is unhurt. "Earn this," Hanks says, vaguely gesturing to the others.

Saving Private Ryan was part of a wave of nostalgic appreciation during the 1990s for the generation that had won World War II. A spate of books, movies, and TV documentaries were other expressions of this phenomenon. On accepting the Oscar for his film, Spielberg thanked his father, a World War II vet, "for showing me that there is honor in looking back and respecting the past."

But respect for the past entails getting it right, and the movie makes some significant errors and omissions. For one, it suggests that the men huddled at the base of the seawall blew up the concrete bunkers on their own. This was not possible. In fact, commanders of destroyers took their ships close to the beaches and fired countless heavy shells into the fortifications, allowing the infantry to move up the hills.

The movie also shows the German soldiers as uniformly expert and professional. But the German army had been decimated by losses in the Soviet Union. The army manning the Normandy defenses included many units composed mostly of old men, boys, or conscripted soldiers from Poland or the Soviet Union. Many surrendered as soon as they encountered American soldiers.

Of the movie's implausible elements, the premise that the U.S. Army high command

ordered a special mission to pluck a grieving mother's son from danger was based on fact. A real Mrs. Niland received telegrams on the same day informing her that three of her sons had been killed in action. Her fourth son, "Fritz," had parachuted into Normandy with the 101st Airborne. The army did in fact snatch him from the front line and return him to safety.

The movie provides a fair rendering of many other elements of the battle: the inaccuracy of aerial bombing, which missed most of the beach fortifications; the confusion caused when hundreds of landing craft failed to reach their destination; the destruction of scores of gliders, which crashed into high hedgerows while attempting to land behind German lines.

Yet through it all, some men, like the captain portrayed by Hanks, drew heroism from some unfathomed depths of the soul. One real soldier at Omaha Beach remembered "a captain and two lieutenants who demonstrated courage beyond belief as they struggled to bring order to the chaos around them."

Saving Private Ryan is not a fully accurate representation of the attack on Omaha Beach, but it depicts—realistically and memorably— how soldiers conferred meaning on the heedless calculus of modern warfare.

Questions for Discussion
- Do generals have the right to order some men to near certain death in order to save others? To save a nation?
- Do soldiers have the right to disobey such orders? Why or why not?

Midway, a tiny Pacific island, mattered only because of its airfield. The Japanese sent a naval task force to invade the island, but in June 1942 U.S. warplanes sank several of the Japanese aircraft carriers accompanying the invasion force. With air cover gone, Japan called off the invasion. Midway marked a turning point in the war in the Pacific.

The navy's aircraft carriers had escaped destruction at Pearl Harbor, a stroke of immense good fortune because the airplane had revolutionized naval warfare. Commanders discovered that carrier-based planes were far more effective against warships than the heaviest naval artillery because of their greater range and more concentrated firepower.

This was demonstrated in May 1942 in the Battle of the Coral Sea. Having captured an empire in a few months without the loss of any warship larger than a destroyer, the Japanese believed the war already won. This led them to overextend themselves.

The Coral Sea lies northeast of Australia and south of New Guinea and the Solomon Islands. Japanese mastery of these waters would cut Australia off from Hawaii and thus from American aid. Admiral Isoroku Yamamoto had dispatched a large fleet of troopships screened by many warships to attack Port Moresby, on the southern New Guinea coast. On May 7–8 planes from the American carriers *Lexington* and *Yorktown* struck the convoy's screen, sinking a small carrier and damaging a large one. Superficially, the battle seemed a victory for the Japanese, for their planes mortally wounded the *Lexington* and sank two other ships, but the troop transports had been forced to turn back—Port Moresby was saved. Although large numbers of cruisers and destroyers took part in the action, none came within sight or gun range of an enemy ship. All the destruction was wrought by carrier aircraft.

Encouraged by the Coral Sea "victory," Yamamoto decided to force the American fleet into a showdown battle by assaulting the Midway Islands, west of Hawaii. His armada never reached its destination. Between June 4 and 7 control of the central Pacific was decided entirely by airpower. American dive bombers sent four large Japanese carriers to the bottom. About 300 Japanese planes were destroyed. The United States lost only the *Yorktown* and a destroyer. Thereafter the initiative in the Pacific war shifted to the Americans, but victory came slowly and at painful cost.

American land forces were under the command of Douglas MacArthur, a brilliant but egocentric general whose judgment was sometimes distorted by his intense concern for his own reputation. MacArthur was in command of American troops in the Philippine Islands when the Japanese struck in December 1941. After his heroic but hopeless defense of Manila and the Bataan peninsula, President Roosevelt had him evacuated by PT boat to escape capture; those under MacArthur's command endured horrific conditions as prisoners of Japan.

Thereafter MacArthur was obsessed with the idea of personally leading an American army back to the Philippines. Although many strategists believed that the islands should be bypassed in the drive on the Japanese homeland, in the end MacArthur convinced the Joint Chiefs of Staff, who determined strategy. Two separate drives were undertaken, one from New Guinea toward the Philippines under MacArthur, the other through the central Pacific toward Tokyo under Admiral Chester W. Nimitz.

Island Hopping

Before commencing this two-pronged advance, the Americans had to eject the Japanese from the Solomon Islands in order to protect Australia from a flank attack. Beginning in August 1942, a series of land, sea, and air battles raged around Guadalcanal Island in this archipelago. Once again American airpower was decisive, although the bravery and skill of the ground forces that actually won the island must not be underemphasized. American pilots, better trained and with tougher planes than the Japanese, had a relatively easier task. They inflicted losses five to six times heavier on the enemy than they sustained themselves. Japanese airpower disintegrated during the long battle, and this in turn helped the fleet to take a heavy toll on the Japanese navy. By February 1943 Guadalcanal had been secured.

In the autumn of 1943 the American drives toward Japan and the Philippines got under way at last. In the central Pacific campaign the Guadalcanal action was repeated on a smaller but equally bloody scale from Tarawa in the Gilbert Islands to

Table 27.2 Turning Points of World War II in the Pacific

December 7, 1941	Japanese sneak-attack on Pearl Harbor; United States declares war
May 1942	Japanese win Battle of the Coral Sea, but invasion of Australia foiled
June 1942	United States wins Battle of Midway; Japanese advance toward Hawaii turned back
February 1943	United States takes Guadalcanal, along the southernmost periphery of Japanese power
February 1945	United States retakes Philippines
June 1945	United States takes Okinawa, near Japanese islands
August 1945	United States drops atomic bombs on Hiroshima and Nagasaki; Japan surrenders

Kwajelein and Eniwetok in the Marshalls. The Japanese soldiers on these islands fought for every foot of ground. They almost never surrendered. But Admiral Nimitz's forces were in every case victorious. By midsummer of 1944 this arm of the American advance had taken Saipan and Guam in the Marianas. Now land-based bombers were within range of Tokyo.

Meanwhile, MacArthur was leapfrogging along the New Guinea coast toward the Philippines. In October 1944 he landed on Leyte, south of Luzon. Two great naval clashes in Philippine waters, the Battle of the Philippine Sea (June 1944) and the Battle for Leyte Gulf (October 1944), completed the destruction of Japan's sea power and reduced its air force to a band of fanatical suicide pilots called *kamikazes*, who tried to crash bomb-laden planes into American warships and airstrips. The *kamikazes* caused much damage but could not turn the tide. In February 1945 MacArthur liberated Manila.

The end was now inevitable. B-29 Superfortress bombers from the Marianas rained high explosives and firebombs on Japan. The islands of Iwo Jima and Okinawa, only a few hundred miles from Tokyo, fell to the Americans in March and June 1945. But such was the tenacity of the Japanese soldiers that it seemed possible that it would take another year of fighting and perhaps a million more American casualties to subdue the home Japanese islands.

World War II Pacific Theatre After the Battle of Midway (June, 1942), the United States began to seize one Pacific island after another, with one task force pushing west from Pearl Harbor, and another moving north from Australia.

Building the Atom Bomb

At this point came the most controversial decision of the entire war, and it was made by a newcomer on the world scene. In November 1944 Roosevelt had been elected to a fourth term, easily defeating Thomas E. Dewey. Instead of renominating Henry A. Wallace for vice president, whom conservatives considered too radical, the Democratic convention had nominated Senator Harry S Truman of Missouri, a reliable party man well-liked by professional politicians. Then, in April 1945, President Roosevelt died of a cerebral hemorrhage. Thus it was Truman who had to decide what to do when, in July 1945, American scientists placed in his hands a new and awful weapon, the atomic bomb.

After Roosevelt had responded to Albert Einstein's warning in 1939, government-sponsored atomic research had proceeded rapidly, especially after the establishment of the so-called Manhattan Project in May 1943. The manufacture of the element plutonium at Hanford, Washington, and of uranium 235 at Oak Ridge, Tennessee, continued, along with the design and construction of a transportable atomic bomb at Los Alamos, New Mexico, under the direction of J. Robert Oppenheimer. Almost $2 billion was spent before a successful bomb was exploded at Alamogordo, in the New Mexican desert, on July 16, 1945. As that first mushroom cloud formed over the desert, Oppenheimer recalled the prophetic words of the *Bhagavad Gita*: "I am become death, the shatterer of worlds."

●●●—⎾Read the **Document**
Einstein, *Letter to President Roosevelt* at **myhistorylab.com**

Should a bomb with the destructive force of 20,000 tons of TNT be employed against Japan? By striking a major city, its dreadful power could be demonstrated convincingly, yet doing so would bring death to tens of thousands of Japanese civilians. Many of the scientists who had made the bomb now argued against its use. Others suggested alerting the Japanese and then staging a demonstration explosion at sea, but that idea was discarded because of concern that the bomb might fail to explode.

Truman was torn between his awareness that the bomb was "the most terrible thing ever discovered" and his hope that using it "would bring the war to an end." The bomb might cause a revolution in Japan, might lead the emperor to intervene, might even persuade the military to give up. Considering the thousands of Americans who would surely die in any conventional invasion of Japan and, on a less humane level,

Hiroshima lies in ruins, destroyed by an atomic bomb.

influenced by a desire to end the Pacific war before the Soviet Union could intervene effectively and thus claim a role in the peacemaking, the president chose to go ahead. The moral soundness of Truman's decision has been debated ever since. On August 6 the Superfortress *Enola Gay* dropped an atomic bomb on Hiroshima, killing about 78,000 persons (including twenty American prisoners of war) and injuring nearly 100,000 more out of a population of 344,000. Over 96 percent of the buildings in the city were destroyed or damaged. Three days later, while the stunned Japanese still hesitated, a second atomic bomb blasted Nagasaki. On August 15 Japan surrendered.

Thus ended the greatest war in history. Its cost was beyond calculation. No accurate count could be made even of the dead; we know only that the total was in the neighborhood of 20 million. As in World War I, American casualties— 291,000 battle deaths and 671,000 wounded—were smaller than those of the other major belligerents. About 7.5 million Soviets died in battle, 3.5 million Germans, 1.2 million Japanese, and 2.2 million Chinese; Britain and France, despite much smaller populations, suffered losses almost as large as did the United States. And far more than in World War I, American resources, human and matériel, had made victory possible.

No one could account the war a benefit to humanity, but in the late summer of 1945 the future looked bright. Fascism was dead. The successful wartime diplomatic dealings of Roosevelt, Churchill, and the Soviet dictator, Joseph Stalin, encouraged many to hope that the communists were ready to cooperate in rebuilding Europe. Out of the death and destruction had come technological developments that seemed to herald a better world as well as a peaceful one. Enormous advances in the design of airplanes and the development of radar (which some authorities think was more important than any weapons system in winning the war) were about to revolutionize travel and the transportation of goods. Improvements in surgery and other medical advances gave promise of saving millions of lives, and the development of penicillin and other antibiotics, which had greatly reduced the death rate among troops, would perhaps banish all infectious diseases.

Above all, there was the power of the atom. The force that seared Hiroshima and Nagasaki could be harnessed to serve peaceful needs, the scientists promised, with results that might free humanity forever from poverty and toil. The period of reconstruction would be prolonged, but with all the great powers adhering to the new United Nations charter, drafted at San Francisco in June 1945, international cooperation could be counted on to ease the burdens of the victims of war and help the poor and underdeveloped parts of the world toward economic and political independence. Such at least was the hope of millions in the victorious summer of 1945.

Wartime Diplomacy

During the course of World War II every instrument of mass persuasion in the country had been directed toward convincing the people that the Soviets were fighting America's battle as well as their own. Even before Pearl Harbor, former Ambassador Joseph E. Davies wrote in his best-selling *Mission to Moscow* (1941) that Joseph Stalin and other communist leaders were "devoted to the cause of peace for both ideological and practical reasons."

Such views of Joseph Stalin were naive, to say the least, but the United States and the Soviet Union agreed emphatically on the need to defeat Hitler. The Soviets repeatedly expressed a willingness to cooperate with the Allies in dealing with postwar problems. The Soviet Union was one of the twenty-six signers of the Declaration of the United Nations (January 1942), in which the Allies promised to eschew territorial aggrandizement after the war, to respect the right of all peoples to determine their own form of government, to work for freer trade and international economic cooperation, and to force the disarmament of the aggressor nations.[1]

In May 1943 the Soviet Union dissolved the Comintern, its official agency for the promulgation of world revolution. The following October, during a conference in Moscow with the Allies, Soviet Foreign Minister V. M. Molotov joined in setting up a European Advisory Commission to divide Germany into occupation zones after the war. That December, at a conference held in Tehran, Iran, Roosevelt, Churchill, and Stalin discussed plans for a new league of nations. When Roosevelt described the kind of world organization he envisaged, the Soviet dictator offered a number of constructive suggestions.

Between August and October 1944, Allied representatives met at Dumbarton Oaks, outside Washington. The chief Soviet delegate, Andrei A. Gromyko, opposed limiting the use of the veto by the great powers on the future **United Nations (UN)** Security Council, but he did not take a deliberately obstructionist position. At a conference held at Yalta in the Crimea in February 1945 Stalin joined Roosevelt and Churchill in the call for a meeting in April at San Francisco to draft a charter for the UN. "We argued freely and frankly across the table," Roosevelt reported later. "But at the end, on every point, unanimous agreement was reached. I may say we achieved a unity of thought and a way of getting along together."

The UN charter drafted at the 50-nation San Francisco Conference gave each UN member a seat in the General Assembly. The locus of authority in the new organization resided in the Security Council, "the castle of the great powers." This consisted of five permanent members (the United States, the Soviet Union, Great Britain, France, and China) and six others elected for two-year terms.

The Security Council was charged with responsibility for maintaining world peace, but any great power could block UN action whenever it wished to do so. The United States insisted on this veto power as strongly as the Soviet Union did. In effect the charter paid lip service to the Wilsonian ideal of a powerful international police force, but it incorporated the limitations that Henry Cabot Lodge had proposed in his 1919 reservation to Article X of the League Covenant, which relieved the United States from the obligation of enforcing collective security without the approval of Congress.

Allied Suspicion of Stalin

Long before the war in Europe ended, however, the Allies had clashed over important policy matters. Since later world tensions developed from decisions made at this time, an understanding of the disagreements is essential for evaluating several subsequent decades.

---

[1]These were the principles first laid down in the so-called Atlantic Charter, drafted by Roosevelt and Churchill at a meeting on the USS *Augusta* off Newfoundland in August 1941.

Much depends on one's view of the postwar Soviet system. If the Soviet government under Stalin was bent on world domination, events fall readily into one pattern of interpretation. If, having endured an unprovoked assault by the Nazis, it was seeking only to protect itself against the possibility of another invasion, these events are best explained differently. Because the United States has opened nearly all its diplomatic records, we know a great deal about how American foreign policy was formulated and about the mixed motives and mistaken judgments of American leaders. This helps explain why many scholars have been critical of American policy and the "cold warriors" who made and directed it. The Soviet Union, for many years, did not let even its own historians into its archives.

It is clear, however, that the Soviets resented the British-American delay in opening up a second front. They were fighting for survival against the full power of the German armies; any American invasion of northern France, even an unsuccessful one, would have relieved some of the pressure. Roosevelt and Churchill would not move until they were ready, and Stalin had to accept their decision. At the same time, Stalin never concealed his determination to protect his country from future attack by extending its frontier after the war. He warned the Allies repeatedly that he would not tolerate any unfriendly government along the western boundary of the Soviet Union.

Most Allied leaders, including Roosevelt, admitted privately during the war that the Soviet Union would annex territory and possess preponderant power in Eastern Europe after the defeat of Germany, but they never said this publicly. They believed that the Soviets would allow free governments to be created in countries like Poland and Bulgaria.

The Polish question was a terribly difficult one. The war, after all, had been triggered by the German attack on Poland; the British in particular felt a moral obligation to restore that nation to its prewar independence. During the war a Polish government in exile was set up in London, and its leaders were determined—especially after the discovery in 1943 of the murder of some 5,000 Polish officers several years earlier at Katyn, in Russia, presumably by the Soviet secret police—to make no concessions to Soviet territorial demands. Public opinion in Poland (and indeed in all the states along Russia's western frontier) was not so much anti-Soviet as anti-Russian. Yet the Soviet Union's legitimate interests could not be ignored.

Yalta and Potsdam

◉ Watch the Video

The Big Three Conference at Yalta at **myhistorylab.com**

At the **Yalta Conference**, Roosevelt and Churchill agreed to Soviet annexation of large sections of eastern Poland. In return they demanded that free elections be held in Poland itself. Stalin agreed, almost certainly without intending to keep his promise. The elections were never held; Poland was run by a pro-Soviet puppet regime.

Stalin apparently could not understand why the Allies were so concerned about the fate of a small country remote from their strategic spheres. That they professed to be concerned seemed to him an indication that they had some secret, devious purpose. Roosevelt, however, was worried about the political effects that Soviet control of Poland might have in the United States. Polish Americans would be furious if the United States allowed the Soviets to control their homeland.

But had Roosevelt described the difficulties to the Polish Americans and the rest of the American people more frankly, their

Churchill, Roosevelt, and Stalin meet at the Yalta, U.S.S.R., conference in February 1945. By April 1945, Roosevelt was dead.

reaction might have been less angry. In any case, when he realized that Stalin was going to act as he pleased, Roosevelt was furious. In July 1945, following the surrender of Germany, the new president, Harry Truman, met with Stalin and Churchill at Potsdam, outside Berlin.[2] At the **Potsdam Conference** they agreed to try the Nazi leaders as war criminals, made plans for exacting reparations from Germany, and confirmed the division of the country into four zones to be occupied separately by American, Soviet, British, and French troops. Berlin, deep in the Soviet zone, had itself been split into four sectors. Stalin rejected all arguments that he loosen his hold on Eastern Europe, and Truman made no concessions. But he was impressed by Stalin.

On both sides suspicions were mounting, positions hardening. Yet all the advantages seemed to be with the United States. Was this not, as Henry Luce, the publisher of *Time* had declared, "the American century," an era when American power and American ideals would shape the course of events the world over? Besides its army, navy, and air force and its immense industrial potential, alone among the nations the United States possessed the atomic bomb. When Stalin's actions made it clear that he intended to control Eastern Europe and to exert influence elsewhere in the world, most Americans expressed resentment tempered by amazement. It took time for them to realize that the war had caused a fundamental change in international politics. The United States might be the strongest country in the world, but the western European nations, victor and vanquished alike, were reduced to their own and America's surprise to the status of second-class powers. The Soviet Union, on the other hand, had gained more influence than it had held under the czars and regained the territory it had lost as a result of World War I and the communist revolution.

---

[2]Clement R. Attlee replaced Churchill during the conference after his Labour party won the British elections.

Milestones

1941	Roosevelt prohibits discrimination in defense plants (Fair Employment Practices Committee)	1943	Roosevelt, Churchill, Stalin meet at Tehran, Iran
	Japan attacks Pearl Harbor	1944	Allies invade Normandy, France (D-Day)
	Roosevelt and Churchill draft Atlantic Charter		Battle of the Bulge exhausts German reserves
1942	Executive Order 9066 sends Japanese Americans to relocation camps	1945	Big Three meet at Yalta Conference
	Japanese take Philippines		Fifty nations draft UN Charter at San Francisco
	Carrier-based planes dominate Battle of Coral Sea		Roosevelt dies; Truman becomes president
	U.S. airpower takes control of central Pacific at Battle of Midway		Germany surrenders (V-E Day)
	U.S. troops invade North Africa		United States tests atom bomb at Alamogordo, New Mexico
1943	Oppenheimer directs Manhattan Project to make atom bomb		Truman, Churchill, Stalin meet at Potsdam
	Race riots rage in Detroit and Los Angeles		United States drops atom bombs on Hiroshima and Nagasaki, Japan
	Allies invade Italy		Japan surrenders (V-J Day)

✓•—Study and Review at **www.myhistorylab.com**

Review Questions

1. What did the U.S. government do to mobilize for war? How did the war affect women and minority groups?
2. Why did FDR order that American citizens of Japanese ancestry be placed in internment camps? What was the Supreme Court's response to the constitutionality of this decision?
3. Why, since Japan attacked first, did FDR decide to commit most American resources to defeating the Germans in Europe? What were the key phases of the war in Europe? Of the war in the Pacific?
4. What role did science and technology play in the war?
5. Should Truman have used atomic bombs against Japan? Why had American relations with the Soviet Union deteriorated by 1945?

Key Terms

Allies 718
D-Day 720

internment camps 715
Potsdam Conference 731

United Nations
  (UN) 729
Yalta Conference 730

Collision Courses, Abroad and at Home: 1946–1960

28

((•—Hear the Audio Chapter 28 at myhistorylab.com

Do you ever drive too fast?

IN 2009 OVER 10,000 PEOPLE BETWEEN THE AGES OF SIXTEEN AND twenty-four were killed in motor vehicle accidents—the leading cause of death among young people. Each month nearly as many Americans died in car crashes as perished at the World Trade Center on September 11, 2001. American traffic fatalities totaled 34,000.

But it could have been worse—and once was. During the decade of the 1970s, a half million Americans died in traffic accidents—over 50,000 each year. Since Henry Ford first rolled out the Model-T, over three and a half million Americans have died on the nation's roads and highways. Despite the carnage, automobiles have become so much a part of American life that few can imagine living without them.

The ascendancy of the automobile over mass transit was well-established during the 1930s. But World War II put more Americans in motion than ever before. Afterwards, car ownership soared. Designers produced faster and heavier cars for "a wartime generation" that was far "bigger, taller and more active" than its predecessors. Americans hurtled along the new superhighways that the federal government built in part for military purposes.

The American nation, too, was rushing into a new era of Cold War confrontation with the Soviet Union. In both countries new weapons loomed larger, each more menacing than the last. By 1960, hundreds of millions of people could be wiped out in an instant. The Cold War between the superpowers turned hot in Korea, the Middle East, and Latin America. Real foreign spies exacerbated fears of domestic subversion.

Postwar complacency soon gave way to racial confrontation at home. African Americans who had helped defeat Nazi racism accelerated demands for fair treatment. First they challenged Jim Crow segregation in the courts. When these initiatives encountered segregationist roadblocks, they turned to nonviolent protests that they knew would likely trigger violent responses.

From 1946 through 1960, Americans lived dangerously in a postwar era of menacing uncertainty.

The Postwar Economy

Economists had feared that the flood of millions of veterans into the job market would cause serious unemployment. But the widespread craving for cars—bigger, faster, and "loaded" with features such as radios and air-conditioners—fueled the postwar economic boom. During the decade of the 1920s American factories had produced 31 million cars. In the 1950s, 58 million rolled off the assembly lines; during the 1960s, 77 million were made. The proliferation of cars contributed to the expansion of related industries, especially oil. Gasoline consumption first touched 15 billion gallons in 1931; it soared to 35 billion gallons in 1950 and to 92 billion in 1970.

Although the car industry was the leading postwar economic sector, war-weary Americans also bought new houses, washing machines, and countless other products. Unable to buy such goods during the war, they used their war-enforced savings to go on a shopping spree that kept factories operating at capacity.

In addition, the government made an unprecedented educational opportunity available to veterans. Instead of a general bonus, which would have stimulated consumption and inflation, in 1944 Congress passed the *GI Bill of Rights*, which made subsidies available to veterans so they could continue their educations, learn new trades, or start new businesses. After the war nearly 8 million veterans took advantage of the education and training grants.

Economic prosperity in the decades after World War II allowed the federal government to increase its military and economic commitments abroad without raising taxes.

Truman Becomes President

When Harry S Truman received the news of Roosevelt's death in 1945, he claimed that he felt as though "the moon, the stars, and all the planets" had suddenly fallen upon him. Although he could not have been quite as surprised as he indicated (Roosevelt was known to have been in extremely poor health), he was acutely conscious of his own limitations.

Truman was born in Missouri in 1884. He served in a World War I artillery unit, and later became a minor cog in the political machine of Democratic boss Tom Pendergast. In 1934 Truman was elected to the U.S. Senate, where he proved to be a loyal but obscure New Dealer. He first attracted national attention during World War II when his "watchdog" committee on defense spending, working with devotion and efficiency, saved the government immense sums. This led to his nomination and election as vice president.

Levittown, New York, in 1949 epitomizes the postwar housing boom.

As president, Truman sought to carry on in the Roosevelt tradition. Curiously, he was at the same time humble and cocky, even brash—both idealistic and cold-bloodedly political. He adopted liberal objectives only to pursue them sometimes by rash, even repressive means. On balance, however, he was a strong and, in many ways, successful president.

But he lost a major battle early on. In June 1947, the new Congress passed the **Taft-Hartley Act**. It outlawed the closed shop (a provision written into many labor contracts requiring new workers to join the union before they could be employed). Most important, it authorized the president to seek court injunctions to prevent strikes that, in his opinion, endangered the national interest.

Truman vetoed the bill, but Congress overrode it. The Taft-Hartley Act made the task of unionizing industries more difficult, but it did not seriously hamper existing unions.

The Containment Policy

Although he was vice president during much of World War II, Truman had been excluded from all foreign policy discussions. He was not granted full security clearance and thus knew little about the Manhattan Project. While FDR had concluded at Yalta that he could charm or otherwise personally cope with the Soviet dictator, Truman resolved to deal with Stalin firmly.

Repeatedly Stalin made it clear that he had no intention of even consulting with Western leaders about his domination of Eastern Europe, and he seemed intent on extending his power deep into war-devastated central Europe. By January 1946 Truman had decided to stop "babying" the Russians.

Truman's problem was that Stalin had far more military divisions than anyone else. Truman had swiftly responded to the postwar clamor to "bring the boys home." In the two years following the surrender of Japan, the armed forces of the United States had dwindled from 6 million to 1.5 million. Stalin, who kept domestic foes out of office by shooting them, ignored domestic pressure to demobilize the Red Army, estimated by U.S. intelligence at twice the size of the American army.

Stalin and the mighty Red Army evoked the image of Hitler's troops pouring across the north European plains. Like Hitler, Stalin was a cruel dictator who championed an ideology of world conquest. George Kennan, a scholarly foreign officer who also had served in Moscow, thought that ideology was more symptom than cause. Marxism, he wrote, provided the intellectual "fig-leaf of morality and respectability" for naked Soviet aggression. In an influential article, "The Sources of Soviet Conduct," published anonymously in the July 1947 issue of *Foreign Affairs*, Kennan argued that the instability and illegitimacy of the Soviet regime generated explosive internal pressures. These forces, vented outward, would cause the Soviet Union to

ПОД ВОДИТЕЛЬСТВОМ ВЕЛИКОГО СТАЛИНА–ВПЕРЕД К КОММУНИЗМУ!

A propaganda poster enshrining Stalin proclaims that he has led his people "Forward to Communism!"

expand "constantly, wherever it is permitted to move" until it filled "every nook and cranny available to it in the basin of world power." A policy of "long-term, patient but firm and vigilant containment" was the best means of dealing with the Soviet Union.

The Atom Bomb: A "Winning" Weapon?

Although Truman authorized use of the atom bomb to force the surrender of Japan, he had hoped that a demonstration of the weapon's power also would inhibit Stalin and serve as a counterweight to the Red Army. Stalin, however, refused to be intimidated. He knew that the American atomic arsenal—slightly more than a dozen bombs in 1947—was insufficient to destroy the Soviet Union's military machine.

The atomic bomb was a doubtful deterrent for another reason. Sobering accounts of the devastation of Hiroshima and Nagasaki and the suffering of the victims of radiation poisoning left many Americans uneasy. Even Truman doubted whether the American people would again "permit" their president to use atomic weapons for aggressive purposes.

In November 1945 the United States suggested that the UN supervise all nuclear energy production, and the General Assembly created an Atomic Energy Commission to study the question. In June 1946 Commissioner Bernard Baruch offered a plan for the eventual outlawing of atomic weapons. Under this proposal UN inspectors operating without restriction anywhere in the world would ensure that no country made bombs clandestinely. When, at an unspecified date, the system was established successfully, the United States would destroy its stockpile of bombs.

Most Americans thought the Baruch plan magnanimous, and some considered it positively foolhardy, but the Soviets rejected it. They would neither permit UN inspectors in the Soviet Union nor surrender the Soviet Union's veto power over Security Council actions dealing with atomic energy. They demanded that the United States destroy its bombs at once. American leaders did not comply; they believed that the atom bomb would be, in Baruch's words, their "winning weapon" for years to come.

A Turning Point in Greece

The strategy of containment began to take shape early in 1947 as a result of a crisis in Greece. Greek communists, waging a guerrilla war against the monarchy, were receiving aid from communist Yugoslavia and Bulgaria. Great Britain had been assisting the monarchists but could no longer afford this drain on its resources. In February 1947 the British informed President Truman that they would cut off aid to Greece.

The British predicament forced American policymakers to confront the fact that their European allies had not been able to rebuild their war-weakened economies. That the Soviet Union was actually discouraging the Greek rebels out of fear of American intervention in the area the policymakers ignored.

Truman asked Congress to approve what became known as the **Truman Doctrine**. If Greece or Turkey fell to the communists, he said, all of the Middle East might be lost. To prevent this "unspeakable tragedy," he asked for $400 million in military and

economic aid to Greece and Turkey. "It must be the policy of the United States to support free peoples who are resisting attempted subjugation by armed minorities or by outside pressures," he said.

•••—[Read the Document

Truman Doctrine, 1947
at **myhistorylab.com**

By exaggerating the consequences of inaction and by justifying his request on ideological grounds, Truman obtained his objective. The result was the establishment of a right-wing, military-dominated government in Greece. In addition, by not limiting his request to the specific problem posed by the situation in Greece, Truman caused considerable concern in many countries.

The threat to Western Europe certainly loomed large in 1947. The entire continent seemed in danger of falling into communist hands without the Soviet Union raising a finger.

The Marshall Plan and the Lesson of History

In a 1946 speech entitled "The Lesson of History," George C. Marshall, army chief of staff during World War II, reminded Americans that their isolationism had contributed to Hitler's unchecked early aggression. This time, Marshall noted, the people of the United States must be prepared to act against foreign aggressors. In 1947 Marshall was named secretary of state. He outlined an extraordinary plan by which the United States would finance the reconstruction of the European economy. "Hunger, poverty, desperation, and chaos" were the real enemies of freedom and democracy, Marshall said. The need was to restore "the confidence of the European people in the economic future of their own countries." Even the Soviet Union and Soviet-bloc nations would be eligible for American aid.

The European powers eagerly seized upon what became known as the **Marshall Plan**, a massive infusion of American aid to rebuild Europe after World War II. European leaders set up a sixteen-nation Committee for European Economic Cooperation, which soon submitted plans calling for up to $22.4 billion in American assistance.

The Soviet Union and its European satellites were tempted by the offer and sent representatives to the initial planning meetings. But Stalin grew anxious that his satellite states would be drawn into the orbit of the United States. He recalled his delegates and demanded that Soviet bloc nations do likewise. Those who hesitated were ordered to report to the Kremlin. "I went to Moscow as the Foreign Minister of an independent sovereign state," Jan Masaryk of Czechoslovakia commented bitterly. "I returned as a lackey of the Soviet government."

In February 1948 a communist coup took over the Czechoslovak government; Masaryk fell (or more likely was pushed) out a window to his death. These strong-arm tactics brought to mind the Nazi takeover of Czechoslovakia a decade earlier and helped persuade Congress to appropriate over $13 billion for the Marshall aid program. Results exceeded all expectations. By 1951 Western Europe was booming.

But Europe was now divided in two. In the West, where American-influenced governments were elected, private property was respected if often taxed heavily, and corporations gained influence and power. In the East, where the Soviet Union imposed its will and political system on client states, deep-seated resentment festered among subject peoples.

In March 1948 Great Britain, France, Belgium, the Netherlands, and Luxembourg signed an alliance aimed at social, cultural, and economic collaboration. The Western nations abandoned their understandable but counterproductive policy of crushing Germany economically. They announced plans for creating a single West German Republic with a large degree of autonomy.

In June 1948 the Soviet Union retaliated by closing off surface access to Berlin from the west. For a time it seemed that the Allies must either fight their way into the city or abandon it to the communists. Unwilling to adopt either alternative, Truman decided to fly

Recipients of Marshall Plan Aid, 1948–1952 Marshall Plan aid was originally offered to the Soviet Union and communist bloc states. Stalin, however, refused to accept American aid and ordered Soviet satellites to refuse, too. All did, except Yugoslavia, whose disobedience infuriated Stalin.

supplies to the capital from Frankfurt, Hannover, and Hamburg. American C-47 and C-54 transports delivered enough food, fuel, and other goods necessary to maintain more than 2 million West Berliners. The **Berlin airlift** put the Soviets in an uncomfortable position; if they were determined to keep supplies from West Berlin, they would have to start the fighting. They were not prepared to do so. In May 1949 they lifted the blockade.

American generals intensified preparation of contingency plans in the event of a Soviet attack.

The Election of 1948

In the spring of 1948 President Truman's fortunes were at low ebb. Public opinion polls suggested that a majority of the people considered him incompetent or worse. The Republicans seemed so sure to win the 1948 presidential election that many prominent

Democrats began to talk of denying Truman the nomination. Two of FDR's sons came out for General Eisenhower as the Democratic candidate. Governor Dewey, who again won the Republican nomination, ran confidently (even complacently), certain that he would carry the country.

Truman's position seemed hopeless because he had alienated both southern conservatives and northern liberals. The Southerners were particularly distressed because in 1946 the president had established a Committee on Civil Rights,

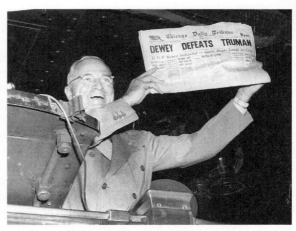

In 1948 the strongly Republican *Chicago Daily Tribune* printed its post-election headlines before all the returns were in. For Truman, it was the perfect climax to his hard-won victory.

which had recommended antilynching and antipoll tax legislation and the creation of a permanent Fair Employment Practices Commission. When the Democratic convention adopted a civil rights plank, the southern delegates walked out. Southern conservatives then founded the States' Rights ("Dixiecrat") party and nominated J. Strom Thurmond of South Carolina for president.

As for the liberals, in 1947 a group that believed Truman's containment policy a threat to world peace organized a new Progressive party and nominated former Vice President Henry A. Wallace. With two minor candidates sure to cut into the Democratic vote, the president's chances seemed minuscule.

Truman launched an aggressive whistle-stop campaign. He excoriated the "do-nothing" Republican Congress, which had rejected his program and passed the Taft-Hartley Act, and he warned labor, farmers, and consumers that if Dewey won, Republican "gluttons of privilege" would do away with all the gains of the New Deal years.

Millions were moved by Truman's arguments and by his courageous fight against great odds. The success of the Berlin airlift during the presidential campaign helped him considerably, as did disaffection among normally Republican midwestern farmers. The Progressive party fell increasingly into the hands of communist sympathizers, driving away many liberals who might otherwise have supported Wallace.

The president reinvigorated the New Deal coalition and won an amazing upset victory on election day. He collected 24.1 million votes to Dewey's 21.9 million, the two minor candidates being held to about 2.3 million. In the Electoral College his margin was a thumping 303 to 189.

Truman's victory encouraged him to press forward with what he called his **Fair Deal** program. He urged Congress to raise the minimum wage, fund an ambitious public housing program, develop a national health insurance system, and repeal the Taft-Hartley Act. However, relatively little of Truman's Fair Deal was enacted into law. Congress approved a federal housing program and measures increasing the minimum wage and Social Security benefits, but these were merely extensions of New Deal legislation.

Containing Communism Abroad

During Truman's second term the confrontation between the United States and the Soviet Union dominated the headlines. To strengthen ties with the European democracies, in April 1949 the North Atlantic Treaty was signed in Washington. The United States, Great Britain, France, Italy, Belgium, the Netherlands, Luxembourg, Denmark, Norway, Portugal, Iceland, and Canada[1] agreed "that an armed attack against one or more of them in Europe or North America shall be considered an attack against them all" and that in the event of such an attack each would take "individually and in concert with the other Parties, such action as it deems necessary, including the use of armed force." The pact established the **North Atlantic Treaty Organization (NATO)**.

In September 1949 the Soviet Union detonated an atomic bomb. When the explosion was confirmed, Truman called for rapid expansion of the American nuclear arsenal. He also asked his advisers to determine whether the United States should develop a new weapon thousands of times more destructive than atomic bombs. The "super" or hydrogen bomb would replicate the fusion process on the surface of the sun. The Atomic Energy Commission argued that there was no military use for hydrogen bombs, which would destroy hundreds of square miles as well as precipitate a dangerous arms race with the Soviet Union. The Joint Chiefs of Staff disagreed. Even if the hydrogen bomb could not be used in battle, they argued, its mere existence would intimidate enemies; and, the military men added, the Soviets would themselves build a hydrogen bomb whether or not the United States did so. (Unbeknownst to American leaders, Stalin had already ordered development of the hydrogen bomb.) On January 31, 1950, Truman publicly announced that "though none wants to use it" he had no choice but to proceed with a hydrogen bomb.

In Asia the effort to contain communism in China had failed utterly. After World War II, Nationalists under Chiang Kai-shek (sometimes spelled Jiang Jieshi) dominated the south; communists under Mao Zedong controlled much of the north. Truman tried to bring Chiang's Nationalists and Mao's communists together. He sent General Marshall to China to seek a settlement, but neither Chiang nor Mao would make significant concessions. In January 1947 Truman recalled Marshall and named him secretary of state. Soon thereafter civil war, suspended during the Japanese occupation, erupted in China.

By the end of 1949 communist armies had administered a crushing defeat to the nationalists. The remnants of Chiang Kai-shek's forces fled to the island of Formosa, now called Taiwan. Mao ruled China. The "loss" of China to communism strengthened right-wing elements in the Republican party. They charged that Truman had not backed the Nationalists strongly enough and that he had stupidly underestimated Mao's dedication to the cause of world revolution.

Containment had relied on American money, materials, and know-how, but not on American soldiers. In early 1950, Truman proposed to pare the budget by further reducing the nation's armed forces. Truman also called for a thorough review of the concept of containment. Dean Acheson, who recently had succeeded George Marshall as secretary of state, supervised the study. In March, it was submitted to the National Security Council, assigned a numerical designation (NSC-68), classified top secret, and sent to the nation's military and diplomatic leaders for review.

---

[1]In 1952, Greece and Turkey joined the alliance, and in 1954 so did West Germany.

NSC-68 called for an enormous military expansion. The Soviet Union, it declared, was engaged in a worldwide assault on freedom. Instead of relying on other nations, the United States itself must develop sufficient military forces to stop communism from spreading *anywhere in the world*. Military spending therefore had to be increased from $14 billion to nearly $50 billion. If the Soviet Union failed to keep up with the American expenditures, it would no longer pose a military threat, and if it attempted to match the high levels of American military spending, its less efficient economic system would collapse from the strain.

The document was submitted to Truman on April 7, 1950. He had planned significant cuts to the defense budget; the prospect of increasing it by 350 percent appalled him. Within a few months, however, events in Korea changed his mind.

Hot War in Korea

After World War II the province of Korea was taken from Japan and divided at 38° north latitude into the Democratic People's Republic in the north, backed by the Soviet Union, and the Republic of Korea in the south, backed by the United States and

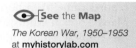

See the **Map**

The Korean War, 1950–1953
at **myhistorylab.com**

the UN. Both powers withdrew their troops from the peninsula. The Soviets left behind a well-armed local force, but the Republic of Korea's army was small and ill-trained.

America's first line of defense against communism in East Asia was to be its island bases in Japan and the Philippines. In a speech in January 1950 Acheson deliberately excluded Korea from what he described as the "defensive perimeter" of the United States in Asia. It was up to the South Koreans, backed by the UN, to protect themselves, Acheson said. This encouraged the North Koreans to attack. In June 1950, when their armored divisions, led by 150 Soviet-made tanks, rumbled across the thirty-eighth parallel, the South Koreans failed to stop them.

Truman was at his family home in Independence, Missouri, when Acheson telephoned with the news of the North Korean attack. On the flight to Washington, Truman recalled how the communists in Korea were acting "just as Hitler, Mussolini, and the Japanese had acted ten, fifteen, and twenty years earlier." "If this were allowed to go unchallenged," he concluded, "it would mean a third world war, just as similar incidents had brought on the Second World War." With the backing of the UN Security Council (but without asking Congress to declare war), he sent American planes into battle.[2] Ground troops soon followed. Truman also ordered the adoption of NSC-68 "as soon as feasible."

Nominally the Korean War was a struggle between the invaders and the United Nations. General MacArthur, placed in command, flew the blue UN flag over his headquarters, and sixteen nations supplied troops for his army. However, more than 90 percent of the forces were American. At first the North Koreans pushed them back rapidly, but in September a front was stabilized around the port of Pusan, at the southern tip of Korea. Then MacArthur executed a brilliant amphibious invasion, landing at the west coast city of Inchon, fifty miles south of the thirty-eighth parallel. Their lines of supply destroyed, the North Koreans retreated in disorder. By October the battlefront had moved north of the 1945 boundary.

---

[2]The Soviet Union, which could have vetoed this action, was at the moment boycotting the Security Council because the UN had refused to give the Mao Zedong regime China's seat on that body.

General MacArthur now proposed the conquest of North Korea, even if it meant bombing "privileged sanctuaries" on the Chinese side of the Korean border. A few of Truman's civilian advisers, the most important being George Kennan, opposed advancing into North Korea, fearing intervention not only by the Red Chinese but also by the Soviets.

Truman authorized MacArthur to advance as far as the Yalu River, the boundary between North Korea and China. It was an unfortunate decision. As the advance progressed, ominous reports came from north of the Yalu. Mao's Foreign Minister warned that the Chinese would not tolerate seeing their neighbors being "savagely invaded by imperialists." Alarmed, Truman flew to Wake Island, in the Pacific, to confer with MacArthur. The general, who had a low opinion of Asian soldiers, assured him that the

The Chinese counteroffensive of November 1950 caught the Americans by surprise and cut off many units. Here, a U.S. Marine rests during the retreat that winter.

Chinese would not dare to intervene. If they did, he added, his army would crush them easily; the war would be over by Christmas.

Seldom has a general miscalculated so badly. Ignoring intelligence reports and dividing his advancing units, he drove toward the Yalu recklessly. Suddenly, on November 26, thirty-three Chinese divisions, hidden along the interior mountains of Korea, smashed through the center of MacArthur's lines. Overnight a triumphant advance became a bloody, disorganized retreat. MacArthur now spoke of the "bottomless well of Chinese manpower" and justified his earlier confidence by claiming that he was fighting "an entirely new war."

The UN army rallied south of the thirty-eighth parallel, and MacArthur then urged that he be permitted to bomb Chinese installations north of the Yalu. He also suggested a naval blockade of the coast of China and the use of Chinese Nationalist troops. Truman rejected these proposals on the ground that they would lead to a third world war. MacArthur, who tended to ignore the larger political aspects of the conflict, attempted to rouse Congress and the public against the president by openly criticizing administration policy. Truman ordered him to be silent. When the general persisted in his criticisms, Truman fired him.

As the months passed and the casualties mounted, many citizens became disillusioned and angry. Military men backed the president almost unanimously. General Omar N. Bradley, chairman of the Joint Chiefs of Staff, said that a showdown with communist China "would involve us in the wrong war, at the wrong place, at the wrong time and with the wrong enemy." In June 1951 the communists agreed to discuss an armistice in Korea, although the negotiations dragged on interminably. The war was unresolved when Truman left office: by the time it was over, it had produced 157,000 American casualties, including 54,200 dead.

Korean War, 1950–1953 In June, North Korea nearly overran South Korea (top maps). But in September MacArthur counterattacked at Inchon and advanced far into North Korea (bottom left). The intervention of the Chinese in November led to a stalemate (bottom right).

If the Korean War persuaded Truman to adopt NSC-68, it also exposed the failings of the policy. By conceiving of communism as a monolithic force it tended to make it so, driving Red China and the Soviet Union into each other's arms. By committing American military forces to potential trouble spots throughout the world, it increased the likelihood they would prevail in none.

The Communist Issue at Home

The Korean War highlighted the paradox that, at the pinnacle of its power, the influence of the United States in world affairs was declining. Its monopoly on nuclear weapons had been lost. China had passed into the communist orbit. Elsewhere in Asia and throughout Africa, new nations, formerly colonial possessions of the Western powers, were adopting a "neutralist" position in the Cold War. Despite the billions poured into armaments and foreign aid, national security seemed far from ensured.

Internal as well as external dangers loomed. Alarming examples of communist espionage in Canada, Great Britain, and the United States convinced many citizens that clever conspirators were everywhere at work undermining American security. Both the Republicans and conservative Democratic critics of Truman's domestic policies were charging that he was "soft" on communists.

There were never more than 100,000 communists in the United States, and party membership plummeted after the start of the Cold War. However, the possibility that a handful of spies could do enormous damage fueled a kind of panic that could be used for partisan purposes. In 1947, hoping to defuse the communists-in-government issue by being more zealous in pursuit of spies than his critics, Truman established a Loyalty Review Board to check up on government employees. The program made even sympathy for a long list of vaguely defined "totalitarian" or "subversive" organizations grounds for dismissal. During the following ten years about 2,700 government workers were discharged, only a relative handful of them for legitimate reasons. A much larger number resigned.

In 1948 Whittaker Chambers, an editor of *Time* who had formerly been a communist, charged that Alger Hiss, president of the Carnegie Endowment for International Peace and a former State Department official, had been a communist in the 1930s. Hiss denied the charge and sued Chambers for libel. Chambers then produced microfilms purporting to show that Hiss had copied classified documents for dispatch to Moscow. Hiss could not be indicted for espionage because of the statute of limitations; instead he was charged with perjury. In January 1950, he was convicted and sentenced to a five-year jail term.

If a distinguished official such as Hiss had been disloyal, anything seemed possible. The case fed the fears of those who believed in the existence of a powerful communist underground in the United States. The disclosure in February 1950 that a British scientist, Klaus Fuchs, had betrayed atomic secrets to the Soviets heightened these fears, as did the arrest and conviction of his American associate, Harry Gold, and two other Americans, Julius and Ethel Rosenberg, on the same charge.

Although they were not major spies and the information they revealed was not crucial, the Rosenbergs were executed, to the consternation of many liberals in the United States and elsewhere. However, information gathered by other spies had speeded the Soviet development of nuclear weapons. This fact encouraged some Republicans to press the communists-in-government issue hard.

McCarthyism

In February 1950 an obscure senator, Joseph R. McCarthy of Wisconsin, introduced this theme in a speech to the even less well-known Ohio County Republican Women's Club of Wheeling, West Virginia. "The reason we find ourselves in a position of impotency," he stated, "is not because our only powerful potential enemy has sent men to invade our shores, but rather because of the traitorous actions of those who have been treated so well by this nation." The State Department, he added, was "infested" with communists.

●•●─[**Read** the **Document**

McCarthy, *Wheeling, West Virginia, Speech* at **myhistorylab.com**

McCarthy had no shred of evidence to back up these statements, as a Senate committee headed by the conservative Democrat Millard Tydings of Maryland soon demonstrated. He never exposed a single spy or secret American communist.

But because of the government loyalty program, the Hiss case, and other recent events, thousands of people were too eager to believe McCarthy to listen to reason. Within a few weeks he was the most talked of person in Congress. When McCarthy's victims indignantly denied his charges, he distracted the public with still more sensational accusations directed at other innocents. Even General Marshall, whose patriotism was beyond question, was subjected to McCarthy's abuse. The general, he said, was "steeped in falsehood," part of a "conspiracy so immense and an infamy so black as to dwarf any previous venture in the history of man."

McCarthy was totally unscrupulous and his crude tactics would have failed if the public had not been so worried about communism. The worries were caused by the reality of Soviet military power, the attack on Korea, the loss of the nuclear monopoly, and the stories about spies, some of them true.

Dwight D. Eisenhower

As the 1952 presidential election approached, Truman's popularity was again at low ebb; he chose not to seek reelection. In choosing their candidate, the Republicans passed over the twice-defeated Dewey and their most prominent leader, Senator Robert A. Taft of Ohio, an outspoken conservative, and nominated General Dwight D. Eisenhower.

Eisenhower's popularity did not grow merely out of his achievements in World War II. His genial personality and evident desire to avoid controversy proved widely appealing. In his reluctance to seek political office, Eisenhower reminded the country of George Washington, whereas his seeming ignorance of current political issues was no more a handicap to his campaign than the similar ignorance of Jackson and Grant in their times. People "liked Ike" because his management of the Allied armies suggested that he would be equally competent as head of the complex federal government. Eisenhower's campaign was also the first to use television effectively. It featured what came to be known as "spots," twenty-second tapes of candidate Eisenhower responding to questions about his opinions on issues, important and trivial. Eisenhower's promise during the campaign to go to Korea if elected to try to bring the war to an end was a political masterstroke.

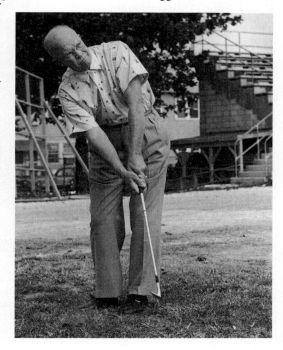

Many critics lampooned Eisenhower for his banal amusements. A popular bumper sticker read: "BEN HOGAN [a famous golfer] FOR PRESIDENT. IF WE'RE GOING TO HAVE A GOLFER FOR PRESIDENT, LET'S HAVE A GOOD ONE." Others have viewed Eisenhower's passion for golf as characteristic of his presidential style: methodical, prudent, and, when in the rough, disarmingly shrewd.

The Democrats nominated Governor Adlai E. Stevenson of Illinois, whose grandfather had been vice president under Grover Cleveland. Stevenson's unpretentiousness was appealing, and his witty, urbane speeches captivated intellectuals. In retrospect, however, it is clear that he had not the remotest chance of defeating the popular Eisenhower.

The result was a Republican landslide: Eisenhower received almost 34 million votes to Stevenson's 27 million, and in the Electoral College his margin was 442 to 89.

On the surface, Eisenhower seemed the antithesis of Truman. The Republicans had charged the Democratic administration with being wasteful and extravagant, and Eisenhower planned to run his administration on sound business principles. He spoke scornfully of "creeping socialism," called for more local control of government affairs, and promised to reduce federal spending to balance the budget and cut taxes. He believed that by battling with Congress and pressure groups over the details of legislation, his immediate predecessors had sacrificed part of their status as chief representative of the American people.

Eisenhower proved to be an excellent politician. He knew how to be flexible without compromising his basic values. His "conservatism" became first "dynamic conservatism" and then "progressive moderation."

Yet his policies toward illegal Mexican immigrants and native Americans proved less than humane. In 1954 he authorized Operation Wetback, which rounded up and deported nearly a million illegal Mexican immigrants. He also sought to weaken New Deal policies that strengthened Native American tribes as political entities. Indian leaders resisted this change, and the policy ended in 1961.

The Eisenhower-Dulles Foreign Policy

The American people, troubled and uncertain over the stalemate in Korea, counted on Eisenhower to find a way to employ the nation's immense strength constructively. The new president shared the general feeling that a change of tactics in foreign affairs was needed. He counted on his secretary of state to solve the practical problems.

His choice, John Foster Dulles, was a lawyer with considerable diplomatic experience. He had been an outspoken critic of Truman's policy of containment. In a May 1952 article in *Life* entitled "A Policy of Boldness," he argued that global military containment was both expensive and ineffective. Instead of waiting for the communist powers to make a move and then "containing" them, the United States would build so many powerful nuclear weapons that the Soviet Union or communist China wouldn't dare take provocative actions. An

An eleven-megaton hyrdrogen bomb is detonated over Bikini Atoll in March 1954. One megaton had the explosive power of 1 million tons of TNT. (The bomb that had destroyed Hiroshima had the equivalent of 12,500 tons of TNT.) An earlier atom bomb test at Bikini Island prompted a French fashion designer to give the name "bikini" to his explosively provocative bathing suit.

immense arsenal of nuclear bombs, loaded on the nation's formidable fleet of bombers, would ensure a **massive retaliation** against any aggressor. Such a "new look" military would be cheaper to maintain than a large standing army, and it would prevent the United States from being caught up in "local" conflicts like the Korean War.

Korea offered the first test of his views. After Eisenhower's post-election trip to Korea failed to bring an end to the war, Dulles signaled his willingness to use tactical nuclear weapons in Korea by showily transferring nuclear warheads from the United States mainland to bomber units stationed in East Asia. Several weeks later, in July 1953, the Chinese signed an armistice that ended hostilities but left Korea divided. The administration interpreted the softening of the Chinese position as proof that the nuclear threat had worked.

Emboldened by his apparent triumph, Dulles again brandished the nation's nuclear arsenal. Chiang Kai-shek had stationed 90,000 soldiers—one-third of his army—in Quemoy and Matsu, two small islands located a few miles from mainland China. In 1954 the Chinese communists began shelling the islands, presumably in preparation to invade them. Chiang appealed for American protection, warning that loss of the islands would bring about the collapse of Nationalist China. At a press conference in 1955 Eisenhower announced his willingness to use nuclear weapons to defend the islands. The Chinese communists backed down.

Massive retaliation succeeded in reducing the defense budget by allowing Eisenhower to pare a half million men from the armed forces. On balance, however, Dulles's strategy was flawed, and many of his schemes were preposterous. Above all, massive retaliation was an extremely dangerous policy when the Soviet Union possessed nuclear weapons as powerful as those of the United States.

McCarthy Self-Destructs

Although the State Department was now controlled by Dulles, a Republican and hard-line anticommunist, Senator McCarthy refused to moderate his attacks on the department. In 1953 television newscaster Edwin R. Murrow cast doubt on McCarthy's methods; soon he and McCarthy were pummeling each other on television.

((•—Hear the Audio
Joseph P. McCarthy Speech
at **myhistorylab.com**

But McCarthy finally overreached himself. Early in 1954 he turned his guns on the army, accusing Pentagon officials of trying to blackmail his committee. The resulting Army-McCarthy hearings, televised before the country, and Murrow's increasingly sharp criticisms, proved the senator's undoing. When the hearings ended in June 1954 after some million words of testimony, his spell had been broken.

The Senate, with President Eisenhower (who despised McCarthy but who considered it beneath his dignity as president to "get into the gutter with that guy") applying pressure behind the scenes, at last moved to censure him in December 1954. Although he continued to issue statements and wild charges, the country no longer listened. In 1957 he died of cirrhosis of the liver.

Asian Policy after Korea

Shortly after an armistice was finally arranged in Korea in July 1953, new trouble erupted far to the south in the former French colony of Indochina. Nationalist rebels led by the communist Ho Chi Minh had been harassing the French in Vietnam, one of the three puppet kingdoms (the others were Laos and Cambodia) fashioned by France in Indochina after the defeat of the Japanese. When China recognized the rebels, who were known as the Vietminh, and supplied them with arms, President Truman countered with economic and military assistance to the French, and President Eisenhower continued and expanded this assistance.

Early in 1954 Ho Chi Minh's troops trapped and besieged a French army in the remote stronghold of Dien Bien Phu. In May the garrison surrendered. Several months later France, Great Britain, the Soviet Union, and China signed an agreement dividing Vietnam along the seventeenth parallel. France withdrew from the area. The northern sector became the Democratic Republic of Vietnam, controlled by Ho Chi Minh; the southern sector remained in the hands of the emperor, Bao Dai. An election to settle the future of all Vietnam was scheduled for 1956.

When it seemed likely that the communists would win that election, Ngo Dinh Diem, a conservative anticommunist, overthrew Bao Dai and became president of South Vietnam. The United States supplied his government liberally with aid. The planned election was never held, and Vietnam remained divided.

Dulles responded to the diplomatic setback in Vietnam by establishing the Southeast Asia Treaty Organization (SEATO), but only three Asian nations—the Philippine Republic (which was granted independence in 1947), Thailand, and Pakistan—joined this alliance.[3]

Israel and the Middle East

Truman and Eisenhower had intervened in the Far East because of a direct communist threat. But as the American love affair with cars turned into an obsession, United States policymakers became increasingly attentive to the Middle East, where seas of oil had been recently discovered. Iran, Iraq, Kuwait, and Saudi Arabia sat upon nearly 60 percent of the world's known reserves.

After World War II, Zionists, who had long sought to promote Jewish immigration to Palestine, intensified their efforts. The slaughter of six million European Jews by the Nazis strengthened Jewish claims to a homeland and intensified pressure to allow hundreds of thousands of Jewish refugees to immigrate to Palestine, which was governed by Great Britain according to a League of Nations mandate. But the influx of Jewish settlers, and their calls for creation of a Jewish state (Israel), provoked Palestinian and Arab leaders. Fighting broke out. President Truman angered Arab leaders by endorsing the partition of the region into an Israeli and a Palestinian state. In 1947, the United Nations voted for partition and on May 14, 1948, the State of Israel was established. Within hours, Truman recognized its sovereignty.

Then Arab armies from Egypt, Jordan, Iraq, Syria, and Lebanon attacked Israel. Although badly outnumbered, the Israelis were better organized and better armed than the Arabs and drove them off with relative ease. Nearly a million local Arabs were displaced, causing a desperate refugee problem in nearby countries.

President Truman had consistently placed support for Israel before other considerations in the Middle East, partly because of the conviction that survivors of the Nazi holocaust were entitled to a country of their own and partly because of the political importance of the Jewish vote in the United States. Dulles and Eisenhower tried to restore

---

[3]The other signatories were Great Britain, France, the United States, Australia, and New Zealand.

balance and mollify the Arabs by deemphasizing American support of Israel. Gas-hungry Americans could ill afford to alienate the Arab world.

In 1952 Colonel Gamal Abdel Nasser emerged as the strongman of Egypt. The United States was prepared to lend Nasser money to build a huge dam on the Nile at Aswan that would provide irrigation and electric power for much of the region. However, Eisenhower would not sell Egypt arms, but the communists would.

For this reason Nasser drifted toward the communist orbit. When Eisenhower then decided not to finance the Aswan Dam, Nasser responded by nationalizing the Suez Canal. This move galvanized the British and French. In conjunction with the French, and without consulting the United States, the British in 1956 decided to take back the canal by force. The Israelis, alarmed by repeated Arab hit-and-run raids, also attacked Egypt.

Events moved swiftly. Israeli armored columns crushed the Egyptian army in the Sinai Peninsula in a matter of days. France and Britain occupied Port Said at the northern end of the canal. Nasser sank ships to block the channel. In the UN the Soviet Union and the United States introduced resolutions calling for a cease-fire. Both were vetoed by Britain and France.

Then the Soviet Union threatened to send "volunteers" to help defend Egypt and launch atomic missiles against France and Great Britain if they did not withdraw. Eisenhower also demanded that the invaders pull out of Egypt. On November 6, only nine days after the first Israeli units had invaded Egypt, British Prime Minister Anthony Eden announced a cease-fire. Israel withdrew its troops.

The United States had won a measure of respect in the Arab countries, but at what cost? Its major allies had been humiliated. Their ill-timed attack had enabled the Soviet Union to recover much of the prestige it had lost as a result of its brutal suppression of a Hungarian revolt that had broken out a week before the Suez fiasco.

When the Soviet Union seemed likely to profit from its "defense" of Egypt in the crisis, the president announced the Eisenhower Doctrine (January 1957), which stated that the United States was "prepared to use armed force" anywhere in the Middle East against "aggression from any country controlled by international communism." In practice, the Eisenhower Doctrine amounted to little more than a restatement of the containment policy.

Eisenhower and Khrushchev

In 1956 Eisenhower was reelected, defeating Adlai Stevenson even more decisively than he had in 1952. Despite evident satisfaction with their leader, however, the American people were in a sober mood. Hopes of pushing back the Soviet Union with clever stratagems and moral fervor were fading. Although the United States detonated the first hydrogen bomb in November 1952, the Soviets followed suit within six months. The Cold War between the superpowers had become yet more chilling.

Stalin died in March 1953, and after a period of internal conflict within the Kremlin, Nikita Khrushchev emerged as the new master of the Soviet Union. Prone to violent tantrums and tearful histrionics, Khrushchev delighted in shocking people with words and gestures. In the most famous of these, he pounded his shoe on the table during a debate at the United Nations. Although a product of the Soviet system, Khrushchev recognized its deep failings and resolved to purge it of Stalinism. He released political prisoners from Stalin's gulags, or political prison camps, and told wide-eyed party functionaries that Stalin had committed monstrous crimes.

Vice President Richard M. Nixon and Soviet leader Nikita Khrushchev engage in a "kitchen debate" over the future of capitalism at a Moscow trade fair in 1959. Although the encounter did little to advance United States-Soviet relations, it established Nixon's credentials as a tough negotiator.

Eisenhower, a seasoned analyst of military capabilities, understood that Khrushchev's antics were meant to conceal the Soviet Union's many weaknesses: the bitter opposition to Soviet rule among peoples of Eastern Europe; the deficiencies of the overcentralized Soviet economy, especially in agriculture; and the bureaucratic stultification of its armed forces. Thousands of American airplanes were based in Europe, northern Africa, and Turkey, placing most Soviet targets within easy range. The United States would win (whatever that meant) any nuclear war.

But this advantage disappeared in the exhaust trail of a Soviet rocket, launched on October 4, 1957, that carried a 184-pound capsule named *Sputnik* far above the atmosphere into earth orbit. Soon, American policymakers knew, Soviet missiles capable of reaching

Table 28.1 The Cold War Escalates

Year	Event	Significance
1947	George Kennan's "Sources of Soviet Conduct"	Outlines rationale for "containment" of Soviet Union
1947	Truman Doctrine	United States supports Greece and Turkey against communist threats
1948	Marshall Plan	United States provides economic aid to Western Europe
1949	Soviet Union detonates atom bomb	Truman calls for development of hydrogen bomb
1950	North Korea invades South Korea	Truman intervenes, as does communist China
1950	NSC-68 adopted	Truman authorizes worldwide expansion of U.S. military to stop Soviet aggression anywhere
1952	United States detonates hydrogen bomb	Soviet Union follows suit, 1953
1953	NSC-68 replaced with "massive retaliation"	Dulles-Eisenhower signal willingness to start a nuclear war to defend American interests
1957	Soviet Union launches *Sputnik*	Shows Soviet capacity to hit American targets with nuclear weapons

American soil would be tipped with nuclear warheads. The nation's far-flung network of bomber defenses had become obsolete, and with it the strategy of massive retaliation.

Eisenhower refused to take chances. He secretly authorized high-altitude American planes to spy on key Soviet military installations. On May 1, 1960, high over Sverdlovsk, an industrial center deep in the Soviet Union, an American U–2 spy plane was shot down by antiaircraft fire. The pilot of the plane survived the crash, and he confessed to being a spy. His cameras contained aerial photographs of Soviet military installations. When Eisenhower assumed full responsibility for the mission, Khrushchev accused the United States of "piratical" and "cowardly" acts of aggression.

Latin America Aroused

Events in Latin America compounded Eisenhower's difficulties. During World War II the United States, needing Latin American raw materials, had supplied its southern neighbors liberally with economic aid.

But as the Cold War progressed, the United States neglected Latin America. Economic problems plagued the region, and in most nations reactionary governments reigned. Radical Latin Americans accused the United States of supporting cliques of wealthy tyrants, whereas conservatives blamed insufficient American economic aid for the plight of the poor.

Eisenhower, eager to improve relations, stepped up economic assistance. Resistance to communism nonetheless continued to receive first priority. In 1954 the government of Jacobo Arbenz Guzman in Guatemala began to import Soviet weapons. The United States promptly dispatched arms to neighboring Honduras. Within a month an army led by an exiled Guatemalan officer marched into the country from Honduras and overthrew Arbenz. Elsewhere in Latin America, Eisenhower, as Truman had before him, continued to support regimes that were kept in power by the local military.

Events in Cuba demonstrated that there was no easy solution to Latin American problems. In 1959 a revolutionary movement headed by Fidel Castro overthrew Fulgencio Batista, one of the most noxious of the Latin American dictators. Eisenhower recognized the Castro government at once, but the Cuban leader soon began to criticize the United States in highly colored speeches. Castro confiscated American property without providing adequate compensation, suppressed civil liberties, and entered into close relations with the Soviet Union. After he negotiated a trade agreement with the Soviet Union in February 1960, which enabled the Russians to obtain Cuban sugar at bargain rates, the United States retaliated by prohibiting the importation of Cuban sugar into America.

Khrushchev then announced that if the United States intervened in Cuba, he would defend the country with atomic weapons. "The Monroe Doctrine has outlived its time," Khrushchev warned. Shortly before the end of his second term, Eisenhower broke off diplomatic relations with Cuba.

Fighting the Cold War at Home

The looming Soviet threat brought the Cold War closer to the American people than ever before. Such fears provided public support for increased spending on defense. In 1955 Eisenhower worried that a Soviet nuclear attack would plunge American cities into chaos. The roads out of threatened cities "would be the breeder of a deadly congestion within hours of an attack," he noted. He therefore backed a federally-funded highway system; this would not only facilitate the evacuation of cities but would also allow the army to mobilize more rapidly. The National Interstate and Defense Highway Act of 1956 became the largest public works project in the nation's history.

This interchange near Seattle was part of the interstate highway system advanced by Eisenhower to facilitate both military transports and civilian evacuations.

The Soviet Union's success in building atomic and hydrogen bombs, and especially in launching an orbiting satellite before the United States, also prompted Eisenhower to initiate a sweeping reform of the nation's schools. "The defense of the nation depends upon the mastery of modern techniques developed from complex scientific principles," he declared. In 1958 he signed the National Defense Education Act. It provided federal aid to promote study of science, mathematics and foreign languages in large, comprehensive (and sometimes anonymous) high schools.

"Godless" communism posed an ideological as well as military threat. In 1954 the Reverend George Docherty warned his Presbyterian congregation in Washington, DC, that "little Muscovites" in the Soviet Union were pledging allegiance to "hammer and sickle" atheism. But an "atheistic American," he intoned, was "a contradiction in terms." Later that day Eisenhower, commenting on the sermon, told a radio audience that whatever their "personal creed," Americans still "believed in a higher power." A few months later he signed a law that added the phrase "one nation under God" to the Pledge of Allegiance. The next year, Congress added "In God We Trust" to the nation's currency.

Watch the Video
Duck and Cover at
myhistorylab.com

Blacks Challenge Segregation

Another front in the Cold War concerned race relations. How could African and Asian leaders be persuaded to reject communism and follow the example of the United States when American blacks were treated so poorly? American diplomats winced when the finance minister of Ghana was refused a meal at the Howard Johnson's, a chain restaurant, in Dover, Delaware. "Colored people are not allowed to eat in here," the manager explained to the African leader. Vice President Nixon declared, "In the world-wide struggle in which we are engaged, racial prejudice is a gun we point at ourselves."

But racial confrontations remained in the news. During and after World War II a demand for change had developed in the South. Its roots lay in southern industrialization, in the shift from small sharecropping holdings to large commercial farms, in the vast wartime expenditures of the federal government on aircraft factories and army bases in the region; in the impact of the GI Bill on southern colleges and universities, and in the gradual development of a southern black middle class.

Black soldiers who had served abroad demanded that they be treated with respect when they returned home. In 1947 Jackie Robinson, a black officer who had been court-martialed—and acquitted—for refusing to move to the back of a segregated military bus during World War II, was ready to integrate major league baseball. When his team—the Brooklyn Dodgers—checked into the Ben Franklin Hotel in Philadelphia, he was refused a room. A week later the Dodgers went to Pittsburgh. When he took his position at second base, the Pirates refused to come onto the field. Only under threat of forfeiting the game would they play against Robinson.

More blacks insisted on their right to vote—and many got it. In 1940 only 2 percent of African Americans in the south were registered to vote; by 1947, that had increased to 12 percent. But white resistance remained formidable. In 1946 Eugene Talmadge, behind in the polls, won his race for governor by promising that if he were elected "no Negro will vote in Georgia for four years."

In this photo opportunity, Phillies manager Ben Chapman refused to shake Jackie Robinson's hand. Instead, he leaned toward Robinson and said quietly, "Jackie, you know, you're a good ballplayer, but you're still a nigger to me." Robinson replied by leading the Dodgers to the pennant and winning Rookie of the Year honors.

The NAACP (the National Association for the Advancement of Colored People) decided that the time had come to challenge segregation in the courts. Thurgood Marshall, the organization's chief staff lawyer, went from state to state filing legal challenges to the "separate but equal" principle laid down in *Plessy v. Ferguson* in 1896 (see Chapter 20). In 1938 the Supreme Court had ordered the University of Missouri law school to admit a black student because no law school for blacks existed in the state. This decision gradually forced some southern states to admit blacks to advanced programs.

In 1953 President Eisenhower appointed California's Governor Earl Warren chief justice of the U.S. Supreme Court. Convinced that the Court must take the offensive in the cause of civil rights, Warren succeeded in welding his associates into a unit on this question. In 1954 an NAACP-sponsored case, **Brown v. Board of Education of Topeka**, came up for decision. Marshall submitted a mass of sociological evidence to show that the mere fact of segregation made equal education impossible and did serious psychological damage to both black and white children. Speaking for a unanimous Court, Warren reversed the *Plessy* decision. "In the field of public education, the doctrine of 'separate but equal' has no place," he declared. "Separate educational facilities are inherently unequal." The next year the Court ordered the states to end segregation "with all deliberate speed."

●●●[Read the Document

Brown v. Board of Education of Topeka, Kansas at **myhistorylab.com**

Flouting the Court's decision, few districts in the southern and border states integrated their schools. As late as September 1956, barely 700 of the South's 10,000 school districts had been desegregated.

Angry jeers from whites rain down on Elizabeth Eckford, one of the first black students to arrive for registration at Little Rock's Central High School in 1957. State troops turned black students away from the school until President Eisenhower overruled the state decision and called in the National Guard to enforce integration.

President Eisenhower thought equality for blacks could not be obtained by government edict. He said that the Court's ruling must be obeyed, but he did little to discourage southern resistance to desegregation.

However, in 1957 events compelled him to act. When the school board of Little Rock, Arkansas, opened Central High School to a handful of black students, the governor of the state, Orval M. Faubus, called out the National Guard to prevent them from entering the school. Unruly crowds taunted the students and their parents. Eisenhower could not ignore the direct flouting of federal authority. After the mayor of Little Rock sent him a telegram saying, in part, "situation is out of control and police cannot disperse the mob," Eisenhower dispatched 1,000 paratroopers to Little Rock and summoned 10,000 National Guardsmen to federal duty, thus removing them from Faubus's control. The black students then began to attend class. A token force of soldiers was stationed at Central High for the entire school year to protect them.

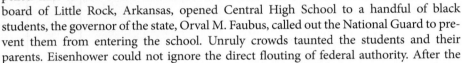

Watch the Video

How did the Civil Rights Movement change American schools? at **myhistorylab.com**

Direct Action Protests: The Montgomery Bus Boycott

While Marshall and the NAACP were dismantling the legal superstructure of segregation, its institutional foundations remained. Blacks increasingly took action on their own.

This change first came to national attention during the Eisenhower administration in the rigidly segregated city of Montgomery, Alabama. On Friday, December 1, 1955, Rosa Parks, a seamstress at the Montgomery Fair department store, boarded a bus on her way home from her job. She dutifully took a seat toward the rear as custom and law required. As white workers and shoppers filled the forward section, the driver ordered her to give up her place to a white passenger. Parks, who was also secretary of the Montgomery NAACP chapter, refused. She had decided, she later recalled, that "I would have to know once and for all what rights I had as a human being and a citizen."

She was arrested. Over the weekend, Montgomery's black leaders organized a boycott. "Don't ride the bus . . . Monday," their mimeographed notice ran. "If you work, take a cab, or share a ride, or walk." Monday dawned bitterly cold, but the boycott was a total success.

Most Montgomery blacks could not afford to miss a single day's wages, so the protracted struggle to get to work was difficult to maintain. Black-owned taxis reduced their rates sharply, and when the city declared this illegal, car pools were quickly organized. Few African Americans owned cars. Although nearly everyone who did volunteered, there were never more than 350 cars available to the more than 10,000 people who needed rides to their jobs and back every day. Nevertheless, the boycott went on.

Late in February the Montgomery authorities obtained indictments of 115 leaders of the boycott, but this move backfired because it focused national attention on the situation. A young clergyman, the Reverend Martin Luther King, Jr., was emerging as the leader of the boycott. A gifted speaker, he became an overnight celebrity. (See American Lives, "Martin Luther King, Jr.," p. 756.) Money poured in from all over the country to support the movement. The boycott lasted for over a year. Finally the Supreme Court declared the local law enforcing racial separation unconstitutional: Montgomery had to desegregate its public transportation system.

This success encouraged blacks elsewhere in the South to band together against segregation. A new organization founded in 1957, the **Southern Christian Leadership Conference (SCLC)**, headed by King, moved to the forefront of the civil rights movement. Other organizations joined the struggle, notably the Congress of Racial Equality (CORE), which had been founded in 1942. The direct action movement was becoming a broad-based nationwide civil rights movement.

The Election of 1960

As the end of his momentous second term approached, Eisenhower somewhat reluctantly endorsed Vice President Richard Nixon as the Republican candidate to succeed him. Nixon had originally skyrocketed to national prominence by exploiting the public fear of communist subversion. In 1947 he was an obscure young congressman from California; in 1950 he won a seat in the Senate; two years later Eisenhower chose him as his running mate.

The Democrats nominated Senator John F. Kennedy of Massachusetts. His chief rival for the nomination, Lyndon B. Johnson of Texas, the Senate majority leader, became his running mate. Kennedy was the son of Joseph P. Kennedy, a wealthy businessman who had served as ambassador to Great Britain under Franklin Roosevelt. During World War II, Kennedy served in the Pacific, captaining a torpedo boat. When the boat was sliced in two by a Japanese destroyer, Kennedy showed personal courage in rescuing his men. Besides wealth, intelligence, good looks, and charm, Kennedy had the advantage of his Irish-Catholic ancestry, a valuable asset in heavily Catholic Massachusetts. After three terms in the House, he moved on to the Senate in 1952.

Watch the Video
Kennedy-Nixon Debate at **myhistorylab.com**

After his landslide reelection in 1958, only Kennedy's religion seemed to limit his political future. No Catholic had ever been elected president. Nevertheless, influenced by Kennedy's victories in the Wisconsin and West Virginia primaries—the latter establishing him as an effective campaigner in a predominantly Protestant region—the Democratic convention nominated him.

Kennedy had not been a particularly liberal congressman. He was not involved in the civil rights movement. He enthusiastically endorsed the Cold War and indicted the Eisenhower administration for falling behind the Soviet Union in the race to build missiles. He admitted frankly that he liked Senator Joseph McCarthy and thought that "he may have something" in his campaign against supposed communists in government. However, as a presidential candidate, he sought to appear more forward-looking. He stressed his youth and "vigor" (a favorite word) and promised to open a **New Frontier** for the country. Nixon ran on the Eisenhower record, which he promised to extend in liberal directions.

MARTIN LUTHER KING, JR.

On December 1, 1955, Rosa Parks was arrested for violating Montgomery's segregation laws. Black leaders immediately made plans to boycott the city buses the following Monday.

On Monday morning, the buses were nearly empty. That afternoon black leaders met to discuss strategy for a public meeting that evening. One minister urged that they keep their plans secret. E. D. Nixon, a railroad porter and president of the local NAACP, jumped to his feet: "How do you think you can run a bus boycott in secret?" Then he lost his temper. "You ministers have lived off these wash-women for the last hundred years and ain't never done nothing for them."

As Nixon was finishing his diatribe, the new minister in town strode into the room. Young, well-dressed Martin Luther King, Jr. was regarded as something of a dandy. Now, all eyes turned to the dapper latecomer. He called on the ministers to act in open and use their names. Someone proposed that King be named president of the protest movement. Nearly everyone agreed.

That evening, hundreds filled the largest Baptist church, with many more spilling onto the lawn and streets. A loudspeaker was set up. Inside, King outlined the situation, and then, slipping into a preaching mode, began to roll off one booming phrase after another. "And you know, my friends, there comes a time when people get tired of being trampled over by the iron feet of oppression," he said in a deep voice. By the time he finished, his words were drowned out by the stomping of feet and the roars of the crowd outside.

King's rhetorical mastery stunned nearly everyone. He was only twenty-six, and had served as a pastor for only a year.

His father had been minister of the largest Baptist church in Atlanta, and Martin's circumstances as a child had been comfortable. He briefly attended a special school run by Atlanta University, then the local public high school before going to Morehouse College in Atlanta. He eventually followed in his father's footsteps.

He attended Crozer seminary in Pennsylvania. After finishing at the top of his class, he went to Boston University, where he earned a doctorate in philosophy. He resolved to become a successful preacher in a big-city church.

In 1953 King married Coretta Scott; the next year he was appointed pastor at Dexter Avenue Baptist Church in Montgomery.

But in the first week of December, 1955, his life had taken an unexpected turn. He would be given the task of forging into a single movement the disparate elements of the black community. He would adapt the passive nonviolence tactics used by Indian nationalist Mohandas Gandhi to gain independence from Britain, and apply them to the American South. He would use the language of Christian brotherhood to reach out to whites. He would lead the movement that would change the nation.

But that was in the future. In December 1955, a convergence of fateful circumstances had pushed him into leadership of a bus boycott. Twelve years later, he would be dead, victim of an assassin's bullet.

The Rev. Martin Luther King, Jr., Coretta Scott King, and their children share a moment of calm in Montgomery, 1956. That year, while King was addressing a mass meeting, his house was bombed; Coretta and the children were unhurt.

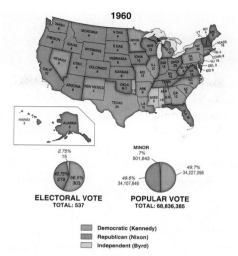

1960

MINOR
.7%
501,643

ELECTORAL VOTE
TOTAL: 537

2.75%
15

40.75%
219

56.5%
303

POPULAR VOTE
TOTAL: 68,836,385

49.7%
34,227,096

49.6%
34,107,646

Democratic (Kennedy)
Republican (Nixon)
Independent (Byrd)

Election of 1960 Like nearly all Democrats since the Compromise of 1877, Kennedy carried most of the South. White Southerners opposed the party of Lincoln, and few black Southerners had been registered to vote.

A series of television debates between the candidates helped Kennedy by enabling him to demonstrate his maturity and mastery of the issues. Although both candidates laudably avoided it, the religious issue was important. His Catholicism helped Kennedy in eastern urban areas but injured him in many farm districts and throughout the West. Kennedy's victory, 303 to 219 in the Electoral College, was paper-thin in the popular vote, 34,227,000 to 34,109,000.

The years since the end of World War II had been dominated by the prospect of war more terrible than anyone could imagine. By the end of 1960 Eisenhower was less concerned about a communist victory than the impact of the arms race on America itself. By then defense expenditures devoured one-tenth of the nation's GNP. In his final speech as president, Eisenhower warned of the "grave implications" resulting from "the conjunction of an immense military establishment and a large arms industry." What Eisenhower called the **military-industrial complex** potentially endangered "the very structure of our society." Could the nation mount a worldwide defense of democracy without endangering that democracy at home?

Milestones

1944	Congress provides subsidies to veterans in GI Bill of Rights
1946	UN creates Atomic Energy Commission
1947	Taft-Hartley Act regulates unions and labor disputes
	Truman announces Truman Doctrine to stop communism's spread
	George Kennan ("X") urges containment policy in *Sources of Soviet Conduct*
1948	Marshall Plan provides funds to rebuild Europe
	Harry S Truman is elected president
	State of Israel is created as Jewish homeland; Arabs declare war
1948– 1949	United States supplies West Berlin during Berlin airlift
1949	United States and eleven other nations form North Atlantic Treaty Organization (NATO)
	Soviet Union detonates atom bomb
1950	North Korea invades South Korea
	NSC-68 calls for massive military buildup
	Alger Hiss is convicted of perjury
	McCarran Act restricts "subversive" activity
	Senator Joseph McCarthy charges that the State Department is riddled with communists

1950	UN counterattack in Korea is driven back by Red Chinese army
1952	Dwight D. Eisenhower is elected president
1953	John Foster Dulles institutes "New Look" nuclear-based foreign policy
	Korean War ends with armistice
1954	Senate holds Army–McCarthy hearings
	United States helps overthrow Arbenz in Guatemala
	French are defeated in Indochina after siege of Dien Bien Phu
	Supreme Court orders school desegregation in *Brown v. Board of Education of Topeka*
	Egypt nationalizes Suez Canal in Suez Crisis
1955	The Rev. Martin Luther King, Jr., leads Montgomery Bus Boycotts
1956	Eisenhower is reelected president
1957	M. L. King, Jr., and followers form Southern Christian Leadership Conference
	National Guard enforces desegregation of Central High School in Little Rock, Arkansas
1959	Fidel Castro overthrows Fulgencio Batista, takes power in Cuba
1960	John F. Kennedy is first Roman Catholic to be elected president

Review Questions

1. The late 1940s and 1950s are often characterized as a period of complacency and consensus. Yet this chapter holds that, in foreign and domestic affairs, it was a period of "menacing uncertainty." What constituted the chief elements of menace?

2. Throughout the period from 1946 to 1960, American presidents sought to "contain" communism. How did Eisenhower's "massive retaliation" differ from Truman's worldwide "NSC-68" containment? How did *Sputnik* influence the Cold War?

3. Why did Truman intervene in Korea, and why did the war end in stalemate?

4. What was the impact of the Cold War on American society?

5. Why did the civil rights movement gain momentum after 1945? On what grounds did the Supreme Court overturn the "separate but equal" ruling in *Brown v. Board of Education* (1954)? Why did African Americans subsequently resort to "direct action" protests?

Key Terms

Berlin airlift *738*
Brown v. Board of Education of Topeka *753*
Fair Deal *739*
Marshall Plan *737*
massive retaliation *747*

military-industrial complex *757*
New Frontier *755*
North Atlantic Treaty Organization (NATO) *740*
NSC-68 *741*

Southern Christian Leadership Conference (SCLC) *755*
Taft-Hartley Act *735*
Truman Doctrine *736*

29 From Camelot to Watergate: 1961–1975

((•—⌐Hear the Audio Chapter 29 at myhistorylab.com

How do you get out of a deep hole?

ON DECEMBER 2, 2009, AS POLLS REVEALED GROWING DISSATISFACTION
with the wars in Iraq and Afghanistan, President Barack Obama promised to withdraw
all U.S. troops from Iraq within two years. But he announced that he would send an additional 30,000 troops to Afghanistan, where the situation had deteriorated.

"I do not make this decision lightly," he said, noting that he had opposed the war in
Iraq. But Afghanistan, he insisted, was different. It had been the home of the Al Qaeda
terrorists who attacked on September 11, 2001. By sending more troops to Afghanistan
now, Obama believed the military would defeat Al Qaeda more quickly. "There are those
who suggest that Afghanistan is another Vietnam," he conceded. "I believe this argument
depends on a false reading of history."

Because nothing in the past is exactly like anything else, all historical analogies are
flawed. But the history of Vietnam suggests that once soldiers have fought and died for
a cause, the task of getting out of a war—short of victory—is not an easy one.

Just before President John F. Kennedy sent the first American troops to Vietnam in 1961,
he confided doubts to an aide: "The troops will march in; the bands will play; the crowds will
cheer. . . Then we will be told we have to send more troops. It's like taking a drink. The effect
wears off, and you have to take another."

By 1963, despite the infusion of some 16,000 U.S. soldiers, South Vietnam was crumbling. In 1965, with a communist takeover imminent, Lyndon Johnson, Kennedy's successor,
increased U.S. troop levels to nearly a half million. Yet victory remained elusive. In 1969,
his successor, Richard M. Nixon, promised to bring an honorable peace to Vietnam; but
American troops remained for another four years.

The long war in Vietnam exposed deep fissures within the nation. Racial divisions
widened into gaping holes. Student protests drew violent responses. Nixon's heated
rhetoric and illegal campaign tactics heightened tensions. And less than a year after he
resigned, communist North Vietnam completed its conquest of South Vietnam. For the
United States, the war ended in failure.

Kennedy in Camelot

Having lampooned the Eisenhower administration as stodgy and unimaginative, President Kennedy made a show of his style and wit. He quoted Robert Frost and Dante. He played and replayed recordings of Winston Churchill, hoping to imprint the great orator's sonorous cadences on his own broad Bostonian vowels. At the instigation of his elegant wife, Jacqueline, Kennedy surrounded himself with the finest intellects at glittering White House galas to honor Nobel Prize winners and celebrated artists.

Kennedy's youthful senior staff boasted impressive scholarly credentials. His national security adviser, McGeorge Bundy, had been dean of the faculty at Harvard. Secretary of Defense Robert McNamara also had taught at Harvard before becoming the first nonfamily member to head the Ford Motor Company.

Kennedy's campaign slogan—"Let's get this country moving again"—was embodied in his own active life. He played rugged games of touch football with the press corps and romped with his young children in the Oval Office. In an article for *Sports Illustrated* entitled "The Soft American" published just after the election, Kennedy complained that television, movies, and a comfortable lifestyle had made too many young people flabby. His earliest presidential initiative was a physical fitness campaign in the schools.

Kennedy's image of youthful vigor was enhanced by the beauty and presence of Jacqueline, whose wide-eyed diffidence was universally admired as regal bearing. The image was enhanced by Lerner and Loewe's musical *Camelot*, which opened a few weeks before the inauguration. Its evocation of King Arthur, who sought to lead his virile young knights in challenges great and good, suggested the Kennedy White House. All Washington seemed aglow with excitement and energy.

Never, too, had the substance of an administration been so closely identified with the style of its president. But the dazzle was misleading. Although quick-witted and intelligent, Kennedy was no intellectual. Nor did the president embody physical fitness. Congenital back problems, aggravated by war injuries, forced Kennedy to use crutches or a cane in private and to take heavy doses of painkillers and amphetamines. The president's permanent "tan" did not result from outdoor exercise, as the public assumed, but from Addison's disease, an often fatal failure of the adrenal glands for which Kennedy gave himself daily injections of cortisone. Though he publicly denied it, Kennedy was chronically ill throughout his presidency.

The Cuban Crises

"The torch has been passed to a new generation of Americans," Kennedy declared in his inaugural address. Its chief task was to stop the spread of communism. While Eisenhower had relied on the nation's nuclear arsenal to intimidate the Kremlin, Kennedy proposed to challenge communist aggression whenever and wherever it occurred. A new breed of cold warrior, Kennedy called on young men and women to serve in the Peace Corps, an organization that he created to mobilize American idealism and technical skills to help developing nations. His was a call for commitment—and action.

Perhaps seduced by his own rhetoric, Kennedy blundered almost immediately. Anti-Castro exiles were eager to organize an invasion of their homeland, reasoning that the Cuban people would rise up against Castro and communism as soon as "democratic" forces provided the necessary leadership. Under Eisenhower the CIA had begun training some

2,000 Cuban exiles in Nicaragua. Kennedy was of two minds about the proposed invasion. Some in his administration opposed it strongly, but his closest advisers, including his brother Robert, urged him to give his approval. In the end he did.

The invaders, 1,400 strong, struck in April 1961. They landed at the Bay of Pigs, on Cuba's southern coast. But the Cuban people failed to flock to their lines, and soon Castro's army pinned the invaders down and forced them to surrender. Because American involvement could not be disguised, the affair exposed the United States to all the criticism that a straightforward assault would have produced, without accomplishing the overthrow of Castro. Worse, it made Kennedy appear impulsive as well as unprincipled. Castro tightened his connections with the Soviet Union.

In June, Kennedy met with Soviet Premier Khrushchev in Vienna. Furious over the invasion of Cuba, Khrushchev blustered about grabbing West Berlin. In August, he abruptly closed the border between East and West Berlin and erected the **Berlin wall**—a barrier of concrete blocks and barbed wire across the city to stop the flow of East Germans into

"Ich bin ein Berliner" (I am a Berliner), Kennedy declared from a balcony in West Berlin in June, 1961, and his words brought a roar of approval from the West Berliners. Gesturing toward the Berlin wall, he called it "the most obvious and vivid demonstration of the failures of the communist system."

the noncommunist zone. At the same time, the Soviets resumed nuclear testing. Khrushchev ordered detonation of a series of gigantic hydrogen bombs, including one with a power 3,000 times that of the bomb that had devastated Hiroshima.

Kennedy followed suit: He announced plans to build thousands of nuclear missiles, known as Minutemen, capable of hitting targets on the other side of the world. He expanded the space program, vowing that an American would land on the moon within ten years. The president called on Congress to pass a large increase in military spending.

In secret, Kennedy also resolved to destroy Castro. He ordered military leaders to plan for a full-scale invasion of Cuba. He also instructed the CIA to undertake "massive activity" against Castro's regime. The CIA devised Operation Mongoose, a plan to slip spies, saboteurs, and assassins into Cuba. Although never officially endorsed by the president, Mongoose operated under the oversight of Robert Kennedy.

In 1962 Khrushchev precipitated the most dangerous confrontation of the Cold War. To forestall the anticipated American invasion of Cuba, he moved tanks, heavy bombers, and 42,000 Soviet troops and technicians to the island. His most fateful step was to sneak several dozen guided nuclear missiles into the country and prepare them for launching. The missiles could have hit most of the eastern United States with nuclear warheads.

On October 14 American spy planes spotted the launching pads and missiles. The president faced a dreadful decision. After the **Bay of Pigs fiasco**, he could not again appear to back down to the communists. But if he invaded Cuba or bombed the Soviet bases and missile sites, Khrushchev would likely seize West Berlin or bomb U.S. missile sites in Turkey. Either action might lead to a full-scale nuclear war and millions of deaths.

On October 22 Kennedy addressed the nation on television. The Soviet buildup was "a deliberately provocative and unjustified change in the status quo." He ordered the American navy to stop and search all vessels headed for Cuba and to turn back any containing "offensive" weapons. Kennedy called on Khrushchev to dismantle the missile bases and remove from the island all weapons capable of striking the United States. Any Cuban-based nuclear attack would result, he warned, in "a full retaliatory response upon the Soviet Union."

For days, Soviet ships steamed toward Cuba and work on the missile launching pads continued. An American spy plane was shot down over Cuba. Khrushchev sent a desperate telegram, suggesting that he was near the breaking point. Robert Kennedy and others engaged in frantic negotiations through intermediaries. Then Khrushchev backed down. He recalled the ships, withdrew the missiles, and reduced his military establishment in Cuba to modest proportions. In response, Kennedy lifted the blockade. He also promised not to invade Cuba, thus ensuring Castro's survival; Kennedy further agreed to withdraw U.S. missiles from Turkey, though this latter concession was not made public at the time.

Immediately the president was hailed for his steady nerve and consummate statesmanship; the Cuban missile crisis was widely regarded as his finest hour. Yet in retrospect it appears that he may have overreacted. The Soviet nuclear threat had been exaggerated. After *Sputnik*, the Soviet long-range missile program flopped, though this was not known at the time. By the summer of 1962 a "missile gap" existed, but it was overwhelmingly in favor of the United States, whose nuclear forces outnumbered those of the Soviet Union by a ratio of seventeen to one. Khrushchev's decision to put medium-range missiles in Cuba signified Soviet weakness rather than impending aggression. Both Kennedy and Khrushchev were sobered by the **Cuban missile crisis**. They signed a treaty outlawing nuclear testing in the atmosphere. But Khrushchev's bluff had been called—a public humiliation from which he never recovered. Within two years, hard-liners in the Kremlin forced him out of office. He was replaced by Leonid Brezhnev, an old-style Stalinist who inaugurated an intensive program of long-range missile development. The nuclear arms race moved to new terrain, uncertain and unimaginably dangerous.

JFK's Vietnam War

Truman's attempt to prevent Ho Chi Minh's communist insurgents from seizing Vietnam failed when the French army surrendered to Ho's troops at Dien Bien Phu in 1954. Eisenhower, equally unwilling to accept a communist victory, then supported creation of an anticommunist South Vietnam, headed by Ngo Dinh Diem, a Vietnamese nationalist who hated the communists. While the United States poured millions of dollars into strengthening Diem's South Vietnam, and especially its army, Ho Chi Minh consolidated his rule in North Vietnam. Those Viet Minh units that remained in the South—they came to be known as Vietcong—were instructed to form secret cells and bide their time. During the late 1950s they gained in strength and militancy.

In May 1959 Ho decided that the time had come to overthrow Diem. Vietcong guerrillas infiltrated thousands of villages, ambushed South Vietnamese convoys, and assassinated government officials. Soon the Vietcong controlled large sections of the countryside, some almost within sight of the capital city of Saigon.

Kennedy sharply increased the American military and economic commitment to South Vietnam. At the end of 1961 there were 3,200 American military personnel in the country; within two years, there were more than 16,000, and 120 American soldiers had been killed. Despite the expanded effort, by the summer

In the summer of 1963, Buddhist monks protested against the rule of Diem (and his brother, the Catholic archbishop of Vietnam) by setting themselves on fire.

of 1963 Diem's regime was in ruins. Unable to persuade Diem to moderate his policies, Kennedy sent word to dissident Vietnamese generals of his willingness to support them if they ousted Diem. On November 1 several of these generals surrounded the presidential palace with troops and tanks, seized Diem, and killed him. Kennedy, though appalled by Diem's death, recognized the new junta. The decision to overthrow Diem was fateful; it committed the United States to finding a solution to a worsening situation in Vietnam.

SNCC – focus s. tms

"We Shall Overcome": The Civil Rights Movement

In February 1960 four African American college students in Greensboro, North Carolina, sat down at a lunch counter at a Woolworth's store. "We do not serve Negroes," they were told. They returned with more and more demonstrators. By the end of the week over a thousand protesters descended on Woolworth's, led by a phalanx of football players from the nearby black college who cleared the way through a throng of Confederate flag-wavers.

This "sit-in" tactic was not new. But the Greensboro students sparked a national movement; students in dozens of other southern towns and cities copied their example.

●●● Read the Document

Charles Sherrod, *SNCC Memorandum (1961)* at myhistorylab.com

Soon more than fifty sit-ins were in progress in southern cities. By the end of 1961 over 70,000 people had participated in such demonstrations. Still another new organization, the **Student Nonviolent Coordinating Committee** (**SNCC**), was founded by black college students in 1960 to provide a focus for the sit-in movement and to conduct voter registration drives in the South, actions that more than any other roused the fury of southern segregationists.

This protracted struggle eventually yielded practical and moral benefits for southern whites as well as blacks. Gradually all but the most unwavering defenders of segregation changed their attitudes. But this took time, and many blacks were unwilling to wait.

Some blacks, contemptuous of white prejudices, were urging their fellows to reject "American" society and all it stood for. In the North, black nationalism became a potent force. Elijah Muhammad, leader of the Black Muslim movement, loathed whites so intensely that he demanded that a part of the United States be set aside exclusively for blacks. He urged his followers to be industrious, thrifty, and abstemious—and to view all whites with suspicion and hatred.

"This white government has ruled us and given us plenty hell, but the time has arrived that you taste a little of your own hell," Muhammad said. He scorned Martin Luther King, Jr., and others who advocated Christian nonviolence. Another important Black Muslim, Malcolm X, put it this way in a 1960 speech: "For the white man to ask the black man if he hates him is just like the rapist asking the raped, or the wolf asking the sheep, 'Do you hate me?'"

Whites pour mustard and ketchup over black students (and one white) who were integrating a lunch-counter.

Ordinary southern blacks became increasingly impatient. In the face of brutal repression by local police, many began to question Martin Luther King's tactic of nonviolent protest. After leading a series of demonstrations in Birmingham, Alabama, in 1963, King was thrown in jail. When local white clergymen, professing themselves sympathetic to the blacks' objectives, nonetheless urged an end to "untimely" protests, which (they claimed) "incite hatred and violence," King wrote his now-famous "Letter from Birmingham Jail," which contained this moving explanation of why he and his followers were unwilling to wait any longer for justice:

> **Watch** the Video
> *Civil Rights Movement* at
> **myhistorylab.com**

> [W]hen you take a cross-country drive and find it necessary to sleep night after night in the uncomfortable corners of your automobile because no motel will accept you; when you are humiliated day in and day out by nagging signs reading "white" and "colored"; when your first name becomes "nigger" and your middle name becomes "boy" . . . then you will understand why we find it so difficult to wait.

Source: Copyright 1963 Dr. Martin Luther King Jr; copyright renewed 1991 Coretta Scott King.

The brutal repression of the Birmingham demonstrations, captured in newspaper photos and on television broadcasts, brought a flood of recruits and money to the protesters' cause. Pushed by all these developments, President Kennedy reluctantly began to change his policy. His administration had from the start given lip service to desegregation and encouraged activists' efforts to register black voters in the South, but when confrontations arose the president hesitated, arguing that it was up to local officials to enforce the law. After Birmingham, however, Kennedy supported a modest civil rights bill.

When this measure ran into stiff opposition in Congress, blacks organized a demonstration in Washington, attended by 200,000 people. At this gathering, King delivered his "I Have a Dream" address, looking forward to a time when racial prejudice no longer existed and people of all religions and colors could join hands and say, "Free at last!" Kennedy sympathized with the Washington gathering but feared it would make passage of the civil rights bill more difficult. As in other areas, he was not a forceful advocate of his own proposals.

> **Watch** the Video
> *Civil Rights March on Washington* at
> **myhistorylab.com**

Tragedy in Dallas: JFK Assassinated

Through it all, Kennedy retained his hold on public opinion. In the fall of 1963 most observers believed he would win a second term. Then, while visiting Dallas, Texas, on November 22, he was shot in the head by an assassin, Lee Harvey Oswald, and died almost instantly.

Kennedy's assassination precipitated an extraordinary series of events. Oswald had fired on the president with a rifle from an upper story of a warehouse. No one saw him pull the trigger. He was apprehended largely because he panicked and killed a policeman across town later in the day. He denied his guilt, but a mass of evidence connected him with the assassination of the president. Before he could be brought to trial, however, he was himself murdered by Jack Ruby, the owner of a Dallas nightclub. The incident took place in full view of television cameras, while Oswald was being transferred from one place of detention to another.

Each day brought new revelations. Oswald had defected briefly to the Soviet Union in 1959, then had returned to the United States and formed a pro-Castro organization in New Orleans. Many concluded that some nefarious conspiracy lay at the root of the tragedy. Oswald, the argument ran, was a pawn—either of communists or anticommunists—whose murder was designed to shield from exposure the masterminds who had engineered the assassination. A special commission headed by Chief Justice Earl Warren was convened to analyze the evidence. After a lengthy investigation, it concluded that Oswald had acted alone.

Instead of dampening charges of conspiracy, the report of the Warren Commission provoked new doubts. As word leaked out about the earlier CIA assassination attempts against Castro, the failure of the Warren Report even to mention Operation Mongoose made the commission suspect, all the more so since several members, including Allen Dulles, former director of the CIA, had known of the operation. While, there is little solid evidence to suggest that Oswald was part of a wider conspiracy, the decision of Dulles and other commissioners to protect CIA secrets engendered skepticism.

One measure of Kennedy's hold on the public imagination was the outpouring of grief that attended his death. Kennedy had given hope to people who had none. Young black civil rights activist Anne Moody, who later wrote *Coming of Age in Mississippi*, was working as a waitress in a segregated restaurant. "Tears were burning my cheeks," she recalled. Her boss, a Greek immigrant, gently suggested she take the rest of the day off. When she looked up, there were tears in his eyes too.

JFK and Jacqueline Kennedy ride in a motorcade with Texas Governor John Connolly and his wife in Dallas, November 22, 1963. Several minutes later, Kennedy was shot and killed; Connolly was wounded.

Lyndon Baines Johnson: The Great Society

John F. Kennedy's death made Lyndon B. Johnson president. From 1949 until his election as vice president, Johnson had been a senator from Texas and, for most of that time, Senate Democratic leader. Many people swore by him; few had the fortitude to swear at him. Above all he knew what to do with political power.

Johnson, who had consciously modeled his career after that of Franklin D. Roosevelt, considered social welfare legislation his specialty. The contrast with Kennedy could not have been sharper. Kennedy's plans for federal aid for education, urban renewal, a higher minimum wage, and medical care for the aged were blocked in Congress by Republicans and southern Democrats. But Kennedy had reacted to these defeats mildly, almost wistfully. He thought the machinery of the federal government was cumbersome and ineffective.

Johnson knew how to make it work. On becoming president, he pushed hard for Kennedy's programs. Early in his career Johnson had voted against a bill making lynching a federal crime, and he also had opposed bills outlawing state poll taxes and establishing the federal Fair Employment Practices Commission. But after he became an important figure in national affairs, he consistently championed racial equality. Bills long buried in committee sailed through Congress. Early in 1964 Kennedy's tax cut was passed. A few months later, an expanded version of another Kennedy proposal became law as the Civil Rights Act of 1964.

The much-strengthened Civil Rights Act outlawed discrimination by employers against blacks and also against women. It broke down legal barriers to black voting in the southern states and outlawed racial segregation of all sorts in places of public accommodation, such as movie theaters, hotels, and restaurants. In addition, unlike presidents Eisenhower and Kennedy, Johnson established agencies to enforce civil rights legislation.

Johnson's success in steering the Civil Rights Act through Congress confirmed his belief that he could be a reformer in the tradition of Franklin Roosevelt. He declared war on poverty and set out to create a Great Society in which poverty no longer would exist.

In 1937 Roosevelt had been accused of exaggeration for claiming that one-third of the nation was "ill-housed, ill-clad, ill-nourished." In fact Roosevelt had underestimated the extent of poverty. Wartime economic growth reduced the percentage of poor people in the country substantially, but in 1960 between 20 and 25 percent of all American families—about 40 million people—were living below the poverty line, a government standard of minimum subsistence based on income and family size.

The presence of so many poor people in an affluent society was deplorable but not difficult to explain. In any community a certain number of people cannot support themselves because of physical, mental, or emotional problems. The United States also included entire regions, the best known being Appalachia, that had been bypassed by economic development and no longer provided their inhabitants with adequate economic opportunities.

Moreover, prosperity and advancing technology had changed the definition of poverty. Telephones, radios and electric refrigerators, and other goods unimaginable to the most affluent Americans of the 1860s, were necessities a hundred years later. But as living standards rose, so did job requirements. Technology was changing the labor market. Educated workers with special skills and good verbal abilities easily found well-paid jobs. Those who had no special skills or were poorly educated went without work.

The Economic Opportunity Act of 1964 created a mixture of programs, among them a Job Corps similar to the New Deal Civilian Conservation Corps, a community

LBJ cultivated the masculine image of a Texas cowboy. Biographers have suggested that Johnson was torn between the expectations of his father, a crude local politician who flouted polite society, and those of his mother, a refined woman who insisted that her son read poetry and practice the violin. Johnson later told biographer Doris Kearns Goodwin that he persisted in Vietnam because he worried that critics would accuse him of being "an unmanly man. A man without a spine."

action program to finance local antipoverty efforts, and a system for training the unskilled unemployed and for lending money to small businesses in poor areas. The programs combined the progressive concept of government aid for those in need with the conservative idea of individual responsibility.

Buttressed by his legislative triumphs, Johnson sought election as president in his own right in 1964. He achieved this ambition in unparalleled fashion. His championing of civil rights won him the almost unanimous support of blacks; his tax policy attracted the well-to-do and the business interests; his war on poverty held the allegiance of labor and other traditionally Democratic groups. His down-home southern antecedents counterbalanced his liberalism on the race question in the eyes of many white southerners.

The Republicans played into his hands by nominating the conservative Senator Barry M. Goldwater of Arizona, whose objective in Congress had been "not to pass laws but to repeal them." As a presidential candidate he favored such laissez-faire policies

Table 29.1 Making a "Great Society"

Assisted Group	Legislation and Provisions
African Americans	Civil Rights Act (1964): Outlawed discrimination in employment, public accommodations, and federally-funded programs
	Voting Rights Act (1965): Federal registrars sent to the South
Elderly	Medicare (1965): Federally-funded medical care for elderly
Low-income people	Economic Opportunity Act (1964): Federally-funded antipoverty programs and agencies
	Medicaid (1965): Federally-funded health care for welfare recipients
	Housing and Urban Development Act: Federally-funded housing projects and rent support
Students	Elementary and Secondary Education Act (1965): Federal support for public and parochial schools for texts and materials, and for Head Start
	Higher Education Act (1965): Federally-funded loans and scholarships for college students

as cutting back on the Social Security system and doing away with the Tennessee Valley Authority. A large majority of voters found Goldwater out-of-date on economic questions and dangerously aggressive on foreign affairs.

In November, Johnson won a sweeping victory, collecting over 61 percent of the popular vote and carrying the whole country except Goldwater's Arizona and five states in the Deep South.

Quickly Johnson pressed ahead with his Great Society program. In January 1965 he proposed a compulsory hospital insurance system, known as Medicare, for all persons over the age of sixty-five. As amended by Congress, the Medicare Act consisted of Part A, hospital insurance for the elderly (funded by increased Social Security taxes), and a voluntary plan, Part B, covering doctors' bills (paid for in part by the government). The law also provided for grants to the states to help pay the medical expenses of poor people, even those below the age of sixty-five. This part of the system was called Medicaid. Before the passage of the Medicare Act, about half of Americans over sixty-five years old had no medical insurance.

Next, Congress passed the Elementary and Secondary Education Act in 1965, which supplied federal funds to school districts; the Higher Education Act (1965), which provided financial aid to college students; and Head Start, a program to prepare poor preschoolers for elementary school. It also provided medical examinations and nutritious meals for children.

Still another important reform was the Voting Rights Act of 1965, pressed through Congress by President Johnson after more brutal repressions of civil rights demonstrators in the South. This law provided for federal intervention to protect black registration and voting in six southern states. It applied to state and local as well as federal elections.

See the **Map**
Impact of the Voting Rights Act of 1965 at **myhistorylab.com**

Other laws passed at Johnson's urging in 1965 and 1966 included the creation of the National Endowment for the Arts and the National Endowment for the Humanities and measures supporting scientific research, highway safety, crime control, slum clearance, clean air, and the preservation of historic sites. Of particular significance was the Immigration Act of 1965, which did away with most provisions of the national-origin system of admitting newcomers. Instead, 290,000 persons a year were to be admitted on the basis of such priorities as job skills and need for political asylum. The law also placed a limit of 120,000 immigrants a year from countries in the Western Hemisphere. Previously, immigration from these countries had been unrestricted.

The Great Society program was one of the most remarkable outpourings of important legislation in American history. On balance, the achievements of the Great Society were far below what President Johnson had promised and his supporters had envisioned. Despite his long political experience, Johnson tried to accomplish too many things too quickly. He relied too heavily on the techniques of political manipulation. Without the crisis atmosphere that had appeared to justify hasty experimentation during the New Deal years, the public judged the results of the Great Society and the president who had shaped it skeptically.

New Racial Turmoil

One reason for skepticism was that the adoption of the Great Society coincided with increasing racial polarization. Black militancy, building steadily during World War II and the

Watch the **Video**
Malcolm X at **myhistorylab.com**

Police watch as the Watts section of Los Angeles burns during riots in August, 1965.

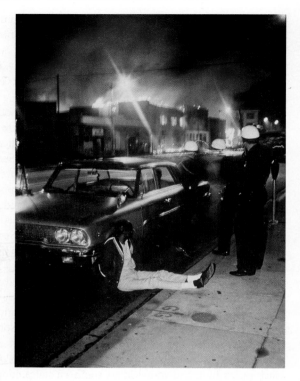

postwar years, burst forth in the mid-1960s. An important illustration was the response of Black Muslims to Malcolm X's 1964 decision to abandon the organization. A trip to the Middle East had exposed him to Islamic doctrines of racial equality and the brotherhood of man. In response he founded the Organization of Afro-American Unity. In 1965, while making a speech in favor of racial harmony, he was assassinated by Black Muslim fanatics.

Even Martin Luther King, Jr., the herald of nonviolent resistance, became more aggressive. "We are not asking, we are demanding the ballot," he said in January 1965. A few weeks after Malcolm's death, King led a march from Selma, Alabama, to Montgomery as part of a campaign to force Alabama authorities to allow blacks to register to vote. King chose Selma because the county in which it was located had a black majority but only 325 registered black voters. He expected the authorities to react brutally, thus attracting public sympathy for the marchers, and he was not disappointed. His marchers were assaulted by state policemen who wielded clubs and tossed canisters of tear gas.

Many African Americans lost patience with nonviolence. "The time for running has come to an end," declared Stokely Carmichael, chairman of the Student Nonviolent Coordinating Committee (SNCC). "It's time we stand up and take over." He began chanting "Black Power!" and other African-Americans chimed in. Black Power caught on swiftly among militants. This troubled white liberals, who feared that Black Power would antagonize white conservatives. They argued that since blacks made up only about 11 percent of the population, any attempt to obtain racial justice through the use of naked power was sure to fail.

●●●—[Read **the Document**

Black Power 1967 at
myhistorylab.com

Meanwhile, black anger erupted in a series of destructive urban riots. The most important occurred in Watts, a ghetto of Los Angeles, in August 1965. A trivial incident brought thousands into the streets. The neighborhood almost literally exploded: For six days Watts was swept by fire, looting, and bloody fighting between local residents and nearly 15,000 National Guardsmen, called up to assist the police. The following two summers saw similar outbursts in scores of cities.

●●●—[Read **the Document**

Watts Riots 1967 at
myhistorylab.com

Then, in April 1968, Martin Luther King, Jr., was murdered in Memphis, Tennessee, by a white man, James Earl Ray. Blacks in more than a hundred cities unleashed their anger in outbursts of burning and looting. The death of King appeared to destroy the hope that his peaceful appeal to reason and right could solve the problems of racism.

The most frightening aspect of the riots was their tendency to polarize society on racial lines. Whites fled to the suburbs in droves. Advocates of Black Power became more determined to separate themselves from white influence; they exasperated white supporters of school desegregation by demanding schools of their own. Extremists formed the Black Panther party and collected weapons to resist the police. "Shoot, don't loot," the radical H. Rap Brown advised all who would listen.

From the "Beat Movement" to Student Radicalism

The increased militancy of many American blacks paralleled the emergence of an increasingly strident attitude among many young people as the "conformist" decade of the 1950s gave way to the "activist" 1960s.

This common characterization, however, is overdrawn. The roots of 1960s' dissent were firmly planted in the 1950s. J. D. Salinger, perhaps the most popular writer of the decade and the particular favorite of college students—*The Catcher in the Rye* (1951) sold nearly 2 million copies—wrote about young people whose self-absorption was a product of their alienation from society. Allen Ginsberg's dark, desperate *Howl*, written in 1955, perhaps the most widely read poem of the postwar era, underscored generational differences. "I saw the best minds of my generation destroyed by madness, starving hysterical naked," the poem begins. In *On the Road* (1957), Jack Kerouac, founder of the **beat** (for "beatific") **school**, described a manic, drug-laced flight from traditional values and institutions. In *Catch-22* (1955), Joseph Heller produced a war novel at once farcical and an indignant denunciation of the stupidity and waste of warfare.

But if the "beats" were a fringe group of poets and musicians, their successors in the 1960s—generally known as hippies—could be found in large groups in every big city in the United States and Europe. They were so "turned off" by the modern world that they retreated from it, finding refuge in communes, drugs, and mystical religions. They were disgusted by the dishonesty and sordid antics of so many of the politicians, horrified by the brutality of Vietnam, appalled by racism, and contemptuous of the smugness they encountered in colleges and universities. But they rejected activism. Theirs was a world of folk songs and blaring acid rock music, of "be-ins," "love-ins," casual sex, and drugs. But the 1960s also witnessed the emergence of a new activism. Many students were frustrated by persistent racism and bigotry, but they regarded these as symptoms of a right-wing "power elite" of corporate executives and military and political leaders—a concept outlined in a book of that title by Columbia sociologist C. Wright Mills. In 1962 a small group of students in the **Students for a Democratic Society (SDS)** put together a manifesto for action at a meeting at Port Huron, Michigan: Their main concerns were racial bigotry, the bomb, and the "disturbing paradoxes" associated with these concerns. SDS sought to wrest power from the "military-industrial" complex and institute a radical socialist government. SDS grew, powered by rising college enrollments and a seemingly unending list of local campus issues. The first great student outburst convulsed the University of California at Berkeley in the fall of 1964. Angry students, many veterans of the 1964 fight for black rights in the South, staged sit-down strikes in university buildings to protest the prohibition of political canvassing on the campus. This free speech movement

((•—[Hear the **Audio**

Timothy Leary, *Going Out*
(1966) at **myhistorylab.com**

A young man perches in a tree with a guitar at Woodstock, a drug- and water-logged music festival that attracted 500,000 to rural New York in 1968.

disrupted the institution over a period of weeks. Hundreds were arrested, the state legislature threatened reprisals, the faculty became involved in the controversy, and the crisis led to the resignation of the president of the University of California, Clark Kerr.

But what transformed student activism from being a local campus irritation to a mass political movement was the decision by Lyndon Johnson to escalate the war in Vietnam.

Johnson Escalates the War

After Diem's assassination in 1963, the situation in South Vietnam worsened. One military coup followed another, and political instability aggravated military incapacity. President Johnson nevertheless felt that he had no choice but to prop up the South Vietnamese regime.

Johnson decided to punish North Vietnam directly for prosecuting the war in the South. In early 1964 he secretly ordered American warships to escort the South Vietnamese navy on commando missions far into the Gulf of Tonkin. After one such mission, American destroyers were fired on by North Vietnamese gunboats. Several nights later during a heavy storm, American ships reported that they were being fired on, though the enemy was never spotted. Using this Tonkin "incident" as pretext, Johnson demanded, and in an air of crisis obtained, an authorization from Congress to "repel any armed attack against the forces of the United States and to prevent further aggression." With this blank check, known as the Gulf of Tonkin Resolution, Johnson authorized air attacks in

•••—[Read the Document

The Gulf of Tonkin Resolution Message at **myhistorylab.com**

From 1965 to 1968, American troops in Vietnam conducted "search and destroy" missions to shatter the insurgents. Here a soldier watches as a village is burned.

The Vietnam War, 1961–1975 As American bombing and "search and destroy" missions spread throughout South Vietnam, North Vietnamese supply lines moved westward, into Laos and Cambodia. U.S. troops and bombers attacked there as well. This destabilized Cambodia, which fell to the brutal Khmer Rouge communists in 1975.

North Vietnam. By the summer of 1965, American bombers were conducting some 5,000 raids each month.

But the hail of bombs on North Vietnam had little effect on the struggle in the South. Worse, the Vietcong expanded the areas under their control. After a fact-finding mission in the war zone, McGeorge Bundy concluded that the prospects were grim for South Vietnam. "The energy and persistence of the Vietcong are astonishing," he reported. "They have accepted extraordinary losses and they come back for more. They show skill in their sneak attacks and ferocity when cornered." If the war was to be won, American soldiers—lots of them—would have to do much of the fighting themselves.

In July 1965 Johnson ordered the first of several huge increases in American ground forces. By the end of 1965, 184,000 Americans were in the field; a year later, 385,000; and after another year, 485,000. By the middle of 1968 the number exceeded 538,000. Each increase was met by corresponding increases from the other side. The Soviet Union and China sent no combat troops, but stepped up their aid, and thousands of North Vietnamese regulars filtered across the seventeenth parallel to fight with the Vietcong guerrillas.

The new American strategy was not to seize any particular battlefield or terrain as in all previous wars, but to kill as many of the enemy as possible through bloody "search and destroy" operations. As the scope of the action broadened, the number of American casualties rose. The United States was engaged in a full-scale war, one that Congress never declared.

The Election of 1968

Gradually the opponents of the war gained numbers and strength. They began to include some of the president's advisers. By late 1967 Secretary of Defense McNamara, who had methodically tracked kill ratios, troop replacement rates, and nearly every other conceivable statistic, concluded that "the figures didn't add up" and the war could not be won. Deeply despondent, he resigned, but did not publicly admit his doubts.

Opposition to the war was especially vehement on college campuses, some students objecting because they thought the United States had no business intervening in the Vietnam conflict, others because they feared being drafted, still others because so many students obtained educational deferments, while young men who were unable to attend college were conscripted.

Then, in November 1967, Eugene McCarthy, a low-keyed, introspective senator from Minnesota, announced his candidacy for the 1968 Democratic presidential nomination. Opposition to the war was his issue.

Preventing Johnson from being renominated seemed impossible. Aside from the difficulty of defeating a "reigning" president, there were the domestic achievements of Johnson's Great Society program: the health insurance program for retired people, greatly expanded federal funding of education and public housing, and the Civil Rights Act. Even Senator McCarthy took his chances of being nominated so lightly that he did not trouble to set up a real organization. He entered the campaign only to "alleviate . . . this sense of political helplessness." Someone, he decided, must step forward to put the Vietnam question before the voters.

Stung by the critics, Johnson ordered General William C. Westmoreland, commander of American forces in Vietnam, to reassure the American people on the course of the war. The general obligingly returned to the United States in late 1967 and told the press that he could see "some light at the end of the tunnel."

Suddenly, early in 1968, on the heels of this announcement, North Vietnamese and Vietcong forces launched a general offensive to correspond with their Lunar New Year (called Tet). Striking thirty-nine of the forty-four provincial capitals, many other towns and cities, and every American base, they caused chaos throughout South Vietnam. They held Hué, the old capital of the country, for weeks. To root insurgents out of Saigon the Americans had to level large sections of the city.

The Tet offensive was essentially a series of raids; the communists did not expect to hold the cities indefinitely, and they did not. Their losses were enormous. Nevertheless the psychological impact in South Vietnam and in the United States made Tet a clear victory for the communists. American pollsters reported an enormous shift of public opinion against further escalation of the fighting. When Westmoreland described Tet as a communist defeat and yet requested an additional 206,000 troops, McCarthy, who was

Table 29.2 Major Events in the Vietnam War, 1961–1968

1961	JFK dispatches thousands of U.S. military "advisers" to South Vietnam
1963	Vietnamese Buddhists rebel; United States supports overthrow of Diem
1964	LBJ obtains Gulf of Tonkin Resolution to expand war
1965	LBJ greatly increases U.S. troop levels
1968	Tet Offensive throughout South Vietnam; LBJ decides not to seek reelection; My Lai Massacre

campaigning in the New Hampshire primary, suddenly became a formidable figure. Thousands of students and other volunteers flocked to the state to ring doorbells on his behalf. On primary election day he polled 42 percent of the Democratic vote. This prompted former attorney general Robert F. Kennedy, brother of the slain president, to declare his candidacy for the Democratic nomination. Like McCarthy, Kennedy opposed Johnson's Vietnam policies but thought his chances of winning were better than McCarthy's.

Confronting this division in the ranks, President Johnson realized he could no longer hope to be an effective president. In a surprising televised announcement, he withdrew from the race. Vice President Hubert H. Humphrey then announced his candidacy, and Johnson threw the weight of his administration behind him.

Kennedy carried several primaries, including California. Immediately after his victory speech in a Los Angeles hotel, however, he was assassinated by Sirhan Sirhan, an Arab nationalist who had been incensed by Kennedy's support of Israel. In effect, Kennedy's death ensured the nomination of Humphrey.

The contest for the Republican nomination was far less dramatic, although its outcome, the nomination of Richard M. Nixon, would have been hard to predict a few years earlier. After his loss to Kennedy in 1960, Nixon ran unsuccessfully for governor of California in 1962, then moved to New York City and joined a prominent law firm. But he remained active in Republican affairs. In 1964 he had campaigned hard for Goldwater. When no other Republican developed extensive support as the 1968 election approached, Nixon entered the race, swept the primaries, and won an easy first-ballot victory at the Republican convention.

Nixon then astounded the country and dismayed liberals by choosing Governor Spiro T. Agnew of Maryland as his running mate. Agnew was a political unknown. Nixon chose him primarily to attract southern votes.

Placating the South seemed necessary because Governor George C. Wallace of Alabama was making a determined bid to win enough electoral votes for his American Independent party to prevent any candidate from obtaining a majority. Wallace was flagrantly anti-black and anti-intellectual. He denounced federal "meddling," the "coddling" of criminals, and the forced integration of schools.

This Republican strategy to win the South heightened the tension surrounding the Democratic convention, which met in Chicago in late August. Humphrey delegates controlled the convention. Several thousand activists, representing a dozen groups and advocating tactics ranging from orderly demonstrations to civil disobedience to indiscriminate violence, descended on Chicago to put pressure on the delegates to repudiate the Johnson Vietnam policy.

In the tense atmosphere that resulted, the party hierarchy overreacted. The mayor of Chicago, Richard J. Daley, whose ability to "influence" election results in a manner favorable to Democrats had often been demonstrated, ringed the convention with policemen to protect it from disruption. This was a reasonable precaution in itself. Inside the building the delegates nominated Humphrey and adopted a war plank satisfactory to Johnson. Outside, however, provoked by the abusive language and violent behavior of radical demonstrators, the police tore into the protesters, in novelist Norman Mailer's graphic phrase, "like a chain saw cutting into wood," while millions watched on television in fascinated horror.

The mayhem in Chicago seemed to benefit Nixon by strengthening the convictions of many voters that the tougher treatment of criminals and dissenters that he and Agnew were calling for was necessary. Those who were critical of the Chicago police tended to blame Humphrey, whom Mayor Daley supported.

Nixon campaigned at a deliberate, dignified pace. He made relatively few public appearances, relying instead on carefully arranged television interviews and taped commercials. He stressed firm enforcement of the law and his desire "to bring us together." As for Vietnam, he would "end the war and win the peace," by just what means he did not say. Agnew, in his blunt, coarse way, assaulted Humphrey, the Democrats, and left-wing dissident groups.

But gradually Humphrey gained ground, and on election day the popular vote was close: Nixon slightly less than 31.8 million, Humphrey nearly 31.3 million. Nixon's Electoral College margin, however, was substantial—301 to 191. The remaining 46 electoral votes went to Wallace, whose 9.9 million votes came to 13.5 percent of the total. Together, Nixon and Wallace received 57 percent of the popular vote.

Nixon as President: "Vietnamizing" the War

When he took office in January 1969, Richard Nixon projected an image of calm and deliberate statesmanship; he introduced no startling changes, proposed no important new legislation. He considered the solution of the Vietnam problem his chief task. Although he insisted during the 1968 campaign that he would end the war on "honorable" terms if elected, he suggested nothing very different from what Johnson was doing.

In office, Nixon first proposed a phased withdrawal of all non-South Vietnamese troops, to be followed by an internationally supervised election in South Vietnam. The North Vietnamese rejected this scheme and insisted that the United States withdraw its forces unconditionally. The intransigence of the North Vietnamese left the president in a difficult position. Nixon could not compel the foe to end a war it had begun against the French nearly a quarter of a century earlier, and every passing day added to the strength of antiwar sentiment, which in turn led to deeper divisions in the country. Yet Nixon could not face up to the consequences of ending the war on the communists' terms.

The president responded to the dilemma by trying to build up the South Vietnamese armed forces so that American troops could pull out without South Vietnam being overrun by the communists. He shipped so many planes to the Vietnamese that within four years they had the fourth-largest air force in the world. He also announced a series of troop cuts.

For a while, events appeared to vindicate Nixon's position. A gradual slowing of military activity in Vietnam had reduced American casualties. Troop withdrawals continued in an orderly fashion. A new lottery system for drafting men for military duty eliminated some of the inequities in the selective service law.

But the war continued. Early in 1970 reports that an American unit had massacred civilians, including dozens of women and children, in a Vietnamese hamlet known as

South Vietnamese women and children were among some 300 apparently unarmed civilians killed in the My Lai Massacre in 1968. Lieutenant William Calley was convicted of murder and sentenced to life in prison. After many appeals, he was released in 1974.

My Lai revived the controversy over the purposes of the war and its corrosive effects on those who were fighting it.

Nixon wanted to end the war but he did not want to lose it. The war's human, economic, and social costs could only vex his days and threaten his future reputation. When he reduced the level of the fighting, the communists merely waited for further reductions. When he raised it, many Americans denounced him in increasingly massive antiwar protests. If he pulled out of Vietnam and the communists won, other Americans would be outraged.

Perhaps Nixon's error lay in his unwillingness to admit his own uncertainty, something the greatest presidents—one thinks immediately of Lincoln and Franklin Roosevelt—were never afraid to do. Facing a dilemma, he tried to convince the world that he was firmly in control of events. Thus he heightened the tensions he sought to relax—in America, in Vietnam, and elsewhere.

The Cambodian "Incursion"

Late in April 1970 Nixon announced that Vietnamization was proceeding more rapidly than he had hoped, that communist power was weakening, and that within a year another 150,000 American soldiers would be extracted from Vietnam. A week later he announced that military intelligence had indicated that the enemy was consolidating its "sanctuaries" in neutral Cambodia and that he was therefore dispatching thousands of American troops to destroy these bases.

Nixon's shocking announcement triggered many campus demonstrations. One college where feeling ran high was Kent State University in Ohio. For several days students there clashed with local police; they broke windows and caused other damage to property. When the governor called out the National Guard, angry students showered the soldiers with stones. During a noontime protest on May 4 the guardsmen, who were poorly trained in crowd control, suddenly opened fire. Four students were killed, two of them women who were merely passing by on their way to class.

Watch the **Video**

Protests Against the Vietnam War at **myhistorylab.com**

While the nation reeled from this shock, two students at Jackson State University were killed by Mississippi state policemen. A wave of student strikes followed, closing down hundreds of colleges, including many that had seen no previous unrest. Moderate students by the tens of thousands joined with the radicals.

The almost universal condemnation of the invasion and of the way it had been planned shook Nixon hard. He backtracked, pulling American ground troops out of Cambodia quickly. But he did not change his Vietnam policy, and in fact Cambodia apparently stiffened his determination. As American ground troops were withdrawn, he stepped up air attacks.

The balance of forces remained in uneasy equilibrium through 1971. But late in March 1972 the North Vietnamese again mounted a series of assaults throughout South Vietnam. Nixon responded with heavier bombing, and he ordered the approaches to Haiphong and other North Vietnamese ports sown with mines to cut off the communists' supplies.

Détente with Communism

But in the midst of these aggressive actions, Nixon and his National Security Adviser Henry Kissinger devised a bold diplomatic offensive, executed in nearly complete secrecy. Nixon and Kissinger made an effective though not always harmonious team. Abandoning a lifetime of treating communism as a single worldwide conspiracy that had to be contained at all costs, Nixon decided to deal with China and the Soviet Union as separate powers and, as he put it, to "live together and work together" with both. Nixon and Kissinger called the new policy détente, a French term meaning "the relaxation of tensions between governments." But détente was not an expression of friendship so much as an acknowledgment that for decades the policy of containment had driven China and the Soviet Union closer together.

First Nixon sent Kissinger secretly to China and the Soviet Union to prepare the way for summit meetings with the communist leaders. Both the Chinese and the Soviets agreed to the meetings. Then, in February 1972, Nixon and Kissinger, accompanied by a small army of reporters and television crews, flew to Beijing. After much dining, sightseeing, posing for photographers, and consultation with Chinese officials, Nixon agreed to promote economic and cultural exchanges and supported the admission of communist China to the United Nations. As a result, exports to communist China increased substantially, reaching $4 billion in 1980. Nixon's visit, ending more than twenty years of adamant American refusal to accept the reality of the Chinese revolution, marked a dramatic reversal; as such it was hailed throughout the world.

In May 1972 Nixon and Kissinger flew to Moscow. This trip also produced striking results. The mere fact that it took place while war still raged in Vietnam was remarkable. More important, however, the meeting resulted in a **Strategic Arms Limitation Treaty (SALT)**. The two powers agreed to stop making nuclear ballistic missiles and to reduce the number of antiballistic missiles in their arsenals to 200. Nixon also agreed to permit large sales of American grain to the Soviet Union.

By the summer of 1972, with the presidential election looming in the fall, Kissinger redoubled his efforts to negotiate an end to the Vietnam War. By October he and the North Vietnamese had hammered out a settlement calling for a cease-fire, the return of American prisoners of war, and the withdrawal of United States forces from Vietnam. Shortly before the presidential election Kissinger announced that peace was "at hand."

Nixon in Triumph

A few days later President Nixon was reelected, defeating the Democratic candidate, Senator George McGovern of South Dakota, in a landslide—521 electoral votes to 17. McGovern carried only Massachusetts and the District of Columbia. McGovern's campaign had been hampered by his tendency to advance poorly thought-out proposals, such as his scheme for funneling money directly to the poor, and by his rather bumbling, low-key oratorical style. The campaign marked the historical breakdown of the coalition that Franklin Roosevelt had fashioned and on which he and his Democratic successors, particularly Truman and Johnson, had ridden to power. Of that coalition, only African Americans voted solidly for McGovern.

Nixon had won over hundreds of thousands of voters who had supported Democrats in earlier elections. The "solid South" was again solid, but this time solidly Republican. Nixon's so-called southern strategy of reducing the pressure for school desegregation and otherwise restricting federal efforts on behalf of blacks had a powerful attraction to northern blue-collar workers as well.

Suddenly Nixon loomed as one of the most powerful and successful presidents in American history. His tough-minded but flexible handling of foreign policy questions, even his harsh Vietnamese policy, suggested decisiveness and self-confidence, qualities he had often seemed to lack in his earlier career. His willingness, despite his long history as a militant cold warrior, to negotiate with the communist nations indicated a new flexibility and creativity. His landslide victory appeared to demonstrate that a large majority of the people approved of his way of tackling the major problems of the times.

But Kissinger's agreement with the North Vietnamese came apart when Nguyen Van Thieu, the South Vietnamese president, refused to sign it. Thieu claimed that the agreement, by permitting communist troops to remain in the South, would ensure his ultimate defeat. To Kissinger's chagrin, Nixon sided with Thieu and resumed the bombing of North Vietnam in December 1972, this time sending the mighty B-52s directly over Hanoi and other cities. The destruction they caused was great, but their effectiveness as a means of forcing concessions from the North Vietnamese was at best debatable.

In January 1973 a settlement was finally reached. As with the October "agreement," the North Vietnamese retained control of large sections of the South, and they promised to

President and Mrs. Nixon dine with Chinese communist officials in Beijing in February 1972. Even Nixon's harshest critics conceded that his initiative in reopening United States-China relations was a diplomatic masterstroke.

release American prisoners of war within sixty days. Thieu assented this time, largely because Nixon secretly pledged that the United States would "respond with full force" if North Vietnam resumed its offensive. Within several months most prisoners of war were released, and the last American troops were pulled out of Vietnam. More than 57,000 Americans had died in the long war, and over 300,000 more had been wounded. Nearly a million communist soldiers and 185,000 South Vietnamese soldiers were reported killed.

In 1973, too, Kissinger was named secretary of state; he shared the Nobel Prize for Peace with a North Vietnamese diplomat for negotiating an end to the Vietnam War.

Domestic Policy under Nixon

When Nixon became president in 1969, the major economic problem he faced was inflation. This was caused primarily by the heavy military expenditures and easy-money policies of the Johnson administration. Nixon cut federal spending and balanced the 1969 budget, while the Federal Reserve Board forced up interest rates to slow the expansion of the money supply. When prices continued to rise, uneasiness mounted and labor unions demanded large wage increases.

In 1970 Congress passed a law giving the president power to regulate prices and wages. Nixon originally opposed this legislation, but in the summer of 1971 he changed his mind and announced a ninety-day price and wage freeze. Then he set up a pay board and a price commission with authority to limit wage and price increases when the freeze ended. These controls did not check inflation completely—and they angered union leaders, who felt that labor was being shortchanged—but they did slow the upward spiral.

In handling other domestic issues, the president was less firm. Like President Kennedy he was primarily interested in foreign affairs. He supported a bold plan for a "minimum income" for poor families, but dropped it when it alarmed his conservative supporters and got nowhere in Congress. But when a groundswell of public support for conserving natural resources and checking pollution led Congress to pass bills creating the **Environmental Protection Agency** (**EPA**) and the Clean Air Act of 1970, he signed them cheerfully.

After his triumphant reelection and the withdrawal of the last American troops from Vietnam, Nixon resolved to change the direction in which the nation had been moving

The Clean Air Act of 1970 mandated reductions in air pollution, arguably the most important environmental legislation passed by the United States during the twentieth century.

for decades. He announced that he intended to reduce the interference of the federal government in the affairs of individuals. People should be more self-reliant, he said, and he denounced what he called "permissiveness." Excessive concern for the interests of blacks and other minorities must end. Criminals should be punished "without pity." No person or group should be coddled by the state.

These aims brought Nixon into conflict with liberals in both parties, with the leaders of minority groups, and with those alarmed by the increasing power of the executive. The conflict came to a head over the president's anti-inflation policy. After his second inauguration he ended price and wage controls and called for voluntary "restraints." This approach did not work. Prices soared in the most rapid inflation since the Korean War. In an effort to check the rise, Nixon set a rigid limit on federal expenditures. To keep within the limit, he cut back or abolished a large number of social welfare programs and reduced federal grants in support of science and education. He even impounded (refused to spend) funds already appropriated by Congress for purposes of which he disapproved.

The impoundment created a furor on Capitol Hill, but when Congress failed to override his vetoes of bills challenging this policy, it appeared that Nixon was in total command. The White House staff, headed by H. R. Haldeman and John Ehrlichman, dominated the Washington bureaucracy. Critics began to grumble about a new "imperial presidency." No one seemed capable of checking Nixon.

The Watergate Break-In and Cover-Up

On March 19, 1973, James McCord, a former agent of both the Federal Bureau of Investigation and the Central Intelligence Agency accused of burglary, wrote a letter to the judge presiding at his trial. His act precipitated a series of disclosures that first disrupted and then destroyed the Nixon administration.

McCord had been employed during the 1972 presidential campaign as a security officer of the Committee to Re-elect the President (CREEP). At about 1 AM on June 17, 1972, he and four other men had broken into Democratic party headquarters at Watergate, a complex of apartments and offices in Washington. The burglars were members of an unofficial CREEP surveillance group known as "the plumbers." Nixon, who was compelled by a need to conceal information about his administration, had formed the group after the Pentagon Papers, a confidential report on government policy in Vietnam, had been leaked to the press. The "plumbers" had been caught rifling files and installing electronic eavesdropping devices.

Two other Republican campaign officials were soon implicated in the affair. Their arrest aroused suspicions that the Republican party was behind the break-in. Nixon denied it.

Most people evidently took the president at his word. He was far ahead in the polls and seemed so sure to win reelection that it was hard to believe he would stoop to burglary to discover what the Democrats were up to. In any case, the affair did not materially affect the election. When brought to trial early in 1973, most of the Watergate burglars pleaded guilty.

McCord, who did not, was convicted by the jury. Before Judge John J. Sirica imposed sentences on the culprits, however, McCord wrote his letter. High Republican officials had known about the burglary in advance and had paid the defendants "hush money" to keep their connection secret, McCord claimed. Perjury had been committed during the trial.

The truth of McCord's charges swiftly became apparent. The head of CREEP, Jeb Stuart Magruder, and President Nixon's lawyer, John W. Dean III, admitted their involvement. Among the disclosures that emerged over the following months were these:

- Large sums of money had been paid to the burglars at the instigation of the White House to ensure their silence.
- Agents of the Nixon administration had burglarized the office of a psychiatrist, seeking evidence against one of his patients, Daniel Ellsberg, who had been charged with leaking the Pentagon Papers to the *New York Times*. (This disclosure led to the immediate dismissal of the charges against Ellsberg.)
- CREEP officials had attempted to disrupt the campaigns of leading Democratic candidates during the 1972 primaries in a number of illegal ways.
- A number of corporations had made large contributions to the Nixon reelection campaign in violation of federal law.
- The Nixon administration had placed wiretaps on the telephones of some of its own officials as well as on those of journalists critical of its policies without first obtaining authorization from the courts.

These revelations led to the dismissal of John Dean and to the resignations of most of Nixon's closest advisers, including Haldeman, Ehrlichman, and Attorney Generals John Mitchell and Richard Kleindienst. They also raised the question of the president's personal connection with the **Watergate scandal**. This he steadfastly denied. He insisted that he would investigate the Watergate affair thoroughly and see that the guilty were punished. He refused, however, to allow investigators to examine White House documents, on grounds of executive privilege, which he continued to assert in very broad terms.

In the teeth of Nixon's denials, John Dean, testifying under oath, stated flatly and in circumstantial detail that the president had ordered him to pay the Watergate burglars to conceal White House involvement; if true, the president had been guilty of obstructing justice, a serious crime.

Dean had been a persuasive witness, but many people were reluctant to believe that a president could lie so cold-bloodedly to the entire country. Therefore, when it came out during later hearings of the Senate committee investigating the Watergate scandal that the president had systematically made secret tape recordings of White House conversations and telephone calls, the disclosure caused a sensation. It seemed obvious that these tapes would settle the question of Nixon's involvement once and for all. Again Nixon refused to allow access to the evidence.

One result of the scandals and of Nixon's attitude was a precipitous decline in his standing in public opinion polls. Calls for his resignation, even for impeachment, began to be heard. Yielding to pressure, he agreed to the appointment of an "independent" special prosecutor to investigate the Watergate affair, and he promised the appointee, Professor Archibald Cox of Harvard Law School, full cooperation.

Cox swiftly aroused the president's ire by seeking access to White House records, including the tapes. When Nixon refused to turn over the tapes, Cox obtained a subpoena from Judge Sirica ordering him to do so. The administration appealed this decision and lost in the appellate court. Then, while the case was headed for the Supreme Court, Nixon ordered the new attorney general, Elliot Richardson, to dismiss Cox. Both Richardson, who had promised the Senate during his confirmation hearings that the special prosecutor would have a free hand, and his chief assistant resigned rather than do as the president directed. The third-ranking officer of the Justice Department carried out Nixon's order.

These events of Saturday, October 20, promptly dubbed the Saturday Night Massacre, caused an outburst of public indignation. Congress was bombarded by thousands of letters and telegrams demanding the president's impeachment. The House Judiciary Committee began an investigation to see if enough evidence for impeachment existed.

Once again Nixon backed down. He agreed to turn over the tapes to Judge Sirica with the understanding that relevant materials could be presented to the grand jury investigating the Watergate affair but that nothing would be revealed to the public. He then named a new special prosecutor, Leon Jaworski, and promised him access to whatever White House documents he needed. However, it soon came out that several tapes were missing and that an important section of another had been deliberately erased.

Then Vice President Agnew was accused of income tax fraud and of having accepted bribes while serving as Baltimore county executive and governor of Maryland. To escape a jail term Agnew admitted in October that he had been guilty of tax evasion and resigned as vice president.

Acting according to the procedures for presidential and vice-presidential succession of the Twenty-Fifth Amendment, adopted in 1967, President Nixon nominated Representative Gerald R. Ford of Michigan as vice president, and he was confirmed by Congress. Ford had served continuously in Congress since 1949 and as minority leader since 1964. His positions on public issues were close to Nixon's; he was an internationalist in foreign affairs and a conservative and convinced Republican partisan on domestic issues.

The Judgment on Watergate: "Expletive Deleted"

Meanwhile, special prosecutor Jaworski continued his investigation of the Watergate scandals. In March 1974 a grand jury indicted Haldeman; Ehrlichman; former attorney general John Mitchell, who had been head of CREEP at the time of the break-in; and four other White House aides for conspiring to block the Watergate investigation. The jurors also named Nixon an "unindicted co-conspirator," Jaworski having informed them that their power to indict a president was constitutionally questionable. Judge Sirica thereupon turned over the jury's evidence against Nixon to the House Judiciary Committee.

In an effort to check the mounting criticism, late in April Nixon released edited transcripts of the tapes he had turned over to the court the previous November. In addition to much incriminating evidence, the transcripts provided the public with a fascinating and shocking view of how the president conducted himself in private. In conversations he seemed confused, indecisive, and lacking in any concern for the public interest. His repeated use of foul language, so out of keeping with his public image, offended millions. The phrase "expletive deleted," inserted in place of words considered too vulgar for publication in family newspapers, overnight became a catchword.

With the defendants in the Watergate case demanding access to tapes that they claimed would prove their innocence, Jaworski was compelled either to obtain them or to risk having the charges dismissed on the grounds that the government was withholding evidence. He therefore subpoenaed sixty-four additional tapes. Nixon refused to obey the subpoena. Swiftly the case of *United States v. Richard M. Nixon* went to the Supreme Court.

In the summer of 1974—after so many months of alarms and crises—the Watergate drama reached its climax. The Judiciary Committee, following months of study of the evidence behind closed doors, decided to conduct its deliberations in open session. While millions watched on television, thirty-eight members of the House of Representatives debated the charges and finally adopted three articles of impeachment. They charged the president with obstructing justice, misusing the powers of his office, and failing to obey the committee's subpoenas. Except in the case of the last article, many of the Republicans on the committee joined with the Democrats in voting aye, a clear indication that the full House would vote to impeach.

On the eve of the debates, the Supreme Court had ruled unanimously that the president must turn over the sixty-four subpoenaed tapes to the special prosecutor. Executive privilege had its place, the Court stated, but no person, not even a president, could "withhold evidence that is demonstrably relevant in a criminal trial."

When the subpoenaed tapes were released and transcribed, Nixon's fate was sealed. Three recorded conversations between the president and H. R. Haldeman just after the Watergate break-in proved conclusively that Nixon had tried to obstruct justice by engaging the CIA in an effort to persuade the FBI not to follow up leads in the case on the spurious grounds that national security was involved.

Read the **Document**

House Judiciary Committee's Conclusion on Impeachment at **myhistorylab.com**

When the House Judiciary Committee members read the new transcripts, all the Republican members who had voted against the impeachment articles reversed themselves. Republican leaders told the president categorically that the House would impeach him and that no more than a handful of senators would vote for acquittal.

Nixon Resigns, Ford Becomes President

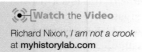

Watch the **Video**

Richard Nixon, I am not a crook at **myhistorylab.com**

On August 8, 1974, Nixon announced his resignation. The resignation took effect at noon on August 9, when Gerald Ford was sworn in as president. "Our long national nightmare is over," Ford declared. Within weeks of taking office, Ford pardoned Nixon for whatever crimes he had committed in office, even any, if such existed, as had yet to come to light.

Whether Nixon's resignation marked the end of one era or the beginning of another is a difficult question. Like most critical moments in human history, it seems in retrospect to have been both. Nixon had extricated the United States from Vietnam—though at tremendous cost in lives and money and to little evident purpose. His détente with the Soviet Union and Red China was surely an early sign of the easing of Cold War tensions characteristic of the decades to follow. Moreover, Nixon's assault on liberals, coming just as public disillusionment with the Great Society programs was mounting, put an end to the liberal era that had begun with the reforms of the New Deal.

Milestones

1951	J. D. Salinger publishes *The Catcher in the Rye*	**1965**	Black Muslim fanatics assassinate Malcolm X
1955	Joseph Heller publishes *Catch*-22	**1968**	Communists strike all over South Vietnam in Tet Offensive
	Allen Ginsberg publishes *Howl*		
1957	Jack Kerouac publishes *On the Road*		Lyndon Johnson withdraws as candidate for reelection
1960	Black college students found Student Nonviolent Coordinating Committee (SNCC)		Martin Luther King, Jr., is assassinated
			Robert F. Kennedy is assassinated
	John F. Kennedy elected President		Richard Nixon is elected president
1961	CIA-trained Cuban exiles launch disastrous Bay of Pigs invasion	**1969**	Nixon announces "Vietnamization" of war
	Soviets build Berlin wall		Apollo 11 lands on the moon
	John F. Kennedy founds Peace Corps	**1970**	Nixon announces "incursion" into Cambodia
	Freedom riders integrate buses in South		
1962	Soviet Premier Khrushchev precipitates Cuban missile crisis		Antiwar student protesters are killed at Kent State University and Jackson State University
	Students for a Democratic Society (SDS) issues Port Huron Statement		Congress passes Clean Air Act and creates Environmental Protection Agency (EPA)
1963	United States supports coup to oust President Ngo Dinh Diem of South Vietnam	**1972**	Nixon's "plumbers" burglarize Democratic national headquarters at Watergate complex
	Martin Luther King, Jr., gives "I Have a Dream" speech during March on Washington		Nixon and Kissinger visit China and Soviet Union
	Lee Harvey Oswald assassinates President Kennedy; Lyndon Johnson becomes president		United States and Soviet Union sign Strategic Arms Limitation Treaty (SALT)
1964	Congress endorses escalation of Vietnam War in Gulf of Tonkin Resolution		Nixon is reelected in landslide
		1973	House Judiciary Committee begins impeachment hearings against Nixon
	Lyndon Johnson is elected president, begins Great Society program		Vice President Spiro Agnew resigns; Gerald Ford is appointed vice president
	Congress passes historic Civil Rights Act		
	Free speech movement disrupts University of California at Berkeley		Last American troops leave Vietnam
1965	Congress passes Immigration Act, ending national quota system		Nixon fires Watergate special prosecutor Archibald Cox (Saturday Night Massacre)
	Medicare Act pays some medical costs for senior citizens and the poor	**1974**	Supreme Court orders release of Nixon's White House tapes
	Congress funds education with Elementary and Secondary Education Act and Higher Education Act		Nixon resigns; Gerald Ford becomes president and pardons Nixon

✓●─⌐Study and **Review** at **www.myhistorylab.com**

Review Questions

1. The introduction emphasizes the difficulties JFK, LBJ, and Nixon had in getting out of the "quagmire" that was the Vietnam War. What might they have done differently? Why did they pursue the course they chose?

2. Why did the escalation of the war from 1961 to 1968 fail to produce a victory? How did Nixon change the Vietnam policies of his predecessors? Why didn't they succeed?

3. How did the war affect American society? What effect did student protests have on the war?

4. How did Johnson's Great Society differ from Franklin D. Roosevelt's New Deal? Which aspects of the Great Society proved most successful? Why did others fall short of expectations?

5. What explains the rise of Black Power during the 1960s? Why did the race riots strike just as the federal government was providing tangible assistance on matters of civil rights, racial discrimination, and poverty?

6. Why did Nixon form the "plumbers" and then obstruct justice following the Watergate break-in? Why did Ford pardon Nixon?

Key Terms

Bay of Pigs fiasco *762*
beat school *771*
Berlin wall *762*
Civil Rights Act
    of 1964 *767*
Cuban missile
    crisis *763*
détente *778*
Environmental Protection
    Agency (EPA) *780*

Great Society *767*
Gulf of Tonkin
    Resolution *772*
Medicare *769*
Strategic Arms Limitation
    Treaty (SALT) *778*
Student Nonviolent
    Coordinating
    Committee
    (SNCC) *764*

Students for a Democratic
    Society (SDS) *771*
Tet offensive *774*
United States v. Richard M.
    Nixon *784*
Voting Rights Act
    of 1965 *769*
Watergate scandal *782*

Running on Empty: 1975–1991

30

((•—Hear the Audio Chapter 30 at myhistorylab.com

Do you pay too much for gas?

DURING THE SUMMER OF 2008, WITH THE PRESIDENTIAL CAMPAIGN in full swing, gas prices topped $4 a gallon. Republican candidate John McCain called for laws allowing oil companies to drill for oil in U.S. coastal waters. Sarah Palin, Governor of oil-rich Alaska and McCain's running mate, put it more succinctly: "Drill, Baby, Drill!"

Senator Barack Obama had opposed offshore drilling. But as gas prices rose, his lead in the polls slipped. With the election less than two months away, Obama reversed course. Now he supported off-shore drilling. Democratic leaders in Congress, scrambling to clamber onto the offshore drilling bandwagon, pushed through a law ending the quarter-century old ban on drilling for oil in federal waters off the Atlantic and Pacific Coasts.

Then, in 2010, a British-owned oil rig forty miles off the coast of Louisiana exploded, killing eleven workers and releasing millions of barrels of crude oil into the Gulf of Mexico. The oil spill was arguably the worst environmental disaster in the nation's history.

For much of the twentieth century, the high cost and environmental risks of offshore oil drilling exceeded the projected profits of such ventures. But that changed in 1970s when the flow of crude oil to the United States and the West was cut off; the price of oil soared. Now offshore drilling made economic sense. Because most of the untapped oil lay beneath the oceans, offshore drilling platforms were built in the North Sea, off the coast of Brazil, and in the Gulf of Mexico.

For a nation dependent on the automobile, the 1970s oil shortage plunged the economy into a deep recession. Factories were closed and workers laid off. A new conservatism prevailed, part of a reaction against the costly measures of LBJ's Great Society. The need for cheap oil, moreover, pushed the United States deeper into the labyrinth of Middle Eastern politics. War would follow.

The Oil Crisis

While most Americans watched, transfixed, as the events of Watergate interred the Nixon presidency, few were aware that a battle on the other side of the world was about to transform their lives. On October 6, 1973, the eve of Yom Kippur, the Jewish Day of Atonement, Egypt and Syria attacked the state of Israel. Six years earlier Israel had trounced the

Egyptians with humiliating ease; it had then seized the Sinai peninsula and the West Bank of the Jordan River, an area including Jerusalem. But now Egypt's armored divisions roared into the Sinai and threatened to slice Israel in half; Syrian troops advanced against Israel farther north.

Israeli Prime Minister Golda Meir pleaded with President Nixon for additional arms and aircraft. The United States immediately airlifted scores of fighter planes and other desperately needed material to Israel. The Israelis recrossed the Suez Canal, cut Egyptian supply

After the Arab oil embargo, gasoline became so scarce that customers were limited to buying ten gallons at a time. This led to long lines at the pumps.

lines, and forced Egypt's president, Anwar Sadat, to capitulate. But the Arab world then aimed its biggest weapon squarely at the United States: It cut off oil shipments to the West.

Deprived of Middle Eastern oil, the American economy sputtered. The price of oil rose to $12 a barrel, up from $3. This sent prices soaring for nearly everything else. Homes were heated with oil, factories were powered by it, utility plants used it to generate electricity, and farm produce was shipped to markets on gas-fueled trucks. The Arab oil embargo pushed up gas prices; service stations intermittently ran out of gasoline; long lines formed at those that remained open.

In the spring of 1974, Henry Kissinger negotiated an agreement that required Israel's withdrawal from some territory occupied since the 1967 war; the Arab nations then lifted the oil embargo. But the principal oil exporting nations—Venezuela, Saudi Arabia, Kuwait, Iraq, and Iran—had learned a valuable lesson: If they limited production, they could drive up the price of oil. After the embargo had ended, their cartel, the **Organization of Petroleum Exporting Countries (OPEC)**, announced another price increase. Gasoline prices doubled overnight.

American automakers who had scoffed at tiny Japanese "boxes" now winced as these foreign competitors claimed the new market for small, fuel-efficient, front-wheel-drive cars. American auto companies were unable to respond to this challenge. As production costs rose, manufacturers needed to sell more of their behemoth models, loaded with expensive options such as air conditioning, power windows, and stereo systems. Because the automobile industry stimulated so many other industries—steel, vinyl, glass, rubber— the nation's manufacturing sector was soon in trouble.

Ford as President

Gerald Ford replaced Nixon as president in the summer of 1974, just as the economy was beginning to deteriorate. At first, the country greeted Ford with a collective sigh of relief. Most observers considered Ford unimaginative, certainly not brilliant. But he was hardworking, and—most important under the circumstances—his record was untouched by scandal.

Ford identified inflation as the chief economic culprit and asked patriotic citizens to signify their willingness to fight it by wearing WIN (Whip Inflation Now) buttons. Almost immediately the economy slumped. Production fell and the unemployment rate rose above 9 percent, about twice the postwar average. The president was forced to ask for tax cuts and other measures aimed at stimulating business activity. This made inflation worse and did little to promote employment.

The Fall of South Vietnam

Depressing news about the economy was compounded by disheartening events in Vietnam. In January 1975, after two years of a bloody "cease-fire", North Vietnam attacked just south of the seventeenth parallel, commencing its two-year plan to conquer South Vietnam. The South Vietnamese army retreated, then fled, and finally dissolved with a rapidity that astonished their attackers.

Ford had always supported the Vietnam War. As the military situation deteriorated, he urged Congress to pour more arms into the South to stem the North Vietnamese advance. The legislators flatly refused to do so, and on May 1, 1975, the Viet Cong and North Vietnamese entered Saigon, which they renamed Ho Chi Minh City. The long Vietnam War was finally over.

Ford versus Carter

Ford's uninspiring record on the economy and foreign policy suggested that he would be vulnerable in 1976. That year the Democrats chose Jimmy Carter, a former governor of Georgia, as their candidate.

Carter had been a naval officer and a substantial peanut farmer and warehouse owner before entering politics. He was elected governor of Georgia in 1970. While governor he won something of a reputation as a southern public official who treated black citizens fairly. Carter's political style was informal. During the campaign for delegates he turned his inexperience in national politics to advantage, emphasizing his lack of connection with the Washington establishment rather than apologizing for it. He repeatedly called attention to his integrity and deep religious faith.

Carter sought to make the election a referendum on morality. After Watergate, an atmosphere of scandal permeated Washington, and aspiring journalists and congressmen trained their sights on Kissinger, who

Georgia governor Jimmy Carter and President Gerald Ford debate in 1976. The campaign featured Carter's candor in a *Playboy* interview: "I've committed adultery in my heart many times." The headline stories often neglected the sentences that followed: "This is something that God recognizes I will do—and I have done it—and God forgives me for it."

remained secretary of state after Nixon's resignation. The most significant of the allegations was his meddling in the affairs of Chile, which in 1970 elected Salvador Allende, a Marxist, as president. After Allende's election, Kissinger called on the CIA to "destabilize" Allende's regime. In 1973, Allende was murdered in a military coup and his government toppled. Carter promised an administration of "constant decency" in contrast to Kissinger's penchant for secret diplomacy and covert skullduggery.

In the Republican primaries, Ford was challenged by Ronald Reagan, ex-governor of California, a movie actor turned politician who was the darling of the Republican right wing. Reagan was an excellent speaker, whereas Ford proved somewhat bumbling on the stump. Reagan, too, hammered away at Kissinger, citing his "immoral" détente with communist China. At Reagan's insistence, the Republican platform denounced "secret agreements, hidden from our people"—another jab at Kissinger.

Both Republican candidates gathered substantial blocs of delegates, but Ford staved off the Reagan challenge. That Ford did not win easily, possessed as he was of the advantage of incumbency, made his chances of election in November appear slim.

When the final contest began, both candidates were vague with respect to issues, a situation that hurt Carter particularly because he had made so much of honesty and straight talk. With both candidates stumbling toward the finish line, pundits predicted an extremely close contest, and they were right: Carter won, 297 electoral votes to 241, having carried most of the South, including Texas, and a few large industrial states. He also ran well in districts dominated by labor union members. The wish of the public to punish the party of Richard Nixon probably was a further reason for his victory.

The Carter Presidency

Carter shone brightly in comparison with Nixon, and he seemed more forward-looking and imaginative than Ford. He tried to give a tone of democratic simplicity and moral fervor to his administration. After delivering his inaugural address he walked with his wife Rosalynn and their daughter Amy in the parade from the Capitol to the White House instead of riding in a limousine. They enrolled Amy, a fourth-grader, in a largely black Washington public school. Soon after taking office he held a "call-in"; for two hours he answered questions phoned in by people from all over the country.

Carter's actual administration of his office did not go nearly so well. He put so many Georgians in important posts that his administration took on a parochial character. The administration developed a reputation for submitting complicated proposals to Congress with great fanfare and then failing to follow up on them. Whatever matter Carter was considering at the moment seemed to absorb him totally—other urgent matters were allowed to drift.

A National Malaise

To Carter, the nation's economic woes were symptomatic of a more fundamental flaw in the nation's soul. In a heralded television speech he complained that "a moral and spiritual crisis" had sapped people's energies and undermined civic pride. Critics responded that the nation needed a president rather than a preacher, and that sermons on the emptiness of consumption rang hollow to those who had lost their jobs.

The economic downturn, though triggered by the energy shortage, had more fundamental causes. In the prosperous postwar decades, many companies had grown too big and complacent, more attuned to the demands of the corporate bureaucracy than the needs of customers. Workers' boredom lowered productivity. Absenteeism at General Motors and Ford had doubled during the 1960s. On an average day in 1970, 5 percent of GM's workforce was missing without explanation, and on Mondays and Fridays 10 percent failed to show up. Two years later simmering discontents among young workers boiled over at the GM assembly division at Lordstown, Ohio. GM had installed robotic welding machines, streamlined the workforce, and accelerated the assembly line: 100 cars passed through the line each hour—40 more than under the previous system. Without authorization from the national UAW, younger workers refused to work at the faster pace, allowing many chassis to pass through untouched and throwing the factory into chaos.

Union membership slipped badly from the high point of the mid–1950s, when over one in three nonagricultural workers belonged to unions; by 1978, the proportion had declined to one in four, and by 1990, one in six. During the 1940s and 1950s, most workers voted to join a union, pay dues, and have the organization bargain for them. By 1978, however, union organizers were losing three-fourths of their campaigns to represent workers; and many workers who belonged to unions were opting to get out. Every year, 800 more union shops voted to rescind their affiliation.

The economic crisis after 1973 was unsettling because, for the first time in the nation's history, the rising tide of unemployment had failed to extinguish inflation. Millions of workers lost their jobs, yet wages and prices continued to rise. The term **stagflation** (a combination of stagnation and inflation) was coined to describe this anomaly. In 1971 an inflation rate of 5 percent had so alarmed President Nixon that he had imposed a price freeze. By 1975 inflation had soared to 11 percent and by 1979, it peaked at a whopping 13 percent; unemployment ranged from 6 to 10 percent, nearly twice the usual postwar level.

Carter had promised to fight inflation by reducing government spending and balancing the budget and to stimulate the economy by cutting taxes, policies that were very much like those of Nixon and Ford. He advanced an admirable if complicated plan for conserving energy and reducing the dependence of the United States on OPEC oil. This plan would raise the tax on

The skyrocketing price of oil caused many to champion nuclear energy. But on March 28, 1979, the failure of a cooling system caused the Three Mile Island nuclear reactor to overheat and generate radioactivity in the Harrisburg region. The reactor was shut down five days later.

gasoline and impose a new tax on "gas guzzlers," cars that got relatively few miles per gallon. But in his typical fashion he did not press hard for these measures.

The federal government made matters worse in several ways. Wages and salaries rose in response to inflation, but taxes went up more rapidly because larger dollar incomes put people in higher tax brackets. This "bracket creep" caused resentment and frustration among middle-class families. "Taxpayer revolts" erupted as many people turned against expensive government programs for aiding the poor. Federal borrowing to cover the deficit pushed up interest rates and increased the costs of all businesses that had to borrow.

Soaring mortgage rates made it difficult to sell homes. The housing slump meant unemployment for thousands of carpenters, bricklayers, and other construction workers and bankruptcy for many builders. Double-digit interest rates also hurt small businesses seeking to expand. Savings and loan institutions were especially hard-hit because they were saddled with countless mortgages made when rates were as low as 4 and 5 percent. Now they had to pay much more than that to hold deposits and offer even higher rates to attract new money.

Bad as inflation was in the mid-1970s, it got worse in 1979 when further instability in the Middle East nearly tripled the price of oil, which now reached $34 a barrel. This sent gasoline far over the $1 a gallon price barrier many had thought inconceivable. Within months Ford stock, at thirty-two in 1978, plummeted to sixteen; its credit rating with Standard and Poor's fell from AAA to an ignominious BBB. Chrysler, the third largest automaker, tottered near bankruptcy and then fell over the edge, saved in mid-fall only by a $1.2 billion federal loan guarantee. From 1978 to 1982, the jobs of one in three autoworkers were eliminated.

"Constant Decency" in Action

In contrast to the shadowy dealings of the Nixon-Kissinger years, Carter promised to conduct a foreign policy characterized by "constant decency." The defense of "basic human rights" would come before all other concerns. He then cut off aid to Chile and Argentina because of human rights violations. He also negotiated treaties with Panama that provided for the gradual transfer of the Panama Canal to that nation and guaranteed the canal's neutrality. But he said little about what was going on in a long list of other nations whose citizens' rights were being repressed.

The president also intended to carry forward the Nixon-Kissinger policy of détente, and in 1979 another Strategic Arms Limitation Treaty (SALT II) was signed with the Soviet Union. But the following winter the Soviet Union sent troops into Afghanistan to overthrow the government there. Carter denounced the invasion and warned the Soviets that he would use force if they invaded any of the countries bordering the Persian Gulf. He withdrew the SALT treaty, which he had sent to the Senate for ratification. He also refused to allow American athletes to compete in the 1980 Olympic games in Moscow.

Carter's one striking diplomatic achievement was the so-called **Camp David Accords** between Israel and Egypt. In September 1978 President Anwar Sadat of Egypt and Prime Minister Menachem Begin of Israel came to the United States at Carter's invitation to seek a peace treaty ending the state of war that had existed between their two countries for many years.

For two weeks they conferred at Camp David, the presidential retreat outside the capital, and Carter's mediation had much to do with their successful negotiations.

In the treaty Israel promised to withdraw from territory captured from Egypt during the 1967 Israeli-Egypt war. Egypt in turn recognized Israel as a nation, the first Arab country to do so. Peace ensured an uninterrupted supply of Arab oil to the United States. The Camp David Accords were the first and, as it turned out, the last significant agreement between Israel and a major Arab state.

The Iran Crisis: Origins

At this point a dramatic shift in Iran thrust Carter into the spotlight as never before. On November 4, 1979, about 400 armed Muslim militants broke into the American embassy compound in Tehran, Iran, and took everyone within the walls captive.

The seizure had roots that ran far back in Iranian history. During World War II, Great Britain, the Soviet Union, and later the United States occupied Iran and forced its pro-German shah into exile, replacing him with his twenty-two-year-old son, Muhammad Reza Pahlavi. But in the early 1950s power shifted to Prime Minister Muhammad Mossadegh, a leftist who sought to finance social reform by nationalizing the mostly American-owned Anglo-Iranian Oil Company.

In 1953, the Iranian army, backed by the CIA, arrested Mossadegh and put the young Pahlavi in power. The fall of Mossadegh ensured a steady flow of cheap oil, but it turned most Iranians against the United States and Shah Pahlavi. His unpopularity led the shah to purchase enormous amounts of American arms. Over the years Iran became the most powerful military force in the region.

The shah's rule was not one of "constant decency." His secret police, the Savak, brutally suppressed liberal opponents. At the same time, Muslim religious leaders were particularly offended by the shah's attempts to introduce Western ideas and technology into Iran. Because his American-supplied army and his American- and Israeli-trained secret police kept the shah in power, his opponents hated the United States almost as much as they hated their autocratic ruler.

Throughout 1977, riots and demonstrations convulsed Iran. When soldiers fired on protesters, the bloodshed caused more unrest, and that unrest caused even more bloodshed. Over 10,000 civilians were killed; many times that number were wounded. In 1978 the whole country seemed to rise against the shah. Finally, in January 1979, he was forced to flee. A revolutionary government headed by a religious leader, the Ayatollah Ruhollah Khomeini, assumed power. Freedom, he said, was the great enemy of Islam. He also claimed that Islam condoned terror: "Islam says: Whatever good there is exists thanks to the sword and in the shadow of the sword! . . . The sword is the key to paradise, which can be opened only for holy warriors."

Khomeini denounced the United States, the "Great Satan," whose support of the shah, he said, had caused the Iranian people untold suffering. When President Carter allowed the shah to come to the United States for medical treatment, militants in Tehran seized the American embassy.

The Iran Crisis: Carter's Dilemma

The militants announced that the Americans at the embassy would be held hostage until the United States returned the shah to Iran for trial as a traitor. They also demanded that the shah's vast wealth be confiscated and surrendered to the Iranian government. President

Carter rejected these demands. Instead Carter froze Iranian assets in the United States and banned trade with Iran until the hostages were freed.

A stalemate developed. Months passed. Even after the shah, who was terminally ill, left the United States for Panama, the Iranians remained adamant. The **Iranian hostage crisis** produced a remarkable emotional response in the United States. For the first time since the Vietnam War the entire country agreed on something.

In 1979 Islamic militants hold an American embassy worker in Tehran.

Nevertheless the hostages languished in Iran. In April 1980 Carter finally ordered a team of marine commandos flown into Iran in a desperate attempt to free the hostages. The raid was a fiasco. Several helicopters broke down when their rotors sucked desert sand into the engines. Another helicopter crashed and eight commandos were killed. The Iranians made political capital of the incident, gleefully displaying on television the wrecked aircraft and captured American equipment. The stalemate continued. When the shah died in exile in Egypt in July 1980, the Iranians made no move to release the hostages.

The Election of 1980

Despite the failure of the raid and the persistence of stagflation, Carter had more than enough delegates at the Democratic convention to win renomination on the first ballot. His Republican opponent in the campaign that followed was Ronald Reagan.

Reagan had grown up a New Deal Democrat, but during and immediately after World War II he became disillusioned with liberalism. As president of the Screen Actors Guild he attacked the influence of communists in the movie industry. After his movie career ended, Reagan did publicity for General Electric until 1960, then worked for various conservative causes. In 1966 he ran for governor of California, and struck a responsive chord by attacking the counterculture. He won the election and was easily reelected.

Both Carter and Reagan spent much of the 1980 campaign explaining why the other was unsuited to be president. Carter defended his record, though without much conviction. Reagan denounced criminals, drug addicts, and all varieties of immorality and spoke in support of patriotism, religion, family life, and other "old-fashioned" virtues. This won him the enthusiastic backing of fundamentalist religious sects and other conservative groups. He also called for increased spending on defense, and he promised to transfer some functions of the federal government to the states and to cut taxes. He insisted at the same time that the budget could be balanced and inflation sharply reduced.

On election day the voting was light, but Reagan received 8 million more votes than Carter. Dissatisfaction with the economy and the unresolved hostage crisis seem to have determined the result. The Republicans also gained control of the Senate and cut deeply into the Democratic majority in the House of Representatives.

Carter devoted his last weeks in office to the continuing hostage crisis. War had broken out between Iran and Iraq in September. The Iraqi president, Saddam Hussein, had hoped to exploit the chaos following the downfall of the shah to seize oil-rich territory in Iran. Early Iraqi victories prompted the Iranians to free the hostages in return for the release of Iranian assets that had been frozen in the United States. After 444 days in captivity, the fifty-two hostages were set free on January 20, the day Reagan was inaugurated.

Reagan as President

Reagan hoped to change the direction in which the country was moving. He demanded steep reductions in federal spending and the deficit, to be accomplished by cutting social expenditures such as welfare, food stamps and student loans, and by turning many functions of the federal government over to the states. The marketplace, not federal bureaucratic regulations, should govern most economic decisions.

He asked Congress to lower income taxes by 30 percent. When critics objected that this would increase the deficit, the president and his advisers reasoned that the tax cut would leave people with more money, which they would invest in productive ways. The new investment would generate more goods and jobs—and, ultimately, taxes for the federal government. This scheme became known as **Reaganomics**.

Helped by the votes of conservative Democrats, Reagan won congressional approval of the Budget Reconciliation Act, which reduced government expenditures on domestic programs by $39 billion.

Congress enacted most of the tax cuts the president had asked for, lowering individual income taxes by 25 percent over three years, but it resisted reducing the politically popular "entitlement" programs, such as Social Security and Medicare, which accounted for about half of the budget. Reagan himself refused to reduce the military budget to bring the government's income more nearly in line with its outlays. Instead he called for a military buildup

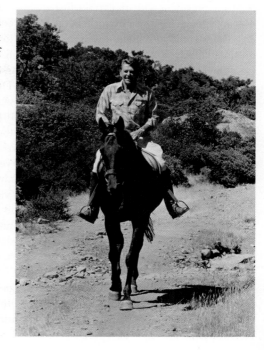

Ronald Reagan rides a horse—a familiar photo opportunity for presidents. (Recall the similar picture of LBJ on page 768.) But Reagan was an amiable cowboy; his smile and sense of humor were his most disarming weapons. In 1966 just after the election, when reporters asked him what sort of governor he would be, Reagan, a former actor, answered, "I don't know. I've never played a governor." Three months into his presidency, moments after he was seriously wounded in an assassination attempt, he took his wife's hand. "Honey," he said, "I forgot to duck." While being wheeled into the operating room, he quipped to the surgeons, "I hope you are all Republicans."

Read the **Document**

Reagan, *Air Traffic Controllers' Strike (1981)* at **myhistorylab.com**

to ensure that the United States would prevail in any war with the Soviet Union, which he called an "evil empire." In particular, he sought to expand and improve the nation's nuclear arsenal. He made no secret of his wish to create so formidable a nuclear force that the Soviets would have to back down in any confrontation. The deficit worsened.

In Central America Reagan sought the overthrow of the left-wing government of Nicaragua and the defeat of communist rebels in El Salvador. He even used American troops to overthrow a Cuban-backed regime on the tiny Caribbean island of Grenada. When criticized for opposing leftist regimes while backing rightist dictators, Jeane Kirkpatrick, U.S. ambassador to the United Nations, explained that "rightist authoritarian regimes can be transformed peacefully into democracies, but totalitarian Marxist ones cannot."

In 1982 the continuing turmoil in the Middle East thrust the Reagan administration into a new crisis. Israel had invaded Lebanon to destroy Palestine Liberation Organization units that were staging raids on northern Israeli settlements. Israeli troops easily overran much of the country, but in the process the Lebanese government disintegrated. Reagan agreed to commit American troops to an international peacekeeping force.

Tragedy resulted in October 1983 when a fanatical Muslim crashed a truck loaded with explosives into a building housing American marines in Beirut. The building collapsed, killing 239 marines. Early the next year, Reagan removed the entire American peacekeeping force from Lebanon.

Four More Years

A sitting president with an extraordinarily high standing in public opinion polls, Reagan was nominated for a second term at the 1984 Republican convention without opposition. The Democratic nomination went to Walter Mondale of Minnesota, who had been vice president under Carter. Mondale electrified the country by choosing Representative Geraldine Ferraro of New York as his running mate. An Italian American and a Catholic, Ferraro was expected to appeal to conservative Democrats who had supported Reagan in 1980 and to win the votes of many Republican women.

Reagan began the campaign with several important advantages. He was especially popular among religious fundamentalists and other social conservatives, and these groups

Watch the **Video**

Reagan Presidential Campaign Ad: A Bear in the Woods at **myhistorylab.com**

were increasingly vocal. Fundamentalist television preachers were almost all fervent Reaganites and the most successful of them were collecting tens of millions of dollars annually in contributions from viewers. One of these, the Reverend Jerry Falwell, founded the **Moral Majority** and set out to create a new political movement. "Americans are sick and tired of the way the amoral liberals are trying to corrupt our nation," Falwell announced in 1979.

During the first Reagan administration, the Moral Majority had become a powerful political force. Falwell denounced drugs, the "coddling" of criminals, homosexuality, communism, and abortion, all things that Reagan also disliked. Falwell also disapproved of forced busing to integrate schools. In addition, Reagan favored government aid to private schools run by church groups, something dear to the Moral Majority despite the constitutional principle of separation of church and state.

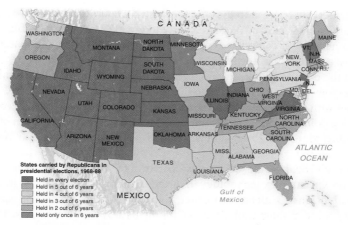

Success of the Republican "Southern Strategy" In 1968, Kevin M. Phillips, a key Nixon strategist, proposed a "southern strategy" to create an "emerging Republican majority." Many doubted that the South, which had long been opposed to the party of Lincoln, could be won over. But in presidential elections from 1968 to 1988, far more southern counties voted Republican than Democratic.

Reagan's support was also drawn from blue collar workers and white Southerners, constituencies that had been solidly Democratic during the New Deal and beyond. The president's personality was another important plus—voters continued to admire his informal yet firm style and his stress on patriotism and other "traditional" virtues.

Most polls showed Reagan far in the lead when the campaign began, and this remained true throughout the contest. Nothing Mondale or Ferraro did or said affected the president's popularity. On election day he got nearly 60 percent of the popular vote and lost only in Minnesota, Mondale's home state, and in the District of Columbia. Reagan's Electoral College margin was overwhelming, 525 to 13.

Reagan's triumph, like the two landslide victories of Dwight Eisenhower in the 1950s, was a personal one. The Republicans made only minor gains in the House of Representatives and actually lost two seats in the Senate.

"The Reagan Revolution"

Reagan's agenda for his second term closely resembled that of his first. In foreign affairs, he ran into continuing congressional resistance to his requests for military support for his anticommunist crusade. This was particularly true after Mikhail S. Gorbachev became the Soviet premier in March 1985. Gorbachev seemed far more moderate and flexible than his predecessors. He began to encourage political debate and criticism in the Soviet Union—the policy known as *glasnost* (openness)—and he sought to stimulate the stagnant Soviet economy by decentralizing administration and rewarding individual enterprise (*perestroika*).

Gorbachev also announced that he would continue to honor the unratified SALT II agreement, whereas Reagan, arguing that the Soviet Union had not respected the limits laid down in the pact, seemed bent on pushing ahead with the expansion and modernization of America's nuclear arsenal. Reagan sought funds to develop an elaborate system of missile defenses. He referred to it as the **Strategic Defense Initiative (SDI)**, although it was popularly known as Star Wars, a reference to the 1977 George Lucas film. SDI would consist of a network of computer-controlled space stations that would detect oncoming enemy missiles and destroy them with speculative high-tech weaponry.

When the president realized that the Soviets were eager for an agreement to limit nuclear weapons, he ceased referring to the Soviet Union as an "evil empire." In October 1986 he met with Gorbachev in Iceland in search of an agreement on arms control. The chief sticking point was SDI. Gorbachev proposed instead the elimination of all nuclear weapons—including SDI. Reagan, however, was determined to push Star Wars, and the summit collapsed.

Congress balked at the enormous cost of Star Wars. Expense aside, the idea of relying on the complex technology involved in controlling machines in outer space for national defense suffered a further setback in 1986, when the space shuttle *Challenger* exploded shortly after takeoff, killing its seven-member crew. This disaster temporarily put a stop to the program.

Reagan's basic domestic objectives—to reduce the scope of federal activity, particularly in the social welfare area; to lower income taxes; and to increase the strength of the armed forces—remained constant. Despite the tax cuts already made, congressional leaders of both parties agreed to the Income Tax Act of 1986, which reduced the top levy on personal incomes from 50 percent to 28 percent and the tax on corporate profits from 46 percent to 34 percent.

[●]Watch the Video

Ronald Reagan on the Wisdom of the Tax Cut at myhistorylab.com

Reagan advanced another of his objectives more gradually. This was his appointment of conservatives to federal judgeships, including Sandra Day O'Connor, the first woman named to the Supreme Court. By 1988 Reagan had appointed three Supreme Court justices and well over half the members of the federal judiciary.

The New Merger Movement

During the Reagan years, the nation began to climb out of the recession of the 1970s. Reagan's policies helped, though often in unpredictable ways. Reagan's relaxed regulation of Wall Street helped precipitate a frenzy of corporate mergers. Deregulation provided the context for the merger movement, but the person most responsible for it was Michael Milken, a shrewd stockbroker of the firm of Drexel Burnham Lambert. Milken specialized in selling "junk bonds," the debt offerings of companies whose existing debts were already high. He persuaded savings and loan associations, insurance companies, pension funds, and other big investors to buy these junk bonds, which, though risky, offered high interest rates. The success of his initial ventures prompted Milken to approach smaller companies, encourage them to borrow immense sums by floating junk bonds, and use the proceeds to acquire larger firms.

In 1985 Ronald Perelman, an aggressive entrepreneur, employed this strategy to perfection. He had recently obtained control of Pantry Pride, a supermarket chain with a net worth of about $145 million. Now he sought to acquire Revlon, a $2 billion cosmetics and health care conglomerate. With Milken's help, Pantry Pride borrowed $1.5 billion and used that capital to buy Revlon. He then paid off Pantry Pride's $1.5 billion in junk bonds ("junk" because the debt so greatly exceeded the $145 million value of Pantry Pride) by selling huge chunks of Revlon. Then he integrated the food component of Revlon into Pantry Pride.

The bond purchasers profited handsomely from the high return on the junk bonds, and Perelman made a fortune from his new food conglomerate. That same year the R. J. Reynolds Tobacco Company purchased Nabisco for $4.9 billion. Three years later this new giant, RJR Nabisco, was itself taken over by Kohlberg, Kravis, Roberts, and Company for $24.9 billion.

Workers at a Nike factory in Indonesia insert soles into sneakers.

During the frenzied decade of the 1980s, one-fifth of the *Fortune* 500 companies were taken over, merged, or forced to go private; in all, some 25,000 mergers and acquisitions were successfully undertaken; their total value was nearly a half-trillion dollars. To make their companies less tempting to cash-hungry raiders, many corporations took on whopping debts or acquired unprofitable companies. By the late 1980s, many American corporations were wallowing in red ink. Debt payments were gobbling up 50 percent of the nation's corporate pretax earnings.

Read the Document

Paul Craig Roberts, *The Supply-Side Revolution (1984)* at **myhistorylab.com**

"A Job for Life": Layoffs Hit Home

Most corporations coped with the debt in two ways: They sold assets, such as factories, offices, and warehouses; or they cut costs through layoffs. U.S. Steel, whose rusting mills desperately needed an infusion of capital, instead spent $5 billion to acquire Marathon Oil of Ohio; that decision meant that nearly 100,000 steelworkers lost their jobs. No firm was immune, nor any worker secure. During the 1980s, the total number of employees who worked for *Fortune* 500 companies declined by three million; nearly one-third of all positions in middle management were eliminated.

Many of the jobs went abroad, where labor costs were lower and unions nonexistent. In 1984 Nike moved sewing operations to Indonesia, where it could hire female workers for fourteen cents an hour. In 1986 the chassis for the Mustang, long a symbol of American automotive style, was built by Mazda in Hiroshima, Japan.

Towering mountains of private corporate debt nearly were overshadowed by the Everest of public debt held by the federal government itself. Reagan's insistence on a sharp cut in personal taxes and a substantial increase in military expenditures produced huge—and growing—annual federal deficits. When Reagan took office, the total federal debt was $900 million; eight years later, it exceeded $2.5 *trillion*.

Corporate Restructuring

Although few perceived it at the time, the economy was undergoing a transformation of historic dimensions. Much as the depression after 1893 had strengthened the nation's economy by wiping out thousands of inefficient steel and machinery firms, the seismic

BILL GATES

"Project Breakthrough! World's First Minicomputer Kit to Rival Commercial Models." This headline in the January 1975 issue of *Popular Electronics* triggered the neurons in Bill Gates's brain. In an instant, he perceived that the revolution had begun. Most earlier computers cost hundreds of thousands of dollars, filled room-sized air-conditioned vaults, and were found in university science centers, government agencies, and corporate headquarters. But this kit cost only $397. The computer (its name—*Altair*—came from a planet in the TV series *Star Trek*), could fit on a desktop. Gates believed that computers like this would soon be as much a part of life as telephones or automobiles. Armed with the slogan, "A computer on every desktop," Gates resolved to become the Henry Ford of the computer revolution (and to become, like Ford, immensely rich). He was twenty years old.

Gates recognized Altair's fatal flaw: It did little more than cause a few lights to blink in complex ways. It lacked internal instructions to convert electrical signals into letters and numbers. He determined to write instructions—the software—to make the personal computer useful. Gates and Paul Allen, a school friend, telephoned Ed Roberts, the president of MITS, manufacturer of the Altair. They told him they had written operating software for the machine. Roberts was skeptical. Scores of programmers had made such claims, he said, but none had actually done it. He told them to bring their software to the company headquarters in Albuquerque, New Mexico, within two months. Allen and Gates were euphoric, but not for long: They had not even begun to write a program for the Altair.

The boys had met in 1967 at Lakeside, an elite private school in Seattle, when Gates was in seventh grade, Allen in ninth. That year, the Lakeside Mothers Club had bought time on a digital training terminal that connected by phone to a company that leased a mainframe computer. Within weeks of its installation, this computer had become Gates's life. He remained in the terminal room after school and late into the evenings, breaking only for Coke and pizza. "He lived and breathed computers," a friend recalled.

Gates learned programming by writing programs and seeing what worked. His first was for playing tic-tac-toe. He also designed a program for student schedules at Lakeside. He placed "all the good girls in the school" (and very few males of any kind) in his own classes—an early manifestation of his penchant for defeating competitors by conniving to eliminate them.

Bill Gates as a young CEO at Microsoft.

Although his father was a wealthy corporate attorney and his mother a prominent socialite, Gates was preoccupied with making money. In high school he took a job tabulating automobile traffic data; this required that he count the holes in a roll of paper punched out when automobiles passed over a hose. He designed a computerized machine to count and analyze the data and he formed a company, Traf-O-Data, to build and market the device. But, Traf-O-Data failed to attract many customers—most municipalities and highway departments lost interest when they learned that the company was run by high school students.

Gates and Allen completed the program just hours before Allen boarded the plane to Albuquerque. (Allen went because he was older and presumably a more credible "corporate" spokesman.) The next morning, Allen fed long rolls of punched yellow paper tape—the software—into an Altair while company executives looked on skeptically. For fifteen minutes the machine clattered away. Misgivings mounted. Then the teletype printed the word, "READY." Allen typed, "PRINT 2 + 2." The teletype spat out "4." The program worked. Gates and Allen had a deal.

Gates dropped out of Harvard and formed a partnership with Allen. They called their company Microsoft and moved to Albuquerque. They wrote operating programs for personal computers introduced by Apple, Commodore, and Radio Shack. Soon money was pouring into Microsoft. In 1979 they moved Microsoft to Bellevue, Washington, near Seattle. Then came the blockbuster.

In 1980 IBM, the world's foremost manufacturer of mainframe computers, belatedly entered the home computer market. IBM approached Gates to write the operating software for its new, state-of-the-art personal computer. IBM intended to keep the computer's specifications secret so that other manufacturers could not copy its design, but Gates shrewdly proposed that IBM make its specifications public. Doing so would allow the IBM personal computer to become the industry standard, giving IBM the edge in developing peripherals—printers, monitors, keyboards, and various applications. IBM agreed. Now Gates's software, called Microsoft-Disk Operating System (MS-DOS), would run every IBM personal computer as well as every computer made by other companies according to the IBM specifications. In a single stroke, Gates had virtually monopolized the market for PC operating software.

Microsoft's sales jumped from $7.5 million in 1980 to $140 million in 1985. Then Microsoft moved into software applications: word processing, accounting, and games. By 1991, Gates was the wealthiest man in the world. In 1994, he and his wife established the Bill and Melinda Gates Foundation; by 2010, it had assets of over $33 billion and gave nearly $2 billion annually to charitable causes, especially education.

Questions for Discussion

- Intelligence, ambition, business sense, or all three? In what ways did Bill Gates's triumph parallel Andrew Carnegie's a century earlier?
- What was the main prerequisite for Gates's triumph?

economic upheavals after 1973 toppled many inefficient manufacturers but created the foundations for more efficient global conglomerates. As weeds grew in the parking lots of the factories of the "Rust Belt" of the Midwest, new technology industries sprouted in the "Silicon Valley" of California, along Route 128 outside of Boston, and in booming cities such as Seattle, Washington, and Austin, Texas.

By the end of the Reagan era, the economy consisted of two separate and increasingly unequal components: a battered sector of traditional heavy industry, characterized by declining wages and diminishing job opportunities; and an advancing high-tech and service sector dominated by aggressive, innovative, and individualistic entrepreneurs. (See American Lives, "Bill Gates," pp. 368–369.) The older corporations that survived the shakeout of the 1980s were leaner and better equipped to compete in expanding global markets.

A worker studies a lighted diagram of an integrated circuit at a California computer factory.

Yet American society was becoming as fractured as the "bipolar" economy from which it drew sustenance. The Reagan tax cuts had disproportionately benefited the wealthy, as had the extraordinary rise of the stock market. Conversely, the economic transformation struck low- or semiskilled wage earners hardest. At the end of Reagan's second term the standard of living of the poorest fifth of the population (40 million people) was 9 percent lower than it had been in 1979, while that of the wealthiest fifth had risen about 20 percent.

Rogue Foreign Policy

Especially during his second term as president, Reagan paid little attention to the details of administration. Thus two major initiatives unfolded of which Reagan himself claimed little knowledge.

The first concerned Nicaragua. In 1979 leftist rebels had overthrown the dictatorial regime of Anastasio Somoza. Because the victorious Sandinista government was supported by both Cuba and the Soviet Union, Reagan was determined to force it from power. He backed anti-Sandinista elements in Nicaragua known as the Contras and in 1981 persuaded Congress to provide these "freedom fighters" with arms.

But the Contras made little progress, and many Americans feared that aiding them would lead, as it had in Vietnam, to the use of American troops in the fighting. In October 1984 Congress banned further military aid to

◆●●─[**Read** the **Document**

Reagan, *Support for the Contras (1984)* at **myhistorylab.com**

the Contra rebels. Reagan then sought to persuade other countries and private American groups to help the Contras (as he put it) keep "body and soul together."

Marine Colonel Oliver North, an aide of Reagan's national security adviser, devised a scheme to indirectly funnel federal money to the Contras. He inflated the price of U.S. weapons, sold them to Iran[1], and secretly transferred the profits to the Contras. This plainly violated the congressional ban on such aid.

When North's stratagem came to light in November 1986, he was fired from his job with the security council. Reagan insisted that he knew nothing about the aid to the Contras. Critics pointed out that if he was telling the truth it was almost as bad since that meant that he had not been able to control his own administration.

Meanwhile, the Soviet invasion of Afghanistan in 1980 enraged Charles Wilson, a Democratic congressman from Texas. (Wilson, a womanizer, heavy drinker, and alleged cocaine-user, was played by Tom Hanks in the movie, *Charlie Wilson's War* [2007]). Wilson persuaded his colleagues to allocate money for the *mujahideen*, Muslim warriors who were trying to drive the Soviets out of their country. Within several years the Afghan tribes, especially Islamist radicals known as the Taliban, were covertly receiving hundreds of millions of dollars in weapons. Muslim insurgents ambushed convoys, mined roads, and engaged in various acts of terrorism. Soviet casualties increased, as did the cost of the war. Soviet generals began referring to the war in Afghanistan as "our Vietnam." In 1989 the Soviets pulled out; in 1996 the Taliban took over Afghanistan and instituted a radical Islamic state.

Assessing the Reagan Revolution

Reagan was not an able administrator; the **Iran-Contra affair** and financial scandals of his administration did not stick to him because he was seldom close enough to the action to get splattered by it. He articulated, simply and persuasively, a handful of concepts—chiefly the "evil" character of Soviet communism, the need to get government off people's backs—and in so doing created a political climate conducive

Mujahideen in Afghanistan stand on top of a Soviet helicopter they shot down with U.S.-supplied Stinger missiles in the early 1980s.

---

[1]Earlier in the Iran-Iraq war, when Iran appeared on the verge of defeating Iraq, Reagan had provided $500 million a year in credits to allow Iraq's Saddam Hussein to buy armaments. If either Iran or Iraq won decisively, it could control the flow of Middle Eastern oil. The United States therefore preferred a stalemate.

to change. Reagan was directly responsible for neither of the great transformations of the late twentieth century—the restructuring of American corporations and the collapse of the Soviet Union. Yet his actions and, indeed, his failures to act indisputably influenced them. His decision to increase military spending and undertake the fantastically expensive SDI ("Star Wars") forced Gorbachev to seek an accommodation with the United States. Reagan's tax cuts precipitated unimaginably large federal deficits, and deregulation unloosed a sordid pack of predators who preyed on the economy. Yet the ensuing Darwinian chaos strengthened those corporations that survived and gave them the muscle to prevail in emerging global markets.

The Election of 1988

The issues that had dominated American politics for over a decade—the Soviet threat, the energy crisis, stagflation—were gone. The presidential election of 1988 initially lacked focus. The selection of Vice President George H. W. Bush as the Republican nomination was a foregone conclusion. Bush, the son of a Connecticut senator, had served as a pilot during World War II and then settled in Texas, where he worked in the family's oil business and became active in Republican politics. From 1971 to 1973 he served as ambassador to the UN and from 1976 to 1977 as director of the CIA. As Republican presidential hopeful, he trumpeted his experience as vice president.

The Democratic race was far more complicated but scarcely more inspiring. So many lackluster candidates entered the field that wits called them "the seven dwarfs." But eventually Governor Michael Dukakis of Massachusetts, stressing his record as an efficient manager, accumulated delegates steadily and won the nomination.

During the campaign, Bush attacked Dukakis as a liberal governor who had been soft on crime. Lee Atwater, campaign manager for Bush, produced and aired a television advertisement showing prisoners, many of them black, streaming through a revolving door. Dukakis's attempts to shift the focus away from crime failed. The presidential campaign became, in effect, a referendum on crime in which Dukakis failed the toughness test. Bush won 54 percent of the vote and carried the Electoral College, 426 to 112.

George H. W. Bush as President

In 1989 President Bush, having attacked Dukakis for being soft on crime, named a "drug czar" to coordinate various bureaucracies, increased federal funding of local police, and spent $2.5 billion to stop the flow of illegal drugs into the nation. Although the campaign generated plenty of arrests, drugs continued to pour in: As one dealer or trafficker was arrested, another took his place. Bush also worked to shed the tough image he had cultivated during the campaign. In his inaugural address he said that he hoped to "make kinder the face of the nation and gentler the face of the world." He also displayed a more traditional command of the workings of government and the details of current events than his predecessor. At the same time he pleased right-wing Reagan loyalists by his opposition to abortion and gun control, and by calling for a constitutional amendment prohibiting the burning of the American flag. His standing in the polls soared.

The Collapse of Communism in Eastern Europe

One important reason for this was the flood of good news from abroad. The reforms instituted in the Soviet Union by Gorbachev led to demands from its Eastern European satellites for similar liberalization. Gorbachev responded by announcing that the Soviet Union would not use force to keep communist governments in power in these nations. Swiftly the people of Poland, Hungary, Czechoslovakia, Bulgaria, Romania, East Germany, and the Baltics did away with the repressive regimes that had ruled them throughout the postwar era. Except in Romania, where the dictator Nicolae Ceausescu was executed, all these fundamental changes were carried out peacefully.

Almost overnight the international political climate changed. Soviet-style communism had been discredited. A Soviet attack anywhere was almost unthinkable. The Cold War was over.

President Bush profited from these developments immensely. He expressed moral support for the new governments but he refrained from embarrassing the Soviets. At a summit meeting in Washington in June 1990 Bush and Gorbachev signed agreements reducing American and Russian stockpiles of long-range nuclear missiles by 30 percent and eliminating chemical weapons.

The Collapse of Communism in Eastern Europe When Gorbachev withdrew Soviet troops from Eastern Europe, the communist regimes there collapsed rapidly. The Soviet Union itself disintegrated.

In 1989 President Bush sent troops to Panama to overthrow General Manuel Noriega, who had refused to yield power when his figurehead presidential candidate lost a national election. Noriega was under indictment in the United States for drug trafficking. After temporarily seeking refuge in the Vatican embassy in Panama, he surrendered to the American forces and was taken to the United States, where he was tried, convicted, and imprisoned.

Meanwhile, in the Soviet Union, nationalist and anticommunist groups demanded more local control of their affairs. President Gorbachev, who opposed this breakup, sought compromise, backing a draft treaty that would increase local autonomy and further privatize the Soviet economy. In August, however, before this treaty could be ratified, hard-line communists attempted a coup. They arrested Gorbachev, who was vacationing in the Crimea, and ordered tanks into Moscow. But Boris Yeltsin, the anticommunist president of the Russian Republic, defied the rebels and roused the people of Moscow. The coup swiftly collapsed. Its leaders were arrested, the communist party was officially disbanded, and the Soviet Union itself was replaced by a federation of states, of which Russia, led by Yeltsin, was the most important. Gorbachev, who had begun the process of liberation, found himself without a job.

The War in the Persian Gulf

Although Reagan had provided economic assistance to Saddam Hussein of Iraq to prevent Iran from winning the Iran-Iraq war, few in the administration were enthusiastic about the Iraqi dictator. For years Saddam had been crushing the Kurds, an ethnic minority in northern Iraq that sought independence. In 1987 the U.S. State Department reported on his "widespread destruction and bulldozing of Kurdish villages." In March 1988, after Kurdish rebels had supported an Iranian advance into Iraq near Halabja, a mostly Kurdish city, Saddam's troops dropped mustard gas, sarin, and other chemical weapons on the city. Some 5,000 civilians died.

In August 1990, Saddam launched an all-out attack on Iraq's tiny neighbor to the south, the oil-rich sheikdom of Kuwait. Saddam hoped to swallow up Kuwait, thus increasing Iraq's already large oil reserves to about 25 percent of the world's total. His soldiers overran Kuwait swiftly, then systematically carried off everything of value they could bring back to Iraq. Within a week Saddam annexed Kuwait and massed troops along the border of neighboring Saudi Arabia.

The Saudis and the Kuwaitis turned to the United States and other nations for help, and it was quickly given. In a matter of days the UN applied trade sanctions against Iraq, and at the invitation of Saudi Arabia, the United States (along with Great Britain, France, Italy, Egypt, and Syria) moved troops to Saudi bases. Many Muslims opposed the presence of non-Muslim troops on Saudi soil; but the Saudi ruling family overruled them, fearing an Iraqi invasion.

By November, Bush had increased the American troops in the area from 180,000 to more than 500,000, part of a larger UN operation. On January 17, the Americans unleashed an enormous air attack, directed by General Norman Schwarzkopf. This air assault went on for nearly a month, and it reduced much of Iraq to rubble. The Iraqi forces, aside from firing a number of Scud missiles at Israel and Saudi Arabia and

[Watch the Video

President Bush on the Gulf War at **myhistorylab.com**

The Middle East In February 1991, combined U.S., British, French, and Arab armies drove Saddam Hussein from Kuwait and invaded Iraq.

setting fire to hundreds of Kuwaiti oil wells, simply endured the rain of destruction that fell on them daily.

On February 23 Bush issued an ultimatum to Saddam: Pull out of Kuwait or face an invasion. When Saddam ignored the deadline, UN troops (most under U.S. command) attacked. Bush called the assault "Desert Storm." Between February 24 and February 27 they retook Kuwait, killing tens of thousands of Iraqis. Some 4,000 Iraqi tanks and enormous quantities of other military equipment were destroyed.

Bush then stopped the attack, and Saddam agreed to UN terms that included paying reparations to Kuwait, allowing UN inspectors to determine whether Iraq was developing atomic and biological weapons, and agreeing to keep its airplanes out of "no-fly" zones over Kurdish territory and other strategic areas. Polls indicated that about 90 percent of the American people approved both the president's management of the **Persian Gulf War** and his overall performance as chief executive. These were the highest presidential approval ratings ever recorded.

President Bush and most observers expected Saddam to be driven from power in disgrace by his own people. Indeed, Bush publicly urged the Iraqis to do so. The Kurds in northern Iraq and pro-Iranian Muslims in the south then took up arms, but Saddam used the remnants of his army to crush them. He also refused repeatedly to carry out the terms of the peace agreement. This led critics to argue that Bush should not have stopped the fighting until Baghdad, the Iraqi capital, had been captured and Saddam's army destroyed.

Deficits

The huge cost of the Persian Gulf War exacerbated the federal deficit. Candidate Bush had promised not to raise taxes. As president he recommitted himself to that objective; in fact he even proposed reducing the tax on capital gains. But like his conservative predecessor, Bush could not control the deficit. Congress obstinately resisted closing local military bases or cutting funding for favored defense contractors. Reducing nonmilitary expenditures, especially popular entitlement programs such as Medicare and Social Security, also proved nearly impossible.

The deficit for 1992 hit $290 billion. Bush had no choice but to join with Congress in raising the top income tax rate from 28 percent to 31 percent and levying higher taxes on gasoline, liquor, expensive automobiles, and certain other luxuries. This damaged his credibility and angered conservative Republicans. "Read my lips," critics muttered, "No more Bush."

Another drain on the federal treasury resulted from the demise of hundreds of federally insured savings and loan institutions (S&Ls). S&Ls had traditionally played an important role in nearly every community, and a secure if sleepy niche in the economy: home mortgages. In the 1980s Congress permitted S&Ls to enter the more lucrative but riskier business of commercial loans and stock investments. This attracted a swarm of aggressive investors who acquired S&Ls and invested company assets in high-yield but risky junk bonds and real estate deals.

In October 1987 the stock market crashed, rendering worthless the assets held by many of the S&Ls. Hundreds were plunged into bankruptcy. In 1988 Michael Milken, the junk bond "guru," was indicted on ninety-eight charges of fraud, stock manipulation, and insider trading. He pleaded guilty, agreed to pay $1.3 billion in compensation, and was sent to jail. Drexel Burnham Lambert, his investment firm, filed for bankruptcy. The junk bond market collapsed.

Because S&L deposits were insured by the federal government, taxpayers were forced to cover the losses. The reserve fund for such purposes—$5 billion—was quickly exhausted. In 1991 Congress allocated $70 billion to close the failing S&Ls, liquidate their assets, and pay off depositors. The Justice Department charged nearly a thousand people for criminal involvement in a mess that, according to most estimates, would eventually cost taxpayers $500 billion.

During the preceding two decades, the American nation, like the automobiles that stretched for blocks in line to buy gasoline during the oil embargo, had been running on empty. The federal government was deeply in debt. Corporations had exhausted their cash reserves. Workers lived in fear of the layoff or bank foreclosure notice. Gone were the fanciful expressions of an earlier era—long and wide-bodied chassis, roaring

V-8 engines, sweeping tail fins, chromium grills like the jaws of a barracuda. Most cars had become simple boxes, trimmed with plastic, whose efficient four-cylinder engines thrummed steadily.

The nation's aspirations, like its cars, had become smaller, more sensible. Politicians muted their rhetoric, rarely issuing grandiose declarations of war against some intractable foe of humanity. Corporate executives spoke of "downsizing" firms rather than building them into empires. And the American people increasingly hunkered down in their own private spaces, which they locked up and wired with alarms.

Milestones

1973	Israel, aided by United States, defeats Egypt and Syria	1981	Iran releases U.S. hostages
1973–1974	Arabs impose oil embargo		Reagan appoints Sandra Day O'Connor to Supreme Court
1974–1976	Gerald Ford serves as president after Nixon's resignation	1981–1988	War persists between Iran and Iraq
		1984	Reagan is reelected president
1975	North Vietnam defeats South Vietnam; Saigon is renamed Ho Chi Minh City.	1985	Mikhail Gorbachev becomes premier of the Soviet Union
1976	Jimmy Carter is elected president	1986	Reagan secretly sells arms to Iran to finance Nicaraguan Contras
1978	Egypt and Israel sign Camp David Accords	1988	Republican George H. W. Bush elected president
1979	Jerry Falwell founds the Moral Majority		
	Muslim militants seize U.S. Embassy in Tehran, Iran	1989	Gorbachev allows Eastern European nations to establish independent democratic governments
	United States recognizes People's Republic of China	1990	Iraq invades Kuwait
1980	Soviet troops invade Afghanistan	1991	UN forces, led by the United States, drive Iraqi forces from Kuwait
	U.S. rescue mission in Iran fails		
	Ronald Reagan is elected president		Soviet Union is dissolved; Boris Yeltsin becomes president of Russia
1980s	Entrepreneurs' merger movement leads to huge corporate debt		

✓●─[Study and Review at www.myhistorylab.com

Review Questions

1. The introduction to this chapter suggests that cheap oil and gas have long been prominent in American politics. How did the oil shortage of the 1970s affect politics? What was its impact on the economy? In what sense was "stagflation" weird?

2. Did Carter realize his hopes for a foreign policy based on "constant decency"?

3. How did Reagan contribute to corporate restructuring? What was the impact of the merger movement on the American economy generally? What new industries emerged in the late 1980s and 1990s?

4. Why did the Soviet Union collapse? What role, if any, did Reagan play in its demise?

5. Why did George H. W. Bush go to war with Iraq? Why, having defeated the Iraqi army, didn't he seize Baghdad and remove Saddam Hussein from power?

Key Terms

Camp David
   Accords *792*
Iran-Contra affair *803*
Iranian hostage
   crisis *794*

Moral Majority *796*
Organization of Petroleum
   Exporting Countries
   (OPEC) *788*
Persian Gulf War *807*

Reaganomics *795*
stagflation *791*
Strategic Defense
   Initiative
   (SDI) *798*

From Boomers to Millennials

31

((•─|Hear the Audio Chapter 31 at myhistorylab.com

Why do you go to college?

EVERY YEAR SINCE 1966, THE UCLA SCHOOL OF EDUCATION HAS surveyed nearly a quarter of a million first-year college students. The college-aged Boomers of the late 1960s were not much different from Millennials in 2009. Then as now, the great majority regarded themselves as "middle-of-the-road" in politics.

But the past forty years have witnessed a widening gulf between Boomers (born from 1946 to 1964) and Millennials (born after 1980). One example relates to life goals. According to the survey, when Boomers were in their freshman year of college, about three-fourths believed that "acquiring a meaningful philosophy of life" was "essential" or "very important." Only a third attached similar importance to "being well off financially." But forty years later the percentages had been nearly reversed. Over three-fourths of the Millennials entering college in 2009 believed that "being well off financially" was "essential" or "very important" while only a third thought it equally important to acquire "a meaningful philosophy of life." (The figures do not add up to 100 percent because respondents could give opinions for more than one statement.) Millennials are far more likely to seek wealth, while Boomers were more likely to seek "a meaningful philosophy of life."

One explanation is that Boomers came of age during a period of unprecedented economic growth. They were free to ponder the meaning of life because they rarely worried about finding a decent job. They could imagine brave new worlds of gender revolution and institutional transformation, of liberal treatment of criminals and immigrants, of a broader reform of society as a whole.

But the protracted recession after 1973 changed the way people looked at things. An infusion of new peoples, a liberalization of attitudes, and a transformation of institutions all suggested that society was becoming unhinged. A period of retrenchment was in order. Marriage and the family were to be preserved in familiar forms; tougher laws must be passed and criminals punished.

Through it all, the sphere of public life contracted; private concerns—such as making money—took precedence over grand social schemes. And public spaces receded as people retreated to their cars and homes, where they could interact with Facebook friends and virtual realities.

The New Immigration

A Pew poll in 2008 unearthed another major attitudinal difference between Boomers and Millennials. When asked whether immigrants strengthened the country with their hard work and talent, or burdened it because they took jobs, housing, and healthcare, the Boomers overwhelmingly (50 percent to 30 percent) regarded immigrants as a burden, while Millennials overwhelmingly (58 percent to 32 percent) thought immigrants strengthened the country. One reason for the attitudinal change is that a far higher proportion of Millennials are themselves immigrants or the children of immigrants.

See the Map
Immigration to the U.S., 1945–1990 at **myhistorylab.com**

Since 1924, immigration to the United States had been governed by a quota system that ensured that the distribution of new immigrants mirrored the nation's existing ethnic patterns (see Chapter 24, p. 632). But the Immigration Act of 1965 eliminated the old system. It instead gave preference to immigrants with specialized job skills and education, and it allowed family members to rejoin those who had immigrated earlier. In 1986, Congress offered amnesty to illegal immigrants who had long lived in the United States and penalized employers who hired illegal immigrants in the future. Many persons legalized their status under the new law, but the influx of illegal immigrants continued. Together, these laws enabled more than 25 million to immigrate to the United States from 1970 to 2000.

Asians, many of whom possessed skills in high-tech fields, benefited most from the abandonment of the "national origins" system. Of the 9 million Asians who immigrated to the United States during these years, most were from China, South Korea, India, Pakistan, and the Philippines. Following the defeat of South Vietnam and the Khmer Rouge takeover of Cambodia, some 700,000 South Vietnamese and Cambodians received refugee status.

From 1970 to 2000 the largest number of immigrants were Latinos, sometimes called Hispanics (16 million). By 2000, the Latino population of the United States (35 million) for the first time exceeded African Americans (34 million). The overwhelming majority of these Spanish-speaking immigrants

Dolores Huerta and César Chávez, leaders of the United Farm Workers, discuss their 1968 strike of grape pickers. They are framed by photographs of Robert Kennedy, campaigning for the Democratic nomination for president, and Mohandas Gandhi, leader of the non-violent protest movement that won independence for India in 1947.

were Chicanos—Mexican Americans who settled in the Southwest. (Of the nation's 35 million Hispanics, 11 million lived in California, and nearly 7 million in Texas; over 42 percent of the population of New Mexico was Latino.) In addition, several million Puerto Ricans came to the mainland United States, most of whom settled in well-established Puerto Rican neighborhoods in northeastern cities. About a million Cuban immigrants arrived in Florida during these years.

●**●●** Read the Document

LBJ Immigration Act of 1975 at **myhistorylab.com**

But immigration was far more complex than the aggregate data suggest. Dearborn, Michigan, headquarters of the Ford Motor Company, is in many ways the prototypical American city. Yet nearly a third of its 100,000 residents are Arab-speaking immigrants from Lebanon, Iraq, Yemen, and Palestine.

About 10,000 Sudanese, refugees from a genocidal war in Africa, have flocked to Omaha, Nebraska, to work in its meatpacking plants. Nearly as many Bosnians, refugees from a civil war in the Balkans, have settled in Boise, Idaho.

In many communities, the new immigrants became a significant political force. Latinos elected Latino mayors in Los Angeles, Miami, Denver, and San Antonio. César Chávez, a pivotal figure in the history of Mexican Americans (Chicanos), succeeded in bringing tens of thousands of Mexicans into his United Farm Workers union. In a series of well-publicized strikes and boycotts, Chávez and the UFW forced wage concessions from hundreds of growers in California, Texas, and the Southwest.

But the infusion of immigrants generated concern. In 1992 Patrick Buchanan, campaigning for the Republican nomination for president, warned that the migration of "millions of illegal aliens a year" from Mexico constituted "the greatest invasion" the nation had ever witnessed. By then, about one-third of the Chicanos in the United States had arrived without valid visas, usually by slipping across the long U.S. border with Mexico. Of particular concern was the fact that the Latino poverty rate—which hovered around 10 percent—was twice the national average. In 1994 California passed Proposition 187, which made illegal immigrants ("undocumented aliens") ineligible for social services, public education, and nonemergency medical services. (The U.S. Supreme Court struck the law down as an infringement of federal powers. In 2001 the Supreme Court ruled that immigrants were entitled to all the protections the Constitution afforded citizens.)

In *Who Are We?* (2004), Harvard political scientist Samuel P. Huntington warned that the massive infusion of Latinos could "divide the United States into two peoples, two cultures, and two languages." Population projections showed that by 2050 whites might become a minority. But Huntington's dichotomy was too simple. Although immigrant groups often lived in distinct neighborhoods—Mexicans on one block and Hondurans on the next—they increasingly reached across national boundaries. Local restaurants offered wide assort-

●**●●** Read the Document

Illegal Immigration Reform and Immigrant Responsibility Act of 1996 at **myhistorylab.com**

ments of ethnic fares, outdoor festivals attracted all peoples, and popular music featured a fusion of styles. Most important, immigrants increasingly ceased to think of themselves as belonging to a particular ethnic group. In 2000, nearly 7 million Americans identified themselves as "multiracial."

BARACK OBAMA

Not many thirty-three-year-olds write a memoir. But Barack Obama, who intended to write a book on race relations, instead explored the meaning of his young life.

The facts were clear enough. He was born on August 4, 1961, in Honolulu, Hawaii. His mother was Stanley (Ann) Dunham, whom a friend described as "Kansas white." His father, Barack Obama, Sr., was a Luo tribesman from Nyanza Province, Kenya, who had come to the University of Hawaii on a program to educate potential leaders of newly independent African nations. The couple had met in a Russian-language course at the university the previous year. Within a few months, Dunham was pregnant. Obama told her that he had been married in Kenya but had since divorced. Ann and Obama married in February, 1961. She was eighteen when she had Barack, Jr.

Her husband, however, had lied. Not only was he still married to a Kenyan, but he had one son by her with another on the way. In 1962, after graduating from Hawaii, he went to Harvard to pursue a graduate degree, leaving Ann and their son in Hawaii. When she went to visit him at Harvard, she brought the infant along. The trip went badly. Her husband had not told his friends about her or his wife in Kenya. Ann returned to Hawaii; it would be another ten years before she or her son saw his father again.

Ann and her son moved into her parents' two-bedroom apartment in Honolulu. She returned to college and her parents often took care of the boy, whom everyone called Barry. Several years later Ann divorced Obama—by then he had taken yet another wife—and she married an Indonesian geologist at the University of Hawaii. In 1967, Ann, her new husband and six-year-old Barry moved to the outskirts of Jakarta, Indonesia, where the family lived in a stucco house on a dirt lane. Chickens and ducks ran around the backyard and two crocodiles lived in a fenced-in pond on the property. Obama's mother had always encouraged her son to adapt to different peoples, but soon her thinking shifted. Now she realized the vast chasm separating the prospects of young people who grew up in Indonesia compared to the United States.

She enrolled in a correspondence course for elementary school children in the United States. At four each morning, she awakened Barry and together they worked through the materials. After he had completed fourth grade in Jakarta, she sent him to Honolulu to live with her parents, promising to follow within a year.

Barry's grandfather arranged for the boy to attend the elite Punahou Academy. He was one of the few African Americans in the school. When some boys teased him about living in the jungle, he invented stories about how his father was a warrior and an African prince. Obama nearly persuaded himself that this fiction was true.

When his father showed up in Honolulu for a month-long visit, Barry was appalled. What would he tell his friends? But he was also confused. His long-absent father proceeded to boss Ann and her parents

Stanley (Ann) Dunham with her son, Barack Obama, age two.

and demanded that Barry work harder in school. When Barry's teacher invited his father to give a lecture on Africa, Barry was mortified. But his father's talk was smooth and gripping. Barry's friends were impressed. His father left soon afterwards. Barry never saw him again.

As a teenager, Barry excelled at basketball; his senior year, he was on the Punahou team that won the state championship. He also wrote poetry. But he lacked motivation and managed only a B– average as a senior. He spent most of his time hanging out with slacker friends. Privately, he brooded over his father's estrangement. He coped with doubts about himself by using marijuana, booze, and cocaine. When one of his friends was busted for drug possession, Obama knew it could have been him.

His first two years at Occidental College in California were more of the same. He did little work. He was nevertheless popular with nearly everyone, navigating among different social groups with ease. "He was a hot, nice, everything-going-for-him dude," one friend recalled. "You couldn't help but like him." But issues of race weighed upon him and his black friends. After some of them teased him for using the name Barry, he began to ask people to call him Barack.

After his sophomore year, Obama transferred to Columbia University in New York. Denied campus housing as a transfer student, he lived in cheap apartments in Harlem. Then something changed. He studied, ran three miles a day, often fasted on Sundays, gave up drinking and drugs (cigarettes proved more difficult), and kept a journal to record his thoughts and poetry.

Late in the fall of his senior year, he received a phone call from Africa. His father was dead. He had been drunk and drove his car into the stump of a gum tree. Even in death, his father remained a mystery to Obama.

Obama later dreamt that he was on a long bus ride that ended up at a jail. He went in and saw his father in a cell, naked but for a cloth around his waist. As Obama entered the cell, his father teased him for being so thin. Obama embraced him and wept. His father then said that he had always loved his son.

When Obama awakened, he was crying.

Perhaps young Barack had at last reconciled with his absent father, enabling him to march toward his destiny with the singular purposefulness that became his trademark. Or perhaps he sensed that he would have to create a meaningful life through achievement of his own.

Whatever the reason, he did achieve. In 1985, after graduating from Columbia, he took a job as a community organizer in Chicago and established job training programs in schools, fought to remove asbestos in housing projects, and campaigned against drug dealers. Then he was admitted to Harvard Law School, named to the *Harvard Law Review*, and elected its president, the first black to hold this prestigious position. Afterwards he returned to Chicago to write a book; it became *Dreams from My Father* (1995), a memoir from which much of this account is taken. (The publisher has refused permission for any quotes from that book to appear in this one.) He taught constitutional law at the University of Chicago while working for a black law firm with strong connections to Chicago politics. In 1996 he ran for the Illinois state legislature and won. It was the beginning of a meteoric ascent in American politics that culminated in Obama's election as president in 2008.

Questions for Discussion

- President Barack Obama identifies himself as black. Do you agree? What is the definition of race in the contemporary United States?
- What explains Obama's transition from being an indifferent student in high school and college to a disciplined achiever?

The Emergence of Modern Feminism

"Boomers"—from the phrase "baby boom"—got that name because so many of their generation were born after World War II, when returning soldiers were reunited with their girlfriends and wives, and when ample job opportunities made it easier to raise families. Boomers' parents married earlier and had children sooner after marriage than at any other time in the twentieth century. By the late 1950s, the birthrate of the United States approached that of teeming India.

An important force in the early lives of Boomers was Dr. Benjamin Spock's *Common Sense Guide to Baby and Child Care*. First published in 1946, Spock's manual sold 24 million copies during the next quarter century. Spock's book guided young parents through the common medical crises of parenthood—ear infections, colic, chickenpox—and also counseled them on psychological issues. A mother's most important job, Spock insisted, was to shore up her children's sense of self by providing continuous support and affection. Women were naturally attuned to nurturing and childcare. Those women who entered the aggressive "men's world" of work would be at odds with their psychological inclinations.

Television picked up on this theme and hammered away at it each week in sitcoms such as Robert Young's ironically titled *Father Knows Best* (1954–1962) and Jackie Gleason's equally ironic take on working-class marriage, *The Honeymooners* (1953–1962). Repeatedly irascible or befuddled patriarchs blundered into family matters, only to be gently eased out of harm's way by their understanding and psychologically savvy wives.

But the reality of the postwar woman was more complicated. Economic expansion generated many new jobs, especially in the burgeoning corporate bureaucracies and retail stores. Women were in high demand because they would work for lower wages than men. Many took jobs, ignoring Spock and cultural conventions. In 1940, only one

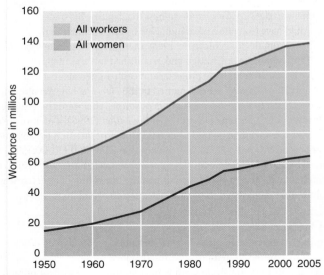

Paid Workforce, 1950–2005, by Gender The number (and percentage) of wage-earning women increased rapidly after 1960. In 1950, for example, fewer than one-third of the paid work force consisted of women; by 2006, the proportion had increased to nearly half.

in four civilian employees was female, one-third of them married. Three decades later, four in ten paid employees were women, two-thirds of them married.

Working women were acutely aware of the fact that men in similar jobs were paid more and had better opportunities for advancement. Women noticed, too, that minorities had improved their situations by fighting publicly. Increasingly activists for women's rights adopted similar strategies; they were the founders of the modern women's liberation movement.

One of its leaders was Betty Friedan, an activist journalist in the labor movement during the 1930s and 1940s who shifted to gender issues in later decades. In *The Feminine Mystique* (1963), Friedan argued that advertisers, popular magazines, and other "authorities" brainwashed women into thinking that they could thrive only at home. They were wrong, Friedan insisted. According to her survey of her classmates at Smith College, many housewives were troubled with vague but persistent feelings of anger and discomfort.

The Feminine Mystique provided what later came to be known as "consciousness raising" for thousands of women. Over a million copies were quickly sold. Friedan was deluged by hundreds of letters from women who had thought that their unease and depression despite their "happy" family life were both unique and unreasonable. Many now determined to expand their horizons by taking jobs or resuming their education.

Friedan had assumed that if able women acted with determination, employers would recognize their abilities and stop discriminating against them. As feminists were outlining plans to strengthen women's claims to fair treatment in the workplace, they won an unexpected victory. In 1964, during a debate on whether to ban racial discrimination in employment, Virginia Senator Howard Smith, seeking to scuttle the law, proposed that women also be protected from discrimination in hiring and promotion. Several congresswomen immediately endorsed the idea and proposed an amendment to that effect. This became Title VII of the Civil Rights Act of 1964.

In 1966 Friedan and other feminists founded the **National Organization for Women (NOW)**. "The time has come for a new movement toward true equality for all women in America and toward a fully equal partnership of the sexes," the leaders announced. In 1967 NOW came out for an equal rights amendment to the Constitution, for changes in the divorce laws, and for the legalization of abortion, the right of "control of one's body."

The **Equal Rights Amendment (ERA)**, which would make it unconstitutional to deny equal rights "on account of sex," had been proposed by the National Woman's party in 1923; by the late 1930s it appeared headed for adoption by Congress. But Eleanor Roosevelt and other women's groups killed the amendment, fearing it would rescind laws that protected poor women and their children. By the late 1960s, however, NOW's campaign for the ERA was yielding dividends. In 1971 the House of Representatives approved the ERA and the Senate followed the next year. By the end of 1972, twenty-two states had raced to go on record to ratify the amendment: What politician could prudently oppose equal rights for women? At the outset of 1973, only sixteen more states needed to ratify ERA before it was added to the Constitution.

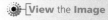

View the Image

Jimmy Carter Signs the House of Representative Resolution for the Equal Rights Amendment, 1972 at **myhistorylab.com**

Feminist activists soon turned to another major goal: legalization of abortion. The Constitution made no reference to abortion. But during the nineteenth century botched surgical abortions that killed many women prompted the American Medical Association to call for the "general suppression" of the practice. By 1900, every state except Kentucky had passed antiabortion laws. Most states granted exceptions when the woman had been impregnated by rape or incest or when a doctor thought it necessary to save the woman's life. In 1967, for example, Governor Reagan of California, an opponent of abortion, signed a law allowing doctors to perform abortions if childbirth would "gravely impair the physical or mental health of the mother." The number of legal abortions in California increased from 5,018 in 1968 to more than 100,000 by 1972.

In 1970, however, feminist activists persuaded the Hawaii legislature to repeal its criminal abortion statute, the first state to do so. Later that year, another battle was waged in New York. It pitted feminists, liberals, and the medical establishment against conservatives and the Roman Catholic Church. The state assembly repealed its antiabortion law by a single vote. Feminists regarded this as a crucial but sobering victory. If a liberal state such as New York had barely mustered a majority in favor of abortion rights, how long would it take for the campaign to prevail elsewhere?

Roe v. Wade

The question soon became moot; the United States Supreme Court took the decision out of the hands of state legislatures. A key factor was a new concept in constitutional law: the "right to privacy." In the nineteenth century, the Catholic Church had persuaded many state legislatures to ban dissemination of information on contraceptives and birth control. Connecticut was one such state. But in 1961 Estelle Griswold, head of Planned Parenthood in Connecticut, opened a birth control clinic to challenge the law. In the case of *Griswold v. Connecticut*, the Supreme Court, headed by Earl Warren, struck down the Connecticut statute, contending that it violated couples' "right to privacy." While conceding that no such term appeared in the Constitution, the Court held that various other constitutional provisions—such as freedom of speech and press and prohibitions against unreasonable searches—together provided an "umbrella" of privacy-related rights. This "right to privacy" protected people from unwarranted intrusions by the state.

Then, in 1969, Norma McCorvey asked her doctor for an abortion. She was unmarried, unemployed, twenty-five years old, and pregnant. Her doctor refused. Abortion, he told her, was illegal in Texas unless performed to save the woman's life. McCorvey's lawyer encouraged her to challenge the law. She consented, using the pseudonym "Jane Roe," and her lawyer filed suit against Henry Wade, the Dallas County prosecutor.

In 1973, after McCorvey had the baby, the U.S. Supreme Court rendered a decision in *Roe v. Wade*. Rejecting any "single" theory of life, the justices maintained that a fetus did not have a "right to life" until the final three months of pregnancy, when it could likely survive without the mother. Until then, the mother's right to "privacy" took precedence. The state could not prevent a woman from having an abortion during the first six months of pregnancy. Most abortions were no longer illegal. A major goal of the feminists had been achieved almost overnight.

The *Roe v. Wade* decision resulted in a rapid expansion of abortion facilities. From 1973 to 1980, the number of abortions performed annually increased from 745,000 to 1.5 million. Abortion had become the nation's most common surgical procedure. The new feminist movement had prevailed on a number of issues that would have been unthinkable a decade earlier.

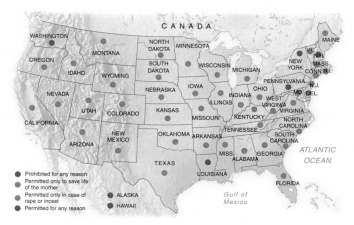

State Laws on Abortion Prior to *Roe v. Wade* (1973) Prior to *Roe v. Wade*, only Hawaii, Alaska, and New York had legalized abortion. Louisiana, Pennsylvania, and New Hampshire prohibited all abortions, while every other state allowed abortions only in cases of rape or incest or to preserve the life of the woman.

Conservative Counterattack

But the *Roe v. Wade* decision also energized a grass-roots conservative movement against abortion, often supported by the Catholic Church, the Mormons, and Protestant groups such as Falwell's Moral Majority (see Chapter 30, p. 796). The right-to-life movement endorsed the presidential campaigns of Ronald Reagan and George H. W. Bush, whose Supreme Court appointments generally favored the right-to-life position. In *Webster v. Reproductive Health Services* (1989) and *Planned Parenthood of Southeastern Pennsylvania v. Casey* (1992), the Supreme Court allowed states to impose

certain conditions, such as tests of viability and waiting periods, before abortions could be performed. But well into the twenty-first century, *Roe v. Wade* remained the law of the land.

Conservatives were more successful in contesting the ERA, which seemed headed to prompt ratification. In 1973 Phyllis Schlafly, a former vice president of the National Federation of Republican Women and publisher of a conservative newsletter, spearheaded a nation-wide campaign against ratification of the ERA. She argued that it would subject young women to the military draft, deprive divorced women of alimony and child custody, and

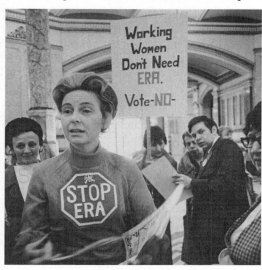

Phyllis Schlafly drew much of her support from working-class women who were left vulnerable by the recession after 1973.

make married women legally responsible for providing 50 percent of household income. As the recession after 1973 dragged the economy down, Schlafly's words struck a responsive chord among anxious housewives and low-wage-earning women who doubted they could survive the recessionary economy on their own. The ratification campaign lost momentum and stalled, falling just three states short. By 1980, the ERA was dead.[1]

The Rise of Gay and Lesbian Rights

The rhetoric of "minority rights" and the example of activists in other movements during the 1960s encouraged gay rights activists to demand that society cease harassing and discriminating against *them*. In 1969, New York City police raided the Stonewall Inn, a popular gay bar in Greenwich Village and arrested the occupants—most of them gays—for "solicitation" of illegal sexual acts. The crowd outside threw rocks and bottles and the police were forced to retreat. The Stonewall riot lasted for several days and marked a turning point in the history of gays and lesbians. No longer would gays in Greenwich Village remain "in the closet"—hidden from view. Public advocacy of their cause strengthened it immeasurably.

●●◖Read the Document

The Gay Liberation Front, Come Out (1970) at **myhistorylab.com**

Gay activists embarked on numerous campaigns to eliminate discrimination against gays. Gay psychiatrists challenged the American Psychiatric Association's longstanding judgment that homosexuality was a treatable mental illness. In 1973 the association's board of directors agreed to remove homosexuality from the standard manual of psychiatric disorders. Disgruntled traditionalists challenged the decision and forced the directors to put the matter up for a vote of the entire membership. In 1974 the members upheld the directors. The next year the American Psychological Association concurred. Homosexuality was not a mental illness.

Gay and lesbian activists also filed suits to eliminate discrimination against gays in education, housing, education, and employment. In response to such pressures, the U.S. Civil Service Commission rescinded its ban on hiring homosexuals. Now gays chose to run openly for public office. In 1977, Harvey Milk, the first openly gay man to run for office in California, was elected supervisor in San Francisco. The next year he led the fight against a California law that would fire gay teachers. Former California governor Ronald Reagan opposed the bill as a violation of human rights, as did President Jimmy Carter; the proposition was defeated by a million votes. Three weeks later Milk was assassinated; he became a martyr to the gay rights movement.

Harvey Milk was the first openly gay candidate to be elected to office in California.

---

[1]Various Supreme Court decisions, such as *Reed v. Reed* (1971), struck down laws that failed to provide "equal protection" of men and women or applied arbitrary standards in making legal distinctions between the rights of men and women.

AIDS

But by the late 1970s, as gays were openly acknowledging and celebrating their sexual identity, many were being struck down by a new disease. World health officials had spotted the outbreak of yet another viral epidemic in central Africa; but no one noticed that this virus had mutated into a more lethal strain and was spreading to Europe and North America. On June 5, 1981, the Centers for Disease Control (CDC) alerted American health officials to an outbreak of a rare bacterial infection in Los Angeles. What made the outbreak distinctive was that this particular infection had struck five healthy young men. All were homosexuals. Within months, all died.

By 1982 the CDC called this new disease **acquired immunodeficiency syndrome (AIDS)**. The CDC learned that AIDS was caused by the **human immunodeficiency virus (HIV)**, a lethal virus that destroys the body's defenses against infection. HIV spreads when an infected person's body fluids come in contact with someone else's. By the end of 1982, the CDC had documented 900 cases of AIDS; the disease was increasing exponentially. In June 1983, when the federal budget approached $1 trillion, Congress finally voted $12 million for AIDS research and treatment.

Not until 1985, when the square-jawed romantic actor Rock Hudson confirmed that he was dying of AIDS, did the subject command widespread public attention. President Reagan, an old friend of Hudson's, publicly acknowledged that the disease constituted a grave health crisis. Congress approved Reagan's call for a substantial increase in AIDS funding. But Reagan's appeal was belated and insufficient. By then, nearly 21,000 Americans had died; by 1999, the total number of AIDS-related deaths approached 400,000.

The AIDS epidemic affected public policy and private behavior. Fear of the disease, and of those who suffered from it, exacerbated many people's homophobia. But the AIDS epidemic also forced most people to confront homosexuality directly and perhaps for the first time, and thus contributed to a deeper understanding of the complexity of human nature. Gay and lesbian organizations, the vanguard in the initial war against AIDS, continued to fight for social acceptance and legal rights.

In this electron microscopic photograph, two human immunodeficiency virus (HIV) cells, in different stages of budding, are emerging from an infected T-lymphocyte human blood cell (pink). The HIV cell that has almost broken free includes RNA (green—the cell's genetic code) and it will reinfect other T-cells. T-cells are part of the body's immune system.

Publicly Gay

Although gays had always served in the military—Milk had been an officer in the navy during the Korean War—they were technically banned. In 1992 President Bill Clinton had promised to end the ban on gays and lesbians in the armed services, but when the Joint Chiefs of the armed forces and a number of important members of Congress objected, he settled for a policy known as "don't ask, don't tell," meaning that such persons would be allowed to enlist only if they did not openly proclaim their sexual preferences. In 2010 Congress voted to openly admit gays and lesbians to the armed forces.

Another long-term objective was same-sex marriage. Why, gay and lesbian couples asked, should they not be allowed to adopt children or receive the legal protections and benefits of marriage? Conservative groups argued that religious texts and moral tradit-ions had defined marriage as heterosexual. In 2006 conservatives, backed by President

Table 31.1 Gender Activist Victories and Conservative Responses

Year	Activist Victory	Consequence	Conservative Response (after 1972)
1964	Title VII, Civil Rights Act of 1964	Prohibited employers from discriminating on account of sex; enforced by federal government	
1965	*Griswold v. Connecticut*	Supreme Court asserted a "right to privacy" to allow dissemination of information on birth control	
1972	Equal Rights Amendment (ERA) approved by Congress	Extended the equal rights protections of Fourteenth Amendment to women	Phyllis Schlafly inaugurated "Stop ERA" campaign (1973), which blocked ratification
1973	*Roe v. Wade*	Supreme Court legalized most abortions	Jerry Falwell's Moral Majority founded; helped elect Ronald Reagan president (1980); named more conservative Supreme Court justices
2000	Vermont recognized same-sex unions	Paved way for a half-dozen states to approve same-sex marriage	George W. Bush-backed proposed constitutional amendment to limit marriage to heterosexuals narrowly defeated in Senate (2006)

George W. Bush, proposed an amendment to the Constitution that would define marriage as "a union between a man and a woman." The measure fell just short of passage in the Senate.

In 2000 Vermont became the first state to recognize same-sex civil unions, providing gay and lesbian couples with some of the legal rights of marriage. In 2004 Massachusetts was the first state to recognize same-sex marriage; within the next five years, a half dozen states passed similar laws. When Washington, DC approved a same-sex marriage law, the Catholic Archdiocese of Washington, DC protested the decision by revising health care benefits of its agencies to avoid covering same-sex couples. But by 2010, according to most opinion polls, a solid majority of Americans favored same-sex marriage. And by a hefty margin, Millennials were far more likely to endorse same-sex marriage than any other age group, including Boomers.

Crime and Punishment

Civil rights protesters who intentionally violated laws rather than work within the law to change it; feminists who flouted conventional gender roles and asserted a right to abortion; gays and lesbians who claimed a right to serve openly in the military and enter into same-sex marriages—all were evidence, at least in the opinion of some, that the nation had lost its moral bearings. Such misgivings had spiked in the late 1960s, as antiwar protests closed down college campuses and race riots ravaged cities. Violent crime increased. Many called for restoration of "law and order." During the 1970s and 1980s conservative activists, borrowing strategies from activist movements on the left, succeeded in implementing many of the goals of the "law and order" movement. They elected officials who passed tougher laws, hired more police, and built additional prisons.

The shift toward capital punishment was symptomatic. No criminal had been executed since 1967. The practice simply had fallen from favor. But in response to the

Narcotics policemen in Bridgeport, Connecticut, arrest a suspect for selling crack near housing projects in 1994.

conservative demand for tough legislation against criminals, legislators rewrote capital punishment statutes in light of the *Furman* decision, depriving juries of discretion in sentencing. The Supreme Court upheld these laws and capital punishment resumed in 1976. Since then, over a thousand convicts have been executed.

Another manifestation of the crackdown on crime was the increase in the nation's prison population. In 1973 the nation's prisons—state and federal—held about 200,000 convicts. By 1990 the number of prisoners exceeded 750,000, and by 2004, 2 million. This required the construction of a 1,000-bed prison every week. In 1995, for the first time, states spent more on prisons than on higher education. By 2010, the United States incarcerated more people than any country in the world, except perhaps communist China, which did not disclose such information.

Crack and Urban Gangs

Several factors intensified the problem of violent crime, especially in the inner cities. One was a shift in drug use. During the 1960s marijuana had become commonly available, especially on college campuses; this was followed by cocaine, which was far more powerful and addictive but so expensive that few could afford it.

During the 1980s growers of coca leaves in Peru and Bolivia greatly expanded production. Drug traffickers in Colombia devised sophisticated systems to transport cocaine to the United States. The price of cocaine dropped from $120 an ounce in 1981 to $50 in 1988.

Still more important was the proliferation of a cocaine-based compound called "crack" because it crackled when smoked. Many users found that it gave an intense spasm of pleasure that overrode all other desires.

The lucrative crack trade led to bitter turf wars in the inner cities; dealers hired neighborhood youths, organized them into gangs, armed them with automatic weapons, and told them to drive competitors away. A survey of Los Angeles county in the early 1990s found that more than 150,000 young people belonged to 1,000 gangs. Violence had become a fact of life. In 1985, before crack had seized hold of the inner city, there were 147 murders in Washington, DC; in 1991, the figure skyrocketed to 482.

Black on black murder had become a significant cause of death for African Americans in their twenties. In 1988 Monsta' Kody Scott, who at age eleven pumped shotgun blasts into rival gang members, returned after prison to his Los Angeles neighborhood. He was horrified: Gangs no longer merely shot their rivals but sprayed them with automatic weapons, seventy-five rounds to a clip, or blew them away with small rockets. By 2010, 30 percent of African American men in their twenties were in prison, or on probation or parole.

Violence and Popular Culture

Conservatives—and plenty of liberals—were also dismayed by the violence of popular culture. They cited as proof the lurid violence of the movie industry, pointing out that in *Public Enemy*, reputedly the most violent film of the 1930s, and *Death Wish*, a controversial vigilante fantasy of 1974, the body count reached eight. But three movies released during the late 1980s—*Robocop, Die Hard*, and *Rambo III*—each produced a death tally of sixty or more, nearly one every two minutes. The trend culminated in *Natural Born Killers* (1994), director Oliver Stone's unimaginably violent "spoof" of media violence. Television imitated the movies as the networks crammed violent crime shows into prime time. In 1991 an exhaustive survey found that by the age of eighteen, the average viewer had witnessed some 40,000 murders on TV.

A new sound called "rap" then emerged from the ghetto. Rap consisted of unpredictably metered lyrics set against an exaggeratedly heavy downbeat. Rap performers did not play musical instruments or sing songs so much as convey, in words and gestures, an attitude of defiant, raw rage against whatever challenged their sense of manhood: other young males; women, whom they derided in coarse sexual epithets; and the police. Predictably, raps such as "Cop Killer" and "Illegal Search" contributed to the charge that rap condoned violence and crime.

The appeal of rap quickly spread beyond black audiences. When Dr. Dre (Andrew Young), founder of a gangsta rap group and head of a record firm, discovered that whites bought more rap CDs than blacks, he promoted the career of a young white rapper, Eminem. Born Marshall Bruce Mathers III, Eminem attracted attention with songs such as "Murder, Murder," "Kill You," "Drug Ballad," and "Criminal." He bashed women, gays, his wife, and nearly everyone else. His lyrics were of such surpassing offensiveness that he became an overnight celebrity and instant millionaire. His fans, whom he treated with scorn, were delighted by the universality of his contempt. The list of those suing him included his mother.

By the 1990s improvements in computer graphics led to the development of increasingly realistic—and violent—video games. "Grand Theft Auto," which by 2005 had sold over 35 million copies and generated over $2 billion, was the subject of a *60 Minutes* special. Journalist Ed Bradley described the game this way: "See a car you like? Steal it. A cop in your way? Blow him away." Bradley recounted the story of Devin Moore, an eighteen-year-old who played the game "day and night" for years. On June 7, 2003, he stole a car; when apprehended he grabbed a gun, killed three policemen, and fled in a police cruiser. When finally caught he said, "Life is like a video game. Everybody's got to die sometime."

America, it seemed, had become seemingly filled with menace. At night, few ventured downtown and many avoided public places. Car alarm systems became standard. The popular phrase—"your home is your castle"—took on an eerie reality. Americans reinforced doors with steel, nailed windows shut, and increasingly hunkered down in their own private spaces, which they locked up and wired with alarms.

From Main Street to Mall to Internet

In 1960 civil rights protesters picketed six stores in Richmond, Virginia. Within several decades, all of the stores had closed. So had most of the luncheonettes, 5 & 10 cent stores, bus stations, and community swimming pools that had been sites of civil rights protests during the late 1950s and early 1960s. Civil rights leaders targeted such facilities because they sought equal access to public spaces downtown, where community life was transacted. There people worked, bought clothing and cars, got their hair cut and cavities filled, paid taxes and filed for driver's licenses, ate meals and brokered deals, watched movies and attended ball games, and engaged in countless other activities. Thirty years later, however, many downtown business districts had been all but abandoned.

In 2007 a storm approaches the mostly abandoned main street of Robert Lee, county seat of Coke County, Texas.

Some blamed the civil rights movement itself. Inner-city protests and the desegregation of city schools, they said, caused many whites to flee to the suburbs. Others cited the rise in crime in the late 1960s. But "white flight" commenced in the late 1940s, long before the civil rights movement and busing disputes, before the race riots and crack infestations. Postwar federal policies played a major role in the demographic upheaval that transformed the cities and gave rise to the suburbs. The G. I. Bill of 1946 offered veterans cheap home mortgages. Real estate developers bought huge tracts of land and built inexpensive houses designed especially for returning

Racial Shifts in St. Louis during the 1950s During the 1950s, the white population of St. Louis declined by more than 200,000, while the black population increased by 100,000. Much of the central core was almost entirely black.

Growth of Suburban St. Louis, 1950–1960 During the 1950s, the suburban townships in St. Louis county west of the city gained nearly 300,000 people, an increase of 73 percent. More than 99 percent of the suburban residents were white.

veterans. Postwar lending policies of the Federal Housing Authority also contributed to the rise of the suburbs, chiefly by rejecting loans in older residential urban areas. Eisenhower's decision to pump money into highway construction (rather than subways and railway infrastructure) also contributed to the growth of suburbs.

Retailers followed consumers, renting space in strip malls along the busy roadways that reached out to the suburbs. Then came the shopping malls. In 1946 there were only eight shopping malls in the nation; by 1972, over 13,000. Mall managers anchored their complexes with national retailers such as Sears and JCPenney. Because such companies bought in large quantities, their stores out-priced locally owned competitors on Main Street. Main Street faded. By the 1980s, retailers such as Sam Walton took the logic of price competition several steps farther. He dispensed with the customary amenities of shopping—attractive displays, pleasant décor, professional salespeople—and built "big box" stores that were little more than shopper-accessible warehouses. Then came another shift. Early in the twenty-first century, shoppers who wearied of pushing carts through dimly lit warehouses and standing in line to pay now had an alternative: They could shop via the Internet, which by 2010 accounted for nearly 10 percent of all retail sales.

Within a half century, shopping had not only become more private, but it also was less social. Big-box stores replaced commissioned salespeople with low-paid checkers. In the past decade improvements in scanner technology allowed retailers to dispense even with checkers. And an increasing number of online consumers shop at home. Increasingly, shopping entails no social interaction whatsoever.

A similar shift from public interaction to private pursuits has characterized many other daily activities. For much of their lives, Boomers regularly visited local banks to make deposits and cash checks. But during the recession of the 1970s banks closed many branches and in subsequent decades hundreds of banks were merged. More branches were closed and tens of thousands of tellers laid off. Rather than drive to distant branches and wait in long lines, banking customers learned to use ATMs and bank online. Banking for Boomers had been a social occasion; for Millennials it became an interaction with a machine.

By the 1970s and 1980s, many service sector jobs had disappeared: milkmen who delivered fresh dairy products; door-to-door salespeople who demonstrated cosmetics, appliances, and encyclopedias; "service station" attendants who pumped gas and checked the oil; bakery owners and candy makers who sold goods they had made themselves. Then in the 1990s, person-to-person interactions in daily life occurred even less frequently. With the advent of the Internet and improved software, many people became their own travel agent, tax preparer, financial adviser, grocer, cosmetician, medical assistant, and bookseller.

From Community to Facebook

Religious institutions have long constituted the bulwark of communities, and the postwar period witnessed a remarkable expansion. By 1990, membership in all churches and synagogues surpassed 148 million, an increase of 60 million during the previous four decades. (The total population during the period increased by nearly 100 million.) With the large influx of Hispanic immigrants, membership in the Roman Catholic Church more than doubled. Membership in mainstream Protestant churches generally declined, but rose solidly in fundamentalist and evangelical churches, such as the Southern Baptist, Pentecostal, Holiness, Assemblies of God, and Church of God in Christ. The Jehovah's Witnesses and the Mormon Church grew as well. In 1990 two-thirds of all Americans reported that they belonged to a church, the highest percentage by far among the major industrial nations of the West.

But the membership numbers were misleading. Since 1970, church attendance among persons younger than sixty has declined about 20 percent. The UCLA survey cited in the introduction to this chapter found that in 1968, 9 percent of entering college freshmen said they never attended church; by 2000, that percentage had more than doubled. By the 1970s, moreover, millions of Americans went to church by turning on the TV. "Televangelists" such as Rex Humbard, Oral Roberts, Jerry Falwell, Pat Robertson, and Jim and Tammy Bakker founded their own churches and educational institutions, supported by direct appeals to viewers. A few established their own colleges, such as Falwell's Liberty University, Oral Roberts University, and Robertson's CBN University (renamed Regent University in 1990). A number of scandals involving prominent televangelists caused disillusionment and widespread defections. On the other hand, the rapid spread of cable television greatly increased the number of available channels, enabling scores of new evangelists to reach out to viewers. Community-based ministers saw congregations shrink; thousands of churches closed their doors for good. Some churches devised "healing rituals" to ease their abandonment of formerly sacred space.

Participation in team sports fell at about the same rate as church attendance. By the first decade of the twenty-first century, more young people played basketball and soccer than in the past, but far fewer played softball, baseball, football, tennis, and league bowling. The fields on which young Boomers often spent much of their lives had been sold to developers or fenced in and locked.

The lack of exercise among Millennials became a source of national concern. In 2010 Surgeon General Regina Benjamin announced that one in three American children was obese. One reason, Benjamin explained, was that youngsters between ages eight to eighteen averaged seven hours and thirty-eight minutes a day on electronic media—watching TV, talking on cell phones, playing video games, and logged into the Internet. That year, First Lady Michelle Obama inaugurated a nationwide antiobesity campaign named—appropriately—"Let's move!"

Some Millennials exercised *while* engaged with electronic media. (Multitasking became a redundant adjective for the Millennial generation.) Since 2000, membership in gyms skyrocketed. And often Millennials could be seen pounding away on treadmills or other exercise machines, staring at TV monitors or listening to music with an earpiece. Not all Millennials are sedentary; but many are nearly always plugged in.

The rise of online learning is an illustration of the transformation of social activities into solitary Internet pursuits. By 2009, over 4 million Americans enrolled in online courses, twice as many as in 2003. For many, especially full-time employees, ease of access compensated for the lack of face-to-face contact with other students. Tim Scott, a twenty-five-year-old clerk in a drugstore who enrolled in technology courses at the University of Phoenix, explained, "This is pretty much the only way I could get a college degree." Online education spread to all walks of life. Some people took courses to learn new languages and career skills, such as "Dental Anthropology," "Clown Education," or

"Golf Course Management." Others logged in to learn new hobbies, such as "building a kayak," "paragliding in the Alps," or "Salsa dancing." Employees were required to take mandatory online courses on company policies and sexual harassment. Although surveys suggest that most online learners prefer classes in which they interact with real people in a classroom, the fact was that often regular classrooms had themselves become anonymous and impersonal. As Harvard Professor Clayton Christensen observed, "Anything beyond the 10th row in a large lecture hall is distance learning."

One reason distance online education took off was that it spared commuting students the hassle of driving to college and finding parking. Such experiences underscored the extent to which cars had become the predominant mode of transportation, another shift from the earlier social context of mass transit to the mostly solitary experience of driving. Bus and train ridership was declining well before the advent of the Boomers; but the postwar population shift to the suburbs accelerated the ascendancy of cars over mass transit. As more drivers—nearly always alone—clogged the highways, traffic jams grew longer. By 2005, the average American spent thirty-eight hours a year stuck in traffic. Although many found repose within the solitary confines of a car, others coped with the loneliness of driving by chatting on their cell phones or texting friends. (A Pew poll in 2010 found that one in three texting teenagers did so while driving a car.)

The postwar suburban home itself was conceived as a private refuge from the hustle and bustle of downtown. But over time suburban homes became still more private. Newer houses were set farther back from the curb; high fences and thick hedges discouraged the over-the-barbecue conviviality of the 1950s suburbs. By the 1990s, many well-to-do people moved into privately owned "gated communities," surrounded by high fences and patrolled by private security guards. Only residents and specified guests were allowed in.

The trend toward increased privacy could be seen even within the home. Young Boomers generally ate dinner in a family dining room and played cards and board games afterwards in the living room. By the mid 1950s, television-watching had become a family affair, and a child's dreaded punishment was to be sent to his or her room after dinner. During the 1980s and 1990s, however, homes became larger and families smaller. Most Millennials had their own bedrooms. By 1975 fewer than half of Americans ate dinner with their whole family; and by 2000, that fraction had slipped to one-third. Family members instead retreated to their own rooms to watch their own television shows or log onto the Internet. (In 2010 the average number of TV sets per household—2.93— exceeded the number of *people* per household—2.88.) For Millennials, the worst punishment was to be deprived of the Internet or their Blackberries.

Millennials withdrew to the privacy of their rooms in order to socialize. David Greenfield of the Center for Internet Studies explained that the Internet was "a socially connecting device that's socially isolating at the same time." For their part, most Millennials thought the Internet improved social relations. "I've outsourced my social life exclusively to Facebook," one Millennial explained in 2009. "My time on Facebook substitutes for face time and has made my life more organized and efficient." In 2010 Facebook reported that the average college student had over 400 Facebook friends. Plenty of users greatly exceeded this average, prompting Facebook in 2008 to rule that friendship rosters would be capped at 5,000. Social connections in excess of 5,000, Facebook officials reasoned, were probably not "actual friends." While bemoaning the cutoff, Jeffrey Wolfe, a real estate broker in San Francisco with 4,447 friends, conceded that keeping up with them could be demanding: "Normally I start hitting it about 10 o'clock at night, and if I do it right, I can be done by 1 a.m."

Some worried that Millennials spent so much time attending to their own circle of Facebook friends (however great in circumference) or logging onto sites dedicated to Lady Gaga, labrador retrievers, or Legos, that they often failed to encounter people with ideas or perspectives different from their own. But others endorsed the Internet as an ideal if somewhat odd way to meet strangers and exchange opinions. *Second Life*, a virtual 3D world populated by some 18 million "residents," was among the innumerable interactive games that allowed strangers to converse and imaginatively interact. In 2009 Linden Lab, the San Francisco company behind the concept, noted that *Second Life* residents had logged over a billion hours on the site and spent a billion dollars buying unreal things (mostly clothing and cars) for their virtual personas, or avatars. One Stanford researcher explained how he had experienced "the most sexually charged non-sexual experience I've ever had" when his avatar was propositioned by another avatar in a "private room" (!).

Virtual communities possessed both the advantages and disadvantages of anonymity. "On the Internet, no one knows you're a dog," as a *New Yorker* cartoon's canine narrator remarked. A 2001 study found that half of the female Avatars in *Second Life* were actually men. Anonymity may help protect people who wish to articulate ideas and explore behaviors that might generate disapproval in "real" settings.

But the anonymity of the Internet also carries risks. Sexual predators target teen chat rooms and social-networking sites. Anonymity, too, allows people to vent frustrations, prejudices, and spite without concern for consequences. In 2006, Lori Drew, a mother in O'Fallon, Missouri, sought to teach a lesson to Megan Meier, a fourteen-year-old whom Drew believed had been spreading rumors about Drew's daughter. Drew created

In *Second Life*, a multi-player online game, these two avatars engage in virtual courtship.

a fictitious MySpace persona of a sixteen-year-old named "Josh," who friended Meier, gained her confidence, and acquired her secrets. But then "Josh" turned on Meier, advising, "The world would be a better place without you." Twenty minutes later, Meier hanged herself in her bedroom closet.

Drew was convicted of a misdemeanor for violating the terms of her MySpace agreement; but a federal judge set the ruling aside: Violation of an Internet agreement did not constitute criminal behavior. State legislatures in Missouri and California immediately passed "anti-cyberbullying" laws. In 2009 Congresswoman Linda Sanchez introduced the "Megan Meier Cyberbullying Prevention Act," but constitutional experts predicted that such laws would be struck down as infringements on free speech and privacy rights.

But what did privacy mean? During the previous four decades, Boomers and Millennials had repeatedly debated and redefined the concepts of private and public. Feminists had asserted a "right to privacy," including a right to an abortion; but the Moral Majority had insisted on the superior "right to life" of the fetus. Gays and lesbians had sought freedom from government harassment; but they also sought public acceptance through adoption of same-sex marriage laws and open acknowledgement of their service in the military. President Reagan and conservatives campaigned to "get government off our backs" and yet they expanded the government's role in prosecuting behavior deemed deviant or immoral. And if public physical spaces were disappearing, Millennials increasingly participated, often from the solitude of a bedroom or study, in a bogglingly public world of the Internet, blithely posting their innermost thoughts (and sometimes photos) on social networking sites.

Greying of the Boomers

On January 1, 2011, when the first Boomer turned sixty-five, nearly one-seventh of the American population was over sixty-five, the customary retirement age. Demographic projections indicated that by the time the Millennials reached sixty-five, one-fifth of the population would be over sixty-five.

The aging of the nation's population had serious economic implications. A substantial proportion of the nation's wealth was shifting from economically productive purposes (educating the young, building and maintaining infrastructure, and creating new businesses and technology) to the less productive task of providing health care and pensions for the elderly.

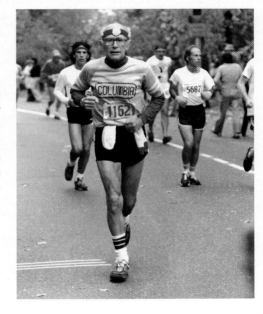

In 1980, sixty-year-old John A. Garraty, co-author of this book, completed his first twenty-six-mile marathon in New York City. He completed his last marathon when he was seventy-two.

Of particular concern was the viability of Social Security, the New Deal program that provided pensions for the elderly. In theory, workers and employers paid into the Social Security Trust Fund; when workers retired, they would draw their "savings" from the Trust Fund. But under pressure from seniors—the highest-voting proportion of the population—Congress increased old-age benefits. As of 2010, the Social Security Trust Fund had $2 trillion in assets, but the projected cost of Social Security by 2050 exceeded $7 trillion. The difference would have to be covered by the contributions made by working Millennials, many of whom worried that the fund would be gone by the time they retired. A 2009 poll by the American Association of Retired Persons (AARP) found that only 31 percent of Americans between the ages of eighteen and thirty-nine believe that Social Security will be available to them on retirement.

Medical advances during the late twentieth century led to an increase in the life span: An American born in 1900 could expect to live to be fifty, while one born in 2000 was projected to live to seventy-seven. But this good news further complicated the transition from Boomers to Millennials.

Compounding the difficulty were attitudinal differences between the generations, such as those cited elsewhere in this chapter. The 2008 Pew poll also found that 75 percent of Millennials had profiles on a social networking site, compared to 30 percent of Boomers; that 38 percent of Millennials had a tattoo, compared to 15 percent of Boomers; and that 23 percent of Millennials had body piercings other than an ear lobe, compared to fewer than 1 percent of Boomers. How Millennials will treat aging Boomers is anyone's guess.

Milestones

1946	Dr. Benjamin Spock publishes *Common Sense Guide to Baby and Child Care*	1969	Stonewall riots mark public assertion of rights of homosexuals
1947	Construction begins on Levittown, New York, first tract-house suburb	1973	Supreme Court legalizes abortion in *Roe v. Wade*
1960	FDA approves sale of birth control pills	1979	Jerry Falwell founds the Moral Majority
1963	Betty Friedan publishes *The Feminine Mystique*	1982	Center for Disease Control identifies new disease, AIDS
1965	Congress passes Immigration Act that ends "national origins" quotas	1989	Supreme Court limits abortion rights in *Webster v. Reproductive Health Services*
	Supreme Court affirms "right to privacy" in *Griswold v. Connecticut*	2000	Vermont recognies same-sex unions
	César Chávez organizes boycott to support grape pickers	2010	Michelle Obama introduces anti-obesity campaign

✓●─│Study and **Review** at www.myhistorylab.com

Review Questions

1. The introduction to this chapter argues that young Boomers were more inclined to look for a "meaningful philosophy of life," while young Millennials were more interested in being "well-off financially." Do you agree? What evidence from the chapter supports your position? What refutes it?

2. What accounted for the emergence of modern feminism in the 1960s? Did it succeed in changing gender roles and if so, how? What explained the emergence of gay and lesbian activism?

3. What were the main components of the conservative movement after 1970? How did it influence culture and society?

4. How did the cultural shift from "downtown" to the suburbs change society more generally? In what sense has life become more or less "private"?

Key Terms

acquired immunodeficiency syndrome (AIDS)   *821*

Equal Rights Amendment (ERA)   *817*

human immunodeficiency virus (HIV)   *821*

National Organization for Women (NOW)   *817*

32 Shocks and Responses: 1992–Present

((•─Hear the Audio Chapter 32 at myhistorylab.com

What will happen to you?

"THOSE WHO FAIL TO LEARN FROM THE PAST ARE DOOMED TO REPEAT it"—This cliché, a favorite of history teachers, contains some truth. The book you are reading, for example, provides some solid guidance: Governments that ignore the wishes of the people probably won't long endure; wars are easier to start than to stop; and investments that seem to be "too good to be true" probably are. But apart from such common-sense observations, history provides few clues about the future.

The first decade of the twenty-first century proves this point emphatically. In 2000 Americans were mostly optimistic, and for good reason. After the dissolution of the Soviet Union in 1991, a new era of peace was dawning. Successive American presidents reduced the nation's armed forces by nearly a million men and women; defense spending (as a proportion of the GNP) was nearly cut in half. Three decades of deficits had come to an end: In 2000 the U.S. Treasury operated at a $250 billion *surplus*. The Congressional Budget Office projected a $4 *trillion* federal surplus for the coming decade.

It didn't happen. The terrorist attack of September 11, 2001 shattered hopes for peace. Within two years, American soldiers were fighting fierce battles in Afghanistan and Iraq. By the end of the decade, over 5,000 U.S. servicemen and women would be dead.

By then, too, an economic earthquake had nearly toppled the nation's major financial institutions. By late 2008 political and economic leaders were spending trillions to prop up banks, investment houses, and insurance firms that "were too big to fail." The federal deficit for the decade approached $4 *trillion*.

More bad news was to come. In early 2010 an oil rig owned by British Petroleum blew up, killing eleven and releasing millions of barrels of oil into the Gulf of Mexico. President Obama called it the nation's worst environmental disaster ever.

By then, *Time* magazine had already pronounced these years "The Decade from Hell." But no one had any inkling of this in 1992.

A New Face: Bill Clinton

William (Bill) Clinton was born William Jefferson Blythe IV, but his father died in a car accident before he was born. Though his stepfather was an abusive alcoholic, at age fifteen Bill legally took his stepfather's name. He graduated from Georgetown, won a Rhodes scholarship to study at Oxford University, and graduated from Yale Law School. He returned to Arkansas and was soon elected state attorney general.

In 1977 Clinton and his wife, Hillary Rodham, joined with James McDougal, a banker, to secure a loan to build vacation homes in the Ozarks. But the development, which they named Whitewater, eventually became insolvent. McDougal illegally covered the debts with a loan from a savings and loan company he had acquired. In 1989 the savings and loan failed, costing the federal government $60 million to reimburse depositors. In 1992 federal investigators claimed that the Clintons had been "potential beneficiaries" of McDougal's illegal activities.

By this time Clinton, now governor of Arkansas, was campaigning in the New Hampshire primary for the Democratic nomination for president. Few voters could make much sense of the financial mess known as the "Whitewater scandal," nor did they have much opportunity to do so: Another, far more explosive story threatened to sink the Clinton campaign. It came out that Clinton had for many years engaged in an extramarital affair with one Gennifer Flowers; Clinton's standing in the polls tumbled.

Watch the Video
Bill Clinton Sells Himself to America: Presidential Campaign Ad, 1992 at **myhistorylab.com**

Hillary Rodham Clinton appeared with her husband on CBS's *60 Minutes* to address the allegations. Bill Clinton indignantly denied Flowers's statements but then issued an earnest if ambiguous appeal for forgiveness. "I have acknowledged causing pain in my marriage," he said. "I think most Americans will know what we're saying; they'll get it." Clinton was right, early evidence of his ability to address the American people directly, but on his own—carefully worded—terms. He finished second in New Hampshire, captured most of the remaining primaries, and won the Democratic nomination with ease. His choice of running mate—Senator Al Gore of Tennessee, a Vietnam veteran, family man, and environmentalist—helped the ticket considerably.

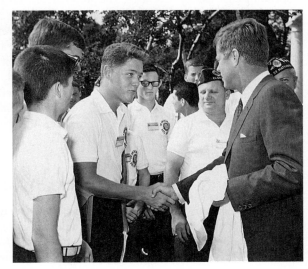

Young Bill Clinton (left) shakes hands with President John F. Kennedy. "The torch has been passed to a new generation of Americans," Kennedy had declared in his inaugural. "Ask not what your country can do for you—ask what you can do for your country," JFK added. Thirty years later, Clinton's inaugural echoed Kennedy's: "Today, a generation raised in the shadows of the Cold War assumes new responsibilities," Clinton declared. "I challenge a new generation of young Americans to a season of service."

The Election of 1992

While Clinton tiptoed through a minefield of personal scandals, President George (Herbert Walker) Bush rested secure in the belief that, after crushing Saddam Hussein and the Iraqi army in the Gulf War, the 1992 election campaign would be little more than a victory lap. But he encountered unexpectedly stiff opposition within the Republican party. Patrick Buchanan, an outspoken conservative, did well enough to alarm White House strategists. Then Ross Perot, a billionaire Texan, announced his independent candidacy. His platform had both conservative and liberal planks. He would avoid raising taxes, and cut government spending by "getting rid of waste." He also supported gun control, backed a woman's right to an abortion, and called for an all-out effort to "restructure" the health care system.

Polls quickly revealed that Perot was popular in California, Texas, and other key states that Bush was counting on winning easily. At the Republican convention in August, Bush was nominated without opposition.

On election day, more than 100 million citizens voted. About 44 million voted for Clinton, 38 million for Bush, and 20 million for Perot. Clinton was elected with 370 electoral votes to Bush's 168. Perot did not win any electoral votes.

A New Start: Clinton as President

Watch the Video
Bill Clinton First Inauguration
at **myhistorylab.com**

Clinton first used his executive authority to strengthen the Supreme Court majority in favor of upholding the landmark case of *Roe v. Wade*. The majority included three conservative justices who had been appointed by Reagan and Bush. Clinton appointed Ruth Bader Ginsberg, a judge known to believe that abortion was constitutional. Clinton indicated that he would veto any bill limiting abortion rights.

The first major test of the president's will came when he submitted his first budget to Congress. He hoped to reduce the deficit by roughly $500 billion in five years, half by spending cuts, half by new taxes. The proposal for a tax increase raised a storm of protest. Even so, the final bill passed by the narrowest of margins. Clinton rightly claimed a victory.

He then turned to his long-awaited proposal to reform the nation's expensive and incomplete health insurance system. A committee headed by his wife had been working for months with no indication that a plan acceptable to the medical profession,

View the Image
Bill Clinton and Al Gore on the South Lawn of the White House, 1993 at **myhistorylab.com**

the health insurance industry, and ordinary citizens was likely to come from its deliberations. The plan that finally emerged seemed even more complicated and possibly more costly than the existing system. It never came to a vote in Congress.

Emergence of the Republican Majority

The Whitewater scandal, which Clinton had managed to brush aside during the campaign, gnawed at his presidency. Public pressure forced Attorney General Janet Reno to appoint a special prosecutor. She named Kenneth W. Starr, a Republican lawyer, to investigate Whitewater and other alleged misdeeds of the Clintons.

More troubles followed. Paula Corbin Jones, a State of Arkansas employee, charged that Clinton, while governor, had invited her to his hotel room and asked her to engage in oral sex. Clinton's attorney denied the accusation and sought to have the case dismissed on the grounds that a president could not be sued while in office. The case commenced a tortuous route through the courts.

Eager to take advantage of Clinton's troubles, Republicans looked to the 1994 congressional elections. Led by Congressman Newt Gingrich of Georgia, they offered voters an ambitious program to stimulate the economy by reducing both the federal debt and the federal income tax. Federally administered welfare programs were to be replaced by block grants to the states. Many measures protecting the environment, such as those making businesses responsible for cleaning up their waste, were to be repealed.

On election day, the Republicans gained control of both houses of Congress. Under the firm direction of Gingrich, now Speaker, the House approved nearly all of the provisions of this **Contract with America**. This appalled Clinton, who vetoed the 1995 budget drafted by the Republicans. When neither side agreed to a compromise, the government for a time ran out of money and shut down all but essential services.

The Election of 1996

The public tended to blame Congress, and particularly Speaker Gingrich, for the shutdown. The president's approval rating rose. But the main issue of the day was the economy, and the upturn during and after 1991 benefited Clinton enormously. By the fall of 1996, unemployment had fallen well below 6 percent, and inflation below 3 percent. Clinton was renominated for a second term without opposition.

A number of Republicans competed in the presidential primaries, but after a slow start Bob Dole of Kansas, the Senate majority leader, won the nomination. His main proposal was a steep reduction of the deficit and a 15-percent income tax cut. Pressed to explain how this could be done without drastic cuts in popular social programs, especially Social Security and Medicare, he gave a distressingly vague reply.

On election day Clinton won an impressive victory, sweeping the Northeast, all the Midwest except Indiana, the upper Mississippi Valley, and the Far West. He divided the South with Dole, who carried a band of states running north from Texas. Clinton's Electoral College margin was substantial, 379 to 159. The Republicans, however, retained control of both houses of Congress.

Clinton Impeached

Although President Clinton steadfastly denied allegations of womanizing, in January 1998 a judge ordered him to testify in Paula Corbin Jones's lawsuit against him. Jones, who sought to strengthen her suit by showing that Clinton had a history of propositioning women, also subpoenaed a former White House intern. Her name was Monica Lewinsky.

Lewinsky and Clinton were separately asked if they had had an affair, and each denied the charge. When word of their alleged relationship was leaked to the press, Clinton declared in a TV news conference, "I did not have sexual relations with that woman, Miss Lewinsky."

Unbeknown to the Clintons, however, Lewinsky had been confiding to Linda Tripp, a former White House employee, and Tripp had secretly tape-recorded some twenty hours of their conversations. Tripp turned these tapes over to special prosecutor Starr, whose investigations of the Clintons' roles in the Whitewater scandal had broadened into a more general inquiry. In the tapes Lewinsky provided intimate details of repeated sexual encounters with the president. Clinton and Lewinsky appeared to have lied under oath. Starr threatened to indict Lewinsky for perjury. In return for immunity from prosecution, she admitted that she had engaged in sexual relations with the president and that he and his aides had encouraged her to give misleading testimony in the Jones case.

When called in August to testify on videotape before the Starr grand jury, Clinton conceded that he had engaged in "inappropriate intimate contact" with Lewinsky. But he insisted, "I have not had sex with her as I defined it." When pressed to supply his own definition, he responded with legalistic obfuscation: "My understanding of this definition is it covers contact by the person being deposed with the enumerated areas, if the contact is done with an intent to arouse or gratify." Because Clinton had not intended to arouse or gratify Lewinsky, he had not "had sex" with her. He allowed that this definition was "rather strange."

Read the Document

Bill Clinton, Answers to the Articles of Impeachment at **myhistorylab.com**

Clinton's testimony infuriated Starr, who made public Lewinsky's humiliatingly detailed testimony and announced that Clinton's deceptive testimony warranted consideration by the House of Representatives for impeachment.

But throughout Clinton's legal battles, opinion polls indicated that two in three Americans approved of his performance as president. Buoyed by the vibrant economy, most Americans blamed the scandal on the intrusive Starr nearly as much as the evasive Clinton. The November election proved disastrous for the Republicans, who nearly lost their majority in the House.

Clinton's troubles, however, were by no means over. Republican leaders in the House impeached Clinton on the grounds that he had committed perjury and had

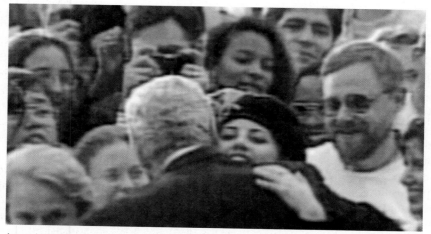

A seemingly anonymous well-wisher from the crowd greets President Bill Clinton. When Clinton was later investigated for having an affair with Monica Lewinsky, a former White House intern, this photograph of the two surfaced. Clinton's lack of discretion struck many as self-destructive.

obstructed justice by inducing Lewinsky and others to give false testimony in the Jones case. The vote closely followed party lines.

The impeachment trial in the Senate began in January 1999. Chief Justice William Rehnquist presided. The Republicans numbered fifty-five, enough to control the proceedings but twelve short of the two-thirds necessary to convict the president and remove him from office. Democrats, while publicly critical of Clinton's behavior, maintained that his indiscretions did not constitute "high crimes and misdemeanors" as specified in the Constitution for removal from office. They prevailed. The article accusing Clinton of perjury was defeated by a vote of fifty-five to forty-five; on the article alleging obstruction of justice, the vote was fifty to fifty. Clinton remained president.

Clinton's Legacy

One reason why Clinton survived was the health of the economy. Few wanted to rock the ship of state when it was stuffed with cash. Until the final months, the Clinton years coincided with the longest economic boom in the nation's history. Clinton deserves considerable credit for the remarkable prosperity of the era. His reducing the federal deficit drove interest rates down, spurring investment and economic growth. By August 1998 unemployment had fallen to 4.5 percent, the lowest level since the 1960s; inflation had eased to a minuscule 1 percent, the lowest level since the 1950s. In 1998 the federal government operated at its first surplus since 1969. In the 2000 fiscal year, the surplus hit $237 billion.

Clinton also supported globalization of the economy. He successfully promoted the **North American Free Trade Agreement (NAFTA)** to reduce tariff barriers; Congress approved NAFTA in 1993. But the new global economy harmed many. Some union leaders bitterly asked how their members could compete against convict labor in China or sweatshop workers in Indonesia or Malaysia. Others complained that the emphasis on worldwide economic growth was generating an environmental calamity. International protests against the World Trade Organization culminated in the disruption of its 2000 meeting in Seattle, when thousands of protesters went on a rampage, setting fires and looting stores.

Clinton's record in foreign affairs was mixed. In 1993 he failed in an effort to assemble an international force to prevent "ethnic cleansing" by Serbian troops against Muslims in Bosnia, formerly part of Yugoslavia. In 1999 critics predicted another debacle when Clinton proposed a NATO effort to prevent General Slobodan Milosevic of Yugoslavia from crushing the predominantly Muslim province of Kosovo, which was attempting to secede. But after several months of intense NATO bombing of Serbia, Milosevic withdrew from Kosovo. Within a year, he was forced out of office and into prison, awaiting trial for war crimes before a UN tribunal.

Clinton labored, as had his predecessors in the White House, to broker peace between Israel and the Palestinians; like his predecessors, he failed. In 1993 Yitzhak Rabin, Israeli prime minister, and Yassir Arafat, leader of the Palestine Liberation Organization, signed an agreement preparing for a Palestinian state. But extremists on both sides shattered the fragile accord. In 1995 Rabin was assassinated by a Jewish zealot. Palestinians, enraged by the construction of Israeli settlements in Palestinian territory, stepped up their campaign of suicide bombings. Israel retaliated with tank and helicopter attacks on suspected terrorist strongholds. The negotiations collapsed. Arafat unleashed a new wave of uprisings, and hardliners, headed by Ariel Sharon, took charge of Israel. Violence intensified on both sides.

Whatever the successes and shortcomings of his administration, the Clinton presidency will always be linked to his relationship with a White House intern and the impeachment proceedings that ensued. Though by no means the first president to stray from matrimonial propriety, Clinton's behavior, in an era when the media thrived on scandal, was symptomatic of an almost willful self-destructiveness.

The Economic Boom and the Internet

A significant part of the prosperity of the 1990s came from new technologies such as cellular phones and genetic engineering. But the most important was the development of a revolutionary form of communication: the Internet.

In the early 1990s, Tim Berners-Lee, a British physicist working at a research institute in Switzerland, devised the software that became the grammar—the "protocols"—of the Internet "language." With this language, the Internet became the World Wide Web (WWW), a conduit for a stream of electronic impulses flowing among hundreds of millions of computers.

The number of Web sites increased exponentially. In 1995 Bill Gates's Microsoft entered the picture with its Windows operating system, which made the computer easy to use. It created a Web browser—Microsoft Internet Explorer—and embedded its software in the Windows 95 bundle.

"Venture capitalists," independent investors seeking to fund emerging "tech" companies, sensed a glittering new economic frontier somewhere down the Internet super-highway, and they poured billions into start-up dot-coms. In 1999 some 200 Internet companies "went public," selling shares in the major stock exchanges. They raised $20 billion easily. In the spring of 2000, with the stock market still surging, a selling wave hit the tech stocks and spilled over to other companies. Stock prices plummeted. In all, some $2 trillion in stock funds disappeared. As the 2000 election approached, many feared that the economy was nearing a recession.

The 2000 Election: George W. Bush Wins by One Vote

During the 2000 campaign, Vice President Al Gore secured the Democratic nomination and chose as running mate Senator Joseph Lieberman of Connecticut, an observant Jew and outspoken critic of Clinton during the impeachment proceedings.

The leading contender was George W. Bush, son of former President Bush. Like his father, Bush graduated from Yale and worked in the family oil business. He headed a group that bought the Texas Rangers baseball team. Although some doubted Bush's abilities, his visible success with the Rangers catapulted him into Texas politics. An effective and personable campaigner, he was elected governor in 1994. Six years later he defeated Senator John McCain of Arizona in a battle for the Republican nomination for president. Bush selected as running mate Dick Cheney, who had served as defense secretary in his father's administration.

The main issue was what to do with the federal surplus, which by some projections would soon exceed $1 trillion. Bush called for a substantial tax cut; Gore wanted to increase spending on education and shore up the Social Security system.

Gore, though knowledgeable, seemed stiff, and he occasionally indulged in self-serving bombast, as when he claimed to have "invented" the Internet. Bush's principal offense was against the English language. "Rarely is the question asked," he once declaimed, "Is our children learning?" His poetic flights of fancy did not stay long aloft, as when he evoked American aspirations for "wings to take dream" and endorsed economic growth to "make the pie higher." However exaggerated or garbled their messages, the candidates spent a record $1 billion getting it to the voters.

Having been inundated with advertisements, many on election night breathed a sigh of relief that the election was finally over. They were wrong. By midnight it appeared that Bush had 246 electoral votes, and Gore, 267, with 270 necessary to win; but Florida, with 25 electoral votes, had not been decided. As returns trickled in, the television networks reversed themselves and declared Florida—and the election—"too close to call." Bush's lead there was 1,784 out of nearly 6 million cast.

After a machine recount, Bush's margin in Florida was reduced to several hundred votes, with Democrats complaining that a punch-card ballot used in some communities was confusing, depriving Gore of thousands of votes; worse, the machines routinely failed to count incompletely punched ballots. Gore's lawyers demanded that the ballots in several predominantly Democratic counties be counted by hand. Republicans countered that Democrats had no right to change voting procedures after the election. They demanded that the hand recounts cease.

The entire election ended up in the courts. On December 12, more than a month after the election, the Supreme Court ruled by a five to four vote that the selective hand recounts violated the Constitution's guarantee of equal protection. Bush's victory stood.

Nationwide, Gore received 51 million votes, Bush, 50.5 million.

The New Terrorism

After the fall of the Soviet Union, American military might seemed unassailable. Military dictators who had been kept afloat by the Soviets or the Americans—and often from both simultaneously—now were obliged to seek the support of the people they had long ruled. This further destabilized the Middle East. The military leaders of Egypt and hereditary rulers of Saudi Arabia, for example, sought to retain the support of Islamic clerics while refraining from accepting an Islamic theocracy—direct rule by Islamic rulers. Arab leaders cultivated popular support by denouncing Israel, which refused to return land seized in the 1967 war. Insofar as Israel relied ultimately on American support, Arab rage was increasingly directed at the United States.

During these years, Islamist terrorists emerged throughout the Middle East, usually in response to the repression of radical Islamic clerics. In 1998 a new figure surfaced from among such groups: Osama bin Laden, son of a Saudi oil billionaire. In 1998, bin Laden published a *fatwa*—a religious edict—to Islamic peoples throughout the world: "To kill Americans and their allies, both civil and military, is an individual duty of every Muslim who is able . . ." By now, bin Laden was protected by an extremist Islamic group, the Taliban, that ruled Afghanistan. (The United States had provided military assistance to the Taliban in its ultimately successful campaign to drive the Soviet Union out of the country a decade earlier. See Chapter 30.) Six months later, bin Laden's terrorist organization—al-Qaeda—had planned and ordered the bombings of the U.S. embassies in Nairobi and Dar es Salaam in Africa, which killed hundreds of people.

September 11, 2001

At 8:40 on the morning of September 11, 2001, Madeline Amy Sweeney, an attendant on American Airlines Flight 11, placed a cell phone call from the galley of the plane to her supervisor in Boston. In a whisper, she said that four Arab men had slashed the throats of two attendants, forced their way into the cockpit, and taken over the plane. She gave him their seat numbers so that their identities could be determined from the passenger log. The supervisor asked if she knew where the plane was headed. She looked out the window and noted that it was descending rapidly. "I see water and buildings." The water was the Hudson River, and the buildings were the skyscrapers of lower Manhattan, foremost among them the 110-story twin towers of the World Trade Center.

The hijackers pushed the throttle to full, and the Boeing 767 was traveling at 500 miles per hour at 8:46 when it slammed into the ninety-sixth floor of the north tower. A fireball, fed by 10,000 gallons of jet fuel, instantly engulfed eight or nine stories.

Fifteen minutes later a second airliner came into view over Manhattan harbor, banked sharply, and plowed into the eightieth floor of the south tower. New York mayor Rudolph Giuliani, who had raced to the scene, asked Fire Chief Peter Ganci, "What should I communicate to people?" "Tell them to get in the stairways," Ganci replied. "I think we can save everyone below the fire." The World Trade Center employed 50,000. As thousands fled the buildings, hundreds of firefighters, Ganci among them, charged up the stairs to rescue those who were trapped.

At 9:30 the White House received word that another hijacked airliner was barreling toward Washington, DC. Secret Service agents rushed Vice President Cheney to an emergency command bunker far below the White House. At 9:35 the airliner plunged into the Pentagon and burst into flames. Cheney telephoned President Bush, who was in Sarasota, Florida. The nation was under attack. Bush authorized the Air Force to shoot down any other hijacked airliners. A few minutes later a fourth hijacked airliner crashed into a field in Pennsylvania after passengers had declared their intention—again by cell phone—to retake the plane.

While television viewers absorbed these shocks, they watched as the upper floors of the World Trade Center towers blackened, like charred matches. At 9:59, the south tower collapsed, followed by the north tower a half hour later, pulverizing millions of tons of concrete and glass and enveloping lower Manhattan in choking dust. Nearly three thousand lay dead in the mountain of rubble, including Chief Ganci and 350 firemen; several hundred more perished at the Pentagon and in the crash of the airliner in Pennsylvania.

Teams of four or five Arabic-speaking men had hijacked each of the planes. Several of the hijackers were quickly linked to the al-Qaeda terrorist network run by bin Laden, who had previously been indicted (but not captured) for the 1998 bombing of U.S. embassies in East Africa and the 2000 attack on the USS *Cole*. Bin Laden operated with impunity in Afghanistan.

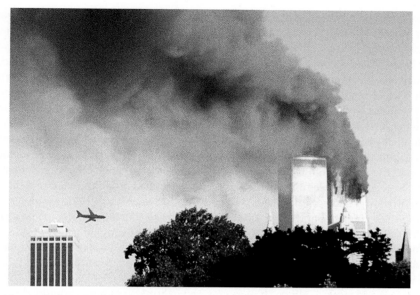

A second jetliner approaches the south tower of the World Trade Center on September 11, 2001. The north tower had already been hit and was engulfed in flames and smoke.

That evening President Bush addressed the nation. He spoke simply and with force. "We will find these people," he said of the terrorists. "They will pay." Any government harboring the terrorists—an obvious reference to the Taliban—would be held equally responsible for the attack.

Read the Document

George W. Bush, Address to Congress (September 20, 2001) at **myhistorylab.com**

Several weeks later, Bush declared that bin Laden would be taken "dead or alive." The president also offered a $25 million reward for his death or capture, an evocation of swift frontier justice that suited the national mood. Within the United States, thousands of Arabs were rounded up and detained; those with visa and immigration violations were imprisoned.

Then more trouble arrived at the capital, this time in the mail. Several letters addressed to government officials included threatening messages and a white powder consisting of billions of anthrax spores, which could prove fatal if touched or inhaled. Thousands of government employees took antibiotics as a precaution, but some spores had seeped out of the envelopes and killed five postal workers and mail recipients.

Bush responded to these multiple threats by creating a Cabinet position, the Office of Homeland Security, and naming Pennsylvania Governor Tom Ridge to direct it. Repeatedly Ridge issued vague warnings of imminent terrorist attacks. How exactly Americans were to protect themselves, he did not say.

America Fights Back: War in Afghanistan

Bush had declared a **war on terror**, a war unlike any other the nation had fought. Al-Qaeda had secret terrorist cells in many countries. Bin Laden was ensconced in remote Afghanistan, protected by thousands of Taliban soldiers who had inflicted heavy losses on Soviet invaders in the 1980s. The source of the anthrax letters proved even more problematic, because the spores resembled a strain developed in American military laboratories.

Bush's challenge was all the greater because of his own stated opposition to ill-defined and far-flung military operations. He had chastised the Clinton-Gore administration for "extending our troops all around the world." He underscored his reticence for such ventures by naming Colin Powell secretary of state. Powell, who had been sobered by his experiences in Vietnam, maintained that U.S. troops should only be deployed when their political objective was clear, military advantage overwhelming, and means of disengaging secure. This became known as the Powell doctrine, and Bush had endorsed it during the campaign. But the proposed war against terror adhered to none of its precepts. Now such scruples did not matter; the president had little choice but to fight.

Powell urged European, Asian, and even Islamic states to crack down on terrorist cells in their countries and to provide assistance in the U.S. military campaign against the Taliban; he also persuaded anti-Taliban factions within Afghanistan to join forces to topple the regime. On September 20 Bush ordered the Taliban to surrender bin Laden and top al-Qaeda leaders; when the Taliban refused, Bush unleashed missiles and warplanes against Taliban installations and defenses.

For several weeks, Taliban soldiers cowered in bunkers as bombs thudded nearby; but they defended their positions when anti-Taliban forces attacked. Then small teams of elite American soldiers, armed with hand-held computers and satellite-linked navigational devices, joined with anti-Taliban contingents, marking Taliban positions with laser spotters and communicating with high-altitude bombers. These planes, circling at 30,000 feet, dropped electronically guided bombs on Taliban troops with uncanny (but not infallible) accuracy. Within weeks the Taliban were driven from power. Only one American soldier was killed by hostile fire. The United States had won the first battles in the war against terror.

The Second Iraq War

In January 2002, after the Taliban had been crushed, President Bush declared that he would not "wait on events while dangers gather." The United States would take "preemptive actions"—war—against regimes that threatened it. He identified Iran, North Korea, and Iraq as an **axis of evil** that warranted scrutiny. Immediately after September 11, he secretly initiated plans to attack Iraq, ruled by Saddam Hussein.

Secretary of State Powell advised Bush not to attack Iraq. If Saddam were driven from power, Powell warned, Bush would become "the proud owner of 25 million people—you'll own it all." Vice President Cheney, Defense Secretary Donald Rumsfeld, and others in the administration insisted that the Iraqis would welcome liberation and embrace democracy.

In September, Bush sought congressional support for an attack on Iraq. "The Iraqi regime possesses chemical and biological weapons," he declared, adding that Saddam also sought nuclear weapons. Congress voted overwhelmingly for the war appropriation.

Bush then called on the United Nations to join the United States. That Saddam had used chemical weapons during the Iran-Iraq war and also against the Kurds was beyond dispute; but following Saddam's defeat in 1991, UN inspectors had destroyed thousands of tons of Iraqi chemical weapons. They doubted that more such weapons had been stockpiled. Bush saw this as proof that Saddam had hoodwinked the inspectors. When the Security Council delayed taking action, Bush formed a coalition to oust Saddam. The United States was joined by Great Britain, Italy, Spain, and a few other countries.

On March 20, 2003, American missiles and bombs pounded Saddam's defenses. The "Shock and Awe" campaign to liberate Iraq had begun. Two armored columns roared across the Kuwaiti border into Iraq, passing burned-out Iraqi tanks from the first Gulf War. British forces moved along the coast toward the oil port of Basra. Television reporters, perched atop Humvees and armored personnel carriers, provided live coverage. The first night, American units advanced halfway to Baghdad.

On April 4, the U.S. Army seized the Baghdad International Airport. The next morning, some 800 American soldiers in tanks and armored vehicles blasted their way into downtown Baghdad. While some Iraqis poured into the streets

"Mission Accomplished" proclaimed the banner on the USS *Abraham Lincoln*, where on May 1, 2004, President George W. Bush declared, "Major combat operations in Iraq have ended." But the war continued for years.

to celebrate, others looted offices, museums, stores, and hospitals. Saddam disappeared and his government evaporated. By mid-April, the Pentagon declared that major combat operations had come to an end.

But Iraq was in chaos. There were too few U.S. troops to preserve order. Islamist radicals, enraged by the American occupation, joined with Saddam's supporters in ambushing occupation forces. The insurgents rammed trucks filled with explosives into police stations, wired cell phones to artillery shells, and detonated them as Americans approached. Others sabotaged oil pipelines and power generators.

2004: Bush Wins a Second Term

The war became the main issue of the presidential campaign. In December 2003 American soldiers captured Saddam, hiding in an underground bunker. Bush's approval rating soared.

By January, however, Senator John Kerry, a Democratic senator from Massachusetts, was gaining in the polls. The son of a diplomat and a graduate of Yale, Kerry appeared accomplished and steady. He had commanded a patrol boat during the Vietnam War and was decorated for courage under fire. In April, he won the Democratic nomination. He chose Senator John Edwards of North Carolina, a wealthy trial lawyer, as his running mate.

In Iraq, the situation deteriorated further. In April the *60 Minutes* news program revealed that American captors had tortured Iraqi captives in the Abu Ghraib prison. Photographs of American soldiers, including women, taunting naked Muslim men fueled the insurgency. Casualties mounted. The cost of the occupation spiraled upward. Worse, American forces failed to find any Iraqi weapons of mass destruction.

At the Democratic convention in July, Kerry emphasized his military service in Vietnam. He criticized Bush for attacking Iraq before capturing Osama bin Laden, who remained at large. He also chided the president for initiating war with insufficient international support, and not sending enough troops to preserve order and rebuild Iraq.

Bush mobilized conservatives and religious fundamentalists by proposing a constitutional amendment that would define marriage as the union between a man and a woman. Kerry endorsed gay rights but endlessly qualified earlier statements in support of same-sex marriage.

Republicans also portrayed Kerry as opportunistic. If Kerry and Edwards thought the war was a mistake, why did they vote for the original war resolution in the Senate? During a debate with Bush, Kerry conceded that he had "made a mistake" in explaining his position on Iraq. "But the president made a mistake in invading Iraq. Which is worse?"

The election, one of the most divisive in recent decades, brought 12 million more voters to the polls than in 2000. Kerry received 57 million votes, 3 million more than Ronald Reagan in his 1984 landslide. But Bush got over 60 million, a record. He also prevailed in the Electoral College, 286 to 252.

Crime: Good News and Bad

The crime wave of the 1980s subsided during the 1990s. By 2009, the homicide rate nationwide was 40 percent below 1991. In many big cities the decline was astonishing. In 1990, for example, 5,641 felonies were committed in New York City's twenty-fourth precinct, near Central Park; in 2009 the number of felonies there had declined to 987.

But if urban crime was down, violence repeatedly jolted the nation. On April 20, 1999, two teenagers wearing trench coats and armed with automatic weapons went on a rampage at Columbine High School in Littleton, Colorado. Before shooting themselves to death, they killed twelve students and a teacher and wounded more than thirty. On October 2, 2006, a thirty-two-year-old truck driver took a dozen Amish schoolgirls hostage and shot and killed six of them. A week earlier, in two separate incidents, a gunman took six girls hostage at Platte Canyon High School at Bailey, Colorado, and shot and killed one; and a fifteen-year-old student at Weston High School in Cazenovia, Wisconsin, shot and killed his principal.

Perhaps inspired by these attacks, a deranged student at Virginia Tech in February 2007 bought a .22 caliber Walther P22 pistol on the Internet. The next month he bought a Glock 19 rapid-fire semiautomatic pistol and acquired ammunition from online vendors and from Wal-Mart and Dick's Sporting Goods. On April 16 he went to another dorm and shot and killed a female student and the resident advisor. After reloading, he entered Norris Hall, an engineering building, chained all three entry doors closed, climbed the stairs to the second floor, and walked up and down the hallway, taking aim at students and teachers and shooting them. Then he put a pistol to his head and committed suicide. The shooting spree at Norris lasted less than ten minutes: He shot over sixty people, killing thirty-three.

The massacre at Virginia Tech was the worst mass killing in recent American history. But each year, about 14,000 Americans are killed with guns. The spate of shootings reignited a heated debate. Proponents of gun control deplored the easy access to such lethal weapons. The National Rifle Association and other defenders of the right to bear arms, affirmed by the Second Amendment to the Constitution, blamed criminals for the mayhem. They insisted that law-abiding citizens needed guns to defend themselves from such evildoers. In 2010 the Supreme Court struck down municipal laws banning handguns in Chicago and the District of Columbia (*McDonald v. Chicago*).

Hurricane Katrina

The Bush presidency was largely shadowed by two events over which he initially had little control: the terrorist attack of September 11, 2001, and Hurricane Katrina, which swept across Florida and into the warm waters of the Gulf Coast in August 2005. On the morning of August 28, the National Weather Service released so dire a warning about Katrina—"devastating damage," "most of the area will be uninhabitable for weeks"— that some broadcasters refused to read it, thinking it might be a hoax. State and federal officials ordered mandatory evacuation of the Louisiana coastline.

Millions fled in their cars, clogging the highways. But of the half million residents of New Orleans, 100,000 remained, many of them poor African Americans who lacked access to automobiles. As rain started to fall that evening, some 10,000 took refuge in the New Orleans Superdome stadium.

Early the next morning Katrina crashed ashore. Within minutes, it destroyed nearly every building in Plaquemines Parish. Winds approaching 150 miles per hour ripped two holes in the Superdome. By afternoon, the hurricane had moved north, dumping more water along the way, swelling the rivers, streams, and canals that emptied into the Gulf. Within hours, rising waters spilled over the banks and collapsed canals. Then the levees at Lake Pontchartrain broke.

Downtown New Orleans after Hurricane Katrina.

By that evening, much of New Orleans was underwater. Some 25,000 people crowded into the Superdome. Food and water grew scarce. Fights broke out. When officials locked the Superdome's doors, the thousands left outside went to the nearby Convention Center, surged past security guards, and took possession of the complex.

Over the next three days, the situation worsened. Over a million people had been displaced from their homes. In the heat and humidity, dead bodies, sewage, rotting food and plants, and factory effluents combined to form a fetid and toxic inland sea. The Convention Center, which now housed 20,000, descended into anarchy. There were reports of rape and murder. Throughout the storm-devastated region, looting became widespread; public order collapsed.

"Mr. President, we need your help," declared Louisiana Governor Kathleen Blanco. But TV crews arrived on the scene long before assistance from the Federal Emergency and Management Agency (FEMA). Television viewers were outraged to see footage of the dead floating in pools of filth or abandoned in wheelchairs.

Yet Michael Chertoff, secretary of Homeland Security (which oversaw FEMA), expressed satisfaction with its efforts. "Considering the dire circumstances that we have in New Orleans, virtually a city that has been destroyed—things are going relatively well," he declared. By then, more than 1,300 were dead.

Many shared in the blame. For decades, engineers had warned that the levees and canals in New Orleans could fail, but little was done to strengthen them. Environmentalists had complained of the overdevelopment and erosion of the coastal marshes and wetlands whose vegetation sponged up excess water, but their warnings, too, had been mostly ignored. Officials in New Orleans had neglected to devise an evacuation plan for those without cars; worse, one-sixth of the police force abandoned the city before the storm struck. In Washington, FEMA director Michael Brown was so worried about making a mistake that he failed to do much at all—the worse mistake possible. Bush erred in publicly complimenting the beleaguered FEMA director: "Brownie, you're doing a heck of a job," a statement so obviously at variance with public perception that it became an instant joke. Within a week Brown was demoted; soon afterward he resigned.

Katrina was not the worst natural disaster in the nation's history. In 1900 a hurricane destroyed Galveston, then the largest city in Texas, killing 10,000. In 1906 an earthquake hit San Francisco, ignited hundreds of fires that burned 500 blocks of the city, and killed 700—a larger proportion of the population than perished in Katrina. But apart from Katrina's terrible human toll, the hurricane pointed up the nation's vulnerability. If Homeland Security could not get buses or water to New Orleans in a timely fashion, how could it protect the nation from determined terrorists or respond effectively should they mount another attack?

Iraq Insurgency and Bush's "Surge"

Bush faltered during Katrina partly because he was distracted by Iraq. Insurgents blew up police stations and marketplaces; saboteurs destroyed power facilities and cut oil pipelines; and rival religious sects, tribes, warlords, and criminal gangs pushed the country toward anarchy.

While coalition forces attempted to halt the violence, political officials laid the foundations for a new Iraqi government. On June 28, 2004, the coalition transferred nominal authority to an Iraqi Governing Council whose chief task was to organize the

In 2006 an Iraqi tribunal convicted Saddam Hussein of murdering his own people and sentenced him to death by hanging. What might have been a defining moment in the emergence of a new Iraq was marred when he was rushed to the gallows and taunted by his executioners.

election of a National Assembly to draft a constitution. On January 30, 2005, nearly 8 million Iraqis went to the polls, almost two-thirds of the eligible voters.

The election, though fraught with irregularities, offered a glimpse of the democratic Iraq that Bush hoped would initiate a broader transformation of the Middle East. But the election also underscored the divisions within Iraq. In the north, the Kurdish majority won most of the seats, but Kurdish leaders sought to form their own state and secede. In the south, the Shiites forged strong ties to the radical Islamic clerics who ruled Iran. The Sunnis dominated the region around Baghdad. Post-Saddam Iraq was on the verge of fracturing into separate nations.

Complicating matters further was the decision by terrorists to wreck the new government by driving a deeper wedge between Sunnis and Shiites. On February 22, 2006, insurgents blew up the golden dome of the Askariya Mosque in Sammara, a Shiite shrine. Enraged Shiites attacked Sunni mosques and clerics, triggering an endless cycle of reprisals. Some Iraqi military and police officers formed extralegal death squads to eliminate Sunni leaders and terrorize their followers. Sunni militias responded in kind.

In the fall of 2006, an Iraqi tribunal convicted Saddam of killing 148 Shiites, the first of several planned trials to chronicle his regime's genocide. But on December 30, 2006, the Iraqi government dispatched Saddam to the gallows. Instead of marking the triumph of law over tyranny, the executioners resembled the Shiite death squads: Hangmen taunted Saddam and chanted the name of Muqtada Al Sadr, a Shiite cleric whose militias caused much of the chaos.

Attacks on security forces and civilians intensified and casualties mounted. As the 2006 U.S. congressional elections approached, the war was costing $2 billion a week; the annual U.S. deficit soared to a half trillion dollars. Democrats, most of whom had voted for the war, increasingly withdrew their support. Some Republicans, too, defected from the president's position.

THREE HEROES

On March 20, 2003, American, British, and NATO forces commenced the assault to drive Saddam Hussein from power. It marked the beginning of the second Gulf War, also known as "Operation Iraqi Freedom." Saddam was swiftly driven from power, but by March 20, 2010, the seventh anniversary of the war, Americans were still fighting in Iraq and Afghanistan. By then, over 5,000 United States service personnel had died, including over 100 women; over 25,000 had been wounded. The following soldiers are a random sample of that group, chosen because they died on the March 20 anniversary of the onset of the war.

Francisco ("Paquito") Martinez, 20

Francisco G. Martinez.

"Paquito" Martinez was born on December 16, 1984, in San Juan, Puerto Rico. He was the son of Francisco Martinez, an army soldier and air force airman, and Carmen R. Hernandez. In 2000 Paquito moved to Ft. Worth, Texas, where he joined his father, "Paco," and his stepmother Maria. His father worked as a computer software engineer. Paquito enjoyed skateboarding, drawing, poetry and Web design. An "army brat," he vowed never to follow his father into military service. But several months after graduating from Eastern Hills High School in 2002, "Paquito" enlisted. He thought he might eventually go into computer-based graphic design.

In 2003 he was stationed in Korea. The next year he was sent to Iraq. He soon had doubts about the war. "I will serve myself, my family, my friends, and my loved ones," he blogged. "I won't serve my country, nor will I serve its leaders."

Later that year he completed a video entitled "Peacefull." Grass sways before a distant hill. In editing the video, Martinez drained it of color. The text is sparse:

> take this time to breathe
> open your mind
> feel your worries flow free

Then a monarch butterfly, in dazzling yellows and orange, wafts across the scene.

> life is what you make of it

On March 20, 2005, while on patrol in Tamin, Iraq, a sniper shot Martinez in the hip, severing an artery; despite trauma surgery, he died within an hour.

Curtis E. Glawson Jr., 24

Curtis E. Glawson Jr.

Curtis E. Glawson was born on June 10, 1982, in Detroit, Michigan. His parents—Yolanda and Curtis Sr.—were both career soldiers. As a child Curtis traveled with his parents from one base to another in Germany, New Mexico, Georgia, and Alabama. He learned to adapt to different people and cultures and made friends quickly; his smile was electric.

Glawson was fast and agile and he excelled in sports. When not engaged in football, baseball, basketball and running, he enjoyed sports-related video games. He was a passionate fan of all Detroit (and Michigan) sports teams. Friends called him Mr. ESPN.

In 2000 Glawson graduated from Daleville high school in Alabama, near Fort Rucker. He immediately enlisted in the army. That fall he was sent to Fort Jackson, South Carolina, where he received advanced training in mechanics. Certified as a light truck mechanic, he was subsequently stationed in Afghanistan, Uzbekistan, and Korea.

In Korea, he met Hyunjung Jang; the couple married at the United States embassy in Seoul in September, 2005.

In February, 2007 he was sent to Baghdad in Iraq. Once, when his unit made a wrong turn, they encountered a group of preteens armed with AK-47 automatic weapons. Although he grew increasingly nervous about his missions, he relished his work. When his mother urged him to beg off dangerous assignments, he replied, "No, momma, I can't do that. I have a job to do."

On the morning of March 20, 2007, Glawson was sent to retrieve a truck that broke down in the outskirts of Baghdad. He went out, fixed it, and brought it back to the motor pool. Later that afternoon, his platoon sergeant asked if Curtis could rescue another disabled vehicle in a dangerous sector. "I'm good to go, sergeant," Glawson replied. "Are you sure?" the officer asked, looking him in the eye. "Always ready, sergeant," Glawson replied.

That journey proved to be his last. As the road wound toward the dusty hills outside Baghdad, an **improvised explosive device (IED)** blew up his vehicle. Glawson was killed instantly. He wanted to be remembered as a loving son, husband, brother, friend, and dedicated soldier.

Daniel J. Geary, 22

Daniel Geary was born on September 12, 1986, the son of Michael Geary, machine foreman, and Agnes Geary, machine operator, in Rome, New York. Daniel was the fourth of seven children. When he was eight, he smelled smoke and pulled his four-year-old sister from a room that was engulfed in flames.

As a teenager, Geary enjoyed paintball, working on his Chrysler Sebring, and bowling. At sixteen, he bowled his first perfect game. He attended Rome Free Academy, a public high school, but dropped out a few weeks before graduation. For a time, he was

Daniel J. Geary.

unsure of what to do with his life. He landed a job at the Turning Stone Casino in Rome, owned by the Oneida Indians. Several months later, however, he resolved to get his diploma. "I was never more proud of him," his mother recalled. In 2006 he returned to school, joined the officer training program, and decided on a career in the military. In June, shortly before receiving his diploma, he enlisted in the Marines and soon subscribed to its motto wholeheartedly: *semper fidelis* (always faithful).

In September, Geary reported to Camp Lejeune, North Carolina, where he met his fiancée. In November, 2008, after a tour of duty on a ship in the Indian Ocean, he was sent to Kandahar, Afghanistan. He was impressed by the mountains that towered above ancient valleys. "Other than people trying to shoot me and blow me up," he told his mother, "you can't believe how beautiful it is over here."

On March 19, 2009, he was part of a team of Marines that caught an enemy bomber near a police station. The next day the team returned to the station to encourage the local police to work harder to capture insurgents. While the others were meeting inside, Geary stood guard, manning a machine gun in a Humvee. Then a car with police markings came through the gate, approached the Humvee and blew up, killing Geary instantly.

Question for Discussion

■ These three soldiers are among the millions who contributed to the American destiny but whose names so often are missing from historical accounts. What other unsung heroes are missing from this book?

When the midterm votes were counted, the Republicans were decisively defeated. Democrats now controlled Congress—and the budget. Several days after the election Bush dismissed Defense Secretary Rumsfeld, acknowledging voter "displeasure with the lack of progress in Iraq." But the president vowed to remain. "America's going to stand with you," Bush promised Iraqi leaders.

Democrats named Nancy Pelosi Speaker of the House of Representatives, the first woman to hold that position. Insofar as the speaker follows the vice president in chain of succession, Pelosi became the highest-ranking woman ever to hold office in the United States. In January 2007, when Bush called for a modest increase in troop levels in Iraq, Pelosi and some prominent Democrats opposed the measure. The Democratic leadership in Congress voted to reduce funding for the war, actions Bush vetoed.

In January, 2007 Bush named General David Petraeus to command a "**surge**" in American troop levels in Iraq. The troops were to remove insurgents from a region, establish military control over it, and build stronger ties with the Iraqi people. Initially, Petraeus made little progress. The losses among American military personnel mounted (see American Lives, "Three Heroes," pp. 850–851). Petraeus shifted more military tasks to the Iraqis and reduced operations that would likely lead to high civilian casualties. He also worked to bring former Sunni leaders into the Iraqi government. By the spring of 2008, the violence in Iraq had declined; the "surge" appeared to be working.

2008: McCain v. Obama

By the spring of 2008 John McCain, a Republican senator from Arizona, was far ahead in the race for the Republican nomination. McCain had piloted a navy fighter-bomber during the Vietnam war. After his plane was shot down over North Vietnam, he was held as a prisoner-of-war for six years; occasionally he was tortured. Now seventy-one, McCain if elected would be the oldest person to serve as a first-term president. Although McCain's positions were similar to those of Bush, McCain had often criticized the president and described himself as a "maverick."

Watch the Video
The Historical Significance of the 2008 Presidential Election at myhistorylab.com

True to his own label, he surprised pundits by naming Sarah Palin, the little-known governor of Alaska, as running mate. Her youth (forty-four) counterbalanced McCain's age. Palin also exhibited a down-to-earth feistiness. She was a new type of feminist: a former beauty queen who hunted and fished; an ardent defender of traditional family values who pursued an extravagantly ambitious career.

Among Democrats, Hillary Clinton, now a senator from New York, emerged as frontrunner. But she was soon eclipsed by Barack Obama, a first-term senator from Illinois (see Chapter 31, American Lives, "Barack Obama"). Clinton had voted for the war in Iraq while Obama opposed it; otherwise they agreed on most issues. Obama won the Democratic nomination and named Joe Biden, a senator from Delaware, as his running-mate.

During the general election McCain pointed out that Obama had failed to serve even a single full term as U.S. senator: Obama, he claimed, was unqualified for the presidency. But McCain's choice of Palin deprived McCain of his strongest issue. Palin had served as governor for only two and a half years; before that she was mayor of tiny Wasilla, Alaska. When critics questioned her experience in foreign affairs, her breezy reply—"You can actually see Russia from land here in Alaska"—cast doubt on McCain's judgment.

Obama criticized the Republican administration for waging war against Iraq, thereby diverting resources that might have crushed the main 9/11 culprits: the

Taliban in Afghanistan and Osama bin Laden, who remained at large. Obama proposed moving troops from Iraq to Afghanistan. He also advocated a major expansion of federally backed health care. McCain sought to send more troops to Iraq: The "war on terror" did not allow retreats. He also criticized Obama's health-care proposal as a major step toward socialized medicine.

As the campaign was heating up, a tremor rocked the foundations of the global economic system. Alarming financial news pushed the campaign out of the headlines.

Republican candidates John McCain and Sarah Palin campaign at Franklin & Marshall University in 2008.

Financial Meltdown

The fault lines of the 2008–2009 crisis extended to the 1990s. At that time the economy appeared to have recovered from the recession that began in 1973. But while the stock market soared, wages lagged far behind. By 2005, for the first time since the Great Depression, the American people spent more than they earned. Mostly they bought houses. But how, without savings, could they afford down payments? Politicians, bankers, and financial "wizards" had devised several solutions. In 2002 President George W. Bush declared that the government should "encourage folks to own their own home." Homeowners, he believed, were more responsible citizens than renters. Leaders in both parties advocated easier lending requirements and prodded the huge federally owned mortgage companies to issue more mortgages. Private mortgage companies followed suit. They reasoned that as house prices increased, the ability of homeowners to repay loans mattered less: A repossessed house could be sold for more than the original mortgage loan.

Granted easier credit, millions of Americans for the first time bought homes. In 1994, 64 percent of U.S. families owned homes; by 2004, the percentage had increased to

Table 32.1 Causes of the 2008–2009 Financial Crisis

Consumers exhaust savings to buy houses
The president and Congress call on federally owned mortgage companies to relax lending requirements
Global investment bankers devise complicated bundles of mortgages and market them globally
Credit-rating agencies grade these mortgage investments as solid and AIG insures them
Lending banks issue mortgages greatly in excess of available reserves
Millions of homeowners fall into debt and cannot make mortgage payments
Collapse of mortgage investments brings down investment banks
Capital evaporates, leading to layoffs and threatening a second Great Depression

69 percent, the highest ever. Housing prices soared. Many homeowners bought bigger ones—"McMansions," in the slang of the day.

Soon banks and mortgage companies had exhausted their capital. Large international investment banks such as Goldman Sachs, Lehman Brothers, and Bear Stearns more than filled the void. They bought tens of thousands of mortgages from the original banks and lending institutions. Lending banks used this revenue to loan out more mortgages—thereby generating more profits (and bonuses). International investment firms chopped up the mortgages like sausages, clumped them into complicated investment bundles, and sold the bundles to investors worldwide. Credit-rating companies, such as Moody's and Standard and Poor's, pronounced the bundles to be sound investments. And many investors bought insurance from the American Insurance Group (AIG) to protect them if the bundles somehow went bad. AIG, perceiving little risk, failed to set aside much money to cover potential losses.

By late 2008, however, millions of homeowners were swamped with bills they could not pay. Total household debt in the United States exceeded $14.5 *trillion*—twenty times more than in 1974. Nearly 10 percent of all American mortgages were delinquent or in foreclosure. Goldman Sachs quietly placed bets that the mortgage bundles it had mass-marketed would lose their value!

Investors suddenly caught on and dumped their mortgage bundles. Panic selling hit financial markets worldwide. Almost overnight, Bear Stearns collapsed and Lehman Brothers went bankrupt. The Dow Jones Industrial Average plunged from over 14,000 to under 9,000; stocks lost $8 trillion. Pension funds, corporate reserves, and personal accounts for retirement and college education lost one-third of their value. AIG, swamped with claims, neared bankruptcy. Its failure would take down many of the world's major banks and investment firms.

Nearly all banks and investment houses ran low on capital; many struggled to stave off bankruptcy. Few could make new loans. But most businesses, hospitals, schools, state and municipal governments relied on short-term loans, which were repaid as revenues came in. In the absence of these customary loans, few employers could pay bills or cover payrolls. A global calamity loomed.

In the final months of 2008, Bush and his chief financial advisers raced to avert catastrophe. Ben Bernanke, head of the Federal Reserve and a scholar of the Great Depression, pleaded with Congress to authorize over $700 billion to buy up the "toxic" mortgage bundles, an indirect way of preserving the banks and global investment firms that had issued them. He also proposed to pump hundreds of billions directly into Goldman Sachs, AIG, and scores of other investment banks. Such companies, he warned, were "too big to fail." Congress seethed at using taxpayers' money to bail out avaricious corporate executives; but political leaders could not risk a second Great Depression.

"Yes We Can": Obama Elected President

The economic crisis caught nearly everyone by surprise. Much of the blame fell on Republicans, whose support for deregulation of financial markets dated from the Reagan era. McCain was especially hurt by the economic meltdown. On September 15, 2008, the day after Lehman Brothers declared bankruptcy, McCain downplayed the crisis, claiming "The fundamentals of our economy are strong." Within a few hours, the stock market fell 500 points. He appeared to be out of touch.

Obama's oft-repeated (albeit vague) insistence on change now acquired new meaning. When confronted with "impossible odds," he insisted, "Americans have responded with a simple creed: Yes we can." The nation was ready for change. On election day, Obama won by over 8 million votes; his victory in the Electoral College was by a 365 to 173 margin.

◉ Watch the Video

The Connection Between Obama & Lincoln at **myhistorylab.com**

Obama's victory stunned foreigners. Nelson Mandela, the black leader of the movement that toppled white rule in South Africa, claimed that Obama's election inspired everyone who wanted "to change the world for a better place." Gordon Brown, prime minister of Great Britain, called Obama's election "a moment that will live in history as long as history books are written."

Obama as President

Only a few weeks after Obama, his wife Michelle, and their two daughters had moved into the White House, he was awarded the Nobel Prize "for his extraordinary efforts to strengthen international diplomacy and cooperation between peoples." Abashed at receiving an award in the expectation that he would earn it, Obama gave the $1.4 million prize to charity. Nevertheless, Obama's intentions of changing the course of American foreign policy were evident. He closed CIA-run secret prisons and banned torture and other means of coercion during interrogation of suspected terrorists. He named Hillary Clinton secretary of state and promised to work more closely with the international community.

In Iraq, Obama proceeded cautiously. He asked Robert Gates, secretary of defense under Bush, to remain in that capacity in his administration. He also announced a plan to withdraw most American troops from Iraq by the fall of 2010.

During his first months as president, however, Obama was mostly absorbed in the financial crisis. Despite repeated promises of change, he retained many of Bush's chief financial advisers; nearly all were Wall Street insiders. Critics grumbled that it made little sense to ask those who had broken the economy to put it back together. But Obama had little choice. No one else understood the complicated mathematical models on which modern trading was based; unfortunately, few Wall Street executives understood them either. Macroeconomics, some economists maintained, had become an elaborate exercise in chaos theory.

By late March 2009 the Dow Jones had fallen below 6,600, down from 14,000 seventeen months earlier. Chrysler declared bankruptcy, followed by General Motors several months later. Huge layoffs ensued. Unemployment rose steadily, surpassing

President-elect Barack Obama, his daughters, and wife, Michelle, celebrate his victory in November, 2008.

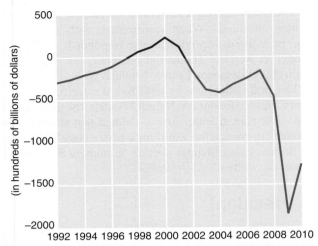

Annual Federal Deficit (and Surplus), 1992–2010 After years of deficits, the federal government operated at a $250 billion surplus in 2000. But the war on terror after 9/11 resulted in massive deficits, which were exacerbated by the financial meltdown after 2008.

10 percent for the first time in several decades. Obama pumped another $700 billion into the struggling economy.

Then word leaked out that hundreds of millions of dollars had been paid in bonuses to executives of Goldman Sachs, AIG, and many of the big banks that had been saved by federal bailouts. Obama railed against their ill-timed greed and slapped the companies with nuisance taxes, but he could do little else. He needed the big financial institutions to help jolt the economy back to life.

By the fall of 2009, the strategy appeared to be working. Employment increased and the stock market rose. Some banks repaid their government loans. Talk of economic collapse abated, partly because predictions varied widely. Some economists insisted that once the stimulus money had been exhausted, employment, wages, and prices would again fall and the nation would slip into a recession—or worse. Others pointed to the projected $1.8 trillion deficit for 2009 and predicted rampant inflation. Insofar as no one had forecast the financial meltdown of 2008–2009, most political leaders discounted *all* economic predictions and simply hoped for the best.

Health Care Reform

By 2009 nearly everyone agreed that medical costs had spun out of control. In 1990, per capital medical expenditures were $3,000; by 2009, they exceeded $8,000. That year, though nearly 18 percent of the nation's gross domestic product went for medical care, some 46 million Americans lacked any coverage whatsoever. When struck by serious illness, they were denied treatment or were hit with staggering bills. More than half of the nation's personal bankruptcies were precipitated by illness.

Obama's goal was twofold: to provide health care to Americans who lacked it and to reduce health care costs. Some advocated a government-run system, such as Franklin Roosevelt had done with old age pensions through Social Security. Many European governments operated health care systems along similar lines. But opposition

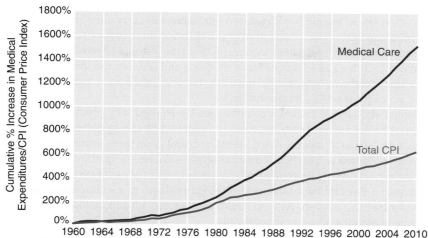

Price Increases - CPI vs. Medical Care (Cumulative % Increase)

The Increasing Cost of Health Care, 1960–2008 (% increase) By the 1990s, health care cost increases greatly exceeded the increase in the Consumer Price Index.

to socialized medicine in the United States was intense. Polls showed that few Americans wanted their doctors to be employees of the federal government.

Supported by Democratic leaders in Congress, Obama proposed a system that combined private and public health insurance. Elderly and poor Americans would continue to be covered by the government; private insurers would continue to insure millions of Americans, but they could not kick people out of their systems when they became ill; companies with more than fifty employees would be required to provide health care insurance for employees and their families or else face stiff penalties; most other persons would be eligible for publicly supported health insurance.

Republicans almost uniformly denounced the plan; they insisted that Americans did not want the federal government to control health care. Republicans instead recommended tax incentives or state initiatives to encourage private employers to broaden coverage. Republicans added that the federal government, with a looming annual deficit of $1.8 trillion, would be hard-pressed to pay for Medicare in the future; to embark on a major new commitment was madness.

The Democrats, despite strong majorities in both houses of Congress, were themselves divided on Obama's plan. The final compromise provided for his reform to be phased in over ten years at a cost of $1 trillion, and coverage would not be universal: By 2019, 24 million people would still lack health insurance, about a third of them illegal immigrants.

In March 2010, Congress approved the measure—the vote in the House was 220 to 207. No Republican voted for the bill. Obama had nevertheless engineered the first major health care reform since 1965, when President Lyndon Johnson signed Medicare into law.

Immigration Reform

Buoyed by this success, Obama turned to immigration. Early in his presidency, he strengthened border security to cut down on illegal immigration from Mexico, an action that angered Mexican leaders (see the introduction to Chapter 11, p. 299).

Yet illegal immigration persisted. In 2010 Arizona governor Jan Brewer, complaining that "the majority of illegal trespassers" were "bringing drugs in," signed the toughest immigration law in the nation. It required immigrants to carry alien registration forms at all times and authorized police to stop and question anyone they suspected of being an illegal immigrant. Legislators in dozens of states introduced similar bills. Obama denounced such laws as a form of racial profiling and ordered the Justice Department to take legal action against the Arizona bill. He also called for a federal initiative to prevent states from acting "irresponsibly."

Obama also steered toward a compromise. He rejected state plans for rounding up and deporting the nation's 11 million illegal immigrants; he also opposed liberal proposals to declare an "amnesty" against illegal immigrants and grant them immediate citizenship. Instead he proposed a "practical, common-sense" solution—a "pathway to citizenship." Illegal immigrants would be granted citizenship only after they admitted they had broken the law, paid a fine and back taxes, and provided evidence of a willingness to assimilate, such as by learning English. As with health care reform, Obama outlined few specifics, preferring to allow Congress to shape the plan.

Republicans bristled; without more effective policing of the border, Obama's "reform" would encourage more illegal immigrants to pour into the country. Many complained that Obama was courting Hispanic voters just a few months ahead of the 2010 congressional elections. The prospects for quick passage of comprehensive immigration reform seemed poor.

Environmental Concerns and Disaster in the Gulf

During his first weeks in office, Obama had pledged a "new era of global cooperation on climate change." Nearly everyone assumed that he intended to push for ratification of the 1997 agreement, signed by more than 130 nations at Kyoto, Japan, to reduce emissions of carbon dioxide and other atmospheric pollutants. The Senate had opposed the Kyoto accords because developing nations—including China, the worst air polluter in the world—were exempted from its costly provisions. President Clinton never submitted the treaty for ratification. In 2001, President George W. Bush withdrew the United States from subsequent negotiations. But in 2006 the mayors of over 200 U.S. cities, struggling with smog and air pollution, signed a Climate Protection Agreement pledging to meet the Kyoto targets for greenhouse gas reductions by 2012. But if Obama intended to move in the direction of the Kyoto agreements, the economic crisis of 2008–2009 changed his mind. With the nation's economy in recession, Obama thought it unwise to impose new environmental restrictions. In late 2009 he quietly withdrew support for an international arrangement on atmospheric pollutants.

By then, political economic realities had already caused Obama to backtrack on another environmental issue. Originally an opponent of oil drilling off the Atlantic coast, he changed his position during the 2008 presidential campaign: The nation needed cheap oil and gasoline (see introduction, Chapter 30, p. 787). On April 21, 2010, disaster struck in the Gulf of Mexico. Workers aboard a British Petroleum (BP) oil platform forty-one miles off the coast of Louisiana were drilling for oil at a depth of 5,000 feet. The drill hit a pocket of methane gas under high pressure; it shot upward through the drilling pipe and exploded, blasting eleven workers from the platform and engulfing it in flames. Oil gushed from the damaged pipe, an upsetting image captured by underwater cameras

A brown pelican surveys the ecological damage caused by the BP oil spill in the Gulf of Mexico in 2010.

and transmitted by streaming video on the Web. The world watched in horror as BP's repeated attempts to cap the well failed; weeks passed as hundreds of millions of gallons of oil spewed into the Gulf, fouling marshes and beaches, killing fish, birds, and aquatic life. Obama called it the "worst environmental disaster America has faced."

Pressure built on him to "do something." Exactly what was unclear. "He can't put on scuba gear and go down and stop this well," observed New York City mayor Michael Bloomberg, a Republican. Obama forced BP to set aside $20 billion to cover damage claims and sacked the director of the Minerals Management Service for failing to adequately inspect the off-shore platforms. He also declared a six-month moratorium on deepwater drilling, pending the inspection of existing platforms.

Opponents of the moratorium included both of Louisiana's senators and its governor, Bobby Jindal, who noted that the oil industry accounted for 17 percent of Louisiana's jobs and much of the state's revenue. Such opposition underscored the dilemma confronting a nation whose thirst for cheap oil was unquenchable. The exhaustion of oil reserves beneath the earth's landmass necessitated offshore drilling; but the environmental risks of deep-sea drilling were all too apparent.

Obama resurrected his campaign goal of promoting alternative sources of energy, such as solar and wind power. But such solutions seemed to lie far in the future. Whether the disaster in the Gulf of Mexico would reinvigorate the environmental movement remained to be seen.

Afghanistan, Again

The economic crisis and the environmental calamity in the Gulf of Mexico notwithstanding, Afghanistan loomed as the dominant issue for Obama's presidency. Few could have imagined such a development in December 2001, when the war in Afghanistan appeared to be over. The Taliban had been driven from power; most of

An Army helicopter arrives to evaluate soldiers wounded after their armored vehicle hit an improvised explosive device (IED) in the Tangi Valley in Afghanistan.

its leaders had been killed or captured or they had fled to Pakistan. Bush shifted his attention to driving Saddam Hussein from power in Iraq; a United Nations commission was given the task of building a new Afghan government.

In late 2001, the commission summoned Afghan leaders who eventually chose Hamid Karzai as interim leader of the nation. Karzai had helped channel American aid to the Taliban when it was fighting the Soviet Union; he later became a staunch opponent of the Taliban and worked with Americans to forge a coalition in opposition to it. As interim leader, Karzai relied on United Nations troops—one-half of them provided by the United States—to enforce the new government's authority.

For a time it appeared that a new Afghanistan was emerging. Hundreds of schools, hospitals, and roads were built; women were granted new rights. In 2004 Karzai defeated twenty-two opponents to become the first democratically elected president of the Islamic Republic of Afghanistan.

But much of the progress was illusory. Karzai's government was weak and riddled with corruption. In the southern sections of Afghanistan, Islamic radicals resurfaced and the former Taliban slipped back into the country, calling on Muslims to fight "infidel" troops. In the north, tribal leaders jockeyed to expand their power. Nearly everywhere, criminal militias vied for control of the lucrative opium trade.

The election scheduled for the fall of 2009 made matters worse. The first round was marred by voting fraud, which UN observers confirmed. During the final campaign the chief opposition candidate withdrew, charging Karzai's government with rigging the outcome. Karzai "won" by default. Enemies of Karzai's regime exploited the controversy.

By late 2009 Obama, who had opposed the "surge" in Iraq, sent another 30,000 troops to Afghanistan. American forces increasingly relied on drones—unmanned planes—to drop guided bombs on suspected enemies in Afghanistan and Pakistan. When the bombs missed the targets and killed civilians, riots ensued and UN casualties mounted.

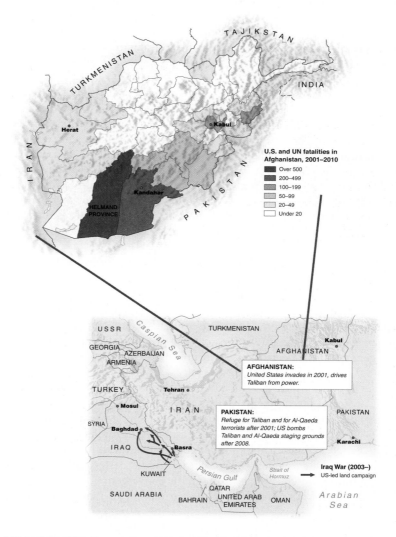

War in Iraq and Afghanistan, 2001–Present Since 2003, the United States has fought two major wars in Central Asia: in Afghanistan, first to drive the Taliban from power and later to suppress an insurgency; and in Iraq, first to crush Saddam Hussein and later to install a democratic government. In Afghanistan, American losses have been heaviest in the southern provinces bordering Pakistan.

For some time, General Stanley McChrystal, commander of the United Nations troops, had chafed at rules of engagement designed to limit civilian casualties. Obama's administration, McChrystal's aides complained to reporters for *Rolling Stone*, was weak and ineffective. The article appeared in June 2010, the month with the heaviest losses of the war. Obama sacked McChrystal for insubordination, replacing him with David Petraeus, architect of the "surge" in Iraq. "We have arrived at a critical point," Petraeus declared on July 4, 2010. "We are in this to win."

A month later secret government documents, leaked to the press, revealed that while Pakistan had pledged to support the war on terror, its intelligence service helped the Taliban plan attacks on American soldiers. Insurgents in Iraq and Afghanistan persisted in blowing up crowded marketplaces, mosques, and government offices. Prospects for victory in the region remained bleak; no one could even imagine what it would look like.

The Persistent Past and Imponderable Future

But the previous eighteen years had shown that human events rarely unfold in predictable ways. The 9/11 terrorist attack, the subsequent wars in Iraq and Afghanistan, the near-collapse of the economy in 2008–2009, Hurricane Katrina, and the massive oil spill in the Gulf of Mexico all shocked the American people. And the surprises were not all bad. No one in 1992 could have predicted that the tidal wave of crime would recede the following decade. For that matter, the relative absence of racial references during the 2008 campaign that resulted in the election of the nation's first African American president would have been unimaginable decades earlier.

But if the past does not enable us to predict the future, what do we ever "learn" from history? Consider an analogy with seismology, the study of earthquakes. Seismologists cannot predict exactly when and where any earthquake will strike, but their study of the underlying forces—the shift and collision of tectonic plates—helps explain the phenomenon. Historians similarly cannot predict the future course of human events. But the study of history can provide insights on the underlying forces that generate historical change. No one predicted, for example, that a particular deep-sea oil well would explode and release millions of barrels of oil into the Gulf of Mexico in the summer of 2010; but the American nation's voracious thirst for oil—a result of many developments during the previous century—led to the demand for the exploitation of deep-water oil resources. Similarly, in the first decades of the twenty-first century Americans fought and died in Iraq and Afghanistan because of a wide variety of historical forces, ranging from a commitment to democratic values and human rights to a demand for cheap Middle Eastern oil. History does not predict the future, which emerges through the convergence of infinite actions and reactions. But history can help reveal the various forces that are heaving beneath the surface of time.

This book was conceived as a reminder that the past is never truly past. It radiates through time. It touches our lives, just as what we do today will influence the future. By connecting to the past, we better understand ourselves and perhaps gain an inkling of what will become of us.

Milestones

1992	Democrat Bill Clinton is elected president
1993	Ruth Bader Ginsberg becomes second woman justice of the Supreme Court
1994	Republicans win control of both houses of Congress
	Congress defeats Clinton's health care reform plan
1996	Democrat Bill Clinton is reelected president; Republicans retain control of Congress
	Measure revamping federal welfare system is passed by Congress and signed by President Clinton
1998	The House of Representatives impeaches Clinton
1999	Clinton acquitted by Senate, Clinton remains in office
	NATO troops, including Americans, are sent to Kosovo to stop Serbian "ethnic cleansing"
	Gun violence in schools escalates; twelve die at Columbine High School in Colorado
2000	Republican George W. Bush is elected president when Supreme Court halts Florida recounts
2001	Terrorists hijack airliners and fly them into the twin towers of the World Trade Center in New York and the Pentagon, killing 3,000
	United States drives Taliban from power in Afghanistan
2002	President Bush prepares for war as he accuses Saddam Hussein of Iraq of developing weapons of mass destruction
2003	United States and United Kingdom attack and defeat Iraq and capture Saddam Hussein
2004	Republican George W. Bush is reelected president
2005	Hurricane Katrina devastates New Orleans and Gulf Coast region
2007	Democrat Nancy Pelosi becomes first woman Speaker of the House
2008	Deranged student kills thirty-three at Virginia Tech
	Democrat Barack Obama is first African American to be elected president
	Collapse of U.S. mortgage markets triggers global financial crisis
2009	Obama implements troop surge in Afghanistan
2010	Congress approves health care bill
	BP-owned rig explodes, killing eleven and spewing oil into the Gulf of Mexico
	Arizona passes law to crack down on illegal immigrants; national debate ensues
	Republicans take control of House of Representatives

✓•⌐Study and Review at www.myhistorylab.com

Review Questions

1. The introduction divides this chapter into two different narrative arcs: the first one—from 1992 to 2001—is mostly positive; the second, from 9/11 through 2010, is said to constitute—as *Time* magazine put it—"The Decade from Hell." What were the "positive" aspects of the period from 1992 to 2001? The "negative" components of the subsequent one? How is this characterization too simple?

2. Bill Clinton was hardly the first president to commit adultery. Why did his indiscretions lead to charges that resulted in an impeachment proceeding? Did his actions constitute "high crimes and misdemeanors"? What were the major achievements of the Clinton presidency?

3. The section of this chapter on the disputed 2000 presidential election is subtitled: "George W. Bush Wins by One Vote." What does that mean? Why did Bush win the election?

4. Why did Islamist terrorists attack on 9/11? Why did George W. Bush go to war against Afghanistan shortly afterwards? Why did he then invade Iraq? What issues in Iraq made it difficult to withdraw United States troops?

5. Hurricane Katrina was a natural disaster. To what extent, however, did human actions—and inactions—aggravate the calamity?

6. Why did global financial markets nearly collapse from 2008–2009? What caused the financial meltdown? What impact did it have on Americans?

7. What factors contributed to Barack Obama being elected president? What were the major elements of his health care reform act and how did he get it through Congress?

8. Why did Obama send American troops back into Afghanistan?

Key Terms

axis of evil *844*
Contract with
     America *837*
improvised explosive
     device (IED) *851*

North American Free
     Trade Agreement
     (NAFTA) *839*

"surge" *852*
war on terror *843*

APPENDIX:
The Declaration
of Independence

In Congress, July 4, 1776

The Unanimous Declaration of the Thirteen United States of America,

When, in the course of human events, it becomes necessary for one people to dissolve the political bonds which have connected them with another, and to assume, among the powers of the earth, the separate and equal station to which the laws of nature and of nature's God entitle them, a decent respect to the opinions of mankind requires that they should declare the causes which impel them to the separation.

We hold these truths to be self-evident: That all men are created equal; that they are endowed by their Creator with certain unalienable rights; that among these are life, liberty, and the pursuit of happiness; that, to secure these rights, governments are instituted among men, deriving their just powers from the consent of the governed; that whenever any form of government becomes destructive of these ends, it is the right of the people to alter or to abolish it, and to institute new government, laying its foundation on such principles, and organizing its powers in such form, as to them shall seem most likely to effect their safety and happiness. Prudence, indeed, will dictate that governments long established should not be changed for light and transient causes; and accordingly all experience hath shown that mankind are more disposed to suffer, while evils are sufferable, than to right themselves by abolishing the forms to which they are accustomed. But when a long train of abuses and usurpations, pursuing invariably the same object, evinces a design to reduce them under absolute despotism, it is their right, it is their duty, to throw off such government, and to provide new guards for their future security. Such has been the patient sufferance of these colonies; and such is now the necessity which constrains them to alter their former systems of government. The history of the present King of Great Britain is a history of repeated injuries and usurpations, all having in direct object the establishment of an absolute tyranny over these states. To prove this, let facts be submitted to a candid world.

He has refused his assent to laws, the most wholesome and necessary for the public good.

He has forbidden his governors to pass laws of immediate and pressing importance, unless suspended in their operation till his assent should be obtained; and, when so suspended, he has utterly neglected to attend to them.

He has refused to pass other laws for the accommodation of large districts of people, unless those people would relinquish the right of representation in the legislature, a right inestimable to them, and formidable to tyrants only.

He has called together legislative bodies at places unusual, uncomfortable, and distant from the depository of their public records, for the sole purpose of fatiguing them into compliance with his measures.

He has dissolved representative houses repeatedly, for opposing, with manly firmness, his invasions on the rights of the people.

He has refused for a long time, after such dissolutions, to cause others to be elected; whereby the legislative powers, incapable of annihilation, have returned to the people at large for their exercise; the state remaining, in the mean time, exposed to all the dangers of invasions from without and convulsions within.

He has endeavored to prevent the population of these states; for that purpose obstructing the laws for naturalization of foreigners; refusing to pass others to encourage their migration hither, and raising the conditions of new appropriations of lands.

He has obstructed the administration of justice, by refusing his assent to laws for establishing judiciary powers.

He has made judges dependent on his will alone, for the tenure of their offices, and the amount and payment of their salaries.

He has erected a multitude of new offices, and sent hither swarms of officers to harass our people and eat out their substance.

He has kept among us, in times of peace, standing armies, without the consent of our legislatures.

He has affected to render the military independent of, and superior to, the civil power.

He has combined with others to subject us to a jurisdiction foreign to our constitution, and unacknowledged by our laws, giving his assent to their acts of pretended legislation:

For quartering large bodies of armed troops among us;

For protecting them, by a mock trial, from punishment for any murder which they should commit on the inhabitants of these states;

For cutting off our trade with all parts of the world;

For imposing taxes on us without our consent;

For depriving us, in many cases, of the benefits of trial by jury;

For transporting us beyond seas, to be tried for pretended offenses;

For abolishing the free system of English laws in a neighboring province, establishing therein an arbitrary government, and enlarging its boundaries, so as to render it at once an example and fit instrument for introducing the same absolute rule into these colonies;

For taking away our charters, abolishing our most valuable laws, and altering fundamentally the forms of our governments;

For suspending our own legislatures, and declaring themselves invested with power to legislate for us in all cases whatsoever.

He has abdicated government here, by declaring us out of his protection and waging war against us.

He has plundered our seas, ravaged our coasts, burned our towns, and destroyed the lives of our people.

He is at this time transporting large armies of foreign mercenaries to complete the works of death, desolation, and tyranny already begun with circumstances of cruelty and perfidy scarcely paralleled in the most barbarous ages, and totally unworthy the head of a civilized nation.

He has constrained our fellow-citizens, taken captive on the high seas, to bear arms against their country, to become the executioners of their friends and brethren, or to fall themselves by their hands.

He has excited domestic insurrection among us, and has endeavored to bring on the inhabitants of our frontiers the merciless Indian savages, whose known rule of warfare is an undistinguished destruction of all ages, sexes, and conditions.

In every stage of these oppressions we have petitioned for redress in the most humble terms; our repeated petitions have been answered only by repeated injury. A prince, whose character is thus marked by every act which may define a tyrant, is unfit to be the ruler of a free people.

Nor have we been wanting in our attentions to our British brethren. We have warned them, from time to time, of attempts by their legislature to extend an unwarrantable jurisdiction over us. We have reminded them of the circumstances of our emigration and settlement here. We have appealed to their native justice and magnanimity; and we have conjured them, by the ties of our common kindred, to disavow these usurpations, which would inevitably interrupt our connections and correspondence. They, too, have been deaf to the voice of justice and of consanguinity. We must, therefore, acquiesce in the necessity which denounces our separation, and hold them, as we hold the rest of mankind, enemies in war, in peace friends.

We, therefore, the representatives of the United States of America, in General Congress assembled, appealing to the Supreme Judge of the world for the rectitude of our intentions, do, in the name and by the authority of the good people of these colonies, solemnly publish and declare, that these United Colonies are, and of right ought to be, FREE AND INDEPENDENT STATES; that they are absolved from all allegiance to the British crown, and that all political connection between them and the state of Great Britain is, and ought to be, totally dissolved; and that, as free and independent states, they have full power to levy war, conclude peace, contract alliances, establish commerce, and do all other acts and things which independent states may of right do. And for the support of this declaration, with a firm reliance on the protection of Divine Providence, we mutually pledge to each other our lives, our fortunes, and our sacred honor.

John Hancock

New Hampshire
Josiah Bartlett
William Whipple
Matthew Thornton

Massachusetts
John Adams
Samuel Adams
Robert Treat Paine
Elbridge Gerry

New York
William Floyd
Philip Livingston
Francis Lewis
Lewis Morris

Rhode Island
Stephen Hopkins
William Ellery

New Jersey
Richard Stockton
John Witherspoon
Francis Hopkinson
John Hart
Abraham Clark

Pennsylvania
Robert Morris
Benjamin Rush
Benjamin Franklin
John Morton
George Clymer
James Smith
George Taylor
James Wilson
George Ross

Delaware
Caeser Rodney
George Read
Thomas McKean

Maryland
Samuel Chase
William Paca
Thomas Stone
Charles Carroll
of Carrollton

North Carolina
William Hooper
Joseph Hewes
John Penn

Virginia
George Wythe
Richard Henry Lee
Thomas Jefferson
Benjamin Harrison
Thomas Nelson, Jr.
Francis Lightfoot Lee
Carter Braxton

South Carolina
Edward Rutledge
Thomas Heyward, Jr.
Thomas Lynch, Jr.
Arthur Middleton

Connecticut
Roger Sherman
Samuel Huntington
William Williams
Oliver Wolcott

Georgia
Button Gwinnett
Lyman Hall
George Walton

The Constitution of the United States of America

Preamble

We the People of the United States, in Order to form a more perfect Union, establish Justice, insure domestic Tranquility, provide for the common defence, promote the general Welfare, and secure the Blessings of Liberty to ourselves and our Posterity, do ordain and establish this Constitution for the United States of America.

Article I

Section 1

All legislative Powers herein granted shall be vested in a Congress of the United States, which shall consist of a Senate and House of Representatives.

Section 2

The House of Representatives shall be composed of Members chosen every second Year by the People of the several States, and the Electors in each State shall have the Qualifications requisite for Electors of the most numerous Branch of the State Legislature.

No Person shall be a Representative who shall not have attained to the Age of twenty five Years, and been seven Years a Citizen of the United States, and who shall not, when elected, be an inhabitant of that State in which he shall be chosen.

Representatives and direct Taxes shall be apportioned among the several States which may be included within this Union, according to their respective Numbers, *which shall be determined by adding to the whole Number of free Persons, including those bound to Service for a Term of Years, and excluding Indians not taxed, three fifths of all other Persons.** The actual Enumeration shall be made within three Years after the first Meeting of the Congress of the United States, and within every subsequent Term of ten Years, in such Manner as they shall by Law direct. The Number of Representatives shall not exceed one for every thirty Thousand, but each State shall have at Least one Representative; *and until such enumeration shall be made, the State of New Hampshire shall be entitled to chuse three, Massachusetts eight, Rhode-Island and Providence Plantations one, Connecticut five, New York six, New Jersey four, Pennsylvania eight, Delaware one, Maryland six, Virginia ten, North Carolina five, South Carolina five, and Georgia three.*

When vacancies happen in the Representation from any State, the Executive Authority thereof shall issue Writs of Election to fill such Vacancies.

The House of Representatives shall chuse their Speaker and other Officers; and shall have the sole Power of Impeachment.

---

*Passages no longer in effect are printed in italic type.

Section 3

The Senate of the United States shall be composed of two Senators from each State, *chosen by the Legislature thereof,* for six Years; and each Senator shall have one Vote.

Immediately after they shall be assembled in Consequence of the first Election, they shall be divided as equally as may be into three Classes. The Seats of the Senators of the first Class shall be vacated at the Expiration of the second Year, of the second Class at the Expiration of the fourth Year, and of the third Class at the Expiration of the sixth Year so that one third may be chosen every second Year; and if Vacancies happen by Resignation, or otherwise, during the Recess of the Legislature of any state, the Executive thereof may make temporary Appointments until the next Meeting of the Legislature, which shall then fill such Vacancies.

No Person shall be a Senator who shall not have attained to the Age of thirty Years, and been nine Years a Citizen of the United States, and who shall not, when elected, be an Inhabitant of that State for which he shall be chosen.

The Vice President of the United States shall be President of the Senate, but shall have no Vote, unless they be equally divided.

The Senate shall chuse their other Officers, and also a President *pro tempore,* in the Absence of the Vice President, or when he shall exercise the Office of President of the United States.

The Senate shall have the sole Power to try all Impeachments. When sitting for that Purpose, they shall be on Oath or Affirmation. When the President of the United States is tried the Chief Justice shall preside: And no Person shall be convicted without the Concurrence of two thirds of the Members present.

Judgment in Cases of Impeachment shall not extend further than to removal from Office, and disqualification to hold and enjoy any Office of honor, Trust or Profit under the United States: but the Party convicted shall nevertheless be liable and subject to Indictment, Trial, Judgment and Punishment, according to Law.

Section 4

The Times, Places and Manner of holding Elections for Senators and Representatives, shall be prescribed in each State by the Legislature thereof; but the Congress may at any time by Law make or alter such Regulations, except as to the Places of chusing Senators.

The Congress shall assemble at least once in every Year, *and such Meeting shall be on the first Monday in December, unless they shall by Law appoint a different Day.*

Section 5

Each House shall be the Judge of the Elections, Returns and Qualifications of its own Members, and a Majority of each shall constitute a Quorum to do Business; but a smaller Number may adjourn from day to day, and may be authorized to compel the Attendance of absent Members, in such Manner, and under such Penalties as each House may provide.

Each House may determine the Rules of its Proceedings, punish its Members for disorderly Behaviour, and, with the Concurrence of two thirds, expel a Member.

Each House shall keep a Journal of its Proceedings, and from time to time publish the same, excepting such Parts as may in their Judgment require Secrecy; and the Yeas and Nays of the Members of either House on any question shall, at the Desire of one fifth of those Present, be entered on the Journal.

Neither House, during the Session of Congress, shall, without the Consent of the other, adjourn for more than three days, nor to any other Place than that in which the two Houses shall be sitting.

Section 6

The Senators and Representatives shall receive a Compensation for their Services, to be ascertained by Law, and paid out of the Treasury of the United States. They shall in all Cases, except Treason, Felony and Breach of the Peace, be privileged from Arrest during their Attendance at the Session of their respective Houses, and in going to and returning from the same; and for any Speech or Debate in either House, they shall not be questioned in any other Place.

No Senator or Representative shall, during the Time for which he was elected, be appointed to any civil Office under the Authority of the United States, which shall have been created, or the Emoluments whereof shall have been encreased during such time, and no Person holding any Office under the United States, shall be a Member of either House during his Continuance in Office.

Section 7

All Bills for raising Revenue shall originate in the House of Representatives; but the Senate may propose or concur with Amendments as on other Bills.

Every Bill which shall have passed the House of Representatives and the Senate, shall, before it become a Law, be presented to the President of the United States; If he approve he shall sign it, but if not he shall return it, with his Objections to the House in which it shall have originated, who shall enter the Objections at large on their Journal, and proceed to reconsider it. If after such Reconsideration two thirds of that House shall agree to pass the Bill, it shall be sent, together with the Objections, to the other House, by which it shall likewise be reconsidered, and if approved by two thirds of that House, it shall become a Law. But in all such Cases the Votes of both Houses shall be determined by yeas and Nays, and the Names of the Persons voting for and against the Bill shall be entered on the Journal of each House respectively. If any Bill shall not be returned by the President within ten Days (Sundays excepted) after it shall have been presented to him, the Same shall be a Law, in like Manner as if he had signed it, unless the Congress by their Adjournment prevent its Return, in which Case it shall not be a Law.

Every Order, Resolution, or Vote to which the Concurrence of the Senate and House of Representatives may be necessary (except on a question of Adjournment) shall be presented to the President of the United States; and before the Same shall take Effect, shall be approved by him, or being disapproved by him, shall be repassed by two thirds of the Senate and House of Representatives, according to the Rules and Limitations prescribed in the Case of a Bill.

Section 8

The Congress shall have Power To lay and collect Taxes, Duties, Imposts and Excises, to pay the Debts and provide for the common Defence and general Welfare of the United States; but all Duties, Imposts and Excises shall be uniform throughout the United States;

To borrow Money on the credit of the United States;

To regulate Commerce with foreign Nations, and among the several States, and with the Indian Tribes;

To establish an uniform Rule of Naturalization, and uniform Laws on the subject of Bankruptcies throughout the United States;

To coin Money, regulate the Value thereof, and of foreign Coin, and fix the Standard of Weights and Measures;

To provide for the Punishment of counterfeiting the Securities and current Coin of the United States;

To establish Post Offices and post Roads;

To promote the Progress of Science and useful Arts, by securing for limited Times to Authors and Inventors the exclusive Right to their respective Writings and Discoveries;

To constitute Tribunals inferior to the supreme Court;

To define and punish Piracies and Felonies committed on the high Seas, and Offences against the Law of Nations;

To declare War, grant Letters of Marque and Reprisal, and make Rules concerning Captures on Land and Water;

To raise and support Armies, but no Appropriation of Money to that Use shall be for a longer Term than two Years;

To provide and maintain a Navy;

To make Rules for the Government and Regulation of the land and naval Forces;

To provide for calling forth the Militia to execute the Laws of the Union, suppress Insurrections and repel Invasions;

To provide for organizing, arming, and disciplining, the Militia, and for governing such Part of them as may be employed in the Service of the United States, reserving to the States respectively, the Appointment of the Officers, and the Authority of training the Militia according to the discipline prescribed by Congress;

To exercise exclusive Legislation in all Cases whatsoever, over such District (not exceeding ten Miles square) as may, by Cession of particular States, and the Acceptance of Congress, become the Seat of the Government of the United States, and to exercise like Authority over all Places purchased by the Consent of the Legislature of the State in which the Same shall be, for the Erection of Forts, Magazines, Arsenals, dock-Yards, and other needful Buildings;—And

To make all Laws which shall be necessary and proper for carrying into Execution the foregoing Powers, and all other Powers vested by this Constitution in the Government of the United States, or in any Department of Officer thereof.

Section 9

The Migration or Importation of such Persons as any of the States now existing shall think proper to admit, shall not be prohibited by the Congress prior to the Year one thousand eight hundred and eight, but a Tax or duty may be imposed on such Importation, not exceeding ten dollars for each Person.

The Privilege of the Writ of Habeas Corpus shall not be suspended, unless when in Cases of Rebellion or Invasion the public Safety may require it.

No Bill of Attainder or ex post facto Law shall be passed.

No Capitation, or other direct, Tax shall be laid, unless in Proportion to the Census or Enumeration herein before directed to be taken.

No Tax or Duty shall be laid on Articles exported from any State.

No Preference shall be given by any Regulation of Commerce or Revenue to the Ports of one State over those of another: nor shall Vessels bound to, or from, one State, be obliged to enter, clear, or pay Duties in another.

No Money shall be drawn from the Treasury, but in Consequence of Appropriations made by Law; and a regular Statement and Account of the Receipts and Expenditures of all public Money shall be published from time to time.

No Title of Nobility shall be granted by the United States: And no Person holding any Office of Profit or Trust under them, shall, without the Consent of the Congress, accept of any present, Emolument, Office, or Title, of any kind whatever, from any King, Prince, or foreign State.

Section 10

No State shall enter into any Treaty, Alliance, or Confederation; grant Letters of Marque and Reprisal; coin Money; emit Bills of Credit; make any Thing but gold and silver Coin a Tender in Payment of Debts; pass any Bill of Attainder, ex post facto Law, or Law impairing the obligation of Contracts, or grant any Title of Nobility.

No State shall, without the Consent of the Congress, lay any Imposts or Duties on Imports or Exports, except what may be absolutely necessary for executing its inspection Laws: and the net Produce of all Duties and Imposts, laid by any State on Imports or Exports, shall be for the Use of the Treasury of the United States; and all such Laws shall be subject to the Revision and Controul of the Congress.

No State shall, without the Consent of Congress, lay any Duty of Tonnage, keep Troops, or Ships of War in time of Peace, enter into any Agreement or Compact with another State, or with a foreign Power, or engage in War, unless actually invaded, or in such imminent Danger as will not admit of delay.

Article II

Section 1

The executive Power shall be vested in a President of the United States of America. He shall hold his Office during the Term of four Years, and, together with the Vice President, chosen for the same Term, be elected, as follows:

Each State shall appoint, in such Manner as the Legislature thereof may direct, a Number of Electors, equal to the whole Number of Senators and Representatives to which the State may be entitled in the Congress: but no Senator or Representative, or Person holding an Office of Trust or Profit under the United States, shall be appointed an Elector.

The Electors shall meet in their respective States, and vote by Ballot for two Persons, of whom one at least shall not be an Inhabitant of the same State with themselves. And they shall make a List of all the Persons voted for, and of the Number of Votes for each; which List they shall sign and certify, and transmit sealed to the Seat of the Government of the United States, directed to the President of the Senate. The President of the Senate shall, in the Presence of the Senate and House of Representatives, open all the Certificates, and the Votes shall then be counted. The Person having the greatest Number of Votes shall be the President, if such Number be a Majority of the whole number of Electors appointed; and if there be more than one who have such Majority, and have an equal Number of Votes, then the House of Representatives shall immediately chuse by Ballot one of them for President; and if no Person have a Majority, then from the five highest on the List the said House shall in like Manner chuse the President. But in chusing the President, the Votes shall be taken by States, the Representation from each State having one Vote; A quorum for this Purpose shall consist of a Member or Members from two thirds of the States, and a Majority of all the States shall be necessary to a Choice. In every Case, after the Choice of the President, the Person having the greatest Number of Votes of the Electors shall be the Vice President. But if there should remain two or more who have equal Votes, the Senate shall chuse from them by Ballot the Vice President.

The Congress may determine the time of chusing the Electors, and the Day on which they shall give their Votes; which Day shall be the same throughout the United States.

No person except a natural born Citizen, *or a Citizen of the United States, at the time of the Adoption of this Constitution,* shall be eligible to the Office of

President; neither shall any Person be eligible to that Office who shall not have attained to the Age of thirty five Years, and been fourteen Years a Resident within the United States.

In Case of the Removal of the President from Office, or of his Death, Resignation, or Inability to discharge the Powers and Duties of the said Office, the Same shall devolve on the Vice President, and the Congress may by Law provide for the Case of Removal, Death, Resignation or Inability, both of the President and Vice President, declaring what Officer shall then act as President, and such Officer shall act accordingly, until the Disability be removed, or a President shall be elected.

The President shall, at stated Times, receive for his Services, a Compensation, which shall neither be encreased nor diminished during the Period for which he shall have been elected, and he shall not receive within that period any other Emolument from the United States, or any of them.

Before he enter on the Execution of his Office, he shall take the following Oath or Affirmation:—"I do solemnly swear (or affirm) that I will faithfully execute the Office of President of the United States, and will to the best of my Ability, preserve, protect and defend the Constitution of the United States."

Section 2

The President shall be Commander in Chief of the Army and Navy of the United States, and of the Militia of the several States, when called into the actual Service of the United States; he may require the Opinion, in writing, of the principal Officer in each of the executive Departments, upon any Subject relating to the Duties of their respective Offices, and he shall have Power to grant Reprieves and Pardons for Offences against the United States, except in Cases of Impeachment.

He shall have Power, by and with the Advice and Consent of the Senate, to make Treaties, provided two thirds of the Senators present concur; and he shall nominate, and by and with the Advice and Consent of the Senate, shall appoint Ambassadors, other public Ministers and Consuls, Judges of the supreme Court, and all other Officers of the United States, whose Appointments are not herein otherwise provided for, and which shall be established by Law: but the Congress may by Law vest the Appointment of such inferior Officers, as they think proper in the President alone, in the Courts of Law, or in the Heads of Departments.

The President shall have Power to fill up all Vacancies that may happen during the Recess of the Senate, by granting Commissions which shall expire at the End of their next Session.

Section 3

He shall from time to time give to the Congress Information of the State of the Union, and recommend to their Consideration such Measures as he shall judge necessary and expedient; he may, on extraordinary Occasions, convene both Houses, or either of them, and in Case of disagreement between them, with Respect to the Time of Adjournment, he may adjourn them to such Time as he shall think proper; he shall receive Ambassadors and other public Ministers; he shall take Care that the Laws be faithfully executed, and shall Commission all the officers of the United States.

Section 4

The President, Vice President and all civil Officers of the United States, shall be removed from Office on Impeachment for, and Conviction of, Treason, Bribery or other high Crimes and Misdemeanors.

Article III

Section 1

The judicial Power of the United States, shall be vested in one supreme Court, and in such inferior Courts as the Congress may from time to time ordain and establish. The Judges, both of the supreme and inferior Courts, shall hold their offices during good Behaviour, and shall, at stated Times, receive for their Services, a Compensation, which shall not be diminished during their Continuance in Office.

Section 2

The judicial Power shall extend to all Cases, in Law and Equity, arising under this Constitution, the Laws of the United States, and Treaties made, or which shall be made, under their Authority;—to all Cases affecting Ambassadors, other public Ministers and Consuls;—to all Cases of admiralty and maritime Jurisdiction;—to Controversies to which the United States shall be a Party;—to Controversies between two or more States;—*between a State and Citizens of another State;*—between Citizens of different States;—between Citizens of the same State claiming Lands under Grants of different States, and between a State, or the Citizens thereof, and foreign States, Citizens or Subjects.

In all Cases affecting Ambassadors, other public Ministers and Consuls, and those in which a State shall be Party, the supreme Court shall have original Jurisdiction. In all the other Cases before mentioned, the supreme Court shall have appellate Jurisdiction, both as to Law and Fact, with such Exceptions, and under such Regulations as the Congress shall make.

The Trial of all Crimes, except in Cases of Impeachment, shall be by Jury; and such Trial shall be held in the State where the said Crimes shall have been committed, but when not committed within any State, the Trial shall be at such Place or Places as the Congress may by Law have directed.

Section 3

Treason against the United States, shall consist only in levying War against them, or in adhering to their Enemies, giving them Aid and Comfort. No person shall be convicted of Treason unless on the Testimony of two Witnesses to the same overt Act, or on Confession in open Court.

The Congress shall have Power to declare the Punishment of Treason, but no Attainder of Treason shall work Corruption of Blood, or Forfeiture except during the Life of the Person attainted.

Article IV

Section 1

Full Faith and Credit shall be given in each State to the public Acts, Records, and judicial Proceedings of every other State. And the Congress may by general Laws prescribe the Manner in which such Acts, Records and Proceedings shall be proved, and the Effect thereof.

Section 2

The Citizens of each State shall be entitled to all Privileges and Immunities of Citizens in the several States.

A Person charged in any State with Treason, Felony, or other Crime, who shall flee from Justice, and be found in another State, shall on Demand of the executive

Authority of the State from which he fled, be delivered up, to be removed to the State having Jurisdiction of the Crime.

No Person held to Service or Labour in one State, under the Laws thereof, escaping into another, shall, in Consequence of any Law or Regulation therein, be discharged from such Service or Labour, but shall be delivered up on Claim of the Party to whom such Service or Labour may be due.

Section 3

New States may be admitted by the Congress into this Union; but no new State shall be formed or erected within the Jurisdiction of any other State; nor any State be formed by the Junction of two or more States, or Parts of States, without the Consent of the Legislatures of the States concerned as well as of the Congress.

The Congress shall have Power to dispose of and make all needful Rules and Regulations respecting the Territory or other Property belonging to the United States; and nothing in this Constitution shall be so construed as to Prejudice any Claims of the United States, or of any particular States.

Section 4

The United States shall guarantee to every State in this Union a Republican Form of Government, and shall protect each of them against Invasion; and on Application of the Legislature, or of the Executive (when the Legislature cannot be convened) against domestic violence.

Article V

The Congress, whenever two thirds of both Houses shall deem it necessary, shall propose Amendments to this Constitution, or, on the Application of the Legislatures of two thirds of the several States, shall call a Convention for proposing Amendments, which, in either Case, shall be valid to all Intents and Purposes, as Part of this Constitution, when ratified by the Legislatures of three fourths of the several States, or by Conventions in three fourths thereof, as the one or the other Mode of Ratification may be proposed by the Congress; Provided *that no Amendment which may be made prior to the Year One thousand eight hundred and eight shall in any Manner affect the first and fourth Clauses in the Ninth Section of the first Article;* and that no State, without its Consent, shall be deprived of its equal Suffrage in the Senate.

Article VI

All Debts contracted and Engagements entered into, before the Adoption of this Constitution, shall be as valid against the United States under this Constitution, as under the Confederation.

This Constitution, and Laws of the United States which shall be made in Pursuance thereof; and all Treaties made, or which shall be made, under the Authority of the United States, shall be the supreme Law of the Land; and the Judges in every State shall be bound thereby, any Thing in the Constitution or Laws of any State to the Contrary notwithstanding.

The Senators and Representatives before mentioned, and the Members of the several State Legislatures, and all executive and Judicial Officers, both of the United States and of the several States, shall be bound by Oath or Affirmation, to support this Constitution; but no religious Test shall ever be required as a Qualification to any Office of public Trust under the United States.

Article VII

The Ratification of the Conventions of nine States, shall be sufficient for the Establishment of this Constitution between the States so ratifying the Same.

Done in Convention by the Unanimous Consent of the States present the Seventeenth Day of September in the Year of our Lord one thousand seven hundred and Eighty seven and of the Independence of the United States of America the Twelfth[†] IN WITNESS whereof We have hereunto subscribed our Names,

George Washington
President and Deputy from Virginia

Delaware
George Read
Gunning Bedford, Jr.
John Dickinson
Richard Bassett
Jacob Broom

Maryland
James McHenry
Daniel of St. Thomas
Jenifer
Daniel Carroll

Virginia
John Blair
James Madison, Jr.

North Carolina
William Blount
Richard Dobbs Spraight
Hugh Williamson

South Carolina
John Rutledge
Charles Cotesworth
Pinckney
Charles Pinckney
Pierce Butler

Georgia
William Paterson
William Few
Abraham Baldwin

New Hampshire
John Langdon
Nicholas Gilman

Massachusetts
Nathaniel Gorham
Rufus King

Connecticut
William Samuel Johnson
Roger Sherman

New York
Alexander Hamilton

New Jersey
William Livingston
David Brearley
Jonathan Dayton

Pennsylvania
Benjamin Franklin
Thomas Mifflin
Robert Morris
George Clymer
Thomas FitzSimons
Jared Ingersoll
James Wilson
Gouverneur Morris

[†]The Constitution was submitted on September 17, 1787, by the Constitutional Convention, was ratified by the Convention of several states at various dates up to May 29, 1790, and became effective on March 4, 1789.

Amendments to the Constitution

Amendment I

Congress shall make no law respecting an establishment of religion, or prohibiting the free exercise thereof; or abridging the freedom of speech, or of the press; or the right of the people peaceably to assemble, and to petition the Government for a redress of grievances.

Amendment II

A well regulated Militia being necessary to the security of a free State, the right of the people to keep and bear Arms, shall not be infringed.

Amendment III

No Soldier shall, in time of peace be quartered in any house, without the consent of the Owner, nor in time of war, but in a manner to be prescribed by law.

Amendment IV

The right of the people to be secure in their persons, houses, papers, and effects, against unreasonable searches and seizures, shall not be violated, and no Warrants shall issue, but upon probable cause, supported by Oath or affirmation, and particularly describing the place to be searched, and the persons or things to be seized.

Amendment V

No person shall be held to answer for a capital, or otherwise infamous crime, unless on a presentment or indictment of a Grand Jury, except in cases arising in the land or naval forces, or in the Militia, when in actual service in time of War or public danger; nor shall any person be subject for the same offense to be twice put in jeopardy of life or limb; nor shall be compelled in any criminal case to be a witness against himself, nor be deprived of life, liberty, or property, without due process of law; nor shall private property be taken for public use, without just compensation.

Amendment VI

In all criminal prosecutions, the accused shall enjoy the right to a speedy and public trial, by an impartial jury of the State and district wherein the crime shall have been committed, which district shall have been previously ascertained by law, and to be informed of the nature and cause of the accusation; to be confronted with the witnesses against him; to have compulsory process for obtaining witnesses in his favor, and to have the Assistance of Counsel for his defence.

Amendment VII

In Suits at common law, where the value in controversy shall exceed twenty dollars, the right of trial by jury shall be preserved, and no fact tried by a jury, shall be otherwise re-examined in any Court of the United States, than according to the rules of the common law.

Amendment VIII

Excessive bail shall not be required, nor excessive fines imposed, nor cruel and unusual punishments inflicted.

Amendment IX

The enumeration in the Constitution, of certain rights, shall not be construed to deny or disparage others retained by the people.

Amendment X*

The powers not delegated to the United States by the Constitution, nor prohibited by it to the States, are reserved to the States respectively, or to the people.

Amendment XI

[Adopted 1798]

The Judicial power of the United States shall not be construed to extend to any suit in law or equity, commenced or prosecuted against one of the United States by Citizens of another State, or by Citizens or Subjects of any Foreign State.

Amendment XII

[Adopted 1804]

The Electors shall meet in their respective states, and vote by ballot for President and Vice President, one of whom, at least, shall not be an inhabitant of the same state with themselves; they shall name in their ballots the person voted for as President, and in distinct ballots the person voted for as Vice President, and they shall make distinct lists of all persons voted for as President, and of all persons voted for as Vice President, and of the number of votes for each, which lists they shall sign and certify, and transmit sealed to the seat of the government of the United States, directed to the President of the Senate;—The President of the Senate shall, in the presence of the Senate and House of Representatives, open all the certificates and the votes shall then be counted;—The person having the greatest number of votes for President, shall be the President, if such number be a majority of the whole number of Electors appointed; and if no person have such majority, then from the persons having the highest numbers not exceeding three

---

*The first ten amendments (the Bill of Rights) were ratified and their adoption was certified on December 15, 1791.

on the list of those voted for as President, the House of Representatives shall choose immediately, by ballot, the President. But in choosing the President, the votes shall be taken by states, the representation from each state having one vote; a quorum for this purpose shall consist of a member or members from two-thirds of the states, and a majority of all the states shall be necessary to a choice. And if the House of Representatives shall not choose a President whenever the right of choice shall devolve upon them, before *the fourth day of March* next following, then the Vice President shall act as President, as in the case of the death or other constitutional disability of the President.—The person having the greatest number of votes as Vice President, shall be the Vice President, if such number be a majority of the whole number of Electors appointed, and if no person have a majority, then from the two highest numbers on the list, the Senate shall choose the Vice President; a quorum for the purpose shall consist of two-thirds of the whole number of Senators, and a majority of the whole number shall be necessary to a choice. But no person constitutionally ineligible to the office of President shall be eligible to that of Vice President of the United States.

Amendment XIII

[Adopted 1865]

Section 1

Neither slavery nor involuntary servitude, except as a punishment for crime whereof the party shall have been duly convicted, shall exist within the United States, or any place subject to their jurisdiction.

Section 2

Congress shall have power to enforce this article by appropriate legislation.

Amendment XIV

[Adopted 1868]

Section 1

All persons born or naturalized in the United States, and subject to the jurisdiction thereof, are citizens of the United States and of the State wherein they reside. No State shall make or enforce any law which shall abridge the privileges or immunities of citizens of the United States; nor shall any State deprive any person of life, liberty, or property, without due process of law; nor deny to any person within its jurisdiction the equal protection of the laws.

Section 2

Representatives shall be apportioned among the several States according to their respective numbers, counting the whole number of persons in each State, excluding Indians not taxed. But when the right to vote at any election for the choice of electors for President and Vice President of the United States, Representatives in Congress, the Executive and Judicial officers of a State, or the members of the Legislature thereof, is denied to any of the male inhabitants of such State, being twenty-one years of age, and citizens of the United States, or in any way abridged, except for participation in rebellion, or other crime, the basis of representation therein shall be reduced in the proportion which the number of such male citizens shall bear to the whole number of male citizens twenty-one years of age in such State.

Section 3

No person shall be a Senator or Representative in Congress, or elector of President and Vice President, or hold any office, civil or military, under the United States, or under any State, who, having previously taken an oath, as a member of Congress, or as an officer of the United States, or as a member of any State legislature, or as an executive or judicial officer of any State, to support the Constitution of the United States, shall have engaged in insurrection or rebellion against the same, or given aid or comfort to the enemies thereof. But Congress may by a vote of two-thirds of each House, remove such disability.

Section 4

The validity of the public debt of the United States, authorized by law, including debts incurred for payment of pensions and bounties for services in suppressing insurrection or rebellion, shall not be questioned. But neither the United States nor any State shall assume or pay any debt or obligation incurred in aid of insurrection or rebellion against the United States, or any claim for the loss or emancipation of any slave; but all such debts, obligations and claims shall be held illegal and void.

Section 5

The Congress shall have power to enforce, by appropriate legislation, the provisions of this article.

Amendment XV

[Adopted 1870]

Section 1

The right of citizens of the United States to vote shall not be denied or abridged by the United States or by any State on account of race, color, or previous condition of servitude.

Section 2

The Congress shall have power to enforce this article by appropriate legislation.

Amendment XVI

[Adopted 1913]

The Congress shall have power to lay and collect taxes on incomes, from whatever source derived, without apportionment among the several States, and without regard to any census or enumeration.

Amendment XVII

[Adopted 1913]

The Senate of the United States shall be composed of two Senators from each State, elected by the people thereof, for six years; and each Senator shall have one vote. The electors in each State shall have the qualifications requisite for electors of the most numerous branch of the State legislatures.

When vacancies happen in the representation of any State in the Senate, the executive authority of such State shall issue writs of election to fill such vacancies: *Provided,*

That the legislature of any State may empower the executive thereof to make temporary appointments until the people fill the vacancies by election as the legislature may direct.

This amendment shall not be so construed as to affect the election or term of any Senator chosen before it becomes valid as part of the Constitution.

Amendment XVIII

[Adopted 1919, repealed 1933]

Section 1

After one year from the ratification of this article the manufacture, sale, or transportation of intoxicating liquors within, the importation thereof into, or the exportation thereof from the United States and all territory subject to the jurisdiction thereof for beverage purposes is hereby prohibited.

Section 2

The Congress and the several States shall have concurrent power to enforce this article by appropriate legislation.

Section 3

This article shall be inoperative unless it shall have been ratified as an amendment to the Constitution by the legislatures of the several States, as provided in the Constitution, within seven years from the date of the submission hereof to the States by the Congress.

Amendment XIX

[Adopted 1920]

The right of citizens of the United States to vote shall not be denied or abridged by the United States or by any State on account of sex.

Congress shall have power to enforce this article by appropriate legislation.

Amendment XX

[Adopted 1933]

Section 1

The terms of the President and Vice President shall end at noon on the 20th day of January, and the terms of Senators and Representatives at noon on the 3d day of January, of the years in which such terms would have ended if this article had not been ratified and the terms of their successors shall then begin.

Section 2

The Congress shall assemble at least once in every year, and such meeting shall begin at noon on the 3d day of January, unless they shall by law appoint a different day.

Section 3

If, at the time fixed for the beginning of the term of the President, the President elect shall have died, the Vice President elect shall become President. If a President shall not have been chosen before the time fixed for the beginning of his term, or if the President elect shall have failed to qualify, then the Vice President elect shall act as President until a President shall have qualified; and the Congress may by law provide for the case wherein neither a President elect nor a Vice President elect shall have qualified, declaring who shall then act as President, or the manner in which one who is to act shall be selected, and such person shall act accordingly until a President or Vice President shall have qualified.

Section 4

The Congress may by law provide for the case of the death of any of the persons from whom the House of Representatives may choose a President whenever the right of choice shall have devolved upon them, and for the case of the death of any of the persons from whom the Senate may choose a Vice President whenever the right of choice shall have devolved upon them.

Section 5

Sections 1 and 2 shall take effect on the 15th day of October following the ratification of this article.

Section 6

This article shall be inoperative unless it shall have been ratified as an amendment to the Constitution by the legislatures of three fourths of the several States within seven years from the date of its submission.

Amendment XXI

[Adopted 1933]

Section 1

The eighteenth article of amendment to the Constitution of the United States is hereby repealed.

Section 2

The transportation or importation into any State, Territory, or possession of the United States for delivery or use therein of intoxicating liquors in violation of the laws thereof, is hereby prohibited.

Section 3

This article shall be inoperative unless it shall have been ratified as an amendment to the Constitution by conventions in the several States, as provided in the Constitution, within seven years from the date of the submission hereof to the States by the Congress.

Amendment XXII

[Adopted 1951]

Section 1

No person shall be elected to the office of the President more than twice, and no person who has held the office of President, or acted as President, for more than two years of a term to which some other person was elected President shall be elected to the office of the President more than once. But this Article shall not apply to any person holding the office of President when this Article was proposed by the Congress, and shall not prevent any person who may be holding the office of President, or acting as President, during the term within which this Article becomes operative from holding the office of President or acting as President during the remainder of such term.

Section 2

This article shall be inoperative unless it shall have been ratified as an amendment to the Constitution by the legislatures of three-fourths of the several States within seven years from the date of its submission to the States by the Congress.

Amendment XXIII

[Adopted 1961]

Section 1

The District constituting the seat of Government of the United States shall appoint in such manner as the Congress shall direct:

A number of electors of President and Vice President equal to the whole number of Senators and Representatives in Congress to which the District would be entitled if it were a State, but in no event more than the least populous State; they shall be in addition to those appointed by the States, but they shall be considered, for the purposes of the election of President and Vice President, to be electors appointed by a State; and they shall meet in the District and perform such duties as provided by the twelfth article of amendment.

Section 2

The Congress shall have power to enforce this article by appropriate legislation.

Amendment XXIV

[Adopted 1964]

Section 1

The right of citizens of the United States to vote in any primary or other election for President or Vice President, for electors for President or Vice President, or for Senator or Representative in Congress, shall not be denied or abridged by the United States or any state by reason of failure to pay any poll tax or other tax.

Section 2

The Congress shall have the power to enforce this article by appropriate legislation.

Amendment XXV

[Adopted 1967]

Section 1

In case of the removal of the President from office or his death or resignation, the Vice President shall become President.

Section 2

Whenever there is a vacancy in the office of the Vice President, the President shall nominate a Vice President who shall take the office upon confirmation by a majority vote of both houses of Congress.

Section 3

Whenever the President transmits to the President pro tempore of the Senate and the Speaker of the House of Representatives his written declaration that he is unable to discharge the powers and duties of his office, and until he transmits to them a written declaration to the contrary, such powers and duties shall be discharged by the Vice President as Acting President.

Section 4

Whenever the Vice President and a majority of either the principal officers of the executive departments or of such other body as Congress may by law provide, transmit to the President pro tempore of the Senate and the Speaker of the House of Representatives their written declaration that the President is unable to discharge the powers and duties of his office, the Vice President shall immediately assume the powers and duties of the office as Acting President.

Thereafter, when the President transmits to the President pro tempore of the Senate and the Speaker of the House of Representatives his written declaration that no inability exists, he shall resume the powers and duties of his office unless the Vice President and a majority of either the principal officers of the executive department or of such other body as Congress may by law provide, transmit within four days to the President pro tempore of the Senate and the Speaker of the House of Representatives their written declaration that the President is unable to discharge the powers and duties of his office. Thereupon Congress shall decide the issue, assembling within 48 hours for that purpose if not in session. If the Congress, within 21 days after receipt of the latter written declaration, or, if Congress is not in session, within 21 days after Congress is required to assemble, determines by two-thirds vote of both houses that the President is unable to discharge the powers and duties of his office, the Vice President shall continue to discharge the same as Acting President; otherwise, the President shall resume the powers and duties of his office.

Amendment XXVI

[Adopted 1971]

Section 1

The right of citizens of the United States, who are 18 years of age or older, to vote shall not be denied or abridged by the United States or any state on account of age.

Section 2

The Congress shall have the power to enforce this article by appropriate legislation.

Amendment XXVII

[Adopted 1992]

No law, varying the compensation for the services of the Senators and Representatives shall take effect, until an election of Representatives shall have intervened.

Glossary

abolitionism (p. 282) Worldwide movement to end slavery. In the United States the term chiefly applies to the antebellum reformers whose cause culminated in the Civil War.

acquired immunodeficiency syndrome (AIDS) (p. 821) A deadly, and very often sexually transmitted disease that emerged in the 1980s and that at first spread chiefly among injection drug users and gay male populations, but soon affected all communities. The disease is a complex of deadly pathologies resulting from infection with the **human immunodeficiency virus (HIV)**. By 2000, AIDS deaths in the United States had surpassed 40,000.

Agricultural Adjustment Act (AAA) (p. 681) New Deal legislation that raised farm prices by restricting output of staple crops. It restricted production and paid subsidies to growers; declared unconstitutional in 1936.

Albany Plan (p. 87) A proposal, drafted in Albany, New York, in 1754 by Benjamin Franklin of Pennsylvania, for a "plan of union" for the collective defense of the British colonies. Because it held the potential for unifying the colonies against its rule, the British government never adopted the plan.

Alien and Sedition Acts (p. 167) Four laws passed by the Federalist-dominated Congress in 1798 directed against sympathizers to the **French Revolution**—chiefly Thomas Jefferson and his **Republican party**. The laws, which stifled dissent and made it more difficult for immigrants to gain citizenship, had lapsed by 1802.

Allied Powers (p. 603) The military alliance during World War I, chiefly consisting of Britain, France, Russia, and Italy, that opposed the **Central Powers**, chiefly Germany, Austria-Hungary, and Turkey.

Allies (p. 718) In the context of United States history, a term that refers to the nations that opposed the **Axis Powers**, chiefly Nazi Germany, Italy, and Japan, during World War II. The Allies included Britain, France (except during the Nazi occupation, 1940–1944), the Soviet Union (1941–1945), the United States (1941–1945), and China.

American Colonization Society (p. 235) An organization, founded in 1816, that proposed to solve the "Negro problem" by transporting freed slaves from the United States to Africa. Although the society purchased land in Africa (Liberia), few African Americans chose to resettle there.

American Federation of Labor (AFL) (p. 472) A union, formed in 1886, that organized skilled workers along craft lines. It focused on workplace issues rather than political or social reform.

American System (p. 216) Kentucky Senator Henry Clay's plan for national economic development; it included protective tariffs, a national bank, and federal subsidies for railroad and canal construction.

Anaconda Plan (p. 381) General Winfield Scott's strategy for defeating the Confederacy; its central elements included a naval blockade and seizure of the Mississippi River valley.

Antifederalists (p. 152) Critics of the Constitution who initially opposed its ratification. By the late 1790s, they generally endorsed states' rights and sought limitations on federal power.

antinomianism (p. 35) A religious doctrine that affirmed that individuals who possessed saving grace were exempt from the rules of good behavior and from the laws of the community. In puritan New England, such beliefs were generally regarded as heresy.

Arminianism (p. 30) A religious doctrine that held that good works and faith could lead to salvation. In puritan New England, this was regarded as heresy akin to Catholicism because it implied that God's will was contingent on the acts of man.

Articles of Confederation (p. 130) The charter establishing the first government of the United States, ratified in 1781. The Articles placed the coercive powers to tax and regulate trade within the individual state governments; the national government, widely criticized for being weak, was superseded by the government established by the Constitution of the United States, effective in 1789.

Ashcan School (p. 545) Artists in the early twentieth century who used as their subject matter the things and people found in city streets and slums. Ashcan artists often supported progressive political and social reform.

Atlanta Compromise (p. 529) A social policy, propounded by black leader Booker T. Washington in 1895, advocating that blacks concentrate on learning useful skills rather than agitate over segregation, disfranchisement, and discrimination. In Washington's view, black self-help and self-improvement was the surest way to economic advancement.

axis of evil (p. 844) A pejorative phrase, coined by President George W. Bush in 2002, referring to states that supported terrorism and sought weapons of mass destruction. He specifically identified Iraq, Iran, and North Korea.

Axis Powers (p. 702) A term for the alliance between Nazi Germany and Italy after 1936 and, after 1940, Japan.

Bacon's Rebellion (p. 59) An armed uprising in 1676, led by Nathaniel Bacon, against Virginia governor Sir William Berkeley. Initially the rebels attacked Indian settlements but later moved against Berkeley's political faction and burned Jamestown, capital of the colony. After Bacon's death that year, the rebellion collapsed.

Bank of the United States (p. 157) Established as a joint public and private venture in 1791 at the behest of Secretary of Treasury Alexander Hamilton, the Bank of the United States served as a depository of government funds, collected and expended government revenue, and issued notes to serve as a national medium of exchange. The bank's charter expired in 1811. A Second Bank of the United States was chartered in 1816.

Bank war (p. 253) The political dispute over whether to renew the charter of the Second Bank of the United States. In 1832, Congress voted to recharter the bank but President Andrew Jackson vetoed the measure and the charter expired in 1836. He argued that the Bank was unconstitutional, a dangerous monopoly, and vulnerable to control by foreign investors.

Bay of Pigs fiasco (p. 762) A military debacle in April 1961, during an American-organized effort to invade Cuba and drive Fidel Castro, the communist ruler, from power. The invasion force of some 1,500 Cuban exiles was routed at the Bay of Pigs, a major embarrassment for President John F. Kennedy.

beat school (p. 771) Also known as "beats," "beatniks," or the "beat generation"—nonconformists in the late 1950s who rejected conventional dress and sexual standards and cultivated avant-garde literature and music.

Berlin airlift (p. 738) U.S. effort to deliver supplies including 2 million tons of food and coal by air to West Berlin in 1948–1949 in response to the Soviet blockade of the city.

Berlin wall (p. 762) Erected by East Germany in 1961 and torn down by a Dutch company in 1989, the wall isolated West Berlin from the surrounding areas in communist controlled East Berlin and East Germany.

Bill of Rights (p. 155) The first ten amendments to the United States Constitution (adopted in 1791); they protected individual liberties and states' rights against the power of the national government.

Black Codes (p. 409) Special laws passed by southern state and municipal governments after the Civil War that denied free blacks many rights of citizenship.

Bland-Allison Silver Purchase Act (p. 534) An 1878 compromise law that that provided for the limited coinage of silver.

Blitzkrieg **(p. 701)** A German tactic in World War II, translated as "lightning war," involving the coordinated attack of air and armored firepower.

Bonus Army (p. 673) A gathering of 20,000 Great War veterans in Washington, DC in June

1932, to demand immediate payment of their "adjusted compensation" bonuses voted by Congress in 1924. Congress rejected their demands, and President Hoover ordered U.S. troops to drive them from the capital.

Boston Massacre (p. 106) A violent confrontation between British troops and a Boston mob on March 5, 1770; the soldiers opened fire and killed five, an incident that inflamed sentiment against the British.

Brown v. Board of Education of Topeka (p. 753) The 1954 Supreme Court decision that held that racially segregated education, which prevailed in much of the South, was unconstitutional. The ruling overturned the doctrine of "separate but equal" that had provided the legal justification for racial segregation ever since the 1896 **Plessy v. Ferguson** Supreme Court decision.

Camp David Accords (p. 792) A 1978 peace treaty between Egypt and Israel, mediated by President Jimmy Carter, signed at Camp David, a presidential retreat near Washington, DC.

carpetbaggers (p. 419) A pejorative term for Northerners who went to the South after the Civil War to exploit the new political power of freed blacks and the disenfranchisement of former Confederates.

Central Powers (p. 603) Germany and its World War I allies—Austria-Hungary, Turkey, and Bulgaria.

Chinese Exclusion Act (p. 434) A law passed by Congress in 1882 that prohibited Chinese immigration to the United States; it was overturned in 1943.

Civil Rights Act of 1964 (p. 767) Legislation outlawing discrimination in public accommodations and employment on the basis of race, skin color, sex, religion, or national origin.

civil rights cases (p. 526) A group of cases in 1883 in which the U.S. Supreme Court declared unconstitutional the Civil Rights Act of 1875, which had prohibited racial discrimination in hotels, theaters, and other privately owned facilities. The Court ruled that the **Fourteenth Amendment** barred state governments from discriminating on the basis of race but did not prevent private individuals, businesses, or organizations from doing so.

Civilian Conservation Corps (CCC) (p. 680) A **New Deal** program to provide government jobs in reforestation, flood control, and other conservation projects to young men between ages eighteen and twenty-five.

Clayton Antitrust Act (p. 566) Legislation that strengthened antitrust laws. Passed in 1914, it outlawed interlocking directorates, exempted labor unions from antitrust laws, and limited the use of injunctions in labor disputes.

Coercive Acts (p. 108) A series of laws passed by Parliament in 1774 to punish Boston and Massachusetts for the destruction of tea during the "Boston Tea Party." Many colonists, who regarded these and similar laws as "intolerable," moved closer toward war.

Columbian Exchange (p. 23) The transfer of plants, animals, and diseases from Europe, Africa, and Asia to and from the Americas after Columbus's fateful voyage in 1492.

Common Sense (p. 117) An influential tract, published by Thomas Paine in January 1776, calling for American independence from Great Britain and establishment of a republican government.

Compromise of 1850 (p. 318) Several laws that together sought to settle several outstanding issues involving slavery. They banned the slave trade, but not slavery in Washington, DC; admitted California as a free state; applied popular sovereignty to the remaining Mexican Cession territory; settled the Texas-New Mexico boundary dispute; and passed a more stringent **Fugitive Slave Act**.

Compromise of 1877 (p. 429) A brokered arrangement whereby Republican and Democratic leaders agreed to settle the disputed 1876 presidential election. Democrats allowed returns that ensured the election of Republican Rutherford B. Hayes; and Republicans agreed to withdraw federal troops from the South, ensuring an end to Reconstruction.

Comstock Lode (p. 441) The first major vein of silver ore in the United States, discovered in the late 1850s, near Virginia City, Nevada.

conquistadores (p. 17) The Spanish term for "conquerors," specifically the explorers, adventurers, and soldiers who crushed the native peoples of the Americas.

Conservation (p. 561) The efficient management and use of natural resources, such as forests, grasslands, and rivers; it represents a "middle-of-the-road" policy as opposed to the uncontrolled exploitation of such resources or the preservation those resources from any human exploiters.

Continental army (p. 115) The regular or professional army authorized by the **Second Continental Congress**, mostly under the command of General George Washington during the Revolutionary War.

Contract with America (p. 837) A pledge, signed by many Republicans running for Congress in 1994, to support conservative reforms limiting federal power and expenditures. Championed by House Speaker Newt Gingrich, it contributed to a Republican electoral victory; but opposition by President William Clinton, a Democrat, prevented passage of much of the contract's legislative agenda.

Copperheads (p. 382) Term that initially applied to northern Democrats who resisted Republican war measures and advocated negotiation with the Confederacy. Later in the Civil War, the term became tantamount to an accusation of treason against the Union.

Crittenden Compromise (p. 373) Legislation proposed by Kentucky Senator John Crittenden during the Secession Crisis in 1860–1861. It called for a constitutional amendment recognizing slavery in all territory south of 36°30' (the "Missouri Compromise line") and an iron-clad amendment guaranteeing slavery in slave states. President-elect Lincoln and the Republicans rejected the proposals.

crop-lien system (p. 423) A system of agriculture in which local landowners and merchants loaned money to farm workers in return for a portion of the harvest of cash crops. By forcing farmers to plant cash crops, the system discouraged diversified agriculture in the South.

Cuban missile crisis (p. 763) The showdown between the United States and the Soviet Union during October 1962, after the Soviet Union had sneaked medium-range nuclear missiles into communist Cuba. After President John F. Kennedy publicly demanded their removal and ordered the blockade of Cuba, Soviet leader Nikita Khrushchev agreed to do so, averting a nuclear war.

Cult of True Womanhood (p. 274) An ideal of middle-class womanhood in the early nineteenth century that asserted that women were naturally pious, pure, and submissive; exemplars of Christian precepts; and best-suited to supervise the moral development of the family.

D-Day (p. 720) June 6, 1944, the day Allied troops crossed the English Channel, landed on the coast of Normandy, and opened a second front in Western Europe during World War II. The "D" stands for "disembarkation"—to leave a ship and go ashore.

***Dartmouth College v. Woodward* (p. 243)** The 1819 Supreme Court case that held that a state charter—in this case, to Dartmouth College—was a contract and that contracts could not be canceled or altered without the consent of both parties, a ruling that strengthened corporations and encouraged investment.

Dawes Severalty Act of 1887 (p. 439) An 1887 law terminating tribal ownership of land and allotting some parcels of land to individual Indians with the remainder of the land left open for white settlement. It included provisions for Indian education and eventual citizenship. The law led to corruption, exploitation, and the weakening of Indian tribal culture. It was reversed in 1934.

détente (p. 778) A French term, meaning the relaxation of tensions, applied to an easing of Cold War antagonisms during the 1970s. Under President Richard Nixon and foreign affairs adviser Henry Kissinger, détente was a strategy to allow the United States to weaken the bonds between the Soviet Union and communist China.

dollar diplomacy (p. 597) A policy of President William Taft to promote American economic penetration to underdeveloped nations, especially in Latin America; it sought to strengthen American influence without requiring the presence of U.S. troops.

Dred Scott decision (p. 360) The 1857 Supreme Court ruling that held that blacks were not citizens and could not sue in a federal court, and, most important, that Congress had exceeded its constitutional authority in banning slavery from the territories. By declaring the Missouri

Compromise unconstitutional, and making future compromises even more difficult, the decision pushed the nation closer to civil war.

Electoral College (p. 150) An assembly of delegates representing each of the states who choose the president of the United States. This mechanism, established by the U.S. Constitution, was regarded as less volatile than allowing voters to elect the president directly.

Emancipation Proclamation (p. 390) A decree by President Abraham Lincoln that freed all slaves in Confederate states that remained in active rebellion on January 1, 1863, when the proclamation went into effect.

Embargo Act (p. 188) A law passed by Congress in 1807 prohibiting all American exports. President Thomas Jefferson, who proposed the law, sought to pressure Britain and France—then at war with each other—into recognizing neutral rights.

encomienda **system (p. 18)** A feudal labor arrangement, imposed in the Spanish colonies of the Americas, by which Spanish settlers were granted a certain number of Indian subjects who were obliged to pay tribute in goods and labor.

Enlightenment (p. 88) An intellectual movement of the eighteenth century that celebrated human reason and scientific advances and expressed doubts about the truth claims of sacred texts.

Environmental Protection Agency (EPA) (p. 780) A federal agency created in 1970 to oversee environmental monitoring and cleanup programs.

Equal Rights Amendment (ERA) (p. 817) A proposed amendment to the U.S. Constitution to outlaw discrimination on the basis of sex. Although first proposed in 1923, the amendment was not passed by Congress until 1972; but the ratification movement fell short and the ERA was not added to the Constitution.

Era of Good Feelings (p. 210) A period from 1817 to 1823 in which the disappearance of the **Federalists** enabled the Republicans to govern in a spirit of seemingly nonpartisan harmony.

Espionage Act (p. 614) A law passed in 1917 that made it a crime to obstruct the nation's effort to win World War I.

Fair Deal (p. 739) President Harry Truman's 1949 program for expanded economic opportunity and civil rights.

Farewell Address (p. 165) President Washington's influential 1796 speech in which he deplored the rise of political factions and warned against "permanent alliances" with foreign nations.

Federal Reserve Act (p. 566) A 1913 law establishing a Federal Reserve Board, which controlled the rediscount rate and thus the money supply; this helped regularize the national banking system.

Federalist Papers **(p. 153)** A series of essays, chiefly written by Alexander Hamilton, James Madison, and John Jay, explaining and defending the national government proposed by the Constitutional Convention of 1787.

Federalists (p. 152) Advocates of a strong national government; they supported ratification of the Constitution and subsequently supported measures to expand federal revenues and functions.

Fifteenth Amendment (p. 419) An amendment (1870), championed by the Republican party, that sought to guarantee the vote to blacks in the South following the Civil War.

First Continental Congress (p. 109) An assembly comprised of delegates from twelve colonies that met in Philadelphia in 1774. It denied Parliament's authority to legislate for the colonies, adopted the Declaration of Rights and Grievances, created a Continental Association to enforce a boycott of British imports, and endorsed a call to take up arms against Britain.

Force Acts (p. 424) Three laws passed by the Republican-dominated Congress in 1870–1871 to protect black voters in the South. The laws placed state elections under federal jurisdiction and imposed fines and imprisonment on those guilty of interfering with any citizen exercising his right to vote.

Fourteen Points (p. 620) A comprehensive plan, proposed by President Woodrow Wilson in January 1918, to negotiate an end to World War I. It called for freedom of the seas, free trade, arms reduction, national self-determination and an end to colonial rule and secret diplomacy.

Fourteenth Amendment (p. 415) An amendment, passed by Congress in 1866 and ratified in 1868, that prohibited states from depriving citizens of the due process or the equal protection of the laws. Although the amendment was a response to discriminatory laws against blacks in the South, it figured prominently in the expansion of individual rights and liberties during the last half of the twentieth century.

Free Soil party (p. 315) A party that emerged in the 1840s in opposition to the expansion of slavery into the territories. Formally organized in 1848, it nominated Martin Van Buren for president. In 1856, Free Soil party members joined with former **Whigs** and other disaffected voters to form the **Republican party**.

Freedmen's Bureau (p. 414) A federal refugee agency to aid former slaves and destitute whites after the Civil War. It provided them food, clothing, and other necessities as well as helped them find work and set up schools.

French and Indian War (p. 92) Fourth in the series of great wars between Britain and France, this conflict (1754–1763) had its focal point in North America and pitted the French and their Indian allies against the British and their Indian allies. Known in Europe as the **Seven Years' War**, this struggle drove the French government from much of North America.

French Revolution (p. 159) The massive and violent social and political upheaval commencing in 1789 that ended the French monarchy, established a republic, expropriated the land and property of the Catholic Church, and culminated in a bloody reign of terror.

Fugitive Slave Act (p. 318) Initially, a 1793 law to encourage the return of runaway slaves; this law was amended, as part of the **Compromise of 1850**, so as to authorize federal commissioners to compel citizens to assist in the return of runaway (fugitive) slaves. The law offended Northerners and its nonenforcement offended Southerners.

Gibbons v. Ogden (p. 244) Supreme Court ruling (1824) that held that no state could pass laws affecting interstate trade, thereby ensuring the federal government's supremacy in interstate commerce.

Glorious Revolution (p. 66) The peaceful accession of William II, a Protestant, and Queen Mary to the British throne in 1688, ending the Catholic rule of James II. Many colonists rebelled against governors who had been appointed by James II and demanded greater political rights.

gold rush (p. 313) Term for the gold-mining boom in the U.S. western territories in the late 1840s and 1850s.

"good neighbor" (p. 665) President Herbert Hoover's policy to promote better relations between the United States and nations in the Western Hemisphere; it declared America's intention to disclaim the right to intervention pronounced in the **Platt Amendment** and the **Roosevelt Corollary**.

Great Awakening (p. 85) A widespread evangelical revival movement of the 1740s and 1750s, sparked by the tour of the English evangelical minister George Whitefield. The Awakening spread religious fervor but weakened the authority of established churches.

Great Compromise (p. 150) Resolved the differences between the New Jersey and Virginia delegations to the Constitutional Convention by providing for a bicameral legislature: the Senate, with equal representation for each state, and the House of Representatives, apportioned by population.

Great Society (p. 767) The sweeping legislative agenda of President Lyndon Johnson; it sought to end poverty, promote civil rights, and improve housing, health care, and education. The program was criticized as costly and ineffective.

greenbacks (p. 382) Paper currency issued by the Union government during the Civil War, resulting in inflation. Whether to continue the issue of greenbacks became a key political issue in the decades after the Civil War.

Gulf of Tonkin Resolution (p. 772) Congressional action, undertaken at President Johnson's request, giving the President the authority to deploy U.S. troops to repel aggression in Southeast Asia. This provided congressional sanction for the escalation of the Vietnam war.

Half-Way Covenant (p. 65) A modification of puritan practice, adopted by many Congregational churches during the 1650s and afterwards, that allowed baptized puritans who had not experienced saving grace to acquire partial church membership and receive sacraments.

Harlem Renaissance (p. 650) A modern artistic and literary movement that celebrated African American life and culture in early twentieth-century Harlem, New York. Among its key figures were Langston Hughes, Richard Wright, and Zora Neale Hurston (literature); Duke Ellington (music); Jacob Lawrence (painting); and Aaron Douglas (sculpture).

Hartford Convention (p. 203) A gathering of New England **Federalists** from December 1814 through January 1815 to channel opposition to Thomas Jefferson and the **War of 1812**. Some participants may have regarded the meeting as preparatory to a secession movement by the New England colonies.

headright (p. 54) A system of land distribution, adopted first in Virginia and later in Maryland, that granted colonists fifty acres for themselves and another fifty for each "head" (or person) they brought with them to the colony. This system was often used in conjunction with indentured servitude to build large plantations and supply them with labor.

Hepburn Act (p. 560) Federal legislation, passed in 1906, that gave the Interstate Commerce Commission sufficient power to inspect railroad companies' records, set maximum rates, and outlaw free passes.

Homestead Act (1862) (p. 396) Federal law granting 160 acres of public land in the West to any settler who would farm and improve it within five years of the grant; it encouraged migration into the Great Plains.

human immunodeficiency virus (HIV) (p. 821) A virus, usually spread through sexual contact, that attacks the immune system, sometimes fatally. HIV, which causes **acquired immunodeficiency syndrome (AIDS)**, first appeared in the United States in the 1980s.

impressment (p. 187) The policy whereby Britain forced people to serve in its navy. The impressment of sailors—even American citizens—on neutral vessels during the Napoleonic Wars outraged Americans and was a major cause of the **War of 1812**.

improvised explosive device (IED) (p. 851) Also known as "roadside bombs," IEDs are homemade bombs that usually consist of captured artillery shells that are wired to a detonator. Either they are exploded remotely or by suicide bombers. IEDs accounted for over a third of the casualties sustained by American and United Nations forces in the Iraq and Afghanistan wars.

indentured servants (p. 55) Individuals working under a form of contract labor that provided them with free passage to America in return for a promise to work for a fixed period, usually seven years. Indentured servitude was the primary labor system in the Chesapeake colonies for most of the seventeenth century.

Industrial Workers of the World (IWW) (p. 546) A militant labor organization, founded in 1905 and inspired by European anarchists, that advocated "abolition of the wage system" and called for a single union of all workers, regardless of trade or skill level; it was repressed during and after World War I.

internment camps (p. 715) Detainment centers, mostly located in western states, that held approximately 110,000 Japanese aliens and American citizens of Japanese origin during World War II.

Interstate Commerce Act (p. 468) Federal law establishing the Interstate Commerce Commission in 1887, the nation's first regulatory agency.

Iran-Contra affair (p. 803) Scandal involving high officials in the Reagan administration accused of funding the Contra rebels in Nicaragua in violation of 1984 Congressional laws explicitly prohibiting such aid. The Contra funding came from the secret sale of arms to Iran.

Iranian hostage crisis (p. 794) Protracted crisis that began in 1979 when Islamic militants seized the American embassy in Tehran, Iran, and held scores of its employees hostage. The militants had been enraged by American support for the deposed Shah of Iran. The crisis, which lasted over a year, contributed to President Jimmy Carter's defeat in his reelection campaign in 1980.

isolationism (p. 575) A national policy that eschews foreign alliances, such as was propounded by George Washington in his "**Farewell Address**." Isolationism was also embraced by part of the **Monroe Doctrine** of 1823 and after the First World War, when the United States refused to join the **League of Nations** and sought to distance itself during the 1930s from the rumblings of another world war. Isolationism ended as national policy when Japan attacked Pearl Harbor on December 7, 1941.

Jacksonian democracy (p. 248) A political doctrine, chiefly associated with Andrew Jackson, that proclaimed the equality of all adult white males—the common man—and disapproved of anything that smacked of special privilege, such as chartered banks.

Jay's Treaty (p. 164) Named after John Jay, the American negotiator, and ratified in 1795, this treaty eased tensions with Great Britain. By its provisions Britain agreed to evacuate forts on the United States' side of the Great Lakes and submit questions of neutral rights to arbitrators.

joint-stock companies (p. 25) Businesses in which investors pooled capital for specific purposes, such as conducting trade and founding colonies. Examples include the English joint-stock companies that founded the Virginia, Plymouth, and Massachusetts Bay colonies.

judicial review (p. 150) A crucial concept that empowered the Supreme Court to invalidate acts of Congress. Although not explicitly propounded in the U.S. Constitution, Chief Justice John Marshall affirmed in *Marbury v. Madison* (1803) that the right of judicial review was implicit in the Constitution's status as "the supreme Law of the Land."

Kansas-Nebraska Act (p. 354) A compromise law in 1854 that superseded the **Missouri Compromise** and left it to voters in Kansas and Nebraska to determine whether they would be slave or free states. The law exacerbated sectional tensions when voters came to blows over the question of slavery in Kansas.

Kentucky and Virginia Resolves (p. 168) Political declarations in favor of states' rights, written by Thomas Jefferson and James Madison, in opposition to the federal **Alien and Sedition Acts**. These resolutions, passed by the Kentucky and Virginia legislatures in 1798, maintained that states could nullify federal legislation they regarded as unconstitutional.

Knights of Labor (p. 471) A national labor organization, formed in 1869 and headed by Uriah Stephens and Terence Powderly, that promoted union solidarity, political reform, and sociability among members. Its advocacy of the eight-hour day led to violent strikes in 1886 and the organization's subsequent decline.

Know-Nothing party (p. 355) A nativist, anti-immigrant and anti-Catholic party that emerged in response to the flood of Catholic immigrants from Ireland and Germany in the 1840s. The party achieved mostly local successes in the Northeast port cities; but in 1856 former President Millard Fillmore, whose Whig party had dissolved, accepted the nomination of southern Know-Nothings but carried only Maryland, a failure that contributed to the movement's decline.

Ku Klux Klan (p. 424) Founded as a social club in 1866 by a handful of former Confederate soldiers in Tennessee, it became a vigilante group that used violence and intimidation to drive African Americans out of politics. The movement declined in the late 1870s but resurfaced in the 1920s as a political organization that opposed all groups—immigrant, religious, and racial—that challenged Protestant white hegemony.

laissez-faire (p. 462) A French term—literally, "to let alone"—used in economic contexts to signify the absence of governmental interference in or regulation of economic matters.

League of Nations (p. 623) A worldwide assembly of nations, proposed by President Woodrow Wilson, that was included in the Treaty of Versailles ending World War I. The refusal of the United States to join the League limited its effectiveness.

Lecompton constitution (p. 362) A proslavery constitution, drafted in 1857 by delegates for Kansas territory, elected under questionable circumstances, seeking admission to the United States. It was rejected by two territorial governors, supported by President Buchanan, and decisively defeated by Congress.

Leisler's Rebellion (p. 73) An uprising in 1689, led by Jacob Leisler, that wrested control of New York's government following the abdication of King James II. The rebellion ended when Leisler was arrested and executed in 1690.

Lend-Lease Act (p. 703) A military aid measure, proposed by President Franklin D. Roosevelt in 1941 and adopted by Congress, empowering the president to sell, lend, lease, or transfer $7 billion of war material to any country whose defense he declared as vital to that of the United States.

Lewis and Clark expedition (p. 184) An exploration of the Louisiana Territory and the region stretching to the Pacific, commissioned by President Jefferson. Commanded by Meriwether Lewis and William Clark, the enterprise (1804–1806) brought back a wealth of information about the region.

Louisiana Purchase (p. 177) An 1803 agreement whereby the United States purchased France's North American Empire, the vast region drained by the Mississippi and Missouri Rivers, for $15 million; it doubled the size of the nation.

Loyalists (p. 120) Sometimes called Tories, the term for American colonists who refused to take up arms against England in the 1770s.

lyceums (p. 294) Locally sponsored public lectures, often featuring writers, that were popular in the nineteenth century.

Manhattan Project (p. 701) The code name for the extensive United States military project, established in 1942, to produce fissionable uranium and plutonium, and to design and build an atomic bomb. Costing nearly $2 billion, the effort culminated in the destruction of Hiroshima and Nagasaki in August 1945.

manifest destiny (p. 303) Originating in the 1840s, a term that referred to support of the expansion of the United States through the acquisition of Texas, Oregon, and parts of Mexico. The term was also used in the 1890s in reference to the conquest of foreign lands not meant to be incorporated into the United States.

Marbury v. Madison (p. 176) An 1803 Supreme Court ruling that declared the Judiciary Act of 1789 unconstitutional and established the precedent for judicial review of federal laws.

Marshall Plan (p. 737) A proposal, propounded in 1947 by Secretary of State George Marshall, to use American aid to rebuild the war-torn economies of European nations. Adopted by Congress in 1948 as the European Recovery Program, it pumped some $13 billion into Europe during the next five years.

massive retaliation (p. 747) The "New Look" military policy of the Dwight D. Eisenhower and Secretary of State John Foster Dulles relying on nuclear weapons to inhibit communist aggression during the 1950s.

Mayflower Compact (p. 31) An agreement, signed aboard the *Mayflower* among the Pilgrims en route to Plymouth Plantation (1620), to establish a body politic and to obey the rules of the governors they chose.

McCulloch v. Maryland (p. 243) An 1819 Supreme Court ruling that state governments could not tax a federal agency—in this case the second Bank of the United States—for "the power to tax involves the power to destroy." The decision affirmed the doctrine of the implied powers of the federal government.

Medicare (p. 769) A social welfare measure, enacted in 1965, providing hospitalization insurance for people over sixty-five and a voluntary plan to cover doctor bills paid in part by the federal government.

mercantilism (p. 81) A loose system of economic organization designed, through a favorable balance of trade, to guarantee the prosperity of the British empire. Mercantilists advocated possession of colonies as places where the mother country could acquire raw materials not available at home.

Mexican War (p. 308) Fought between the United States and Mexico from May 1846 to February 1848, the Mexican War greatly added to the national domain of the United States; see also **Treaty of Guadalupe Hidalgo**.

military-industrial complex (p. 757) A term, popularized by President Dwight D. Eisenhower in his 1961 farewell address, for the concert of interests among the U.S. military and its chief corporate contractors.

Missouri Compromise (p. 218) A legislative deal, brokered in 1820, that preserved the balance of slave and free states in the Union by admitting Missouri as a slave state and Maine as a free state; it also banned slavery from that part of the Louisiana Territory north of 36°30'.

Monroe Doctrine (p. 207) A foreign policy edict, propounded by President James Monroe in 1823, declaring that the American continents were no longer open to European colonization or exploitation and that the United States would not interfere in the internal affairs of European nations.

Moral Majority (p. 796) A term associated with the organization by that name, founded in 1979 by the Reverend Jerry Falwell to combat "amoral liberals," drug abuse, "coddling" of criminals, homosexuality, communism, and abortion.

muckraker (p. 545) A term for progressive investigative journalists who exposed the seamy side of American life at the turn of the twentieth century by "raking up the muck."

mugwumps (p. 524) A group of eastern Republicans, disgusted with corruption in the party, who campaigned for the Democrats in the 1884 elections. These anticorruption reformers were conservative on the money question and government regulation.

National American Woman Suffrage Association (NAWSA) (p. 554) An organization, founded in 1890, that united the National Woman Suffrage Association, headed by Elizabeth Cady Stanton and Susan B. Anthony, and the American Woman Suffrage Association, headed by Lucy Stone. After ratification of the Nineteenth Amendment granting women the vote in 1920, the NAWSA became the League of Women Voters.

National Association for the Advancement of Colored People (NAACP) (p. 571) A national interracial organization, founded in 1909, that promoted the rights of African Americans. Initially it fought against lynching, but from 1955 through 1977, under the leadership of Roy Wilkins, it launched the campaign that overturned legalized segregation and it backed civil rights legislation. The NAACP remains the nation's largest African American organization.

National Grange of the Patrons of Husbandry (p. 467) A farmers' organization, founded in 1867 by Oliver H. Kelley, that initially provided social and cultural benefits but then supported legislation, known as the Granger laws, providing for railroad regulation.

National Organization for Women (NOW) (p. 817) An organization, founded in 1966 by Betty Friedan and other feminists, to promote equal rights for women, changes in divorce laws, and legalization of abortion.

National Origins Act (p. 632) A federal law, passed in 1929 that curtailed immigration, especially from southern and eastern Europe and Asia.

National Recovery Administration (NRA) (p. 680) A New Deal agency, established in 1933, to promote economic recovery, that promulgated industry-wide codes to control production, prices, and wages.

nationalism (p. 135) An affinity for a particular nation; in particular, a sense of national consciousness and loyalty that promotes the interests and attributes of that nation over all others.

nativism (p. 486) A fear or hatred of immigrants, ethnic minorities, or alien political movements.

Navigation Acts (p. 82) Seventeenth-century Parliamentary statutes to control trade within the British empire so as to benefit Britain and promote its administration of the colonies.

Neolithic revolution (p. 4) The transition from a hunter-gather economy to one mostly based on the cultivation of crops.

neutrality acts (p. 698) Legislation affirming nonbelligerency in the event of war. In relation to American history, such legislation was passed in 1794 to preclude American entanglement in the Napoleonic Wars; similar laws were passed just before and after World War I, especially during the 1930s.

New Deal (p. 679) A broad program of legislation proposed by President Franklin D. Roosevelt to promote recovery from the Great Depression and provide relief for those in distress.

New Freedom (p. 564) Democratic candidate Woodrow Wilson's term in the 1912 presidential campaign for a proposed policy that would restore competition by breaking up the trusts and punishing corporations that violated rules of business conduct.

New Frontier (p. 755) President John F. Kennedy's term for a revitalized national agenda, particularly in relation to foreign policy and space exploration.

new immigration (p. 485) Reference to the influx of immigrants to the United States during the late nineteenth and early twentieth century predominantly from southern and eastern Europe.

New Jersey Plan (p. 148) The proposal to the Constitutional Convention of 1787 by New Jersey delegate William Paterson to create a federal legislature in which each state was represented equally. The concept became embodied in the United States Constitution through the Senate, in which each state has two representatives, though this was counterbalanced by the House of Representatives, in which each state's representation is proportional to its population.

New Nationalism (p. 563) Progressive candidate Theodore Roosevelt's term in the 1912 presidential election for an expansion of federal power to regulate big business and enact legislation to promote social justice.

Niagara movement (p. 570) A response by W. E. B. Du Bois and other blacks, following a meeting in Niagara Falls in 1905, in opposition to Booker T. Washington's advocacy of black accommodation to white prejudice; these leaders drafted a political program to achieve equal opportunity, equal justice, and an end to segregation that led to the founding of the **National Association for the Advancement of Colored People (NAACP)**.

North American Free Trade Agreement (NAFTA) (p. 839) A 1993 accord signed by Canada, Mexico, and the United States to reduce and eventually eliminate barriers to trade, including tariffs, among the signatories.

North Atlantic Treaty Organization (NATO) (p. 740) A military mutual-defense pact, formed in 1948, by the United States, Canada, and ten European nations, including Great Britain, France, and West Germany; the Soviet Union countered with the formation of the Warsaw Pact among communist regimes in Eastern Europe.

Northwest Ordinance (p. 137) A 1787 measure of the Continental Congress, passed according to the **Articles of Confederation**, to provide for governance of the region north of the Ohio River and the eventual admission of up to five territories—ultimately the states of Ohio, Indiana, Illinois, Michigan, and Wisconsin. The ordinance also prohibited slavery in the region and reserved lands for Indians.

NSC-68 (p. 741) A secret policy statement, proposed by the National Security Council in 1950, calling for a large, ongoing military commitment to contain Soviet communism; it was accepted by President Harry Truman after the North Korean invasion of South Korea.

nullification (p. 261) A doctrine, forcefully articulated by John C. Calhoun in 1828, asserting that a state could invalidate, within its own boundaries, federal legislation the state regarded as unconstitutional.

Open Door policy (p. 593) A policy, propounded by Secretary of State John Hay in 1899, affirming the territorial integrity of China and a policy of free trade.

Organization of Petroleum Exporting Countries (OPEC) (p. 788) A cartel of oil-producing nations in Asia, Africa, and Latin America that gained substantial power over the world economy in the mid- to late-1970s.

Ostend Manifesto (p. 351) A confidential 1854 dispatch to the U.S. State Department from American diplomats meeting in Ostend, Belgium, suggesting that the United States would be justified in seizing Cuba if Spain refused to sell it to the United States. When word of the document was leaked, Northerners seethed at this "slaveholders' plot" to extend slavery.

Paleolithic revolution (p. 1) Period 750,000 years ago when humans devised simple stone tools, inaugurating life based on hunting and gathering.

Pendleton Act (p. 523) An 1883 law bringing civil service reform to federal employment; it classified many government jobs and required competitive exams for these positions.

People's (Populist) party (p. 531) The People's party of America was an important "third party," founded in 1891, that sought to unite various disaffected groups, especially farmers. The party nominated James B. Weaver for president in 1892 and in 1896 joined with the Democratic party in support of William Jennings Bryan for president.

Persian Gulf War (p. 807) The 1991 war following Iraq's takeover of Kuwait; the United States and a coalition of allies defeated the army of Iraqi leader Saddam Hussein but failed to drive him from power.

Platt Amendment (p. 589) A law, passed in 1901 and superseding the **Teller Amendment**, which stipulated the conditions for the withdrawal of

American forces from Cuba; it also transferred ownership of the naval base at Guantanamo Bay to the United States.

***Plessy v. Ferguson* (p. 526)** Supreme Court ruling (1896) that held that racial segregation of public accommodations did not infringe on the "equal protection" clause of the Constitution; this "separate but equal" doctrine was overturned by *Brown v. Board of Education* in 1954.

popular sovereignty (p. 314) The principle of allowing people to make political decisions by majority vote. As applied to American history, the term generally refers to the 1848 proposal of Michigan Senator Lewis Cass to allow settlers to determine the status of slavery in the territories.

Potsdam Conference (p. 731) A wartime conference (April 1945) held in occupied Germany where Allied leaders divided Germany and Berlin into four occupation zones, agreed to try Nazi leaders as war criminals, and planned the exacting of reparations from Germany.

pragmatism (p. 513) A philosophical system, chiefly associated with William James, that deemphasized abstraction and assessed ideas and cultural practices based on their practical effects; it helped inspire political and social reform during the late nineteenth century.

predestination (p. 30) The Calvinist belief, accepted by New England puritans, that God had determined who would receive eternal grace at the dawn of time; nothing people did during their lifetime could alter their prospects of salvation.

Progressivism (p. 543) A cluster of movements for various forms of social change—some of them contradictory—during the early twentieth century; progressives generally opposed corruption and inefficiency in government, monopoly power among corporations, and wayward behavior among immigrants and others.

Protestant Reformation (p. 24) A religious movement of the sixteenth century initially focused on eliminating corruption in the Catholic Church; but under the influence of theologians Martin Luther and John Calvin, it indicted Catholic theology and gave rise to various denominations that advanced alternative interpretations.

puritans (p. 30) A term, initially derisive, referring to English religious dissenters who believed that the religious practices and administration of the Church of England too closely resembled those of the Catholic Church; many migrated to Massachusetts Bay after 1630 to establish a religious commonwealth based on the principles of John Calvin and others.

Quakers (p. 39) Adherents of a religious organization founded in England in the 1640s who believed that the Holy Spirit lived in all people; they embraced pacifism and religious tolerance, and rejected formal theology. In the decades after 1670, thousands of Quakers emigrated to New Jersey and Pennsylvania.

Radical Republicans (p. 382, 412) A faction within the Republican party, headed by Thaddeus Stevens and Benjamin Wade, that insisted on black suffrage and federal protection of the civil rights of blacks. After 1867, the Radical Republicans achieved a working majority in Congress and passed legislation promoting Reconstruction.

Reaganomics (p. 795) A label pinned on President Ronald Reagan's policies of tax cuts, social welfare cuts, and increased military spending; it generated huge federal deficits, but also promoted the reorganization of large corporations.

"reconcentration" camps (p. 580) A term that referred to the Spanish refugee camps into which Cuban farmers were herded in 1896 to prevent them from providing assistance to rebels fighting for Cuban independence from Spain.

"red scare" (p. 628) Public hysteria over Bolshevik influence in the United States after World War I; it led to the arrest or deportation of thousands of radicals, labor activists, and ethnic leaders.

Republican party (p. 356) One of the original two political parties, sometimes called "Democratic Republican," it was organized by James Madison and Thomas Jefferson and generally stood for states' rights, an agrarian economy and the interests of farmers and planters over those of financial and commercial groups, who generally supported the **Federalist** party; both of the original parties faded in the 1820s. A new Republican party emerged in the 1850s in opposition to the extension of slavery in the territories. It also adopted most of the old Whig party's economic program. The party nominated John C. Fremont for president in 1856 and Abraham Lincoln in 1860.

romanticism (p. 288) A loosely defined aesthetic movement originating in the late eighteenth century and flowering during the early nineteenth century; it encompassed literature, philosophy, arts, and music and enshrined feeling and intuition over reason.

Sanitary Commission (p. 398) A private and voluntary medical organization, founded in May 1861, that sought to improve the physical and mental well-being of Union soldiers during the Civil War.

scalawags (p. 419) White southern Republicans—mainly small landowning farmers and well-off merchants and planters—who cooperated with the congressionally imposed Reconstruction governments set up in the South following the Civil War.

Scopes trial (p. 643) Also called the "Monkey Trial," it was a celebrated 1924 contest that pitted Darwinian evolutionists against fundamentalist "Creationists." John T. Scopes, a teacher charged with defying Tennessee law by teaching evolution, was found guilty and fined $100.

Second Continental Congress (p. 114) A gathering of American Patriots in May 1775 that organized the **Continental army**, requisitioned soldiers and supplies, and commissioned George Washington to lead it.

Second Great Awakening (p. 275) A wave of religious enthusiasm, commencing in the 1790s and lasting for decades, that stressed the mercy, love, and benevolence of God and emphasized that all people could, through faith and effort, achieve salvation.

second party system (p. 263) A term for the political contention between the Democratic party, as rejuvenated by Andrew Jackson in 1828, and the **Whigs**, who emerged in response to Jackson.

Sedition Act (p. 614) Federal legislation, first passed in 1798 and expired in 1801, that placed limits on freedom of speech during wartime. Another such act was passed in 1918 and led to the imprisonment of Socialist Eugene V. Debs and others during World War I.

Seneca Falls Convention (p. 287) A meeting, held at Seneca Falls, New York in 1848, that affirmed that "all men and women are created equal" and sought the franchise (vote) for women.

settlement houses (p. 495) Community centers, founded by reformers such as Jane Addams and Lillian Wald beginning in the 1880s, that were located in poor urban districts of major cities; the centers sought to Americanize immigrant families and provide them with social services and a political voice.

Seven Years' War (p. 93) The global conflict, sometimes known as the **French and Indian War**, that lasted from 1756 to 1763 and pitted France and its allies against Britain and its allies. Britain ultimately prevailed, forcing France to surrender its claims to Canada and all territory east of the Mississippi River.

Shakers (p. 277) A religious commune founded by Ann Lee in England that came to America in 1774. Shakers practiced celibacy, believed that God was both Mother and Father, and held property in common.

sharecropping (p. 422) A type of agriculture, frequently practiced in the South during and after Reconstruction, in which landowners provided land, tools, housing, and seed to a farmer who provided his labor; the resulting crop was divided between them (i.e., shared).

Shays's rebellion (p. 145) An armed rebellion of western Massachusetts farmers in 1786 to prevent state courts from foreclosing on debtors. Nationalists saw such unrest as proof of the inadequacy of the federal government under the **Articles of Confederation**.

Sherman Antitrust Act (p. 469) A federal law, passed in 1890, that outlawed monopolistic organizations that functioned to restrain trade.

Sherman Silver Purchase Act (p. 534) An 1890 law that obliged the federal government to buy and coin silver, thereby counteracting the deflationary tendencies of the economy at the time; its repeal in 1894, following the Depression of 1893, caused a political uproar.

social Darwinism (p. 464) A belief that Charles Darwin's theory of the evolution of species also applied to social and economic institutions an practices: The "fittest" enterprises or individuals prevailed, while those that were defective naturally faded away; society thus progressed most surely when competition was unrestricted by government.

Social Gospel (p. 495) A doctrine preached by many urban Protestant ministers during the early

1900s that focused on improving living conditions for the city's poor rather than on saving souls; proponents advocated civil service reform, child labor laws, government regulation of big business, and a graduated income tax.

Social Security Act (p. 689) A component of Franklin Roosevelt's **New Deal**, it established in 1935 a system of old-age, unemployment, and survivors' insurance funded by wage and payroll taxes.

Southern Christian Leadership Conference (SCLC) (p. 755) A civil rights organization, founded in 1957 by Martin Luther King, Jr. and his followers, that espoused Christian nonviolence but organized mass protests to challenge segregation and discrimination; it played a major role in support of the **Civil Rights Act of 1964** and the **Voting Rights Act of 1965**.

Specie Circular (p. 262) An edict, issued by President Andrew Jackson in 1836, obliging purchasers of public land to do so with gold coins rather than the paper currency issued by state banks; it caused the speculative boom in real estate to collapse and exacerbated a financial panic the following year.

spoils system (p. 252) A term, usually derisive, whereby newly elected office-holders appoint loyal members of their own party to public office.

Square Deal (p. 559) The phrase, initially employed by President Theodore Roosevelt in 1904, to describe an arbitrated settlement between workers and an employer, but more generally employed as a goal to promote fair business practices and to punish "bad" corporations that used their economic clout unfairly.

stagflation (p. 791) A term coined in the 1970s to describe the period's economic downturn and simultaneous deflation in prices.

Stamp Act Congress (p. 101) A meeting in New York City of delegates of most of the colonial assemblies in America to protest the Stamp Act, a revenue measure passed by Parliament in 1765; it was a precursor to the Continental Congress.

Strategic Arms Limitation Treaty (SALT) (p. 778) A treaty, signed by the United States and the Soviet Union in 1972, restricting the testing and deployment of nuclear ballistic missiles, the first of several such treaties.

Strategic Defense Initiative (SDI) (p. 798) The concept of a space-based missile defense system—popularly known as "Star Wars," after the movie by that name—proposed by President Ronald Reagan in 1983. Controversial and costly, the concept was never fully realized.

Student Nonviolent Coordinating Committee (SNCC) (p. 764) A civil rights organization, founded in 1960, that drew heavily on younger activists and college students. After 1965, under the leadership of Stokely Carmichael and then H. Rap Brown, the group advocated "Black Power."

Students for a Democratic Society (SDS) (p. 771) An organization created by leftist college students in the early 1960s; it organized protests against racial bigotry, corporate exploitation of workers, and, especially after 1965, the Vietnam war.

"surge" (p. 852) The sudden increase in troop strength that appeared to have been used successfully against the Iraq insurgency in 2007. President Barack Obama similarly adopted a surge in 2009 to stabilize a deteriorating situation in Afghanistan.

Taft-Hartley Act (p. 735) A 1947 federal law that outlawed the closed shop and secondary boycotts and obliged union leaders to sign affidavits declaring that they were not communists.

Tariff of Abominations (p. 193) An exceptionally high tariff, passed in 1828, that provoked Vice President John C. Calhoun to write the "South Carolina Exposition and Protest"—a defense of the doctrine of **nullification**.

Teapot Dome scandal (p. 659) A scandal during the administration of Warren Harding in which the Secretary of the Interior, Albert Fall, accepted bribes from oil companies that then leased the Teapot Dome federal oil reserve in Wyoming.

Teller Amendment (p. 582) A rider to the 1898 war resolution with Spain whereby Congress pledged that it did not intend to annex Cuba and that it would recognize Cuban independence from Spain.

temperance movement (p. 281) A reform movement of the nineteenth and early twentieth centuries in which women and ministers played a major role and that advocated moderation in the use of alcoholic beverages, or, preferably, abstinence. The major organizations included the American Temperance Society, the Washingtonian movement, and the Women's Christian Temperance Union (WCTU).

Ten Percent Plan (p. 411) A measure drafted by President Abraham Lincoln in 1863 to readmit states that had seceded once 10 percent of their prewar voters swore allegiance to the Union and adopted state constitutions outlawing slavery.

tenement (p. 489) Four- to six-story residential apartment house, once common in New York and certain other cities, built on a tiny lot with little regard for adequate ventilation or light.

Tennessee Valley Authority (TVA) (p. 683) A **New Deal** agency that built and operated dams and power plants on the Tennessee River; it also promoted flood control, soil conservation, and reforestation.

Tet offensive (p. 774) A wide-ranging offensive, launched by North Vietnamese and Vietcong troops throughout South Vietnam in February 1968. It failed to cause the South Vietnamese government to collapse, but persuaded many Americans that the war was not winnable. President Lyndon B. Johnson announced his decision not to run for reelection several months later.

Thirteenth Amendment (p. 413) Passed in 1865, this amendment declared an end to slavery and negated the Three-fifths Clause in the Constitution, thereby increasing the representation of the southern states in Congress.

Three-Fifths Compromise (p. 149) The provision in the Constitution that defined slaves, for purposes of representation in the House of Representatives and state tax payments, not as full persons, but as constituting only three-fifths of a person.

Trail of Tears (p. 259) The name for the 1838 forced removal of Cherokee and other Indians from Georgia and the western Appalachians to Indian Territory in Oklahoma and nearby regions.

transcendentalism (p. 288) A diverse and loosely defined philosophy that promoted a mystical, intuitive way of looking at life that subordinated facts to feelings. Transcendentalists argued that humans could transcend reason and intellectual capacities by having faith in themselves and in the fundamental benevolence of the universe. They were complete individualists.

Transcontinental Treaty (p. 207) Also called the Adams-Onís Treaty. Ratified in 1821, it acquired Florida and stretched the western boundary of the Louisiana Territory to the Oregon coast.

Treaty of Guadalupe Hidalgo (p. 312) Signed in 1848, this treaty ended the **Mexican War**, forcing that nation to relinquish all of the land north of the Rio Grande and Gila Rivers, including what would eventually become California, in return for monetary compensations.

Treaty of Tordesillas (p. 17) Negotiated by the pope in 1494, this treaty resolved the territorial claims of Spain and Portugal; in the Western Hemisphere Portugal was granted Brazil, while Spain was granted nearly all of the remaining lands.

triangular trade (p. 69) An oversimplified term for the trade among England, its colonies in the Americas, and slave markets in Africa and the Caribbean.

Truman Doctrine (p. 736) A foreign policy, articulated by President Harry Truman in 1947, that provided financial aid to Greek and Turkish governments then under threat by communists rebels.

underground railroad (p. 348) A support system established by antislavery groups in the upper South and the North to help fugitive slaves who had escaped from the South to make their way to Canada.

Underwood Tariff (p. 566) A 1913 reform law that lowered tariff rates and levied the first regular federal income tax.

United Nations (UN) (p. 729) An international organization, founded in 1945, that sought to promote discussion and negotiation and thereby avoid war; it was joined by nearly all nations.

***United States v. Richard M. Nixon* (p. 784)** A Supreme Court ruling (1974) that obliged President Richard Nixon to turn over to the Watergate special prosecutor sixty-four White House audiotapes; these helped prove that Nixon had known about the cover-up of the Watergate burglary.

utopian (p. 278) Any of countless schemes to create a perfect society.

Virginia Plan (p. 148) An initiative, proposed by James Madison of Virginia, calling on the

Constitutional Convention to declare that seats in the federal legislature would be proportionate to a state's population, a concept that caused smaller states to propose a New Jersey plan in which each state would have the same number of representatives. The controversy was resolved in the Great Compromise.

Voting Rights Act of 1965 (p. 769) Federal legislation that empowered federal registrars to intervene when southern states and municipalities refused to let African Americans register to vote.

Wade-Davis bill (p. 412) An 1864 alternative to Lincoln's "**Ten Percent Plan**," this measure required a majority of voters in a southern state to take a loyalty oath in order to begin the process of Reconstruction and guarantee black equality. It also required the repudiation of the Confederate debt. The president exercised a pocket veto, and it never became law.

Wagner Act (p. 688) Officially the National Labor Relations Act and sometimes called Labor's Magna Carta, it gave workers the right to organize and bargain collectively. It also created the National Labor Relations Board to supervise union elections and stop unfair labor practices by employers.

War Hawks (p. 196) Young congressional leaders who in 1811 and 1812 called for war against Great Britain as the only way to defend the national honor.

War Industries Board (WIB) (p. 612) A federal agency, established during World War I, that reorganized industry for maximum efficiency and productivity.

War of 1812 (p. 197) A war fought by the United States and Britain from 1812 to 1815 over British restrictions on American shipping.

war on terror (p. 843) Initially, a worldwide campaign to catch and prosecute those guilty of the September 11, 2001, attacks; as terrorist attacks spread throughout the world, the war became defined far more broadly.

Watergate scandal (p. 782) A complex scandal involving attempts to cover up illegal actions taken by administration officials and leading to the resignation of President Richard Nixon in 1974.

Webster-Ashburton Treaty (p. 301) A treaty between the United States and Britain, signed in 1842, that settled the controversy of the Maine-Canada boundary. The treaty allowed Canada to build a military road from Halifax to Quebec while the United States got most of the disputed territory.

Whigs (p. 264) Originally a reference to British politicians who sought to exclude the Catholic Duke of York from succession to the throne in the 1760s; in the United States after the 1830s, it referred to a political party that opposed the Jacksonian Democrats and favored a strong role for the national government, especially in promoting economic growth.

Whiskey Rebellion (p. 162) A violent protest by western Pennsylvania farmers who refused to pay the whiskey tax proposed by Alexander Hamilton. In 1794, the rebels threatened to destroy Pittsburgh; by the time the Union army had arrived, the rebels had dispersed.

Wilmot Proviso (p. 314) A proposed amendment to an 1846 appropriations bill that banned slavery from any territory the United States might acquire from Spain. It never passed Congress, but generated a great debate on the authority of the federal government to ban slavery from the territories.

woman suffrage (p. 553) The right of women to vote, ensured by the passage and ratification of the Nineteenth Amendment (1920).

Works Progress Administration (WPA) (p. 685) A **New Deal** agency, established in 1935 and run by Harry Hopkins, that spent $11 billion on federal works projects and provided employment for 8.5 million persons.

XYZ Affair (p. 167) A political furor caused by French diplomats who in 1797 demanded a bribe before they would enter into negotiations with their American counterparts; some **Federalists**, furious over this assault on national honor, called for war.

Yalta Conference (p. 730) A wartime conference (February 1945) held in the Russian Crimea, where the **Allies**—Franklin Roosevelt, Winston Churchill (Britain), and Josef Stalin (Soviet Union)—agreed to final plans for the defeat and joint occupation of Germany; it also provided for free elections in Poland, but such elections were never held.

Young America movement (p. 351) The confident enthusiasm, infused with a belief in the nation's "**manifest destiny**," that spread rapidly during the 1850s.

Credits

Index

Note: Italicized letters *f*, *m*, and *n* following page numbers indicate figures (photos, illustrations, and graphs), maps, and footnotes, respectively.